ThisBook Comes With Lots of
FREE Online Resources

Nolo's award-winning website has a page dedicated just to this book. Here you can:

KEEP UPO DATE. When there are important changes the information in this book, we'll post updes.

GET DISCUNTS ON NOLO PRODUCTS. Get discounts hundreds of books, forms, and software.

READ BLG. Get the latest info from Nolo authors' bs.

LISTEN TODCASTS. Listen to authors discuss tiy issues on topics that interest you.

WATCH VOS. Get a quick introduction to a legal topic our short videos.

And that's not all.
Nolo.com contains thousands of articles on everyday legal and business issues, plus a plain-English law dictionary, all written by Nolo experts and available for free. You'll also find more useful **books, software, online apps, downloadable forms,** plus a **lawyer directory.**

With
Downloadable FORMS

NOLO
LA for ALL

Get forms and mor
www.nolo.com/back-
PAT.html

19th Edition

Patent It Yourself

Your Step-by-Step Guide to Filing at the U.S. Patent Office

**Patent Attorneys David Pressman
and David E. Blau**

NINETEENTH EDITION	AUGUST 2018
Editor	DAVID GOGUEN
Cover Design	SUSAN PUTNEY
Book Design	TERRI HEARSH
Proofreading	IRENE BARNARD
Index	JULIE SHAWVAN
Printing	BANG PRINTING

ISSN: 1554-9925 (print)
ISSN: 2371-9966 (online)
ISBN: 978-1-4133-2539-3 (pbk)
ISBN: 978-1-4133-2540-9 (epub ebook)

This book covers only United States law, unless it specifically states otherwise.

Please note

We believe accurate, plain-English legal information should help you solve many of your own legal problems. But this text is not a substitute for personalized advice from a knowledgeable lawyer. If you want the help of a trained professional—and we'll always point out situations in which we think that's a good idea—consult an attorney licensed to practice in your state.

Acknowledgments

My deep thanks go to my clients, and other inventors whose creativity and genius I so greatly admire and envy. My readers have given me much valuable feedback and suggestions, and I am grateful to them as well.

I also thank the staff at Nolo, including Richard Stim, Steve Elias, Stephanie Harolde, and Ralph Warner for their ideas, contributions, and support, and, especially, Terri Hearsh for substantially improving the look and feel of the book.

Finally, I thank my wife Roberta for her unflagging support and contributions.

—David Pressman

Thanks go to David Pressman for his insight and hard work making this book possible and keeping it relevant, to Thomas Tuytschaevers for his kind assistance and advice throughout the process, and to Janet Portman and David Goguen at Nolo for gently pushing me along when it was needed.

Thanks also to Elizabeth de Armond for teaching me to be an organized writer, and to Timothy Holbrook for teaching me the importance of patent law.

Finally, thanks to Peter, Evelyn, and Christina Blau for their unfailing patience and support (and for Christina's amazing cooking).

—Dave Blau

About the Authors

David Pressman is a member of the California and Patent and Trademark Office bars. He's had over 45 years' experience in the patent profession, as a patent examiner for the U.S. Patent Office, a patent attorney for Philco-Ford Corp., Elco Corp., and Varian Associates, as a columnist for *EDN* Magazine and Entrepreneur.com, and as an instructor at San Francisco State University. He contributed the Patent, Trademark and Copyright entries to the *World Book Encyclopedia*. He's also an inventor, with two patents issued. When not writing, dabbling in electronics, programming, inventing, or playing his trumpet, he practices as a patent lawyer in San Francisco. Originally from Philadelphia, he has a B.S. in Electrical Engineering from Pennsylvania State University. He spent his first year in law school at the University of Pennsylvania and completed his second and third years at George Washington University, where he served on the *Law Review* and received a Juris Doctor degree. He is also active in the general semantics and vegetarian movements. His mother, Mildred Phillips, was also a writer, having composed lyrics for numerous published songs, including Bill Haley's "Mambo Rock."

David E. Blau is a patent attorney at Daly, Crowley, Mofford & Durkee in Canton, Massachusetts, and is a member of the U.S. Patent and Trademark Office and Massachusetts bars. Dave received his B.S. from the California Institute of Technology, with majors in both Mathematics and Engineering & Applied Science. Prior to law school, he worked for the government as a mathematician, for a number of private companies writing software to perform scalable content storage and distribution and back-office online commerce functions, and co-founded a Web design business. He received his J.D. from the Chicago-Kent College of Law with a certificate in Intellectual Property, and has practiced patent law in the Boston area ever since. Outside the practice of law, Dave is a scuba diver and a licensed private pilot who hopes to get his instrument rating someday.

Table of Contents

Appendixes

Nondisclosure Agreement

Invention Disclosure

Provisional Application for Patent Cover Sheet—PTO SB/16

Application Data Sheet—PTO AIA/14

Positive and Negative Factors Evaluation

Positive and Negative Factors Summary

Consultant's Work Agreement

Searcher's Worksheet

Drawing Reference Numerals Worksheet

Declaration for Utility or Design Patent Application Using an Application Data Sheet
—PTO AIA/01

Declaration for Utility or Design Patent Application—PTO AIA/08)

Supplemental Sheet for Declaration—PTO AIA/10

Utility Patent Application Transmittal—PTO AIA/15

Fee Transmittal—PTO SB/17

Credit Card Payment Form—PTO 2038

Information Disclosure Statement Cover Letter

8 How to Use the Downloadable Forms on the Nolo Website 611

Index 615

Your Legal Companion

Patent It Yourself allows you, the inventor, to patent and commercially exploit your invention by yourself. It provides:

- instructions for inventing and documenting an invention, and how and when to file a Provisional Patent Application
- step-by-step guidance for obtaining a U.S. patent, together with tear-out or downloadable forms that are necessary for each step of the process
- an overview of the procedures and requirements for getting patent protection abroad and concrete suggestions for finding the necessary resources to help you do this
- an overview of the alternative and supplementary forms of protection available for inventions, such as trade secrets, copyrights, trademarks, and unfair competition law, and
- detailed information and advice on how to commercially evaluate, market, and license your invention.

One purpose of this book is to save you money. According to the American Intellectual Property Association, the *average* cost of preparing a minimally complex patent application is approximately $8,500; preparing a relatively complex application—for example, an application for a chemical, biotech, mechanics, electronics, or data processing invention—may cost between $11,500 and $15,500. You may not be able to afford these fees, and even if you can, it still pays to do it yourself. By following the instructions set out in this book, you'll not only save on attorneys' fees, but you'll be personally involved in every step of the patenting process. After all, you know your invention better than anyone else!

A. You Don't Have to Use a Patent Attorney

The laws contain no requirement that you must have a patent attorney to file a patent application, deal with the PTO concerning the application, or to obtain the patent. In fact, PTO regulations (*Manual of Patent Examining Procedure* (MPEP), Section 707.07(j)) specifically require patent examiners to help inventors in *pro se* (no lawyer) cases. Many hundreds of patent applications are filed and successfully prosecuted each year by *pro se* inventors.

B. A Layperson Can Do a Quality Job

Keep in mind that the quality of a patent is dependent upon four basic factors:

1. whether the patent application contains a full, clear, and accurate description that tells how to make and use the invention
2. whether the reach of the patent (technically covered in the patent "claims") is as broad as possible, given the state of prior developments in the field
3. whether the application "sells" the advantages of the invention, and
4. how an applicant handles correspondence with the PTO.

Fortunately, it takes no special legal expertise to do an excellent job for these, especially if you utilize the many checklists we have provided throughout this book.

C. Using an Attorney

Even if you do choose to work with an attorney, or have one available to you through the process, you'll find that this book allows you to take an active role in the process, do a better job of monitoring your attorney (no trivial consideration), and greatly adds to your understanding of the ways in which the law is willing to protect your invention. No matter how competent an attorney is, the client who understands what's going on will always obtain better service. Indeed, many corporate legal departments use this book to educate their inventors and support personnel to deal with patent attorneys and to protect their inventions more effectively.

D. Should You Do It Yourself?

Even though many if not most inventors can file and handle their own patent application, the big question is should you do so on your own or hire an expert?

Patent It Yourself—Quick-Start Guide

If you don't have the time to read *Patent It Yourself* from cover to cover,
this Quick-Start Guide will tell you where to look to accomplish a specific task.

Task	What to Read or Do
You've invented something and you want to protect it.	Read Chapter 1, which introduces the basic tasks—that is, recording the invention (by filing a Provisional Patent Application), evaluating the commercial potential, searching for patentability, applying for a patent, and marketing it.
You have a patent and want to license or sell it.	Read Chapter 11 on Marketing.
You have a patent that may be infringed.	Read Chapter 15 to learn how to determine whether it's infringed and how to go after the infringer.
You have a patent and want to maintain it.	Read Chapter 15 on Maintenance Fees.
You have a patent and want to sell or license it.	Reach Chapter 16 on Assignments and Licensing.
You want to learn about all forms of intellectual property.	Read Chapters 1 and 7.
You want to determine whether your invention will sell.	Read Chapter 4 on Evaluating Commerciality.
You want to see if your invention is patentable.	Read Chapters 5 and 6 on Patentability and Searching.
You want to get a monopoly on your invention abroad.	Read Chapter 12 on Foreign Patenting.
You have a pending patent application and want to learn how to deal with the Patent Office.	Read Chapter 13 on Patent Application Prosecution and Chapter 14 on Branches of Your Application.
You want to see more reference sources for inventors.	Read Appendix 2, Resources.
You need a name for something or a definition of a patent-legal term.	See Appendix 3, Glossaries.
You need to determine a time limit.	See Appendix 6, Timing Chart.
You need a patent form.	See Appendix 7, Forms.

The cost factor alone may dictate your decision for you if you can't afford the $5,000 to $15,000 most attorneys now charge to prepare a patent application on a simple invention.

On the other hand, if you're fortunate enough to afford an attorney and you either don't have enough time to do it yourself, you don't think you'll be able to write a detailed description of your invention in conjunction with drawings, (or you aren't diligent and committed enough to complete projects in a reasonable time or in a fairly high-quality manner), then perhaps you should use an attorney in conjunction with *Patent It Yourself*, to monitor and enhance the attorney's work.

The above can be expressed by the following proportion:

$$\text{DIY} \; \alpha \; \frac{\text{AT} \cdot \text{WA} \cdot \text{D} \cdot \text{DC}}{\text{AF}}$$

which means you should be inclined to *Do It Yourself* in direct proportion to your *Available Time*, your *Writing Ability*, your *Diligence*, and your *Desire to Control* things, and in inverse proportion to your *Available Funds*. While this proportion isn't even an approach at precision, it provides the appropriate criteria and how to use them when making the do-it-yourself versus hire-an-attorney decision.

The best answer for some inventors may be to do some of both. Using this approach, diligent inventors will do much of the patent work themselves, only consulting with an attorney at an hourly rate if snags develop, or to check the patent application before submission.

E. How to Use *Patent It Yourself*

The book is organized primarily for chronological use, starting with an overview of the entire intellectual property field (which includes patents, trademarks, copyright, and trade secret law). Then it sequentially covers the steps most inventors will take to monopolize

and profit from their inventions. Throughout the book references are made to several forms. A blank copy of each is also located in Appendix 7 for your use, and all forms can be downloaded from the Web page listed in Appendix 7.

We refer throughout to intellectual property laws, and rules made by the agencies that implement those laws. Laws passed by Congress form the United States Code (USC), and are organized by topic into titles and sections. Title 35 contains the federal patent laws—you may become very familiar with it! These laws define your rights. Using legal citation, title 35, section 102 is written "35 USC 102."

Regulations or rules provide the procedures that must be followed to secure those rights. These rules are issued by government agencies, including the United States Patent and Trademark Office and the Copyright Office, and are organized in the Code of Federal Regulations (CFR). Title 37 of the CFR includes the regulations relating to patents, trademarks, and copyrights. Part 1 is concerned with patent rules. Using legal citation, title 37, section 1.111 is written "37 CFR 1.111," and is sometimes called "Patent Rule 111."

Many abbreviations are used throughout *Patent It Yourself* to save space and spare you the tedium of repeatedly reading long phrases. If at any time you need to refresh your memory about an abbreviation, please refer to Appendix 1, Abbreviations Used in *Patent It Yourself*.

Appendix 3 provides two dictionaries. The first is a list of technical terms used in the preparation of patent applications (Glossary of Useful Technical Terms). The second list provides definitions for many of the terms used throughout this book (Glossary of Legal Terms).

The law is constantly changing. We try to update the important changes in each printing, but in the meantime you can get updates at www.nolo.com.

Welcome to the world of intellectual property! Good luck and successful inventing!

Introduction to Patents and Other Intellectual Property

Inventor's Commandment 1

Prior to deciding how to proceed with any creation, you should learn and be familiar with the various forms of intellectual property, including utility patents, design patents, trademarks, copyright, trade secrets, and unfair competition, so that you will be able to select and employ the proper form(s) of coverage for your creation.

In this chapter we'll first introduce you to the world of "intellectual property" (IP) law, including not only patents, but trademarks, copyright, trade secrets, and so on. Although you may think that a patent is the only form of protection available for your creation, there are many other forms of IP that may be available to help you. We strongly recommend that you become familiar with and consider all forms of IP, since you may find that you can use one or more of the other forms of IP in addition to or instead of a patent. This chapter presents an overview of the types of IP, including patents. Of course, we'll honor the title of this book in subsequent chapters, which will focus on how to obtain and profit from a patent.

A. What Is a Patent and Who Can Apply for It?

Before we start, to show the importance of patents to a society, consider what Mark Twain said about patents way back in 1889:

> *"That reminds me to remark, in passing, that the very first official thing I did, in my administration—and it was on the very first day of it, too—was to start a patent office; for I knew that a country without a patent office and good patent laws was just a crab, and couldn't travel any way but sideways or backways."*

> —*A Connecticut Yankee in King Arthur's Court,*
> *Chapter IX, "The Tournament."*

Have you ever thought about why the standard of living in the United States is so high? I believe it's due in part to the United States patent system, which stimulates the creative genius in the U.S. As Lincoln said, "The patent system added the fuel of interest to the fire of genius."

What is a patent? It's an exclusive right granted by the government to an inventor.

What is the nature of the patent right? A patent gives its owner—the inventor or the person or business to whom the inventor legally transfers the patent—the right to exclude others from making, using, selling, or importing the invention "claimed" in the patent deed for approximately 17 to 18 years, provided three maintenance fees are paid. (See Chapter 9 for more on patent claims, and Chapter 15 for more on maintenance fees.) You can use this right to exclude others by notifying infringers of your patent, or if that fails, by filing a patent infringement lawsuit in federal court.

Important Definitions

While these definitions may seem elementary, we provide them here because many inventors confuse these terms, and so that you will know exactly what we mean when we use these terms later.

Also, in the patent world, a single word or comma can make the difference between allowance or rejection of a set of claims, or whether a court will hold that a device infringes a patent. All patent practitioners consider it important and usually essential to use words and punctuation precisely and accurately.

An **invention** is any new and useful process, machine, manufacture, or material composition, or an improvement to one of these, developed by a human.

A **patent application** is a set of papers that describe an invention, suitable for filing in a patent office to apply for (or in the case of a Provisional Patent Application, establish a date to apply for) a patent on the invention.

A **patent** is a grant from a government that confers upon an inventor the legal right to exclude others from making, using, selling, importing, or offering an invention for sale for a fixed duration. (We encounter many beginning inventors who refer to a patent application as a "patent." If we feel they won't take offense, we usually correct them gently to start them on the path of accurate word usage.)

Who can apply for a patent? Anyone, regardless of age, nationality, mental competency, state or history of incarceration, or any other characteristic, so long as he or she is a true inventor of the invention. Even dead or insane persons may apply through their personal representative. (See Chapter 16 for more on patent ownership.)

Who can use a patent? A patent is a form of personal property, and can be sold outright for a lump sum, or its owner can give anyone permission to use the invention it covers ("license it") in return for royalty payments. (More on this in Chapter 16.)

B. The Three Types of Patents

There are three types of patents—utility patents, design patents, and plant patents. Let's briefly look at each.

- **Utility Patents:** As we'll see in Chapters 8 to 10, a utility patent, the main type of patent, covers inventive *function*. Examples of utility inventions are Velcro hook-and-loop fasteners, new drugs, electronic circuits, software that is tied to some form of hardware, semiconductor manufacturing processes, new bacteria, newly discovered genes, new animals, plants, automatic transmissions, Internet techniques and methods of doing business (provided they are not abstract ideas), and virtually anything else under the sun that can be made by humans.

  To get a utility patent, one must file a patent application that consists of a detailed description telling how to make and use the invention, together with claims (formally written sentence fragments) that define the invention, drawings of the invention (if warranted), other formal paperwork, and a filing fee. Again, only the actual inventor can apply for a utility (or any other) patent. The front or abstract page of a typical utility patent is illustrated in Fig. 1A.

- **Design Patents:** As discussed in more detail in Chapter 10, a design patent (as opposed to a utility patent) covers inventive *appearance*: the unique, decorative shape or visible surface ornamentation of an article of manufacture. Thus, if a lamp, a building, a computer case, or

a desk has a truly unique shape, its design can be patented. Even computer screen icons and an arrangement of printing on a piece of paper can be patented.

The design must be for an article that is different from an object in its natural state; thus, a figure of a man would not be suitable for a design patent, but if the man is an unnatural position, this can be patented. For an example, see patent Des. 440,263 (2001) to Norman.

However, the uniqueness of the shape must be purely ornamental or aesthetic, not functional. If the design is functional, then only a utility patent is proper, even if it is also aesthetic. A useful way to distinguish between a design invention and a utility invention is to ask, "Were the novel features added to make the device *work* better or *look* better?" Or, ask, "Will removing the novel features substantially impair the function of the device?"

Three examples will illustrate the difference between a design invention and a utility invention. The first is a jet plane with a constricted waist for reducing turbulence at supersonic speeds. Although the novel shape is attractive, its functionality makes it suitable for a utility patent only. The second example is a woodshop wall clock that is shaped like a circular saw blade. Changing the shape of this invention does not change how it functions, so a design patent is indicated. The third example is a uniquely-shaped wearable shoe-phone. The wearable *functionality* of the phone is suited to a utility patent, while the *appearance* of the shoe is suited to a design patent; the inventor may apply for both kinds of patent.

Sometimes the state of the art, rather than the nature of the novelty, will determine whether a design or utility patent is proper for an invention. If a new feature of a device performs a novel function, then a utility patent is proper. However, if the state of the art is such that the general nature of the feature and its function is old, but the feature has a novel shape that is an aesthetic improvement, then only a design

United States Patent [19]

Holmes

[11]	Patent Number: **4,949,887**
[45]	Date of Patent: **Aug. 21, 1990**

[54] **INSULATED MULTI-USE SEAT CUSHION WITH CLOSABLE HAND AND FOOT OPENINGS**

[76] Inventor: **William A. Holmes**, 209 Highland Ave., Piedmont, Calif. 94611-3709

[21] Appl. No.: **132,982**

[22] Filed: **Dec. 15, 1987**

Related U.S. Application Data

[63] Continuation-in-part of Ser. No. 867,453, May 28, 1986, abandoned.

[51] Int. Cl.⁵ A61G 1/00
[52] U.S. Cl. **224/151**; 224/205; 224/236; 2/66; 2/202; 126/204; 297/188
[58] Field of Search 224/151, 153, 202, 205, 224/257, 206, 207, 236, 237; 2/66, 91, 93, 108, 202, 203; 383/61, 110, 98, 99, 8; 128/382; 190/107, 102; 5/417–421; 297/230, 188, 192, 219; 126/204, 207, 208

[56] **References Cited**

U.S. PATENT DOCUMENTS

273,523	3/1883	Havasy	....	190/102
1,137,049	4/1915	Bushwick	....	190/107
2,835,896	5/1958	Giese	....	2/66
3,460,740	8/1969	Hagen	....	383/110
3,793,643	2/1974	Kinoshita	....	2/66
4,423,834	1/1984	Rush	....	224/151

4,604,987	8/1986	Keltner	.... 5/421

Primary Examiner—Linda J. Sholl
Attorney, Agent, or Firm—David Pressman

[57] **ABSTRACT**

An insulated hollow cushion has a neck strap (30), an interior portion (72) sufficiently large to accommodate a portable heating source and/or hot and cold foods (74, 76), two side slits through which hands can be inserted for warmth, sealable flaps (16, 20) for closing the side slits when insulation is desired, a slit (36) at the top of the cushion for insertion of items into the cushion's interior, a closeable top flap (28) to seal the top opening for insulation purposes, and a closeable top small flap (56) to insulate the gap between a user's ankles when such user's feet are inserted through the top slit. The side flaps can be insulated so that they can be tucked into the side openings to narrow these openings to provide a tight seal when small hands are inserted into these openings. The insulating layer within the front (10) or the back panel can have multiple perforations (92) over an area thereof and this area can be covered, uncovered, or partially covered by a releasably closable flap (84), thereby to provide a "heat window" which allows maximum transmission of heat (or cold) from an internal hot (or cold) source, or partial transmission, or no more transmission than would occur through an intact insulated wall.

20 Claims, 6 Drawing Sheets

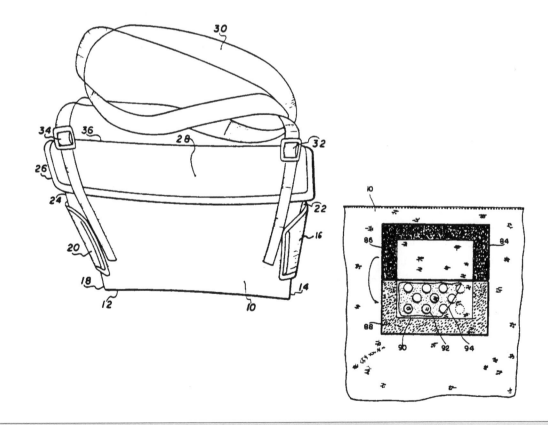

Fig. 1A—Utility Patent Abstract Page

The Life of an Invention

Although most inventors will be concerned with the rights a patent grants during its monopoly or in-force period, the law recognizes four "rights" periods in the life of an invention. These four periods are as follows:

1. **Patent Application Not Yet Filed:** Since March of 2013, if two inventors file patent applications on the same patentable invention, the PTO will award a patent to the first inventor to file, even if the other inventor conceived and built and tested the invention first. An exception occurs if the second inventor to file (Sally) can prove that the first inventor to file (Fred) "derived" (stole, acquired, or misappropriated) the invention from Sally, then the patent will go to Sally.

    During this period, the invention should be treated as a "trade secret"—that is, kept confidential. This gives the inventor the legal right to sue and recover damages against anyone who illegally learns of the invention—for instance, through industrial spying. For this reason, inventors should document their inventions properly. Good documentation practice is covered in Chapter 3.

2. **Patent Pending—Patent Application Filed but Not Yet Issued:** After a patent application is filed, the invention is "patent pending." During the patent pending period, including the one-year period after a Provisional Patent Application is filed, the inventor's rights are the same as described in Period 1 above, with one exception noted below.* Otherwise, the inventor has no rights whatsoever against infringers—only the hope of a future monopoly, which doesn't commence until a patent issues.

    Most companies that manufacture a product that is the subject of a pending patent application will mark the product "patent pending" in order to warn potential copiers that if they copy the product, they may have to stop later (and thus scrap all their molds and tooling) if a patent issues. The Patent and Trademark Office (PTO) by law must keep all patent applications preserved in secrecy until the application is published or the patent issues (whichever comes first). The patent pending period usually lasts from one to three years.

3. **In-Force Patent—Patent Issued but Hasn't Yet Expired:** After the patent issues, the patent owner can bring and maintain a lawsuit for patent infringement against anyone who makes, uses, or sells the invention without permission. A utility patent's in-force period lasts from the date it issues until 20 years from the filing date of its first Regular Patent Application, provided maintenance fees are paid. (Chapter 14 provides more detail about filing multiple applications for an invention with several points of novelty.) Plant patents last just as long, but don't require maintenance fees. Neither does a design patent, however a design patent remains in force for 15 years from the day it was granted, regardless of when the application was initially filed.

    Nearly every initial utility or plant patent is guaranteed an in-force period of at least 17 years—20 years from filing, less three years that the PTO is granted to examine the application. To assure this 17-year term, the patent will be extended, if necessary, to compensate for delays resulting from failures by the PTO in processing the patent application. Also, once the patent issues, it becomes a public record or publication that can block others who file later from getting patents on the same or similar inventions—that is, it becomes "prior art" to anyone who files after its filing date.

4. **Patent Expired:** After the patent expires (20 years after the filing date, or sooner if a maintenance fee isn't paid), the patent owner has no further rights, although infringement suits can be brought for any infringement that occurred during the patent's in-force period. An expired patent remains a valid "prior-art reference" (as of its filing date) forever.

---

* Under the 18-month publication statute (see Section Q2), an inventor whose application is published prior to issuance may obtain royalties from an infringer from the date of publication, provided the application later issues as a patent and the infringer had actual notice of the published application.

patent will be proper. A design patent application consists primarily of drawings, along with formal paperwork and a filing fee.

- **Plant Patents:** A plant patent covers inventive *cultivation*. Since plants change characteristics through cross-breeding, a plant patent covers only plants that can be reproduced asexually (that is, using grafts, cuttings, or spores). Sexually reproducible plants (that is, those that use pollination), can be protected under the Plant Variety Protection Act (7 USC 2321). If a plant also has a useful function, it may be protected by a utility patent, no matter how it reproduces.

  Plant patents are a comparatively recent innovation (1930). Luther Burbank, the great botanist of Santa Rosa, California, goaded Congress to act, stating, "We plant inventors cannot patent a new plum, though the man who makes an automobile horn can get a patent and retire to Southern California and wear silk underclothes the rest of his life."

C. The Novelty and Unobviousness Requirement

An invention is not an invention unless it is new. But workers sometimes engage in workmanlike or routine problem-solving, and their creations, while technically new, are obvious and shouldn't earn the strong protection of a patent monopoly—at least, according to Congress! To uphold these policies, an examiner at the Patent and Trademark Office (PTO) applies these "novelty" and "unobviousness" requirements of the patent laws to each patent application.

The novelty requirement is easy to satisfy: Your invention must be different from what is already known to the public. Any difference, however slight, will suffice. (Note: When we refer to your invention, we are referring to the way it is "claimed" in your patent. The claims, as we'll discuss later in Chapter 9, define your invention.)

Novelty, however, is only one small hurdle to overcome. In addition to being novel, the examiner must also be convinced that your invention is "unobvious." This means that at the time you came

up with your invention, it would have been considered unobvious to a person skilled in the technology (called "art") involved in your creation. As we'll see in Chapter 5, unobviousness is best shown by new and unexpected, surprising, or far superior results, when compared with previous inventions and knowledge ("prior art") in the particular area of the invention. (In addition to being novel and unobvious, utility inventions must also be "in a statutory class" and be useful. More on this later.)

D. How Long Do Patent Rights Last?

How long can you, the patent owner, exclude others from infringing the exclusive rights granted by your patent? Utility and plant patents expire 20 years from the earliest date of filing a Regular Patent Application, while design patents last 15 years from the date of issuance. The terms of patents for certain products whose commercial marketing has been delayed due to regulatory review (such as for drugs or food additives) can be extended beyond the statutory period.

While the term of a patent is calculated from its filing date, the monopoly period it creates—its in-force period—doesn't start until the patent issues. Effective June 2000, every initial utility patent is guaranteed an in-force period of at least 17 years. The patent term will be extended for as long as necessary to compensate for any of the following:

- any delay caused by the PTO failing to examine a new application within 14 months from filing
- any delay caused by the PTO failing to take any of the following actions within four months:
  - reply to an amendment or to an appeal brief
  - issue an allowance or Office Action after a decision on appeal, or
  - issue a patent after the issue fee is paid and any required drawings are filed
- any delay caused by the PTO failing to issue a patent within three years from filing, unless the delay was due to the applicant filing a continuation application or buying a delay to reply to an Office Action, or
- any delay due to secrecy orders, appeals, or interferences.

The patent's in-force or enforceable monopoly period starts when the patent issues, usually about one to three years after the application is filed. From the date of filing to issuance (termed the "pendency period") the inventor has no rights, with one exception: If the patent application is published, an inventor will gain some "provisional" rights against an infringer. An inventor may obtain royalties from an infringer from the date of publication provided (1) the application later issues as a patent; and (2) the infringer had actual notice of the published application. When, and if, the patent later issues—whether or not the application was published—the inventor will obtain the right to prevent the continuation of any infringing activity that started during the pendency period. Relevant time periods are indicated in "The Life of an Invention," above, and in the chart in Appendix 6.

E. Patent Filing Deadlines

As we'll see in more detail in Chapter 5, under current law in the United States you must file your patent application within one year after you first commercialize, publish, or reveal without restriction details of the invention. However foreign countries don't have this one-year grace period, so there's some disadvantage if you sell or publish before filing. For this reason, your safest route is to file a complete U.S. patent application before you publish or commercialize your invention. You are permitted to file a "provisional patent application" (PPA) describing your invention in detail, in accordance with the instructions in Chapters 3 and 8. (No claims, discussed in Chapter 9, are needed.) This PPA can be used, under most circumstances, to defeat or block a patent application or invention of someone else who may subsequently file a patent application on the same invention. However, to obtain the benefit of the PPA's filing date, a regular patent application must be filed within one year after the PPA's filing date—more on this in Chapters 7 and 8.

Under the new First-to-File (FTF) law, effective 2013 Mar 16, if anyone (except the inventor or someone who obtained details of the invention from the inventor) first discloses by commercialization, publication, or other relevant details of the invention to the public, then it is too late to file a valid patent application on the invention. That's because the disclosure will be considered prior art to the patent application. However if the actual inventor or someone who obtained details of the invention from the inventor makes the disclosure, then the actual inventor may file a valid patent application up to one year after the disclosure. However, we still recommend that after FTF takes effect you file a patent application (PPA or RPA) on your invention before any public disclosure in the U.S. That's because a public disclosure before filing will destroy your foreign-filing rights and anyone who sees your disclosure may file their own application on it before you file, thus requiring an expensive and uncertain derivation proceeding.

F. Patent Fees

How much will it cost to get a patent? Assuming you use this book and don't use any patent attorneys or agents, and not including costs of drawings, typing, photocopying, and postage, the only fees you'll have to pay are government fees.

As part of the changes under the "First to File" law, the PTO was given the authority to set these fees to recover actual costs the agency incurs. Thus, the fees change on an irregular basis. The amounts of these fees for the current year (2018) are listed on the PTO Fee Schedule in Appendix 4. The PTO always lists current fees on its website, www.uspto.gov.

As indicated in the Schedule, most PTO fees are three-part: large entity, small entity, and micro entity. The large entity fees are generally paid by large corporations, while the small entity fees, which are half the large entity fees, are generally paid by start-ups and growing companies. Micro entity fees are typically for solo inventors. For more on this, see Chapter 10, Section E5.

The names of these fees and the circumstances when they're due are as follows:

- **Provisional Filing Fee:** To file a provisional patent application, you'll have to pay a *PPA Filing Fee.*

A PPA cannot become a patent, but gives you a year to file a utility application that can.

- **Regular Filing Fee:** To file a nonprovisional utility, design, or patent application, you must pay a *Patent Application Filing Fee*. This fee has three components—filing fee, search fee, and examination fee—that are different for each type of patent, but all three must be paid before the PTO will begin examining your application.

- **Issue Fee:** To have the PTO issue your utility, design, or plant patent, you must pay a *Patent Application Issue Fee*.

- **Maintenance Fee:** To keep your utility patent in force for its full statutory term, you must pay the PTO three maintenance fees, as follows:
    - *Maintenance Fee I*, payable 3.0 to 3.5 years after issuance
    - *Maintenance Fee II*, payable 7.0 to 7.5 years after issuance, and
    - *Maintenance Fee III*, payable 11.0 to 11.5 years after issuance.

Under the America Invents Act (AIA) if you file your application in paper form (not online) there is a paper-filing surcharge and if you are a "micro entity" you'll be able to get a 75% reduction on most fees. (See Chapter 10 for the definition of a micro entity.)

G. Patents Are Like Property

The patent right extends throughout the entire U.S., its territories, and possessions. A patent is transferable by sale or gift, by will, or by descent (under the state's intestate succession, or "no-will" laws). The patent rights can also be licensed; that is, you can own the patent and grant anyone else, including a company, the right to make, use, or sell your invention in exchange for the payment of fees, called "royalties" (more on licensing in Chapter 16). As mentioned, the patent right is granted by the federal government, acting through the Patent and Trademark Office (a division of the Department of Commerce), in Alexandria, Virginia. The patent right is recognized and enforced by the U.S. (federal) courts.

H. How Patent Rights Can Be Lost

The patent right isn't an absolute monopoly for the period that it is in force (from the date of issuance until the expiration date—20 years from date of filing).

It can be lost if:

- utility patent maintenance fees aren't paid
- it can be proved that the patent either (a) fails adequately to teach how to make and use the invention, (b) improperly describes the invention, or (c) contains claims that are legally inadequate
- one or more prior-art references (earlier patents or other publications) are uncovered that show that the invention of the patent wasn't new or wasn't different enough when the invention was made
- the patent owner engages in certain defined types of illegal conduct, that is, commits antitrust or other violations connected with the patent, or
- the patent applicant committed "fraud on the Patent and Trademark Office (PTO)" by failing to disclose material information, such as relevant prior-art references, to the PTO during the period when the patent application was pending.

In short, the patent monopoly, while powerful, may be defeated and is limited in scope and time.

I. What Rights a Patent Grants, and the Prior-Art Reference Value of a Patent

The patent grant gives its owner—one or more individuals, a partnership, corporation, or other entity to which an inventor has "assigned" (legally transferred) the invention—the right to file, maintain, and recover in a lawsuit against any person or legal entity (infringer) who makes, uses, or sells the claimed invention, or an essential part of it. If the patent owner wins the lawsuit, the judge will issue an injunction (a signed order) against the infringer, ordering the infringer not to make, use, or sell the invention any more. Also, the judge will award the patent owner damages—money to compensate the patent owner for loss due to the infringement. The amount of the damages is often the equivalent to a reasonable royalty (say 5%), based on the infringer's sales. However, if the patent owner can convince the judge that the infringer acted in bad faith—for example, infringed intentionally with no reasonable excuse—the judge can triple the damages and make the infringer pay the patent owner's attorneys' fees.

In addition to bringing in licensing income and enabling a manufacturer to charge more for a unique product, patents also have other uses. Some inventors file for and obtain patents mainly for vanity, or the prestige a patent brings. Others use patents to impress (and obtain financing from) investors. And many organizations obtain large portfolios of patents simply to assert them as a defense against any company that charges the organization with patent infringement.

When I'm Used as an Offensive Weapon	When I'm Used as a Prior-Art Reference
1. My claims can be used to stop infringers and/ or obtain damages from them.	1. My specification and drawings constitute prior art, just like any magazine article or book. They can be used to prevent others from getting a patent on what I disclose.
2. My offensive rights start when I issue (or when my application is published— See Section D, above), and expire 20 years from my filing date, provided my maintenance fees are paid.	2. I'm effective as of my filing date and I remain effective as prior art forever.
3. My powers are based solely upon my claims.	3. My claims are irrelevant. Think of me simply as a book, a magazine article, or any other publication.

Fig. 1B—A Patent Can Be Used as an Offensive Weapon or as a Prior-Art Reference

The value of patents cannot be overestimated. As Dr. Edwin Land, the inventor and founder of Polaroid, stated, "The only thing that keeps us alive is our brilliance. The only way to protect our brilliance is patents." For a more concrete example, consider that in 2000 the PTO granted over 2,800 patents to IBM, which now holds about 19,000 U.S. patents. These patents generated over $1.5 billion in revenue! In fiscal year 2005 (from 2005 July 1 to 2006 Jun 30), inventors filed 400,000 patent applications in the PTO and this rate is increasing by 6% to 10% per year!

Since the patent defines the invention monopoly very precisely, the patent owner can use the patent only against supposed infringers who make, use, or sell things or processes that fall within the defined monopoly. This means that not everyone who makes something like your invention will be an infringer; you can validly sue only those whose products or processes fall within the scope of the claims in your patent. (See Chapters 9, 13, and 15 for more on claims.)

In addition to its above-described use as an offensive weapon, a patent also provides a prior-art reference that will block others from getting a patent on anything disclosed in the patent. In this respect, a patent is like a periodical (magazine) article or book. This dual nature of a patent is illustrated in Fig. 1B.

J. What Can't Be Patented

Despite the large number of things that can be patented, there are some "inventions" that the law will not allow to be patented. You can't patent any process that can be performed mentally. The reason is that the law doesn't wish to limit what people can do essentially with just their brains. The same rule applies to abstract ideas; inventions that aren't reducible to or practicable in hardware form, or inventions that don't involve the manipulation of hardware or symbols (words, letters, numbers) to produce a useful result; naturally occurring articles; business forms and other printed matter per se (not associated with some hardware); scientific principles in the abstract (without hardware); inventions that won't work to produce the result claimed for them (such as perpetual motion machines); abstract algorithms that merely crunch numbers without a useful result; human beings (such as cloned humans); and atomic energy inventions. Also, while medical procedures can be patented, the patent law prevents lawsuits from being filed against performing such procedures. The AIA also prevents tax-avoidance schemes from being patented. (See Chapters 5, 8, 9, and 13 for more information.)

 NOTE

Computer Program Note. Computer programs cannot be patented per se. The reason is that running a program is using the computer for its intended purpose, which is not inventive. If the program merely manipulates numbers, such as calculating π, or merely provides a better algorithm to perform a calculation, then it can't be patented. However, the program can be patented if it improves the operation of the computer itself. For instance, if the program controls a display, a memory, a keyboard, any other hardware or process, or if it processes or analyzes a signal that represents a physical quantity in an unconventional way, then it can be patented. Computer programs and algorithms per se (without hardware) can alternatively be protected by copyright, and sometimes by trade secret law.

With respect to designs, as explained, the PTO won't grant design patents on:
- any design whose novelty has significant functional utility (use a utility patent)
- ornamentation that is on the surface only, rather than forming an integral part of a device, or
- any device that has a shape that exists in nature.

K. Some Common Patent Misconceptions

Over the years that we've practiced patent law, we've come across a number of misconceptions that laypersons have about patents. As part of our effort to impart what a patent is, we want to clear up a few of the most common here at the outset.

Common Misconception: A patent gives its owner the right to practice an invention.

Fact: If you come up with an invention, you may practice (make, use, and sell) it freely, with or without a patent, provided that it's not covered by the claims of another's "in-force" patent, that is, a patent that is within its 20-year term. If you have a patent on an improvement invention such as a triode (three-element vacuum tube) and someone holds a patent on a basic invention such as a diode (two-element vacuum tube), your patent will not give you any defense if the owner of the basic patent charges you with infringement. However if the owner of the basic patent wants to use your improvement invention, you may be able to work out a cross-license to avoid having to stop using and selling your own invention.

Common Misconception: Once you get a patent, you'll automatically be rich and famous.

Fact: A patent is like a hunting license: It's useful just to go after infringers. If the invention isn't commercialized, the patent is usually worthless. You won't get rich or famous from your patent unless you or someone else gets the invention into widespread commercial use. In this connection, we've met many inventors who tell us that times are rough and they need to get a patent quickly to lift them out of poverty and make things better. We always have to throw cold water on their hopes by telling them that no one should ever depend on a patent to change their life since few patents ever make money for their inventors, and even when they do, it usually takes years for a patented invention to bear fruit. It's okay to pursue your invention and a patent so long as you realize that this path is usually a long shot and time-consuming road to success.

Common Misconception: If a product has been patented, it's bound to be superior.

Fact: Although Madison Avenue would like you to believe this, in reality a patent merely means the invention is significantly different, not necessarily superior.

L. How Intellectual Property Law Provides "Offensive Rights" (and Not Protection) to Inventors

Many people speak of a patent as a form of "protection." The fact is that, as stated, a patent is an offensive weapon, rather than "protection," which is a defensive shield. To properly benefit from a patent, as we'll see in Chapter 15, the patent owner must sue or threaten to sue anyone who trespasses on the right. The patent doesn't provide any "protection" in its own right and does not give its owner a defense if the inventor infringes an earlier patent. Although the word "protection" is in common usage for all types of intellectual property, it's more accurate to say that a patent—as well as a copyright, trade secret, and trademark—gives its owner "offensive rights" against infringers. In other words the patent, copyright, trade secret, or trademark provides a tool with which you can enforce a monopoly on your creation. The distinction between protection (a defense) and offensive rights is as important in intellectual property law as it is in football or basketball: while a good defense may be valuable, you'll need a powerful offense to win the game or stop the infringer.

To help you keep this distinction in mind, we try consistently to use the term "offensive rights" instead of "protection." However, if we slip up from time to time, please remember that by protection we only mean that inventors have the right to affirmatively come forward and invoke the court's help in preventing infringement by others.

Common Misconception: If you make or sell a device on which you have a patent, your patent will protect you against the infringement claims of others.

Fact: A patent is for offensive use only and has no value in defending against infringement charges from other patents, except that your patent sometimes will have value in a counterattack if the other patent owner infringes your patent.

Common Misconception: If a product, such as a tooth whitener, says "patented," no one else can make a product with a similar function.

Fact: Most patents cover only one specific aspect or version of a product, rather than the basic function of the product. For instance, the patent on the tooth whitener may cover only a specific composition, and many other compositions that perform the same function (albeit in an inferior—or superior—way) may exist that don't infringe the patent.

M. Alternative and Supplementary Offensive Rights

As you probably realize, there are several alternative and often overlapping ways to acquire offensive rights on intellectual property. Let's think of these as different roads to the same destination. While the immediate filing of your patent application is one of these roads, it is only one. The purpose of this chapter is to provide you with a map to the other roads and to help you decide which is the best way to travel, given your circumstances.

The value of your invention can sometimes be better monopolized by using one of the other forms of intellectual property and can almost always be enhanced by simultaneously using a patent with one or more of these other forms—such as unique trade dress, a good trademark, and copyright-covered labels and instructions—and by maintaining later improvements as a trade secret.

N. Intellectual Property—The Big Picture

"Intellectual property" (sometimes called "intangible property") refers to any product of the human mind or intellect, such as an idea, invention, expression, unique name, business method, industrial process, or chemical formula, which has some value in the marketplace, and that ultimately can be reduced to a tangible form, such as a computer, a chemical, a software-based invention, a gadget, a process, etc. Intellectual property law, accordingly, covers the various legal principles that determine:

- who owns any given intellectual property
- when such owners can exclude others from commercially exploiting the property, and

- the degree of recognition that the courts are willing to afford such property (that is, whether they will enforce the owner's offensive rights).

In short, intellectual property (IP) law determines when and how a person can capitalize on a creation. In recent years the role of IP has expanded greatly and will continue to do so as our society becomes more dependent upon technology and information.

Formerly, patents were the most significant part of IP law, so most attorneys who handled trademarks, copyright, trade secrets, and unfair competition, as well as patents, called themselves "patent attorneys." Nowadays, the nonpatent forms of IP law have become far more significant, so most patent attorneys now call themselves IP attorneys. This term has engendered some confusion, because many attorneys who aren't licensed to practice patent law (they only do trademark, copyright, etc.) call themselves IP attorneys. To practice patent law before the PTO, one must pass a separate "agent's exam" given by the PTO. Thus if you need someone to represent you before the PTO and you encounter an attorney who is merely identified as an "IP attorney," you must ask the attorney (or check the PTO's site) to see if the attorney is licensed to practice before the PTO.

Over the years, intellectual property law has fallen into several distinct subcategories, according to the type of "property" involved:

- **Patent Law** provides offensive rights with regard to inventions. As indicated earlier, we have three types of patents: utility, design, and plant.
- **Trademark Law** provides rights with regard to symbols (for example, a word, design, or sound) used to identify a brand of goods or services. Examples of trademarks are *Ivory*, *Coke*, *Nolo*, the *Mercedes-Benz* star, and the *NBC* chimes. With regard to advertising slogans, while the courts generally do not regard them as trademarks, they will afford them trademark rights provided their owners have used them consistently as brand names on the goods and not just in the media. Slogans are primarily covered by copyright law and unfair competition (see below).

- **Copyright Law** provides rights with regard to expressive works, such as books, songs, and movies. It grants authors, composers, programmers, artists, and the like the right to pre vent others from copying or using their original expression without permission and to recover damages from those who do so. Copyright law gives me offensive rights against anyone who copies this book without my permission.
- **Trade Secret Law** provides offensive rights with regard to private knowledge that gives the owner a competitive business advantage—for example, manufacturing processes, magic techniques, and formulae. Methods of producing laser light shows and fireworks are trade secrets. Unless its owner makes substantial efforts to keep the knowledge secret, any trade secret rights will be lost.
- **Unfair Competition Law** affords offensive rights to owners of nonfunctional mental creations that don't fall within the rights offered by the four types of law just discussed, but which have nevertheless been unfairly copied by competitors. For example, "trade dress" (such as *Kodak*'s yellow film package), a business name (such as *Procter & Gamble Co.*), a unique advertising slogan (for example, "Roaches check in but they don't check out"), or a distinctive packaging label (such as Duracell's copper-top energy cells) may all enjoy offensive rights under unfair competition principles.

Having covered patent law earlier in this chapter, let's now wade a little deeper into the other forms of intellectual property law, all of which are shown and briefly depicted in Fig. 1C—The Intellectual Property Mandala, below.

Many clients have come to us with an invention or idea, asking if there were some easier and quicker way to protect their invention than the seven methods discussed in the IP mandala, above. Alas, we always have to disappoint them. We have included in this chapter all of the IP techniques that exist. There are no additional or secret weapons in the IP arsenal, so you will have to work with what we have.

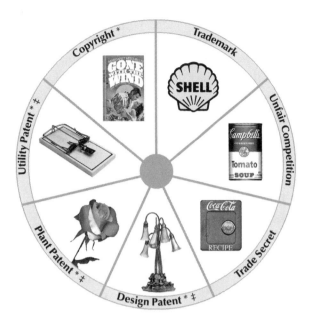

* One must obtain a governmental certificate (patent or registration) to enforce any offensive rights.

‡ Timing is crucial: application must be filed within one year after public exposure.

Fig. 1C—The Intellectual Property Mandala

O. Trademarks

This is the most familiar branch of intellectual property law. On a daily basis, everyone sees, uses, and makes many decisions on the basis of trademarks. For instance, you probably decided to purchase your car, your appliances, much of the packaged food in your residence, your magazines, your computer, and your watch on the basis of their trademarks, at least to some extent. We believe that trademarks originated in 16th century Britain when silversmiths began putting their initials on their products. Naturally, disreputable competitors seeking to capitalize on a well-known silversmith's reputation soon came along and counterfeited the "trade mark" on copycat silverware. Judges were called upon to punish and stop the counterfeiters of the mark and lo, trademark law was born!

1. Trademarks Defined

In its most literal meaning, a trademark is any word or other symbol that is consistently attached to, or forms part of, a product or its packaging to identify and distinguish it from others in the marketplace. In other words, a trademark is a brand.

An example of a word trademark is *Kodak,* a brand of camera. In addition to words, trademarks can be other symbols, such as designs or logos (the Nike swoosh), sounds (the NBC chimes), smells, and even colors. For example, the PTO granted a trademark registration on a specific color used for a line of dry-cleaning ironing pads. (*Qualitex Co. v. Jacobson Products Co., Inc.,* 115 S.Ct. 1300 (1995).) The shape of an object (such as the truncated, contrasting, conical top of Cross pens) can even be a trademark, provided (1) the shape doesn't provide a superior function, and (2) the shape has become associated in the minds of the purchasing public with the manufacturer (known in trademark terms as "secondary meaning").

Many patented goods or processes are also covered by trademarks. For example, *Xerox* photocopiers have many patents on their internal parts, and also are sold under the well-known *Xerox* trademark. Without the patents, people could copy the internal parts, but *Xerox* would still have a monopoly on its valuable and widely recognized trademark.

The term "trademark" is also commonly used to mean "service marks." These are marks (words or other symbols) that are associated with services offered in the marketplace. Examples of service marks include the letters "NBC" (broadcast network services), the Blue Cross–Blue Shield emblem (medical/insurance services), and the words, Café Gratitude (restaurant services).

Two other types of trademark are: "certification marks," the identifying symbols or names used by independent groups, boards, or commissions that certify the quality of goods or services—such as the Good Housekeeping Seal of Approval; and "collective marks," identifying symbols or names showing membership in an organization—for example, the FDIC symbol indicates that a bank is a member of the government-insured banking network.

An important third category of business identifier that is often confused with trademarks is called a "trade name." In the law, trade name is the word or words under which a company does business, while a trademark is the word or other symbol under which a company sells its products or services. To understand this better, let's use *Procter & Gamble* as an example. The words *Procter & Gamble* are a trade or company name, while *Ivory* is a trademark, that is, a brand name for *Procter & Gamble*'s white soap. However, the media often refer to trademarks as trade names. Also, many companies such as *Ford*, use the same words as a trade name and a trademark, so the difference sometimes becomes academic.

Trademarks, such as *Ivory*, enjoy offensive rights under both federal and state trademark laws. The trade name *Procter & Gamble*, however, enjoys offensive rights primarily under state law (corporation registrations, fictitious name registrations, and unfair competition law). However, a federal law can also be used to slap down a trade-name infringement as a "false designation of origin" (17 USC 1125).

2. Monopoly Rights of a Trademark Owner

Briefly, the owner of a trademark may or may not be entitled to legal offensive rights depending on how distinctive (or strong) the law considers the trademark. Trademarks that are arbitrary (*Apple* computers), fanciful (*Double Rainbow* ice cream), or coined terms (*Kodak*) are considered strong, and thus entitled to a relatively broad scope of offensive rights. On the other hand, marks that describe some function or characteristic of the product (such as "*RapidCompute* computers" or "*RelieveIt*" for an analgesic) are considered weaker and won't enjoy as broad a scope of offensive rights. Although the above differences may seem somewhat arbitrary, they really aren't. The courts give fanciful, coined, or other arbitrary marks a stronger and broader monopoly than descriptive marks because descriptive marks come close to words in common usage and the law protects everyone's right to use these. Also, the owner of a "famous" mark can prevent anyone from diluting the mark—that is, blurring or tarnishing its distinctiveness—even if the diluting mark is not used on similar goods or services.

In addition to the strong/weak mark dichotomy, trademark owners may be denied offensive rights if the trademark becomes commonly used to describe an

---

Protection of Domain Names

A domain name is a unique "address" that connects your computer with a website. But a domain name can be more than an address; it is often the identifier for a business. A domain name may even function as a trademark (and may infringe another company's trademark). Registering a domain name does not guarantee your exclusive use of that term in commerce and—because each domain name must be unique—it is impossible for two different businesses to have the same domain name.

Keep in mind that even if a company owns a federally registered trademark, someone else may still have the right to own a domain name that includes that trademark. For example, many different companies have federally registered the trademark Executive for different goods or services. All of these companies may want http://www.executive.com, but the first one to purchase it—in this case, a software company—is the one that acquired the domain name.

When registering a domain name, a company should be sure that nobody else is using it as a trademark for similar goods and services. If another business is selling similar goods or services with a similar name, the use of the domain name can be terminated under trademark law. In addition, a domain name can be challenged if the owner is a cybersquatter—someone registering, trafficking in, or using a domain name with the intent to profit in bad faith from the goodwill of a trademark belonging to someone else. Domain name owners can sue under the Anticybersquatting Consumer Protection Act (ACPA—15 USC 1125(d)), or can arbitrate under ICANN's Uniform Dispute Resolution Policy (UDRP). While you can't recover damages from the infringer under a UDRP arbitration, the procedure is less expensive and less time-consuming (it usually takes about three to six months).

The easiest way to check if a domain name is available is at one of the dozens of online websites that have been approved to register domain names. A listing of these website registrars can be accessed at the ICANN site (http://www.icann.org). ICANN is the organization that oversees the process of approving domain name registrars. For more information, review *Trademark: Legal Care for Your Business & Product Name*, by Stephen Fishman (Nolo).

entire class of products, that is, it becomes "generic." For example, "aspirin," once a trademark that enjoyed strong offensive rights, became a generic word (no offensive rights) for any type of over-the-counter painkiller using a certain chemical. Why? Because its owner used it improperly as a noun (such as "Buy *Aspirin*") rather than as a proper adjective (such as "Buy *Aspirin* (brand) analgesic"), and the public therefore came to view it as synonymous with the product it described.

3. Relationship of Trademark Law to Patent Law

As indicated above, trademarks are very useful in conjunction with inventions, whether patentable or not. A clever trademark can be used with an invention to provide it with a unique aspect in the marketplace so that purchasers will tend to buy the trademarked product over a generic one. For example, consider the *Crock Pot* slow cooker, *Ivory* soap, and the *Hula Hoop* exercise device. These trademarks helped make all of these products successful and market leaders even though they were not granted any basic patent. In short, a trademark provides brand-name recognition to the product and a patent provides a tool to enforce a monopoly on its utilitarian function. Since trademark rights can be kept forever (as long as the trademark continues to be used), a trademark can be a powerful means of effectively extending a monopoly initially created by a patent.

4. Overview of How Offensive Rights to Trademarks Are Acquired

Here's a list of steps you should take if you come up with a trademark and you want to acquire offensive rights to it and use it properly. Because this is a patent book, we haven't covered this topic in detail.

a. Preserve Your Mark as a Trade Secret Until You Use It

As we explain in Subsection d, below, you must take certain actions before you can acquire offensive rights in a mark. This means that during the developmental stage you must treat your trademark as a trade secret so that others won't adopt your proposed mark and use it first. (See Section Q, below, for an overview of acquiring offensive rights to trade secrets.)

b. Make Sure the Mark Isn't Generic or Descriptive

Ask yourself if the mark is generic or descriptive. A generic mark is a word or other symbol that the public already uses to designate the goods or service on which you want to use the mark. Thus you can't acquire offensive rights on "The Pill" for a birth-control pill, since it's already a generic term. A descriptive mark is similar to a generic mark in that it describes the goods, but hasn't yet gotten into widespread public use. For instance, if you came up with a new electric fork, you cannot acquire offensive rights in the mark *Electric Fork*, since it merely describes the product.

c. Make Sure Your Mark Isn't Already in Use

It's essential to select a mark that is not in use by someone else. The goodwill you develop around the mark may go up in smoke in the event of a trademark infringement contest and you may be liable for damages as well. Even if your proposed mark isn't identical to the already-used mark, the other mark's owner can prevent you from using it if, in the eyes of the law, there is a likelihood of customer confusion. Even if there's no such likelihood, the owner of a famous mark can block a mark that is likely to tarnish the reputation of the famous mark. To determine if your mark is already in use, you'll have to make a trademark search or hire someone to do it for you.

A complete trademark search should cover registered and unregistered (common law) marks. You can search all pending and registered trademarks for free at the PTO's website (www.uspto.gov) and you can search all marks (registered and not) on a good search engine, such as Google or Bing. You can also make free searches in *The Thomas Register* in any library or online at www.thomasnet.com, and in *Gale's Trade Name Directory* and *MacRae's Blue Book* (most libraries). For those interested in adopting a website or domain name, Network Solutions, Inc. (InterNIC), has an online search site at www.internic. net. Complete searches of registered and unregistered marks can be ordered through the following companies:

- Compumark, (www.compumark.com/trademark-searching), 800-692-8822, and
- The Trademark Company, (www.thetrademark company.com), 344 Maple Avenue, West, #151, Vienna, VA 22180-5612, 800-906-8626.

However, you can search all pending and registered trademarks for free at the PTO's website (www.uspto. gov), which contains a searchable database of all pending and registered U.S. trademarks.

d. Use or Apply to Register Your Trademark

The first to actually use or file an intent-to-use (ITU) application to register the trademark owns it—that is, acquires offensive rights against infringers. Actual use means shipping goods or advertising services that bear the trademark (not just use in advertising). If an ITU application is filed, the trademark owner must actually use the mark before it can be registered. As a trademark owner, you can validly sue a person who later uses a similar mark for similar goods in a context that is likely to mislead the public. Contrary to popular belief, trademarks do not have to be registered for offensive rights to be acquired: Any entity that uses a mark has common law (judge-made law) rights and has superior rights over infringers of the mark, provided the entity is the first to use the mark and it's a valid mark. However, as explained in Subsection e, just below, registration can substantially add to these offensive rights.

e. Use and Register Your Trademark

If you apply to register your mark federally on the basis of your intent to use it, you will, as stated, eventually have to actually use it on your goods to get it registered. You must thus follow through by actually using it and proving such use as part of your registration application. To federally register a trademark, use the online registration procedures at the PTO website (www.uspto.gov).

If you do adopt and use a trademark on your goods before applying for registration, you should register it in your state trademark office if it's used exclusively in your state, and/or the PTO if it's used across a territorial or international border. Once your mark is federally registered, it will be much easier to sue infringers. The federal registration will cause the court to presume that you have exclusive ownership of the mark and the exclusive right to use it. If you don't register your trademark and it's infringed, you'll have much more difficulty when you go to court.

To register a trademark in your state, call or write to your Secretary of State in your state's capital for a trademark application form and instructions; the cost will be from about $50 to $120.

Trade Group Registration of Trademarks

Instead of (or in addition to) registering your trademark with one or more state trademark offices and the U.S. Patent and Trademark Office (PTO), you can register it with an appropriate specific trade organization. Similarly, movie titles can be registered with a movie industry association and websites and domain names for email addresses can be registered with Internet services. So if you intend to use a trademark in a given industry, check with the industry's main association to see if you can register your mark with them as an alternative or in addition to a PTO or state registration.

f. Use Your Trademark Properly

The law considers it very important to use a trademark properly once you've adopted it as a brand name for your goods. Before it's registered, you should indicate it's a trademark by providing the superscript "TM" after the mark, for example, LeRoy™ Shoes. If it's a service mark, such as a restaurant name or a name for a service business, use the "SM" superscript—for example, "Alice's^{SM} Restaurant." Once the mark is federally registered, provide the superscript "®" or indicate that the mark is registered in the PTO—such as "Reg. U.S. Pat. & TM. Off."

Word trademarks should always be used as brand names on any literature. That is, they should be used as adjective modifiers in association with the general name of the goods to which they apply, and shouldn't be used as a substitute for the name of the goods. For example, if you're making and selling can openers and have adopted the trademark *Ajax*, always use the words "can opener" after *Ajax* and never refer to an *Ajax* alone. Otherwise, the name can become generic and be lost, as happened to "cellophane" and "aspirin," and as could soon happen to *Xerox*. (Doesn't it somehow feel more natural to use the word "Xerox" than "photocopy," or "Kleenex" rather than "tissue"?)

5. What Doesn't Qualify as a Trademark (for the Purpose of Developing Offensive Rights)

The courts won't enforce trademark offensive rights, nor will the PTO or state trademark offices grant trademark registrations, on the following:

- lengthy written matter (copyright is the proper form of coverage here)
- slogans that are merely informational or laudatory, such as "Proudly made in the U.S.A."
- trade names not being used as a trademark or service mark
- immoral, deceptive, or scandalous matter*
- governmental emblems, personal names, or likenesses without consent
- marks that they consider close enough to existing marks as to be likely to cause confusion
- pure surnames or purely geographical designations
- generic terms, or
- descriptive words that do not distinguish a company's products or services.

* Recently, the Supreme Court threw out a prohibition against granting "disparaging" marks. (*Matal v. Tam*, 137 S. Ct. 1744 (2017)).

P. Copyright

A copyright is another offensive right given by law, this time to an author, artist, composer, or programmer. It empowers the holder of a copyright registration to sue in federal court and to have the court issue an injunction ordering the defendant, if found liable, to cease publishing or copying the registered literary, dramatic, musical, artistic, or software works. While a patent can effectively provide offensive rights on a technological application of an idea, a copyright covers only the author's or artist's particular way of expressing an idea. Thus, while a copyright can provide offensive rights on the particular arrangement of words that constitute a book or play, it can't cover the book's subject matter, message, or teachings. Put otherwise, you are free to publish any of the ideas, concepts, and information in this (or any) book, provided that you write it in your own words. But if you copy the specific wording, then you'll infringe the copyright on this book.

Some specific types of works that are covered by copyright are books, poetry, plays, songs, catalogs, photographs, computer programs, advertisements, labels, movies, maps, drawings, sculpture, prints and art reproductions, game boards and rules, and recordings. One yogi has even filed a lawsuit for infringement claiming others have copied his yoga poses. Certain materials, such as titles, slogans, lettering, ideas, plans, forms, useful things, nonoriginal material, and noncreative material (such as a list of names and telephone numbers) can't be covered through copyright. U.S. government publications, by law, aren't covered by copyright and may almost always be freely copied and sold by anyone, if desired.

The 1998 "Digital Millennium Copyright Act" supplements the Copyright Act and provides criminal penalties for those who provide technology that can circumvent copyright protection. (It leaves a "safe harbor" for Internet Service Providers who merely provide access to infringing materials.) It also provides a way to protect original boat hull designs.

While we provide a brief overview of copyright principles in the rest of this section, more complete discussions of this subject are available in *The Copyright Handbook: What Every Writer Needs to Know* (for written works), by Stephen Fishman (Nolo).

	Design Patent	Copyright
Permissible for all of the following:	The aesthetic aspects of articles of manufacture, such as jewelry, furniture, musical and other instruments, and fabrics.	Literary and artistic content of written materials, lectures, periodicals, plays, musical compositions, maps, artworks, software, reproductions, photographs, prints, labels, translations, movies, sculpture.
Disadvantages:	Must prepare a formal application with ink drawings, must prosecute before the PTO with legal briefs, large filing fee and issue fees, lasts only 15 years, takes a long time (one to three years) to secure rights.	Gives a narrow scope of offensive rights, no doctrine of equivalents, no protection of concepts (only particular form of expression thereof), only good against proven actual copiers (not independent creators).
Advantages:	Broader scope of offensive rights, including doctrine of equivalents (see Chapter 15), can cover concepts, good against independent creators.	Only need fill out a simple form with samples of the actual work, no formal drawings needed, no need for legal briefs, only small filing fee, no issue fee, lasts a very long time (life + 70 years or 95–120 years), instant offensive rights.
Can't be used for:	Articles where the novel features have a utilitarian function (use utility patent); writings, flat artwork, photos, maps, drawings, programs, prints, labels, movies (use copyright); surface ornamentation, or objects with a shape which appears in nature.	Utilitarian articles, unless the aesthetic features are separable from and can exist independently of the article (toys aren't considered utilitarian), machines, processes, systems, concepts, principles, or discoveries.
Recommended for:	The aesthetic shape or layout of utilitarian articles.	Articles of manufacture that aren't utilitarian, or if utilitarian, have aesthetic aspects that can be separated and exist independently, jewelry, furniture, fabrics, literary content of written materials, lectures, periodicals, plays, maps, musical compositions, artworks, software, reproductions, photographs, prints, labels with artwork, translations, movies, sculpture.

Fig. 1D—Design Patents Compared to Copyrights

1. What Is Copyright?

Now that we've seen what a copyright covers, what exactly is a copyright? As stated, a copyright is the offensive right that the government gives an author of any original work of expression (such as those mentioned above) to exclude others from copying or commercially using the work of expression without proper authorization.

To obtain copyright rights, the expressive nature of the work must be "original" to the creator, and not merely the result of extended effort. Thus, in 1991, the Supreme Court held that a telephone company that compiled, through much work, an alphabetical directory of names and addresses could not prevent another publisher from copying the directory, since the names and addresses as such were not "original" to the company. (*Feist Publications Inc. v. Rural Telephone Service Co.,* 111 S.Ct. 1282 (1991).) Also, a copyright cannot cover any system, method, process, concept, principle, or device, although it can cover a specific explanation or description of anything.

The copyright springs into existence the instant the work of expression first assumes some tangible form, and lasts until it expires by law (the life of the author plus 70 years, or for works made for hire, 95 years from publication or 120 years from creation, whichever is shorter). A work made for hire is one made by an employee in the course of the employment or by an independent contractor under a written work-made-for-hire contract.

How to Secure Offensive Copyright Rights in a Work

While no longer necessary for works published after March 1, 1989, it's still advisable first to place the familiar copyright notice (for example, Copyright © 2010 Amanda Author) on each published copy of the work. This tells anyone who sees the work that the copyright is being claimed, who is claiming it, and when the work was first published. (The year isn't used on pictures, sculptures, or graphic works.) This notice prevents an infringer from later claiming that the infringement was accidental.

Next you should register the work with the U.S. Copyright Office. If done in a timely manner, registration makes your case better if and when you prosecute a court action (for example, you can get minimum statutory damages and may be awarded attorney fees). It's useful to distinguish between steps (a) and (b), placing the copyright notice on the work and actually getting a copyright registration. Thus we suggest that you don't say, "I copyrighted my program," but rather say, "I put a copyright notice on my program," or "I applied for (or received) a copyright registration on my program."

---

2. Copyright Compared With Utility Patent

The process involved in obtaining a patent differs significantly from that of registering a copyright. A copyright is deemed to exist automatically upon creation of the work, with no registration being necessary unless you want to sue an infringer. On the other hand, to obtain patent rights, an application must be filed with the PTO, and that office must review, approve, and issue a patent.

If a copyright is registered with the Copyright Office (which technically is part of the Library of Congress) on any copyrightable material, a certificate of registration will be granted without any significant examination as to the work's novelty. The PTO (part of the U.S. Department of Commerce), on the other hand, makes a strict and thorough novelty and unobviousness examination on all patent applications and won't grant a patent unless it considers the invention novel and unobvious.

Finally, with some exceptions, the two forms of offensive rights cover types of creation that are mutually exclusive. Simply put, things that are entitled to a patent are generally not entitled to a copyright, and vice versa. However, it's important to understand that there is a small gray area where this generalization isn't necessarily true. A few creations that are both functional and expressive may be eligible for both types of coverage.

3. Areas Where Patent and Copyright Law Overlap

Let's look at these principal areas where you may be able to obtain offensive rights on intellectual property under either patent or copyright coverage, or both.

a. Computer Software

Computer programs are the best example of a type of creative work that may qualify for both a patent and copyright protection.

Viewed in the abstract, a computer program is simply an algorithm: a sequence of steps that, if performed in the right order, produces an intended result. In this view, a program is an unpatentable abstract idea. However, from another perspective, a computer or other device programmed to implement the algorithm is a tangible thing that is functionally different from other computers and devices that do not perform the algorithm. And a CD or DVD that stores the program has a different physical pattern of pits or grooves than other CDs and DVDs. (More on this topic in Chapters 5 and 9.)

Why patent a program as opposed to simply registering a copyright on it? Because the patent affords up to 20 years of broad, hard-to-design-around offensive rights for the program, even if an infringing program is created independently.

What is the drawback? It takes about two years, a considerable amount of work, and a fair amount of money, even if you do it all yourself, to obtain a patent. Because much software becomes obsolete in a much shorter time, your software may not be worth protecting by the time the patent issues. Thus, you often don't need the full term of coverage a patent offers, and money spent on obtaining one may well be wasted.

While copyrighting of programs is relatively inexpensive as well as easy to accomplish, the coverage gained isn't as broad as is offered by a patent. This is so because copyright covers only the particular way the program is written, not what it does. For instance, all major word processing programs accomplish pretty much the same tasks (such as cursor movement, screen and print formatting, search and find functions, and moving text from one location to another) but each does so through a differently expressed program, and thus each is entitled to separate copyright status. Also, a copyright isn't available against independent creators—that is, those who write a similar or even identical program without copying it from the copyrighted program. Patents, on the other hand, can be used to sue independent creators of the patented invention—that is, even if the infringer never heard of or had access to the invention.

So when choosing whether to rely on copyright or a patent for software that is tied to or transfers hardware to a machine or apparatus, the software author must weigh the broader offensive rights that a patent brings against the expense and time in obtaining one. Likewise, the ease with which copyright is obtained must be counter-balanced by the narrow nature of its coverage.

There is one further drawback to copyright for programs: If you do choose to rely on copyright rather than a patent to cover your program, and you don't publicly use it, sell it, or make it otherwise publicly known, you take the risk that someone else may patent it in the meantime.

b. Shapes and Designs

The inventor may also have a choice of utility patent or copyright in areas where an object's shape or design is both functional and aesthetic. Consider, for example, a new alphabet with letters that are attractive, yet which also provide more efficient, unambiguous spelling (such as the efficient alphabet that Shaw used to write *Androcles and the Lion*), or which are easier to read in subdued light. Patent or copyright can be used. The former will afford broader coverage to whatever principles can be identified and the latter will be cheaper, quicker, and easier to obtain, but limited to the specific shapes of the letters. Note that unlike design patents, copyright can be used to cover some aesthetic shapes even if they also have a significant function.

In many areas both forms of coverage can be used together for different aspects of the creation. Thus in parlor games, the game apparatus, if sufficiently unique, can be patented, while the gameboard, rules, box, and design of the game pieces can be covered by copyright. The artwork on the box or package for almost any invention can be covered by copyright, as can the instructions accompanying the product. Also the name of the game (for example, *Dungeons & Dragons*) is a trademark and can be covered as such.

If the invention can also be considered a sculptural work, or if it's embodied or encased in a sculptural work, copyright is available for the sculpture. However, copyright can't be used for a utilitarian article, unless it has an aesthetic feature that can be separated from and can exist independently of the article. This rule, known as the "separability requirement," is very important in copyright law.

Of course, to emphasize our earlier point, both copyrights and patents generally have their exclusive domains. Assuming they don't have any aesthetic components, patents are exclusive for machines, compositions, articles, processes, and new uses per se. On the other hand, copyrights are exclusive for works of expression, such as writings, sculpture, movies, plays, recordings, and artwork, assuming they don't have any functional aspects.

c. Copyright Compared to Design Patents

There's considerable overlap here, since aesthetics are the basis of both forms of coverage. Design patents are used mainly to cover industrial designs where the shape of the object has ornamental features and the shape is inseparable from, or meaningless if separated from, the object. For example, a tire tread design, a computer case, and the workshop clock shaped like a saw blade (see Section B, above) are perfect for a design patent, but a surface decal, which could be used elsewhere, is not. In other words, if the work is purely artistic, a design patent is improper. Copyright, on the other hand, can be used for almost any artistic or written creation, whether or not it's inseparable from an underlying object, so long as the aspect of the work for which copyright is being sought is ornamental and not functional. This means copyright can be used for pure surface ornamentation, such as the artwork on a can of beans, as well as sculptural works where the "art" and the object are integrated, such as a statue. For instance, the shape of a toy was held to be properly covered by copyright since the shape played no role in how the toy functioned and since a toy wasn't considered to perform a useful function (although many parents who use toys to divert their children would disagree). The same principle should apply to "adult toys," provided they are strictly for amusement and don't have a utilitarian function.

What are the differences in the coverage afforded by design patents and copyright? Design patents are relatively expensive to obtain (the filing fee is higher, and an issue fee is required—see Fee Schedule in Appendix 4), formal drawings are required, a novelty examination is required, and the rights last only 15 years. However, a design patent offers broader rights than a copyright in that it covers the aesthetic principles underlying the design. This means that someone else coming up with a similar, but somewhat changed design would probably be liable for patent infringement.

Copyright, on the other hand, provides relatively narrow offensive rights (minor changes in all of the artwork's features will usually avoid infringement), the government fee for registration is very small (see Fee Schedule), the term is long (the life of the creator plus 70 years, or a flat 95 or 120 years for works classified as made-for-hire). And as no novelty examination is performed, you're virtually assured of obtaining a copyright registration certificate if you file.

It has been said that a design patent is basically a copyright with the teeth of a patent because it can cover similar areas as copyright but provides broader offensive rights.

Because the distinctions between design patents and copyrights are especially confusing, I've provided a comparison chart to summarize the distinctions between these two forms in Fig. 1D.

4. When and How to Obtain Copyright Coverage

If you desire to obtain coverage for a copyrightable invention, program, creation, or for instructions, packaging, or artwork that goes with your invention, you don't need to do anything until the item is distributed or published. This is because, as mentioned, your copyright rights arise when your work is first put into tangible form. And, although there is no requirement for a copyright notice on your work before it's generally distributed to the public, I strongly advise you to put the proper copyright notice on any copyrightable material right away, since this will give anyone who receives the material notice that you claim copyright in it and they shouldn't reproduce it without permission.

When your material is distributed to the public, it's even more desirable (though no longer mandatory for works published after March 1, 1989) that you place a copyright notice on it to notify others that you claim copyright and to prevent infringers from claiming they were "innocent" and thus entitled to reduced damages. This notice should consist of the word "Copyright," followed by a "c" in a circle © (or a "p" in a circle for recordings and records), followed by the year the work is first published (widely distributed without restriction), followed by the name of the copyright owner. Thus the copyright notice on this book appears as "Copyright © 2014, 2016, and 2018 by David Pressman and Nolo. All Rights Reserved."

If anyone infringes your copyright (that is, without your permission someone copies, markets, displays, or produces a derivative work based on your original work) and you want to go to court to prevent this from happening and collect damages, you first have to register your work with the U.S. Copyright Office. If you register the work within three months of the time your item is distributed or published, or before the infringement occurs, you may be entitled to attorney fees, costs, and damages that don't have to be proved by you (called "statutory damages"). All things considered, we strongly advise you to register your work as soon as it's published if you think you're entitled to copyright coverage. The Copyright Office, Washington, DC 20559, provides free information and forms on copyright. Call 202-707-9100 or visit www.copyright.gov.

For more information on copyright law, consult Stephen Fishman's *The Copyright Handbook: What Every Writer Needs to Know* (Nolo).

Q. Trade Secrets

This section provides a basic definition of trade secrets, distinguishes trade secret protection from patents, lists the advantages and disadvantages of trade secret versus patenting, and tells you how to acquire and maintain trade secret rights.

1. Definition

Thanks to the intense coverage of the high-tech industry by the media, the term "trade secret" has become virtually a household word. You've probably heard of the case where an employee of a biotech (gene splicing) company was arrested when he tried to sell his employer's secrets to some FBI undercover agents.

What are these trade secrets and why are they valuable enough to warrant corporations paying millions of dollars to high-priced attorneys to protect them? In a sentence, a trade secret is any information, design, device, process, composition, technique, or formula that is not known generally and that affords its owner a competitive business advantage.

Among the items considered as trade secrets are:

- chemical formulas, such as the formula for the paper used to make U.S. currency
- manufacturing processes, such as the process used to form the eyes in sewing needles and the process for adhering PTFE (sold under the trademark Teflon) to a frying pan
- "magic-type" trade secrets, such as the techniques used to produce laser light shows, magician's illusions, and fireworks, and
- chemical recipes that involve both formulas and processes, such as the recipes for certain soft drinks, cosmetics, chemicals, and artificial gems; for example, Chatham, Inc., can actually make precious gems such as rubies, emeralds, and sapphires, and it relies almost exclusively on trade secrets to protect its valuable technology.

Even if the ingredients of a chemical are publicly known, the method of combining the ingredients and their sources of supply can still be a trade secret.

Obviously, since these types of information and know-how can go to the very heart of a business and its competitive position, businesses will often expend a great deal of time, energy, and money to guard their trade secrets.

When we refer to trade secrets in this book, we mean those that consist of technical information, such as in the examples given above. However, virtually every business also owns "business-information" type trade secrets, such as customer lists, names of suppliers, and pricing data. The law will enforce rights to both types of trade secrets, provided the information concerned was kept confidential and can be shown to be nonpublic knowledge and truly valuable.

More so than in any of the other intellectual property categories, the primary idea underlying trade secrets is plain common sense. If a business knows or has some information that gives it an edge over competitors, the degree of offensive rights that the law will afford to the owner of a trade secret is proportional to the business value of the trade secret and how well the owner actually kept the secret. If a company is sloppy about its secrets, the courts will reject its request for relief. Conversely, a company that takes reasonable measures to maintain the information as a secret will be afforded relief against those who wrongfully obtain the information. These central factors underlying trade secrets have profound implications for those who are seeking patents, as I discuss below.

Acquisition of Offensive Rights in Intellectual Property

If Your Creation Relates To:	Acquire Offensive Rights By:
An Invention. The functional aspect of any machine, article, composition, or process or new use of any of the foregoing—such as circuits, gadgets, apparatus, machinery, tools, devices, implements, chemical compositions, and industrial or other processes or techniques that one could discover from final product, toys, game apparatus, semiconductor devices, buildings, receptacles, and vehicles, scientific apparatus, abrasives, hardware, plumbing, parts, alloys, laminates, protective coatings, drugs,[1] timekeeping apparatus, cleaning implements, filters, or anything else made by humans where the novel aspects have a functional purpose.	Utility patent (use the rest of this book). File the utility patent application as soon as possible, but within one year of offer of sale or publication, and get a patent.
Design. Any new design for any tangible thing where the design is nonfunctional and is part of and not removable from the thing, such as a bottle, a computer case, jewelry, a type of material weave, a tire tread design, a building or other structure, any article, item of apparel, furniture, tool, computer screen icon, etc.	Design patent. File a design patent application as soon as possible, but within one year of offer of sale or publication, and get a design patent.
Plant. Any asexually reproduced plant.[2]	Plant patent (see PTO Rules 161–167).
Trademark. Any signifier, whether a symbol, sign, word, sound, design, device, shape, smell, mark, etc., used to distinguish goods (trademark) such as "Ajax"[TM] tools or distinguish services (service mark) such as FedEx. The signifier cannot be generic, for example, "electric fork," and cannot be descriptive unless adequate sales or advertising demonstrate secondary meaning.	Using it as a trademark with "[TM]" or "[SM]" superscript and then registering it in state and/or federal trademark offices. Also, you can apply to register federally before using, based upon your intent to use the mark.
Copyright. Any book, recording, computer program, work of art, musical work, dramatic work, choreographic work, graphic work, motion picture, videotape, map, architectural drawing, gameboard box and game instructions, etc.	Placing a correct copyright notice on the work, e.g., "© 1991 M. Smith"; apply for copyright registration, preferably within three months of publication.
Trade Secret. Any information whatever that isn't generally known that will give a business advantage or is commercially useful, such as formulae, ideas, techniques, know-how, designs, materials, processes, etc.	Keep it secret; establish standard operating procedures and keep good records so you can prove you kept it secret. Have employees sign "nondisclosure" or "keep-confidential" agreements and identify it as proprietary information or a trade secret (see Chapter 3) and limit its dissemination using appropriate means.
Unfair Competition. Any distinctive design, slogan, title, shape, color, trade dress, package, business layout, etc.	Using it publicly as much as possible, in advertising, etc., so as to establish a "secondary meaning" to enable you to win an unfair competition lawsuit. (See above.)

[1] Orphan drugs (those useful in treating rare diseases) can be covered under the Orphan Drug Act, 21 USC 360; write to the Food and Drug Administration for details.

[2] Sexually reproduced plants can be monopolized under the Plant Variety Protection Act, 7 USC 2321; write to Plant Variety Protection Office, National Agriculture Library, Room 500, 10301 Baltimore Boulevard, Beltsville, MD 20705. Also, both types of plants (sexually and asexually reproducible) can be covered by utility patent.

Legal Remedies for Misappropriation of Various Types of Intellectual Property	
Underlying Mental Creation	Legal Remedy for Misappropriation
Invention (machine, article, process, composition, new use)—covered by federal utility patent law.	Patent infringement litigation in federal court.
Industrial or aesthetic design—covered by federal design patent law.	Patent infringement litigation in federal court.
Brand name for a good or service; certification or collective mark or seal—covered by common law, or state or federal trademark law.	Trademark infringement litigation either before or after registration in state or federal court. Also, trademarks can be recorded with U.S. Customs and Border Protection to prevent the importation of goods with infringing marks.
Writings, music, recordings, art, software, sculpture, photos, etc.—covered by federal copyright law.	Copyright infringement litigation, after registration, in federal court.
Confidential technical or business information, not known by competitors—covered by state and federal trade secret law.	Trade secret litigation in state or federal court.
Distinctive trade dress, informative slogans, novel business layout, etc.—covered by common law, state and federal trademark and unfair competition laws.	Unfair competition or trademark litigation in state or federal court.

2. Relationship of Patents to Trade Secrets

Assuming that you have kept your invention secret, you can rely on trade secret principles to enforce rights on the invention. If your invention is maintained as a trade secret and you put it into commercial use, you must file a patent application within one year of the date the invention was used commercially. If you wait over a year, any patent that you ultimately obtain will be held invalid if this fact is discovered (and you will lose trade secret protection because your invention will have been published during the application process).

The PTO treats patent applications as confidential, so it is possible to apply for a patent and still maintain the underlying information as a trade secret—at least for the first 18 months of the application period. The PTO will publish your patent application 18 months after the earliest claimed filing date, but they will not publish it if, at the time of filing, you include a Nonpublication Request (NPR), stating that it will not be foreign-filed. (The NPR is included by checking a box on the Application Data Sheet—see Chapter 10 for more information. The 18-month publication statute was enacted in order to make U.S. patent laws more like those of foreign countries.) If you don't request nonpublication, your application will be printed verbatim after 18 months and all of your secret "know-how" becomes public and the trade secret status of your application will be lost. If you file an NPR and later file the application in a foreign jurisdiction, you must rescind the NPR within 45 days of the later filing or you will lose your U.S. application.

If you file an NPR, the information in your patent application will become publicly available only if and when a patent issues.

However, if a patent is refused so that your application is *not* published, the competition will still not know about your invention and any competitive advantage inherent in that fact can be maintained. The trade secret will remain intact. If the PTO allows your patent application, but you wish, instead of getting a patent, to preserve your invention as a trade secret, you can still choose not to pay the issue fee so that no patent will issue.

What happens if your application is not published after 18 months and a patent later issues? This public disclosure doesn't usually hurt the inventor, since the patent can be used to prevent anyone else from commercially exploiting the underlying information.

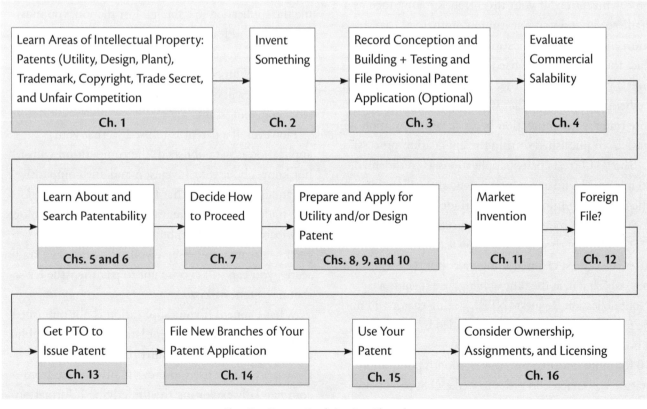

! CAUTION

If you maintain an invention as a trade secret and put it into commercial use, you *must* file any patent application within one year of the date you first used it commercially. If you wait over a year, any patent that you do ultimately obtain will be held invalid if this fact is discovered. (More on the "one-year rule" in Chapter 5, Section E.)

The following material discusses the pros and cons of each form of offensive rights.

3. Advantages of Trade Secret Protection

Often we advise people to choose trade secret rights over those afforded by a patent, assuming it's possible to protect the creation by either. Let's look at some of the reasons why:

- The main advantage of a trade secret is the possibility of perpetual protection. While a patent is limited by statute to 20 years from filing and isn't renewable, a trade secret will last indefinitely if not discovered. For example, some fireworks and sewing needle trade secrets have been maintained for decades.
- A trade secret can be maintained without the cost or effort involved in patenting.
- There is no need to disclose details of your invention to the public for trade secret rights (as you have to do with a patented invention).
- With a trade secret, you have definite, already-existing rights and don't have to worry about whether your patent application will be allowed.
- Because a trade secret isn't distributed to the public as a patent is, no one can look at your trade secret and try to design around it, as they can with the claims of your patent.
- A trade secret can be established without naming any inventors, as must be done with a patent application. Thus no effort need be made to determine the proper inventor and a company needn't request its inventor-employee to assign (legally transfer) ownership of the trade secret to it, as is required with a patent application.

Learn Areas of Intellectual Property: Patents (Utility, Design, Plant), Trademark, Copyright, Trade Secret, and Unfair Competition **Ch. 1**	Invent Something **Ch. 2**	Record Conception and Building + Testing and File Provisional Patent Application (Optional) **Ch. 3**	Evaluate Commercial Salability **Ch. 4**

Learn About and Search Patentability **Chs. 5 and 6**	Decide How to Proceed **Ch. 7**	Prepare and Apply for Utility and/or Design Patent **Chs. 8, 9, and 10**	Market Invention **Ch. 11**	Foreign File? **Ch. 12**

Get PTO to Issue Patent **Ch. 13**	File New Branches of Your Patent Application **Ch. 14**	Use Your Patent **Ch. 15**	Consider Ownership, Assignments, and Licensing **Ch. 16**

Fig. 1E—Patent Exploitation Flowchart

- A trade secret doesn't have to be a significant, important technological advance, as does a patented invention. In particular, innovative (and non-technical) business practices or insights that provide a competitive advantage are often better protected as trade secrets.
- A trade secret can cover more information, including many relatively minor details, whereas a patent generally covers but one broad principle and its ramifications. For example, a complicated manufacturing machine with many new designs and that incorporates several new techniques can be covered as a trade secret merely by keeping the whole machine secret. To cover it by patent, on the other hand, many expensive and time-consuming patent applications would be required, and even then the patent wouldn't cover many minor ideas in the machine.
- Trade secret rights are obtained immediately, whereas a patent takes a couple of years to obtain, in which time rapidly evolving technology can bypass the patented invention.

4. Disadvantages of Trade Secret Versus Patenting

Before you stop reading this book, please understand that we spent three years writing it and thousands of hours updating it for a good reason. Or put more clearly, there are many circumstances in which trade secret rights have significant disadvantages. In these contexts, using the rights provided by a patent is essential.

The main reason that trade secrets are often a poor way to cover your work is that they can't be maintained when the public is able to discover the information by inspecting, dissecting, or analyzing the product (called "reverse engineering"). Thus mechanical and electronic devices that are sold to the public can't be kept as trade secrets. However, the essential information contained in certain chemical compositions sold to the public (cosmetics, for example), and in computer programs (assuming they're distributed to the public in object code form), often can't be readily reverse engineered, and thus can be maintained as trade secrets. However, because very

sophisticated analytic tools are now available, such as chromatographs, Auger analyzers, spectroscopes, spectrophotometers, scanning electron microscopes, and software decompilers, most things can be analyzed and copied, no matter how sophisticated or small they are. And remember, the law generally allows anyone to copy and make anything freely, unless it is patented or subject to copyright coverage, or unless its shape is its trademark (a historical example is the shape of "Fotomat" huts in the 1970s and 80s), or unless its shape has become so well-known or distinctive as to be entitled to trade dress rights. (See Section R, below.)

Strict precautions must always be taken and continually enforced to maintain the confidentiality of a trade secret. If your trade secret is discovered either legitimately or illegally, it's generally lost forever, although you do have rights against anyone who purloins your trade secret by illegal means. You can sue the thief and any conspirators for the economic loss you suffered as a result of the thief's actions. In practice this amount can be considerable, since it will include the economic value of the trade secret.

Since an individual who steals a trade secret rarely has sufficient assets to compensate for the loss, the trade secret owner will often pursue the thief's new employer or whatever business purchased the secrets—usually an entity with deeper pockets. Under this approach, the trade secret owner must demonstrate the employer or business knew or had a reason to know that the secret was acquired improperly. For example, when some Hitachi employees purloined some IBM trade secrets, IBM sued Hitachi as well as the individuals concerned and actually obtained millions of dollars in compensation from Hitachi. In addition, a trade secret is more difficult to sue on and enforce than a patent. A patent must be initially presumed valid by the court, but a trade secret must be proven to exist before the suit may proceed.

A trade secret can be patented by someone else who discovers it by legitimate means. For instance, suppose you invent a new formula, say for a hair treatment lotion, and keep it secret. Jane M., who is totally unconnected with you and who has never even heard of your lotion, comes up with the same formula and decides to patent it, which she does successfully. She can legitimately sue and hold you liable for infringing her patent with your own invention!

There is one exception to this principle. If you are charged with infringement of a method patent, but you invented and were commercially using the method as a trade secret at least one year before the effective filing date of a patent, you will have what is known as "prior-user rights," a full defense to the infringement charge. This is also true (and may invalidate the interloper's patent) if you sold a product produced by the method before the patent's effective filing date.

What conclusion should you draw from this discussion? Because offensive rights connected with trade secrets continue as long as the trade secret itself is maintained, and because infringement of patents on "trade-secretable" inventions is difficult to discover, if you have an invention that can be kept as a trade secret for approximately 20 years, you may be better off doing so than obtaining a patent on it.

5. Acquiring and Maintaining Trade Secret Rights

After we explain the differences between trade secret and patents, inventors will often say to me, "I've decided trade secret is the way to go; how do I get one?" The inventor is pleased to learn that as stated, acquiring and maintaining trade secret rights involves only simple, commonsense procedures and doesn't require any governmental or bureaucratic paperwork. All that is necessary is that the inventor take reasonable precautions to keep the information confidential. Also, an employer should have all employees who have access to company trade secrets sign an agreement to keep the information confidential; see Fig. 16A (in Chapter 16) for a typical employment agreement regarding trade secrets and other employer rights. Over the years the courts have devised a number of tests for determining what these reasonable precautions should be and whether a trade secret owner has taken them.

Most states now have a statute that makes the theft of a trade secret a criminal offense as well as a civil action (for instance, the Uniform Trade Secrets Act, California Civil Code 3246 et seq.). Moreover, there is now a federal statute for the same purpose (Economic Espionage Act, 18 USC 1831 et seq.).

If you're interested in further reading on the subject, review *Nondisclosure Agreement for Inventors,* an eForm kit available for download at www.nolo.com. (Also, see Appendix 2, Resources: Government Publications, Patent Websites, and Books of Use and Interest.)

R. Unfair Competition

The area of "unfair competition" is the most difficult to explain. Although anyone who is creative, or is in a competitive business, will encounter unfair competition problems or questions from time to time, any attempts to define this area are necessarily fraught with confusion. And no wonder! The scope of unfair competition law is nebulous in the first place and is regularly being changed by judges who make new and often contradictory rulings.

1. When Unfair Competition Principles Create Offensive Rights

Fortunately, this is a patent book rather than a law school course. And, for the purpose of this book, all you really need to understand about unfair competition law can be summarized in several sentences:

- An unfair competition situation exists when one business either (a) represents or offers its goods or services in such a way as to potentially cause the class of buyers who purchase the particular type of goods or services to confuse them with goods or services offered by another business, or (b) is unjustly enriched as a result of using the fruits of the other business's labor or creativity.
- Unfair competition law is available as a source of offensive rights under common law (judge-made law) rights, the federal "false-designation-of-origin" statute (15 USC 1125(a)), and state unfair

competition statutes. One example of a state statute is California's Consumer's Legal Remedies Act (Civil Code 1750-1784 and Calif. Code of Civil Procedure 1770), which prohibits 20 categories of illegal acts, including passing off goods or services as those of another or with a deceptive representation, such as a false designation of geographical origin.

- Unfair competition can be used to cover such items as advertising symbols, methods of packaging, slogans, business names, "trade dress" (that is, anything distinctive used by a merchant to package or house its goods, such as the yellow container that has come to be identified with *Kodak* film), and titles. Also, Bette Midler successfully sued an advertising agency for using a singer whose voice sounded like Ms. Midler's. Mother Fuddrucker's restaurants sued a competitor that copied Mother's distinctive restaurant layout. And the owners of the Pebble Beach, California, golf course sued a golf course in Texas for copying Pebble Beach's distinctive layout. In other words, when the characteristics of a product or service aren't distinctive or defined enough to be considered a trademark, then unfair competition may be the appropriate way to cover it.

- If an injured party can prove that a business has engaged in unfair competition, a judge will issue an injunction (legal order) prohibiting the business from any further such activity or defining what the business can and can't do. Further, the court may award compensation (monetary damages) to the injured business (that is, the business that lost profits because of the public's confusion).

2. How Does the Law of Unfair Competition Affect You?

There are several ways in which the law of unfair competition can affect you.

- If you already have a product or service you find has been copied or pirated, and the traditional methods (patents, copyrights, trademarks, and trade secrets) are no help (perhaps because it's not patentable or it's too late to patent it, it doesn't qualify under the copyright or trademark laws, or it doesn't qualify as a trade secret), you still may be able to get relief under the law of unfair competition.

- If you're contemplating coming out with a product or service, try to make it as distinctive as reasonably possible in as many ways as reasonably possible so that you'll easily be able to establish a distinctive, recognizable appearance (termed in the law as "secondary meaning"). For example, you would be wise to use unique and distinctive packaging ("trade dress"), unique advertising slogans and symbols, a unique title, a distinctive business name, and a clever advertising campaign. And the more you advertise and expose your product, and the more distinctive (different) it is, the stronger your unfair competition rights will be.

3. Comparison of Unfair Competition With Design Patents

Some inventors confuse the trade dress area of unfair competition law with design patents. Trade dress refers to the distinctive appearance of a business, a product, or product packaging, where the appearance distinguishes the product or business from other similar products or businesses but isn't significant or specific enough to be considered a trademark. The coloring of a package or label, or the layout of a business, are good examples of distinctive trade dress.

Patentable designs, on the other hand, relate to the appearance of an article that enhances its aesthetic appeal, which is more than mere surface ornamentation and which is novel and unobvious. Examples are a modernistic lamp design and the pattern of a fabric. While trade dress can be mere coloring, surface ornamentation, or a general appearance, a design-patentable invention has to be a shape or appearance of a specific article which is more than a surface appearance, which relates to the overall appearance of the article, and which is different enough to be considered unobvious.

S. Acquisition of Offensive Rights in Intellectual Property—Summary Chart

The "Acquisition of Offensive Rights in Intellectual Property" chart, above, summarizes how an inventor or creator should acquire offense rights in every type of intellectual property.

T. Summary of Legal Remedies for Misappropriation of Various Types of Intellectual Property

Now that you're familiar with all of the types of intangible property, the "Legal Remedies" chart above summarizes how to select the appropriate remedy for any type of intellectual property dispute.

The enforcement of an intellectual property right requires considerable knowledge and experience. For background on intellectual property disputes (and to save money when consulting an attorney), consult the Nolo texts, below.

- **Copyright.** *The Copyright Handbook: What Every Writer Needs to Know,* by Stephen Fishman.
- **Trademark.** *Trademark: Legal Care for Your Business & Product Name,* by Stephen Fishman.
- **Trade Secrets.** *Patent, Copyright & Trademark: An Intellectual Property Desk Reference,* by Richard Stim.

U. Invention Exploitation Flowchart

To make it easier to use this book, we recommend you follow a five-step procedure after you invent something. The procedure can be conveniently summarized by the initials RESAM (Record it, Evaluate commercial potential, Search it, Apply for a patent, and Market it). Fig. 1E shows these steps and the other overall steps for exploiting your invention and where the chapter's instructions for these steps are found.

V. Summary

The law recognizes seven ways in which intellectual property can be monopolized or clothed with offensive rights: utility patents, design patents, plant patents, trademarks, copyright, trade secrets, and unfair competition.

Utility Patents provide a government-sanctioned monopoly on utilitarian inventions. The monopoly lasts 20 years from filing, provided three maintenance fees are paid. The U.S. Patent and Trademark Office (PTO) will grant patents only on inventions that are (a) in a statutory class (machines, articles, processes, compositions, and new uses), (b) useful, (c) novel, and (d) unobvious. The PTO charges filing and issue fees and requires a formal description of the invention with drawings, forms, and claims (legal definitions of the invention). Patents provide offensive rights but are not needed to practice one's own invention and do not protect an inventor who infringes the patents of others. After a patent expires, its monopoly no longer exists.

Design Patents provide a government-sanctioned monopoly on aesthetic or ornamental inventions; the monopoly lasts 15 years from issuance. No maintenance fees are required. The PTO will grant patents only on designs that are ornamental, involve more than mere surface ornamentation, not a natural object, novel, and unobvious. The PTO charges filing and issue fees and requires a brief description of the design with drawings and forms.

Plant Patents provide a government-sanctioned monopoly on asexually reproduced plants; the monopoly lasts 20 years from filing. No maintenance fees are required. The PTO will grant patents only on plants that are novel and unobvious. The PTO charges filing and issue fees and requires a brief description of the plant with drawings and forms.

Trademarks are signifiers (such as brand names) for goods or services. Mere use of a mark confers the user with common law monopoly rights, but it's better to register the mark with a state trademark office (intrastate use) or the PTO (interstate use). Before using, make a search of the proposed mark, considering the goods or service and the strength of mark. If confusion is not likely and the mark is not generic, the government will register it. Descriptive marks are registrable provided that the user can demonstrate sufficient sales or advertising. Before federal registration, use the mark with a "TM" superscript (^{TM}) and as a proper adjective followed by common name of goods. After registration, use the ® superscript. One can also apply to the federal government for an intent to use the mark, but one must show actual use before the PTO will register the mark.

Copyright covers works of authors, artists, photographers, composers, programmers, etc. Copyright covers only a particular form of expression of an idea, but not an idea per se. Copyright is not good for forms, TMs, slogans, methods, lists, formulae, utilitarian articles (unless artwork is separable from article), etc. On published versions of work, it's desirable to include a © notice. Copyrights last for life of the author plus 70 years, or 95 years from the date of publication in the case of a work made for hire. The work should be registered with the Copyright Office before or after publication to secure full rights.

Trade Secrets cover novel information that has some commercial advantage and is not generally known. The information must be kept secret. Trade secret rights will be lost if the secret is discovered by reverse engineering from the final product. Usually only chemical formulae, industrial and commercial processes, and programs with controlled distribution are covered by trade secrets. Trade secrets have a theoretically perpetual term, incur little cost, and provide definite, immediate rights. Patents are preferable over trade secrets as they can be used against independent creators, can't be avoided by reverse engineering, and enjoy more respect in the business and scientific community.

Unfair Competition is a catchall category based on judge-made law and "false-designation-of-origin" statutes to cover trade names, slogans, trade dress, unfair practices, unjust enrichment, "palming off," etc.

The Science and Magic of Inventing

Inventor's Commandment 2

To invent successfully, be aware of problems you encounter and seek solutions. Also, take the time to study and investigate the practicality of new phenomena whether they occur by accident or flash of insight. Persevere with any development you believe has commercial potential.

Before we get to patents, the primary subject of this book, we provide this chapter to discuss inventions and inventing. Why do this? To begin, you may be a first-time inventor and thus have no experience in the real world of protecting and patenting inventions. We believe that you'll be a better inventor if you understand and become familiar with some successful inventors and the invention process. Also, we believe that too many first-timers get discouraged before they try enough. To inspire you to hang in there, we include here some past success stories. Hopefully, when you see that many other small, independent inventors have found their pot of gold, you'll be stimulated to press on.

Inventing can not only be profitable, but it provides things that enhance our lives, making them more interesting, pleasurable, exciting, rewarding, and edu-cational. As the noted Swiss psychologist, Piaget, once said, "We learn most when we have to invent." Re-member that everything of significance, even the chair you're probably seated in now, started with an idea in someone's brain. If you come up with something, don't dismiss it; it could turn out to be something great!

Common Misconception: The day of the small inventor is over; an independent inventor no longer has any chance to make a killing with his or her invention.

Fact: As you'll see by the examples given later in this chapter, many small, independent inventors have done extremely well with their inventions. Billions of dollars in royalties and other compensation are paid each year to independent inventors for their creations. In fact 73% of all inventions that have started new industries have come from individual inventors. So,

don't be a victim of the "no-use-going-on-with-it-because-surely-someone-has-invented-it-already" syndrome. While we recommend that you don't rush blindly ahead to patent your work without making a sensible investigation of prior inventions and your creation's commercial potential (in the ways we discuss later), we urge you not to quit without giving your invention a fair chance.

Another reason for this chapter is that many inventors come up with valuable inventions, but they haven't developed them sufficiently so that they can be readily sold. If their creations could be improved with further work, they'd have a far greater chance of success. So here we'll also give some hints about such things as improving your inventions, solving problems about workability, and drawbacks.

If you've already made an invention, or are even in the business of inventing, we believe the techniques in this chapter that increase your creativity and provide additional stimulation will help you to make more and better inventions. On the other hand, we also recognize that the information in this chapter may not be particularly helpful to the experienced inventor or the corporate inventor—after all, you're already firmly in the inventing business. If you would rather skip this information for now, go to Chapter 3, where our discussion of record keeping should prove of value to even the most seasoned of inventors.

A. What We Mean by "Invention"

In its most general sense, an invention is a solution to a problem. For the purpose of this book, an invention is any thing, process, or idea that isn't generally and currently known; which, without too much skill or ingenuity, can exist in or be reduced to tangible form or used in a tangible thing; which has some use or value to society; and which you or someone else has thought up or discovered.

Note that under this definition, an invention can be a process or even an idea, so long as it can be made tangible in some way, "without too much skill or ingenuity." On the other hand, the definition eliminates fantasies and wishes, such as time-travel or perpetual motion machines, since these obviously (at least to us) can't be made tangible.

An invention must have some use or value to society; otherwise what good is it, and how will you sell it? It must be generally unknown anywhere in the world (at the time you invent it), and it must have been thought up or discovered by you or someone else—otherwise it doesn't really have inventive value.

While you may think that an invention must be a major development to be successful, the truth is that most successful inventions are evolutionary rather than revolutionary. For example, the basic concept of the transistor was invented in the 1930s, but was not feasible enough to be successful until Drs. Brittain, Bardeen, and Shockley made some evolutionary but successful improvements in the late 1940s.

Why do we bother to define the term invention in such detail? So you'll begin to understand it and have a better feel for it, as well as to define the limits of its usage in this book. As you'll see, our primary concern is with inventions that qualify for a patent (that is, patentable inventions). However, nonpatentable inventions can also be valuable as long as society finds them at least somewhat special and useful.

B. Inventing by Problem Recognition and Solution

Now that you know what an invention is, how do you make one? Most inventions are conceived by the following two-step procedure: (1) recognizing a problem, and (2) fashioning a solution.

Although it may seem like duck soup, recognizing a problem often amounts to about 90% of the act of conceiving the invention. As one wise person said, "To be an inventor is to perceive need." In these situations, once the problem is recognized, conceiving the solution is easy. Consider some of the Salton products—the home peanut butter maker, for instance, or the plug-in ice cream maker for use in the freezer. In both cases, once the problem was defined (the need for an easy homemade version of a product normally purchased at the store) implementing the solution merely involved electrification and/or size reduction of

an existing appliance. Once the problem was defined, any competent appliance designer could accomplish its solution. True, during the implementation of the idea, that is, the design of the actual hardware, designers and engineers often contribute the very aspects of the invention that make it ingenious and patentable. Still, the main ingredient leading to a successful outcome for most inventions consists of recognizing and defining the problem that needs to be solved. Although Edison seemed to contradict this when he said that inventing is 10% inspiration and 90% perspiration, he was referring to the whole experience of inventing, including conception, making a practicable model, and licensing or selling the invention. Here, we're referring just to the conception part of inventing—what Edison called "inspiration."

Of course, in some contexts, the recognition of a problem plays no part in the invention. Most improvement inventions fall into this category, such as, for example, the improvement of the mechanism of a ballpoint pen to make it cheaper, more reliable, stronger, etc. But in general, you will find it most effective to go about inventing via the two-step process of identifying a problem and solving it. Or, as famed inventor Jacob Rabinow said, "You invent because something bothers you."

Let's look at some simple inventions that were made using this two-step process and that have been commercially implemented. We delineate the problem P and solution S in each instance. Where we know an Independent Inventor was responsible, we add an II.

1. **Grasscrete.** P Wide expanses of concrete or asphalt in a parking lot or driveway are ugly. S Make many cross-shaped holes in the paving and plant grass in the earth below so that the grass grows to the surface and makes the lot or driveway appear mostly green; grass is protected from the car's tires because of its subsurface position.

2. **Intermittent Windshield Wipers.** P In drizzles, the slowest speed of windshield wipers was unnecessarily fast, and merely slowing the wipers was unsatisfactory, since a slow sweep was annoying. S Provide a "drizzle" setting where the windshield wipers made normally fast sweeps but

paused after each sweep. (Dr. Robert Kearns, Ⅲ. Dr. Kearns's brilliantly ingenious solution earned him and his estate over $50 million in royalties, after he sued Ford, Chrysler, and others, as dramatized in the movie, *Flash of Genius*.)

3. **Buried Plastic Cable-Locator Strip.** Ⓟ Construction excavators often damage buried cables (or pipes) because surface warning signs often are removed or can't be placed over the entire buried cable. Ⓢ Bury a brightly colored plastic strip parallel to and above the cable; it serves as a warning to excavators that a cable is buried below the spot where they're digging. (This is a "new-use" invention since the plastic strip per se was obviously already in existence.)

4. **Magnetic Safety Lock for Police Pistols.** Ⓟ Police pistols are often fired by unauthorized persons. Ⓢ A special safety lock inside the pistol releases only when the pistol is held by someone wearing a finger ring containing a high-coercive-force samarium-cobalt magnet.

5. **Wiz-z-er™ Gyroscopic Top.** Ⓟ Gyroscopes are difficult to get running: they require the user to wind a string around a shaft surrounded by gimbals and then pull it steadily but forcefully to set the rotor in motion. Ⓢ Provide an enclosed gyro in the shape of a top with an extending friction tip that can be easily spun at high speed by moving it across any surface. (Paul Brown, Ⅲ. Mr. Brown came up with this great invention because, while at a party, he had repeated difficulty operating a friend's son's gyro. His first royalty check from Mattel was five times his annual salary!)

6. **Dolby® Audio Tape Hiss Elimination.** Ⓟ Audio tapes played at low volume levels usually have an audible hiss. Ⓢ Frequency-selective companding of the audio during recording and expanding of the audio during playback to eliminate hiss. (Ray Dolby, one of the most successful Ⅲs of modern times.)

7. **Xerography.** Ⓟ Copying documents required messy, slow, complicated photographic apparatus. Ⓢ Xerography—the charging of a photosensitive surface in a pattern employing light reflected from the document to be copied and then using this charged surface to pick up and deposit black powder onto a blank sheet. (Chester Carlson, Ⅲ. When Mr. Carlson, a patent attorney, brought his invention to Kodak, they said it could never be commercially implemented and rejected it. Undaunted, he brought it to The Haloid Co., which accepted it and changed its name to Xerox Corporation; the rest is history.)

8. **Flip-Top Can.** Ⓟ Cans of beverage were difficult to open, requiring a church key or can opener. Ⓢ Provide the familiar flip-top can. (Ermal Frase, Ⅲ.)

9. **FM, CW, and AGC.** Ⓟ Information wasn't conveyable by radio due to noisy, limited frequency response and fade-out of AM reception. Ⓢ Provide CW, FM, and AGC circuitry, familiar to all electronic engineers. (Edwin Howard Armstrong, Ⅲ, the genius of high fidelity.)

10. **Thermostatic Shower Head.** Ⓟ Shower takers sometimes get burned because they inadvertently turn on the hot water while standing under the shower. Ⓢ Provide a thermostatic cut-off valve in the supply pipe. (Alfred M. Moen, Ⅲ.)

11. **VCR Plus.** Ⓟ In the days before streaming and "on-demand" movies, most people were too lazy or too put off by technical matters to learn how to enter a date, time, and channel into their VCR. Ⓢ With VCR Plus, each program was assigned a special code number in the newspaper TV listings and the VCR owner needed merely enter the number and transmit it to the VCR.

12. **Organic Production of Acetone.** Ⓟ During WWI, the U.K. desperately needed acetone to make explosives, since its normal source was cut off. Ⓢ Use an anaerobic bacterium to produce acetone from locally available corn mash. (Dr. Chaim Weizmann, Ⅲ. This invention helped save one nation and start a new one: It was instrumental in helping the U.K. and the Allies survive WWI and defeat the Germans. The U.K. rewarded Weizmann with the Balfour Declaration, which helped lead to the eventual formation of the State of Israel.)

13. **Grocery Shopping Cart.** Ⓟ Shoppers in grocery stores used their own small, hand-carried wicker baskets and bought only the small amounts that they could carry in the baskets, thereby necessitating several trips to the grocery and causing sales to be relatively low per customer visit. Ⓢ Provide a "grocery cart," that is, a large wire basket in a frame on wheels so that it can be rolled about and carry a large amount of groceries. (Sylvan Goldman, Ⅱ. When Mr. Goldman first introduced his carts (about 1925), shoppers wouldn't use them and stores wouldn't buy them despite his extensive efforts. He eventually found a way to get his carts accepted: He hired crews of "shoppers" to wheel the carts about and fill them in his store, and also hired a woman to offer the carts to entering shoppers. Goldman then made millions from patents on his cart and its improvements (nesting carts and airport carts). This illustrates the crucial value of perseverance and marketing genius.)

14. **Belt Loops.** Ⓟ Until 1922, men's pants (then called pantaloons) were held up by either unsightly suspenders or an awkward rope tied around the top of the pants. Ⓢ Provide "loops" at the top of the pants so that a "belt" could be inserted through the loops. (Unknown inventor).

The inventors of these inventions necessarily went through the problem-solution process (though not necessarily in that order) to make their invention. Even if an inventor believes the invention came spontaneously, you'll usually find that problem-solution steps were somehow involved, even if they appear to coalesce.

So, if you either don't have an invention or want to make some new ones, you should begin by ferreting out problem or "need" areas. This can often be done by paying close attention to your daily activities. How do you or others perform tasks? What problems do you encounter and how do you solve them? What needs do you perceive, even if they're as simple as wanting a full month's calendar on your calendar watch? Ask yourself if something can't be done more easily, cheaply, simply, or reliably, if it can't be made lighter, quicker, stronger, etc. Write the problems down and keep a list. Make sure you take the time to cogitate on the problems or needs you've discovered.

Sometimes the solution to the problem you identify will be a simple expedient, such as electrification or reduction in size. Generally, however, it will be more involved, as in some of the examples listed above. But you don't have to be a genius to come up with a solution. Draw on solutions from analogous or even nonanalogous fields. Experiment, meditate, look around. When a possible solution strikes you, write it down, even if it's in the middle of the night. History records a great number of important scientific and conceptual breakthroughs occurring during sleep or borderline-sleep states.

Also, remember that sometimes the "problem" may be the ordinary way something has been done for years, and which no one has ever recognized as a problem. Consider shower heads. Although essentially the same device operated satisfactorily for about 50 years, the inventor of water-massaging shower heads recognized the deficiency of an ordinary constant spray that didn't create any massage effect. He thus developed the water-massaging head that causes the water to come out in spurts from various head orifices, thereby creating the massaging effect.

Don't hesitate to go against the grain of custom or accepted practice if that's where your invention takes you. Many widespread erroneous beliefs have abounded in the past which were just waiting to be shattered. The medical field, in particular, had numerous nonsensical practices and beliefs, such as the use of "poudrage" (pouring talcum powder onto the heart to stimulate it to heal itself), bloodletting, and blistering, and the belief that insanity could be cured by drilling holes in the head to let the demons out. In more recent times the medical establishment believed that ulcers were caused by stress and spicy foods, but Drs. Barry J. Marshall and J. Robin Warren of Australia discovered that a bacterium was the culprit, earning them a Nobel prize. As *Forbes* magazine noted (2005 Nov 14) "great breakthroughs very often come from outsiders, entrepreneurial folk, not part of the establishment of mainstream thought."

You'll probably find the going easier if you invent in fields with which you're familiar. In this way you won't tend to "reinvent the wheel." Also, think about uncrowded fields or newly emerging ones where you will find ample room for innovation. But even if you work in an established area, you will find plenty of opportunity for new inventions.

Many inventors have discovered problems (and come up with solutions) by observing current events in the media. A number of years ago there were problems with medical personnel being stuck and infected by hypodermic needles that slipped or were used against them by disturbed patients. The result—a rash of patents on safety needles. Current problem areas such as terrorism, voting machines, alternative energy, identity theft and credit card fraud, and guerrilla warfare are creating potential markets for inventive individuals. For example, a market exists for a simple, tamper-proof, easy-to-use voting machine or a foolproof way to vote online. If you have technical ability, another way to invent is to "follow the cutting edge." Biotechnology, nanotechnology, alternative energy, energy conservation, and water purification are current hot areas.

One important principle to successful inventing is to remember the acronym KISS (Keep It Simple, Stupid!). If you can successfully eliminate just one part from any mass-produced machine, its manufacturer (or a competing manufacturer!) will be overjoyed: the cost of the machine will be reduced, it will be lighter, and, of course, it will be more reliable. Another way to look at this is Sandra Bekele's (an inventor-friend) admonition to (figuratively) "eliminate the corners." Or, to quote jazz great Charlie Mingus, "Anybody can make the simple complicated. Creativity is making the complicated simple."

Lastly, says highly successful toy inventor Richard Levy, don't go into inventing for money alone; you've got to enjoy the game and the hunt to make it all truly worthwhile.

C. Inventing by Magic (Accident and Flash of Genius)

When we don't understand how something is done, we sometimes call it "magic." Inventions made by "magic" don't involve the problem-solution technique that we just described; rather, they usually occur by "accident" or by "flash of genius." The PTO and the courts really don't care how you come up with an invention, so long as they can see that it wasn't already accomplished and it looks substantially different from what's been done before. In the hopelessly stilted language of the law, "Patentability shall not be negatived by the manner in which the invention was made." (35 USC 103.)

Many famous inventions have resulted from accident or coincidence. For example, Charles Goodyear invented rubber vulcanization when he accidentally added some sulphur to a rubber melt. In the late 1800s, a chemist supposedly accidentally left a crutcher (soap-making machine) on too long, causing air to be dispersed into the soap mixture. He found that the soap floated when it hardened, thus giving birth to floatable soap bars, such as Ivory® brand. In the 1890s the brothers W.K. and J.H. Kellogg, who ran a health sanitarium in Battle Creek, Michigan, accidentally left some of their health bread dough out overnight. They tried to salvage the stale dough by rolling it into loaves but found that it flaked into small pieces. Instead of discarding the flakes, J.H. fed them to his patients, who loved them, so they refined, ramified, and marketed them, eventually selling them as Kellogg's Cornflakes. In 1912, another chemist, Jacques Brandenberger, accidentally mixed some chemicals together and spilled them, finding they hardened to a flexible, transparent sheet (later known as "cellophane"). When Alexander Fleming accidentally contaminated one of his bacterial cultures with a mold, he was sufficiently alert and scientifically minded to notice that the mold killed the bacteria, so he carried this discovery forward and isolated the active ingredient in the mold, which later was named penicillin. (He chose not to patent it, so he got the fame, but not the fortune.)

And in 1948, Georges de Mestral, after taking a walk in the forest of his native Switzerland, noticed some cockleburs had stuck to his pants. Being of scientific mind, he removed and examined them and figured out why they adhered so well. He applied his newly discovered knowledge and as a result invented and made a fortune from hook-and-loop fasteners, which his company sold under the trademark Velcro.

In 1938 chemist Roy Plunkett, while experimenting with refrigerant fluids at a DuPont lab in New Jersey, left some fluorine-based gas in a freezer and came back to find a solid, slippery polymer that was extremely resistant to bonding and to which nothing would stick. Known initially as PTFE, it later earned billions for DuPont under the trademark Teflon.

The law considers the fact that these inventions came about by total accident, without the exercise of any creativity by their "inventors," legally irrelevant. All other things being equal, a patent on cellophane would be just as strong as one on nylon (another former trademark), the result of 12 years' intensive and brilliant work by duPont's now-deceased genius, Dr. Wallace Carothers of Wilmington, Delaware.

Since we don't understand how the "magic" occurs, we can't tell you or even suggest how to invent by accident. Please remember, however, that in case you ever come up with an accidental development, take the time and apply the effort to study, analyze, and try to "practicalize" it. If it has potential value, treat it like any other invention; the law will.

The other type of "magical" invention we'll refer to as the product of a "flash of genius." While "flash of genius" inventions inherently solve a need, the inventive act usually occurred spontaneously and not as a result of an attack on any problem. Some examples of this type are the electric knife and the previously discussed Salton inventions which actually created their own need, the Pet Rock (not a real invention by traditional definitions, but rather a clever trademark and marketing ploy, but highly profitable just the same), Bushnell's "Pong" game, the Cabbage Patch dolls, Ruth Handler's Barbie Dolls, and a client's Audochron® clock, which announces the time by a series of countable chimes for the hours, tens of minutes, and minutes. With these inventions, the inventor didn't solve any real problem or need, but rather came up with a very novel invention which provided a new type of amusement or a means for conspicuous consumption (showing off).

Although we don't understand how the creativity in these types of cases occurs, we suggest several techniques for stimulating and unlocking such creativity. Using these techniques, many inventors have come up with valuable inventions and profitable ideas and marketing ploys.

"Chance favors only the prepared mind."

—*Louis Pasteur*

D. Making Ramifications and Improvements of Your Invention

Once you've made an invention, write down the problem and solution involved. Then, try to ramify it—that is, to do it or make it in other ways so it will be cheaper, faster, better, bigger (or smaller), stronger, lighter (or heavier), longer- (or shorter-) lasting, or even just different. Why ramify?

1. Most inventors usually find that their initial solution can be improved or made more workable.

2. By conceiving of such improvements first, you can foreclose future competitors from obtaining patents on them.

3. Even if you believe your first solution is the best and most workable, your potential producers or manufacturers may not see it that way. So, it's best to have as many alternatives handy as possible.

4. When you apply for a patent, the more ramifications you have, the easier it will be to make your patent stronger.

5. Conversely, if the broad concept or initial embodiment of your invention is "knocked out" by a search of the "prior art" made by you, your searcher, or the examiner in the Patent and Trademark Office, you'll have something to fall back on, so you'll still be able to get a patent.

6. Ramifications often help you understand your basic invention better, see it in a new light, see new uses or new ways to do it, etc.

7. Ramifications can be held back and introduced later, after the basic invention has been "milked" commercially, thereby prolonging the profits, as duPont did with its Teflon®II. Be sure to try to patent the ramifications as soon as possible, however, to foreclose someone else from doing so.

In some situations, you'll find that you won't be able to ramify beyond your basic conception. But give it a try anyway, and make sure you record in writing any ramifications you do come up with as soon as possible.

One way to make ramifications is to pretend that a part of your device can't be made due to a law or crucial material shortage and then try to come up with a replacement.

In addition to making ramifications to your invention, you should, after you've finished with filing a patent application or you've gotten it out on the market, try to make improvements—that is, more substantial changes. Why? There are several reasons: (1) To extend your monopoly and keep the gravy flowing longer; (2) To enhance your credibility as an inventor—if you have several patents it will make any infringer look worse in litigation and make it easier for you to win your lawsuit; (3) Improvement patents cut off avenues that another company can use to design around your base patent; (4) A bank or financier will be more likely to lend you money if you have several patents.

E. Solving Creativity Problems

Unfortunately, hardly any invention ever works right or "flies" the first time it's built. You need to build and test it to be aware of the working problems. If you don't, the first builder, whoever it is, will inevitably face them. If this is a corporation to which you've sold or licensed your invention, it's sure to create problems. If your first construction doesn't work, don't be discouraged; expect problems and expect to solve them through perseverance. If you don't believe me, consider Edison's views on this subject:

> *"Genius? Nothing! Sticking to it is the genius! Any other bright-minded fellow can accomplish just as much if he will stick like hell and remember nothing that's any good works by itself. You've got to make the damn thing work!… I failed my way to success…. Genius is one percent inspiration and ninety-nine percent perspiration."*

If you show your invention to someone and you get static in return, don't necessarily get discouraged; the history of invention abounds with quotes from naysayers who were proved to be disastrously wrong.

The enlightening book *303 of The World's Worst Predictions*, by W. Coffey, is full of amusing and insightful erroneous quotes. Here are a few teasers:

> *"Everything that can be invented has been invented."*
>
> —**U.S. Patent Office Director, urging President McKinley to abolish the Office (1899)**

> *"What, sir? You would make a ship sail against the wind and currents by lighting a bonfire under her decks? I pray you excuse me. I have no time to listen to such nonsense."*
>
> —**Napoleon Bonaparte to Robert Fulton, after hearing Fulton's plans for a steam engine–driven boat**

> *"I think there is a world market for about five computers."*
>
> —**Thomas J. Watson, IBM President (1956)**

> *"Man won't fly for a thousand years."*
>
> —**Wilbur Wright to Orville after a disappointing experiment in 1901**

Many have analyzed the creative process, but so far no one has come up with a foolproof recipe or technique for innovating. However, almost all writers recommend that, unless you already have a "flash of genius," you first thoroughly prepare and familiarize yourself with the field, always keeping an open mind. Thereafter, some writers recommend you wait a while (allot an incubation period) to let your mind digest and work on the problem. Following incubation, work on the problem again and insight may come, sometimes in bits and pieces. "To discover something you've never seen before, walk the same path you walked yesterday." (R.W. Emerson.) Alternatively, some experts recommend that, after preparation, one make a concentrated effort, which may lead to frustration and withdrawal. But be patient, since the insight, which may be an image or a fantasy, will usually come thereafter. Of course follow-through is necessary to implement and profit from the insight or fantasy.

If you have creativity problems, such as how to make that great idea work, here are some specific techniques you can use to enhance your creativity, and hopefully solve that problem.

Frame It Differently: One of the most effective ways to solve a problem is to "frame" the problem properly. Framing is another way of describing the way in which one looks at a situation. A common example of framing a problem occurs when you try to move a bulky sofa through a small doorway. If the first way doesn't work, frame the problem differently by turning the sofa upside down and trying again. Or take another example: If you have an apparatus that includes a lever, and you can't find a design shape for the lever that the machine will accommodate, look at the situation another way; perhaps you can redesign the apparatus to eliminate the lever altogether!

Use Your Right Brain: In the course of trying to solve a problem with an invention, you may encounter a brick wall of resistance when you try to think your way logically through the problem. Such logical thinking is a linear type of process (that is, one step follows another), which utilizes our rational faculties, located in the left side of our brains. This works fine when we're operating in the realm of what we know or have experienced. However, when we need to deal with new information, ideas, and perspectives, linear thinking will often come up short. On the other hand, creativity by definition involves the application of new information to old problems and the conception of new perspectives and ideas. For this you will be most effective if you learn to operate in a nonlinear manner, that is, use your right brain or creative faculties. Stated differently, if you think in a linear manner, you'll tend to be conservative and keep coming up with techniques which are already known. This, of course, is just what you don't want.

One way to engage your right-brain faculties in a search for a creative solution to your quandary is to pose the problem in clear terms and then forget about it and think of something completely different. For example, if you can't fit that lever in your apparatus, think of a different activity, or just take a break (how about a nice boating trip or a hike in the woods). Your subconscious will work on the problem while you're "away." Then come back to the problem and force your different activity onto your problem. In other words,

try to think of the apparatus and your boating trip or hike simultaneously. You may find that a solution appears by magic (for example, you may realize a way to design the machine without the lever!).

Let Go of Assumptions: If you adhere to assumptions, you'll never innovate, since innovation, by definition, is the adoption of something new, the embarkation on an untrodden path. As Erich Fromm said, "Creativity requires the courage to let go of [assumed] certainties." So if you've got a problem, try to see what assumptions are boxing you in (they're usually hidden) and then let them go or try to cancel them—think "outside the box"—and see what you come up with.

Meditation: Another way to bring out your creativity is to meditate on the problem or meditate merely to get away from the problem. Either will help. As strange as it seems, some experts say that creativity can be enhanced during reverie by listening to a largo movement from a baroque symphony. At least you'll enjoy it! Also, the use of biofeedback machines can induce or teach deep relaxation with enhanced alpha, or even theta brain waves, a very effective stimulus to creativity.

Dreams: Some creative people find dreams the most effective way of all to solve problems. Or as Edison said: "I never invented anything; my dreams did."

Elias Howe solved the basic problem of his sewing machine in a dream. He saw some tribal warriors who ordered him to come up with a solution or they would kill him. He couldn't make a solution, so the warriors then threw their spears at him. When the spears came close, he saw that each had a hole near its tip. He awoke from the nightmare in terror, but soon realized the symbology: He put a hole near the tip of his bobbin needle and passed the thread through. Again, the rest is history.

Similarly, Mendeleev came up with the periodic table of the elements in a dream.

To stimulate creative dreaming, first immerse yourself in the problem near bedtime. Then forget about it—do something completely different and go to sleep. Your subconscious will be able to work on the problem. You'll most likely have a dream with an inspiration or insight. Then remember the dream and evaluate the insight to find out if it's correct (sometimes it won't be!).

Note that you'll forget most dreams, so keep a dream diary or notebook handy, by your bedside. Also, you'll find a pen with a built-in flashlight is also helpful. Before you go to bed, repeat fifteen times, "I'll remember my dreams." Whenever you do dream, wake up (you'll find it possible to do this if you intend to do so beforehand) and write your dreams down promptly. Once they are written down, forget about them, go back to sleep, and try to figure them out in the morning. Sometimes a week or more will pass before the meanings become clear. Or talk your dreams over with an equally inventive friend and see if he or she can get the meaning—sometimes talking about it helps.

While sleep dreams are usually the most productive, often daydreams will bring valued insight. So, don't dismiss your daydreams either!

Good luck. And pleasant dreams!

Computerized Creating: As strange as it may seem, computer technology can be used to enhance creativity, solve problems, bust through conceptual roadblocks, and get into the recesses of your memory. Several "mindware" or "CAT" (computer-aided thinking software) programs and books for this purpose exist, and I believe they can be of significant help in this area. The programs work by first asking you to enter lots of details of your problem or area and then they rearrange the details and suggest lots of modifications and permutations for you to consider. To find these programs and books, simply search "idea generator" in any search engine.

The Hot Tub Method: This has been used by many creative geniuses, starting with Archimedes who discovered the principle of volumetric measurement while in his tub. It works like this: When you relax in a hot tub for a long period, the heat on your body mellows you out and dilates your blood vessels so as to draw blood from your analytical brain, allowing your creative subconscious to come to the fore.

Unstructured Fanaticism: As "excellence guru" Tom Peters states, structured planners rarely come up with the really great innovations; monomaniacs who pursue a goal with unstructured fanaticism often do. So let yourself go and become an unreasonable lunatic—it may do the trick!

Group Brainstorming: If all else fails, get a group of friends or trusted associates together (or on a computer network) and throw the problem to the group. For some unknown reason, a group of people working together often come up with more good ideas than the same individuals working separately. This synergistic method is often used in corporations with great success. The use of others to help innovate has been called "leveraging knowledge," since one's knowledge and abilities are multiplied by others in a group. There is even brainstorming software available now.

Increase Self-Confidence: Those with more self-confidence and self-esteem tend to be more venturesome, and hence more creative. If you suffer from low self-confidence or low self-esteem, you may wish to explore local courses or read some self-improvement books.

20 Questions: Dixie Hammond of Focus Works in Van Nuys, California, suggested 20 questions you can ask to encourage ideas:

1. What if …?
2. Can we improve …?
3. How will a customer benefit?
4. Are we forgetting anything?
5. What is the next step?
6. What can we do better?
7. What do you think about …?
8. How can we improve quality?
9. How can we streamline?
10. What should we modify?
11. What should we replace?
12. What should we add?
13. What should we eliminate?
14. Can we make any new assumptions?
15. What will make it work?
16. What other ideas do you have?
17. What issues should we explore?
18. What patterns can you see?
19. How can we simplify?
20. Why?

Idea Tools: Most inventions don't work well as originally developed. Here are some suggestions for modifying your invention to make it work better:

- **Divide:** Divide it into smaller components or separate functions.

- **Combine:** Combine separate ideas, parts, or functions.
- **Simplify:** Simplify it—for example, by making it smoother, or streamlined.
- **Substitute:** Use different materials, parts, functions, or ingredients.
- **Add:** Add additional parts, movement, color, flavor, sound, functions, textures, or ingredients.
- **Subtract:** Remove parts or steps.
- **Reverse:** Reverse the mode of operation or position, or transpose cause and effect.
- **Minimize:** Make it smaller, lighter, or lower.
- **Maximize:** Make it bigger, stronger, better, higher, in multiples; exaggerate it.
- **Redesign:** Redesign the exterior or interior, change the symmetry, speed, shape, function, or perspective; give it new meaning.

F. Contact Other Inventors

In recent years, many inventors' organizations have developed or sprung up in order to provide inventors with information and ideas, model makers, lists of searchers, speakers, patent attorneys, etc., as well as to sponsor various seminars and trade fairs where inventions can be exhibited. One or more of these organizations may provide you with invaluable assistance in your inventing efforts.

One of the oldest and most well-known groups of inventors is the Minnesota Inventors Congress (www.minnesotainventorscongress.org). Inventors' organizations have a reputation for honesty and provide reasonable value for the membership or other fees charged, but check for yourself before investing a significant amount of your time or money. A listing of inventor organizations, can be found at Inventor's Digest Online, www.inventorsdigest.com. (Click on "Resources.")

You can also find inventors' groups in your area by asking the Patent and Trademark Resource Center close to you. You can find a listing of PTRCs in Chapter 6 or by visiting the PTO website (www.uspto.gov) and clicking on "Support Centers" under the "Learning and Resources" tab.

If you wish to subscribe to an online mailing inventors' group, Invent NET (www.inventnet.com) is excellent.

G. Beware of the Novice Inventor's "PGL Syndrome"

As the late successful inventor Paul Brown (he created the "Wizzzer" toy top among others) discovered, many novice inventors have a very different attitude from experienced inventors. He called this attitude the "PGL (Paranoia, Greed, Laziness) syndrome." Let's discuss the components of Mr. Brown's syndrome in more detail, since each usually is a significant hindrance for inexperienced inventors.

Paranoia: Extremely common with inexperienced inventors, paranoia (excessive suspicion of other people's motives) makes them afraid to discuss or show their invention to others—some even go as far as refusing to disclose it to a patent attorney. We do advise some measure of caution with unpatented inventions. However, once you record your invention properly (as discussed in Chapter 3), you can and should disclose it to selected persons, provided you take adequate measures to document whom you've disclosed it to and when. Don't be as paranoid as my friend Tom who invented a very valuable stereo movie invention but kept it totally to himself out of fear of theft, only to see it patented and commercialized by someone else.

Greed/Overestimation: Most people have heard fabulous stories of successful inventors who've collected millions in royalties. For example Los Angeles orthopedic surgeon and independent inventor Dr. Gary Michelson was awarded $1.35 *billion* in a settlement with Medtronic Inc. over some spinal fusion inventions. As a result, some novice inventors think that their invention is worth millions and demand an unreasonably large royalty or lump-sum payment for their creation. This is seldom wise. It is much better to set your sights at a reasonable level (see Chapter 16) so you won't miss out on commercial opportunities.

Laziness: Some novice inventors believe that all they need to do is show their invention to a company, sign a lucrative contract, and let the money roll in. Unfortunately it hardly ever happens so easily. To be successful, you usually have to record your invention properly, build and test a working model (desirable but not always necessary), file a patent application, seek out suitable companies to produce and market the invention, and work like crazy to sell the invention to one of these companies.

H. Don't Bury Your Invention

If you believe that you have what will turn out to be a successful idea, but you have doubts because it's very different, or you get negative opinions from your friends, consider that Alexander Graham Bell was asked by an irate banker to remove "that toy" from his office. The "toy" was the telephone. Or if that doesn't convince you, ponder these words of Mark Twain, Albert Einstein, and John Shedd:

"The man with a new idea is a crank—until the idea succeeds."

—*Mark Twain*

"For an idea that does not at first seem insane, there is no hope."

—*Albert Einstein*

"Opportunities are seldom labeled."

—*John Shedd*

And as a successful inventor, Nolan Bushnell, *(Pong)* said, "Everyone who's ever taken a shower has an idea. It's the person who does something about it who makes a difference."

Don't forget that, in addition to making money if you're successful, an invention can create jobs, make our lives easier and more interesting, and eliminate drudgery. Consider the Linotype® machine, where each machine eliminated 90 manual typesetters and their arduous task and spawned a new industry and profession. Then came the computer, where each modern computer replaced nine Linotype machines, spawned another new industry and gave almost anyone the ability to create typeset documents. If you still doubt the value of inventors and inventions, consider this: without inventors and their inventions, we would still be living the way we lived 50,000 years ago!

We hope you've received our message in this chapter loud and clear. If you have a worthwhile invention, and you scrupulously follow all the advice and instructions given in this and the succeeding chapters, and persevere, we believe you'll have a very good chance of success.

"Each invention leads to new inventions and each discovery to new discoveries; invention breeds invention, science begets science, the children of knowledge produce their kind in larger and larger families; the process goes on from decade to decade, from generation to generation."

—*Alfred Korzybski*

I. Summary

The day of the lone inventor is not over; many successful inventions and industries have been started by independent inventors.

Most inventions are created after recognizing a problem and finding a solution. However, inventions are also made by "magic" (accident and flash of genius), the process of which is not easily analyzed.

If you make an invention, try to conceive of ramifications to enhance its value. If you have trouble solving invention problems, persevere, frame the problem differently, use nonlinear techniques, let go of assumptions, try meditation, employ your dreams, the computer, use brainstorming, inventors' organizations, and other techniques. Beware of the novice inventors' PGL Syndrome (paranoia, greed, laziness). Above all, persevere!

Documentation and the PPA

Inventor's Commandment 3

In case you later need to prove you are the inventor of an invention and the date when you invented it, after you conceive of the invention, you shouldn't proceed to develop, build, or test it, or reveal it to others, until you (1) write in ink or type a clear description of your invention on paper, (2) sign and date the same, and (3) have this document signed and dated by two trustworthy people who have "Witnessed and understood" your write-up.

Inventor's Commandment 4

(1) For commercial evaluation reasons, and in case of an invention dispute, try to build and test your invention (if at all possible) as soon as you can, (2) keep full and true written, signed, and dated records of all the efforts, correspondence, and receipts concerning your invention, especially if you build and test it, and (3) have two others sign and date that they have "Witnessed and understood" your building and testing. (As an alternative—or in addition—to documenting, building, and testing in this manner, you can use the PTO's Provisional Patent Application program, but be aware of the disadvantages and limitations of the PPA.)

A. Introduction

There are two distinct and important reasons why all inventors should document all of their work. The first has to do with the inventing process itself. The second involves the possibility that you will need to prove that you are the inventor and when you made the invention.

B. Documentation Is Vital to the Invention Process

It takes more than a good idea to sustain the invention process. It is absolutely essential to keep good, sound, and complete records, for two sets of reasons, the invention process (explained below) and to prove inventorship and date if ever necessary.

1. Good Engineering Practice

Good engineers and technicians record their developments in chronological order so that they can refer back to their engineering diary at any time— days, weeks, months, or even years later. First, this enables them to avoid running up the same blind alley twice. Second, good records will shed light on subsequent developments, will allow the inventor to find needed data and details of past developments, and will provide a base for new paths of exploration and ramifications, especially if failures have occurred.

2. Psychological Stimulus

Many of us come up with great ideas, especially when we're engaged in some other activity (including dreaming), and we forget to write them down. If we could get into the habit of writing down our thoughts on a piece of paper, later on we'd find that piece of paper there to bug us, almost forcing us to do something about it. So, keep a small pencil or pen and paper with you at all times, and write down your thoughts as soon as they occur.

3. Analysis Stimulus

WWII Admiral Raborn once said, "If you can't write it down, you don't really know what you are doing."

Putting a description of your idea in writing forces you to think about it and crystallize it into communicable form. Note that no matter how great your idea, and no matter how much of the work you do yourself, you'll never be able to make a nickel from it until you can communicate it to others, for example, to get a patent, to license it, or to sell the product.

"Writing forces you to think and get your thoughts straight."

—*Warren Buffett*

C. Documentation Has Legal Implications

There are several reasons why it's legally important promptly and properly to record your conception of your invention.

1. Proof in Case of Theft

If someone sees or hears about your invention and attempts to "steal" it by claiming it as his or her own invention (in actuality, a rare occurrence), there will probably be a lawsuit or other proceeding (a derivation proceeding for applications filed on or after 2013 Mar 16) in which the true and first inventor must be ascertained. In such a proceeding, the side with the earliest, best, and most convincing evidence will win. 'Nuff said!

2. Proof in Case of Confusion of Inventorship

Often several engineers or friends will be working on the same problem, and if inventorship isn't promptly recorded, memories fade and there will be confusion as to who is (are) the actual inventor(s). Also, bosses and other supervisors have been known to claim inventorship, or joint inventorship, in an employee's invention. If all inventors promptly recorded their inventions, signed and dated them, and got them witnessed and dated, preferably by coworkers (including bosses), there would be very few cases of such confusion of inventorship.

3. Supporting Tax Deductions

Once you make an invention and spend any money on your creation, the IRS considers that you are "in business," thus enabling you to file a "Schedule C" or "Schedule E" (Form 1040) with your tax return to deduct all expenditures you made for your invention, from even ordinary income (not investment income) that you received. The IRS will be far more inclined to allow these deductions (assuming you're audited) if you can support them with full, clear, and accurate records of all of your invention activities, including, but not limited to, conception, building, and testing, and expenditures for tools, plastics, other materials, models, etc.

4. Avoidance of Ownership Disputes

Suppose you make an invention in a specific area—say bicycles—and later you go to work for a company engaged in this area—say a bicycle manufacturer. If you haven't already filed a patent application on your bike, you'll have a very hard time proving you already made the invention before your employment with this company if you haven't kept a proper record. In this situation and in many others, the company (or an individual or other organization with whom you deal) will likely claim ownership of your prior invention under your employment (or other) agreement unless you have the "paper" to prove prior invention.

D. Trade Secret Considerations

An invention can qualify as a trade secret, at least for the first 18 months of the patent application period. After 18 months, the PTO will publish the patent application unless the applicant files, at the time of filing, a Nonpublication Request (NPR). Applications that are not published after 18 months will remain as trade secrets until the patent issues. Keeping an invention secret can provide its owner with certain obvious commercial advantages, and the owner may have recourse in the courts against any person who improperly discloses the secret to others.

Whether your invention is to be patented or kept as a trade secret (you can decide later), you should first record it properly so that you can prove that you invented it and that you did so as of a certain date. Since you can keep your notebook confidential, at least for the time being, no loss of any potential trade secret protection will result from your making a proper record of your conception.

CAUTION

Remember that while recording your invention can be vital in the situations outlined above, it provides only limited rights, since it won't give you any weapon to use if anyone independently comes up with your creation, or if anyone copies your invention once it's out on the market. To acquire full offensive rights in these situations, you need to obtain a patent on your invention. Only a patent will give you rights against independent creators of your invention and those who copy it once it's out on the market.

E. Record Conception and the Building and Testing of Your Invention

After you conceive of your invention you should record the conception in a lab notebook or an invention disclosure as explained below. After recording conception, you should try to build and test your invention as soon as you can and keep detailed and adequate records of your efforts.

1. Keep Good Records of Building and Testing Activity

The building and testing of an invention can be as (or even more) important than its conception, and faithfully keeping a journal of those activities can be vital proof of your invention in case of theft, confusion of inventors, and the need to establish tax deductions. However, the recordation of your efforts to build and test your invention is no longer necessary to obtain a patent, except if a special situation occurs that requires you to prove your development efforts.

EXAMPLE: On 2013 March 23 (after the First-to-File law took effect), Millie invents a new hands-free computer pointing device that uses eye motions, thereby eliminating the need for a mouse. She writes up the details of her creation, signs and dates it, and has two witnesses sign and date it, thereby documenting conception. She builds and tests it and then writes up a description of the device and its operation and documents this

in the same way. Harry, a janitor in her lab, sees her invention while performing his duties. Harry tells his brother Jake, who files a patent application on the device in his name. A few months later Millie files her patent application. The PTO rejects Millie's application on Jake's earlier filing date. Millie files a derivation proceeding against Jake and his earlier-filed application and shows her earlier records of conception and building and testing before Jake's filing date and also shows that Jake's brother Harry had access to her invention. The Patent Trial and Appeal Board finds that Jake derived the invention from Millie and can either order Millie's name to be substituted for Jake's in Jake's application or Jake's application to be rejected as anticipated by Millie's earlier work.

Note: It is not necessary to prove building and testing to win a derivation proceeding, although it will surely help. If you can't or don't build and test, your record of conception will be sufficient.

2. Keep Your Building and Testing Activity Confidential

If, as part of the testing of your invention, you have to order any special part or material, or if you have to reveal to or discuss your invention with anyone to get it built or documented, be cautious about how and whom you contact. And when you do make any specific revelation, have the recipient of the information about your invention (the receiving party) sign a Nondisclosure Agreement ("NDA") (see Appendix 7).

Getting the Agreement Signed

Model makers and machine shops are used to signing these agreements. When you make an appointment to show your invention and you wish to have the recipient sign the agreement before viewing, it's only courteous and proper business practice to advise the recipient that you are bringing along a nondisclosure agreement (NDA) before signing. Don't spring the agreement in a surprise manner.

The agreement is completed by specifically identifying the confidential materials (documents or hardware) (the "Confidential Information"), and the name of the recipient (the Receiving Party; you're the Disclosing Party). Have the Receiving Party fill in, sign, and date the bottom of the agreement. Give a copy of the signed NDA to the Receiving Party, as well as any extra copies that may be needed if any other persons in the Receiving Party's organization are to sign also.

Note that if you are lending confidential materials to the Receiving Party, the agreement refers to the delivery of materials to the Receiving Party as a "loan." This will give you maximum rights if the Receiving Party makes unauthorized use of or refuses to return the materials.

It's also desirable to document everything you transact with the receiving party by sending a confirmatory email after each transaction and getting receipts or acknowledgments for everything you do lend or deliver. In other words get and make a full "paper trail" of your activities.

This agreement will cover almost all situations where you need to disclose your invention or deliver proprietary materials under an NDA. However, it isn't cast in stone: If, for example, you are making more than a loan of the materials, feel free to redraft the agreement, for example, by changing "loaned" to "delivered."

> **CAUTION**
>
> **About NDAs:** While it's desirable to have receiving parties sign an NDA, note that if a receiving party steals or copies your invention (rare for uncommercialized inventions), your NDA will be of little value unless (a) you have the funds to hire an attorney to sue the invention thief, or (b) your case is strong and worthwhile enough that you can get an attorney to take it on a contingent-fee basis. Even then the thief can (a) raise defenses that may defeat your suit (nothing is certain in the law), (b) show that you have no actual monetary damages, and (c) be judgment proof (that is, have no assets to pay you for your damages). It's best to investigate (or "vet") your receiving party beforehand by getting references and making sure that he or she is a responsible person or organization.

F. How to Record Your Invention

There are several ways to record your invention, discussed below, together with examples.

1. The Lab Notebook

The best way to record inventorship is by using a blank or lab notebook. Preferably, it should have a thick cover, with the pages bound in permanently, such as by sewing or gluing or a closed spiral binding. Also, the pages should be consecutively numbered. Lab notebooks of this type are available at engineering and laboratory supply stores, and generally have crosshatched, prenumbered pages with special lines at the bottom of each page for signatures (and signature dates) of the inventor and the witnesses. As should be apparent, the use of a bound, paginated notebook that's faithfully kept up provides a formidable piece of evidence if your inventorship or date of invention is ever called into question. A bound notebook with consecutively dated, signed, and witnessed entries on sequential pages establishes almost irrefutably that you are the inventor—that is, the first to conceive the invention—on the date indicated in the notebook. Lab notebooks can be purchased through Fisher Scientific (www.fishersci.com) or Scientific and Engineering Notebook Company. (www.snco.com).

If you don't have or can't get a formal lab notebook like this, a standard bound letter-paper-size crackle-finish school copybook will serve. Just number all of the pages consecutively yourself, and don't forget the frequent dating, signing, and witnessing, even though there won't be special spaces for this. Date each entry in the notebook as of the date you and your coinventor(s), if any, make the entries and sign your name(s). If you made the entries over a day or two before you sign and date them, add a brief candid comment to this effect, such as, "I wrote the above on July 17, 2016, but forgot to sign and date it until now." Similarly, if you made and/or built the invention some time ago, but haven't made any records until now, again state the full, specific, and truthful facts and date the entry as of the date you write the entry and sign it. For example, "I thought of the above invention while trying to open a can of truffles at my sister's wedding reception July 23 (2015), but didn't write any description of it until now when I read *Patent It Yourself.*"

2. How to Enter Technical Information in the Notebook

Fig. 3A is an example of a properly completed notebook page showing the recordation of conception, and Fig. 3B shows recordation of building and testing.

The sketches and diagrams should be clearly written (preferably double-spaced) in ink to preclude erasure and later-substituted entries. Your writing doesn't have to be beautiful and shouldn't be in legalese. Just make it clear enough for someone else to understand without having to read your mind. Use sketches when and wherever possible since readers will find these far easier to comprehend than words. Many inventors have told me they put off writing up their invention in a notebook or invention disclosure because they didn't know the proper "legal" terms to use, or had writer's block. However, as indicated, legalese isn't necessary or desirable. There are two very good ways to bypass writer's block:

- Rely mostly on sketches, with brief labels explaining the parts and their functions.
- Make sketches, describing them orally to a friend, and record your oral description with a tape recorder. Then go back and transcribe your description.

Do not leave any large blank spaces on a page—fill the page from top to bottom. If you do need to leave space to separate entries, or at the bottom on a page where you have insufficient space to start a new entry, draw a large cross over the blank space to preclude any subsequent entries, or, more accurately, to make it clear that no subsequent entries could have been made in your notebook.

If you make a mistake in an entry, don't attempt to erase it; merely line it out neatly and make a dated note why it was incorrect. The notation of error can be made in the margin adjacent to the correct entry, or it can be made several pages later, provided the error is referred to by page and date. Don't make cumulative changes to a single entry. If more than one change

is required, enter them later with all necessary cross-references to the earlier material they supplement. Refer back to earlier material by page and date.

If possible, make all entries directly in the notebook, or copy them there from rough notes on the day the notes were made. If this isn't possible, make them as soon as practicable with a notation explaining when the actual work was done, when the entries were made, and why the delay occurred.

If you've made an invention several months ago, and are now going to record it because you've just read this book, you should date the entries in the notebook when you actually write them, but you should also write when you actually made the invention and explain the delay with honesty and candor! Since the notebook is bound, you will have to handwrite the entries in it. Again, don't worry about the quality of your prose—your goal is only to make it clear enough for someone else to understand; use labeled sketches or the tape recorder/transcription techniques given above if writer's block occurs. If handwriting is difficult for you, or if your handwriting is illegible, you can use an Invention Disclosure form, described below.

3. What Should Be Entered in the Notebook

Your notebook should be used as a "technical diary"—that is, you should record in it anything you work on of technical significance, not just inventions. The front of the notebook should have your name and address and the date you started the notebook. When you record the conception of your invention, you and anyone who later sees the notebook will find it most meaningful if you use the following headings:

- Title (what your invention is called)
- Purpose (what purpose the invention is intended to serve)
- Description (a functional and structural description of the invention)
- Sketch (an informal sketch of the invention)
- Ramifications (include all ramifications of the invention that you have conceptualized; If you fail to include a ramification and one of your witnesses thinks of it, the witness may have to be named as a coinventor if you file a patent application)

TITLE: Self-Adjusting Can Opener   23

PURPOSE: To provide a can opener that self-adjusts to any size can.

DESCRIPTION: The can opener has a sliding clamp with a locking groove at its edge
[etc.] … I conceived of this while I was at my friend Roberta's wedding last Sunday
and saw the caterer having trouble opening small and large cans with several
openers…

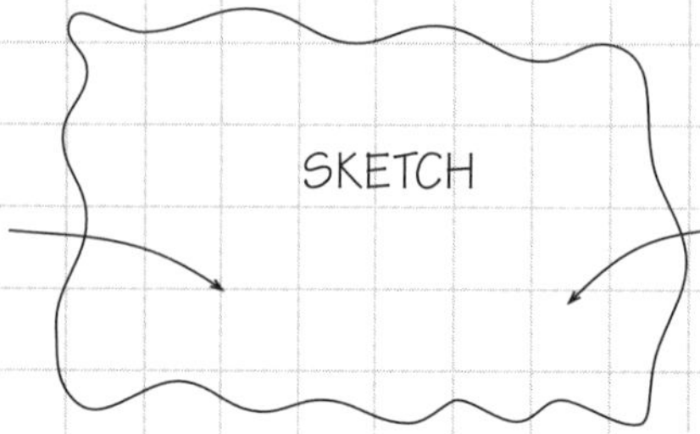

Locking groove   SKETCH   Sliding clamp

RAMIFICATIONS: Instead of the locking groove, a special notch could be used as follows:

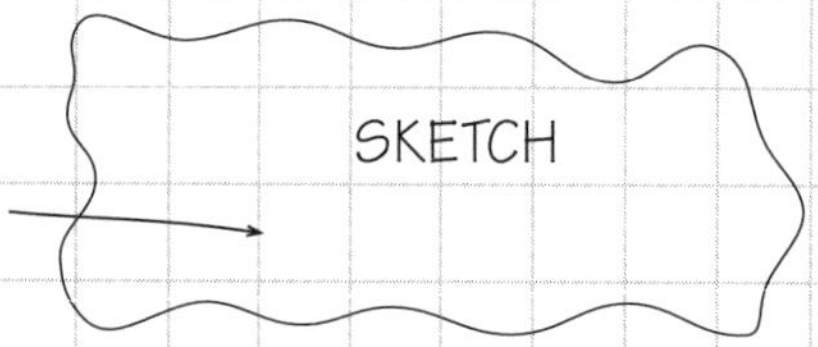

Notch   SKETCH

POSSIBLE NOVEL FEATURES: The sliding clamp with a raised frammis arm is believed
entirely new. Also, [etc.]…

ADVANTAGES: This can opener would eliminate the need for separate can openers for
different sized cans, thereby providing economy, ease of use, [etc.]…

INVENTOR: DATED:

Irma Inventor   *20xx/8/25*

THE ABOVE CONFIDENTIAL INFORMATION IS WITNESSED AND UNDERSTOOD:

Wilfred Witness   *20xx/9/25*

Alberta Attestor   *20xx/9/25*

Fig. 3A—Properly Completed Notebook Page Showing Conception

TITLE: Self-Adjusting Can Opener — Building & Testing   27

REFERENCE: Conception recorded on page 23.

DESCRIPTION: A working model of this opener was made for me by Fred Smith of
    Model Makers, Inc., starting Sept. 1. It was finished Sept. 13. It was made of
    cold-rolled steel, 13 mm. thick, with brass bearings [etc.]…

Here is the photo we took on Sept. 15:

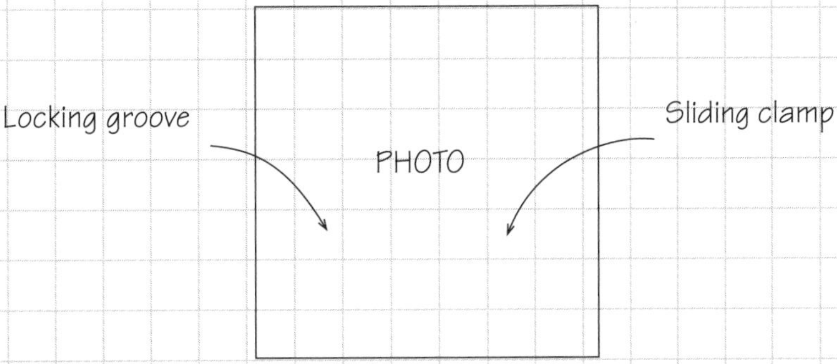

Locking groove   PHOTO   Sliding clamp

RAMIFICATIONS: We also tried a nylon hinge, but it did not work because…

TEST DESCRIPTION: We tried the opener on fifty different cans, from size __
    to size __ …

TEST RESULTS: For the size __ cans, the opener worked as well as the Ajax brand,
    opening each can in an average time of 8.3 seconds, the same as we obtained with
    the Ajax brand. [etc.]…

INVENTOR: DATED:

Irma Inventor   *20xx/9/27*

THE ABOVE CONFIDENTAL INFORMATION IS WITNESSED AND UNDERSTOOD:

Steve Elias   *20xx/9/27*

Fred Friendly   *20xx/9/27*

Fig. 3B—Properly Completed Notebook Page Showing Building and Testing

- Novel features (include all possible novel features of the invention)
- Closest known prior art (the closest known existing approach of which you're aware), and
- Advantages (of the invention over previous developments and/or knowledge—see the example in Fig. 3A).

Don't forget to sign and date your conception and have two witnesses also sign and date the record of conception.

To record the subsequent building and testing of your invention at a later page of the notebook, you will find it most useful to record the following items:

1. Title and Back Reference
2. Technical Description
3. Photos and/or Sketches
4. Ramifications
5. Test Description
6. Test Results
7. Conclusion.

Fig. 3B (above) shows a properly done lab notebook record of the building and testing of an invention. Don't forget to sign and date, and have your witnesses also sign and date, the building and testing record, as well as the conception record. (See Section 5, below.)

If you're skilled enough to conceive, build, and test your invention all at once, just combine all of the items of Figs. 3A and 3B as one entry in your notebook.

Record as much factual data as possible; keep conclusions to a minimum and provide them only if they are supported by factual data. Thus, if a mousetrap operated successfully, describe its operation in enough detail to convince the reader that it works. Only then should you put in a conclusion, and it should be kept brief and with an opinion. For example, "Thus this mousetrap works faster and more reliably than the Ajax brand." Sweeping, opinionated, self-congratulating, or immodest statements tend to give an impartial reader a negative opinion of you or your invention. However, it's useful to include the circumstances of conception, such as how you thought it up and where you were. This makes your account believable and helps refresh your memory later.

Word all entries so that they're complete and clear in themselves—that is, so that anyone can duplicate your work without further explanation. While you shouldn't use the lab notebook as a scratch pad to record every calculation and stray concept or note you make or think about, you also shouldn't make your entries so brief as to be of no value should the need for using the notebook as proof later arise. If you're in doubt as to whether to make an entry, make it; it's better to have too much than too little.

Also, you'll find it very helpful to save all of your "other paperwork" involved with the conception, building, and testing of an invention. Such paperwork includes correspondence and purchase receipts. These papers are highly trustworthy and useful as evidence, since they are very difficult to falsify. For example, if you buy a thermometer or have a machine shop make a part for you, you should save receipts and canceled checks from these expenditures since they'll tie in directly with your notebook work.

4. How to Handle Computer Printouts, Large or Formal Sketches, Photos, Charts, or Graphs Drawn on Special Paper

If you have any computer printouts or any other items that by their nature can't be entered directly in the notebook by hand, you should make or enter them on separate sheets. These, too, should be signed, dated, and witnessed and then pasted or affixed in the notebook in proper chronological order. The inserted sheet should be referred to by entries made directly in the notebook, thus tying them in to the other material. Photos or other entries that can't be signed or written should be pasted in the notebook and referenced by legends (descriptive words, such as "photo taken of machine in operation") made directly in the notebook, preferably with lead lines that extend from the notebook page over onto the photo, so as to preclude a charge of substituting subsequently made photos (see Fig. 3B). The page the photo is pasted on should be signed, dated, and witnessed in the usual manner.

If an item covers an entire page, it can be referred to on an adjacent page. It's important to affix the items to the notebook page with a permanent adhesive, such as white glue or nonyellowing (frosty) transparent tape. If you have to draw a sketch in pencil and want to make a permanent record of it (to put in your notebook) without redrawing the sketch in ink, simply make a photocopy of the penciled sketch: voilà—a permanent copy!

If you make any drawings, photos, or prints that are too large to paste in your notebook, then you have two choices. You can fold them to notebook size and glue them into the notebook so that they can be unfolded and examined without removing them from the notebook. Or you can leave them separate from the notebook, but refer to, and describe them in the notebook. In either case, be sure to sign, date, and get witnesses to sign and date these large documents.

5. Witnessing the Notebook

The witnesses chosen should be as impartial and competent as possible, which means they shouldn't be close relatives or people who have been working so closely with you as to be possible coinventors. A knowledgeable friend, business associate, or professional will make an excellent witness, provided he or she has the necessary technical ability or background to understand the invention. Generally, a witness who understands what the invention does and how it's made and used will be adequate. But if the invention is technically complex, it's best to get a witness who understands the invention's underlying theory. The witness should also be someone who's likely to be available later. Obviously, a person who's seriously ill, or of very advanced age, wouldn't be a good choice. Don't ask your patent attorney (if you are using one) to perform this function, since the courts and the PTO won't allow an attorney to represent someone and also be that person's witness.

If the invention is a very simple mechanical device, practically anyone will have the technical qualifications to be a witness. But if it involves advanced chemical or electronic concepts, obviously a person with an adequate background in the field will have to be used. The witness need not understand the theory behind the invention, but should be knowledgeable enough to understand what it does and how it works. If called upon later, the witnesses should be able to testify to their own knowledge that the physical and/or chemical

facts of the entry are correct. Thus they shouldn't just be witnesses to your signature, so you should not use a notary or a layperson who just witnesses your signature, as do witnesses to a will. Rather the witnesses should actually read or view and understand the actual technical subject material in the notebook, including the actual tests if they are witnessing the building and testing (Fig. 3B). Obviously, then, you should call in your witnesses to observe your final tests and measurements so that they can later testify that they did witness them.

Should You Have Your Notebook Entries or Disclosure Notarized?

Many inventors ask if they should take their notebook or disclosure to a notary and sign it before the notary and have the document notarized. While notarization is slightly better than no witnesses at all, notarization is far inferior to live witnesses. Why? In the U.S. system of jurisprudence, the triers of fact (judge or jury) base their decisions primarily on the testimony of live witnesses, who are subject to cross examination and who understand the document in question and are not merely a "signature witness."

While one witness may be sufficient, the law gives much greater credence to two. If both are available, your case will be very strong. Also having two witnesses will enhance the likelihood of at least one of them being available to testify at a later date. Also, if a dispute occurs between two inventors, the one with the greater number of witnesses will prevail, assuming all other considerations are substantially a wash.

Some notebooks already contain, on each page, a line for the inventor's signature and date, together with the words "Witnessed and Understood" with lines for two signatures and dates. If your notebook doesn't already contain these words and signature lines, merely write them in as indicated in Figs. 3A to 3C. To really tie down the trade secret status of your invention, you should add the words "The above confidential information is" just before the words "Witnessed and Understood," as has been done on

Form 3-2 and on Figs. 3A, 3B, and 3C. You and the witnesses should sign and enter the date on the appropriate lines at the end of your description of the conception of your invention and at the end of your description of your building and testing.

6. What to Do With the Notebook

Now that you've made those nice notebook records of conception and hopefully building and testing, what should you do with the notebook? Nothing, except to keep it in a safe place in case it's ever needed (hopefully not!).

G. Another Way to Record Conception or Building and Testing— The Invention Disclosure

Suppose you conclude that for some good reason it's too difficult or inconvenient for you to keep a notebook or technical diary. There's a second, albeit somewhat inferior, way for you to record the conception or building and testing of your invention. This is by using a document called an "Invention Disclosure."

Despite its formidable name, an Invention Disclosure is hardly different from a properly completed notebook entry of an invention. It should be a complete record of your invention, including a title, its purpose(s), advantages, a detailed description of it, in sufficient detail so that one having ordinary skill in the field of your invention will be able to make and use it, possible novel features, ramifications, details of its construction if you built it, and results obtained, if any. As with the notebook, include sketches when and wherever possible. While it might better be called an "Invention Record," in the arcane world of patents it's called a "disclosure," since an inventor often uses it to disclose an invention to others to get their opinion, have them develop it, and show what progress is being made. These entries should be made on a separate sheet of paper that has no other information on it except details of your invention and your name and address. For your convenience, Appendix 7 provides an Invention Disclosure form, and

Fig. 3C illustrates how the form should be completed to record conception.

Since an Invention Disclosure isn't bound, the writing on it can, and preferably should, be printed or typed. But if you do write rather than type, just make sure your handwriting is legible. A sheet of professional or personal letterhead (if you have it) is suitable for an Invention Disclosure. Otherwise print your name, address, and telephone number at the top (or bottom, after your signature). Business letterhead is okay if the invention is to be owned by your business. If the disclosure runs to more than one page, you should write the title of your invention on the second and each succeeding page, followed by the word "continued," numbering each page and indicating the total number of pages of the entire disclosure—for example, "Page 1 of 3."

As before, the description of your invention should be signed and dated by you, marked "The above confidential information is Witnessed and Understood," and signed and dated, preferably by two witnesses, who, as before, are technically competent to understand your invention and who actually do understand and have witnessed the subject matter you have entered on your Invention Disclosure. If you use more than one page, each should be signed and dated by both the inventor and the witnesses. Again, to guarantee the trade secret status of your invention, you should make sure the words "The above confidential information is" appear just before the words "Witnessed and Understood."

As with the notebook, if you conceive of an invention on one date and build and test the invention later, you should make two separate invention disclosures. Also, as with the notebook, keep the disclosure in a safe place.

TIP

If you've conceived of or have effectively built and tested your invention on a computer, you must print out a hard copy on paper so that you and your witness can sign it properly. Computer records (absent hard-copy printouts) are too impermanent to be given legal credibility.

Invention Disclosure

Sheet __1__ of __1__

Inventor(s): _____Irma Inventor_____

Address(es): _____1919 Chestnut St., Philadelphia, PA 19103_____

Title of Invention: __Self-Adjusting Can Opener__

To record **Conception**, describe: 1. Circumstances of conception, 2. Purposes and advantages of invention, 3. Description, 4. Sketches, 5. Operation, 6. Ramifications, 7. Possible novel features, and 8. Closest known prior art. To record **Building and Testing**, describe: 1. Any previous disclosure of conception, 2. Construction, 3. Ramifications, 4. Operation and Tests, and 5. Test results. Include sketches and photos, where possible. Continue on additional identical copies of this sheet if necessary; inventors and witnesses should sign all sheets.

I thought of this can opener while at my friend Roberta's wedding last Sunday. I saw the caterer having trouble opening small and large cans with several openers. Thinking there was a better way, I recalled my Majestic KY3 sewing machine clamp and how it was adjustable and thought to modify the left arm to accommodate a can opener head.

My can opener will work with all sizes of cans and is actually cheaper than the most common existing one, the UR4 made by Ideal Co. of Racine, WI.

My can opener comprises a sliding clamp 10, a pincer groove 12, [etc.] as shown in the following sketch:

Sketch:

Operation: The user operates the can opener in the same way as any squeeze-and-turn opener for any size can.

Instead of sliding clamp 10, I can use a special notch as follows:

I believe that the combination of sliding clamp 10 and pincer groove 12 is a new one for can openers. Also I believe that it may be novel to provide a frammis head with my whatsit.

The Acme KZ122 can opener, mfgd. by Acme Kitchenwares of Berkeley, CA, and p. 417 of "Kitchen Tools & Their Uses" (Ready Publishers, Phila. 1981) show the closest can openers to my invention, in addition to the devices already mentioned.

Inventor(s): ____Irma Inventor____ Date: _20XX_ / _Jul_ / _6_

Date: _____ / _____ / _____

The following understand, have witnessed, and agree not to disclose the above confidential information:

____Griselda Hammelfarb____ Date: _20XX_ / _Jul_ / _7_

____Neonore Zimla____ Date: _20XX_ / _Jul_ / _10_

Fig. 3C—Invention Disclosure (Form 3-2 in Appendix 7)

H. The Provisional Patent Application— A Substitute for Building and Testing, With Some Disadvantages

Suppose you don't have the facilities, skill, or time to build and test your invention, and you are not in a position to file a complete utility patent application right away. In this case you may file a Provisional Patent Application (PPA) that will serve as a legal alternative to building and testing a utility invention. (The PPA is not available for design patents.) This proves to the PTO that, at the very least, you conceived your invention on or before the day you filed the PPA.

Let's explore the PPA and the advantages and disadvantages of using it.

1. What a Provisional Patent Application (PPA) Is

A PPA is a less formal version of, and usually shorter than, a regular patent application. It is used to establish an early filing date for a later-filed Regular Patent Application (RPA). A PPA must contain:

1. a detailed description of the invention telling how to make and use it
2. drawing(s), if necessary to understand how to make and use the invention
3. a cover sheet, fee transmittal form (prepared automatically if the PPA is filed electronically), and Certification of Micro-Entity Status (if paying the micro-entity fee)
4. a fee (micro entity (ME), small entity (SE), or large entity—see Appendix 4, Fee Schedule), and
5. a return receipt postcard (not required if PPA is filed electronically).

In actuality the term "PPA" is a misnomer, since it is a simple document deposit, not an application (a request for something). Since a PPA is not even a true application, it is not and should never be called a patent.

2. What a PPA Is Not

A PPA is not a regular patent application (RPA) and therefore cannot by itself result in a patent. For those readers already familiar with the regular patent application process described in Chapter 8, the PPA, unlike an RPA, does not require:

- a Patent Application Declaration (PAD)
- an Information Disclosure Statement (IDS)
- patent claims
- an abstract or summary
- a description of the invention's background, or
- a statement of the invention's advantages.

If you don't file an RPA within a year of your PPA's filing date, your PPA will go abandoned and will be of little value. Also, your PPA cannot provide a filing date for subject matter that is not disclosed in it.

3. What a PPA Accomplishes

Once you file a PPA, you will be considered to have acquired an effective filing date, assuming that:

- an RPA (and optionally one or more foreign patent applications) are filed on the invention within one year, and
- the PPA fully describes the invention claimed in the RPA.

Being able to claim the PPA's filing date allows you to overcome any prior-art reference that is cited in opposition to your application and has a publication or filing date that is after your filing date.

4. Advantages of a PPA Over Building and Testing

In addition to the benefits of an early filing date, the PPA gives you the right to claim that your invention has "patent pending" status. In common parlance this means that you can publish, sell, or show your invention to others without fear of theft or loss of any domestic rights. This is because anyone who sees and steals your invention after you file your PPA would have a later filing date than yours.

Assuming you prepare it properly, there are other advantages to using a PPA in place of actually building and testing the invention. These are:

- You need not keep meticulous records of whatever building and testing you do accomplish.
- You need not obtain witnesses.
- You can be certain that your PPA will provide excellent proof of inventorship.
- You will be certain that your PPA's early filing date can be relied upon, provided your

description of the invention in the PPA is legally sufficient as described below.

- You can file a technical article (which you might have written anyway) as a PPA. (But remember, the article, to be adequate for a PPA, must fully disclose how to make and use the invention claimed in the RPA. As stated, the RPA must be filed within one year.)

- You can file a PPA, then within one year, file an RPA, which has the practical effect of delaying examination of the RPA and extending—up to one year—your patent's expiration date. In other words a PPA gives you a filing date that does not start your 20-year patent term. Pushing your patent monopoly term ahead a year can be profitable if your invention is ahead of its time and is likely to have its best sales 20 years from now—for example, as often happens with drugs.

- If you've filed an RPA and wish to restart your 20-year term, you can do so by converting the RPA to a PPA and then filing a second RPA. To make the conversion, file a petition (a simple request letter will do) with the prescribed conversion fee within one year of the RPA's filing date. The PPA will take the first RPA's filing date. Then file the second RPA, also within one year of the first RPA's filing date. The second RPA should claim the benefit of the PPA's filing date. The second RPA will expire 20 years from its own filing date, so you've restarted your 20-year term about a year later, albeit at a price.

- You can refer to your invention as patent pending once you've filed a PPA. This can be a marketing advantage, especially with companies that will not discuss any invention that is not patent pending.

- Suppose you file a PPA and then, within a year, you file an RPA that claims the benefit of the PPA's filing date. If your RPA issues as a patent it will be effective as a prior-art reference as of its PPA's filing date.

- If you are able to license or sell your invention before it is time to file an RPA, your licensee or buyer will have the opportunity to prepare and file the RPA using their own lawyers.

- Preparing an RPA after you've prepared a PPA will give you a second opportunity to perfect your application.

- If you file a PPA and thereafter make any changes in the invention, you can file additional PPAs to cover the changes. You can claim the benefit of as many PPAs as you want in any RPA(s) you file, so long as all PPAs you claim priority from were filed within a year preceding the RPA's filing date.

- You can put multiple inventions in a single PPA and claim the benefit of these in separate RPAs, provided the RPAs are filed within a year after the PPA was filed.

5. Disadvantages of the PPA

Alas, every silver box seems to contain a cloud. The disadvantages of filing a PPA are as follows:

1. You may tend to forgo building and testing and lose the concomitant advantages, such as determining whether the invention is operable, practical, or useful, and having a working prototype to demonstrate to prospective manufacturers.

2. Your PPA may fail to contain a full a description of how to make and use the invention or any embodiment of it. In this case, you won't be able to rely on the PPA's filing date for the invention or any embodiment.

3. You may unintentionally forgo foreign protection. This is because you cannot wait one year after filing the RPA, as is usually done, to foreign file. Instead you must make your foreign filing decision, as well as your regular U.S. filing decision, within one year after your PPA is filed. As I will discuss in Chapter 12, foreign filing is extremely expensive and few foreign filers ever earn their outlay back.

4. You may try to license or interest a manufacturer in your invention in the approximately ten-month period between the time you file the PPA and the time you must begin preparation of your RPA. Since ten months is usually too short a period to license an invention, you may get discouraged and fail to file an RPA and thus give up a potentially valuable invention.

5. If you file an RPA that claims the date of your PPA, and you do not file a Nonpublication Request (see Chapter 10), at the time you file the RPA, your RPA will be published 18 months after you file the PPA, or about six months after you file the RPA. You may not want your application published so early as it will end trade secret status.

Note that the PTO has published the following cautions regarding PPAs:

- PPAs are not examined on their merits.
- The date of a PPA cannot be claimed if an RPA has not been filed within one year.
- A PPA cannot claim the benefit of an earlier application (foreign or domestic).
- The disclosure of a PPA must be clear and complete enough so that an ordinary person skilled in the field of the invention can make and use the invention.
- All contributors to the inventive subject matter of the PPA must be named in the PPA.
- The RPA must name at least one inventor that was named in the PPA.
- In order for an RPA to claim the date of the PPA, the PPA must be filed with the proper fee and must be complete.
- If the basic fee is not paid with the PPA, the fee can be paid later, but the PTO charges a penalty fee.
- PPAs are not available for designs.
- No subject matter can be added once the PPA is filed.
- No patent will result from the PPA unless an RPA is filed within a year or the PPA itself is converted to an RPA.

6. PPA Misconceptions

There are many common misconceptions circulating about what a PPA can accomplish. Here are some.

Common Misconception: The PTO will read and examine and reject or approve your PPA.

Fact: The PTO will never examine or read your PPA unless you need to rely on its date and ask the PTO to do so in order to obtain the benefit of the PPA's filing date.

Common Misconception: After filing your PPA, the PTO will grant you a provisional patent.

Fact: The PTO will never "accept," "grant," or "reject" your PPA on any substantive ground. There is no such thing as a "provisional patent" and your PPA will be discarded if you don't file an RPA within one year that claims the benefits of the PPA's date.

Common Misconception: You can modify your invention after filing a PPA and still claim its benefits.

Fact: If you have an invention in your RPA that isn't in your PPA, you will simply not be able to obtain the benefit of your PPA's filing date for that invention, if you ever need it. If you have an invention in your PPA that isn't in your RPA, the PTO won't care. You can put any and all inventions you want into a PPA and you can do the same with your RPA. (However if your RPA claims multiple inventions the PTO will require you to restrict the claims to one invention.)

Common Misconception: Filing a PPA provides the right to stop others.

Fact: A PPA is a simple placeholder that confers no rights, except the right to rely on its date if it's prepared properly and you file an RPA within a year.

7. How to Prepare and File a PPA

Ideally, the more your PPA resembles the RPA you file within the following year, the more you can be assured that you will be able to claim the PPA's filing date. For that reason, my general recommendation is that you follow the basic rules for writing an RPA set out in Chapter 10. But, since your PPA will not be examined by the PTO unless and until you file an RPA—and then only to see whether it adequately describes the invention being claimed in the RPA—your description need not:

- be a polished presentation (it should be clearly written and understandable)
- contain claims, or
- be typed in any particular format.

As explained below, there are two ways to file a PPA with the PTO: (a) electronically using the PTO's EFS-Web procedures over the Internet (preferred), and (b) by mail (includes personal delivery in case you live near the PTO in Alexandria, Virginia). Whether preparing a PPA for electronic filing or mail, you will need to:

- prepare drawings, if necessary (these need not be polished, but should be understandable)
- prepare a complete description of the structure and operation of your invention
- prepare a PPA cover sheet and (if filing by mail) a fee transmittal
- prepare a Certification of Micro-Entity Status (if paying the micro-entity fee)
- (if filing by mail) prepare a receipt postcard and check or credit card authorization, and
- (if filing electronically) prepare an Application Data Sheet (ADS) (although it's desirable to include an ADS if filing by mail, as well).

PPAs: The Long and the Short

You can fully describe your invention by supplying the information contained in the Description and Operation sections of the Specification in the RPA (and drawings, if necessary). In others words, if you follow the instructions for drafting these two sections in Chapter 8, you will have an adequate PPA.

Generally, a richer or more fulsome PPA is recommended. This should include information contained in other sections of the RPA (the Background, Objects and Advantages, Drawing Figures, Reference Numerals, Summary, Description, Operation, at least one Claim, and the Abstract). If you follow the instructions for drafting these sections in Chapters 8 and 9, you will have a more-than-adequate PPA.

To give you an idea of the difference between the bare-bones and recommended PPA, compare two PPAs on the same invention: Fig. 3D provides an example of the bare-bones approach; while Fig. 3E shows a preferred, fulsome PPA. (An RPA filed on this invention issued as Pat. No. 6,018,830 on 2000 Feb 1, and is titled Adjustable Sleeping Bag With Drawcords.)

In keeping with our recommendation that you make your PPA look as much like your RPA as feasible, prepare your drawings and description as described in Chapter 8. Although you legally don't need to include the Background, Advantages, Description of Drawing Figures, List of Reference Numerals, Summary, Conclusion, or Abstract parts of the specification, it won't hurt if you do, and including these parts will make your PPA that much more effective if it is later relied upon. Your drawings can be informal drawings; they need not be inked or done carefully with a CAD program, but they (and the description) must be in permanent form (no pencil).

You also don't need to include any claims (discussed in Chapter 9). However, if possible, it is a good idea to draft some claims before filing the PPA, since this exercise will help you determine whether your detailed description includes everything necessary about your invention. Also some foreign jurisdictions may require that the application contain a claim to obtain priority.

CAUTION

Provide a Full Description of Your Invention. While it need not be well written or use any legalese, your "description" MUST comply with the full disclosure requirements—that is, it MUST clearly teach how to make and use the invention and it MUST disclose the best mode or version you currently prefer, if it has several modes or versions. To this end, carefully review and follow the material in Chapter 8.

Your description should be written in as simple terms as possible so that a lay judge can understand it or can be easily taught to understand it. If the invention is technical or abstruse, start your description from ground zero, assuming your reader knows nothing about the field, and then gradually move up to the minimum technical level necessary, defining all technical terms. In addition, your invention must be in a statutory class (see Chapter 5, Section C, for more on statutory classes). For software inventions, this means that the invention must be intimately involved with hardware.

Provisional Patent Application of

Robert H. Howe

for

TITLE: ADJUSTABLE SLEEPING BAG WITH DRAWCORDS

DESCRIPTION

FIG. 1 is a perspective view taken from the user's right side of a sleeping bag 11 constructed in accordance with the invention. An upper portion 12 of the bag has a drawcord 14, circumferentially mounted within a fabric casing sleeve 15, and secured by cord lock 16. Such cord arrangements are repeated at each of locations 19, 20, 21, and 22. Each sleeve 15 and each contained drawcord 14 extends only across the upper portion of the bag, from a zipper 17 on the right side of the bag, to a corresponding location 18 (FIG. 2) on the left side. The bottom portion of the bag (not shown) has no drawcords. The drawcords are made of stretchable elastic or nonstretchable material (nylon), while the sleeves are preferably made of the same material as the bag's outer shell, e.g., nylon or rayon. Such sleeves may be sewed, glued, or thermally bonded to the outside of the outer shell.

FIG. 2 is a left perspective view of the bag, showing left-side seam 18 and showing drawcord 14 mounted within sleeve 15 and secured by cord lock 16 at locations 19, 20, 21, and 22. Note that each sleeve 15 and its contained drawcord extends only over the top portion of the bag, from seam 18 to zipper 17.

FIG. 3 is a lateral cross-section through bag 11 at location 19 showing zipper 17, side seam 18, and drawcord 14 relaxed and secured by cord lock 16 while mounted within fabric casing sleeve 15. Sleeve 15 is sewn to outer shell fabric 25. Inner lining fabric 24 and insulation 23 are not compressed since drawcord 14 is relaxed. An occupant 26 of the bag is shown in a horizontal position; note that the bag fits loosely around the occupant and that there is a lot of air space between occupant 26 and the bag. A conventional underlying insulating pad or mat 27, e.g., of foam is used under the bag.

FIG. 4 is a lateral cross-section through sleeping bag 11 at location 19 with drawcord 14 tightened and secured by cord lock 16. Inner lining fabric 24 and insulation 23 are gathered together where they are surrounded by tightened drawcord 14. Note that the

Fig. 3D—Provisional Patent Application Without Embellishments

bag now fits relatively closely or tightly around occupant 26 and that there is very little air space left between occupant 26 and the bag. Insulating pad 27 is again shown under the bag.

OPERATION

In operation one uses the bag in a normal manner with insulating pad 27 under the bag. The user can, when desired, increase the warmth of the bag by tightening the drawcords and securing them with cord lock 16 (FIGS. 3 and 4). When the drawcords are tightened, five effects increase the bag's warmth:

(1) Insulating layer 23 and the inner lining fabric 24 surrounding occupant 26 become thicker.

(2) This increase in thickness also makes the bag less susceptible to the user narrowing the insulation by body movement, e.g., by poking the insulation with an elbow.

(3) The surface area of outer shell fabric 25 exposed to cold air is reduced.

(4) Since the drawcord extends only over upper portion 12 of the bag, lower portion 13 does not tend to be raised from pad 27 beneath the bag to be exposed to cold air.

(5) The air space between occupant 26 and the bag is reduced.

When the user wishes to increase the inner volume of the bag to provide greater freedom of movement (at some loss of insulating ability), it is only necessary to relax the drawcords (FIG. 3) and allow the bag to expand.

Fig. 3D—Provisional Patent Application Without Embellishments (continued)

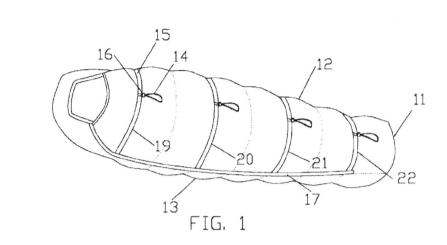

FIG. 1

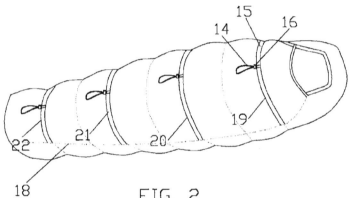

FIG. 2

FIG. 4

FIG. 3

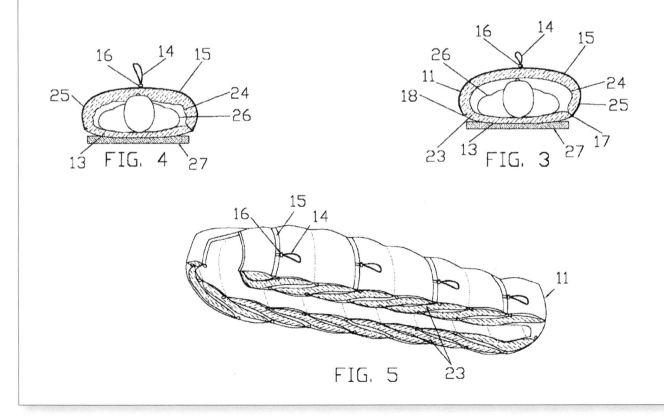

FIG. 5

Fig. 3D—Provisional Patent Application Without Embellishments (continued)

Provisional Patent Application of

Robert H. Howe

For

TITLE: ADJUSTABLE SLEEPING BAG WITH DRAWCORDS

CROSS-REFERENCE TO RELATED APPLICATIONS: None.

FEDERALLY SPONSORED RESEARCH: None.

SEQUENCE LISTING: None.

BACKGROUND

This relates to sleeping bags, specifically to insulated sleeping bags having means that allow users to adjust the insulating ability and internal volume of the bags. Sleeping bags can be uncomfortable, and when they're uncomfortable, they can deny their users much-needed rest. Sleeping bag comfort is largely a matter of warmth— that is, providing the bag's user with the correct amount of insulation to suit the existing conditions—and a matter of providing the user with adequate freedom of movement. These two aspects of sleeping bag comfort can work against each other. For similarly shaped bags, the more room there is inside a bag, the more freedom of movement its user has. However, the more room inside a bag, the more air space the user's body is required to heat and the more outer bag surface is exposed to the cold. Most sleeping bags provide comfort in only a rather narrow range of temperatures. So, sleeping bag manufacturers have long sought means of effectively adjusting the suitability of sleeping bags to fit a wider range of temperatures.

Both U.S. Pat. No. 2,350,410 to Matthesius (1944) and U.S. Pat. No. 1,583,419 to Perl (1926) show sleeping wraps for infants. These bags have side cords which are tied around the upper portion of each of the wraps after an infant is placed on top of the wrap and the flat sides of the wrap are folded around the infant. With both of these wraps the cords are primarily to allow one to complete closure of the wraps. Therefore, they should not be considered sleeping bags but rather, what they clearly are—sleeping wraps for infants. Perl states, "the straps 15 will serve to prevent the possible moving and kicking of the infant from dislodging the cover portion."

Fig. 3E—Provisional Patent Application With Embellishments

2

Both wraps are flat, it is presumed, because it is easier and safer to lay a sometimes struggling, usually writhing infant on a flat surface and fold and tie the sides around the infant than it is to insert the infant into a bag. While the cords of these two wraps may be drawn more or less tightly about the infant before tying, neither wrap is adapted for simple adjustment of its internal volume.

One method used to optimize the warmth and roominess of a sleeping bag is shown in U.S. Pat. No. 5,473,779 to Kramer (1995), where nonadjustable, permanently attached bands of elastic material are incorporated into the portion of the bag surrounding the user's knees and legs. The object is to provide increased freedom of movement while still reducing the inner volume of the bag to optimize bag warmth. However the greater freedom of movement is provided only to the knees and legs. The bag cannot be adjusted to adapt it for cooler or warmer temperatures.

The lower portions of insulated sleeping bags are typically less insulated than the upper portions of the same bags because bag manufacturers rely on bag users to employ well-insulated mats under the sleeping bags. Bag manufacturers rely on such mats for good reasons—they are cheap, effective, and not as compressed by the weight of the user as is the insulation contained in the lower portion of a sleeping bag. If a good insulating mat is not placed under a sleeping bag, it is likely that more warmth will be lost to the ground by conduction than will be lost by convection to the air above the sleeper.

However even if a good ground pad is used with the bag shown in U.S. Pat. No. 4,888,828 to Tatsuno (1989), its effectiveness will be reduced. This is because Tatsuno uses nonadjustable elastic members that are permanently sewn into the bag in circumferential rings spaced axially along the bag. These rings totally encircle the bag and the bag's user and this presents a problem. By totally encircling the bag, each elasticized member pulls an area of the lower portion of the bag up and away from the underlying insulated pad. Thus, these areas are no longer insulated by full contact with the underlying insulating mat as they would otherwise be, but are instead exposed to cold air.

Roach, in U.S. Pat. No. 4,894,878 (1990) shows a bag with a liner whose circumferential dimension can be reduced by a zipper to create increased overlap of the bag's insulating batts and hence more insulation. However, it is difficult to reach an inside zipper to make the necessary adjustment.

Hunt, in U.S. Pat. No. 3,857,125 (1974) shows an insulated bag with inner and outer shell layers that are differentially cut, except in a small portion of the bag, that provides more freedom of movement for the user's shoulders. This differential

Fig. 3E—Provisional Patent Application With Embellishments (continued)

3

cut, Hunt claims, minimizes compression of the insulation when body pressures are exerted against the outer shell. Hunt also claims that the inner shell provides self-adjusting inward lofting of the insulation in the shoulder and chin areas. Hunt's bag provides a hood that surrounds the user's face. Hunt positions the adjustable end of a drawcord used to tighten this hood at one side of the user's face and sews the drawcord to the bag at the other side of the user's face. This, it is claimed, allows the user to independently adjust the tightness of that part of the hood that is above the face. While the effectiveness of providing separate adjustability in areas that are so close together is debatable, one thing is certain: Hunt's bag in no way addresses the need for a bag with adjustability in the fit of the upper insulation.

Demini Sports, of Amsterdam, Holland, has sold a sleeping bag since the early 1970s with drawcords which encircle the bag at spaced locations along the bag. However these bags suffer from the same defect as Tatsuno's, above. I.e., since the means for compressing the bag completely encircle it, they draw the lower portion of the bag away from the underlying insulating ground pad, which, as stated, users normally provide under this type of bag.

In conclusion, insofar as I am aware, no sleeping bag formerly developed provides volume adjustability to a user without the defect of drawing the lower portion of the bag away from the underlying insulating ground pad.

SUMMARY

An improved sleeping bag has adjustable drawcords attached to the outer shell fabric. These drawcords extend only over the top portion of the bag. Cord locks are provided to tighten the drawcords to any desired degree of warmth. The drawcords are encased in drawcord sheaths extending only across the upper portion of the bag. This allows a user to reduce the inner air space of the bag without reducing the effectiveness of the insulation of the lower portion of the bag and without the discomfort of inner encircling drawcords.

Accordingly several advantages are to provide an improved sleeping bag, to provide means of increasing the warmth of a sleeping bag during cooler weather, to provide a bag with increased freedom of movement during warmer weather, and to provide a more user-friendly, yet economical sleeping bag. Still further advantages will become apparent from a study of the following description and the accompanying drawings.

Fig. 3E—Provisional Patent Application With Embellishments (continued)

4

DRAWINGS

FIG. 1 is a perspective right-side view of a sleeping bag constructed in accordance with the invention, showing the upper half of the bag.

FIG. 2 is a perspective left-side view of the sleeping bag of FIG. 1.

FIG. 3 is a lateral cross-sectional view of the sleeping bag of FIGS. 1 and 2 with the drawcord relaxed.

FIG. 4 is a lateral cross-sectional view of the sleeping bag of FIGS. 1 and 2 with the drawcord tightened.

FIG. 5 is a perspective view of the bag taken from above, showing its insulation.

DETAILED DESCRIPTION

FIG. 1 is a perspective view taken from the user's right side of a sleeping bag 11 constructed in accordance with one embodiment. An upper portion 12 of the bag has a drawcord 14, circumferentially mounted within a fabric casing sleeve 15, and secured by cord lock 16. Such cord arrangements are repeated at each of locations 19, 20, 21, and 22. Each sleeve 15 and each contained drawcord 14 extends only across the upper portion of the bag, from a zipper 17 on the right side of the bag, to a corresponding location 18 (FIG. 2) on the left side. The bottom portion of the bag (not shown) has no drawcords. The drawcords are made of stretchable elastic or nonstretchable material (nylon), while the sleeves are preferably made of the same material as the bag's outer shell, e.g., nylon or rayon. Such sleeves may be sewed, glued, or thermally bonded to the outside of the outer shell.

FIG. 2 is a left perspective view of the bag, showing left-side seam 18 and showing drawcord 14 mounted within sleeve 15 and secured by cord lock 16 at locations 19, 20, 21, and 22. Note that each sleeve 15 and its contained drawcord extends only over the top portion of the bag, from seam 18 to zipper 17.

FIG. 3 is a lateral cross-section through bag 11 at location 19 showing zipper 17, side seam 18, and drawcord 14 relaxed and secured by cord lock 16 while mounted within fabric casing sleeve 15. Sleeve 15 is sewn to outer shell fabric 25. Inner lining fabric 24 and insulation 23 are not compressed since drawcord 14 is relaxed. An occupant 26 of the bag is shown in a horizontal position; note that the bag fits loosely around the occupant and that there is a lot of air space between occupant 26 and the bag. A conventional underlying insulating pad or mat 27, e.g., of foam is used under the bag.

Fig. 3E—Provisional Patent Application With Embellishments (continued)

5

FIG. 4 is a lateral cross-section through sleeping bag 11 at location 19 with drawcord 14 tightened and secured by cord lock 16. Inner lining fabric 24 and insulation 23 are gathered together where they are surrounded by tightened drawcord 14. Note that the bag now fits relatively closely or tightly around occupant 26 and that there is very little air space left between occupant 26 and the bag. Insulating pad 27 is again shown under the bag.

REFERENCE NUMERALS

11 sleeping bag

12 upper portion of sleeping bag

13 lower portion of sleeping bag

14 drawcord

15 fabric casing sleeve

16 cord lock

17 zipper

18 side seam

19 sleeve location

20 sleeve location

21 sleeve location

22 sleeve location

23 insulation

24 inner lining fabric

25 outer shell fabric

26 occupant

27 insulating pad

Fig. 3E—Provisional Patent Application With Embellishments (continued)

6

OPERATION

In operation one uses the bag in a normal manner with insulating pad 27 under the bag. The user can, when desired, increase the warmth of the bag by tightening the drawcords and securing them with cord lock 16 (FIGS. 3 and 4). When the drawcords are tightened, five effects increase the bag's warmth:

(1) Insulating layer 23 and the inner lining fabric 24 surrounding occupant 26 become thicker.

(2) This increase in thickness also makes the bag less susceptible to the user narrowing the insulation by body movement, e.g., by poking the insulation with an elbow.

(3) The surface area of outer shell fabric 25 exposed to cold air is reduced.

(4) Since the drawcord extends only over upper portion 12 of the bag, lower portion 13 does not tend to be raised from pad 27 beneath the bag to be exposed to cold air.

(5) The air space between occupant 26 and the bag is reduced.

When the user wishes to increase the inner volume of the bag to provide greater freedom of movement (at some loss of insulating ability), it is only necessary to relax the drawcords (FIG. 3) and allow the bag to expand.

CLAIM

1. A sleeping bag, comprising:

- an upper portion which will overlie the body of an occupant when said occupant is in a horizontal position in said sleeping bag, and

- a lower portion which underlies the body of said occupant, said lower and upper portions being joined at opposite sides of said sleeping bag,

- at least one drawcord attached to said upper portion of said sleeping bag, said drawcord not extending onto said lower portion of said sleeping bag, said drawcord having two ends which are attached to said respective opposite sides of said sleeping bag,

whereby (a) during cold weather, an occupant of said sleeping bag can tighten and clamp said drawcord so that the inner volume and the exposed outer surface area of said sleeping bag can be reduced in order to better insulate said occupant, (b) contact

Fig. 3E—Provisional Patent Application With Embellishments (continued)

7

between said lower portion and any underlying flat insulated pad will not be reduced when said drawcord is tightened, and (c) said occupant of said sleeping bag can relax the tension on said drawcord during warmer conditions and thereby increase the volume of air within said sleeping bag adjacent said occupant of said sleeping bag in order to give said occupant more freedom of movement.

ABSTRACT

A sleeping bag (11) design for providing adjustability of the inner volume and outer exposed surface area of the bag comprises sheathed drawcords (14), preferably elastic, attached only to the top or upper portion of the bag and secured by cord locks (16). A user of the bag can tighten the drawcords during cold weather, thereby providing a warmer bag by reducing the inner volume and the exposed outer surface area of the bag without reducing the thermal protection provided to the lower portion of the bag by an underlying flat insulated pad, as would be the case with drawcords fully encircling the bag. During warmer weather, the user can relax the drawcord adjustment, thereby providing the user with more freedom of movement. Thus a considerably more versatile sleeping bag is provided—that can be adjusted to provide more warmth during cold weather or more freedom of movement during warmer weather.

Fig. 3E—Provisional Patent Application With Embellishments (continued)

Qualifying as a Micro Entity

As of March 2016, inventors paying patent fees at the U.S. Patent and Trademark Office (USPTO), can choose from Column A (Regular Fee), Column B (Small Entity Status), or Column C (Micro-Entity Status). If the filer qualifies for small entity status, the USPTO offers a half-price discount, and a filer that qualifies as a micro entity receives a 75% discount on most fees. The goal of this multi-tiered system is to provide a break for smaller companies and independent inventors, and to encourage innovation.

Qualifying as a Small Entity. To qualify as a small entity you must either be an individual, a small business concern having no more than 500 employees (or affiliates), a university, or a 501(c)(3) nonprofit organization.

If you qualify as a small entity, you need only verify that status by executing a declaration when paying the fee. If, however, you are obligated to license or assign the patent to a bigger entity that doesn't qualify as a small entity—for example, you license your patent to Microsoft—then you could not claim small entity status. Improperly claiming small entity status is considered inequitable conduct and can result in the loss of patent rights.

Qualifying as a Micro Entity. To qualify as a micro entity, the filer must meet small entity requirements and must also meet the following criteria:

(1) The applicant has not been named as the inventor on a total of more than four utility patents (regular utility patents, not provisional patent applications), design patents or plant patents. This also does not include certain international PCT applications and applications owned by a previous employer. In addition, the applicant had to have had a gross income in the previous year of less than three times the median household income reported by the Bureau of the Census (The median household income has been around $57,000 for the past few years.) In the event that the patent application has been assigned, the assignee had to have a gross (not net) income of less than three times the U.S. median household income; or

(2) the majority of the patent filer's employment income is from an Institution of Higher Learning, or the applicant has assigned, or is obliged to assign the patent to an Institution of Higher Learning. An Institution of Higher Learning is a public or nonprofit accredited institution that admits postsecondary students for programs of not less than two years.

How Do You Determine Micro-Entity Status for Multiple Inventors? The rules apply individually to each joint inventor. So, no joint inventor can have been named as an inventor on more than four applications, and no joint inventor can have a gross income (as defined by the IRS) exceeding three times the median household income for the preceding calendar year. (In recent years, the median has been about $57,000, so three times the median is approximately $170,000.)

If you have several inventions, you can put them all into the PPA, even if they're not related. If you know of several embodiments of any invention, put them all in, even if you have doubts about the operability of any embodiment. The PTO will never read your PPA unless they need to verify that it supports an invention or embodiment that you are claiming in an RPA that you file within one year after you file the PPA. As with the invention disclosure, include as many embodiments of your basic invention as you can think of, even if some may not work. For more information on preparing a Provisional Patent Application, review either *Patent Pending in 24 Hours*, by Richard Stim and David Pressman (Nolo), or check Nolo's online provisional patent program (www.nolo.com) that assists in the drafting of a PPA.

Now that you've prepared your PPA (long or short) including the description, drawings, and optionally a claim, you need to prepare a Provisional Application for Patent Cover Sheet document (Cover Sheet). Preparing the Cover Sheet is very easy. Go to the PTO's site (www.uspto.gov), click on the "Patents" tab, then click on "Patent forms." Next, click on the link that says "Patent Forms for Applications Filed

On or After September 16, 2012." From there you'll see a screen that lets you select forms to download, including form SB/16, Provisional Application for Patent Cover Sheet. Scroll through the forms or use the "CTRL + F" keyboard function to locate form SB/16. (While you're at it also download and save the form SB/15A if you are an independent inventor and will be paying micro-entity fees, and download form AIA/14 Application Data Sheet because you'll need this too.) Open the AIA/14 form and fill it out (using your computer) with your name, city, state, and country. Click "Add" to add any additional inventors. Then type the title. Leave "Attorney Docket Number" blank or just put a short reference to your invention if you have filed or plan to file other PPAs. If you have a PTO Customer Number type it in the box, but if not, click "Firm or Individual Name" and some blanks will appear where you fill in your name(s), mailing address, and phone. Click the appropriate button regarding a U.S. government contract. If you haven't assigned (legally transferred) and are not legally obligated to assign the invention to a company with over 500 employees, check "No" under "Entity Status." If you are assigning the invention to an entity with 500 or less employees, check, "Applicant asserts small entity status under 37 CFR 1.27." If you qualify as a micro entity (ME), check the box, "Applicant certifies micro-entity status under 37 CFR 1.29" and complete and include Form SB/15B (for independent inventors) or SB/15A (for institutions of higher learning). (See "Qualifying as a Micro Entity," above.) Type your name and date in the blocks at the end (leave the attorney's Registration Number blank), and sign the form in the Signature block. If there are two or more inventors, only one inventor need sign. You can sign the form using your computer by typing an "S" (slash-sandwiched) signature such as follows: "/Mildred Phillips/" or you can print the form, sign it in ink, and scan it back to PDF.

With your PPA, Cover Sheet (Form SB/16), and Certification of Micro-Entity Status (Form SB/15A or SB/15B) prepared, let's now go on to filing the PPA electronically.

a. Filing Electronically

The PTO's Internet Electronic Filing System (EFS-Web) enables patent applications, amendments, and other documents to be filed over the Internet. Prior to filing you must convert your documents to the Portable Data Format (PDF). There are obvious advantages to online filing. You can (1) file an application anytime and from anywhere that has Internet access, (2) obtain instant confirmation of receipt of documents and a Serial Number and Filing Date from the PTO, (3) send an application to the PTO without having to go to the post office to pay for and get an Express Mail receipt or having to wait for a postcard receipt, and (4) file an application without having to prepare an application transmittal, a fee transmittal, receipt postcard, or check or Credit Card Payment Form (CCPF).

Become a Registered eFiler (If Time Permits)

If you can wait several weeks to file, become a registered eFiler. You'll have to fill out a form to obtain a customer number, and send a notarized certificate to the PTO, obtain access codes, but as a registered eFiler you'll be able to track your application's progress and file additional documents or corrections. To register, go to the PTO's Electronic Business Center page (www.uspto.gov/learning-and-resources/support-centers/patent-electronic-business-center) and navigate from there to instructions for becoming a registered eFiler, e.g., click on "New Users" under the "New to Patents?" section, and follow the detailed instructions. If you can't wait several weeks, you can use EFS-Web to file an application as an unregistered eFiler and register later.

To file your PPA electronically (whether you're a registered eFiler or not), follow the following steps:

- **Convert and Save Your Application to PDF Format:** Convert all documents: (1) the PPA (Drawings, and Specification and optionally including Claims and Abstract), (2) the Cover Sheet (Form SB/16), and (3) Certification of Micro-Entity Status (Form SB/15A if an independent inventor).

If you are scanning documents, set the scan to black-and-white at a resolution of 300 DPI for good clarity. Put all of the PDF application computer files into a separate PDF Application Holding Folder with a suitable name (for example, Derailleur PPA PDFs).

- **(Recommended) Prepare a PDF Application Data Sheet:** When filing electronically, the USPTO gives you a choice to either prepare your ADS ahead of time or the USPTO will generate an ADS electronically when you file your EFS application. If you want to prepare the ADS ahead of time (recommended), download a fillable EFS Application Data Sheet (PTO Form AIA/14) from the PTO's site. The PTO provides detailed instructions (Instructions for Application Data Sheet 37 CFR 1.76) for completing the ADS, and you should download and use them. You can find this 16-page guide at the PTO's forms page (www.uspto.gov/patent/patents-forms). Download and follow the instructions. Leave the Publication Information, Representative Information, Domestic Benefit … , and Foreign Priority sections blank because PPAs are not published and you're filing pro se (no attorney), and you can't claim benefit of any earlier domestic or foreign applications. Leave the Assignee section blank unless you are assigning (legally transferring) the application to another entity. You can sign the form on the computer using an S-signature (see above). Check both of the Opt-Out boxes. Leave the attorney's Registration Number blank. The program will automatically fill in the header blanks. Then, save the completed form using a suitable name, such as *ADS.pdf*, in your PDF Application Holding Folder with your other PDF application forms.

TIP

Before uploading your electronic filing documents, take a dry run using the PTO's Simulated EFS for Unregistered eFilers at www.uspto.gov/ebc/portal/sandbox/efs0-3-0.htm, or for Registered eFilers at www.uspto.gov/ebc/portal/sandbox/efs0-4-0.htm.

- **Sign On:** Go to www.uspto.gov/patents-application-process/applying-online/about-efs-web. If you haven't registered as an eFiler, click on "Launch EFS-Web Unregistered eFiler" and fill in your name and email, select, "New application/proceeding," then select "Utility," and then choose, "Provisional," and click "Continue."

- **Application Data:** On the Application Data page fill in the title of the invention, a docket number for the application of your choosing (optional, but a suitable docket number can be something like "Krypton Derailleur"), and your name and Customer Number or address. It's best to copy this data electronically from your Data Sheet so that everything will be consistent. Click "Continue."

- **Attach PDF Files:** In the Attach Documents page click the Browse button and find your PDF Application Holding Folder that contains the PDF files of your application. Select one of your PDF application files, e.g., the ADS file, click open, and you should see it in the Files To Be Submitted box adjacent the Browse button. Then open the Category pull-down menu adjacent the middle window and select Application Part. Then open the rightmost pull-down menu and select Application Data Sheet. (Make sure the No button opposite "Does your PDF file contain multiple documents?" is checked, because it's more difficult to work when everything is in one PDF document.) Then click the Add File button and another row of three windows will open. When you choose to upload your Certification of Micro-Entity Status PDF, be sure to choose "Entity Status Correspondence" from the Category dropdown menu. Then, choose the type of certification (gross income or education) from Document Description. Repeat the above steps for each of your other PDF application files (that is, *CoverLetter.pdf*, *Dwgs.pdf*, and *Spec.pdf*), selecting the Document Description in the third window for each. When you've attached all of the PDF files in your PDF Application Holding Folder, click the Upload & Validate button at the bottom.

- **Review Documents:** After a few minutes, you'll eventually get a Review Documents page, which should show all of the documents you've attached. Make sure your entire application (drawings, specification, and data sheet) is there and there are no errors. If any errors are indicated, you'll have to go back and fix them. One common error message is that the PDF file of your drawings contains embedded fonts. To fix this delete the PDF file of your drawings from the site and go back to your *Dwgs.pdf* file, open it, and convert it to PDF again using a PDF conversion program such as *CutePDF*. This new PDF will be an "image" PDF that will not have embedded fonts. Upload the new PDF and the problem should be resolved. Once everything is okay click "Continue."
- **Calculate Fees:** On the Calculate Fees page, select your entity size, which will usually be *Micro Entity*, and click the Calculate button. Your subtotal and total filing fee will be entered in the applicable boxes. Click "Continue."
- **Submit Application:** This page will list all of your PDF files, a *Fee-Info.pdf* file, and the filing fee. If everything is okay, click the Submit button at the bottom to bring up a Congratulations! page with an assigned Application Number, Confirmation Number, and Total Fees due. Click the YES! I want to pay now button at the bottom.
- **Review Fees and Select Payment Method:** Unless you have a PTO Deposit Account or are set up for EFT, select "Charge Credit Card," then "Start online payment process" to bring up the payment page. Fill out the blanks and click the Confirm button at the bottom.
- **Acknowledgment Receipt:** If everything is okay you'll get an Acknowledgment Receipt, which is analogous to the receipt postcard which was used for mailed filings. The Acknowledgment Receipt will list the Application (Serial) Number, the Confirmation Number, the application data and parts that you've filed. Congratulations! You've bypassed the post office, filed an application electronically, and have gotten an instant filing acknowledgment, including a Serial Number. Select Print This Page to print the page for your records. In several weeks you'll get an official filing receipt by mail, as usual.

b. Filing by Mail

If you plan to file by mail (not recommended), your PPA should contain the following parts assembled in this order:

- Receipt Postcard
- PPA Cover Sheet—PTO Form SB/16
- Fee Transmittal—PTO Form SB/17
- Certification of Micro-Entity Status—PTO Form SB/15A or 15B (if paying micro-entity fees)
- Filing Fee—PTO CCPF Form 2038 (if paying by credit card) or check
- Application Data Sheet (ADS) Form AIA/14 (optional but desirable)
- Drawings, and
- Specification (optionally including Claims and Abstract).

Preparing the Cover Letter, ADS, and Fee Transmittal is not difficult. For the cover letter, fill out and print Form PTO/SB/16 (which you can download from the PTO's site). Then, fill out the Fee Transmittal (Form PTO/SB/17, also on the PTO's site). Fill out the ADS (PTO/AIA/14) as instructed above. You can find current fees at the PTO website.

Read the Cover Letter form and fill in the name(s) and legal residences of the inventor(s), a title, the number of sheets of specification, and the number of sheets of drawing. The title and name(s) of the inventor(s) are tentative and can be changed later, so long as one inventor named in the PPA is also named in the RPA and that inventor's invention is claimed in the RPA and fully disclosed in the PPA. However, if your RPA contains any essential information that isn't in your PPA, you may not be able to rely on your PPA. So again, be sure your description is adequate and complete.

You are entitled to file as a micro entity (ME) if you are an independent inventor or institution of higher education that meets certain requirements (see "Qualifying as a Micro Entity"). If you file as an ME, you can pay one-quarter the fees of a large entity.

Alternatively, if you don't qualify as an ME, you may be able to file as small entity (SE) and pay one-half the fees of a large entity. Complete the "Check or Credit Card" line (the fee schedule is in Appendix 4). If there are coinventors, only one inventor's signature and address is required.

If you want to get an instant filing date, obtain a Priority Mail Express envelope and label from your post office and complete the Priority Mail Express section. File your PPA as soon as possible.

Make a complete copy of all papers of your PPA and mount them in a separate "legal" file.

Attach a check or Credit Card Payment Form for the appropriate filing fee and a stamped receipt postcard. Address the front of the postcard to yourself and list on the back all of the papers you're sending for the PPA. Fig. 3F provides an example of a completed postcard. If you don't have any postcards, just use a blank 4" x 6" card (preferably colored, so it can be spotted more readily if mixed with other mail) and a postcard-rate stamp.

Provisional Patent Application of Ignatz Inventor and Imogene Inventress for "[Title of Invention]" consisting of ten sheets of specification, three sheets of drawing, cover letter, ADS fee transmittal, $65 check (or Credit Card Payment Form) for filing fee, and receipt postcard filed today.

Fig. 3F—Back Side of Exemplary Receipt Postcard for PPA

Mail all papers to the address on the cover letter—that is, Mail Stop Provisional Patent Application, Commissioner for Patents, P.O. Box 1450, Alexandria, VA 22313-1450. If you use Priority Mail Express (advisable), you can consider your PPA filed as soon as you receive the Priority Mail Express receipt from the postal clerk. About two weeks after you mail the PPA, you'll receive your postcard back, stamped with its date of receipt in the PTO and a serial number that the PTO has assigned to your PPA. If you use regular mail, the date stamped on your postcard will be the filing date of your PPA. Clip your postcard to your PPA cover letter.

About a month later, you'll receive an official filing receipt from the PTO for your PPA. The filing receipt will contain your PPA's serial number, its date, the names of the inventor(s), the title, etc. It will usually contain the notation "Foreign Filing License Granted [date]," which means the PTO hasn't classified your invention as restricted due to national security.

c. After You File Your PPA

After you get the official filing receipt (which may take a month or more), you will never hear from the PTO again regarding the PPA. The ball is now in your court to file a timely RPA and to refer to your PPA if you ever need to rely on its date. Mount this in the file with your PPA. Now determine the date that is ten months after your PPA's filing date and mark this date on your calendar to remind you to consider following through with an RPA and possible foreign patent applications. If you don't file an RPA referring to your PPA within a year of your PPA's filing date, the PTO will forever disregard it.

8. How to Effectively Extend the PPA's One-Year Period to Two Years

While the patent statutes state that an RPA must be filed within one year of the PPA's filing date in order to obtain the benefit of such date, there is a way to effectively extend this one-year period to two years by filing in incomplete RPA within one year with a special form and then completing the RPA by the end of the second year. This practice, called the "Extended Missing Parts Pilot Program," is provided by the PTO to circumvent the one-year PPA statutory period. As of this writing, this program will run until Jan 2 2019. The PTO intends to make a decision before that date on whether the Extended Missing Parts Pilot Program offers sufficient benefits to the patent community for it to be made permanent or whether the PTO should permit the program to expire. Here's how to effectively extend the period to two years:

1. File your PPA as usual, being sure that it has a full disclosure on how to make and use the invention, in accordance with the patent laws (see Chapter 8).

2. Before the end of the one-year period, the anniversary of the PPA's filing date, file an RPA based on the PPA. Be sure to include an ADS that claims priority to your PPA. The RPA must meet all the requirements explained in later chapters, and if your PPA was thorough and contained all of the parts required of an RPA (e.g., full disclosure and at least one claim), your RPA can be a copy of the PPA. File the RPA in the normal manner, but when paying the filing fees for the RPA, pay only the relatively small basic filing fee and do not pay the Search or Examination fees. Be sure to include an executed oath or declaration (unless obtaining them would delay your filing), a specification (with an abstract and at least one claim), drawings if required, and an application-size fee, a sequence listing, and an English translation, if required.

3. As part of the RPA, include a completed PTO/AIA/421, available on the PTO's website. The form requires the signatures of all inventors and date; use several forms if multiple inventors are involved.

4. After filing the RPA, the PTO will send you a "Notice to File Missing Parts," which will give you 12 more months to file the Search and Examination fees.

5. File, by the due date on the "Notice to File Missing Parts," the Search and Examination fees and whatever else is needed, such as the rest of a full set of claims and any other missing parts to complete the RPA. When you complete the filing of the RPA, this will be your effective filing date and you will have delayed the actual filing of the complete RPA to 2 years from the filing date of the PPA.

9. PPA Checklist

If you do decide to file a PPA, here is a checklist to go through before you file it electronically or by mail to make sure that you've done everything correctly. Many errors can be avoided if you assemble everything and wait a day and check everything again before filing.

PPA Checklist

☐ The specification and drawings clearly teach how to make and use all embodiments of the invention that you might later want to claim.

☐ Although it's not strictly necessary, your PPA should be in the format of an RPA, insofar as possible, so that it includes all the parts of an RPA's specification and is written as well and as clearly as an RPA should be. For the same reason, your PPA should comply with the Drawings and Specification checklists in Chapter 8.

☐ It is recommended that your PPA contain at least one claim so that you will become familiar with claims and the scope of offensive rights they provide, and also prevent any challenge to your PPA by foreign patent offices for failure to claim the invention as of your earliest filing date. Chapter 9 contains full instructions for drafting claims and checklist for the claims.

☐ If filing by mail, the PPA Cover Letter is completed, including Priority Mail Express section, to avoid possibility of loss in the mail and to get an instant filing date. If filing electronically the PTO's Data Sheet is completed and saved as a PDF file where you can easily retrieve it.

☐ If filing by mail you've included a return receipt postcard with all papers being sent listed on the back.

☐ You've completed an ADS if filing electronically. (Also desirable if filing by mail.)

☐ If filing by mail you've included a completed Fee Transmittal form and Certification of Micro-Entity Status (if paying the lowest fees for independent inventors).

☐ If filing by mail you've included a Check or Credit Card Payment Form for the filing fee. If a check is used, it is payable to "PTO." Ensure that adequate funds on deposit or adequate credit are available. If filing electronically you have typed the credit card number accurately and adequate credit is available.

☐ If filing by mail the parts are assembled in the above order. If filing electronically or by mail you've made hard copies for your file.

☐ If filing by mail, envelope is addressed to:
Mail Stop PPA Commissioner for Patents
P.O. Box 1450
Alexandria, VA 22313-1450

(Again, it is not necessary to file an Information Disclosure Statement or any prior art with your PPA.)

10. PPAs and Foreign Filing

As we'll learn in Chapter 12, there are two types of foreign jurisdictions in the patent world: those that are members of the Paris Convention and those that are not. If you file a PPA and then file in any Convention jurisdiction (for example, the European Patent Office, Patent Cooperation Treaty (PCT), the U.K., France, China, Japan, Canada, Mexico, Russia, etc.) within a year, your application in the Convention jurisdiction will be entitled to the priority of your PPA's filing date. Thus, after you file a PPA, you can then freely publish and sell your invention without loss of any rights in any foreign Convention jurisdiction, provided you file in the foreign Convention jurisdiction within a year. Unfortunately, non-Convention countries (for example, Ethiopia, Eritrea, and Somalia in the Horn of Africa, Myanmar, and various island nations including Fiji, Maldives, and Micronesia) do not provide any priority, so you must file in these countries before you publish or offer your invention for sale publicly, as fully explained in Chapter 12.

11. What If You Make Changes to the Invention?

Note that you're not allowed to amend or add anything to your PPA. Thus, if you make any changes or improvements to the invention after filing a PPA, you should file a subsequent PPA to record any changes (unless they are minor, such as a change in material). Also, if the date is close to the one-year limit from the filing date of the PPA, it probably isn't worth filing a second PPA; instead, put the changes in the RPA. Your RPA can claim the benefit of more than one PPA and several RPAs may claim the benefit of one or more PPAs. Also, if a PPA contains several inventions, the RPA need not contain them all. Conversely, the RPA may contain several inventions even if its PPA contains only one. In this case the RPA will be entitled to the benefit of the PPA's date for only the invention(s) disclosed in the PPA.

I. Don't Sit on Your Invention After Documenting It

While documenting your invention and the building and testing of it are very important, obviously such documentation, no matter how carefully done and how thorough, will be of no value whatsoever unless you follow through and take further steps to exploit your invention. Keep in mind that whatever method or methods you use to document are not as important as filing a patent application and getting the invention to market so that you can profit from your creativity.

J. Don't Use a "Post Office Patent" to Document Your Invention

There's a myth that you can document the date you conceived of your invention (or even protect your invention) by mailing a description of your invention to yourself by certified (or registered) mail and keeping the sealed envelope. In fact, the law regards the use of a "Post Office Patent" as tantamount to worthless and no substitute for the signatures of live witnesses on a description of your invention. The PTO's Patent Trial and Appeal Board, which has great power in these matters, has specifically said that it gives a sealed envelope little evidentiary value.

K. Summary

Documentation of an invention is important to protect your legal right to assist in your creation of the invention. You should record conception of the invention, then build and test it, if at all possible, and then record your building and testing. You may record conception and building and testing in a lab notebook or by means of an invention disclosure. In either case you, the inventor, should sign and date the document and have it witnessed and dated.

You may also file a provisional patent application (PPA) to obtain patent pending status. The PTO will never read the PPA unless you need to rely on its date later to obtain an earlier date for a regular patent application (RPA). The filing fee for a PPA is relatively small and it need not have claims or the formality of an RPA, but to be effective, the PPA must clearly and fully teach how to make and use the invention. To obtain the benefit of the PPA's filing date, the RPA and any foreign applications must be filed within one year and claim the benefit of the PPA. You may convert an RPA to a PPA and vice versa. Your RPA may claim the benefit of several PPAs. A PPA can contain several inventions, but you can rely on only those that the PPA fully and clearly discloses. You should not use a "post office patent" to document your invention.

Will Your Invention Sell?

Inventor's Commandment 5

Don't spend substantial time or money on your creation until you have thoroughly evaluated it for commercial potential. You should proceed only after you are convinced that your creation can be sold profitably for a significant period of time.

A. Why Evaluate Your Invention for Salability?

Congratulations! If you've gotten this far, you've made an invention and have properly recorded your conception by a notebook or disclosure.

Now it's time to do two more things before proceeding: (1) evaluate your invention for commercial potential and (2) make a patentability search. While you can do these in any order, we recommend that you do the commercial evaluation first, as it is usually easier or cheaper than the search.

Why is a commercial evaluation so important? Because you won't want to invest further labor or take on financial risks unless you feel you have some reasonable chance that your efforts and expenditures will be justified. We recommend that you be reasonably confident that your invention is likely to make you at least $100,000 in profits or royalties, or at least 20 times the cost of what you plan to spend for searching, building a model, and patenting.

Keep in mind that if you come up with a technical breakthrough in a high-tech field, or a highly novel invention, you should consider patenting it even though you don't think it has immediate commercial value. That's because you may be able to license or sell your early patent very profitably some years later, and it will block later inventors from patenting it.

Common Misconception: Anyone who gets a patent will be assured of fame and fortune.

Fact: Fewer than one out of ten patented inventions make any money for their owners, mainly because the inventor did not adequately assess the commercial

prospects of the inventions at the outset and because the inventor did not promote and market the invention adequately thereafter.

"It is to be remembered, that the pursuit of wealth by means of new inventions is a very precarious and uncertain one; a lottery where there are many thousand tickets for each prize."

—Eli Whitney

CAUTION

Test Marketing May Prevent You From Obtaining a Patent. Before 2013 Mar 16, an inventor could test market an invention for one year before filing a patent application. Under the First-to-File patent law (effective 2013 Mar 16), that is no longer the case. Test marketing before you file will destroy your right to file a valid patent application. The exception is that if you have filed a provisional patent application (PPA), you have a year to test market the embodiments described in the PPA. But you must file a regular patent application (RPA) within one year to obtain the benefit of your PPA's date.

B. Start Small but Ultimately Do It Completely

When you evaluate your invention for commercial potential, try to do it on a small scale at first in order to avoid a wasted expenditure. For example, if you make metal parts as part of building a prototype to test operability, try to have them made of wood or cardboard by an economical prototyping technique. Also you may be able to make a virtual (computer-world) prototype. Similarly, prior to conducting extensive interviews, try to consult with a single expert to be sure you're not way out in left field. If your initial, small-scale investigation looks favorable and you don't run into any serious impediments, we advise that you then do it carefully, completely, and objectively, using the techniques of this chapter.

If after you do the full evaluation your idea looks like it has great commercial potential, but some other factor such as patentability or operability doesn't look too promising, don't make any hasty decision to drop it. Continue to explore the negative areas. On the other hand, if after a careful evaluation you are truly convinced that your invention won't be successful, don't waste any further time on it. Move on.

C. You Can't Be 100% Sure of Any Invention's Commercial Prospects

There's only one question you need to answer in commercially evaluating your invention: If my invention is manufactured and sold, or otherwise commercially implemented (for example, as a process that is put into commercial use), and assuming it's promoted properly, will it generate a significant profit? Unfortunately, no one can ever answer this question with certainty. The answer will always depend on how the invention is promoted, how well it's designed, how well it's packaged, the mood of the market, the timing of its commercial debut, and dozens of other intangible factors. For example, if the Pet Rock came out now, rather than in the 1960s, it might be a complete dud. Similarly, if bottled water was marketed in the '60s, rather than in current times, it probably would not have had as much success. Most marketing experts say that five "P" factors must all be "right" for a new product to make it: Production, Price, Position (its place in the market), Promotion, and Perseverance.

In addition to the "Five Ps," the packaging (outer box as well as the shape of the device itself) can be crucial to its success. Consider the Audochron clock, which indicates the time by three successive groups of countable chimes. Given this technical feature only, the clock probably wouldn't have sold too well. But a talented designer put the works in a futuristic case shaped like a flattened gold sphere on a pedestal in which a plastic band at the center of the sphere lit with each chime. As a result, it became a status symbol and sold relatively large quantities at a high price; it even appeared in *Architectural Digest*, shown in a photo of a U.S. president's desk!

The trademark you select for your invention can also make a big difference as to whether it's a commercial success. If you doubt this, consider Vaseline's hand lotion. The lotion would very likely have been just another member of the bunch, consigned to mediocre sales, had not some clever marketing person come up with the trademark *Intensive Care*. This helped make it a sales leader. Ditto for the *Hula-Hoop* exercise device and the *Crock Pot* slow cooker, both of which certainly weren't hurt by evocative names. Even something as dull as roach traps were blasted into marketing stardom by the trademark *Roach Motel* and its brilliant ad campaign ("Roaches check in, but they don't check out").

D. Take Time to Do a Commercial Feasibility Evaluation

Despite the marketing uncertainties, most experts believe that you can make a useful evaluation of the commercial possibilities of an untested invention if you take the time to do some scientific and objective work in four areas:

- the positive and negative marketing factors attached to your invention
- consultation with experts, potential users of the invention, marketing people, and others
- research into prior developments in the same area as your invention, and
- the operability of an actual construction of the invention.

Let's take a look at each.

1. The Positive and Negative Factors Test

Every invention, no matter how many positive factors it seems to have at first glance, inevitably has one or more significant negative ones. To evaluate the positive and negative factors objectively, carefully consider each on the list below. Using Form 4-1, Positive and Negative Factors Evaluation Sheet (we provide a downloadable version on this book's companion page; see Appendix 7 for details), assign a commercial value or disadvantage weight to each factor on a scale of –100 to +100, according to your best, carefully considered estimate. If the factor is irrelevant to your invention, assign a weight of 0.

For example, if an invention provides overwhelming cost savings in relation to its existing counterparts, assign a +80 or higher to the "Cost" factor (#1) in the positive column. But if it requires a high capital expenditure (tooling) to build, a –50 would be appropriate for this factor (#45), and so on.

The following balance scale analogy will help you to understand the positive and negative factors evaluation: Pretend the positive factors are stacked on one side of a balance scale and the negative factors are stacked on the other side, as indicated in Fig. 4A.

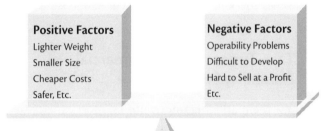

Fig. 4A—Conceptual Weighing of Positive v. Negative Factors Here

If the positive factors (those given a weight from +1 to +100) strongly outweigh the negative (those from –1 to –100), you can regard this as a "go" indication, that is, the invention is commercially viable. Obviously this balance scale is just an analogy. It can't be used with any true quantitative accuracy because no one has yet come up with a way to assign accurate and valid weights to the factors. Nevertheless, you'll find it of great help in evaluating the commercial prospects of your invention. Before you begin your evaluation, read through the following positive and negative factors.

You should consider each factor carefully, especially if you assign a negative value, even if the negative value is merely due to the need to change or design and produce new production equipment. I've seen inventions and developments that were better in every way than what already existed, but which weren't used solely because the improvement didn't justify the cost of replacing existing production equipment, or the cost associated with manufacturing and promoting the device.

The factors of your invention with negative values are generally more important and require more consideration than do those with positive values, since if your invention fails, it will obviously be one or more of the negatives that causes it. On the other hand,

the positive factors will be of great value to you when convincing a patent examiner as to your invention's patentability, or when selling the invention to a potential licensee.

2. Factors Affecting the Marketability of Your Invention

1. **Cost.** Is your invention cheaper or more expensive to build or use than current counterparts? An example where making something more expensive to build would be an advantage is a credit or eligibility card; a more expensive card would be more difficult to counterfeit.

2. **Weight.** Is your invention lighter (or heavier) in weight than what is already known, and is such change in weight a benefit? For example, if you've invented a new automobile or airplane engine, a reduction in weight is a great benefit. However, if you've invented a new ballast material, obviously an increase in weight (provided it doesn't come at too great a cost in money or bulk) is a benefit.

3. **Size.** Is your invention smaller or larger in size or capacity than what is already known, and is such change in size a benefit?

4. **Safety/Health Factors.** Is your invention safer or healthier to use than what is already known? Clearly there's a strong trend in government and industry to improve the safety and reduce the possible chances for injury, harm, and product liability suits in most products and processes, and this trend has given birth to many new inventions. But beware, some safety devices cause more harm than they prevent: For example, antilock brakes have caused more skids and accidents than conventional brakes, because users tend to pump them, although they are supposed to be pressed continuously.

5. **Speed.** Is your invention able to do a job faster (or slower) than its previous counterpart, and is such change in speed a benefit? This advantage is important in software inventions.

6. **Ease of Use.** Is your invention easier (or harder) to use or learn to use than its previously known counterpart? An example of a product where an

increase in difficulty of use would be a benefit is the childproof drug container cap. This advantage is also important if you have a software innovation.

7. **Ease of Production.** Is your invention easier or cheaper (or harder or more expensive) to manufacture than previously known counterparts? Or can it be mass-produced, whereas previously known counterparts had to be made by hand?

8. **Durability.** Does your invention last longer (or wear out sooner) than previously known counterparts? Generally, a long-lasting invention is an advantage. However, keep in mind that many products, such as disposable razors, have earned their manufacturers millions by lasting for a shorter time than previously known counterparts.

9. **Repairability.** Is it easier to repair than previously known counterparts?

10. **Novelty.** Is your invention at all different from all previously known counterparts? Merely making an invention different may not appear to be an improvement per se, but it's often a great advantage: It provides an alternative method or device for doing the job in case the first method or device ever encounters difficulties (such as from government regulation), and in case the first device or method infringes a patent that you want to avoid infringing. It also provides something for ad people to crow about.

11. **Convenience/Social Benefit/Mechanization.** Does your invention make living easier or more convenient? Although you may question the ultimate wisdom of such gadgets as the electric knife, the remote-control TV, and the digital-readout clock, millions of dollars have been made from devices that save labor and time (even though the time required to earn the after-tax money to buy the gadget is often greater than the time saved by using it). Even if the invention has one or more serious drawbacks, if it mechanizes a manual operation, it may still fly. Consider the Epilady leg-hair remover: Even though its rotating spring ripped out leg hairs in an extremely painful manner, it became a great success because it eliminated shaving and depilatories.

At the same time, many industries have been kick-started by making an existing invention easier and more convenient to use. For example, Henry Ford didn't invent the automobile; George Eastman didn't invent the camera; and Steve Jobs and Steve Wozniak didn't invent the computer. However, all of these individuals created new industries by making existing inventions much easier to use.

12. **Reliability.** Is your invention apt to fail less or need repair less often than previously known devices?

13. **Ecology.** Does your invention make use of what previously were thought to be waste products? Does it reduce the use of limited natural resources? Does it produce fewer waste products, such as smoke and waste water? If so, you have an advantage that is very important nowadays and that should be emphasized strongly.

14. **Salability.** Is your invention easier to sell or market than existing counterparts?

15. **Appearance.** Does your invention provide a better-appearing design than existing counterparts?

16. **Viewability.** If your invention relates to eye use, does it present a brighter, clearer, or more viewable image? For example, a color TV with a brighter picture, or photochromic eyeglasses that automatically darken in sunlight were valuable inventions.

17. **Precision.** Does your invention operate or provide greater precision or more accuracy than existing counterparts?

18. **Noise.** Does your invention operate more quietly? Does it eliminate or turn unpleasant noise into a more acceptable sound? (Noise-canceling headphones fit this bill.) Or does it make noise in a desirable situation—for example, a device that produced a warning sound when a Blu-Ray disk was inserted in the wrong manner might be desirable.

19. **Does your invention emanate fewer (or more) unpleasant fumes or odors?** For example, the public would benefit by adding an unpleasant odor to a poisonous or harmful substance (as when public utilities add mercaptan sulphur to heating and cooking gas to alert users when leaks occur).

20. **Taste.** If your invention is edible or comes into contact with the taste buds (for example, a pill or a pipe stem), does it taste better? Even a foul taste can be an advantage, such as for poisons to prevent ingestion by children, and for telephone cables to deter chewing by rodents.

21. **Market Size.** Is there a larger market for your invention than for previously known devices? Because of climatic or legal restrictions, for example, certain inventions are only usable in small geographical areas. And because of economic factors, certain inventions may be limited to the relatively affluent. If your invention can avoid these restrictions, your potential market may be greatly increased, and this can be a significant advantage.

22. **Trend of Demand.** Is the trend of demand for your device increasing? Of course you should distinguish, if possible, between a trend and a fad. The first will provide a market for your invention while the second is likely to leave you high and dry unless you catch it in the beginning stages.

23. **Seasonal Demand.** Is your invention useful no matter what the season of the year? If so, it may have greater demand than a seasonal invention, such as a sailboat.

24. **Difficulty of Market Penetration.** Is your device an improvement of a previously accepted device? If so, it will have an easier time penetrating the market and obtaining a good market share than a device that provides a completely new function.

25. **Potential Competition.** Is your invention so simple, popular, or easy to manufacture that many imitators and copiers are likely to attempt to copy it or design around it, or try to break your patent as soon as it's brought out? Or is it a relatively complex, less popular, hard-to-manufacture device, which others wouldn't be likely to produce because of such factors as the large capital outlay required for tooling and production? However, don't assume that something that's easy to copy is not worth patenting, since patents on simple devices are upheld and enforced successfully all the time.

26. **Quality.** Does your invention produce or provide a higher quality output or result than existing counterparts? For example, Blu-Ray discs provide much better audio and video quality than VHS recordings.

27. **Excitement.** (The Neophile and the Conspicuous Consumer/Status Seeker.) If your invention can provide consumer excitement, either through sheer newness or through evidence of a costly purchase, it has a decided advantage. That's because purchasing cutting-edge gadgets, such as a friendly robotic rug vacuum, excites some humans. These purchasers are "neophiles" (lovers of the new); their excitement comes from having and showing off their new "toy." At the same time, purchasers of expensive products exhibit "status seeking" behavior when they show off an expensive or unique item that they've acquired.

28. **Ability to Acquire Status.** Closely related to the preceding factor (Excitement), a product's ability to acquire a desirable or prestigious status will make it very successful and more profitable once it acquires a desired status among one or more groups. As Kevin Maney explains in his book, *Trade-Off: Why Some Things Catch On, and Others Don't* (Broadway), this is why some teens will pay $3 for a smartphone ring tone that announces their taste but will balk at paying 99 cents for the full song. Maney says that products like the iPhone, Tiffany's jewelry, certain concert tickets, and first-class airline seats can command a larger profit because of their desired status. But bear in mind that a product's status can diminish if the product or service becomes too popular or convenient.

29. **Markup.** If your invention is in an excitement category (that is, if it's very different, novel, innovative, or luxurious), it can command a very high markup, a distinct selling advantage.

30. **Inferior Performance.** Yes, we're serious! If your invention performs worse than comparable things that are already available, this can be a great advantage, if put to the proper use. Consider the 3M Company's fabulously successful Scotch Post-It note pads: Their novelty is simply that they have a strip of stickum that is inferior to known adhesives, thus providing removable self-stick

notes. Here the invention may not be so much the discovery of an inferior adhesive as the discovery of a new use for it.

31. **"Sexy" Packaging.** If your invention is or comes in a "sexy" package, or is adaptable to being sold in such a package, this can be a great advantage. Consider the Hanes L'eggs stockings, where the package (shaped like an egg) made the product!

32. **Miscellaneous/Obviation of Specific Disadvantages of Existing Devices.** This is a catchall to cover anything we may have missed in the previous categories. Often the specific disadvantages that your invention overcomes will be quite obvious; they should be included here, nonetheless.

33. **Long Life Cycle.** If your invention has a potentially long life cycle, that is, it can be made and sold for many years before it becomes obsolete, this is an obvious strong advantage that will justify capital expenditures for tooling and conducting a big ad campaign.

34. **Related Product Addability.** If your invention will usher in new product lines, as did the personal computer, with disk drives, printers, and software, this will be an important advantage.

35. **Satisfies Existing Need.** If your invention will satisfy an existing, recognized need, such as preventing drug abuse, avoiding auto collisions, combating terrorism or crime, or preventing airplanes from catching fire upon crashing, your marketing difficulties will be reduced.

36. **Legality.** Does your invention comply with, or will its use fail to comply with, existing laws, regulations, and product and manufacturing requirements? Are administrative approvals required? If your invention carries legal difficulties with it, its acceptance will be problematic no matter how great its positive advantages are. Also, if the legality of a product is questionable, its manufacturer, distributor, or retailer will have difficulty in obtaining product liability insurance.

37. **Operability.** Is it likely to work readily, or will significant additional design or technical development be required to make it practicable and workable? Usually problems of operability will become abundantly clear when you try to build a working model. Many great-looking inventions such as the turbine automobile engine turned out to be "techno-fizzle" when built and tested.

38. **Development.** Is the product already designed for the market, or is additional engineering, material selection, and appearance work required?

39. **Profitability.** Because of possible requirements for exotic materials, difficult machining steps, great size, and so on, is your invention likely to be difficult to sell at a profit, or at an acceptable price level?

40. **Obsolescence.** Is the field in which your invention is used likely to be around for a long time or die out soon? If the latter, most manufacturers won't be willing to invest money in production facilities.

41. **Incompatibility.** Is your invention likely to be compatible or incompatible with existing patterns of use, customs, and so on?

42. **Product Liability Risk.** Is your invention in a "safe" area, such as a ruler, or in a problem area, such as drugs, firearms, contact sports, and automobiles? If so, the risks of lawsuits against the manufacturer, due to product malfunction or injury from use, are likely to be greater than average. For example, a client of ours invented an ingenious, economical, and highly useful device for preventing a revolver from being accidentally fired. But, alas, though he tried everywhere, he couldn't get any company to take it on because they were afraid of product liability lawsuits if the device ever failed.

43. **Market Dependence.** Is the sale of your invention dependent on a market for other goods, or is it useful in its own right? For example, an improved television tuner depends on the sale of televisions for its success, so that if the television market goes into a slump, the sales of your tuner certainly will fall also.

44. **Difficulty of Distribution.** Is your invention easy to distribute, or is it so large, fragile, or perishable that it will be difficult or costly to distribute?

45. **Service Requirements.** Is your invention free from service requirements or will it require frequent servicing and adjustment? If the latter, this is a distinct disadvantage.

46. **Production Facilities.** Almost all inventions require new production facilities, a distinct disadvantage.

This is because the manufacture of anything new requires new tooling and production techniques. But some inventions require only a modest change or no change, a tremendous advantage.

47. **Inertia Need Not/Must Be Overcome.** There's a risk in introducing any new product. When any invention is radically different, potential manufacturers, users, and sellers manifest tremendous inertia, regardless of the invention's value. An example of a great invention that so far has failed because of user inertia is the Dvorak typewriter keyboard, which, although much faster and easier to use, was unable to overcome the awkward but entrenched Qwerty keyboard.

48. **Minor/Great Technical Advance.** In the '60s, we got a client a very broad patent on a laser pumped by a chemical reaction explosion. We were very pleased with this patent. However, it was so advanced at the time that the technology behind it was not implemented until a military program adopted it in the 1980s. Unfortunately, the patent expired in the meantime. The same goes for the computer mouse patent, which expired in 1980, just before the concept became popular, and the roller-blade skates, the patent for which expired in 1985, just before the roller-blade craze started. An FRB-Dallas survey found that major innovations like the telephone, radio, dishwasher, color TV, microwave oven, VCR, computer, and cellphone took an average of 11.4 years to be owned by 25% of all U.S. households. The moral? Even if you have a great invention, make sure it can be commercially implemented within about 17 years.

49. **Learning Required.** If consumers will have to undergo substantial learning in order to use your invention, this is an obvious negative. An example: the early personal computers. On the other hand, some inventions, such as the automatically talking clock, make a task even easier to do and thus have an obvious strong advantage.

50. **Difficult/Easy to Promote.** If it will be difficult, expensive, or will require a long time to promote and market your invention, e.g., because it's technically complex, has subtle advantages, or is very expensive, large, or awkward, you've got an obvious disadvantage. But if it solves an omnipresent problem and is cheap and easy to market, this is a clear advantage.

51. **Lack/Presence of Market.** If no market already exists for your invention, you'll have to convince the public that they need it—that is, that you have a "product in search of a market." While not a fatal flaw, and while this type of invention can be most profitable, you (or your licensee) will have to be prepared to expend substantial sums on promotion.

52. **Crowded/Wide Open Field.** If the field is already crowded, you'll have an uphill battle.

53. **Commodities.** If you've invented a new commodity—such as a better plastic, solvent, or grain—you'll face stiff price competition from the established, already streamlined standards.

54. **Combination Products.** If you've invented a "combination product"—that is, a product with two inventions that don't really groove together, like a stapler with a built-in beverage cup holder, people won't be beating a path to your door. On the other hand, the clock-radio was just the ticket.

55. **Entrenched Competition.** Despite its overwhelming advantages, Edison had a terrible time promoting his lightbulb because the gas companies fought him bitterly.

56. **Instant Anachronism.** A clever inventor in Oakland, California, invented a wonderful dictionary indexing device that made it much faster to look up any word. However, he was unable to sell it to any dictionary publisher because computerized devices are replacing the dictionary. His clever invention was an "instant anachronism."

57. **Prototype Availability.** Although the presence or absence of a prototype should not affect the marketability or commercial success of your invention, in reality it will! If you have a prototype available, or can make one, you'll find that your invention will be far easier to market.

58. **Broad Patent Coverage Available.** Keep this factor in mind and come back to it after you evaluate patentability. Obviously, if you can obtain broad

patent coverage on your invention, this will affect profitability, because if you're the only source for a device that performs a certain function you'll be able to charge more than you would in a competitive situation. A legal monopoly is a capitalist's dream!

59. **High Sales Anticipated.** If you can anticipate a high sales volume for your invention—for example, for a device like the Hula-Hoop that is relatively simple, cheap, and easy to market—this will be a very positive factor.

60. **Visibility of Invention in Final Product.** If your invention is highly visible in or essentially constitutes the entire final product—for example the sneakers with heels that light up when walking—this will be a distinct marketing advantage to entice buyers who love the new. On the other hand, if the invention is hidden in the final product, such as a stronger frame for an automobile, this factor will not be a plus in marketing.

61. **Ease of Packaging.** If your invention is easy to package—for example, a small gadget that can be put in a cheap blister package—this will be a great aid in marketing. However, if it's difficult and expensive to package, such as a bicycle or hockey stick, this will obviously be a negative factor.

62. **Youth Market.** Young people have substantial discretionary income and tend to spend more in many product areas than the rest of the population. If your invention is something that will appeal to children or young adults, it may command more sales than something that is not attractive to this age group.

63. **Part of a Trending Activity.** If your invention is trending among consumers, such as a low-carbohydrate product, or an identity-theft preventer, it will be far easier to sell. For example, a few years ago when the lottery was legalized in California, a spate of lottery-number selection products appeared and sold briskly until the public's interest simmered down.

64. **Will a Contingent Fee Litigator Take Your Case?** A contingent fee litigator will take your case for a cut of the recovery, usually measured by lost profits/

sales. Before filing your patent application consider whether, if your issued patent is infringed, will there likely be enough sales of the infringing device to get a litigator to represent you on a contingent-fee arrangement. If there aren't enough sales, or if the infringers are fly-by-night, irresponsible operators, most litigators won't take your infringement case on a contingent fee basis. This is true even if you have a strong patent that is clearly infringed. In other words, the law is far more accessible when substantial amounts are likely to be recovered.

Now that you have a grasp of the factors that can influence the commercial viability of an invention, complete Form 4-1 by assigning a weight to each listed factor, either positive or negative. Also list and assign weights to any other factors you can think of which we've omitted. Then compute the sum of your factors and determine the difference to come up with a rough idea of a net value for your invention. We suggest that you continue to pursue inventions with net values of 50 and up, that you direct your efforts elsewhere if your invention has a net value of less than 0, and that you make further critical evaluation of inventions with net values between 0 and 50.

The list has many other valuable uses:

- Using the list may cause you to focus on one or more drawbacks that are serious enough to kill your invention outright.
- The list can be used to provide a way of comparing two different inventions for relative value so that you'll know which to concentrate more effort on.
- It can be used to "sell" your invention to the PTO or a judge if your patent is ever involved in litigation. As we'll see, an invention must be unobvious to be patentable, and unobviousness is best proved by new and unexpected (superior) results of the type listed above.

You now should extract all factors on the list of Form 4-1 that have any value other than 0 and write these factors and their weights on Form 4-2, the Positive and Negative Factors Summary Sheet (we provide a downloadable version on this book's companion page; see Appendix 7 for details). This sheet, when completed, will provide you with a concise summary of the advantages and disadvantages of your invention. You can use it in at least four valuable ways:

1. To provide you with a capsule summary of your invention for commercial evaluation purposes;
2. To help you prepare the "selling" parts of your patent application;
3. To help you to sell or license your invention to a manufacturer; and
4. To help you to get the PTO to grant you a patent.

Don't hesitate to update or redo Forms 4-1 and 4-2 if more information comes to mind.

E. Check Your Marketability Conclusions Using the Techniques of Consultation and Research

Once you reach some tentative conclusions about the commercial viability of your invention, it's time to get a reality check.

1. How to Go About It

If your evaluation gives the positive side the edge, we recommend that you extend your investigation by doing some consultation and research. If you continue to get positive signs, extend your search still further until you've learned all you can about the field of your invention. This knowledge will also be of great benefit when you make your patentability search, prepare your application, market your invention, and deal with the PTO.

TIP

Don't disclose ideas and information without utilizing appropriate confidentiality safeguards as discussed below; otherwise you may lose rights.

Start by asking both nonprofessionals and experts in the particular field of invention for an opinion, and by researching the relevant literature. Nonprofessionals can often be an excellent source of information and advice, especially if your invention is a consumer item that they are likely to have an opportunity to purchase if it's ever mass-produced. Consult your lay friends and associates, that is, those who have no special expertise in the field in which you are interested, but whose opinion you trust and feel will be objective. Often you may find it valuable not to tell them that you are the inventor so you'll get a more objective evaluation. You may also want to inquire as to what price they'd be willing to pay. It's especially helpful if you've built a working model so you can show it to them and ask if they'd buy it and for what price.

Experts to be consulted in the particular field of your invention include any and all of the following who can supply you with relevant feedback:

- salespeople and buyers in stores that sell devices similar to yours
- engineers, managers, or technicians in companies in the field of your invention
- scholars, educators, or professors who do research in the area of your invention, and
- friends who are "in the business."

Naturally you may not know all of these experts. Getting to them will require the creative use of the contacts you do have so as to arrange the proper introductions. Once you do, however, most people will be flattered that you've asked for their advice and pleased to help you.

If you can afford to pay for an evaluation, you may want to consider using an independent invention evaluation service. One university-based service we believe is reputable is the Wisconsin Innovation Service Center (www.wisconsinsbdc.org/wisc).

After you show your invention—preferably a working model—note the initial reaction of whomever you show it to. If you hear a "Well, I'll be damned!" or "Why didn't I think of that!" you know you're on the right track. However if a consultant rejects your idea, don't blindly accept the rejection; try to find out the reason and whether it's valid. Some people don't like anything new, so develop a thick skin and an analytical approach. Keep in mind the words of Charles Brower: "A new idea is delicate. It can be killed by a sneer or a yawn; it can be stabbed to death by a quip and worried to death by a frown on the right man's brow."

For your literature search, we suggest that you start with an Internet search, or by locating a research librarian who's familiar with the area of your concern. Large technical and business libraries and those associated with major universities are obvious places to start. The library literature that you should investigate includes product directories, "how-to" books, catalogs, general reference books, and patents if they are available. Product catalogs are also helpful.

Remember that the purpose of the literature search isn't to determine whether your invention is new or patentable, but rather to give you additional background in the field so you can evaluate the positive and negative factors listed above. However, while you're doing your literature search, you may find that your invention was publicly known before you invented it: you'll either have to drop the invention, or try to make a new invention by improving your first effort. You'll be surprised how much better a feel you'll have for your invention once you've done some research and become familiar with the field.

TIP

This search isn't the equivalent of the "patent search" that occurs before you apply for your patent. Covered in the next chapter is the more formal patent search, which obviously will provide you with considerably more background in the area of your invention.

2. Precautions to Take During Consultation

If you do show your invention to others or discuss it with them to any extent, a degree of care is mandatory to preserve the trade secret status of your invention and to prevent theft of your ideas, or to prove it in case it occurs. (See Chapter 1 for more on trade secrets.) Remember that any of the agreements discussed below are only as good as the parties who have signed them. Thus you shouldn't disclose your invention to anyone you don't trust or whom you feel will not be reliable. Suing someone for breaching a nondisclosure agreement is no substitute for picking a trustworthy person in the first place.

Here are some good alternatives that can be used to protect your invention from being misappropriated by others:

- Have disclosees sign a receipt or logbook entry indicating that they have seen your invention. The logbook entry can be simply a page in your inventor's notebook that says at the top, "The undersigned have seen and understood Tom Brown's confidential [name of invention] as described on pages ___ of this book, on the dates indicated. The undersigned agrees to maintain confidentiality."
- Ask those to whom you show your invention to sign and date your disclosure as witnesses. Witnesses can hardly ever claim that they invented independently of you if they're on record as having witnessed your invention.
- Get your consultants to sign the Nondisclosure Agreement (Form 3-1). However, it may be difficult for you to ask someone who's doing you a favor to sign this agreement.
- Although inferior to the other devices listed above, send a confirming or thank-you letter before and/ or after your consultation so you'll have a written, uncontradicted record that you showed your invention to the person on a specific date and that you asked it to be kept confidential. A confirmatory after-the-fact letter can simply say, "Thanks very much for looking at my [name of invention] at your office last Wednesday, July 3. This letter is to confirm that you agreed that the details of my [name of invention] should be maintained in strictest confidence. Thanks for your cooperation. Sincerely, [your name]." Make a copy of any such letter and keep a copy for your records.

While care in disclosing your invention is necessary to prevent loss of its trade secret status and theft, don't go overboard with precautions. Many new inventors get such a severe case of "inventor's paranoia" (the "P" in the "PGL Syndrome" discussed in Chapter 2) that they're afraid to disclose their brainchild to anyone, or they're willing to disclose it only with such stringent safeguards that no one will want to look at it! In practice, most stolen inventions are taken only after they're out on the market and proven successful. This is because thieves are most interested in sure things.

F. Now's the Time to Build and Test It (If Possible)

Now that you have completed the conceptual process of your invention, it's time to build and test a working model (prototype), or engage someone who will do it for you for a fee.

1. Why Do It?

If you haven't already done so, it's very desirable to build and test a working model (prototype) of your invention, if at all possible. The reasons: A working model will give you something real to show your marketing consultants, plus valuable information about operability, cost, technical problems, and most of the other factors on the positive and negative factors list. If it's impractical to build a working model, often a nonworking model, or scale model, will give you almost as much valuable data. It's also possible to build a "virtual prototype" (computer simulation).

CAUTION

Publication May Cause a Loss of Patent Rights. Under the First-to-File (FTF) rules (effective 2013 Mar 16), an inventor who authorizes publication of his or her invention—for example, the inventor posts details of the invention at a website—has a one-year period to file a patent application. Nevertheless, it is unwise for an inventor to publish before filing because the inventor will lose foreign filing rights and another person may see the publication and file their own application on it before the true inventor files, thus requiring an expensive and uncertain derivation proceeding.

2. If You Use a Model Maker, Use a Consultant's Agreement

If you can't build and test it yourself, many model makers, engineers, technicians, and teachers are available who will be delighted to do the job for you for a fee, or for a percentage of the action. Also there may be a workshop in your area that will supply you with tools, space, and assistance for a fee. If you do use a model maker or consultant, you should take precautions to protect the confidentiality and proprietary status of your invention. There's no substitute for checking out your consultant carefully by asking for references (assuming you don't already know the consultant by reputation or referral).

In addition, have your consultant sign a copy of the Consultant's Work Agreement (you can find Form 4-3 in Appendix 7). Note that this Agreement includes fill-in blanks to describe the names and addresses of the inventor and consultant, the name of the project or invention (such as "New Sweater-Drying Form"), detailed description of the work to be done (such as "build a wire-frame, plastic-covered, sweater-drying collapsible form in accordance with plans in attached Exhibit A—finished form to operate smoothly and collapse to 14" x 23" x 2" (or less) size"), and manner of payment (for example—⅓ at start, ⅓ upon construction, and ⅓ on acceptance by you, the Contractor), and which state's law should govern (pick the state where you reside if the Consultant is out-of-state).

Note that we've provided (see paragraph 7) that any changes in the work to be performed or payment to be made shall be in writing. We've done this because we've been involved in many disputes where the Consultant does additional or more difficult work and wants more money, but the parties' memories differ as to what changes were agreed to, if any.

The Agreement also requires the Consultant to perform in a timely manner or you can void the Agreement and pay only 50%, or have the Consultant pay an agreed-upon penalty for every day he or she is delinquent.

3. What If the Consultant Invents?

Since many consultants are quite clever, they often come up with patentable improvements, ramifications, or even better versions of the basic invention that they're hired to build, test, or develop. This naturally brings up the issue of who will own and be able to use the Consultant's inventions. Having been involved in many disputes in this area, we know that an ounce of prevention—that is, a prior stipulation as to who will own any inventions the Consultant makes—can prevent many misunderstandings, arguments, and even lawsuits later on.

With this end in mind, we've written the agreement to require the Consultant to disclose all innovations made to you, to sign any patent applications that you choose to file on the Consultant's inventions, and also to assign such inventions to you. Note also that the inventions that belong to you (the Contractor) are those that arise out of the Consultant's work under the agreement, even if conceived on the Consultant's own time. This is a customary clause in employment agreements (see Chapter 16) and is provided so that the Consultant won't be able to claim that a valuable invention made under the agreement isn't yours because it was made on the Consultant's time. Generally the Consultant will be a sole inventor (who should be the only one named in the patent application if the Consultant's invention can exist independently of yours), and a joint inventor with you if the invention is closely related to or improves on yours. (More on inventorship in Chapter 10.) This is because all of the true inventor(s) must be named as inventor(s) in all patent applications no matter who owns the application. We provide a downloadable assignment form and a Joint Owners' Agreement on this book's companion page (see Appendix 7 for details).

G. The Next Step

If you decide to go ahead, your next step is to search for prior art and confirm your invention's patentability under the patent laws. To do this, you should first learn the basic four legal requirements for getting a patent. (See Chapter 5.) Then, if it meets the first two of these requirements, make a formal patent search (see Chapter 6) to determine if it's sufficiently novel to satisfy the other two requirements. When you make this search, you'll also obtain valuable commercial information about prior developments in the area of your invention. E.g., if you've invented a new electric

fork and your search shows 30 patents on electric forks and you've never seen any of these in the market, you should seriously question the commercial feasibility of this concept, even if it's patentable.

If, on the other hand, your commercial evaluation leaves you uncertain, though you feel there's good potential, wait a while before proceeding. The passage of time may give you a new perspective that can make your decision easier. If after a couple of weeks you still can't make up your mind, it's probably best to proceed to the next step (the determination of patentability, including a search). If this determination discloses that your invention is already known or otherwise unpatentable, that's the end of the road. But if it shows that you have a patentable invention, you should probably attempt to patent and market it rather than let a potentially valuable and profitable idea die without being given its day in the sun.

H. Summary

You should carefully evaluate the salability of your invention before filing a patent application, because a patent alone will not make you rich or famous— the invention must also become a success in the marketplace. Test marketing is a valuable activity, but keep in mind that under the new patent law (FTF), marketing, use, sale, or showing before filing will destroy your foreign-filing rights and will place your U.S. rights in jeopardy. (An exception occurs if the inventor publishes the invention, in which case, such publication will destroy only foreign rights and the inventor can delay U.S. filing for up to a year after publication. In general, such publication is not recommended.) Also consult with experts and consumers, but take precautions against invention theft by using a nondisclosure agreement and other safeguards. Building a prototype is invaluable for obtaining commercial and technical information, but if you use a model maker, you must also take precautions by using the Consultant's Agreement.

Is It Patentable?

Inventor's Commandment 6

One-Year Rule: It used to be that you had one year to file a patent application after your invention was made public—either through publication, public use or sale.

After 2013 Mar 16, the "one-year rule" disappeared with one exception: if you (or someone who obtained the details of the invention from you) disclosed the invention, you still have one year to file a provisional patent application (PPA) or regular patent application (RPA). If you miss that deadline, then your disclosure will be considered as prior art (and a bar) to your patent application.

Inventor's Commandment 7

To evaluate or argue the patentability of any invention, use a two-step process. First, determine what novel features (§ 102) the invention has over the closest prior-art reference(s). Novelty can be a new physical (hardware) feature, a new combination or rearrangement of two separate old features, or a new use of an old feature. Second, determine if the novel feature(s) is unobvious, that is, does it produce any new and unexpected results or otherwise indicate unobviousness (§ 103).

Here we deal with the specific subject of what's legally patentable and what's not. Over many decades, both Congress and the courts have hammered out a series of laws and accompanying rules of interpretation that the PTO and the courts (and hence you) must use to separate the patentable wheat from the unpatentable chaff.

A. Patentability Compared to Commercial Viability

If you assessed the commercial potential of your invention and your invention received a passing grade, your next question probably is, "Can I get a patent on it?" The answer to this question is important because you're likely to have a difficult time commercially exploiting an invention that isn't patentable, despite its commercial feasibility. You may be able to realize value from an invention by selling it to a manufacturer as a trade secret (a difficult sale to make!), or by selling it yourself using a clever trademark, or (in some cases) by relying on copyright protection and unfair competition laws (as explained in Chapter 1). But such approaches are usually inferior to the broad offensive rights that a patent offers. If your invention fails to pass the tests of this chapter, reconsider its commercial prospects and whether other areas of intellectual property will provide adequate offensive rights in the absence of a patent. You should consider the commercial viability and patentability tests separately, since commercial success and patentability don't always coincide. Your invention should pass both tests before you file a patent application on it.

B. Legal Requirements for a Utility Patent

The legal requirements for a utility patent can be represented by a mountain having four upward sections (see Fig. 5A), each of which represents a separate test that every invention must pass to be awarded the patent. The PTO is required by statute to examine every utility patent application to be sure it passes each of these tests. If it passes, the PTO must award the inventor(s) a patent.

The four requirements and the pertinent respective statutes are:

1. **Statutory Class:** Will the PTO consider that the invention fits into one of five classes established by Congress? (35 USC 101.) Or put specifically, will the PTO regard it as either a:
   - process or method, including a new use
   - machine
   - article of manufacture
   - composition, or
   - improvement on one of the first four?
2. **Utility:** Can the invention properly be regarded as a useful one? (35 USC 101.)

3. **Novelty:** Will the PTO consider that the invention is novel—that is, does it have any aspect or feature that is different in any way from all previous inventions and knowledge, called the "prior art"? (35 USC 102.)

4. **Unobviousness:** Will the PTO consider that the invention is unobvious from the standpoint of someone who has ordinary skill in the specific technology involved in the invention—that is, does it provide one or more new and unexpected results? (When dealing with design patents, the question becomes: Will the PTO consider the design unobvious in an ornamental or aesthetic sense?) (35 USC 103.)

As Fig. 5A shows, the first three tests are represented by relatively short steps. The last one, unobviousness, is relatively high. This reflects the challenge facing patent applicants. In other words, the PTO will find that most inventions (1) fit within at least one statutory class, (2) have utility (or ornamentality for designs), and (3) possess novelty. However, most of patent applications that fail (almost half of all patent applications that are filed) are rejected by the PTO because of an objection that the invention is obvious.

Design and Plant Patents

Design patent applications must cover a new, original, and ornamental design for an article of manufacture, (35 USC 171), and are examined in the same way and must pass the same novelty and unobviousness tests as utility patent applications, except that the "better functioning" tests that are used to evaluate unobviousness (explained later in this chapter), are not used, since only the aesthetics of a design invention are relevant.

Plant patent applications are subject to the same legal requirements as utility patent applications (35 USC 161), except that the statutory class requirement (first test) is obviously not relevant: plants provide their own statutory class. Since plant patents are relatively rare and are of very specialized interest, we don't go into detail except to set forth the additional legal requirements for getting one. They are: (1) the plant must be asexually reproduced; and (2) the plant must be a new variety. These may include cultivated spores, mutants, hybrids, and newly found seedlings, but should not be a tuber, propagated plant, bacterium, or a plant found in an uncultivated state. You may also obtain a monopoly on a sexually reproduced plant under the Plant Variety Protection Act. (For more information, see Chapter 1.)

Plants, if they are man-made (or elements of man-made plants), can also be covered by utility patents. These plants can be reproduced either sexually (by seeds) or asexually (by grafts, cuttings, or other human means). Utility patents have also been issued for elements of plants, such as proteins, genes, DNA, buds, pollen, fruit, plant-based chemicals, and the processes used in the manufacture of these plant products. To obtain a utility patent on a plant, the plant must be made by humans and must satisfy the statutory requirements (utility, novelty, and unobviousness). The patent must describe and claim the specific characteristics of the plant for which offensive rights are sought. Sometimes the best way to meet this requirement is to deposit seeds or plant tissue at a specified public depository. Many countries have International Depository Authorities for such purposes.

Although a utility patent for a plant is harder and more time-consuming to acquire than a plant patent, a utility patent is a stronger form of offensive right. For example, a plant covered by a utility patent can be infringed if it is reproduced either sexually or asexually. By contrast, a plant patent can be infringed only if it is reproduced asexually from the actual plant protected by the patent.

Because the utility patent owner can thoroughly prevent others from making and using the invention, does this mean the buyer of a patented seed cannot sell the resulting plants to the public? No, because according to patent law, the seed's purchaser can sell the resulting plants but cannot manufacture the seed line.

PATENT #1,234,567

Is it unobvious?
(Does the novelty
produce any new and
unexpected results?)

Does it have any novelty?
(Is there a new physical feature, a
new combination of separate old
features, or a new use of an old feature?)

Is it useful?

Is it in a statutory class?
(Process, machine, manufacture, composition, new use?)

**Fig. 5A—Patentability Mountain
The Four Legal Requirements for
Getting a Utility Patent**

Fig. 5B—Patent Authorities

Let's now look at each of these requirements in more detail.

C. Requirement #1: The Statutory Classes

The PTO must consider your invention to fall into one of the five statutory classes for it to be patentable. Fortunately, the five statutory categories established are very broad and comprehensive. To give you an idea how broad, the Supreme Court has stated that "anything under the sun that is made by man" falls within the classes, except for laws of nature, natural phenomena, abstract ideas, and humans. (*Diamond v. Chakrabarty*, 447 U.S. 303 (1980); *Diamond v. Diehr*, 450 U.S. 175 (1981); *Bilski v. Kappos* (2010); *Alice Corp v. CLS Bank* (2014).)

So the statutory class requirement is rarely an issue. Accordingly, you'll usually be able to squeeze most inventions into at least one category. In many instances an invention will fit into more than one category, since they overlap. This isn't a problem, since you don't have to specify the category to which your invention belongs when you file your patent application.

However, as we'll discuss below, there are significant court-created "judicial exceptions" to subject matter eligibility that preclude the patenting of some inventions, so your patent must claim an invention that falls into one of the statutory classes without falling into one of the judicial exceptions. Otherwise, the PTO may reject it under Section 101 as "nonstatutory subject matter."

Let's discuss the five statutory classes in more detail.

The Patent Laws

Congress derives its power to make the patent statutes from the broad wording of the U.S. Constitution (Art. 1, Section 8), which states:

"The Congress shall have power ... to promote the Progress of Science and useful Arts, by securing for limited Times to Authors and Inventors the exclusive Right to their respective Writings and Discoveries."

The patent statutes, passed by Congress to implement this Constitutional provision, can be found in Title 35 of the United States Code (35 USC).

The statutes, in turn, authorize the PTO to issue its Rules of Practice (which are relatively broad, and are found in 37 CFR (Code of Federal Regulations) 1.1, etc.).

The PTO also publishes specific rules for patent examiners in the *Manual of Patent Examining Procedure* (MPEP) (see Appendix 2, Resources).

Fig. 5B illustrates the relationship between these authorities. The complete MPEP is available on the PTO's website and it includes the patent statutes and the PTO's Rules of Practice.

1. Processes, Including Software

Also termed "methods," processes are ways of doing or making things that involve more than purely mental manipulations. Processes always have one or more steps, each of which expresses some activity and manipulates or treats some physical thing. Thus patents have been granted on a method of gripping a golf club and a method of using a keyboard.

a. Conventional Processes

Examples of conventional processes are heat treatments, chemical reactions for making or changing something, and ways of making products or chemicals. The PTO has even granted patents on processes for combing the hair to cover a bald area, analyzing essays for plagiarism, and for feeding chickens a special diet that results in better eggs. Although surgical operations can still be patented, it no longer makes sense to take this step, since the law exempts medical practitioners from infringing any patent on a medical procedure per se.

b. Software

Unfortunately, since 2014 it has become more difficult to obtain a patent on software because of the so-called "judicial exceptions" to patentability. Laws of nature, natural phenomena, and abstract ideas are not eligible for patenting because they are the basic tools of scientific and technological work. As the courts have said, monopolization of those tools through the grant of a patent might tend to impede innovation more than it would tend to promote it. In its 2014 *Alice* decision, the Supreme Court ruled that a particular software claim was just a conventional, computerized implementation of a financial technique, thus tantamount to claiming the technique itself as an abstract idea. Since then, the PTO and the courts have been vigorous in denying software applications.

But just because an invention uses software, that doesn't make it automatically unpatentable. Software and other computerized inventions, including Internet-based inventions, are patentable as a process if they do "something more" than simply use a general-purpose computer (GPC) in a conventional way. The first hurdle that a software patent application must overcome: GPCs are designed to run generic software! They are also designed to gather, receive, store, and retrieve generic data, perform arbitrary computations, and communicate data with other GPCs, along with a host of other functions. Taking an algorithm or non-computerized process and saying "apply it on a GPC as software" is no longer patentable after *Alice*. This is true even for computer algorithms that you are the very first person to create, and even if a computer can perform the process much faster or more efficiently than was previously known. But the Supreme Court was very careful to say that some software could still be patentable. So how do the PTO and the courts resolve this apparent contradiction?

Software is patentable if it solves a technological problem or limitation in a GPC or the Internet itself. Examples of this sort of software upheld as patentable since 2014 include improving how hyperlinks work, improving how a database stores data, improving how Internet content is filtered, and improving how distributed data are stored and retrieved. One way to think of the difference is to ask, "Does my invention improve computer or Internet technology generally, not just a particular computation?" If you can answer yes, then the software is likely patentable.

The other way software is patentable is when its use is unconventional. Recently, the Federal Circuit patent appeals court ruled eligible a software process for animating lip movements synchronized to spoken dialogue, because the process used software animation "rules" not performed by human animators. Thus, the use of computer software did not merely implement a non-computerized technique, but improved it in a non-conventional way. And, software is patentable on an unconventional or special-purpose computer, such as an embedded system (like an implanted medical device), or a distributed data storage or computational system (like a supercomputer). To avoid a PTO rejection for ineligibility, the claims should call out the unconventional nature of the process or the computer. (Claiming is discussed below in Chapter 9.)

c. Business Methods

In its 2010 *Bilski* decision, the Supreme Court stated that "a business method is simply one kind of 'method' that is, at least in some circumstances, eligible for patenting." However, as mentioned above, if the business method consists of purely mental steps or an algorithm, merely implementing that algorithm using software does not provide the "something more" needed to convert the method into a patentable process. Various courts have held as unpatentable "fundamental economic practices" including contract manipulation and mitigating risk, and "certain methods of organizing human activity" including managing relationships, satisfying or avoiding legal obligations, marketing and sales practices, behavior management, and so on. So, while a business method patent is not prohibited by law, getting one in practice is very difficult. If your invention stems from solving a business problem, think about technological hurdles you had to overcome to make it work, and frame the invention in terms of overcoming those hurdles.

2. Machines

Machines are devices or things used for accomplishing a task. Like processes, they usually involve some activity or motion that's performed by working parts, but in machines the emphasis is on the parts or hardware, rather than the activity per se. Put differently, while a process involves the actual steps of manipulation of an item or work piece (the machine that does the manipulation is of secondary import), a machine is the thing that does the manipulating and the steps or manner of its operation, and the process itself, or material worked upon, are of lesser import.

Examples of machines are cigarette lighters, robots, sewage treatment plants, clocks, all electronic circuits, automobiles, automatic transmissions, boats, rockets, telephones, TVs, computers, VCRs, disk drives, printers, lasers, photocopiers, and a layout for a bank. Many machine inventions can also be claimed as a process and/or as a machine. For instance, an electric circuit or a weaving machine can be claimed in terms of its actual hardware and/or as a process for manipulating an electrical signal or weaving fabrics.

While most software inventions are claimed and regarded as processes, they can usually also be claimed and regarded as machines. A computer whose operation is improved using software is a new machine, after all, and is thus patentable. You may claim patentable software as both a process or method, and as a machine.

Conversely, claiming "means for" carrying out a new computation is no longer good enough, since the PTO will try to interpret those "means" as covering a GPC. Unless you also disclose a non-conventional device to run the software (or more generally, perform the process), the PTO can and will reject your application.

> **TIP**
>
> **There are no clear lines between the five statutory classes.** The important thing to realize is that it doesn't matter as long as your invention fits into at least one of them. Put differently, you needn't be able to tell a machine from a process to qualify for a patent.

3. Manufactures

Manufactures, sometimes termed "articles of manufacture," are items that have been made by human hands or by machines. This excludes naturally occurring things, like rocks, gold, shrimp, and wood, or slightly modified naturally occurring things, like a shrimp with its head and vein removed. But if you discover a new and unobvious use for a naturally occurring thing, such as a way to use the molecules in a piece of gold as part of a computer memory, you can patent the invention as a new use (see below), or as a machine (the gold with the necessary hardware to make it function as a memory).

Manufactures are relatively simple things that don't have working or moving parts as prime features. Clearly, you will see some overlap between the machine and the manufacture categories. Many devices, such as mechanical pencils, cigarette lighters, and electronic circuits can be classified as either. Examples of manufactures are erasers, desks, houses, wires, tires, books, cloth, chairs, containers, transistors, dolls, hairpieces, ladders, envelopes, buildings, floppy disks, knives, hand tools, and boxes. The PTO has even issued a patent on a vitamin-fortified egg.

4. Compositions of Matter

Compositions of matter are items such as chemical compositions, conglomerates, aggregates, or other chemically significant substances that are usually supplied in bulk (solid or particulate), liquid, or gaseous form. Examples are road-building compositions, all chemicals, gasoline, fuel gas, glue, paper, soap, drugs, microbes, animals (nonhuman), food additives, plastics, and even chicken eggs with high vitamin E (U.S. Pat. No. 5,246,717) (1993).

Although, as stated, naturally occurring things such as wood and rocks can't be patented, purified forms of naturally occurring things, such as medicinals extracted from herbs, can be. One inventor even obtained a composition of matter patent on a new element he discovered. And recently, genetically altered plants, microbes, and nonhuman animals have been allowed under this category. Although genes have been patented, the Supreme Court ruled in 2012 that a DNA gene process was unpatentable. In that case, a Utah company was the first to extract and isolate two genes apart from the human body. The Supreme Court ruled that the company could not acquire a patent on the genes because the subject matter occurred naturally and was therefore not subject to patent protection. The Supreme Court hypothesized that the creation of a synthetic version of the genes might be patentable. (*Association for Molecular Pathology v. Myriad Genetics, Inc.* 569 U. S. 12-398 (2013).)

Compositions are usually homogeneous chemical compositions or aggregates whose chemical natures are of primary importance and whose shapes are of secondary import, while manufactures are items whose physical shapes are significant, but whose chemical compositions are of lesser import.

5. New Uses of Any of the Above

A new-use invention is a new and unobvious process or method for using an old and known invention, whether it be an old and known process, composition, machine, or article. The inventive act here isn't the creation of a new thing or process per se, but the discovery of a new use for something that already exists.

If you discover a new and unobvious (unrelated) use of any old invention or thing, you can get a patent on your discovery. For example, suppose you discover that your Venetian blind cleaner can also be used as a seed planter. You obviously can't get a patent on the physical hardware that constitutes the Venetian blind cleaner, since you didn't invent it—someone already patented, invented, and/or designed it first—but you can get a patent on the specific new use (seed planting) of the old hardware. In other examples, one inventor obtained a patent on a new use for aspirin: feeding it to swine to increase their rate of growth. Another inventor got a patent on the new use of a powerful vacuum to suck prairie dogs out of the ground. Note, however, that if your invention has any new hardware, your invention probably should be claimed as new hardware, rather than (or in addition to) a new use of old hardware.

New-use inventions are relatively rare and technically are a form of, and must be claimed as, a process. (35 USC 100(b).) However, we have assigned them as a distinct category to make them more prominent. (See Chapter 9 for a discussion of patent claims.)

6. Examples of Inventions That Don't Fit Within a Statutory Class

The following are examples of "inventions" that don't fit within any statutory class and hence are non-statutory subject matter that cannot be patented:

- Processes that could be performed solely with one's mind (such as a method of meditation or a method of speed-reading)
- Naturally occurring phenomena and articles, even if modified somewhat, such as a shrimp with its head and veins removed

- Laws of nature, including abstract scientific or mathematical principles (John Napier's invention of logarithms in 1614 was immensely innovative and valuable, but it would never get past the bottom level of the patentability mountain. However, Napier's "bones" (rods used to multiply by adding) would clearly be statutory subject matter.)

- An arrangement of printed matter without some accompanying instrumentality; printed matter per se isn't patentable, but a printed label on a mattress telling how to turn it to ensure even wear, or dictionary index tabs that guide you to the desired word more rapidly, have been patented as articles of manufacture.

- Methods that have no practical utility, that is, that don't produce any useful, concrete, and tangible result—for example, a method for extracting π. Tax-avoidance schemes may be useful but are also not patentable.

- Computer programs per se, naked computer instructions, or algorithms that don't manipulate hardware such as the algorithm for extracting π

- Ideas per se. Thoughts or goals not expressed in concrete form or usage are obviously not assignable to any of the five categories above. If you have an idea, you must show how it can be made and used in tangible form so as to be useful in the real world, even if only on paper, before the PTO will accept it. For example, an idea for a burping doll can be effectively patented by patenting a doll with a burping mechanism.

- Electrical signals. Transitory electrical signals were held not patentable subject matter since they are not a composition or manufacture. (*In re Nuijten* (Fed. Cir. 2007).)

D. Requirement #2: Utility

To be patentable your invention must be useful. Problems are seldom encountered with the literal utility requirement; any usefulness will suffice, provided the usefulness is functional, and not aesthetic. Utility is occasionally an issue in the chemical area when an inventor tries to patent a new chemical for which a use hasn't yet been found but for which its inventor will likely find a use later. If the inventor can't state (and prove, if challenged) a realistic use, the PTO won't grant a patent on the chemical. A chemical or mechanical intermediate that can be used to produce another useful chemical or useful hardware item is itself regarded as useful—for example, a novel paper blank that can be formed into an insulated cup is considered useful. Software-based inventions usually satisfy the utility requirement, since virtually all software has a utilitarian function, even if used to create aesthetic designs on an idle monitor or to evaluate golf scores or mutual fund assets. The main problem with software-based inventions is that they may not fall (or may not be claimed in a way so that they fall) into a statutory class, as noted in the previous section. Nonetheless, a software invention should be tested for utility just like any other invention just in case it falls into one of the "legally not useful" categories listed below.

Notwithstanding the fact that virtually all inventions are useful in the literal sense of the word, the courts and Congress have decided that some types of inventions are "not useful" as a matter of law, and patents on them are accordingly denied by the PTO. Let's look at this more closely.

1. Unsafe New Drugs

The PTO won't grant a patent on any new drug unless the applicant can show that not only is it useful in treating some condition, but also that it's relatively safe for its intended purpose. Put another way, the PTO considers an unsafe drug useless. Most drug patent applications won't be allowed unless the Food and Drug Administration (FDA) has approved tests of the drug for efficacy and safety, but drugs that are generally recognized as safe, or are in a "safe" chemical category with known safe drugs, don't need prior FDA approval to be patentable. For example, one inventor was able to patent the use of chili peppers to treat baldness since chilies were known to be safe.

2. Whimsical Inventions

Occasionally, the PTO will reject an application for a patent when it finds the invention to be totally whimsical, even though "useful" in some bizarre sense. Nevertheless, in 1937 the PTO issued a patent on a rear windshield (with tail-operated wiper) for a horse (U.S. Pat. No. 2,079,053). They regarded this as having utility as an amusement or gag.

Most patent attorneys have collections of humorous patents. Below are several from our collection:

- a method of exercising a cat (U.S. Pat. No. 5,443,036—1995),
- a lawnmower attachment for a child's tricycle (U.S. Pat. No. 4,455,816—1984),
- animal ear protectors (U.S. Pat. No 4,233,942 —1980),
- a figure-eight-shaped device to hold your big toes together to prevent sunburned inner thighs (U.S. Pat. No. 3,712,271—1973), and
- dentures with individual teeth shaped like the wearer's head (U.S. Pat. No. 3,049,804—1962).

3. Inventions Useful Only for Illegal Purposes

An important requirement for obtaining a patent, which Congress hasn't mentioned, but which the PTO and courts have brought in on their own initiative (by stretching the definition of "useful"), is legality. For example, inventions useful solely for illegal purposes, such as disabling burglar alarms, safecracking, copying currency, and defrauding the public, might be incredibly useful to some elements in our society, but the PTO won't issue patents on them. However, most inventions in this category can be described or claimed in a "legal" way. For example, a police radar detector would qualify for a patent if it's described as a tester to see if a radar is working or as a device for reminding drivers to watch their speed.

4. Immoral Inventions

In the past, the PTO has—again on its own initiative —included morality in its requirements. But, in recent years, with increased sexual liberality, the requirement is now virtually nonexistent. Thus the PTO now regularly issues patents on sexual aids, gags, and stimulants.

5. Nonoperable Inventions, Including Perpetual Motion Machines

Another facet of the useful requirement is operability. The invention must appear to the PTO to be workable before they will allow it. Thus, if your invention is a perpetual-motion machine, or a metaphysical-energy converter, or, more realistically, a very esoteric invention that looks technically questionable (it looks like it just plain won't work or violates some well-accepted physical law), your examiner will reject it as lacking utility because of inoperability. In this case you would either have to produce a logical, technical argument refuting the examiner's reasons (you can include affidavits or declarations of witnesses and experts and test results), or bring the invention in for a demonstration to prove its operability.

Operability is rarely questioned, since most patent applications cover inventions that employ known principles or hardware and will obviously work as described. If the examiner questions operability, however, you have the burden of proof. And note that all patent examiners have technical degrees (some even have Ph.D.s), so expect a very stringent test if the operability of your invention is ever questioned.

Despite the foregoing, the PTO occasionally issues a patent on what appears to be a perpetual-motion-like machine, as they did in 1979 (U.S. Pat. No. 4,151,431). This raises an important point. The fact that a patent is granted doesn't mean that the underlying invention will work. It only means that the invention as described on paper appeared to a patent examiner to work (or that the examiner couldn't figure out why it wouldn't work).

The PTO, however, has become more careful about perpetual-energy or perpetual-motion machines. Some years ago, it denied an inventor a patent on a perpetual-energy machine. The inventor took the case to the courts, but lost after the National Bureau of Standards, acting as a court expert, found the machine didn't have an efficiency of over 100%.

It's a common misconception that the PTO won't "accept" patent applications on perpetual-motion machines: The PTO will accept the application for filing since filing and docketing are clerical functions. However, the examiner (a degreed professional) will almost certainly reject it later as inoperative (giving reasons) after a formal examination.

6. Nuclear Weapons

The invention must not be a nuclear weapon; such inventions aren't patentable because of a special statute. However, if you've invented a doomsday machine, don't be discouraged: You can be rewarded directly by filing an application with the DOE (Department of Energy), formerly the Atomic Energy Commission.

7. Theoretical Phenomena

Theoretical phenomena per se, such as the phenomenon of superconductivity, the transistor effect, or the discovery of logarithms aren't patentable per se. You must describe and claim a practical, realistic, hardware-based version of your invention for the PTO to consider it useful.

8. Aesthetic Purpose

If the invention's sole purpose or "function" is aesthetic, the PTO will reject it as lacking utility; such inventions should usually be the subject of a design patent application. A beautiful vase of unique design, a computer case whose unique shape does not make the computer operate better, and a computer program for producing a low-brightness design on an idle computer monitor, where the only novelty is the aesthetic uniqueness of the design, are examples of inventions which the law considers to lack statutory utility. However, if the design has a functional purpose then statutory utility would be present. For

example, if the shape of the vase makes it easier and safer to lift, or if the shape of the computer case makes it cheaper to manufacture, or if an airplane has a unique type of fairing that enables it to fly at supersonic speeds without buffeting, then the PTO will hold there is utility.

9. Tax-Avoidance Schemes

Section 14 of the America Invents Act (AIA) reads as follows: "[A]ny strategy for reducing, avoiding, or deferring tax liability, whether known or unknown at the time of the invention or application for patent, shall be deemed insufficient to differentiate a claimed invention from the prior art." However inventions for other aspects of taxation, such as facilitating preparation of tax returns, are considered acceptable.

10. Human Organisms

Section 33 of the AIA states that no patent may issue on any human organism. So even if your daughter Alberta is another Einstein, you can't patent her.

E. Requirement #3: Novelty

Now let's look at the novelty requirement of a patent. Like "unobviousness," this requirement is often misunderstood.

1. Prior Art

Your invention must be novel in order to qualify for a patent. In order for your invention to meet this novelty test it must have some physical or method-step difference over all prior developments that are available to the public anywhere in the world. In the realm of patent law, these prior developments and concepts are collectively referred to as "prior art." Unfortunately, like many things in the law, the determination of what is prior art can be quite complex and involved.

Reduction to Practice

The building and testing of an invention is called a "reduction to practice," a term that had great importance under the previous First-to-Invent patent system. The filing of a patent application, while not an actual reduction to practice, was termed a "constructive" reduction to practice because the law interpreted it in the same way it did an actual reduction to practice. The filing of a valid Provisional Patent Application (PPA) also qualified as a constructive reduction to practice.

a. What Is Prior Art?

According to the patent laws, the term "prior art" means generally the state of knowledge existing or publicly available before the date of your earliest patent application. This includes any knowledge that was made publicly available prior to the filing date, unless such knowledge came from the inventor and was not disclosed over a year before the filing date. Prior art also includes a U.S. patent application of another inventor, that is based on an earlier foreign or domestic application and is entitled to the earlier application's filing (priority) date; the earlier application's filing date is the prior-art date. Finally, prior art includes prior use and on-sale activities of the invention, even if done in another country.

b. Date of Your Invention Under FTF

Under the new FTF system, things are a lot simpler and conform to the laws of the rest of the world's countries, but are harder on small entities and independent inventors.

Under FTF, the previous "one-year rule" (which permitted filing of an application within one year of publication or sale) is essentially dead, so generally anything publicly known before your filing date is prior art. The exception: any disclosure that came from you or was derived from you, the inventor, and was not made over a year before the filing date is not considered prior art to you but it is prior art to anyone else. Thus under FTF, the "date of invention" is the actual filing date of a PPA or an RPA. An inventor

will not be able to rely on any date earlier than the filing date of their PPA or RPA, unless the application is based on an earlier domestic or foreign application and is entitled to the filing date (priority) of such an earlier application. An inventor can rely on an earlier domestic application (parent application) for an earlier filing date if the present application is a continuation, continuation-in-part, or divisional application. An inventor can rely on an earlier foreign application for an earlier filing date if the present application is based on the foreign application filed in a "Paris Treaty" jurisdiction (discussed in Chapter 11) and claims the benefit of ("priority") of the foreign application.

c. Specifics of Prior Art

Now that we've broadly defined prior art, let's take a closer look at what it typically consists of, per 35 USC 102.

i. Prior Printed Publications Anywhere

Any printed publication, written by anyone, and from anywhere in the world, in any language, is considered valid prior art if it was published before you filed your present application. (Under current law, if the printed publication originated from the inventor, it is not considered prior art unless it was published over one year before the filing date.) The term "printed publication" thus includes U.S. and foreign patents, published U.S. patent applications (effective as of their filing date), books, magazines (including trade and professional journals), Russian (or former U.S.S.R.) Inventor's Certificates, and publicly available technical papers and abstracts. Even photocopied theses, provided they were made publicly available by putting them in a college library, will constitute prior art. The PTO has even used old Dick Tracy comic strips showing a wristwatch radio as prior art!

TIP

Computer Tip. While the statute speaks of "printed" publications, we're sure that information on computer-information utilities or networks would be considered a printed publication, provided it was publicly available.

The "prior printed publications" category is the most important category of prior art and will generally constitute most of the prior art that you'll encounter. And most of the prior printed publications that the PTO refers to (cites) when it's processing your application, and that you will encounter in your search, will be patents and pre-grant publications of patent applications, mainly from the U.S.

ii. U.S. Patents Filed by Others Prior to Your Application's Filing Date

Any U.S. patent that has a filing date (or claims priority of a PPA that has a filing date) earlier than your filing date is considered valid prior art. This is so even if the patent issues after you file your application.

TIP

A Common Misconception is that only in-force patents (that is, patents that haven't yet expired) count as prior art. This isn't true. Any earlier patent, even if it was issued 150 years ago and has long since expired, will constitute valid prior art against an invention. Otherwise, patents would have a lesser status than other publications.

iii. Prior Publicly Available Knowledge or Use of the Invention in the U.S.

Under current law, prior public knowledge is prior art if it occurred before you filed your present application and was not made by the inventor in a patent application or was made by the inventor over a year before the application's filing date. For example, an earlier heat-treating process used openly by a blacksmith in a small town, although never published or widely known, is a prior public use that will defeat your right to a patent on a similar process. It has been held that allowing even one person to use your invention without restriction will constitute public use. With respect to public knowledge, an example would be if you gave a talk at a publicly accessible technical society. Recently, even a showing of a kaleidoscope without restriction at a party with 30 attendees was held to be prior public knowledge. Or as one writer commented, "Throw a party and lose your patent rights!"

For still another example of a public use, suppose that you invented a new type of paint and you use it to paint your building in downtown San Francisco. Under the First-to-File rules, if the paint did not originate from the inventor and the paint was left on for even one day before the inventor files a patent application on the paint, then the patent application will be invalidated if the painting is discovered. That's because the paint will be considered prior art to the patent application. If the paint did originate from the inventor, the inventor has a year from the date the painting was done to file a valid patent application. Put another way, if an inventor (or someone who obtained details of the invention from the inventor) uses or discloses the invention publicly, then the inventor has up to one year to file a valid patent application on the invention. (But see the Experimental Exception described below.)

This public-use-and-knowledge category of prior art is almost never used by the PTO since they have no way of uncovering it; they search only patents and other publications. Occasionally, however, defendants (infringers) in patent lawsuits happen to uncover a prior public use that they then rely on to invalidate the patent.

TIP

Experimental Exception. Under court decisions, if the prior public use was for bona fide (good faith) experimental purposes, it doesn't count as prior art. Thus suppose, in the "painted San Francisco building" example above, that you painted your building to test the durability of your new paint: each month you photographed it, kept records on its reflectivity, wear resistance, and adhesion. In this case, you must file a patent application before you start any nonexperimental use. We recommend that you avoid public exposure or use of your invention until after filing your application, unless public experimentation is unavoidable.

iv. Your Prior Foreign Patents

Any foreign patent (this includes Russian (or former U.S.S.R.) Inventor's Certificates) of yours or your legal representatives that issued before your U.S. filing date and that was filed over a year before your U.S. filing date is valid prior art. This category is generally pertinent to non-U.S. residents who start the patenting process in a foreign country. If you're in this class, you must file your U.S. application either within one year after you file in the foreign country or before your foreign patent issues. However, if you want to get the benefit of a foreign filing date for your U.S. application, you should file in the U.S. within the one year after your foreign filing date. (See Chapter 12.)

v. Prior U.S. Inventor

The patent application of the inventor who files first will be prior art to the later filing inventor and the first-to-file inventor will get the patent, unless the second inventor to file can prove, in a derivation proceeding, that the first-to-file inventor derived the invention from the second to file.

Common Assignee or Joint Research Agreement. However, there is a little-used exception: If your invention clears Section 102 (that is, it is novel) and the prior inventor and you were obligated to assign your inventions to the same person or organization, or both of you were parties to a joint research agreement and your application is amended to disclose the parties to the agreement, then the prior inventor's work won't be considered prior art under Section 102. (See PTO Rule 104(c)(4).)

vi. Prior Sale or On-Sale Status in the U.S.

Under Section 102, the law also considers certain actions by humans to be "prior art," even when no paper records exist. These actions involve the "sale" or "on-sale" category. Suppose you (or anyone else) offer to sell, actually sell, or commercially use your invention, or any product embodying your invention, in the U.S. Any offer, sale, or commercial use of an invention before the filing date of the application will defeat the application, unless the activity comes from the actual inventor, in which case the inventor has a year from the start of the activity to file a valid application.

TIP

The type of sale or offer of sale that would bar your patent application must be a commercial offer to sell, or a sale of actual hardware or a process embodying the invention. Such an offer or sale will defeat a later-filed application (unless it came from the inventor) or will start the one-year period running, even if the invention has not yet been built. This is true so long as it has been drawn or described in reasonable detail. On the other hand, an offer to license, or sell, or an actual sale or license of the invention in concept form or a patent application on the invention (not hardware) to a manufacturer will not defeat a later-filed application.

If someone sells hardware embodying the invention, that will be prior art. However if someone goes to a manufacturer and offers to sell or license the invention in concept form or a patent application on the invention (not hardware), or actually makes a sale or license of the invention in concept form or a patent application on the invention (not hardware), then this is not prior art.

Abandonment

If you "abandon" your invention by finally giving up on it in some way, and this comes to the attention of the PTO or any court charged with ruling on your patent, your application or patent will be rejected or ruled invalid.

EXAMPLE: You make a model of your invention, test it, fail to get it to work, or fail to sell it, and then consciously drop all efforts on it. Later you change your mind and try to patent it. If your abandonment becomes known, you would lose your right to a patent. But if you merely stop work on it for a number of years because of such reasons as health, finances, or lack of a crucial part, but intend to pursue it again when possible, the law would excuse your inaction and hold that you didn't abandon.

d. Summary of Prior Art

If these prior-art rules seem complicated and difficult to understand, you're not alone. All you really need to remember is that relevant prior art usually consists of:

- any published writing (including any patent) that was made publicly available anytime before the date you file
- any U.S. patent that has a filing or PPA date earlier than your date of filing
- any relevant invention or development (whether described in writing or not) existing before you filed, or
- any public or commercial use, sale, or knowledge of the invention before the date you file, unless the activity came from the actual inventor.

2. Any Physical or Method Step Difference Whatsoever Will Satisfy the Novelty Requirement

Any novel feature, no matter how trivial, will satisfy the novelty requirement. For example, suppose you've "invented" a bicycle that is painted yellow with green polka dots, each of which has a blue triangle in the center. Assume (this is easy to do) that no bicycle has been painted this way before. Your bicycle would thus clearly satisfy the requirement of novelty.

Rarely will an investigation into your invention's patentability (called a "patentability search") reveal any single prior invention or reference that could be considered a dead ringer. Of course, if your search does produce a dead-ringer reference for your invention—that is, an actual device or published description showing all the features of your invention and operating in the same way for the same purpose—obviously your patentability decision can be made immediately. Your invention lacks novelty over the "prior art." Another way of saying this is that your invention has been "anticipated" by a prior invention or conception and is thus definitely unpatentable. The concepts of anticipation and prior art are discussed below in more detail in Requirement #4—unobviousness.

The law generally recognizes three types of novelty, any one of which will satisfy the novelty requirement of Section 102: (1) physical (hardware or method) difference, (2) new combination, and (3) new use.

a. Physical Differences

This is the most common way to satisfy the novelty requirement. Here your invention has some physical or structural (hardware or method) difference over the prior art. If the invention is a machine, composition, or article, it must be or have one or more parts that have a different shape, value, size, color, or composition than what's already known.

It's often difficult for inventors to distinguish between a physical difference and a new result. When asked, "What's physically different about your invention?" inventors usually reply that theirs is lighter, faster, safer, cheaper to make or use, portable, and so on. However, these factors are new results or advantages, not physical or method step differences, and are primarily relevant to unobviousness (see Section F), not to novelty. That is, they won't help your invention satisfy the novelty requirement. Again, a new physical feature must be a hardware (including operational) difference—for example, a part with a different shape, a different material, a different size, a different arrangement of the components, etc.

Even omitting an element can be considered novel. For example, if a machine has always had four gears, and you find that it will work with three, you've satisfied the novelty requirement.

Also, the discovery of a critical area of a given prior-art range will be considered novel. That is, if a prior-art magazine article on dyeing states that a mordant will work at a temperature range of 100–150 degrees centigrade and you discover that it works five times better at 127–130 degrees centigrade, the law still considers this range novel, even though it's technically embraced by the prior art.

A physical difference can also be subtle or less apparent in the hardware sense, so that it's manifested primarily by a different mode of operation. Here are some examples: (a) an electronic amplifying circuit that looks the same, but that operates in a different mode—say Class A rather than Class B; (b) a circuit that is the same physically but is under the control of different software; (c) a pump that looks the same, but that operates at a higher pressure and hence in a different mode; and (d) a chemical reaction that takes place at a substantially different temperature or pressure. All of these will be considered novel, even though they appear the same to the eye.

 NOTE

Processes Note. If your invention is a new process, you don't need any novel hardware; your physical novelty is basically your new way of manipulating old hardware. Any novel step or steps whatever in this regard will satisfy the physical novelty requirement.

b. New Combinations

Many laypersons believe that if an invention consists entirely of old components, it can't be patented. A moment's thought will show that this couldn't be true since virtually all inventions are made of old components. Thus, the PTO will consider your invention novel even if two or more prior-art references (actual devices or published descriptions) together account for all of your invention's physical characteristics. That is, if your invention is a new combination of two old features, the law will consider it novel. (Note that for two or more old references to be legally combinable to prevent your invention from being patented, the actual hardware or parts of the references don't have to be physically combinable: only the concepts inherent in the parts need be usable together.) For example, suppose you invent a bicycle having a frame made of a new carbon-fiber alloy and the prior art includes a patent from 1870 showing your exact bicycle and a magazine article from *Technology Today* from 2005 showing your exact carbon-fiber alloy: Even though these two references taken together show every feature of your invention, your invention still is considered to be novel under Section 102 of the

patent laws since you're the first to "combine" the two old concepts. That is, your bicycle would clearly be considered novel since it has a new physical feature: a frame that is made, for the first time, of a carbon-fiber alloy. For your invention to be considered as lacking novelty and thus subject to rejection under Section 102, all of its physical characteristics must exist in a single prior-art reference. This is often referred to as the "single document rule"; in other words if two separate documents are necessary to show your invention, it is novel under Section 102. But keep in mind, just because it's novel, useful, and fits within a statutory class, doesn't mean the bicycle is patentable. It still must surpass the tough test of unobviousness (covered in the following section).

Another type of new combination which inventors frequently overlook is the new arrangement: If you come up with a new arrangement of an old combination of elements, the PTO will consider this a new combination that will satisfy the novelty requirement. For example suppose you invent an automatic transmission where, for the first time, the torque converter is placed after the gears, rather than before; the PTO will consider that this new arrangement has novelty over the previous arrangement.

"Invention consists in avoiding the constructing of useless combinations and in constructing the useful combinations which are in the infinite minority. To invent is to discern, to choose."

—Henri Poincaré

c. New Use

If you've invented a new use for an old item of hardware, or an old process, the new use will satisfy the novelty requirement, no matter how trivial the newness is. For example, Dorie invents a new vegetable cooker that, after a search, she discovers is exactly like a copper smelter invented by one Jaschik in 1830. Dorie's cooker, even though identical to Jaschik's smelter, will be considered novel, since it's for a different use. (If your invention involves novel physical hardware, technically it can't be a new-use invention.)

If you're the type of person who thinks ahead, you're probably asking yourself, "Why are they bothering with novelty—isn't this requirement inherent in unobviousness—that is, if the invention is found to be unobvious won't it also be found to be novel?" Well, you're 100% correct. If an invention is unobvious, *a fortiori* (by better reason) it must be novel. However, the law makes the determination in two steps (Sections 102 and 103), and most patent professionals have also found it far easier to first determine whether and how an invention satisfies the novelty requirement and then determine if it can be considered unobvious.

F.   Requirement #4: Unobviousness

We're now entering what's probably the most misunderstood and difficult-to-understand, yet most important, issue in patent law—that is, is your invention unobvious? Let's start with a "common misconception."

Common Misconception: If your invention is different from the prior art, you're entitled to get a patent on it.

Fact: Under Section 103 of the patent laws, no matter how different your invention is, you're not entitled to a patent on it unless its difference(s) over the prior art is considered "unobvious" by the PTO or the courts. Because Section 103 is the heart of all patent laws, we are reproducing the first paragraph—the essence of the section—here under the AIA:

35 USC 103 Conditions for patentability; non-obvious subject matter.

> *"A patent for a claimed invention may not be obtained, notwithstanding that the claimed invention is not identically disclosed as set forth in Sec. 102, if the differences between the claimed invention and the prior art are such that the claimed invention as a whole would have been obvious before the effective filing date of the claimed invention to a person having ordinary skill in the art to which the claimed invention pertains. Patentability shall not be negated by the manner in which the invention was made."*

Most of the time a patentability search will produce one or more prior-art references that show devices similar to your invention, or that show several, but not all, of the physical features of your invention. That is, you will find that your invention has one or more features or differences that aren't shown in any one prior-art reference. However, even though your invention is physically different from such prior art (that is, it clears Section 102 as Section 103 states), this isn't enough to qualify for a patent. To obtain a patent, the physical (or use) differences must be substantial and significant. The legal term from Section 103 for such a difference is that it must not be "obvious" or, commonly, it must be "unobvious" or "nonobvious." That is, the differences between your invention and the prior art must not be obvious to one with ordinary skill in the "art" or field of the invention. Because this concept is so important, let's examine it in detail.

1.   Unobvious to Whom?

It doesn't tell anyone much to say an invention must be unobvious. The big question is, unobvious to whom? Under Section 103, you can't get a patent if a person having ordinary skill in the field of your invention would consider the idea of the invention "obvious" at the time you came up with it.

The law considers "a person having ordinary skill in the art to which said subject matter pertains" to be a mythical worker in the field of the invention who has (1) ordinary skill, but who (2) is totally omniscient about all the prior art in his or her field. This is a pure fantasy, since no such person ever lived, or ever will, but realistically there's no other way to come even close to any objective standard for determining nonobviousness.

Let's take some examples. Assume that your invention has to do with electronics—say an improved flip-flop circuit. A Person Having Ordinary Skill In The Art (PHOSITA) would be an ordinary, average logic-circuit engineer who's intimately familiar with all prior-art logic circuits. If your invention relates to the fields of business or the Internet, say a new method of detecting phishing (attempted fraudulent discovery of a password), a PHOSITA would be an Internet software engineer of ordinary skill. If your invention has to do with chemistry, say a new photochemical process, a PHOSITA, a typical photochemical engineer with total knowledge of all photochemical processes, would be your imaginary skilled artisan. If your invention is mechanical, such as an improved cigarette lighter or belt buckle, the PTO would try to postulate a PHOSITA as a hypothetical cigarette-lighter engineer or belt-buckle designer with ordinary skill and comprehensive knowledge. If your invention is a design, say for a computer case, the PTO would invent a hypothetical computer-case designer of ordinary skill and full knowledge of all existing designs as the PHOSITA.

2. What Does "Obvious" Mean?

Most people have trouble interpreting Section 103 because of the word "obvious." If after reading our explanation you still don't understand it, don't be dismayed. Most patent attorneys, patent examiners, and judges can't agree on the meaning of the term. Many tests for unobviousness have been used and rejected by the courts over the years. The courts have often referred to "a flash of genius," and this colorful phrase became the title of a 2008 movie about the efforts of Dr. Robert Kearns to obtain compensation and recognition from Ford for manufacturing vehicles with intermittent windshield wipers, which the court held infringed his patent 3,351,836 (1967). Another colorful term that has been used is "a synergistic effect (the whole is greater than the sum of its parts)." One influential court said that unobviousness is manifested if the invention produces "unusual and surprising results." Foreign countries commonly require an "inventive step." Technically, none of these tests is used any longer. This is because the U.S. Supreme Court, which has final say in such matters, decreed in the famous 1966 case of *Graham v. John Deere*, (383 U.S. 1, 148 USPO 459 (1966)); MPEP 2141, that Section 103 is to be interpreted by taking the following steps:

1. Determine the scope and content of the prior art.

2. Determine the novelty of the invention.
3. Determine the level of skill of artisans in the pertinent art.
4. Against this background, determine the obviousness or unobviousness of the inventive subject matter.
5. Also consider secondary and objective factors such as commercial success, long-felt but unsolved need, and failure of others.

Unfortunately, while in theory the Supreme Court has the last word, in practice it added nothing to our understanding of the terms "obviousness" and "unobviousness." In the crucial step (#4), the court merely repeated the very terms (obvious and unobvious) it was seeking to define. Therefore, most attorneys and patent examiners continue to look for new and unexpected results that flow from the novel features when seeking to determine if an invention is obvious.

Despite its failure to define the term "obvious," the Supreme Court did add an important step to the process by which "obviousness" is to be determined. In Step #5, the court made clear that objective circumstances must be taken into account by the PTO or courts when deciding whether an invention is or isn't obvious. The court specifically mentioned three such circumstances: commercial success, long-felt but unsolved need, and failure of others to come up with the invention.

So, although your invention might not, strictly speaking, produce "new and unexpected results" from the standpoint of one with "ordinary skill in the art," it still may be considered unobvious if, for instance, you can show that the invention has enjoyed commercial success.

Normally, before you file a patent application you won't be able to consider commercial success as a factor in determining patentability. Any sale by anyone who is not associated with the inventor will invalidate any later filed patent application. Again, in order to prevent theft and avoid problems, it is recommended that you file before you sell. Although you usually can't consider commercial success before you file, you can argue commercial success later to the examiner during the prosecution phase if your invention is commercially successful by then.

Under the reasoning of the *John Deere* case, then, to decide whether or not your invention is obvious, you first should ask whether it produces "new and unexpected results" from the standpoint of one skilled in the relevant art. If it does, you've met the test for patentability. However, if there's still some doubt on this question, external circumstances may be used to bolster your position.

 TIP

If you feel your head spinning, don't worry. It's natural. Because these concepts are so abstract, there's no real way to get a complete and comfortable grasp on them. However, if you take it slowly (and take a few breaks from your reading), you should have a pretty good idea of when an invention is and isn't considered "unobvious."

3. Examples of Obviousness and Unobviousness

First, for some examples of unobvious inventions, consider all of the inventions listed in Chapter 2: the magnetic pistol guard, the buried plastic cable, the watch calendar sticker, "Grasscrete," the Wiz-z-er top, the shopping cart, etc. These all had (Section 102) physically novel features that (Section 103) were considered unobvious because they produced new, unexpected results—that is, results that weren't suggested or shown in the prior art.

Although generally you must make a significant physical change for your invention to be considered unobvious, often a very slight change in the shape, slope, size, or material can produce a patentable invention that operates entirely differently and produces totally unexpected results.

> **EXAMPLE:** Consider the original centrifugal vegetable juicer composed of a spinning perforated basket with a vertical sidewall and a nonperforated grater bottom. When vegetables, such as carrots, were pushed into the grater bottom, they were grated into fine pieces and juice that were thrown against the cylindrical, vertical sidewall of the basket. The juice passed through the perforations and was recovered in a container but the pieces clung to the sidewalls, adding weight to the basket and closing the perforations, making the machine impossible to run and operate after a relatively small amount of vegetables were juiced. Someone conceived of making the side of the basket slope outwardly so that while the juice was still centrifugally extracted through the perforated side of the basket, the pulp, instead of adhering to the old vertical side of the basket, was centrifugally forced up the new sloped side of the basket where it would go over the top and be diverted to a separate receptacle. Thus the juicer could be operated continuously without the pulp having to be cleaned out. Obviously, despite the fact that the physical novelty was slight— that is, it involved merely changing the slope of a basket's sidewall—the result was entirely new and unexpected, and therefore was considered unobvious.

In general such a relatively small physical difference (changing the slope of the wall of a basket in a juicer) will require a relatively great new result (ability to run the juicer continuously) to satisfy the unobviousness requirement. On the other hand, a relatively large physical difference will need only minor new results for the PTO to consider it unobvious. That is, in Fig. 5A (The Patentability Mountain) the height of the fourth step can be shortened if the height of the third step is increased.

As indicated, new-use inventions don't involve any physical change at all in the old hardware. However, the new use must be (1) a different use of some known hardware or process, and (2) the different use must produce new, unexpected results.

> **EXAMPLE:** Again consider the Venetian blind cleaner used as a seed planter, and aspirin used as a growth stimulant, discussed above. In both instances, the new use was very different and provided a totally unexpected result: thus both inventions would be patentable. Also, in another interesting new-use case, the patent court in Washington, DC, held that removing the core of an ear of corn to speed freezing and thawing was unobvious over core drilling to speed drying.

The court reasoned that one skilled in the art of corn processing could know that core removal speeds drying without realizing that core removal could also be used to speed freezing and thawing. Accordingly, the court held that the *new* result (faster freezing and thawing) was *unexpected* since it wasn't described or suggested in the prior art.

The courts have held that the substitution of a different, but similarly functioning, element for one of the elements in a known combination, although creating a "novel" invention, won't produce a patentable one unless the results are unexpected. For example, consider the substitution, in the 1950s, after transistors had appeared, of a transistor for a vacuum tube in an old amplifier circuit. At first blush this new combination of old elements would seem to the uninitiated to be a patentable substitution, since it provided tremendous new results (decreased power consumption, size, heat, weight, and far greater longevity). However, you'll soon realize that the result, although new, would have been entirely foreseeable and expected since, just as in the carbon-fiber/bicycle case, the power reduction and reduced-weight advantages of transistors would have been already known as soon as a transistor made its appearance. Thus, although substituting them for tubes provided many new results, it didn't provide the old amplifier circuit with any unexpected new results. Accordingly, the PTO's Patent Trial and Appeal Board held the new combination to be obvious to a PHOSITA at the time.

A factor that works against inventors is that to most people, many inventions seem obvious once they understand the key ideas. So sometimes we have to convince the patent examiner, a potential licensee, or even a judge, not to use hindsight and to try to view the problem without knowledge of the invention in order to understand why it's actually unobvious.

If you're still a bit misty about all this, put yourself in the shoes of an electronic engineer who, at the time of the replacement of the vacuum tube with the transistor, was skilled in designing vacuum tube circuits and was currently designing a flip-flop circuit. Along comes this newfangled "transistor" that uses no heater and weighs one-tenth as much as a comparable tube, but which provides the same degree of amplification and control as the tube did. Do you think that it wouldn't be obvious to the engineer to try substituting a transistor for the tube in that flip-flop circuit? Similarly, the PTO would consider obvious the substitution of an integrated circuit for a group of transistors in a known logic circuit, or the use of a known radio mounting bracket to hold a loudspeaker enclosure instead of a radio. The patent appeals court held that "the routine substitution of modern electronics to an otherwise unpatentable invention typically creates a prima facie [on its face] case of obviousness." (In *re Comiskey*, 499 F.3d 1365 (Fed. Cir. 2007).)

The PTO will also consider as obvious the mere carrying forward of an old concept, or a change in form and degree, without a new result. For instance, when one inventor provided notches on the inner rim of a steering wheel to provide a better grip, the idea was held to be obvious because of medieval sword handles that had similar notches for the same purpose. And the use of a large pulley for a logging rig was held nonpatentable over the use of a small pulley for clotheslines. These situations are known as "obviousness by analogy."

On the other hand, one inventor merely changed the slope of a part in a papermaking (Fourdrinier) machine; as a result the machine's output increased by 25%—a dramatic, new, and unexpected result that was held patentable.

In the recipe field it's usually difficult to come up with an unobvious invention, since most ingredients and their effects are known.

EXAMPLE: Lou comes up with a way to make mustard-flavored hot dog buns—admix powdered mustard with the flour. Even though Lou's recipe is novel, the PTO will almost certainly hold it to be obvious to a PHOSITA since the result of the new combination was entirely foreseeable and expected.

In sum, the PTO will usually hold that substitution of a different material, shape, color, or size is obvious. But if the substitution provides *unexpected* new results, the law will hold it to be unobvious.

The courts and the PTO will also usually consider the duplication of a part obvious unless it can see new results. For instance, in an automobile, the substitution of two banks of three cylinders with two carburetors was held obvious over a six-cylinder, single-carburetor engine, since the new arrangement had no unexpected advantages. However, the use of two water turbines to provide cross flow to eliminate axial thrust on bearings was held unobvious over a single turbine; again, an *unexpected* new result.

Similarly, making devices portable, making parts smaller or larger, faster or slower, effecting a substitution of equivalents (a roller bearing for a ball bearing), making elements adjustable, making parts integral, separable (modular), or in kit form, and other known techniques with their known advantages, will be held obvious unless new, unexpected results can be shown.

Occasionally an inventor will believe that an invention should be considered patentable because it is disposable. As a general rule, that assumption is incorrect. Making products disposable is an old and obvious expedient that has been done with cameras, razors, ballpoint pens, and cigarette lighters. Further, the term "disposable" is too vague to be used in a claim anyway since everything ultimately wears out and thus is disposable. (See Chapter 9 for more information about claims language.) However if you have found a new and unobvious way to make a product more cheaply so that it can be discarded and a new one purchased at a relatively low expense, then the novel way of making it can be patentable.

EXAMPLE: Elaine discovers a new, cheap paper material that can be used to make soft, wearable underwear more cheaply so that it can be discarded after one day's use and at relatively low expense. Elaine's underwear or other garments made of her new paper material is probably patentable, as is the new paper material per se.

CAUTION

If you create what you believe to be a valuable invention, but it seems simple and obvious to you, don't assume automatically that it's legally obvious. Some very simple inventions, like the vegetable juicer and the Fourdrinier machine, have been granted very valuable patents!

NOTE

Design Patent Tip. In design cases, the design must have novel features, and the PTO must be able to regard these as unobvious to a designer of ordinary skill (a PHOSITA). If the design involves the use of known techniques that together don't produce any new and unexpected visual effect, then the PTO will consider it obvious. But if they produce a startling or unique new appearance, then the PTO will hold it to be unobvious. Since only the ornamental appearance and not the function of a design is relevant, the degree of novelty of the design will be the main determinant of unobviousness: a high degree of novelty will always be patentable, while a low degree of novelty will encounter rough sledding unless you can set forth reasons why it has a very different appearance or visual effect.

4. Secondary Factors in Determining Unobviousness

As mentioned, if the new and unexpected results of your invention are marginal, you *may* still be able to get a patent if you can show that your invention possesses one or more secondary factors that establish unobviousness. The PTO and the courts usually give these secondary factors much less weight than the "new and unexpected results" factor, but they still should be considered, especially in close cases. While the Supreme Court listed only three secondary factors in the *John Deere* case, we have compiled a list of 12 basic and nine combinatory secondary factors that the PTO and the courts actually consider. In the real world, these secondary factors must generally be dealt with only if the PTO makes a preliminary finding of obviousness or if your invention is attacked as being obvious. However, when deciding whether your invention is legally entitled to a patent, you'll have a much better idea of how easy or difficult it will be to obtain if you apply these secondary factors to your invention.

SKIP AHEAD

If you're sure that your invention is unobvious, feel free to skip directly to Section 7.

Although some of these secondary factors may appear similar, try to consider each independently, since the courts have recognized subtle differences between them. As part of doing this, remember that lawyers like to chop large arguments into little ones so that it will appear that there are a multitude of reasons for their position rather than just one or two. While this approach may seem silly, it's nevertheless a fact (however sad) that the PTO and courts are used to hearing almost exclusively from lawyers (and, in the case of the PTO, from highly specialized patent agents). Accordingly, the general rule is, the more arguments you can use to claim unobviousness, the better your chances will be of getting a patent.

Now let's look at the secondary factors in detail.

Factor 1. Previous failure of others

If the invention is successful where previous workers in the field were unable to make it work, this will be of great help to your application. For instance, many previous attempts were made to use electrostatic methods for making photocopies, but all failed. Chester Carlson (a patent attorney himself) came along and successfully used an electrostatic process to make copies. This greatly enhanced his case for the patentability of his dry (xerographic) photocopying process.

Factor 2. Solves an unrecognized problem

Here the essence of your invention is probably the recognition of the problem, rather than its solution. Consider the showerhead that automatically shuts off in case of excess water temperature discussed

in Chapter 2. As the problem was probably never recognized in the prior art, the solution would therefore probably be patentable.

Factor 3. Solves an insoluble problem

Suppose that for years those skilled in the art had tried and failed to solve a problem and the art and literature were full of unsuccessful "solutions." Along you come and finally find a workable solution, such as a cure for the common cold: you'd probably get a patent.

EXAMPLE: Potato chips used to be sold in relatively expensive, heavy cardboard boxes that manufacturers thought were necessary to protect against chip breakage. Yet, many chips still broke. Someone thought of packaging the chips in plastic bags that were far cheaper, lighter, and actually reduced the amount of breakage. This invention also satisfies Factor 12.

Factor 4. Commercial success

If your invention has attained commercial success by the time the crucial patentability decision is made, this militates strongly in favor of patentability. Nothing succeeds like success, right?

Factor 5. Crowded art

If your invention is in a crowded field (art)—that is, a field that is mature and that contains many patents, such as electrical connectors or bicycles— a small advance will go farther toward qualifying the invention for a patent than it will in a new, blossoming art.

Factor 6. Omission of element

If you can omit an element in a prior invention without loss of capability, this will count a lot, since parts are expensive, unreliable, heavy, and labor-intensive. A good example is the elimination of the inner tube in tires.

Factor 7. Unsuggested modification

If you can modify a prior invention in a manner not suggested before, such as by increasing the slope in a paper-making machine, or by making the basket slope in a centrifugal juice extractor, this act in itself counts for patentability.

Factor 8. Unappreciated advantage

If your invention provides an advantage that was never before appreciated, it can make a difference. One inventor came up with a gas cap that was impossible to insert in a skewed manner. It was held to be patentable since it provided an advantage that was never appreciated previously.

Factor 9. Solves prior inoperability

If your invention provides an operative result where before only inoperability existed, then it has a good chance for a patent. For instance, suppose you come up with a jet fuel additive that prevents huge fires in case of a plane crash; you've got it made, since all previous fire suppressant additives have been largely unsuccessful.

Factor 10. Successful implementation of ancient idea where others failed

Consider the Wright brothers' airplane. For millennia humans had wanted to fly and had tried many schemes unsuccessfully. The successful implementation of such an ancient desire carries great weight when it comes to getting a patent.

Factor 11. Solution of long-felt need

Suppose you find a way to prevent tailgate-type automobile crashes. Obviously you've solved a powerful need and your solution will be a heavy weight in your favor on the scales of patentability.

Factor 12. Contrary to prior art's teaching

If the prior art expressly teaches that something can't be done or is impractical—for example, humans can't fly without artificial propulsion motors—and you prove this teaching wrong, you've got it made. For example, one inventor realized that packaging potato chips in inexpensive bags (compared to more expensive boxes) actually decreased the amount of breakage. This contrarian discovery militated strongly in favor of unobviousness.

5. Secondary Factors in Determining Unobviousness of Combination Inventions

Inventions that combine two or more elements known in the prior art can still be held patentable, provided that the combination can be considered unobvious— that is, it's a new combination and it produces new and unexpected results. In fact, most patents are granted on such combinations since very few truly new things are ever discovered. So let's examine some of the factors used especially to determine the patentability of "combination inventions" (that is, inventions that have two or more features that are shown in two or more prior-art references).

SKIP AHEAD

The following material is conceptually quite abstract and difficult to understand, even for patent attorneys. We're presenting it in the interest of completeness. However, if you wish, you can safely skip it for now and proceed directly to Section 7. If the PTO or anyone else suggests that two or more prior-art references, taken together, teach that your invention is obvious, come back and read it then.

Factor 13. Synergism (2 + 2 = 5)

If the results achieved by your combination are greater than the sum of the separate results of its parts, this can indicate unobviousness. Consider the pistol trigger release (Chapter 2) where a magnetic ring must be worn to fire the pistol. The results (increased police safety) are far in excess of what magnets, rings, and pistols could provide separately.

EXAMPLE: For another example, suppose that a chemist combines, through experimentation, several metals that cooperate in a new way to provide added strength without added density. If this synergistic result wasn't reasonably foreseeable by a metallurgist, the new alloy would almost certainly be patentable.

Generally, if your invention is a chemical mixture, the mixture must do more than the sum of its components. For this reason, food recipes are difficult to patent unless an ingredient does more than its usual function or produces a new and unexpected result. Or, if you come up with a new technique of cooking that produces a new and unexpected result—for example, a cookie that is chewy inside and crisp outside—you've got a good chance of prevailing. Similarly, if you combine various mechanical or electrical components, the courts and the PTO will usually consider the combination patentable if it provides more than the functions of its individual components.

As an example of an unpatentable combination without synergism, consider the combination of a radio, waffle iron, and blender in one housing. While novel and useful, this combination would be considered an aggregation and obvious, since there's no synergism or new cooperation: the combination merely provides the sum of the results of its components and each component works individually and doesn't enhance the working of any other component. On the other hand, the combination of an eraser and a pencil would be patentable (had it not already been invented) because the two elements cooperate to increase overall writing speed, a synergistic effect. The same would hold true for mounting loudspeakers in a plastic insulating picnic box, where new cooperation results: the box holds the food and provides a baffle for the speakers.

Factor 14. Combination unsuggested

If the prior art contains no suggestion, either expressed or implied, that the references should be combined, this militates in favor of patentability.

Examiners in the PTO frequently are assigned to pass on patent applications for combination inventions. To find the elements of the combination claimed, they'll make a search, often using a computer, to gather enough references to show the respective elements of the combination. While the examiners frequently use such references in combination to reject the claims of the patent application on unobvious grounds, the law says clearly that it's not proper to do so unless the references themselves, or the prior art in general rather than an applicant's patent application, suggests the combination or that the results are predictable.

EXAMPLE: Arthur B. files a patent application on a pastry-molding machine. The examiner cites (or your search reveals) one patent on a foot mold and another on a pastry mold to show the two elements of the invention. It wouldn't be proper to "combine" these disparate references since they're from unconnected fields and thus it wouldn't be obvious to use them together against this invention.

An example of where the law would consider it obvious to combine several references is the case where, as discussed, you make a bicycle out of the lightweight carbon-fiber alloy and, as a result, your bicycle is lighter than ever before. Is your invention "unobvious"? The answer is "No," because the prior art implicitly suggests the combination by mentioning the problem of the need for lighter bikes and the lightness of the new alloy. Moreover, the result achieved by the combination would be expected from a review of existing bicycles and the new lightweight alloy. In other words, if a skilled bicycle engineer were to be shown the new, lightweight alloy, it would obviously occur to the engineer to make a bicycle out of it since bicycle engineers are always seeking to make lighter bicycles.

In *KSR v. Teleflex* (2007), the U.S. Supreme Court made it easier for the PTO or the courts to reject claims or hold patents invalid if those patents are based on a combination of references. Prior to this, the cases held that an invention should not be held obvious over several prior-art references unless there is a suggestion, motivation, or teaching that the references can or should be combined. This case held that there must be some apparent reason in the prior art to justify combining the references. For example, the existence of a problem can make it obvious to try various solutions. The prior art doesn't have to be directed to the precise problem, so long as the references still perform their same functions. If you argue that the combination was not suggested by the prior art, state (if applicable) that the problem solved by your invention is different and the references perform new functions in your combination and the result you achieve was not predictable.

Factor 15. Impossible to combine

This is the situation where prior-art references show the separate elements of the inventive combination, but in a way that makes it seem they would be physically impossible to combine. Stated differently, if you can find a way to do what appears to be physically impossible, then you can get a patent. For example, suppose you've invented the magnetic pistol release. The prior art shows a huge magnetic cannon firing release attached to a personnel shield. Since the step from a cannon to a small handgun is a large one, physical incompatibility might get you a patent—that is, it would be physically impossible to use a huge cannon shield magnet on a small and very differently shaped trigger finger. Note, however, that sometimes by analogy the large can properly be used on the small if a mere change in size is all that's required.

Factor 16. Different combination

Here your combination is A, B, and C, and the prior-art references show a different, albeit possibly confusingly similar combination, say A', B, and C. Since your combination hadn't been previously created, you've got a good case for patentability even though your creation is similar to an existing one. Again the last analogy holds: a personnel shield for a cannon, even though it has a magnetic firing release, is so far different from a finger ring that the prior-art combination must be regarded as different from that of the invention.

Factor 17. Prior-art references would not operate in combination

Here the prior-art references, even if combined, wouldn't operate properly, such as due to some incompatibility. Suppose you've invented a radio receiver comprising a combined tuner-amplifier and a speaker, and the prior art consists of one patent showing a crystal tuner and an advertisement showing a large loudspeaker. The prior-art elements wouldn't operate if combined because the weak crystal tuner wouldn't be able to drive the speaker adequately; thus a combination of the prior-art elements would be inoperative. This would militate strongly in favor of patentability.

Factor 18. References teach away from combining

If the references themselves show or teach that they shouldn't be combined, and you're able to combine them, this militates in favor of patentability. For example, suppose a reference says that the new carbon-fiber alloy should only be used in structural members that aren't subject to sudden shocks, but you were able to make a bike out of the carbon-fiber alloy. If you're able to use it successfully to make a bike frame, which is subject to sudden shocks, you should be able to get a patent.

Factor 19. Awkward, involved combination

Suppose that to make your inventive combination, it takes the structures of three prior-art patents, one of which must be made smaller, another of which must be modified in shape, and the third of which must be made of a different material. These factors can only help you.

Factor 20. References from a different field

If the references show structures that are similar to your invention, but are in a different technical field, this militates in favor of unobviousness and hence of patentability.

Factor 21. Easier to assemble or manufacture

If the novel feature(s) of your invention make it easier or cheaper to assemble or manufacture, this is an important advantage which can be used to prove unobviousness.

6. How Does a Patent Examiner Determine "Unobviousness"?

When patent examiners turn to the question of whether an invention is unobvious, they first make a search and gather all of the patents that they feel are relevant or close to your invention. Then they sit down with these patents (and any prior-art references you've provided with your patent application) and see whether your invention, as described in your claims (see Chapter 9), contains any novelty (novel physical features, new combination, or new use) that isn't shown in any reference. If so, your invention satisfies Section 102—that is, it is novel.

Next they see whether your novelty produces any unexpected or surprising results. If so, they'll find that the invention is unobvious and allow your patent application. If not (this usually occurs the first time they act on your case), they'll reject your application (sometimes termed a "shotgun" or "shoot-from-the-hip" rejection) and leave it to you to show that your new features do indeed produce new, unexpected results. To do this, you can use as many of the reasons listed above that you feel are relevant. If you can convince the examiner, you'll get your patent.

If a dispute over unobviousness actually finds its way into court, however, (a common occurrence) both sides will present the testimony of patent lawyers or technical experts who fit, or most closely fit, the hypothetical job descriptions called for by the particular case. These experts will testify for or against obviousness by arguing that the invention is (or isn't) new and/or that it does (or doesn't) produce unexpected results.

7. Weak Versus Strong Patents

Although this section covers the basic legal requirements for obtaining a patent on an invention, there is, in reality, an additional practical requirement. If the claims in your patent are easy to design around or are so narrow as to virtually preclude you from realizing commercial gain, it's virtually the same as if a patent had been denied you in the first place. The importance of proper claiming cannot be overemphasized. For example, if you claim an improved fan that blows air at 30 miles per hour, and your competitor sells a fan that blows air at 29 or 31 MPH, then their fan will not infringe your patent.

8. The Inventor's Status Is Irrelevant

An inventor's status and personal qualifications are totally irrelevant. An invention need merely meet the four legal criteria The applicant must qualify as a true inventor of the invention but his, her, or their age, sex, citizenship, country of residence, mental competence, health, physical disabilities, nationality, race, creed, religion, state of incarceration, degree of education, amount or time spent inventing, and so on, are irrelevant. The PTO issued a patent on a glider to a death row inventor (U.S. Pat. No. 6,260,795). Even a dead or insane person can apply (through a legal representative, of course).

Common Misconception: If a person invents something by accident, the law won't consider it to be as good an invention as if a genius had come up with it through years of hard, brilliant work.

Fact: The mental abilities of the inventor and the manner of making an invention are totally irrelevant to patentability. The invention is looked at in its own right as to whether or not it would be obvious to one skilled in the art; the way it was made or the qualifications or competence of the applicant are never considered by the PTO.

G. The Patentability Flowchart

To get a better grasp of the admittedly slippery concept of unobviousness and the role it plays in the patent application process, consider Fig. 5C— The Patentability Flowchart. This flowchart is like a computer programmer's flowchart, except that all blocks have been made rectangular to use space more efficiently. In addition to presenting all of the criteria used by the PTO and the courts for determining whether an invention is unobvious, the chart also incorporates the first three tests (statutory class, usefulness, and novelty) of Fig. 5A. Review this chart and the following description of it well, since it sums up the essence of this crucial chapter. Also, you'll want to use this chart when making your search and when prosecuting your patent application. This chart has been designed to cover and apply to anything you might come up with, so you can and should use it to determine the patentability of any utility invention whatever.

Box A (Statutory Class): Assuming that you've made an invention, first determine, using the criteria discussed above, whether you can reasonably classify your invention in one of the five statutory classes indicated without being considered a law of nature, natural phenomenon, or abstract idea. If not, take the "No" output of Box A to the Box X on the left bottom of the chart.

As indicated in Box X, the PTO will probably refuse to grant you a patent, so see if you can gainfully use another form of coverage (such as trade secret, copyright, design patent, trademark, or unfair competition, as discussed in Chapters 1 and 7). If this possibility also fails, you'll have to give up on the creation and invent something else. If the invention can be classified within a statutory class ("Yes" output of Box A), move on to Box B.

Box B (Utility): Now determine, again using the criteria above, whether the invention has utility, including amusement. If not, move to Box X. If so, move on to Box C.

Box C (Novelty): Here's the important novelty determination. If an invention has any physical features that aren't present in any single prior-art reference, or if it is a new combination or rearrangement of old features, or a new use of an old feature or old hardware, no matter how trivial, it will clear Section 102—that is, it has novelty: take the "Yes" output to Box D. If not, it lacks novelty, so take the "No" output and go to Box X again.

Box D (Unobviousness Due to New and Unexpected Results): This is the heart of the chart. You should now determine whether the novelty of your invention would be unobvious to a PHOSITA, that is, does the novelty produce any new and unexpected result ("N&UR")? Use the criteria and examples presented in Sections F1 through F4, above. If you definitely feel that your invention does not provide any N&UR, take the "No" output from Box D to Box X. On the other hand, if your answer is a clear "Yes" (you're sure you have N&UR), it's likely you'll be able to get a patent. While not mandatory, it is recommended that you obtain additional reasons for patentability to boost your confidence by taking the "Yes" output to Box E to consider the "secondary" factors.

If, however, at this point you can't come up with a clear "Yes" or "No" as to N&UR—that is, your invention falls somewhere between these two extremes— it can still qualify for a patent if it has one or more secondary factors. In this case, follow the broken-lined "Possibly" output of Box D to Box E to determine whether your invention qualifies for a patent, even though it doesn't produce any N&UR. From here on, if you took the "Yes" output of Box D, you'll follow a solid-line route, but if you took the "Possibly" output, you'll follow the broken-line route.

Boxes E, F, and G (Other Factors): No matter whether you take the "Yes" = solid line or "Possibly" = broken line route from Box D, you should next answer all of the questions in Box E. Then move to Box F, which tells you to answer all of the questions in Box G if you have a combination invention, or to go directly to the end of Box G if it's not a combination invention. The more questions in Boxes E and G to which you can answer "Yes," the better your chances will be. No matter how you go through Boxes E to G, there are four possibilities, identified below as 1 (A&B) and 2 (A&B).

1. N&URs exist ("Yes" from Box D—solid-line route):
   A. If you answered "Yes" to Box D and to one or more questions in Boxes E and G (there are N&URs and one or more secondary unobviousness factors), take the "Yes"/solid-line output from Box G to Box H, where you'll see that the PTO is very likely to grant you a patent.
   B. If you were not able to answer "Yes" to any question in Boxes E and F (there are N&URs, but no secondary unobviousness factors), take the "No"/solid-line output from Box G to Box I, where you'll see that you'll still be likely to get a patent, based on your N&URs (Box D).

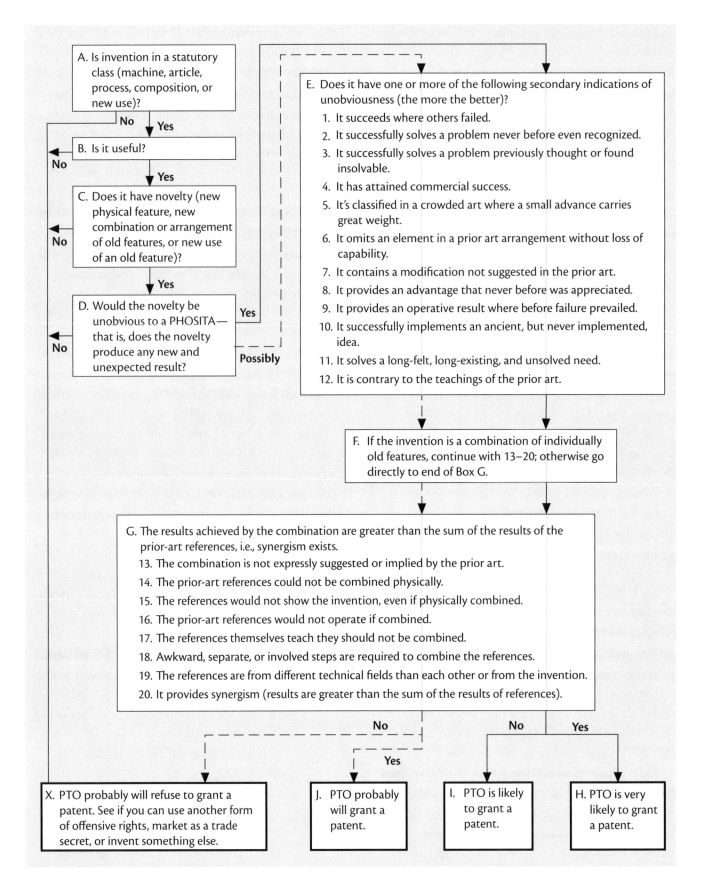

Fig. 5C—The Patentability Flowchart

2. Possible N&URs ("Possibly" from Box D—broken-line route):

   A. If you answered "Possibly" to Box D and "Yes" to one or more questions in Boxes E and G (you're unsure about N&URs but you have one or more secondary unobviousness factors), take the "Yes"/broken-line output from Box G to Box J, where you'll see that the PTO will still probably grant you a patent.

   B. If you answered "Possibly" to Box D, but were not able to answer "Yes" to any question in Boxes E and G (you're unsure about N&URs and there are no secondary unobviousness factors), take the "No"/broken-line output from Box G to Box X, where you'll see that you probably won't be able to get a patent. Don't give up though, if you still think you might be able to prove some secondary factors later, such as commercial success after it hits the market.

H. Don't Make Assumptions About the Law

If you encounter an issue you don't know the answer to and can't find the answer in this book, don't act on any assumptions, because you could suffer for acting on an incorrect assumption. True examples:

- LeRoy assumed that—because a regular patent application had to have at least one claim to be entitled to a filing date—his application, which had four independent claims, counted as four patent applications. He then advertised that he had four patents pending that covered his invention.
- Griselda assumed that if a prior patent showed her invention, but didn't claim it, then she was entitled to get claims to this invention allowed in her patent application.

If you can't find the answer to an issue, you look further, ask a patent attorney, call the PTO's Help Desk at 800-786-9199, or ask an inventors' organization.

I. Summary

The law has four requirements for getting a patent: (1) the invention must be in a statutory class—a machine, an article, a process, a composition, or a new use of the first four; (2) it must be useful (safe, not illegal, operable, and not a nuclear weapon); (3) it must be novel—that is, it must be different in some way from every single item or prior art (prior art means any publication, public use, or public knowledge before the date you file a patent application or Provisional Patent Application); and (4) the novel features must be unobvious to one with ordinary skill in the art—that is, it must produce new and unexpected results or have one or more of the secondary factors of unobviousness.

Search and You May Find

A patentability search is a review of the prior art surrounding your invention. You are looking for a pre-existing invention, device, or publication that would demonstrate that your invention is *not* new or that it is obvious to others in the field. In other words, you're looking for evidence that could prevent you from obtaining a patent. In this way, a patentability search is a paradox, because you're looking for something you hope you won't find! The Patent and Trademark Office (PTO) doesn't require a patentability search, but patent practitioners recommend that all inventors make (or have made) such a search prior to deciding whether to file a patent application.

A. Why Make a Patentability Search?

Here are 14 reasons for making a patentability search.

1. To Determine Whether You Can Get a Patent

The main reason for making a patentability search of your invention is to discover if the PTO will be likely to grant you a patent on your invention. If your search indicates that your invention is likely to qualify for a patent, you can go ahead with your development, marketing, and other work on the invention with far more confidence that your efforts will eventually produce positive results.

If your patentability search indicates that a patent isn't likely to be granted, think about whether to proceed. Most manufacturers won't invest in tooling, producing, and marketing something that their competition can freely copy, and perhaps even sell at a lower cost. (Though there are exceptions as explained in Chapter 7.)

2. To Avoid Needless Expenditures and Work

It makes sense to do a relatively small amount of work—a patentability search—entailing a modest expenditure in order to gain useful information that may well allow you to avoid wasting considerable time and/or spending a relatively large amount of money preparing a patent application.

3. To Provide Background to Facilitate Preparation of Your Patent Application

You'll find it easier to prepare a patent application if you make a patentability search. A search will bring out prior-art references (prior publications including patents and literature) in the field of your invention. After reading these, you're likely to learn much valuable background information that will make the task of writing your patent application easier. Patent attorneys almost always routinely review some sample patents from the field of an invention before they begin preparation of a patent application, in order to give them a "feel for the art."

4. To Know Whether to Describe and Draw Components

A patent application must contain a detailed description of your invention, in sufficient detail to enable a person with ordinary skill in the "art" involved to make and use it. If your invention has certain components with which you aren't familiar, you won't have to take the trouble to draw and describe these in detail if you find them already described in prior-art publications, including patents.

5. To Provide More Information About Operability and Design

When you make a search, you will almost always find patents in the field of your invention, possibly on inventions similar to yours. A reading of these patents will give you valuable technical information about your invention, possibly suggesting ways to make it work better and improve its design, or possibly indicating technical approaches that you should avoid.

6. To Obtain Commercial Information

The patents and other references that you uncover in your search will give you valuable commercial information about similar developments to your invention. For instance, suppose you see many patents on inventions that produce the same result as yours, and you know from your familiarity with the field that none of these has attained commercial success. In this event, you might want to reconsider the wisdom of pushing ahead with your own invention. Or you might conclude that you can do better, because the prior inventions were not commercially exploited properly or because they did not operate properly due to lack of proper components, proper materials, excessive costs, etc.

7. To Obtain Possible Express Proof of Unobviousness

Sometimes a search will uncover references that actually "teach away" from your invention—for example, by suggesting that your approach won't work. You can cite such a reference to the PTO to help convince the examiner to regard your invention as unobvious. For instance, suppose you've invented a bicycle frame made of a new carbon-fiber alloy that makes your bike far lighter and stronger than any previously made. Ordinarily, the substitution of a known alternative material (here a carbon-fiber alloy for steel) would not be patentable, since the substitution would not provide any *unexpected* results or advantages. But suppose during your search you find a prior-art reference (such as an article in *Metallurgic Times*) that states that carbon-fiber should not be used for bicycle frames because it cannot absorb shocks. If you find that such alloys can be used successfully, you can cite this reference to the PTO to show that you've turned a past failure into success. Thus you'll have express, positive proof that your invention provides unexpected results and is unobvious.

8. To Define Around the Prior Art to Facilitate Prosecution

By familiarizing yourself with the prior art, you'll be able to tailor and define the general thrust, structure, and advantages of your patent application around such art and its deficiencies. This will save you work and arm you with the proper terminology and support that you may need later in the "prosecution" stage (that is, the stage where you actually try to obtain a patent from the PTO).

> **EXAMPLE:** LeRoy invented a sturdy but edible, baked scoop for dips, including salsa. His search turned up a patent to Minerva on a similarly shaped cereal product, but which was too fragile for scooping dips. As a result of the knowledge gleaned from his search, LeRoy was able to direct his patent application to the novelty of his scoops by knocking the fragility of Minerva's product and explaining and stressing the strength of his scoops with actual (quantitative) performance figures. This enabled him to distinguish and "sell" his invention over Minerva's product and get a patent.

9. To Learn Your Invention's Novel Features so as to Expedite Prosecution

After making a thorough search of the prior art, you'll be able to find out which of your invention's features are novel, enabling you to recite, stress, and direct your patent application to all of those features and advantages. Also, you can tailor your claims to such novel features so as to preclude an early "final action," expedite the ultimate allowance of your case, and avoid the need to narrow the claims.

10. To Facilitate Licensing or Sale of Your Invention

When you attempt to sell or license your invention rights, your potential licensees will want to know if your patent application will be likely to get through the PTO. You can answer their concern, at least partially, by showing them your search results, providing some confidence in your invention and possibly speeding up and facilitating negotiations.

11. To Find Out What You've Really Invented

Many inventors don't realize or understand exactly what they've invented until they see a search report. Indeed, many inventors get a severe case of "search shock" when their "major advance" turns out to be relatively minor. If this happens, don't give up on your brainchild, since your minor advance may be extremely valuable and vital. On the other hand, occasionally an inventor, believing that the invention is a relatively small advance and that its basic broad idea must have already been invented, is very pleased and surprised to learn from the search results that the invention's a gold mine instead of a nugget!

12. To Get a Stronger Patent

A PTO examiner will usually make a better search than you or a professional searcher will be able to do. Nevertheless, some examiners, at certain times, may miss a highly relevant reference. If anyone uncovers such a reference later, after you get your patent, and brings this reference to the attention of the PTO or any court, it may cast a cloud over, or even invalidate, your patent. However, if you find such a reference in your search, you can (and must) make a record of it in the PTO's file of your patent application, tailor your claims around it, and avoid any potential harm it may cause you later, thus making your patent stronger and less vulnerable.

13. To Get Your Patent Application Examined Ahead of Turn

It's not always a wise idea to get your patent application expedited (see Chapter 10). But, if you really need to speed things up, you'll be entitled to get it examined ahead of its turn if you've made a preexamination search.

14. To Determine If Your Invention Will Infringe Any In-Force Patents

You may wish to know if your invention—if made, used, sold, offered for sale, or imported—will infringe any existing patents, especially if you're considering manufacturing the invention. A search and study of the claims of all relevant in-force patents will reveal this.

B. When Not to Search

Despite our inventor's commandment about doing a patent search prior to filing, there are at least two situations where you can "skip the search."

If you are dealing in a very new or arcane field with which you're very familiar, obviously a search is highly unlikely to be profitable. For example, if you're a biotech engineer who reads all the journals and patents to keep abreast of the state of the art, the newness of your field makes it highly unlikely that you will find any early "prior art." Or, if you make semiconductors and have up-to-the-minute knowledge of all known transistor-diffusion processes, and you come up with a breakthrough transistor-diffusion process, a search will probably not produce any reference showing your idea. Before deciding not to search, however, you should be reasonably certain that you or someone else with whom you are in contact knows all there is to know about the field in question, and that you are fairly confident there is no obscure reference that shows your invention.

In addition, if you've made an improvement to an earlier invention that you've already searched, and you feel the search also covered your improvement, there's obviously no need to make a second search.

TIP

Designs. Generally it's not worth searching design inventions, since the cost and time required to make the search is greater than the time and cost to prepare a design patent application. However, if you believe that some of the reasons expressed, above, are relevant to your situation, you should make a search of your design. Also, you must search your design invention if you want to petition to have your design application examined right away on the "Rocket Docket." (See Chapter 10.)

Common Misconception: There's no reason to make a patentability search prior to filing a patent application because the PTO will make one anyway.

Fact: Even though the PTO will make a search, there are many good reasons (see the 14 reasons, above) to make a search before filing.

C. The Two Ways to Make a Patentability Search

Basically, there are two ways to get your search done: have someone do it for you or do it yourself. If you're a conscientious worker with the necessary free time, and you have access to a search facility (or adequate computer search capability), doing the search yourself is the best way to ensure that it is done thoroughly. This will also save you money and enable you to accumulate valuable information.

However, you may have very good reasons for hiring a professional searcher—for example, you live far from any search facility or you don't have enough time. Also, there's the procrastination factor: half the time the only way some of us will ever get a job done, even though we're capable of doing it, is to turn it over to a pro. If for geographical or other reasons you choose to hire a searcher, you'll find advice on choosing one below. Even if you do use a searcher, read through the instructions on do-it-yourself searching in order to understand what you're paying for and to be able to recognize whether the searcher has done a thorough job.

It's generally not a wise idea to rely on the computer completely, however, because computer searches can miss valuable prior art unless you use the same search words that are in the relevant prior patents. If you do the patentability search yourself, there are three subpossibilities:

1. You can search using the EAST computer system in the PTO in Alexandria, Virginia (definitely the best database)
2. You can do an online search at home or at work, alone or combined with a professional search, or

3. You can do a PubWEST or online search in a local Patent and Trademark Resource Center. Further, wherever you search, there are two types of searches that you can make:
   - **By Classification:** You can make a search of all patents in a particular class and subclass (classification search).
   - **By Keyword:** You can also search for keyword combinations in all patents (keyword search).

Paper Patents Are No Longer Searchable

In the past, inventors and searchers were able to walk into the PTO and search paper patents, either in the public search room or the examining division. Nowadays, the computer has supplanted paper patents for search purposes.

D. The Quality of a Patent Search Can Vary

Your patentability search can never be perfect because there is no way to search unpublished pending patent applications. (A patent application that is based on an RPA or PPA that was filed before your date of invention is valid prior art against your application, even if the patent issues after you file.)

Other reasons why your search may not be perfect are:
- some prior-art references can be missing from the database you're searching
- most patent computer searches do not contain foreign, nonpatent, or exotic references (such as theses, service manuals, magazines, textbooks, etc.)
- very recently issued patents may not have been placed in the computer's database yet
- a relevant reference (patent or nonpatent) may be described using terms that you would not use, or even think of, or
- the technology you are trying to find may have been used publicly without being published before your invention.

E. How to Hire a Patent Professional

Here are some suggestions for how to find and work with a patent professional.

1. Lay Patent Searchers

A lay patent searcher is not licensed to represent inventors before the PTO, (that is because they are usually engineers but not patent agents or patent attorneys). Lay searchers, as well as attorney-agent patent searchers, can be located via online search. Others advertise in periodicals, such as the *Journal of the Patent and Trademark Office Society*, a publication for patent professionals edited and published by a private association of patent examiners, or *Inventor's Digest*. Although there are many good lay searchers, attorneys and agents understand the concept of nonobviousness better and thus dig in more places than might at first appear necessary. However, lay searchers charge about half of what most attorneys and agents charge. Nevertheless, before hiring *any* searcher, find out about the searcher's charges, technical background, on-the-job experience, usual amount of time spent on a search, and where the searcher searches (in the PTO's main search room in the examining division and/or using the EAST system). Most importantly, ask for the names of some clients, preferably in your city, so that you can check with them. Lay searchers do not have to be licensed by any governmental agency, so you should exercise more care in selecting one and you should be aware that they're not allowed to express opinions on patentability.

2. Patent Agents

A "patent agent" is an individual with technical training (generally an undergraduate degree in engineering or science) who is licensed by the PTO to prepare and prosecute patent applications. A patent agent can conduct a patent search and is authorized to express an opinion on patentability, but cannot represent you in court, cannot handle trademarks, and cannot handle licensing or infringement suits.

How to Use a Lawyer or Agent

Here are some tips:

- Make sure the practitioner sends you a copy of every document (letter or official paper) that they generate for you or receive on your behalf.
- Save every paper you receive from the practitioner in a file, keeping official papers, bills, and letters separate.
- Make sure you understand everything the practitioner does or proposes to do for you and why the practitioner is taking this course of action. Almost every possible action is explained in this book, but if not, ask the practitioner to explain it to you.
- Find out in advance the cost of every task the practitioner intends to perform for you and make sure the practitioner understands that you need to approve each and every fee in advance. Have the practitioner agree to obtain your advance approval if any fee will be exceeded. You don't want any open billing. Also make sure the practitioner agrees to send you bills with disbursements itemized and kept separate from the practitioner's fees and that the bills state the basis (time or fixed rate) for the practitioner's fees.
- If you can't communicate with the practitioner, feel that the practitioner is not acting competently, ethically, or honestly, or don't understand what the practitioner is doing and are unable to obtain an adequate explanation, find another practitioner and dismiss the old practitioner. You should have obtained and kept a copy of your papers, but even if you haven't, you are entitled to obtain a copy of your file. In most states you are entitled to the copy without charge, even if you owe the attorney money. Legally, the file belongs to you. Also you are entitled to dismiss your attorney at any time (with rare exceptions).

Although many agents will serve you better, all other things being equal, use an attorney rather than an agent for searching (and patent application work), since most patent attorneys have experience in licensing and litigation that will usually lead them to make wider and stronger searches for possible use in adversarial situations. However, always consider the competence of the individual, how much time he or she will spend with you, and how well you get along.

3. Patent Attorneys

A "patent attorney" or "patent lawyer" is an individual with technical training (generally an undergraduate degree in engineering or science) who is licensed to practice both by the PTO and the attorney-licensing authority (such as the state bar, state supreme court, etc.) of at least one state. A "general" lawyer licensed to practice in one or more states, but not before the PTO, can handle copyrights and trademarks but is not authorized to prepare patent applications or use the title "patent attorney." An intellectual property attorney handles trademarks and copyrights and may or may not be licensed by the PTO to prepare and file patent applications.

4. Finding Patent Agents and Attorneys

All patent agents and attorneys registered to practice before the PTO are listed on the PTO's website at https://oedci.uspto.gov. For patent search purposes, you will want to find an attorney or agent in the Alexandria, Virginia, area (a suburb of Washington, DC). Most patent attorneys and agents who do searching in the PTO can be found in the District of Columbia section, or the Virginia section of the PTO's attorney directory under ZIP codes 22202 or 22301–22336. Pick one or more of these and then call or write to say you want a search made in a particular field. (Generally, hiring an attorney in your locality to do the search is a very inefficient and costly way to do the job, because the attorney or agent will have to hire an associate in or travel to Alexandria to make the search for you.)

Finding a good patent professional often involves more than checking a list. The best way is by personal referral. Another way to check an attorney or agent is to look at the patents they've prepared. You can find these online on the PTO site by entering the attorney's name and reading some of the recent patents. If you do find someone who seems good, make an appointment to discuss the broad outlines of your problem.

Ask what undergraduate degree the attorney has (almost all have undergraduate degrees in engineering or a science); you don't want to use a mechanical engineer to handle a complex computer circuit.

Your next question should be, "Will the professional help you help yourself or demand a traditional attorney-client relationship (attorney does it all and you pay for it)?" Many corporate-employed and retired patent professionals will be delighted to help you with your search, preparation, and/or prosecution of your patent application. Using this approach, you can do much of the work yourself and have the professional provide help where needed at a reasonable cost.

How to Find "Discount" Patent Attorneys and Agents

Active patent professionals (attorneys and agents) are either in private practice (a law firm or solo practice) or employed by a corporation or the government. Most patent professionals in private practice charge about $100 to $600 an hour. But many corporate-employed or semiretired patent professionals also have private clients and charge considerably less than their downtown counterparts. If you want or ever need to consult a local patent professional, you'll save money by using one of these "discount" patent professionals; their services are usually just as good or better than those of the full-priced law firm attorneys. Also, since they have much less overhead (rent, books, secretaries), they'll be more generous with their time (except that patent professionals employed by the federal government are not allowed to represent private clients). Look in the geographical region listing of PTO's attorney directory (https://oedci.uspto.gov) or search by ZIP code for corporate-employed or retired (but still licensed) patent professionals in your area.

When it comes to fees, you should always work these out in advance. Some patent professionals charge a flat fee for searches (and also for patent applications and amendments); others charge by the hour. If you plan to do much of the work yourself, you'll want hourly billing. If you do agree to hourly billing, be sure to first obtain an estimate of the maximum number of hours and an agreement to notify you in advance if this will be exceeded. Many patent attorneys are used to corporate clients who use an open-ended billing arrangement—that is, they bill by the hour without providing any limit or flat fee arrangement. With this system, you can quickly become liable for far more than you may want to spend. Also, be sure it's clear who will pay for other costs associated with prosecuting a patent, such as copies, postage, drafting, filing fees, etc.

When you visit a patent attorney or agent, remember that they're not an oracle of knowledge: Don't expect to be able to lay a prototype or sketch of your invention on their desk and say, "What do you think of this?" and have them instantly tell you its commercial value and give you an opinion on patentability. First, they usually are not qualified to do a commercial evaluation. Second, they can't give you an opinion on patentability without making and analyzing a search.

F. How to Prepare Your Searcher

You'll want to use your patent searcher to maximum efficiency. Do this by sending your searcher easily understandable drawings (they can be informal sketches as long as they are clear) with a clear and complete description of your invention and the drawings. Be sure to disclose all embodiments, variations, and ramifications so that these will be searched. You won't compromise any trade-secret status of your invention (or start the one-year clock running) by such a letter since by law it's considered a confidential communication. If you wish any type of particular emphasis applied to any aspect of your search, be sure to inform the searcher of this fact. If your notebook record of your invention or your invention disclosure is clear enough, you can merely send the searcher a copy. Fig. 6A is an example of a proper search request letter from an inventor and Figs. 6B (a, b, c) are copies of the attachments to the search request letter of Fig. 6A.

You don't need to have a patent agent or a patent attorney sign a Keep-Confidential Agreement, because registered (PTO-licensed) patent professionals are strictly bound by the PTO's rules to keep all client communications confidential. However, if you feel

insecure, or you are using a layperson to search, you certainly can ask your searcher to sign Form 3-1. In any case, you should always keep a "paper trail" of all disclosures you make to anyone.

G. Analyzing the Search Report

After you send out your search request, the searcher will generally take several weeks to perform the patentability search, obtain copies of the patents and other references that the searcher feels are relevant, and report back. Most search reports have four parts:

1. A description of your invention provided by the searcher to assure you that the searcher has understood your invention and to indicate exactly what has been searched.
2. A list of the patents and other references discovered during the search.
3. A brief discussion of the cited patents and other references, pointing out the relevant parts of each.
4. A list of the classes, subclasses, or keywords searched and the examiners consulted, if any.

The searcher will enclose copies of the references (usually U.S. patents, but possibly also foreign patents, magazine articles, etc.) cited in the search report and enclose a bill. Most searchers charge separately for the search, the reference copies, and the postage. If you've paid the searcher a retainer, you should be sent a refund unless your retainer was insufficient. In this case, you'll receive a bill for the balance you owe.

> **EXAMPLES:**
> - Fig. 6C is an example of a typical, competently done search report sent by Samuel Searcher, Esq., in response to Millie Inventress's letter of Fig. 6A.
> - Fig. 6D(a) is a copy of page 1 (the drawing) of the Gabel patent cited in the search report.
> - Fig. 6D(b) is a copy of page 2 of Gabel (the first page of Gabel's specification).
> - Fig. 6D(c) is a copy of page 1 of the Le Sueur patent cited in the search report.

You should now read the searcher's report and the references carefully. Then, determine whether your invention is patentable over the references cited in the search report. Let's use Millie's search report as an example of how to do this.

Millie Inventress
1901 JFK Boulevard
Philadelphia, PA 19103

2016 Jan 22
Samuel Searcher, Esq.
2001 Jefferson Davis Highway
Arlington, VA 22202

Patentability Search: Inventress: Napkin-Shaping Ring

Dear Mr. Searcher:

As we discussed on the phone yesterday, you were highly recommended to me as an excellent searcher by Jacob Potofsky, Esq., who is a general attorney here and a cousin of my friend, Shirley Jaschik. You said that you would be able to make a full patentability search on my above invention, including an examiner consultation and a search in the examiner's files to cover foreign and nonpatent references, for $1,000, including patent copies and postage. I have enclosed this amount as full payment in advance, per your request. You said that you would mail the search report (without an opinion on patentability) and references to me within three weeks from the date you receive this letter.

Enclosed are three sheets of drawings from my notebook (I have properly signed, witnessed, and dated records elsewhere); these sheets clearly illustrate my napkin-shaping ring invention. As you can see from the prior-art Figs 1 (A and B), previous napkin rings were simple affairs, designed merely to hold a previously rolled or folded napkin in a simple shape. In contrast, the napkin ring of my invention, shown in Fig 2, and made of metal or plastic, has a heart-shaped outer member 12, an inner leg 14, and two curved-back arms 16. As shown in Fig 3, it is used by introducing a corner 8 of a cloth napkin 10 between an end 4 of leg 4 and the adjacent portion of outer member 12. When napkin 10 is pulled partially through the ring, as indicated in Fig 4, it will be forced to assume the shape of the space between arms 16 and outer portion 12, as indicated.

Thus my napkin-shaping-and-holding ring can be used to make a napkin have an attractive, graceful shape when it is laid flat and placed adjacent to a place setting, as indicated in Fig 5. The extending portion of the napkin can also be folded up and around, as indicated in Fig 6-A, so that the napkin and its ring can be stood upright.

In addition to the specific shape shown, you should of course search the broader concept of my invention, namely a ring-shaped outer member with an inwardly extending tongue or leg that can be used to shape napkins pulled partially through the structure. I believe that I have provided you with sufficient information to fully understand the structure and workings of my invention so that you can make a search, but if any further information is needed, please don't hesitate to call me.

I understand that you will, in accordance with the ethics of your profession, keep all details of my invention strictly confidential, except to consult an examiner.

Most sincerely,

Millie Inventress

Millie Inventress (215-776-3960)
Encs.: $1,000 check, 3 sheets of drawings
(My file: Search.ltr)

Fig. 6A—Inventor's Search Request Letter to Patent Searcher

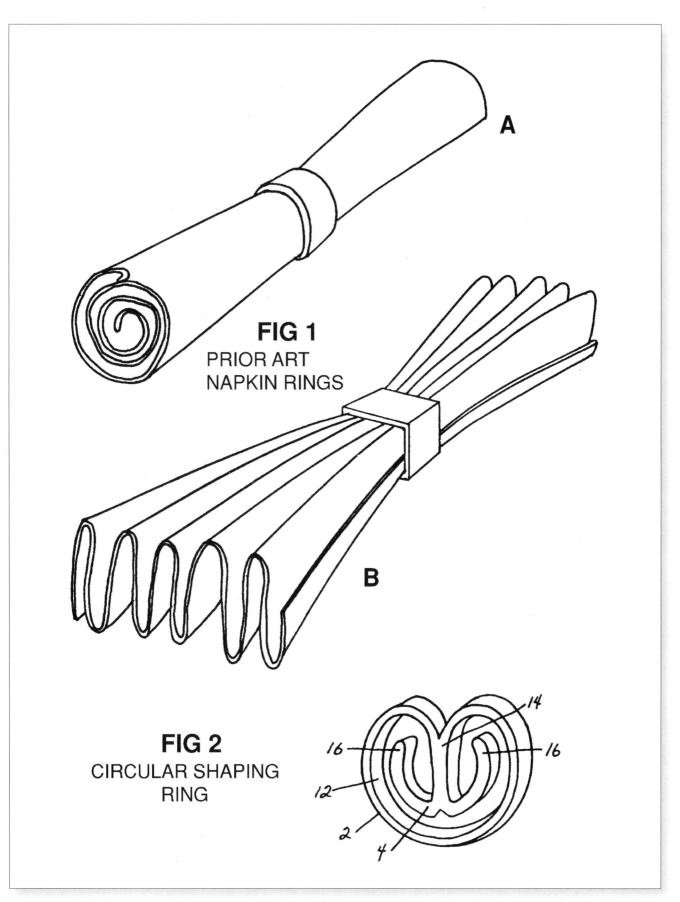

A

FIG 1
PRIOR ART
NAPKIN RINGS

B

FIG 2
CIRCULAR SHAPING
RING

14

16

16

12

2

4

Fig. 6B(a)—Drawing of Invention, Part a

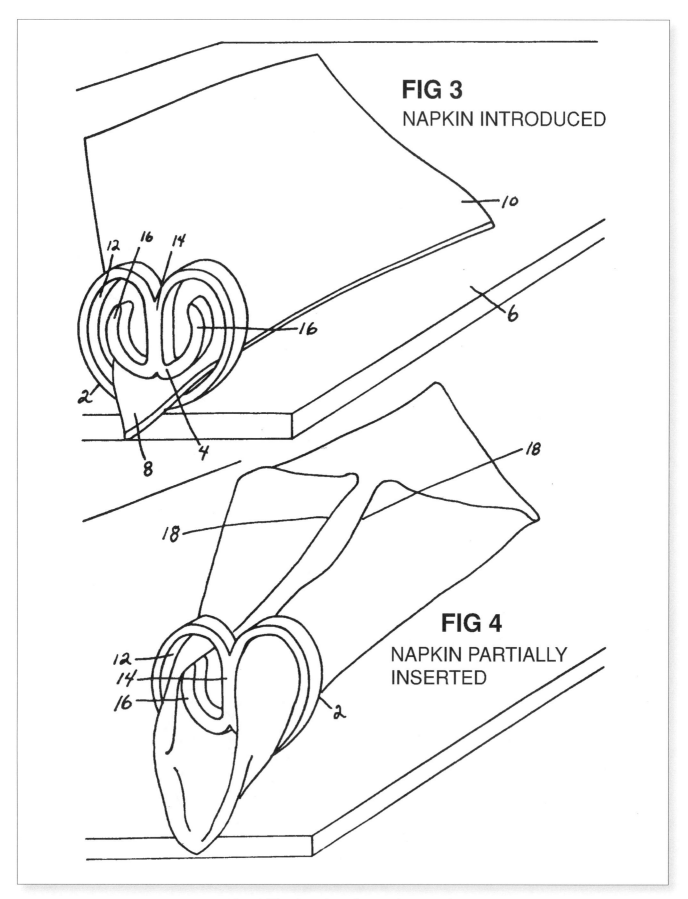

Fig. 6B(b)—Drawing of Invention, Part b

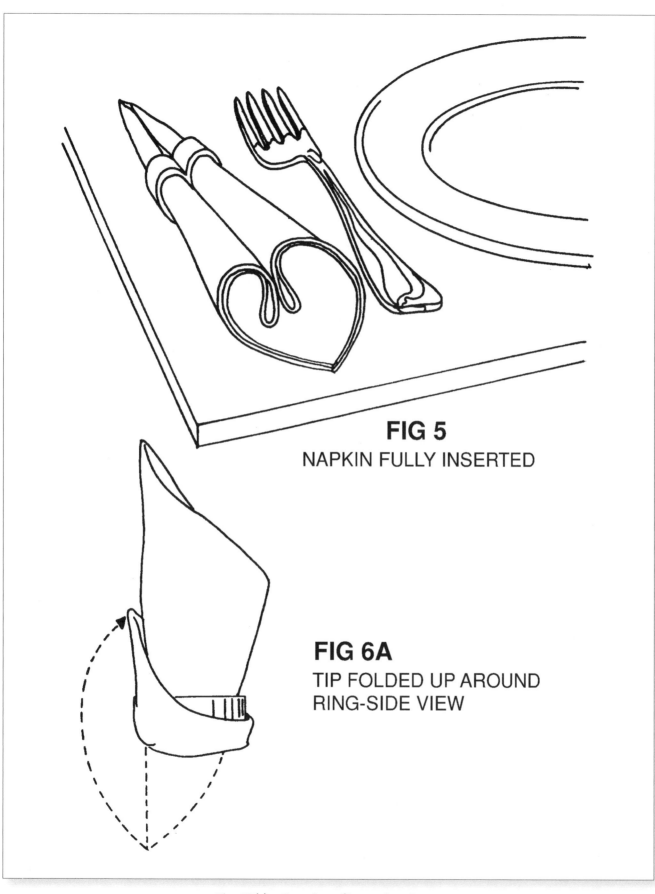

FIG 5
NAPKIN FULLY INSERTED

FIG 6A
TIP FOLDED UP AROUND
RING-SIDE VIEW

Fig. 6B(c)—Drawing of Invention, Part c

SAMUEL SEARCHER
Patent Attorney
2001 Jefferson Davis Highway
Arlington, VA 22202
703-521-3210
2016 Feb 21

Ms. Millie Inventress
1901 JFK Boulevard
Philadelphia, PA 19103

Search Report: Inventress: Napkin-Shaping Ring

Dear Ms. Inventress:

In response to your letter of Jan. 22, I have made a patentability search of your above invention, a napkin-shaping ring comprising an outer portion with an inwardly extending leg and flared-back arms at the end of the leg. I have also searched the broader concept of an annular member with an inward cantilevered leg for shaping a napkin that is drawn therethrough. My bill for $900, the total cost of this search, including the references and postage, is enclosed and is marked "Paid"; I thank you for your check and enclose a refund of $100.

I searched your invention in the following classes and subclasses in the actual examining divisions: 40/21, 40/142, D44/20, and 24/8. In addition, I consulted Examiner John Hayness in Group Art Unit 353 regarding this invention. Otherwise, I kept your invention strictly confidential. In my search, I thought the following references (all U.S. Patents) were most relevant, and I enclose a copy of each: **Bergmann**, 705,196 (1902); **Gabel**, 1,771,328 (1930); **Hypps**, 3,235,880 (1966); and **Le Sueur**, 3,965,591 (1976).

Bergmann shows a handkerchief holder that comprises a simple coiled ring with wavy portions.

Gabel is most relevant; she shows a curtain folder comprising a folded metal device through which a curtain (already partially folded) is inserted and then pulled through and ironed at the exit end.

Hypps shows a necktie and holding device.

Le Sueur shows a napkin ring with magnetically attachable names.

I could not find any napkin-shaping devices as such and Examiner Hayness was not aware of any either. However, be sure to consider the Gabel patent carefully, as it appears to perform a somewhat similar function, albeit for curtains.

It was my pleasure to serve you. I wish you the best of success with your invention. Please don't hesitate to call if you have any questions.

Most sincerely,

Samuel Searcher

Samuel Searcher
Encs: $100 Check, Bill, and References

Fig. 6C—Patent Searcher's Search Report

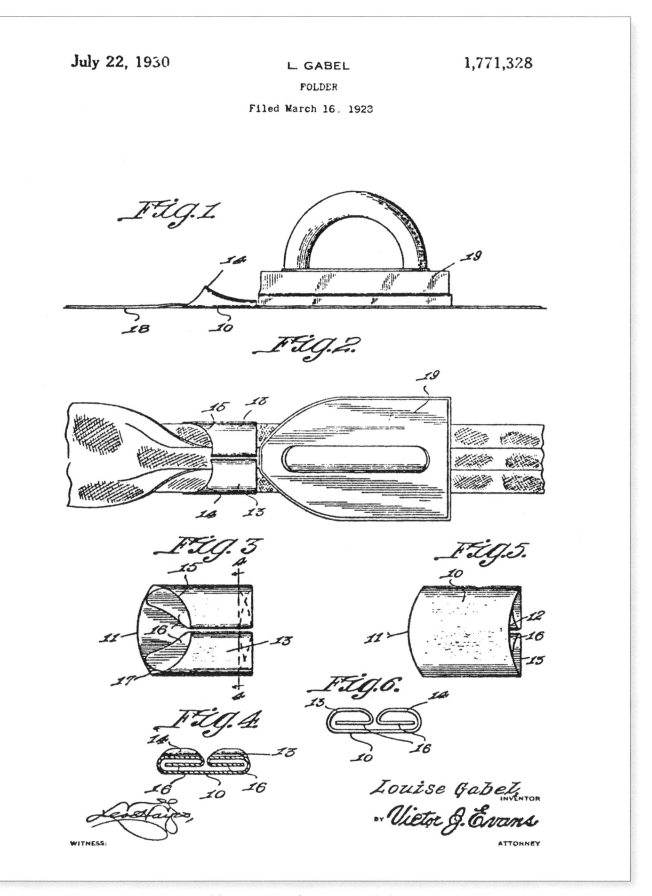

Fig. 6D(a)—Drawing of Prior-Art Gabel Patent

Patented July 22, 1930

1,771,328

UNITED STATES PATENT OFFICE

LOUISE GABEL, OF COLUMBUS, NEBRASKA

FOLDER

Application filed March 16, 1928. Serial No. 262,243.

This invention relates to cloth holding devices and more particularly to a device adapted for holding cloth in the form of plaits while ironing and sewing.

5 An other object of the invention comprehends an enlarged entrance opening in one end of the device within which the cloth may be introduced.

A further object of the invention contem-
10 plates tongue members adapted to form creases in the cloth.

An additional object of the invention consists of a portion removed from the discharge end of the device whereby binding action of
15 a sad iron therewith is obviated while pressing the cloth.

With the above and other objects in view, the invention further consists of the following novel features and details of construc-
20 tion, to be hereinafter more fully described, illustrated in the accompanying drawing and pointed out in the appended claim.

In the drawing:—

Figure 1 is a side elevation of the inven-
25 tion while in use and followed by a sad iron.

Figure 2 is a top plan view of Figure 1.

Figure 3 is a top plan view of the invention per se.

Figure 4 is a sectional view taken on line
30 4—4 of Figure 3.

Figure 5 is a bottom plan view of the invention.

Figure 6 is a front elevation of the invention per se.

35 Referring to the drawing in detail, wherein like characters of reference denote corresponding parts, the reference character 10 indicates a plate member having a curved outwardly projecting forward end 11 and
40 a concaved inner end 12.

The sides of the plate are bent upon themselves upwardly and inwardly upon the plate to provide horizontally disposed guide members 13.

45 As illustrated in Figures 1, 3, 4 and 6, the outermost end, namely 11, is flared to provide an enlarged entrance and to accomplish such construction the outermost ends of the
50 guide members 13 are upwardly flared, as in-

dicated at 14 and concaved, as indicated at 15 upon the foremost edges thereof.

Tongues 16, carried by the guide members 13, are extended reversely thereof and dis-
posed in spaced relation to the upper side of 55 the plate member 10. The side edges of the tongues being also spaced from the guide members. The foremost ends of the tongues 16 are rounded, as indicated at 17, and projected forwardly for greater distances than 60 the adjacent ends of the guide members 13.

In the use and operation of the invention, lengths of cloth, such as indicated at 18, of a desired width, are partially folded along the side edges thereof and the strip per se 65 laid upon the upper side of the plate member 10. The folded portions of the strip be-
ing adapted to repose upon the upper sides of the tongues 16 and to be projected within the spaces as defined between the tongues and the 70 guide members. Due to the fact that the outermost end of the device is flared, an en-
larged entrance is provided by means of which the cloth may be readily introduced and fed. The rounded portions 17 for the 75 tongues also permit ease in the drawing of the cloth through the device or the sliding of the device upon the cloth. As illustrated in Figures 1 and 2 of the drawing, a sad iron, such as indicated at 19, may travel upon 80 the cloth 18 immediately behind the device to press the folded side edges or plaits of the cloth. By the same token, the invention could be used in the formation of dif-
ferent kinds of braids and etc., and to ef- 85 fectively feed the cloth or strip to a sewing machine, in the event the plaits are to be held against displacement from the strip per se.

The concaved portion 12, upon the inner-
most end of the strip 10, is adapted to pre- 90 vent binding action of the sad iron 19 there-
with when the latter closely pursues the plate member. Such construction will also prevent injury to the strip and plaits. 95

Although I have shown, described and il-
lustrated my invention as being primarily adapted for use in the manufacture of plaits, it is to be obviously understood that the invention could be effectively employed for 100

Fig. 6D(b)—Specification of Prior-Art Gabel Patent

United States Patent [19]

Le Sueur

[11] **3,965,591**

[45] **June 29, 1976**

[54] **NAPKIN RING**

[75] Inventor: **Alice E. J. Le Sueur,** Cobble Hill, Canada

[73] Assignee: **The Raymond Lee Organization,** New York, N.Y. ; a part interest

[22] Filed: **Nov. 26, 1974**

[21] Appl. No.: **527,216**

[52] **U.S. Cl.**.. **40/21 R**
[51] **Int. Cl.²**.. **G09F 3/14**
[58] **Field of Search**.................. 40/142 A, 63, 21 A, 40/21 B, 10; 63/2; 24/8

[56] **References Cited**
UNITED STATES PATENTS

198,065   12/1877   Annin .... 63/1 X

2,600,505   6/1952   Jones .... 40/142 A
2,653,402   9/1953   Bonagura .... 40/21 A

FOREIGN PATENTS OR APPLICATIONS

1,308,888   10/1962   France 40/142

Primary Examiner—Louis G. Mancene
Assistant Examiner—Wenceslao J. Contreras
Attorney, Agent, or Firm—Howard I. Podell

[57]   **ABSTRACT**

An open cylindrical napkin ring fitted with magnetic means for attaching an identifying name or set of initials in a recess on the outside of the ring.

3 Claims, 4 Drawing Figures

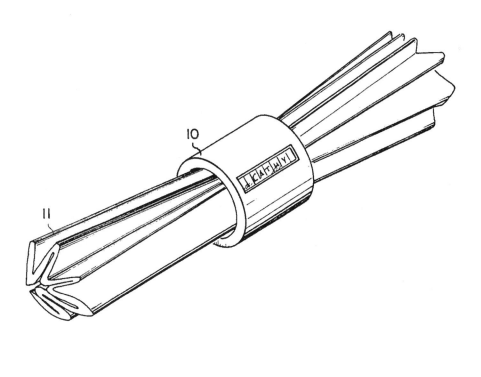

Fig. 6D(c)—Abstract Page of Prior-Art Le Sueur Patent

PATENT DOCUMENT KIND CODES

With new number formats as they appear on documents published on or after January 2, 2001. For a full explanation of document kind codes see WIPO Standard ST.16, available at http://www.wipo.int/scit/en.

New Number Format

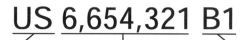

US 6,654,321 B1

country code   document number   document code

Document Type	Before Jan. 2, 2001	On or After Jan. 2, 2001	
	Number Format	Code	Number Format
Utility Patents			
Issued patent (no pre-grant publication)	5,123,456	B1	US 6,654,321 B1
Issued patent (with pre-grant publication)	NA	B2	US 6,654,322 B2
Application (first publication)	NA	A1	US 2001/0001111 A1
Second or subsequent republication of an application	NA	A2	US 2001/0002222 A2
Correction of a published application	NA	A9	US 2001/0003333 A9
Plant Patents			
Issued patent (no pre-grant publication)	Plant 11,000	P2	US PP12,345 P2
Issued patent (with pre-grant publication)	NA	P3	US PP12,345 P3
Application (first publication)	NA	P1	US 2001/0004444 P1
Second or subsequent republication of an application	NA	P4	US 2001/0005555 P4
Correction of a published application	NA	P9	US 2001/0006666 P9
Design Patents	Des. 456,789	S	US D654,321 S
Reissue Patents	RE36,543	E	US RE12,345 E
Reexaminations			
Reexamination certificate issued from first reexamination of a patent (utility, plant, design or reissue)	B1 5,123,456 B1 Plant 11,000 B1 Des. 123,456 B1 RE12,345	C1	US 6,654,321 C1 US PP12,345 C1 US D654,321 C1 US RE12,345 C1
Reexamination certificate issued from second reexamination of a patent	B2 5,123,456 etc.	C2	US 6,654,321 C2 etc.
Reexamination certificate issued from third reexamination of a patent	B3 5,123,456 etc.	C3	US 6,654,321 C3 etc.
Other Patent Documents			
Statutory invention registration (SIR) documents	H1,234	H1	US H2345 H

Created: 1/16/01 MJW

Fig. 6D(d)—Patent Document Kind Codes

Note from Fig. 6B that the napkin-shaping ring of the invention has an annular (ring-shaped) outer member with an inwardly projecting leg. The leg has flared-back arms at its free end. When a folded napkin is drawn through the ring, tip first, the arms and annular member will shape the napkin between them in an attractive manner, as indicated in Fig. 6B(c).

Of the four previous patents cited, let's assume that only Gabel and Le Sueur are of real relevance. Gabel, a patent from 1930, shows a curtain folder comprising a bent sheet-metal member. A curtain is folded slightly and is drawn through the folder that completes the folding so that the curtain can be ironed when it is drawn out of the folder. Le Sueur, a patent from 1976, shows a napkin ring with a magnetized area for holding the letters of the name of a user.

Now, as part of analyzing this sample search report, we'll use the master flowchart reproduced below, as Fig. 6E. If any part of this chart confuses you, reread the part of Chapter 5 that explains each box in detail.

Okay, now let's work our way through the chart:

Box A: Millie's napkin-shaping ring can be classified within a statutory class as an article (or even a machine, since it shapes napkins).

Box B: It clearly has usefulness, since it provides a way for unskilled hostesses or hosts to give their napkins an attractive, uniform shape.

Box C: We must now ask whether the invention is novel—that is, physically different from any single reference. Clearly it's different from Le Sueur because of its inwardly extending leg 14. Also, it's different from Gabel because, comparing it with Gabel's Fig. 6, it's rounder and it has a complete outer ring with an inwardly extending leg, rather than a folded piece of sheet metal. It's important to compile a list of the differences (novel features) that the invention has over the prior-art references, not the differences of the references over your invention.

Box D: The question we must now ask is, "Do the novel features (the roundness of the ring, the inwardly extending leg, and the flared-back arms) provide any new and unexpected results?" After carefully comparing Gabel with Millie's invention, we can answer with a resounding "Yes!" Note that Gabel states, in her

column 2, lines 62 to 66, that the strip of cloth is first partially folded along its side edge and then it is placed in the folder. In contrast, Millie's shaping ring, because of its roundness and leg, can shape a totally unfolded napkin—see Millie's Figs. 3 and 4. This is a distinct advantage, since Millie's shaper does all of the work automatically—the user does not have to specially fold the napkin. While not an earthshaking development or advance, clearly Millie's ring does provide a new result and one that is unexpected, since neither Gabel, Le Sueur, nor any other reference teaches that a napkin ring can be used to shape an unfolded napkin. Thus we take the solid-line "Yes" output of Box D to Box E.

Box E: Although not mandatory, we next check the secondary factors (1 to 22) listed in Boxes E, F, and G.

Reading through these factors, we find first that factor 2 in Box E applies—that is, the invention solves a problem (the inability of most persons to quickly and neatly fold napkins so that they have an attractive shape) that was never before even recognized. Also, we can provide affirmative answers to factors 8 and 11, since the invention provides an advantage that was never before appreciated and it solves a long-felt, but unsolved need—the need of unskilled persons to shape napkins quickly and gracefully (long felt by the more fastidious of those who hate paper napkins, at least).

Boxes F and G: Since two references are present, and each shows some part of Millie's invention, we have to answer "Yes" to Box F and proceed to Box G to consider the possible effect that a combination of these would have on the question of obviousness ("combinatory unobviousness"). In Box G we see that factors 13, 15, 18, 19, and 21 can reasonably be argued as relevant to Millie's invention. The invention has synergism (factor 21), since the results (automatic napkin folding) are greater than the sum of the references; the combination of the two references is not suggested (factor 13) by the references themselves; and even if the two references were combined, Millie's inward leg would not be shown (factor 15). The references are complete and fully functional in themselves, and hence teach by implication that they should not be combined (factor 18). And it would be awkward, requiring redesign and tooling, to combine

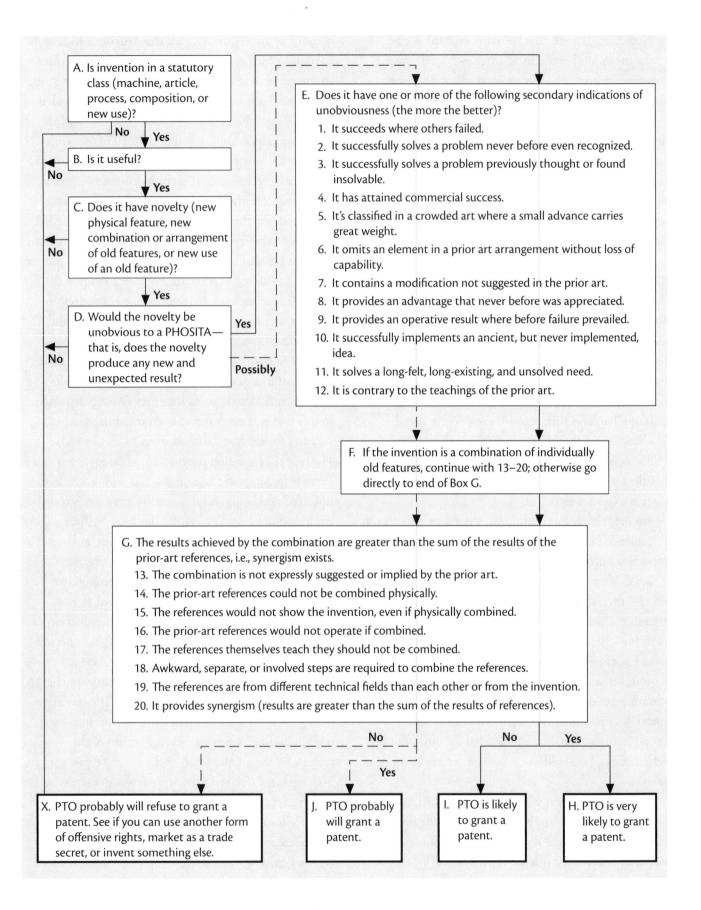

A. Is invention in a statutory class (machine, article, process, composition, or new use)?

No / Yes

B. Is it useful?

No

Yes

C. Does it have novelty (new physical feature, new combination or arrangement of old features, or new use of an old feature)?

No

Yes

D. Would the novelty be unobvious to a PHOSITA—that is, does the novelty produce any new and unexpected result?

Yes

No

Possibly

E. Does it have one or more of the following secondary indications of unobviousness (the more the better)?

1. It succeeds where others failed.
2. It successfully solves a problem never before even recognized.
3. It successfully solves a problem previously thought or found insolvable.
4. It has attained commercial success.
5. It's classified in a crowded art where a small advance carries great weight.
6. It omits an element in a prior art arrangement without loss of capability.
7. It contains a modification not suggested in the prior art.
8. It provides an advantage that never before was appreciated.
9. It provides an operative result where before failure prevailed.
10. It successfully implements an ancient, but never implemented, idea.
11. It solves a long-felt, long-existing, and unsolved need.
12. It is contrary to the teachings of the prior art.

F. If the invention is a combination of individually old features, continue with 13–20; otherwise go directly to end of Box G.

G. The results achieved by the combination are greater than the sum of the results of the prior-art references, i.e., synergism exists.

13. The combination is not expressly suggested or implied by the prior art.
14. The prior-art references could not be combined physically.
15. The references would not show the invention, even if physically combined.
16. The prior-art references would not operate if combined.
17. The references themselves teach they should not be combined.
18. Awkward, separate, or involved steps are required to combine the references.
19. The references are from different technical fields than each other or from the invention.
20. It provides synergism (results are greater than the sum of the results of references).

No

No Yes

Yes

X. PTO probably will refuse to grant a patent. See if you can use another form of offensive rights, market as a trade secret, or invent something else.

J. PTO probably will grant a patent.

I. PTO is likely to grant a patent.

H. PTO is very likely to grant a patent.

Fig. 6E—Patentability Flowchart

the references (factor 19). Thus we can with conviction state that several secondary factors are present, so we take the solid-line "Yes" output of Box G to Box H.

Next, (**Box H**) we see that the PTO is very likely to grant a patent, and our determination on patentability is accordingly positive.

In fact, this exercise is a real case: An examiner initially rejected an application for the napkin-shaping ring as unpatentable over Gabel and Le Sueur. However, he agreed to grant a patent (U.S. Pat. No. 4,420,102) after an argument was filed, forcefully stating the above considerations.

TIP

Although we have analyzed the search report to determine whether Millie's invention was patentable, it's important to remember that a weak patent isn't much better than no patent. So in addition to reaching a decision on patentability, you should also walk the extra mile to determine whether your patent is likely to be of broad enough scope to make it economically worthwhile (see Chapter 4).

Note that we have done our own patentability evaluation—the four-part list, above—and that the search report of Fig. 6C didn't include an opinion on patentability. There are several reasons for this.

First, if your searcher is a layperson (not a patent attorney or agent), the searcher is not licensed to give opinions on patentability since this constitutes the practice of law.

Second, even if your searcher is an attorney or agent, the searcher usually won't provide an opinion on patentability because most searchers are used to working for other patent attorneys who like to form their own opinions on patentability for their clients.

Third, if the searcher's opinion on patentability is negative, a negative written opinion might be damaging to your case if you do get a patent, sue to enforce it, and the opinion is used as evidence that your patent is invalid. This would occur, for example, if your court adversary (the defendant infringer) obtains a copy of the opinion by pretrial discovery (depositions and interrogatories), shows it to the judge, and argues

that since your own search came up with a negative result, this militates against the validity of your patent. However, a negative written opinion can be "worked" in court—that is, distinguished, explained, rebutted, etc.—so if you want the searcher's opinion on patentability in addition to the search, most patent attorney/agent searchers will be glad to give it to you without extra charge, or for a slight additional cost of probably not more than $300 to $600.

Fourth, armed with the knowledge you've gained from Chapter 5, you should be able to form your own opinion on patentability by now; the exercise will be insightful to your invention.

Fifth, note that there's no certainty in the law. No one can ever say for certain that you'll be able to get a patent before you get it since no search can cover pending patent applications, and human responses (how your examiner will react) are very unpredictable. So take any prediction with a grain of salt.

In any case, don't hesitate to ask any questions about the searcher's practices in advance, and be sure to specify exactly what you want in your search. It's your money and you're entitled to buy or contract for whatever services you desire.

H. Computer Searching

In addition to (or instead of) hiring someone else to search for you, you may perform computer-aided searching yourself. While a computer can come in very handy when searching your invention, it is important to recognize that the computer is only a tool, so bear in mind what computer searching can and cannot do, and have a plan before you sit down at the keyboard.

Computer searching is a delicate balance between your precious resources (time and patience) and a level of thoroughness. It is impossible for you to read over 10 million issued patents (and counting) to learn whether someone else has thought of your invention first. It is probably infeasible to read even just the patents that cover your technology (say, bicycles). You need to find and study only the references that are most relevant to your invention, and that by itself can be challenging.

So how should you search? You should do both types of searches (Keyword and Classification) to supplement each other because each has some deficiencies. If you do a Classification search you may use the wrong classification and if you do a Keyword search you may not search with the same keywords as the patent attorneys who wrote the relevant patents.

Keyword searches can be done for combinations of keywords in the texts—specification, claims, abstract, or title—of prior patents. To make a computer Keyword (or Boolean) search, you select a combination of keywords to describe your invention, e.g., "bicycle" and "carbon fiber alloy." The computer will look through its database for any patent that contains all of these words. When it finds any patents that contain your keywords in the combination you specified in your search request, it will display these patents, regardless of their classifications.

If the computer reports too much data for you to conveniently examine—say it's found 200 patents with your words in combination—you should first look at one or two of the patents to see if your invention is shown in an earlier patent (that is—your invention has been "knocked out"). If so, your search is over. If not, you'll need to narrow your search. This is easy. Simply add one or more additional keywords, say "frame," or some details of the alloy, and redo the search with these increased keywords until you've few enough patents to manually review conveniently. Also, you can narrow the search by using narrower (more specific) keywords.

On the other hand, if you get too specific, the computer is likely to report no patents, or just one or two. If this occurs, you'll need to broaden your search. This is just as easy. Merely remove one or more keywords, or broaden your present keywords, and redo the search until you get back what you want. For example, you can eliminate "bicycle" or substitute "frame" for "bicycle" to broaden the search. In summary, to broaden your search (pull out more prior art), you should use fewer keywords, and to narrow your search (pull out less prior art), you should use more keywords.

To make a Classification search, you first have to find the appropriate Classes and Subclasses where the concepts of your invention might be found. After you get the appropriate Classes and Subclasses, you have to browse through every patent in each Subclass to search for the possibly novel concepts of your invention. All of this can be done on a computer terminal.

The data that you search by computer—that is, the texts and drawing of patents—is available for free from the PTO and from several online sites. The latter are private companies that in turn get this data in the form of machine-readable tapes as a byproduct of the patent printing process from the Government Printing Office, which prints all patents. As of this writing, one free service—Google Patents—has used optical character recognition (OCR) to incorporate the data from all patents since 1836 into its database (although the U.S. first granted patents in 1790, the patent numbering system did not begin until 1836). Google's patents are pretty accurate and they do provide the first way to search all patents on the Internet. Presently, the PTO's examiners use computer searching (the EAST search system) almost exclusively. As a result, we're getting better examinations and stronger patents.

1. Available Computer Search Resources

Now that you get the general idea, how do you go about making a computer search? There are two ways to gain access to a computer search service's database:

- Via a personal computer with Internet access—the PTO's and the EPO's websites are completely free, while for others you'll have to make a suitable agreement.
- Via an existing terminal that is dedicated to patent searching, such as at a large company, law firm, the PubWEST system at a PTRC, or the EAST system at the PTO.

On the Internet the PTO itself provides free Keyword searches in bibliographic format (name, title, assignee, city, state, date, etc.) back to 1976 and by patent number and current classification back to 1790. To use this service, visit patft.uspto.gov.

You can use the "Quick Search" or "Advanced Search" links to make the search using the instructions to follow. If you simply want to look up a patent by its number, go to the "Patent Number Search" link.

The EPO (https://worldwide.espacenet.com) provides Quick and Advanced search capabilities in three languages (English, German, and French), but for patentability searches only the Quick search in English is necessary. Searches can be made in four databases: Worldwide (which covers European countries, EPO, and U.S. patents); Japanese; EP (EPO patents); or WIPO (World Intellectual Patent Organization, which administers the PCT databases. (See Chapter 12 for more on the PCT.) To search all databases, search just the Worldwide and Japanese databases). To make a search, type the appropriate keyword combinations in the keyword box with a suitable connector—for example, bicycle AND plastic OR wood. The dates of the databases vary; see the site for more information.

- Google Patents (https://patents.google.com) is an excellent resource that includes U.S. patents back to the beginning.
- ArchPatent.com (www.archpatent.com) is an excellent site with powerful search and filtering capabilities and intuitive search interfaces. You can search by keywords, classification, and a combination of the two.
- FreePatentsOnline.com (www.freepatentsonline.com) is another free search site that can search U.S. patents and patent applications back to the beginning. It has excellent search limiting capabilities.
- Patents.com (www.patents.com) is a free search site that searches U.S. patents and patent applications and European patents back to 1975.

Here are five fee-based organizations that offer computer searching of patent records. Several of the "for fee" databases also provide foreign patent information.

- Derwent Innovation (https://clarivate.com/products/derwent-innovation), from Clarivate Analytics, is a commercial database of patents from more than 50 patent-issuing authorities.

- Total Patent (www.lexisnexis.com/totalpatent), formerly known as LEXPAT, is a commercial patent database offering extensive prior-art searching, plus patent optimization tools.
- Questel (www.questel.com) provides a collection of intellectual property databases, as well as consulting and legal services.
- InnovationQ (ip.com) is a service that uses "concept" or "semantic" searching (methods that are perhaps more thorough than traditional Boolean searching), and includes many databases.
- Washpat (www.washpat.com) uses proprietary search tools and delivers search results in about a week.

2. Vocabulary Associated With Computer Searches

If you're going to do any patent searching, you should learn these terms now:

- A **File** is the actual name of the patent search database provided by the service.
- A **Record** is a portion of a file; the term is used to designate a single reference, usually a patent within a database.
- A **Field** is a portion of a record, such as a patent's title, the names of the inventors, its filing date, its patent number, its claims, etc.
- A **Term** is a group or, in computerese, a "string," of characters within a field—for example, the inventor's surname, one word of the title of a patent, etc., are terms.
- A **Command** is an instruction or directive to the search system that tells it to perform a function. For example, "Search" might be a command to tell a system to look for some key search words in its database.
- **Keywords** or a **Search Terms** are the word combination that are actually searched. "Bicycle" and "carbon fiber alloy" are the keywords for our example above.
- A **Qualifier** is a symbol that is used to limit a search or the information that the search displays for your use. Normally no qualifier would be used

in patentability searches, but if you're looking for a patent to a certain inventor, you could add a qualifier that limits the search to the field of the patentee's name.

- A **Wild Card Symbol** is an ending that is used in lieu of a word's normal ending in order to broaden a keyword. The wild card cuts off immaterial endings so that only word roots are searched. For example, if we were searching Millie's annular napkin-shaping ring, we would want our search to include the words "annular" and "annulus." Thus, instead of using both keywords and the Connector Symbol "or" (see below), we might search for "annul*" where "*" was a wild card symbol that tells the computer to look for any word with the root "annul" and any ending.

- **Connector Words** are those (such as "or," "and," and "not") that tell the computer to look for certain defined logical combinations of keywords. For instance, if you issued a command telling the computer to search for "annulus or ring and napkin," the computer would recognize that "or" and "and" were connector words and would search for patents with the words "annulus" and "napkin," or "ring" and "napkin," in combination. (Note that when you get to writing your claims (Chapter 9), "or" and "not" are generally forbidden.)

- **Proximity Symbols** are those that tell the computer to look for specified keywords, provided they are not more than a certain number of terms apart. Thus, if you told the computer to search for "napkin w/5 shaping" it would look for any patent that contained the words "napkin" and "shaping" within five words of each other, the symbol "w/5" meaning "within five words of." If no proximity symbol is used and the words are placed adjacent to each other—such as "napkin shaping"—the computer will pull out only those patents that contain these two words adjacent to each other in the order given. However, if a connector word is used—such as "napkin and shaping"—the computer will pull out any patent with both of these words, no matter where they are in the patent and no matter in what order they appear.

3. Think of Alternative Search Terms and Get the Classification

No matter what search system you use, be prepared with a well-thought-out group of keywords and all possible synonyms or equivalents. Use a thesaurus or a visual dictionary to get synonyms. Thus, to search for Millie's napkin-shaping ring, in addition to the obvious keywords "ring," "annular," "napkin," and "shaping," think of other terms from the same and analogous fields. In addition to napkin, you could use "cloth." Or, in addition to shaping, you could use "folding" or "bending." In addition to "annulus" or "ring," you could try "device," etc. Also compile a list of all possible Class and Subclass combinations where patents on developments similar to your invention might be classified. To obtain relevant class-subclass combinations, you'll need to use the *Classification Index*, *Manual*, and *Definitions* as explained in Section I, part 2a, below.

4. Using the Computer

From here on, simply follow the computer's instructions for gaining access to and using the database. Write down the number, Inventor, and date of all relevant patents without any consideration of obviousness. Then analyze them later, at your leisure.

Photo by Randy Rabin, Searcher

Searching at an EAST terminal at the PTO

5. Using Computer-Generated References to Work Backward and Forward

After making a computer search and obtaining a group of relevant references generated by the computer, it's possible (and very easy) to use these references to work back and forward and obtain additional, earlier relevant references that antedate the computer's database. How? To work backward, simply look at and/or order each of the "References Cited," which are listed on the abstract page (see Fig. 6D(c)) or at the end of the patent in each computer-selected patent. These references (usually patents) were cited by the PTO during prosecution of the patent and are usually very relevant. You can even look up the "References Cited" in the additional references to go back even earlier, thereby making a "tree" of references. However, the PTO didn't list the "References Cited" before the 1950s.

Another way to work backward, using a hybrid approach, is to find a patent close to your invention using the computer and then find the U.S. Class of the patent (it's 40/21R in Fig. 6D(c)) and then search all patents in this class at a PTRC, or order a list and search them online back to 1971 and in a PTRC for earlier patents.

To work forward, look up any close patent on the EAST system and check the "Patents which cite this patent" for each close patent.

I. Do-It-Yourself Searching

Searches should be made primarily in patent databases, rather than in general reference or scientific files, because there are about ten times as many devices and processes shown in the patent files as in textbooks, magazines, etc. That's because commercial practicability is not a requirement for patentability. All PTO examiners make most of their searches in the patent files for these reasons, so you should also. However, if you have access to a good nonpatent database, such as a good technical library in the field of your invention, you can use this as a supplement or alternative to your search of the patent files.

1. Getting Started at the PTO

The best place to make a search of the patent files is in the PTO unless you have access to the files of a large company that specializes in your field. This is because the PTO's search facilities have all U.S. patents arranged on computers (the PTO's EAST system) in an easily searchable manner by classification or keyword. For example, all patents that show bicycle derailleurs can be located by searching the "derailleur" subclass or searching this keyword. All patents that show flip-flop circuits can be located by searching the "flip-flop" subclass or by searching this keyword. All patents to diuretic drug compositions can be located similarly, etc. The PTO no longer keeps foreign patents and paper literature classified along with U.S. patents according to subject matter, however, but you still should search these areas. Always keep in mind that foreign patents are valid prior art in the U.S.

Here are a few things to know about the PTO:

The PTO is technically part of the Department of Commerce (headquartered in Washington) but operates in an almost autonomous fashion.

The PTO employs about 8,000 examiners, all of whom have technical undergraduate degrees in such fields as electrical engineering, chemistry, or physics. Many examiners are also attorneys. The PTO also has about an equal number of clerical, supervisory, and support personnel. The Commissioner for Patents is appointed by the president, and most of the higher officials of the PTO have to be approved by Congress. Most patent examiners are well paid; a journeyman examiner (ten years' experience) usually makes $80,000 to $125,000 a year.

Assuming you do go to the PTO, get a pass and go to the public search room to use the EAST system.

The PTO gives classes on using the EAST system periodically, so it's best to take one of these classes before you start. However it is possible to make a search on EAST without formal instruction. If you need help with your search or the EAST system, you can ask any of the search assistants in the search room. For help with the search (not the EAST system) you can also ask an examiner in the actual examining division that is in charge of your art area. E.g., if you've invented a bicycle, you may go ask a "bicycle examiner" for assistance. You won't be endangering the security of your invention if you ask any of these people about your search and give them all the details of your invention. They see dozens of new inventions every week, are quite used to helping searchers and others, and would be fired if they ever stole an invention. Also, the PTO's rules forbid employees from filing patent applications. In theory a PTO employee could communicate an invention to a friend or relative who could file, but it's very unlikely to occur because such a relationship could be easily discovered during patent litigation.

2. How to Do the Search—EAST Search at PTO and Internet Searches on PTO's Site

The PTO's EAST (Examiner Automated Search Tool) is available only at the PTO's Public Search Facility at Madison East, 1st Floor, 600 Dulany St., Alexandria, VA 22314, tel. 571-272-3275. Hours are Monday to Friday 8 a.m. to 8 p.m. As stated, EAST requires some training and skill to use. The PTO has about 250 EAST terminals in the public search room and gives free four-hour training sessions once per month. Also, often a user at an adjacent terminal or a search assistant can help a new user with the basics to get the new user started.

EAST is the best search tool because it can perform keyword or classification searches. In terms of speed, it is superior to a paper search because you can flip through patents displayed on the computer monitor faster than you can with the actual paper copies. You can also use EAST to do "forward" searches—that is, if a relevant patent is found, EAST can find and search through all later-issued patents in which the relevant patent is cited (referred to) as a prior-art reference. Further, it can do "backward" searches—that is, it can search through all previously issued patents that are cited as prior art in the relevant patent. You can also use EAST to search European and Japanese patents.

The PTO does not charge to use EAST, but it does charge for printing out copies of patents. The PTO began issuing patents in July 1790, but in 1836 lost all of these early patents in a fire. Some of those 10,000 patents, which were not numbered, have been recovered and are now known as the "X" patents. After the fire, the PTO started numbering patents (Patent 1 issued in July 1836). As of March 2018 the PTO had issued just over 9,900,000 utility patents, and the number will likely be over 10 million when you read this.

Explanations for EAST are not provided because EAST generally requires hands-on training and will be used by readers located near the PTO.

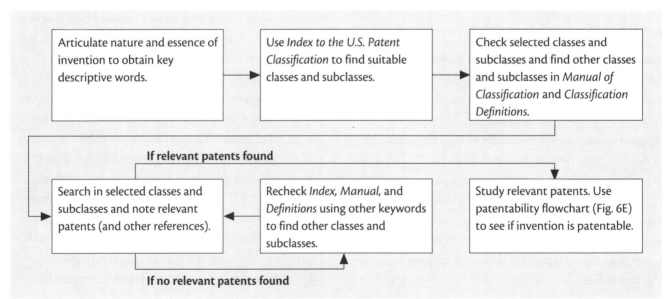

Fig. 6F—Searching Process for Paper Patents

a. Classification Searching

There are seven basic steps to take when conducting a Classification search of patents; these are depicted in Fig. 6F and are summarized below and then are explained in detail:

Step 1: Write out the nature and essence of your invention, using as many different terms as you can think of to describe it. The PTO describes this step concisely as, "Brainstorm key words related to the purpose, use, and composition of the invention."

Step 2: Find potentially relevant classification(s) for your invention. Do this by looking up your keywords in the *Index to the U.S. Patent Classification*. You can do this on EAST or online at www.uspto.gov/web/patents/classification/uspcindex/indextouspc.htm.

Steps 3 and 4: Check the accuracy of the classification(s) in the Class Schedule and Class Definitions in the *Manual of Classification* on EAST or on the Internet at www.uspto.gov/web/patents/classification.

Step 5: Search the patents and published patent applications in your list of relevant classes.

Step 6: Carefully review each patent in the relevant classes and subs to see whether it is relevant, that is, does it come close to the hardware, steps, or purpose of your invention? Write down the numbers, dates, and first Inventor of any patents that are relevant and obtain copies of them to study later.

Step 7: For each relevant patent that you find, check the "References Cited" in the patent to work backward and check the "Field of Search" to find additional relevant classes and subs.

Step 1: Write Out the Nature and Essence of Your Invention

As with any other classification or indexing system, your success will depend on the degree to which the words and phrases you use to define your invention coincide with the terms used by the classifier or indexer. For this reason, you should first figure out several ways to describe your invention. Start by writing down all the physical features of your invention in a brief, concise format so that you'll know exactly what to look for when searching.

For example, if you're searching a bicycle with a new type of sprocket wheel, write down "bicycle, sprocket wheel," and briefly add the details and as many alternative terms as you can think of, such as gear, chain, drive linkage, etc. If you're searching an electronic circuit, write down in a series of phrases like the foregoing or, in a very brief sentence, the quintessence of your invention, such as "flip-flop circuit with unijunction transistors" or some other very brief and concise description. Do the same whether your invention is a mechanical, electronic, chemical, business, Internet, or method invention.

Form 6-1 is a Searcher's Worksheet that you can use to facilitate your searching, and Fig. 6G is a completed version of Form 6-1 that you might produce if you had searched Millie Inventress's invention. Note that the invention description part of the worksheet contains a concise description of the invention for easy reference.

Once you've written a concise description of your invention, think of some alternative keywords or phrases to add to your description. Don't hesitate to define your invention in still additional ways that may come to you during your search. Then, take your worksheet with this brief description and the drawing(s) of your invention to the public search room. Even if you're not going to do your search there, use that room to find out how your invention is classified.

Step 2: Find the Relevant Classifications for Your Invention

To find the places to search your invention using the Internet, you'll need its most relevant search classification (referred to as class and subclass). To obtain this, your first step is to review the PTO's classifications website at www.uspto.gov/web/patents/classification/uspcindex/indextouspc.htm. Next, you will use various reference publications:

- the *Index to the U.S. Patent Classification*
- the *Manual of Classification*, and
- the *Classification Definitions*.

Searcher's Worksheet

Sheet ___1___ of ___1___

Inventor(s): ___Millie Inventress___

Invention Description (use keywords and variations): ___Napkin folder-Annular member with inner leg,___

___flared-back arms___

Selected Search Classifications

Class/Sub	Description	Checked	Comments
40-21	Napkin holders	✓	very relevant—the right place
40-142	misc. tableware	✓	mostly utensils—not too good
044-20	Napkin holders	✓	somewhat relevant
24-8	Shaping devices	✓	N.G.

Patents (and Other References) Thought Relevant

Patent # or Title	Name or Country	Date	Class/Sub	Comment
705, 196	Bergmann	1902	40-142	Plain ring
1,771,328	Gabel	1930	40-21	Curtain shaper
3,235,880	Hypps	1966	40-21	Fancy ring
3,965,59	LeSueur	1976	40-21	Ring with magnetic letters
				Consulted Examiner
				Hayness, John Ext. 353

Searcher: ___S. Searcher___   Date: ___2016-1-12___

Fig. 6G—Completed Searcher's Worksheet (Form 6-1 in Appendix 7)

Gun   INDEX TO CLASSIFICATION - **G**   Gyroscope

	Class	Subclass
Billy club	42	1.16
Blowgun	124	62
Bore inspection	356	241.2
Breakdown type	42	40
Cane gun	42	52
Cattle slaughter type	42	1.12
Control calculators	235	400+
Gun training mechanism	89	41.01+
Motor operated	89	41.02+
Cotton	536	35+
Composition containing	149	94+
Over 10%	149	96+
Design	D22	100+
Grease	D08	14.1
Pistol	D22	104+
Racks	D06	552+
Sights	D22	109
Toy	D21	572+
Dummy	42	106
Ejectors	42	25
Electrically operated		
Firearms	42	84
Lighting devices	362	110+
Ordnance	89	135
Electron	313	441+
Extractors	42	16+
Firing mechanisms	42	69.01
Revolver	42	65
Upward tilting breech	42	41+
Flare	42	1.15
Fluid pressure adapter	124	58
Foob, ie fire out of battery	89	42.03
Gatling type	89	12
Grenade launchers	42	105
Gun engaging means	102	483+
Handles	89	1.42
Heaters	89	1.12
Howitzer	89	
Implement combined	42	90+
Indicators	42	1.01
K gun	89	1.1
Knife combined	42	53
Loading	89	45
Lubricating or caulking type	D08	14.1
Machine gun	89	9+
Toy	D21	573
Magazine	42	87+
Making	42	49.1+
Mechanical	124	
Mount	89	37.01+
Training mechanism	89	41.01+
Mounted	89	
Movable chambers		
Firearms	42	39.5

	Class	Subclass
Ordnance	89	155
Multiple barrel	89	1.41
Nonrecoil	89	1.7
Pen and knife	42	1.09
Port ship	114	173+
Stopper	114	175
Portable	42	
Powder		
Ammunition loading with	86	
Bags	102	282
Engine starters	123	183.1
Engines	123	24 R
Forms	102	283+
Racks	211	64
Rapid fire	124	72+
Recoil operated	89	162
Recoilless	89	1.7
Rests	42	94
Revolver	42	59+
Safety mechanism	42	70.01+
Automatic guns	89	137+
Revolvers	42	66
Semiautomatic	89	4.05+
Shields	89	36.01+
Deflected ray tube	356	253+
Shotguns	42	
Sidearms	D22	
Sights	42	111+
Design	D22	109
Design,telescopic	D16	132
Optical system	356	247+
Stocks	42	71.01+
Teargas	42	1.08
Telescopic gunsight	D16	132
Toy simulating	42	54+
Ammunition	102	281
Machine gun or projector	124	29
Non-detonating	446	473
With sound	446	405+
Training in gunnery	434	16+
Trigger protectors	42	70.07
Underwater	42	1.14
Walking cane combined	4	515+
Water gun	124	56+
Toy	D21	572
Water pistol	222	79
Well tubing perforator	175	2
Y gun	89	1.1
Gussets		
Garment	2	275
Gut or Gut Treatment	8	94.11
Splitter	83	932*
Guttapercha	525	331.9+
Gutter	405	119+

	Class	Subclass
Eaves trough	52	11+
Electric conductor underground		
structure	174	39
Road and pavement	404	2+
Support design	D08	363
Guy	52	146+
Bed spring and frame	52	272
Gymnastic Devices	482	23+
Coin controlled apparatus	194	
Design	D21	797
Gypsum	423	554
Calcining	106	722+
Coating or plastic compositions		
containing	106	772+
Alkali metal silicate	106	611
Gyrating		
Reciprocating sifter		
Actuating means	209	366+
Horizontal and vertical shake	209	326
Horizontal shake	209	332
Gyratory Crusher		
Jaw crushers rotary component	241	207+
Parallel flow through plural zones	241	140
Series flow through plural zones	241	156
Gyro Stabilized		
Article support	248	183.1
Furniture for ships	114	119
Gyroplane (See Aircraft)	244	17.11+
Gyroscope	74	5 R+
Acceleration measuring and testing	73	504.03
Aerial camera combined	396	13
Aircraft control	244	79
Direction indicator	33	318+
Gimbals	248	182.1+
Gun sight combined	89	202
Gyroscopic compass	33	324+
Telemetric system combined	340	870.07+
Gyroscopic light valve,		
photoelectric	250	231.12
Monorail rolling stock	105	141+
Suspended	105	150+
Rotary	73	504.08
Rotors	74	5.95
Rotors and flywheels	74	5.95
Ship antiroll	114	112
Ship stabilizer	114	122
Ship steering	114	144 R
Speed responsive devices	73	504.01
Torpedo	114	24
Torpedo steering	114	24
Toy	446	233+
Transmission	74	64
Velocity measuring and testing	73	504.02

Fig. 6H—Sample Page of *Index to Classification*

These three publications can be accessed online via the PTO website (including at www.uspto.gov/web/patents/classification). Let's look at each publication in detail.

Index to the U.S. Patent Classification

This will be your main reference tool. If you want to do some of the research yourself before going to the PTO, the Index can be searched online. The *Index* also lists the classes alphabetically. Let's assume that you've invented a gymnastic exercising apparatus. The first thing to do is to look in the *Index* under "Gymnastic Devices." We come to page 9 (Fig. 6H), a typical page from the Index. It shows, among other things, that "Gymnastic Devices" are classified in class 482, subclass 23.

Manual of Classification

Now that we've found the class and subclass numbers, it's time to turn to the *Manual of Classification*, which lists the classes of invention numerically. This manual is used as an adjunct to the *Index*, to check your selected classes, and to find other, closely related ones. Each of the 430 classes has its own page(s), together with about 300 to 400 subclasses under each class heading, for a total of about 140,000 subclasses. The *Manual* lists design as well as utility classes; the classes are not in any logical order. To see where class-subclass 482/23 fits, let's look at the first page that covers class 482. Fig. 6I is a copy of this page. It shows the first part of "Class 482—Exercise Devices." Note that subclass 23 in this class covers "Gymnastic." Under 482/23 are further subclasses that may be of interest; these cover trapezes and rings, horizontal bars, etc.

Classification Definitions

To check our selected class and subclass still further, we next consult a third source, known as the *Classification Definitions*. At the end of each subclass definition is a cross-reference of additional places to look that correspond to such subclass.

Fig. 6J shows the classification definition for class/subclass 482/23. This definition is actually a composite assembled from several pages of the *Definitions*—that is,

it includes definitions for class 482 per se and subclasses 23–26. Note that the class definition (482 per se), as well as many of the subclass definitions contain cross-references to other classes and subclasses. You should consider these when selecting your search areas.

Getting Classification From the PTO or a PTRC

You can get a free, informal mail-order classification of your invention for search purposes by sending a copy of your invention disclosure, with a request for suggestions of one or more search subclasses, to Search Room, Patent and Trademark Office, Washington, DC 20231. However, unless you're really stuck in obtaining subclasses, don't use this method, because you have the interest in and familiarity with your invention to do a far better job if only you put a little effort into it.

Also, to save time if you intend to go to the PTO in Alexandria, you can get the search classifications locally, online, or at a PTRC (Patent and Trademark Resource Center) by using its CD-ROM CASSIS (Classification And Search Support Information System). Instructions will be provided at the computer or by the librarian.

Be sure to spend enough time to become confidently familiar with the classification system for your invention. Check all of your subclasses in the *Manual of Classification* and the *Class Definitions* manual to be sure that you've obtained all of the right ones. Usually, two or more subclasses will be appropriate. For example, suppose your gymnastic device uses a gear with an irregular shape. Naturally, you should search in the gear classes as well as in the exercising device classes. Note that the cross-references in the exercising device classes won't refer you to "gears," since this is too specific—the cross-references in the PTO's manuals are necessarily general in nature. It's up to you to consider all aspects of your particular invention when selecting search categories.

Searching analogous classes is usually very beneficial, as well. For example, consider an automobile steering wheel that you've improved by adding finger ridges to improve the driver's grip. In addition to searching in

CLASS 482 EXERCISE DEVICES   482 - 1

1	**HAVING SPECIFIC ELECTRICAL FEATURE**
2	.Electrical energy generator
3	.Pace setting indicator
4	.Equipment control
5	..Amount of resistance
6	...Regulates rate of movement
7	..Rate of movement
8	.Monitors exercise parameter
9	..To create or modify exercise regimen
10	**FOR HEAD OR NECK**
11	.Face (e.g., jaw, lip, etc.)
12	**FOR THRUSTING A POINTED WEAPON (E.G., A FENCING FOIL, ETC.) OR SIMULATION THEREOF**
13	**FOR IMPROVING RESPIRATORY FUNCTION**
14	**FOR TRACK OR FIELD SPORT**
15	.Jumping, vaulting, or hurdling
16	..Crossbar or support therefor
17	...Including height adjustment feature
18	..Vaulting pole or stop
19	.Starting block for runner
20	.Throwing
21	..Discus
22	..Shot-put
23	**GYMNASTIC**
24	.Trapeze or rings
25	.Vaulting or pommel horse
26	.Projector
27	..Trampoline
28	...Having foldable frame
29	...With disparate structure
30	..Spring board
31	...Spring external to board
32	...Movable fulcrum
33	.Tower or pole for swinging upon
34	.Bar or rope for balancing upon
35	.Play area climbing or traversing arrangement (i.e., for use by children)
36	..Having upright array of horizontally extending elements
37	.Arm or hand type climbing arrangement
38	.Horizontal bar
39	..Attached to vertical wall or associated structure
40	...Door or door jamb
41	..Parallel bars

42	...Separately adjustable
43	..Harness for supporting user
44	**HAND, WRIST, OR FINGER**
45	.Involving wrist rotation
46	..About axis perpendicular to forearm
47	.Having individual structure engaging each finger used
48	..Finger loop
49	.Grip
50	..Having weight feature (e.g., dumbbell, etc.)
51	**INVOLVING USER TRANSLATION OR PHYSICAL SIMULATION THEREOF**
52	.Stair climbing
53	..Utilizing fluid resistance
54	.Treadmill for foot travel
55	.Swimming
56	..Out of water type
57	.Bicylcling
58	..Utilizing fluid resistance
59	...Gas
60	..Completely detached from user support
61	..Stand for converting bicycle
62	..Including upper body exercise feature
63	..Utilizing specific resistance generating structure
64	...Flywheel with braking band
65	...Wheel with edge engaging braking roller
66	.Occupant propelled support frame having movement facilitating feature for foot travel
67	..Armpit engaging
68	..Rolling
69	.Occupant suspended from above (e.g., by a body harness, etc.) for foot travel
70	.Having separate foot engaging members reciprocating on parallel guide tracks, e.g., Nordic skiing simulator, etc.
71	.Alpine or towed skiing
72	.Rowing
73	..Utilizing fluid resistance
74	.Jogging accessory
75	.Elevated walking device (e.g., stilts, etc.)
76	..Stilt having specific step
77	.Bouncing device
78	.User inside device

Fig. 6I—Sample Page of *Manual of Classification*

CLASS 482, EXERCISE DEVICES

SECTION I - CLASS DEFINITION

This class provides for apparatus intended to be operated by a human user for the purpose of: (a) facilitating the conditioning or developing of a muscle of the user by repetitive or continuous activity of the user or, (b) participating in a track, field, gymnastic, or athletic activity, unless by analogy of structure or by other function the apparatus is classified elsewhere.

(1)   Note. In some of the definitions of subclasses hereunder, the phrase "significance is attributed" is used to describe a function that is the primary use of the structure of patents therein. The structure of the apparatus may be capable of use for other purposes, but the claimed disclosure of the patent so placed indicates the intended primary function of the structure as that described by the title and definition of the subclass.

(2)   Note. Conditioning or developing a muscle includes helping a user, e.g., an infant or invalid, to walk or learn how to walk unless provided for elsewhere. See Subclass References to the Current Class, below.

23   **GYMNASTIC:**
This subclass is indented under the class definition. Subject matter wherein significance is attributed to the use of the apparatus for an acrobatic purpose by the user.

(1)   Note. The terms "gymnastic" and "acrobatic" have come to denote and describe various pieces of equipment such as a trapeze, bar, vaulting horse, diving board, trampoline, etc., that are used in physical activities known by similar names. These activities are characterized by extreme movements of the user, who uses the equipment as a fulcrum or starting area to launch bodily through space, swing therefrom, or perform other such physical activity thereon. The significance of the apparatus is more in the activity for which the apparatus is used than in the structural differences between the apparatus (see the Class Definition, (1) Note).

SEE OR SEARCH THIS CLASS, SUBCLASS:
109,   for a club type exercise device which may be used for juggling.

SEE OR SEARCH CLASS:
273,   Amusement Devices: Games, particularly subclasses 441+ for a game apparatus dealing with physical ability.

24   **Trapeze or rings:**
This subclass is indented under subclass 23. Subject matter wherein the acrobatic apparatus is either (1) a short, horizontal, swingable bar suspended at each end by a flaccid strand, e.g., a rope, etc., or (2) a pair of annular objects each suspended by a flaccid strand, e.g., a rope, etc., about which the user may move in an acrobatic manner.

SEE OR SEARCH ·THIS CLASS, SUBCLASS:
143+,   for a suspension device from which the user may freely hang.

SEE OR SEARCH CLASS:
472,   Amusement Devices, particularly subclasses 118+ for an amusement swing.

25   **Vaulting or pommel horse:**
This subclass is indented under subclass 23. Subject matter wherein the acrobatic apparatus is (1) a supported body used for jumping over

or for another acrobatic purpose, i.e., a vaulting horse or (2) a supported body with a pair of handles mounted thereon for an acrobatic purpose, i.e., a pommel horse.

SEE OR SEARCH THIS CLASS, SUBCLASS:
16+,   for a track or field sport in which a user jumps, vaults, or hurdles over a crossbar.
34,   for a bar or rope for balancing upon.
38+,   for a horizontal bar used for a gymnasts purpose.

26   **Projector:**
This subclass is indented under subclass 23. Subject matter wherein the acrobatic apparatus

December 2004 Edition

Fig. 6J—Sample Page of *Classification Definitions*

the obvious area (automobile steering wheels), consider searching in any other areas where hand grips are found, such as swords, tools, and bike handlebars.

Fortunately, the cross-references in the *Class Definitions* manual will be of great help here. Note how Sam Searcher, Esq., has completed the "Selected Search Classifications" section of the search worksheet with appropriate classes to search for prior art relevant to Millie Inventress's invention.

Steps 3 and 4: Check the Accuracy of the Relevant Classifications

Check the accuracy of the classifications you found in Step 2 by reviewing the Class Schedule and Class Definitions. Remove any classes and subs that you feel aren't relevant to your invention.

Step 5: Search the Patents and Note Any Relevant Prior Art (Patents and Other Publications) Under Your Classification

After obtaining a list of classes and subclasses, you search through the actual patents in these classes on the Internet (or at the patent office). The PTO recently completed a transition to paperless files, so you no longer need to navigate your way through four acres of shelves to find the exact printed patent you need. Online, go to patft.uspto.gov and click "Quick Search," enter the first class and sub in the "Term 1" box, and hit "Search." Do this for each relevant class and sub under Issued Patents and Patent Applications.

The computer will search according to your class and subclass and present you with a list of patents. As you flip through the patents on the monitor (it's far easier on EAST!), you may at first find it very difficult to understand the patents and to make your search. Don't be discouraged! You'll find it easier to understand newer patents (see Le Sueur—Fig. 6D(c)), because they have an abstract page up front that contains a brief summary of the patent and the most relevant figure or drawing.

You'll find that the older patents (see Gabel—Fig. 6D(a)) have several sheets of unlabeled drawings and a closely printed description, termed a "specification," after the drawings. However, even with older patents, you can get a brief summary of the patent by referring to the summary of the invention, which is usually found in the first or second column of the specification. Near the end of each patent, you'll find the claims. These are formally worded, legalistic sentence fragments that usually come after and are the object of the heading words "I [or "We"] claim." The claims define the legal scope of offensive rights held by the owner of the patent.

In recent years, the PTO added "Patent Document Kind Codes" to the numbers of patents and their other publications, in accordance with international practice. Fig. 6D(d) provides a list of these codes.

Common Misconception: If the claims of a prior patent don't cover your invention, you're free to claim it in your patent application.

Fact: The claims of a patent are there solely to define the monopoly or scope of offensive rights held by the owner of the patent. Patent owners use claims mainly in licensing or in court to determine whether the patent is infringed—that is, whether the hardware that an alleged infringer makes, uses, or sells violates the patent. Thus, when you encounter a relevant patent during a search, you should not fall into the "claims trap," that is, you should not read its claims. You should treat the patent like any other publication (book, magazine article, etc.) to see if the patent's description (the written part other than the claims) or drawings disclose (anticipate) your invention, or any part of it. (According to the patent statutes, the entire written part of a patent or patent application—that is, the description, claims abstract—is called the "specification." However, some practitioners refer to just the description as the "specification" and consider the claims a separate part.) Because the patent's claims merely repeat what's already in the description and drawings, they won't contain anything new, so you need not even read the patent's claims to understand the full technical disclosure of any patent. The description and drawings will almost always contain more than what is in the claims anyway. So even if a patent's claims don't cover your invention, its description and drawings may still disclose your invention. Since the patent is a prior publication as of its filing date, it can thus anticipate your invention, even

Anticipation Versus Infringement

Many inventors have asked me, "How can an expired patent block me from patenting my invention?" That is, how can an expired patent be a valid prior-art reference?

If a patent ceased to be prior art when it expired then anyone could repatent the wheel, the sewing machine, etc. The misconception that a patent ceases to be a prior-art reference when it expires represents a confusion of *anticipation* with *infringement*. They are entirely separate areas in patent law and should be considered independently.

Anticipation is a situation that occurs when a proposed or new invention is discovered or found anywhere in the "prior art" (prior public use or prior publications, including the specification of any in-force or expired U.S. or foreign patent, any prior book, periodical article, etc.). Since the existence of the prior art proves the invention isn't new, the putative invention is said to be anticipated by the prior art and thus can't be patented. (35 USC 102.)

Infringement is a situation that occurs only when the claims of an in-force patent "read on" a product or process. If so, then the product or process *infringes* (violates) the patent and the patent owner may be able to negotiate licensing royalties from the infringer, or successfully sue the infringer for money damages and/or an injunction ordering the infringer to cease infringing. (35 USC 271.) (Note that a patent application can't infringe anything.)

If an invention is anticipated by a prior-art reference, that does not necessarily mean that it would infringe the reference, since the reference may be (a) a periodical article or book, which can't be infringed, (b) a foreign patent, which can't be infringed by activity in the U.S., or (c) an expired U.S. patent, which can no longer be infringed. Even if an invention is anticipated by an in-force U.S. patent, the invention usually will not infringe the patent. Why? Because the patent's claims usually will not read on the invention, most likely because the patentee was not able to get broad enough claims allowed due to even earlier prior art. The PTO is never concerned with and never takes any action with regard to any infringement; their main concern is to find anticipations to prevent the issuance of patents on old inventions.

EXAMPLE: In the early part of the 20th century, J.A. Fleming invented a two-element vacuum tube—the diode—that rectified alternating current. Then Lee De Forest added a third element—a control grid—to the diode, making a triode, which was capable of amplifying signals. Even though triodes infringed the diode patent, the Patent Office granted De Forest a patent since the PTO is not concerned with infringements. Although De Forest was not able to manufacture his triode without infringing Fleming's diode patent, Fleming was not able to make triodes without infringing De Forest's patent. Cross-licensing —in which the parties exchanged rights to their respective patents—solved the problem, enabling each to practice the other's invention.

---

if it doesn't claim your invention. (If you were free to claim an invention that a prior patent disclosed but did not claim, that would make patents worth less as prior art than other publications, such as magazine articles!)

Another reason for not reading the claims of searched patents is that they're written in such stilted legalese that they're difficult to understand. Nevertheless, some searchers do like to read claims of patents to get a quick "handle" on the patent's technical content. Also, if you make an *Official Gazette* search in a Patent and Trademark Resource Center or regular library, you'll have to rely on claims for the most part, since most of the OGs contain only a single claim of each patent.

If you do read the claims, keep in mind three considerations:

1. If a prior-art patent shows (that is, describes) but doesn't formally claim your invention, this doesn't mean you're free to claim it.

2. A patent contains much more technical information than what's in its claims; all of this technical information can be used as prior art, just as if the patent were an article in a technical magazine. Thus, you should use the claims only to get a "handle" on the patent; you should not regard them as a summary or synopsis of the patent's disclosure.

3. The scope of coverage you will likely be able to obtain for your invention (see Section J, below) will usually be narrower than the scope of the claims of the closely relevant prior-art patents you uncover.

Common Misconception: If your invention is covered by the claims of a prior patent, you will be liable as an infringer if you file a patent application on the invention.

Fact: Neither a patent application nor its claims can infringe a prior patent. Only the manufacture, use, sale, offer for sale, or importation of an invention in physical form can infringe. And, as previously stated, the PTO has absolutely no concern about patent infringements.

Don't think about obviousness as you search because this may overwhelm you and detract from the quality of your investigation. Rather, at this stage, try to fish with a large net by merely looking for the physical features of your invention.

As you search, keep a careful record of all patent classes and subclasses you've searched, as indicated in Fig. 6G, above. Probably 95% of the references you encounter when you search will not be relevant. If you find relevant patents or other art, write their numbers, dates, names, or other identification, and order or download copies later. Although you need only the number to order a patent, write the issue date, first inventor's name, and classification as well, to double-check later in case you write down a wrong number.

If you do find an important relevant reference, don't stop; simply asterisk it (to remind you of its importance) and continue your search to the end.

When you note a relevant reference, also write down its most relevant features to refresh your memory and save time later.

If you still don't find any relevant patents, double-check your search classes using *Classification Definitions*, the *Manual of Classification*, and some help from a patent examiner or assistant in the search room. If you're reasonably sure you're in the right class and still can't find any relevant references, write down the closest ones you can possibly find, even if they're not relevant. This will establish that you made the search, what the closest art is, and how novel your invention is, and you'll have references to cite on your Information Disclosure Statement (discussed in Chapter 13); you should never finish any search without coming up with at least several references. If you do consult examiners, write their names in the comments section of the worksheet.

In each subclass, you'll find patents that are directly classified there, and "cross-references" (XRs), patents primarily classified in another subclass, but also classified in your subclass because they have a feature that makes the cross-reference appropriate. Be sure to review the cross-references as well as the regular patents in each subclass.

The public search room at the PTO has printers for making instant printouts of patents for a per-page fee, but if you don't need instant copies, you can download patent copies for a fee on EAST or for free online. You can also acquire a copy of a patent as follows:

- To download a copy of any patent from the free patent sites, go to either Google Patents (https:// patents.google.com)
- Free Patents Online (www.freepatentsonline. com), or
- Pat2PDF (www.pat2pdf.org).

These sites will deliver a PDF copy of the entire patent to your computer desktop.

Step 6: Review the Prior Art to See Whether It Anticipates Your Invention or Renders It Obvious

After you've made your search and obtained the numbers of all the pertinent references, obtain copies and study them. Write a brief summary of each relevant patent, even if it has an abstract, to force you to really understand it. Then, determine if your invention is patentable over the patents you've found. Follow the steps described earlier in this chapter for analyzing the search report when your search is done by someone else to determine whether the prior art renders your invention obvious.

Step 7: Obtain Additional Patents and Classifications

To extend your search further and make it more complete, look at each relevant patent that you found in order to find additional patents and classifications that may be relevant. First check the "References Cited" on the first (or Abstract) page of each patent to find additional patents and other references cited against this patent while it was pending. Look up and check these patents to see if they're also relevant and if so, determine if they anticipate or render your invention obvious. Then check the "Field of Search" on the Abstract page to find additional relevant classes and subs and check the patents in these classes as you did above. It's a lot of work and will take some time, but you'll save a lot of money.

b. Keyword Searching (PubWEST versus Google Patents)

In addition to making a classification search, you can perform a keyword search of your invention on EAST, the Internet, or on PubWEST (Web-based Examiner Search Tool) terminals at all PTRCs. (The PubWEST search engine is not available to the general public on the Internet.) Unfortunately, PubWEST takes some time to learn, and it's probably not worth learning unless you are a frequent patent searcher. Google Patents is far easier to use and provides many of the same features as PubWEST, plus some features that PubWEST lacks.

J. The Scope of Patent Coverage

Although you'd probably like things to be simpler, the determination of whether your invention is patentable will rarely be a "yes" or "no" one, unless your invention is a very simple device, process, or composition. Many inventions are complex enough to have some features, or some combination of features, that will be different enough to be patentable. However, your object is not merely to get a patent, but to get *meaningful* patent coverage—that is, offensive rights that are broad enough that competitors can't "design around" your patent easily. Designing around a patent is the act of making a competitive device or process that is equivalent in function to the patented device but that doesn't infringe the patent.

Often you won't be able to get broad coverage because many "modern" inventions are actually old hat—that is, the basic ideas were known many years before and the real inventions are actually just improvements on old ones. Simply put, you'll often find a search will indicate that your invention, while valuable, may be less of an innovation than you thought it was. You'll thus have to determine whether or not your invention is sufficiently innovative to get meaningful patent protection. In other words, your scope of coverage will depend upon how close the references that your search uncovers are to your invention—that is, how many features of your invention are shown by the references, and how they are shown. In the end, your scope of coverage will actually depend upon the breadth of the claims that you can get the PTO to allow, but this is jumping the gun at this stage.

For an example, let's take a simple invention. As stated, in a simple invention patentability will usually be a black or white determination, and you won't have much of a problem about your scope of coverage. Suppose you've just invented a magnetically operated cat door—that is, you provide a cat with a neck-worn magnet that can operate a release on a cat door. Your search references fail to show any magnetically operated pet release door. Thus, the neck magnet and the magnetic door release are the novel features of your invention. To get a patent, your invention would have to be limited to these specific features, since neither could be changed or eliminated while producing the same result. However, there is no harm in limiting the invention to these features, since it would be difficult for anyone to "design around" them—that is, it would be difficult or impossible for anyone to provide the same result (a cat-operated door release) without using a neck magnet and a magnetic release.

With other inventions, however, your scope of coverage won't be so broad—that is, it won't be as difficult for someone to design around it. For example, suppose you invented the centrifugal vegetable juicer mentioned previously in Chapter 5—that is, a juicer with a sloping side basket permitting the solid pulp to ride up and out so that juicing could continue without having to empty the pulp from the basket.

If the prior art were not "kind" to you—that is, your search uncovered a patent or other publication that showed a juicer with a basket with sloping sides and with a well at the top to catch and hold the pulp—your application would not be allowed if you claimed just the sloping sides (even though it would be superior to the prior art due to the complete elimination of the pulp). To get the patent, you would have to also claim another feature (say, the trough shape). Thus, by having access to the prior art you would know enough to claim your invention less broadly.

Also, suppose you've invented the napkin-shaping ring of Fig. 6B. Suppose further that Gabel did not exist and that your search uncovers only the Le Sueur patent (see Fig. 6D(c)), which shows a plain, circular napkin ring. You'd be entitled to relatively broad coverage, since your novel features are themselves broad: namely, a ring with inner parts that can shape a napkin when it is pulled through the ring.

However, assuming the Gabel patent does exist and your search uncovers it as well as Le Sueur, what are your novel features now? First, your device has a circular ring with a leg extending inwardly from the ring; neither Gabel nor Le Sueur, nor any possible combination of these references, has this combination. Second, your invention has the flaring arms that shape the napkin; these are attached to the end of the inner leg; the references also lack this feature. Thus to distinguish over Le Sueur and Gabel, you'll have to rely on far more specific features than you'd have to do if only Le Sueur existed. Hence your actual invention would be far narrower, since you'll have to limit it to the novel features that distinguish it from Gabel as well as Le Sueur. Unfortunately, this will narrow your scope of coverage, because competitors can design around you more easily than they could do if only Le Sueur existed.

As you've probably gathered by now, your scope of coverage will be determined by what novel features you need to use to distinguish your invention over the prior art and still provide new results that are different or unexpected enough to be considered unobvious. The fewer the novel features you need, the broader your invention or scope of coverage will be. Stated differently, if you need many new features, or very specific features, to define over the prior art and provide new results, it will usually be relatively easy for a competitor to use fewer or alternative features to provide the same results without infringing your patent.

You should make your scope of coverage determination by determining the fewest number or the broadest feature(s) you'll need to distinguish patentability over the prior art. Do this by a repetitive narrowing trial-and-error process: First, see what minimum feature(s) you'll need to have some novelty over the prior art—that is, enough to distinguish under Section 102 (Box C of Figs. 5C and 6E)—and then see if these would satisfy Section 103 (Boxes D, E, and G)—that is, would they provide any unexpected new results?

If you feel that your minimum number of features are enough to ascend the novelty slope of the Patentability Mountain (pictured in Chapter 5), but would not be sufficient to climb the big nonobviousness slope—that is, you don't have enough features to provide new and unexpected results—then try narrowing your features or adding more until you feel that you'll have enough to make it to the patentability summit.

Common Misconception: If a search shows that your invention is not patentable, you may not manufacture or sell it.

Fact: Even if it's not patentable, you usually still can make and sell it because the prior-art reference(s) that make it not patentable probably are either expired patents or don't claim your invention. (For more on how to determine if a prior, in-force patent's claims cover you, see Chapter 15.)

TIP

This is another one of those aspects of patent law that may have your head spinning. Fortunately, the material covered here under determining the scope of your protection is also discussed in the different context of drafting your claims. (See Chapter 9.) By the time you read this book thoroughly, you will understand all of this a lot better.

After you evaluate your search results, you'll have a pretty good idea of the minimum number of novel features that are necessary to sufficiently distinguish your invention over the prior art. If you're in doubt that you have enough such features, or if you feel that you'd have to limit your invention to specific features to define structure that would be considered unobvious over the prior art, it probably isn't patentable, or even if patentable, it isn't worth filing on, since it would be easy to design around. One possibility, if you can't make a decision, is to pay for a professional's opinion.

On the other hand, if you've found nothing like your invention in your search, congratulations. You probably have a very broad invention, since, with the eight million plus patents that have issued thus far, one or more features of almost all inventions are likely to be shown in the prior art.

K. Patent and Trademark Resource Centers

As you may know, Patent and Trademark Resource Centers are scattered around the country and are listed below in Fig. 6K. Before going to any PTRC, call to find out their hours of operation and what search facilities they have.

1. Searching at a PTRC

Searching at a PTRC is less useful than searching at the PTO or the Internet because the EAST system at the PTO has far more capabilities than the PubWEST search facilities available at the PTRCs or the Internet searches, which are available on any computer. However the obvious advantage of the latter two is that they are local.

If we could assign percentage values to the various types of searches: a good examiner's search might be estimated at 90% (that is—it has about a 90% chance of standing up in court), a good search by a nonexaminer in the PTO at 80%, and a good search in a PTRC or on the Internet at 70%. (Unfortunately, as in business, there's no certainty in the law.) If your invention is in an active, contemporary field, such as a computer mouse, you should reduce the value of the two nonexaminer types of searches somewhat, due to the fact that patent applications in this field are more likely to be pending.

To make a Classification search at a PTRC in addition to using PubWEST or the Internet, you can also make an *Official Gazette* (OG) search. You should go through the same four steps given above. First, articulate your invention (in the same manner as before), and second, use the reference tools to find the relevant classes and subclasses. The third step is a review of the patents in the selected classes and subclasses. And finally, you should analyze all relevant prior-art references for their effect on your invention's patentability.

For Recent Years the *Official Gazette* Is Available in Electronic Format Only

The *Official Gazette (Patents)* (OG) was a weekly publication (paperback book) that listed the main facts (patentee, assignee, filing date, classification) plus the broadest claim and main drawing figure of every patent issued that week. It also contained pertinent notices, fees, and a list of all PTRCs (Fig. 6K). The OG notices and patents are published each week only at the PTO's website, under Official Gazette Notices and Official Gazette for Patents, respectively. Also, the complete patents are available online elsewhere on the PTO's website each week.

If you make an OG search you can search the paper (book) copies of the OGs up to about ten years ago (when the PTO stopped printing paper copies); thereafter you will have to search for them on the

Internet. Each patent entry you find will contain only a single claim (or abstract) and a single figure or drawing of the patent, as indicated in Fig. 6M (a typical page from an OG).

Note that for each patent, the OG entry gives the patent number, inventor's name(s) and address(es), assignee (usually a company that the inventor has transferred ownership of the patent to), filing date, application serial number, international classification, U.S. classification, number of claims, and a sample claim or abstract. If the drawing and claim look relevant, go to the actual patent, order or download a copy of it, and study it at your leisure.

Remember that the claim found in the *Official Gazette* is not a descriptive summary of the technical information in the patent. Rather, it is the essence of the claimed invention. The full text of the patent will contain far more technical information than the claim. So, even if a patent's *Official Gazette* claim doesn't precisely describe your invention, the rest of the patent may still be relevant.

> **EXAMPLE:** When recently performing a PTRC search, a client of ours passed over a patent listed in the OG because the single drawing figure appeared to render the patent irrelevant. In fact, another drawing figure in the passed-over patent (but not found in the OG) anticipated our client's invention and was used by the PTO to reject his application (after he had spent considerable time, money, and energy preparing and filing it). The moral? Take an OG search with a grain of salt. Note well that a figure of the patent that isn't shown in the OG may be highly relevant; thus it's best to search full patents.

To make an OG search of the patents in class 272, subclass 109 (Fig. 6L), start with the first patent in this list, D-262,394X. The "D" means that the patent is a design patent and the "X" means that this patent is a cross-reference. To view patent D-262,394, look on the PTO's website under "Patent Number Searching." You'll find the patent, D-262,394, was issued in 1980. If you find it relevant, print it out and write its identifying data down on your Searcher's Worksheet, Form 6-1.

The second patent in the list, RE-25,843, is a reissue patent. (Reissues are discussed in Chapter 14.) For now, all you have to know is that reissues are also available on the PTO's site. Locate the patent, print it out, and list it on your worksheet if you feel it's relevant.

All of the rest of the patents in subclass 109 are regular utility patents in numerical and date order. Start with patent 9,695, which issued in the middle 1800s. You'll be able to view it easily online, in an old paper OG, or on microfilm or microfiche. Look at the patent in the usual manner to see if it's relevant. If so, write its data on your worksheet.

The Internet has full copies of patents readily accessible on any of the above sites—(each patent usually consists of several pages). You can look at the full text of each patent, one by one, in a similar manner as you looked at their abstracts in the OGs. If you find that the patent is relevant, you can download and print a copy of the whole patent, or just its relevant parts, on the spot.

Alternatively, if you don't want to interrupt the flow of your searching, you can save your patent numbers and print out copies later.

After you've completed Step 3, the review of patents, then perform Step 4, the analysis and decision, in exactly the same manner as outlined above.

L. Problems Searching Software and Business Inventions

Many software experts have recently complained that the PTO has been issuing patents on software and business method inventions that aren't novel and nonobvious over the prior art. There is much validity to this charge—that is, many software and business patents really don't claim a novel and nonobvious invention and could be invalidated by a proper search. Part of the problem is due to differences in the PTO's database of software patents. As a result, some people even want to do away with software patents. That might be a case of throwing out the baby with the bathwater.

Reference Collection of U.S. Patents Available for Public Use in Patent and Trademark Resource Centers

The following libraries, designated as Patent and Trademark Resource Centers (PTRCs), receive patent and trademark information from the U.S. Patent and Trademark Office. Many PTRCs have on file patents issued since 1790, trademarks published since 1872, and select collections of foreign patents. All PTRCs receive both the patent and trademark sections of the *Official Gazette* of the U.S. Patent and Trademark Office and numerical sets of patents in a variety of formats. Patent and trademark search systems in the CASSIS optical disk series are available at all PTRCs to increase access to that information. It is through the optical disk systems and other depository materials that preliminary patent and trademark searches may be conducted through the numerically arranged collections.

Each PTRC offers reference publications that outline and provide access to the patent and trademark classification systems, as well as other documents and publications that supplement the basic search tools. PTRCs provide technical staff assistance in using all materials.

All information is available for use by the public free of charge. However, there may be charges associated with the use of online systems, photocopying, and related services.

Since there are variations in the scope of patent and trademark collections among the PTRCs, and their hours of service to the public vary, anyone contemplating use of these collections at a particular center is urged to contact that center in advance about its collections, services, and hours.

For the latest list of PTRCs, go to www.uspto.gov/learning-and-resources/support-centers/patent-and-trademark-resource-centers-ptrcs, and click on "PTRC Locations by State."

State	Name of Resource Center	Telephone
Alabama	Auburn University Libraries*	334-844-1737
	Birmingham Public Library	205-226-3620
Alaska	Fairbanks: Keith B. Mather Library	907-474-2636
Arizona	Phoenix: State Library of Arizona*	602-926-3870
Arkansas	Little Rock: Arkansas State Library*	501-682-2053
California	Los Angeles Public Library*	213-228-7220
	Riverside: Orbach Science Library	951-827-3316
	Sacramento: California State Library	916-654-0261
	San Diego Public Library	619-236-5800
	San Francisco Public Library*	415-557-4400
	San Jose Public Library	408-808-2000
	Sunnyvale Public Library	408-730-7300
Colorado	Denver Public Library	720-865-1363
Connecticut	Fairfield: Sacred Heart University, Ryan-Matura Library	203-371-7726
Delaware	Newark: University of Delaware Library	302-831-2965
DC	Washington: Howard University Libraries	202-806-7252
Florida	Fort Lauderdale: Broward County Main Library*	954-357-7444
	Miami–Dade Public Library*	305-375-2665
	Orlando: University of Central Florida Libraries	407-823-2562

State	Name of Resource Center	Telephone
Georgia	Atlanta: Georgia Institute of Technology, Library and Information Center	404-385-7185
Hawaii	Honolulu: Hawaii State Library*	808-586-3477
Illinois	Chicago Public Library	312-747-4450
	Macomb: Western Illinois University Libraries	309-298-2722
Indiana	Indianapolis: Marion County Public Library	317-269-1741
	West Lafayette: Siegesmund Engineering Library	765-494-2872
Iowa	Davenport: Public Library	563-326-7832
Kansas	Wichita: Ablah Library, Wichita State University*	800-572-8368
Kentucky	Louisville Free Public Library	502-574-1611
	Highland Heights: Northern Kentucky University, W. Frank Steely Library	859-572-5457
Louisiana	Baton Rouge: Troy H. Middleton Library, Louisiana State University	225-388-8875
Maine	Orono: Raymond H. Fogler Library, University of Maine	207-581-1678
Maryland	College Park: Engineering and Physical Sciences Library, University of Maryland	301-405-9157
	Baltimore: University of Baltimore	410-837-4554

* WEST (Web-based Examiner Search Tool—better searching) subscriber.

▲ EAST (Examiner Assisted Search Tool) subscriber.

Fig. 6K—List of Patent and Trademark Resource Centers

State	Name of Resource Center	Telephone
Massachusetts	Amherst: Physical Sciences Library, University of Massachusetts	413-545-2765
	Boston Public Library*	617-536-5400 Ext. 4256
Michigan	Ann Arbor: Art, Architecture & Engineering Library, University of Michigan	734-647-5735
	Big Rapids: Ferris State University, Ferris Library for Information, Technology & Education	231-592-3602
	Detroit Public Library (has APS Image Terminals)*▲	313-481-1391
	Houghton: Michigan Technical University, Van Pelt and Opie Library	906-487-2500
Minnesota	Hennepin County Library	612-543-8000
Mississippi	Jackson: Mississippi Library Commission	601-432-4111
Missouri	Kansas City: Linda Hall Library*	816-363-4600 Ext. 724
	St. Louis Public Library*	314-352-2900
Montana	Butte: Montana Technical Library of the University of Montana	406-496-4281
Nebraska	Lincoln: Engineering Library, University of Nebraska–Lincoln*	402-472-3411
Nevada	Reno: University of Nevada-Reno, Mathewson-IGT Knowledge Center	775-784-6500 Ext. 257
New Hampshire	Concord: University of New Hampshire School of Law	603-513-5130
New Jersey	Newark Public Library	973-733-7779
	Piscataway: Library of Science & Medicine, Rutgers University	732-445-2895
New Mexico	Las Cruces: New Mexico State University	575-646-5792
New York	Albany: New York State Library	518-474-5355
	Buffalo and Erie County Public Library	716-858-7101
	New York Public Library, Science Industry & Business Library	212-592-7000
	Rochester Public Library	716-428-8110
North Carolina	Charlotte: J. Murrey Atkins Library, University of North Carolina at Charlotte	704-687-0494
North Dakota	Grand Forks: Chester Fritz Library, University of North Dakota	701-777-4629

State	Name of Resource Center	Telephone
Ohio	Akron: Summit County Public Library	330-643-9075
	Cincinnati and Hamilton County Public Library	513-369-6932
	Cleveland Public Library*	216-623-2870
	Dayton: Paul Laurence Dunbar Library, Wright State University	937-775-3521
	Toledo/Lucas County Public Library*	419-259-5209
Oklahoma	Stillwater: Oklahoma State University Edmon Low Library*	405-744-6546
Pennsylvania	Philadelphia: The Free Library of Philadelphia*	215-686-5394
	Pittsburgh: Carnegie Library	412-622-3138
	University Park: Physical and Mathematical Sciences Library, Pennsylvania State University	814-865-7617
Puerto Rico	Bayamón: University of Puerto Rico Learning Resources Center	787-993-0000 Ext. 3222
	Mayaguez General Library, University of Puerto Rico	787-832-4040 Ext. 2023
Rhode Island	Providence Public Library	401-455-8027
South Carolina	Clemson University Libraries	864-656-5168
South Dakota	Rapid City: Devereaux Library, South Dakota School of Mines & Technology	605-394-1275
Tennessee	Nashville: Stevenson Science & Engineering Library, Vanderbilt University	615-322-2717
Texas	Austin: McKinney Engineering Library, University of Texas at Austin	512-495-4511
	College Station: West Campus Library, Texas A&M University	979-845-2111
	Dallas Public Library*	214-670-1468
	Houston: The Fondren Library Rice University*	713-348-5483
	Lubbock: Texas Tech University	806-742-2282
	San Antonio Public Library	210-207-2500
Utah	Salt Lake City: Marriott Library, University of Utah*	801-581-8394
Vermont	Burlington: Bailey/Howe Library, University of Vermont	802-656-2542
Washington	Seattle: Engineering Library, University of Washington*	206-543-0740
West Virginia	Morgantown: Evansdale Library, West Virginia University*	304-293-4695
Wisconsin	Madison: Wendt Commons Library, University of Wisconsin, Madison	608-262-0696
	Milwaukee Public Library	414-286-3051
Wyoming	Cheyenne: Wyoming State Library	307-777-7281

* WEST (Web-based Examiner Search Tool—better searching) subscriber.

▲ EAST (Examiner Assisted Search Tool) subscriber.

Fig. 6K (continued)—List of Patent and Trademark Resource Centers

Many, if not most, future technological progress will occur in software, but without the incentive of a patent monopoly, software developers will not have an adequate incentive to innovate. There are many other arguments in favor of software patents, but they're beyond the scope of this book.

If you agree and want to support the continued existence of software patents, keep your eyes peeled for any legislative developments and do whatever you can to support the continued existence of software patents. Also if you have a software invention, be aware of the difficulty in doing a good search of your invention. If you search your invention in the PTO database there will be a greater chance that your search will not catch all of the relevant prior art.

One software patent resource is the Source Translation and Optimization patent website (www.bustpatents. com). The STO is directed by Gregory Aharonian, one of the PTO's most vocal critics. The site provides critiques, legal reviews, CAFC rulings, file wrappers, and infringement lawsuits relating to software patents. The STO also offers a free email newsletter.

M. Searches on the Internet

Free patent searching systems are useful tools for conducting fair-to-good patent searches on inventions using recent technologies and for making free searches for inventions in older technologies. If you are willing to spend the time to do a thorough job, you can make a fairly complete search online. However, if you are unwilling or unable to spend the time, hire a searcher, because it requires diligence to conduct a thorough patent search on the Internet.

1. Google Patents

Google Patents (https://patents.google.com) provides the most complete, most accurate, and fastest way to make online searches. Simply enter the keywords and all possible variations you can think of and it will search the entire U.S. patent database and return all relevant patents.

Fig 6N is Google Patents' main page. It is your gateway to about eight million searchable patents and patent applications dating back to 1836. To search from this page, enter your key search terms, such as "bicycle" and "fiberglass." You'll get a list of patents that have all of your search terms. Click on a patent to get a new page with all of the parts of the patent and a link to download a PDF of the patent. The main search page also links to a help site and to an Advanced Patent Search.

The Google Patents Advanced Search page (Fig. 6O) is where you can refine your search to look for patents with all of your keywords, an exact phrase, only one of a group of words, or omitting a word. Also it can be used to search for patents by number, title, inventor, assignee, or a specific U.S. or international classification. You can restrict the search to U.S. patents or published U.S. patent applications, utility, design patents, etc., or by a date or issue or filing date range. All of these helpful features are free. Thank you, Google!

2. PTO Search With EPO Supplement

The PTO's system can be used to make Keyword patentability searches of U.S. patents back to 1976 and U.S. patent applications back to March 2001 when they were first published. You can also use it to make Classification searches by patent number or class and subclass of U.S. patents from 1790 to the present. It cannot be used to make a patentability search of any patents before 1976. The PTO's URL for searching services is http://patft.uspto.gov. The PTO's servers have been vastly improved, so that you can easily and quickly download and view the images of any patent back to 1790. As stated, to print any patent you will find it faster and easier to use any of the services listed above, which can deliver PDFs of entire patents, rather than one page at a time. Everything is free on the PTO's website, except for orders of patents to be sent by mail. Fig. 6P shows the main page of the PTO's search website—note that you can make the three types of searches of either patents or patent applications. In order to view and print the actual images of patents on this

LISTING **CLASS 272** REEL NO. 7 PAGE 19

105		* 107	* 109	* 109	* 110
80	1,701,026	1,134,008	1,747,352X	3,659,844X	3,754,758
53	1,709,832	1,492,976	1,779,905	3,735,979X	3,834,695
01	1,785,968	1,570,185	1,914,555	3,764,446X	3,837,641X
98X	1,793,898	1,947,025X	1,918,559X	3,778,054X	3,880,422
13X	1,990,497	1,958,807X	1,928,089X	3,785,642X	3,896,858X
28X	2,004,172	2,223,091	2,048,587X	3,825,252X	3,923,302
36	2,144,962	2,640,699X	2,107,377	3,857,561X	4,084,814
22X	2,165,749X	2,864,201X	2,167,696X	3,857,563X	
44	2,323,510	3,312,472X	2,169,710X	3,874,657X	**111**
31	2,341,473	4,121,826X	2,262,761X	3,891,207X	
97	2,505,784		2,324,970X	3,895,795X	D 175,729X
92	2,534,159	**108**	2,496,748	3,912,262	159,301
62	2,890,048		2,572,149X	3,915,451	971,003
16X	2,900,187	450,759	2,595,111X	3,937,461	1,001,300X
18	2,937,871	807,770	2,652,966X	3,947,023X	1,407,642
10X	2,978,692X	1,036,138	2,671,229X	3,966,200	1,419,191X
09	3,010,321X	1,805,121X	2,706,632X	3,969,871X	1,537,686X
22	3,244,421X	1,936,687	2,722,360X	3,971,561X	1,747,721
06	3,400,928	1,997,958X	2,738,189X	3,981,500X	2,000,250
82	3,401,931	2,117,938	2,771,465X	4,014,057X	2,197,600X
91	3,494,615	3,548,420X	2,795,423	4,026,547	2,343,204X
88X	3,608,897	3,759,513	2,829,892X	4,037,834X	2,646,280X
64	3,665,452X	3,884,465X	2,858,132X	4,125,257	2,855,201
64	3,724,843	4,121,826X	2,859,967X	4,137,583X	2,939,704
00X	3,731,298X		2,885,233X	4,147,129X	3,062,542
81	3,746,335	*(109)*	2,897,013X	4,147,828X	3,083,964
67	3,799,542		2,944,815	4,204,719X	3,173,415X
32	3,809,392X	D 262,394X	2,953,376X	4,210,322	3,339,920
17	4,089,519	RE 25,843	3,006,645	4,216,958	3,404,884
12	4,134,583X	9,695	3,044,773X	4,225,131	3,416,792X
48		174,499	3,085,357	4,274,626	3,485,493X
04	**106**	233,273	3,105,082X	4,275,880X	3,545,747X
24		233,274	3,106,395X	4,325,546X	3,547,439
94X	610,131X	233,540	3,204,259X	4,340,215	3,570,847
16X	649,885	233,541	3,205,888X	4,340,216	3,570,848
80	1,122,157	451,411	3,207,511X	4,344,617	3,580,568
88	1,552,442	649,914	3,211,452X	4,350,721X	3,582,068
68X	1,569,395	664,414	3,242,509X	4,410,175X	3,589,716
34X	1,731,686	802,338	3,251,076X		3,616,126X
	1,994,089	811,417	3,262,134X	**110**	3,658,325
	2,036,524X	907,075	3,284,819X		3,722,881
	2,044,092	932,413	3,319,273X	D 198,923X	3,754,757
66	2,122,023	932,902	3,372,920	D 199,984X	3,781,931X
01	2,180,384	998,634	3,379,439X	1,085,505X	3,806,118X
54	2,196,610	1,003,797	3,391,414X	1,100,180X	3,837,644X
26	2,214,464	1,013,687	3,399,407	1,141,292X	3,850,428X
22X	3,163,421X	1,015,208	3,405,939X	1,462,910X	3,944,654
00	3,181,864X	1,126,082	3,409,294X	1,865,095X	3,990,697
78	3,746,334	1,128,201	3,419,270X	1,907,451	4,105,201
65	3,942,793X	1,130,813	3,432,163	1,916,809X	4,133,524
20X	4,084,813	1,142,137X	3,433,477X	2,198,537	4,183,521X
99	4,333,643	1,177,473X	3,459,611X	2,723,855X	4,197,839X
37X	4,337,940	1,204,329X	3,526,911X	2,906,531X	4,204,719X
14X	4,404,053X	1,256,734	3,580,569	2,949,298X	4,258,915
07		1,479,830	3,598,406X	3,246,893X	4,272,073
70	**107**	1,501,823X	3,628,790X	3,250,532	4,278,250X

CLASS 272

112	* 113
D 155,940X	D 173,173
D 208,924X	D 176,999
D 212,021X	D 187,138
D 214,572X	D 187,380
239,970X	D 187,381
450,187	D 187,656
775,309	D 198,532
786,672	D 218,455
950,100	D 218,460
1,485,135	D 218,765
1,585,748	D 224,029
1,670,390	D 224,796
1,676,061	D 227,381
2,240,407	D 227,792
2,303,223X	D 231,557
2,365,117	D 232,4..
2,429,939	D 238,694
2,706,632X	D 250,723
2,800,105X	D 250,783
2,838,307	D 250,784
2,929,627	170,495
2,977,118	209,511
3,032,344	7..,550
3,090,617X	796,159
3,156,465	821,391
3,342,484X	1,126,082
3,445,108	1,185,176
3,483,999X	1,351,053
3,501,140X	1,471,465
3,506,261	1,488,244
3,526,399	1,488,245
3,547,435X	1,488,246
3,563,539X	1,707,854
3,598,406X	1,765,361
3,606,315	1,822,786
3,638,602X	1,877,833
3,642,277	1,901,964
3,771,784X	1,917,018
3,782,718	1,929,822
3,794,316	2,126,636
3,837,642X	2,151,403
3,982,754X	2,206,581
4,018,437X	2,222,119
4,077,403X	2,500,425
4,116,433X	2,584,742
4,149,712	2,620,185
4,159,113	2,648,538
4,161,998X	2,648,539
4,272,073X	2,704,667
4,278,250X	2,720,430
4,335,538X	2,723,853
4,355,633X	2,768,828
4,372,552	2,795,423
	2,843,379
113	2,883,192
	2,886,317

Fig. 6L—List of Patents in Class 272-109 From Microfilm Printout

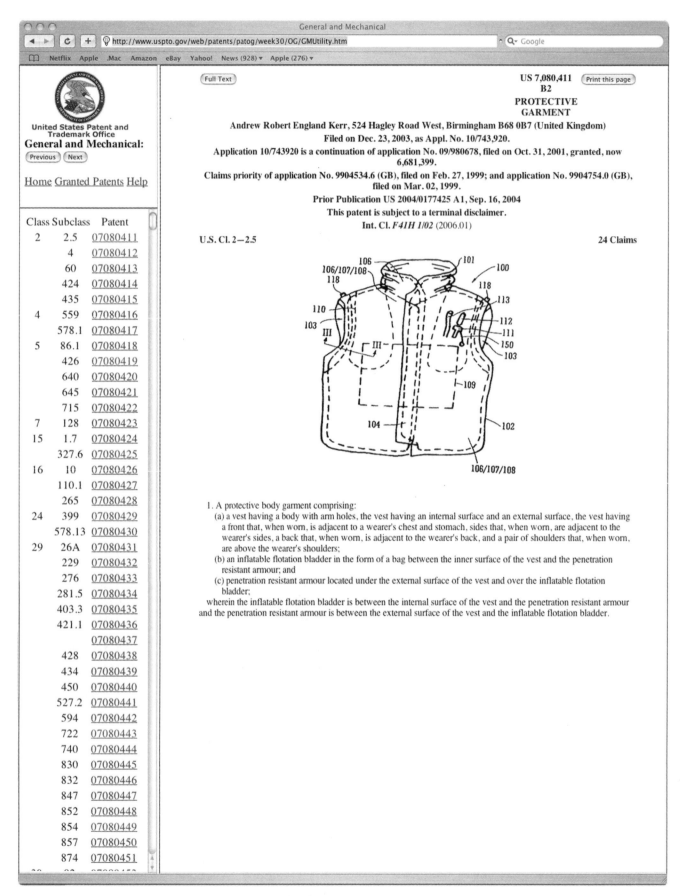

Fig 6M– Example From Online Publication of *Official Gazette* Showing Patent Illustration and Sample Claim

website you may need to download the AlternaTIFF viewer or use one of the free services listed above. You can do a rough extension of your patentability search of U.S. patents back to the 1920s at the EPO's site (https://worldwide.espacenet.com). In addition, this site also provides a searchable database for some foreign patents.

3.   Limitations of the PTO and Other Systems

The fact that the PTO website only permits you to search patents issued since 1971 or 1976 (while the Google search site goes all the way back to 1836), creates an extremely important limitation. All previous inventions (prior art) are relevant when determining whether a new invention qualifies for a patent. Therefore, to be effective, a patent search must cover the earliest prior art that might show your invention. Since patentability searches of the PTO system can be made back only to 1976, you can have confidence in your search results on the PTO's site only if your invention technology—for example an Internet invention—wasn't around prior to 1971 or 1976. For a low-tech invention that requires searching back beyond the 1971 date (for instance, a bicycle) these systems will only provide a fraction of the total prior art for that invention. Thus you should use Google's patent search site to search back to the first numbered U.S. patent, which issued in 1836. Even so, be aware that on some very old patents, Google's optical character recognition (OCR) produces garbled results, so your keywords may not match.

A second limitation is the fact that you must depend on keywords and the PTO's classification system. Traditional patent searching uses just the classification scheme to find relevant prior art. This scheme is the result of humans grouping like inventions together and does not depend on the whimsy of which search terms you select. The keyword system, on the other hand, requires you to come up with the right words in your search request. However, patents are often written with legal-sounding terms or technical jargon in place of otherwise ordinary terms. For example, a patent for a telephone may be titled "Full Duplex Voice

Fig. 6N—Google Patents (Main Page)

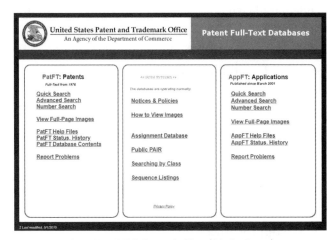

Fig. 6O—Google Patents Advanced Search

Fig. 6P—PTO Search Site (Main Page)

Telecommunication Device." Such a patent may never be found with "telephone" as the search term. This limitation is inherent in any computerized searching system based on search terms. The disadvantages of the keyword search system can to some extent be overcome by following the tips described below as well as by using the logic implicit in the Boolean search technique and supplementing your Keyword search with a Classification search.

4. The Ways to Search the PTO's Website

There are three ways to make a search on the PTO's website (Quick, Advanced, and Patent Number).

a. PTO Patent Number Search

To make a patent number search (better termed a patent lookup by number) on the PTO's website, go to the main search page (Fig. 6P) and click "Number Search," which will take you to the "Patent Number Search" page shown in Fig. 6Q. Then enter the number of the patent you want to view. Note that utility patents need no prefix while design, plant, and reissue patents, and defensive publications (see Chapter 7) require the prefixes indicated.

Next, click "Search," which will take you to the "Full Text Display" page (see Fig. 6R). This page displays the entire text of the patent and all of its bibliographic data. However, only the first page of this text is shown. Scroll down to see the rest of the patent. Any of the text can be copied and pasted into a word processor for editing. This page does not display any of the drawings of the patent displayed, however.

Finally, click "Images" near the top of the page and the first (or abstract) page of the actual patent appears (see Fig. 6S). Note that in addition to the first page of the patent, some extraneous information (the PTO's logo and some navigation buttons) also appears at the top and left side of the abstract page. The buttons are used to display other pages of the patent.

If you need to obtain copies of any patent, it's best to use one of the private patent copy supply services listed above because the PTO's server can download only one page of a patent at a time. If you do want to get a copy of any patent from the PTO's site, print out the actual images using the above procedure; don't print the text version or the patent page with the extraneous information. To print just the patent images, simply click the printer icon (not shown) near the top right corner of the image itself. (Don't click "Print" on your computer's toolbar above the page.)

The above procedure can be used to look up patent applications; just use the right-hand side as seen in Fig. 6P. If you do make a patentability search, you should search both patents and published patent applications.

b. PTO Quick Search

The PTO's "Quick Search" page allows you to enter and search two simple Boolean terms, such as bicycle AND aluminum (as shown in Fig. 6T). Note that "All Fields" is selected in the Field 1 and Field 2 boxes; this is where you should make all Boolean searches. Also note that "1976 to present" is displayed in the "Select years" box.

Fig. 6U shows the results of the quick search of Fig. 6T. Note that the search yielded 7,110 patents, which is too large a number to handle, so the search will have to be narrowed by using more specific search terms.

Note that Fig. 6T displays the first 21 patents. Scrolling down and visiting subsequent page links can show the rest. To view any patent that looks interesting, click its title or number. Again, the same procedure can be used to search patent applications (use the information on the right-hand side of Fig. 6P).

Also note that in addition to the AND Boolean operator, the operators OR and ANDNOT are available. Further, nested expressions, such as *tennis* AND (*racquet* OR *racket*) are available. If you enter this query, you will retrieve a list of all patents that contain both the terms tennis and either *racket* or *racquet* somewhere in the document. For another example, consider the search terms *television* OR (*cathode* AND *tube*). This query would return patents containing either the word *television* OR both the words *cathode* AND *tube*. A third example is the search expression *needle* ANDNOT ((*record* AND *player*)

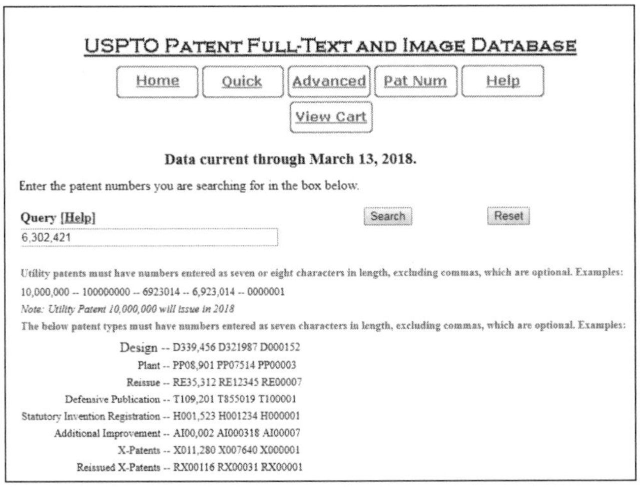

Fig. 6Q—PTO Patent Number Search Page

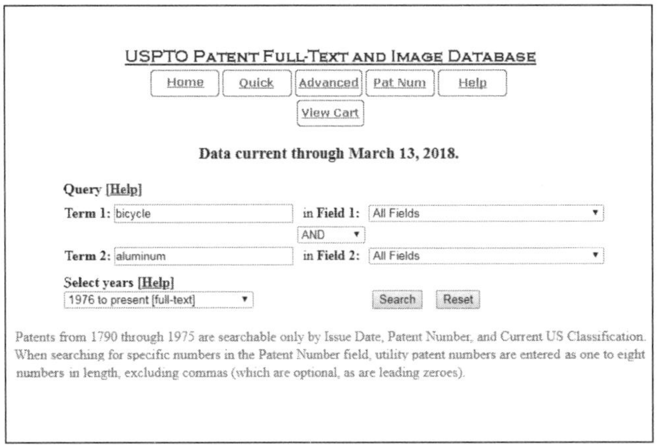

Fig. 6T—Quick Text Search Page

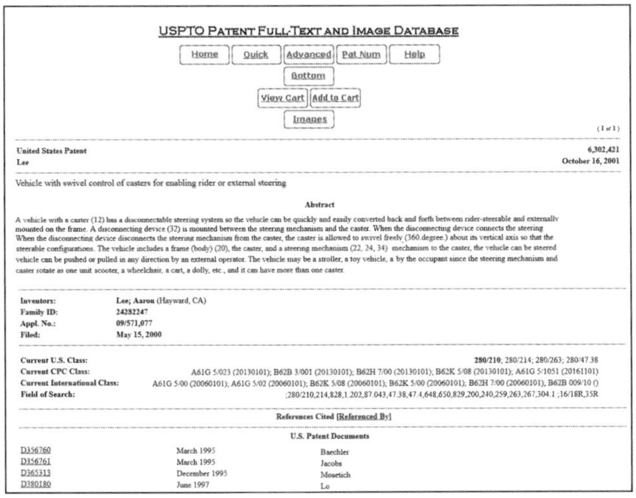

Fig. 6R—PTO Patent Full Text Display (Page 1)

Fig. 6U—PTO Quick Text Search Results Page

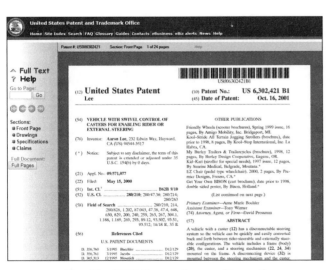

Fig. 6S—PTO Patent Image (Page 1)

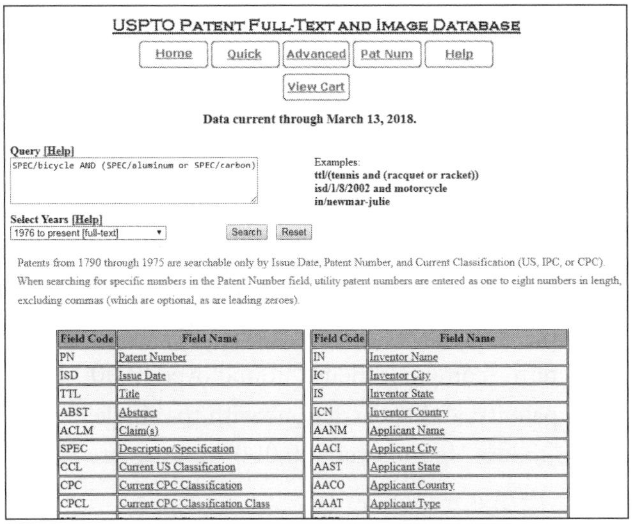

Fig. 6V—PTO Advanced Search Page

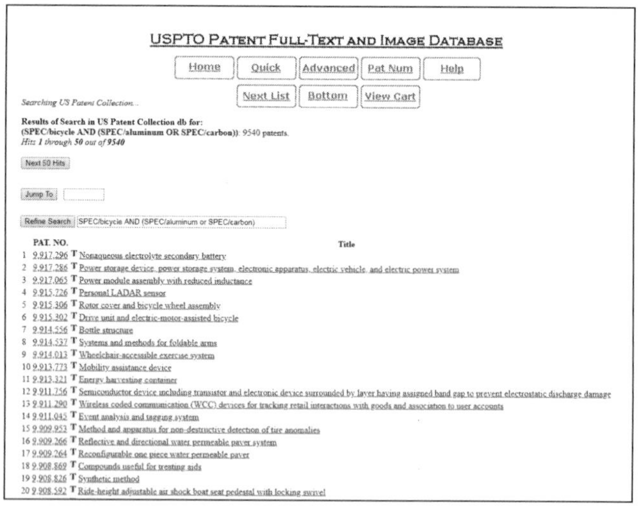

Fig. 6W—PTO Advanced Search Results (Page 1)

OR sewing). This complex query will generate a list of hits that contain the word needle, but not contain any references to sewing. In addition, none of the hits would contain the combination of record AND player.

c. PTO Advanced Search

Despite its name, the "Advanced Search" page (see Fig. 6V) really doesn't offer any more capabilities than the "Quick Search" page. The "Advanced Search" page is simply more difficult to use since it requires that you enter the search query in free form. The field must be manually typed (see Fig. 6V). Note that the field codes must be typed before the search terms. Fig. 6W shows part of the results of the advanced search of Fig. 6V.

5. Important Searching Tips

Your searching can be more productive and accurate if you follow these important tips:

1. *Less is more.* The fewer words used to define a search, the broader the results, and vice versa. For example, in 2016, a search done with the three-word term "ergonomic computer mouse" found 62 U.S. patents; a search done with the two-word term "computer mouse" found over 12,000 U.S. patents; and a search done with the single term "mouse" found over 400,000 U.S. patents.

2. *Use alternative terms.* A variety of different terms are often used in patents to describe similar inventions, so search with as many alternative terms as you can think of. For example, a computer mouse is also referred to as a "computer input device" or a "pointing device."

3. *Make good use of the Boolean connectors*, AND, OR, and ANDNOT, to connect words or terms in a box in any of the search methods, except for Patent Number Search. For example, "ergonomic AND mouse" can be entered in the Simple Text Search box. When Boolean connectors are used, multiple-word terms must be enclosed in quotes. For example, "ergonomic AND 'pointing device'" will search for all patents that have the word "ergonomic" AND the expression "pointing device." Boolean connectors can also be used to search for inventions with alternative terms simultaneously. For example, "computer mouse OR 'pointing device'" finds all patents with either the word "ergonomic" OR the expression "pointing device."

4. *Use wild cards.* Use the asterisk (*) as a wild card to represent any character or characters. For example, John* finds patents by all inventors with the first or last name starting with John, and ending with any character or characters, including John, Johnny, Johnson, and Johnston. Use the question mark (?) as a wild card to represent any single character. For example, ?am finds ram, cam, jam, etc.

5. *Inventor Names.* Always enter inventor names last-name first, for example, Edison Thomas.

6. *Class and References.* If you find a relevant patent, click on the Intl. Class and U.S. Class links to display patents for potentially similar inventions, and the U.S. References link to view the patents specifically cited as being similar.

Information on using more advanced search techniques can be found by clicking the search language link in the Advanced Text Search page.

N. NPL (Non-Patent Literature) Searches

While patent databases are the best place to make preexamination searches of inventions, additional prior art can sometimes be found by making a search of Non-Patent Literature, which the PTO calls NPL. NPL includes periodicals, textbooks, websites (current and obsolete), published theses, product manuals, advertisements, etc. Remember that any publication dated earlier than your date of invention can be valid prior art against your invention. There are many excellent places to search for NPL. Here are a few:

- **General Search Engines:** Internet search engines, including Google (www.google.com) and Yahoo (www.yahoo.com) can be used in the same manner as any of the Keyword patent searches above: you enter keyword combinations in the search box (e.g., "bicycle" and "carbon fiber alloy") and examine the NPL that the engine returns. If you get too many references, add or narrow your keywords to narrow the search and if you don't get enough references, use fewer and/or broader terms to broaden your search.
- **Specialized Search Engines:** A scientific search engine such as Google Scholar (https://scholar.google.com) will filter out nonscientific sites to speed searching.

Lastly, don't forget about Wikipedia (www.wikipedia.org), a free online encyclopedia that provides a great introduction and summary of practically any subject under the sun. It's a great place to start and to obtain a picture of the overall landscape before you drill down using one or more search engines.

O. Summary

There are many reasons to perform a patentability search for your invention: to save needless work and expenditures; to facilitate patent application preparation prosecution; to learn more about your invention; and to facilitate licensing. To possibly avoid making a full search, make a quick preliminary search yourself in stores and catalogs.

If you hire someone to make a search, hire a competent, experienced searcher, preferably a patent agent or attorney, and prepare your searcher with a full description of your invention. In order to analyze a search report, read the cited patents and other references carefully and determine what novel features your invention has and whether these are nonobvious.

All patent searches must now be made on a computer. To search, use (a) a Patent Resource Center's computer search facilities, (b) the Internet with a personal computer, namely the free website services of Google, the PTO, and the EPO (or use a fee-based commercial service), or (c) the EAST system in the PTO. Computer searches should be made using either Keywords by looking for patents with combinations of appropriate keywords or the PTO's Classification system where you can review all the patents in a particular subject-matter class. If you make a computer search, and you have a low-tech invention, make sure the computer's database extends all the way back to 1836.

What Should I Do Next?

After making your commercial evaluation and search, consider the following alternatives before proceeding or dropping the invention: File a Provisional Patent Application (PPA), file a Regular Patent Application (RPA), test the market* for up to a year and then consider filing, keep it a trade secret, file a design patent application, use a clever trademark, use copyright coverage, and/or use distinctive "trade dress."

* You may test market for a year but only if the inventor, or one who obtained details of the invention from the inventor, does the marketing. However test marketing is not advisable because of loss of foreign patent rights and the possibility of invention theft.

Now that you have an idea of the patentability and commercial status of your invention, it is time to make a plan for acquiring legal rights. You might think that your next step would be to prepare and file a patent application, but that's not necessarily the case. Review the Invention Decision Chart (Fig. 7) to simplify and organize the alternatives.

A. Fig. 7—Invention Decision Chart

The numbers in parentheses in the following discussion refer to the boxes on the chart in Fig. 7A. While there are six final options, several of these can be reached by several routes. Under the First-to-File rules of the America Invents Act (which went into effect in 2013), any marketing before filing by anyone other than the inventor or one who obtained details of the invention from the inventor will defeat any rights to a patent on the invention marketed. If the inventor, or one who obtained details of the invention from the inventor, publicly discloses the invention, the inventor has one year from the date of disclosure to file a patent application. That's an issue if you, or your company, or

associates want to test market for up to a year before filing. Beware: if you test market before filing you may lose foreign rights and increase the possibility of theft and an expensive and uncertain derivation proceeding.

B. Drop It If You Don't See Commercial Potential (Chart Route 10-12-14-X)

Assuming that you've invented something (Box 10) and recorded the conception properly (Box 12), you should then proceed to build and test your invention as soon as practicable, or consider filing a Provisional Patent Application, provided you're aware of all of the disadvantages of the Provisional Patent Application (PPA) (Box 12). If building and testing would be difficult, you should wait until after you evaluate your invention's commercial potential (Box 14), or patentability (Box 16). But always keep the building and testing as a goal; it will help you to evaluate commercial potential. What's more, as you'll find, a working model can be extremely valuable when you show the invention to a manufacturer.

Your next step is stated in Box 14—investigate your invention's commercial potential using the criteria of Chapter 4. Assuming you decide that your invention has little or no commercial potential, your answer to the commercial question is "No," and you would thus follow the "No" line from Box 14 to the ultimate decision, Box X, which says "Invent something else."

While you may be disappointed at having spent time and effort recording your invention, investigating its commercial potential, building and testing it, or searching it, your time and effort were definitely not wasted. You haven't failed in any way—unless you failed to learn a lesson from your experience. Edison had 3,000 failures, yet he regarded these as positive experiences since he learned 3,000 things he didn't know before. Armed with what you learned, you'll have a better chance at success and will encounter smoother sailing with your next invention.

"Our greatest glory is not in never falling, but in getting up every time we do."

—Confucius

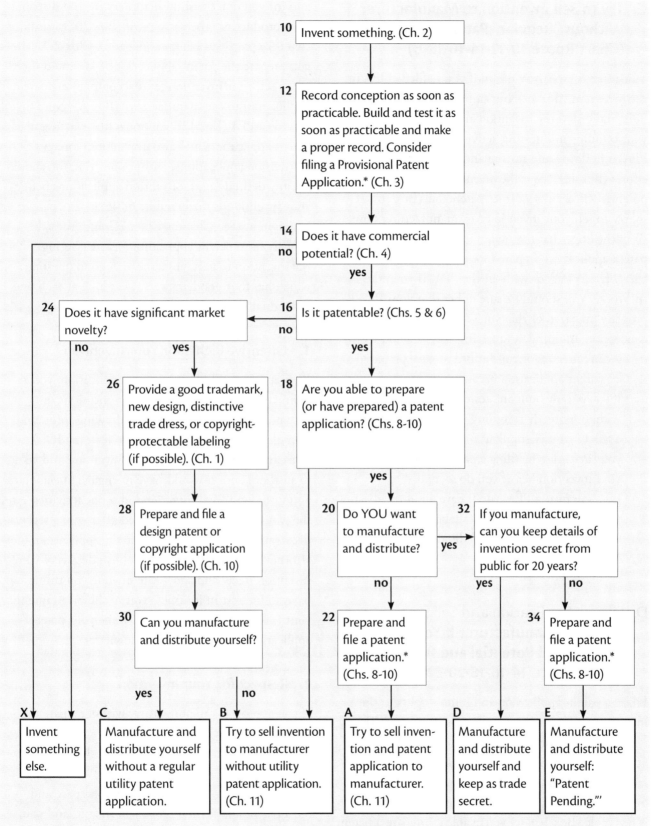

10 Invent something. (Ch. 2)

12 Record conception as soon as practicable. Build and test it as soon as practicable and make a proper record. Consider filing a Provisional Patent Application.* (Ch. 3)

14 Does it have commercial potential? (Ch. 4) — **no**

yes

16 Is it patentable? (Chs. 5 & 6) — **no**

24 Does it have significant market novelty?

yes

26 Provide a good trademark, new design, distinctive trade dress, or copyright-protectable labeling (if possible). (Ch. 1)

18 Are you able to prepare (or have prepared) a patent application? (Chs. 8-10)

yes

28 Prepare and file a design patent or copyright application (if possible). (Ch. 10)

20 Do YOU want to manufacture and distribute? — **yes**

32 If you manufacture, can you keep details of invention secret from public for 20 years?

no

yes / **no**

30 Can you manufacture and distribute yourself?

22 Prepare and file a patent application.* (Chs. 8-10)

34 Prepare and file a patent application.* (Chs. 8-10)

yes / **no**

X Invent something else.

C Manufacture and distribute yourself without a regular utility patent application.

B Try to sell invention to manufacturer without utility patent application. (Ch. 11)

A Try to sell invention and patent application to manufacturer. (Ch. 11)

D Manufacture and distribute yourself and keep as trade secret.

E Manufacture and distribute yourself: "Patent Pending."'

* If you filed a Provisional Patent Application, you must file a regular patent application and any desired foreign convention applications within one year—see Chapter 3. (File non-Convention applications before invention is made public or any patent issues on it.)

Fig. 7A—Invention Decision Chart

C. Try to Sell Invention to Manufacturer Without "Regular" Patent Application (Chart Route 10-12-14-16-18-B)

This route is especially useful if you've filed a PPA on the invention (Box 12), but can also be used if you've built and tested the invention and properly recorded your building and testing activities. After filing a PPA or building and testing and recording your efforts (Box 12), see if the invention has commercial potential (Box 14) and if it's patentable (Box 16). If so, try to sell your invention to a manufacturer (Box B) in the hope that the manufacturer will have the patent application prepared for you, either on the basis of your PPA or without the PPA. If you take this route, you should be sure either that your PPA is properly prepared or that you've properly documented conception, building, and testing. Use this route only if you can't prepare or can't afford to have prepared a regular patent application because:

- if you've only built and tested the invention without properly recording your activities, you run a risk of an unscrupulous manufacturer stealing your invention by filing a patent application on your invention before you do so, and
- if you've filed a PPA, you'll have all of the disadvantages of the PPA. (See Chapter 3 for a discussion of the advantages and disadvantages of filing a PPA.)

D. File an Application and Sell It to or License a Manufacturer If You See Commercial Potential and Patentability (Chart Route 14-16-18-20-22-A)

Filing a patent application and selling rights to the invention is the usual route for most inventors. This is because inventors seldom have the capability to establish their own manufacturing and distribution facilities. If (a) your invention has good commercial potential (Box 14), (b) your decision on patentability is favorable (Box 16), (c) you're able to prepare a patent application (Box 18) (or have one prepared for you),

and (d) you don't wish to manufacture and distribute your product or process yourself (Box 20), your next step is to prepare a patent application (Box 22). After you prepare the patent application, you should then try to sell your invention (and accompanying patent application) to the manufacturer (Box A). Note that if you file a PPA (Box 12), you must file your "regular" patent application, and also any desired foreign convention applications, within one year. You should file any desired non-Convention applications before your invention is made public or before any patent issues on it. (See Chapter 12 on "Going Abroad.")

Why file a patent application before offering the invention to a manufacturer? A good question, which has four good answers. Let's look at each one individually.

1. Offensive Rights for Your Invention

By preparing and filing a patent application, you've defined your invention and its ramifications in very precise terms, made formal drawings of it, and formally established your claim to it in the PTO. Thus anyone who later sees your invention and wants to steal or adopt it would have to engage in elaborate and (usually) illegal forgeries and other activities. And, the would-be thief will have filed after you, a serious disadvantage. Thus once you file the application, most attorneys agree that you may publish details of your invention freely and show it to anyone you think may have an interest in it (unless you've chosen to maintain your invention as a trade secret while your patent application is pending—see below).

2. Respect for Your Invention

If you approach a manufacturer without a patent application, they may not think you're a serious player. A manufacturer to whom you show the invention, seeing that you have thought enough of your invention to take the trouble to prepare and file a patent application on it, will treat it, and you, with far more respect and give it much more serious consideration than if you offer an unfiled invention.

3. You Have Rights Even If You Sign a Manufacturer's Waiver

Most manufacturers to whom you offer an invention will not deal with you unless you first waive (give up) certain potential claims that might arise from the transaction (such as being able to charge the manufacturer with stealing your idea in the event this occurs). Simply put, signing a waiver if you haven't already filed a patent application will put you at the complete mercy of the company to whom you show your invention. Fortunately, however, such waivers do not involve your giving up your rights under the patent laws. Thus, having a patent application on file, in this context, affords you powerful rights against underhanded dealing by the manufacturer (assuming the patent subsequently issues). One inventor, Stephen Key, has said that a patent application levels the playing field, giving an inventor the power to play ball with corporate America.

4. You'll Be Offering More So You'll Get More

Most manufacturers want a proprietary or privileged position—that is, a position that entitles them to a commercial advantage in the marketplace that competitors can't readily copy and obtain. A patent provides a very highly privileged position: a 17- to 18-year (approximately) monopoly. Thus if you have a patent application that already covers your invention, manufacturers may be far more likely to buy your invention (with its covering patent application) than if you offered them a "naked" invention on which they have to take the time and trouble to file a patent application for you themselves.

TIP

An Exception. Although, as stated, it's usually best to file your patent application as soon as possible, it may be to your advantage to delay and keep the invention secret or take your chances approaching manufacturers "naked" if your invention is so innovative that it's not likely to be commercialized for many years. Gordon Gould, the inventor of the laser, did this unintentionally when he delayed in filing his patent application because he mistakenly believed he needed a working model to file. His mistake worked to his great advantage, however, since his delay postponed his monopoly period so that it coincided with the laser's commercial period, thereby turning what would have been a worthless patent into pure gold.

Common Misconception: You shouldn't patent your invention, since someone will see your patent, copy your invention, and make it more cheaply.

Facts: Copiers rarely use patents as a basis for their activities. Usually they copy successful products in the marketplace by reverse engineering. They'll be less likely to do this if it is patented, and a patent will enable you to sue them to stop their production or importation, or get royalties from them.

E. If You Have Commercial Potential Without Patentability, License or Sell Your Invention to a Manufacturer Without Filing (Chart Route 16-24-26-28-30-B)

If your invention isn't patentable (that is—the decision in Box 16 is negative), don't give up; there's still hope. Many fortunes have been made on products that weren't patentable. For instance, the Apple computer made its designer-promoters, Jobs and Wozniak, multimillionaires, yet lacked any significant inventive concepts and never was awarded a major patent. Ditto for Henry Ford's automobile and George Eastman's Kodak camera.

Thus you should now decide, on the basis of your commercial potential and patentability evaluations, whether your invention nevertheless possesses "significant market novelty" (Box 24). If so, it may in fact be quite profitable if introduced to the market. Put differently, if your patentability search produces close prior art, but not a dead ringer, this indicates that probably no one has tried your specific, particular idea before, although someone has come close enough to preclude you from getting a patent. However, if you feel, looking back on your commercial-potential and patentability evaluations, that it doesn't have significant market novelty—that is, there's little chance of commercial success—then there isn't much hope and you'll have to try again (Box X).

Assuming that your invention does have significant market novelty (Box 24) but does not qualify for a utility patent, there are several ways that you can use to obtain proprietary rights on your invention and make it more attractive to potential manufacturers. Let's take a closer look at these.

1. Record Conception Properly

While recording conception won't provide you with any rights against independent creators, or "reverse engineers," it will establish (a) you as the inventor, and (b) the date of your invention, so you'll be able to prove that you invented it and when you did so. This may be of great help in stopping any invention thieves who copy it illegally before it's out.

2. Provide a Clever Trademark

One good way to make your invention more attractive is to provide a clever trademark for it (Box 26). A trademark is a name or other signifier for a product. A clever trademark can be a very powerful marketing tool—that is, a tool that will greatly enhance the value and salability of your invention and give you added proprietary rights to sell to a manufacturer. Examples of clever, suggestive trademarks are *Ivory* for a soap and *HushPuppies* for shoes. Also consider *Sunkist* citrus fruit, *Shasta* soft drinks, *Roach Motel* roach traps, *Heavyhands* exercise weights, and *Sun Tea* beverage.

If you think the mark is valuable and that you (or a company that will license the product) will be able to offer a product with the mark within a year or so, then you can file an Intent-to-Use trademark application with the PTO to begin the process of registering the mark.

3. Provide a Unique Patentable Design

If the invention that fails to qualify for a utility patent is a tangible product, the second trick to obtaining proprietary rights is to create a distinctive design (Box 26). Then, perhaps, a design patent can be obtained. By distinctive design, we're referring to a shape or layout that is unique and different from anything you've seen so far. The design, in this case, doesn't mean the function or internal structure of the product, but only its outward, nonfunctional, ornamental, aesthetic shape or layout that makes it distinct visually.

For example, the D-shaped *Heavyhands* weights and Dizzy Gillespie's trumpet with its upwardly bent bell section are excellent examples of valuable design inventions. If you've invented a computer, a new case shape can be a design invention. For a bicycle, a new frame shape design would be a design invention. From abacuses to zithers, from airplanes to zippers, almost every humanly made object under the sun can be redesigned or reshaped in a new way so that it can be covered by a design patent and also can be made more attractive to potential buyers.

However, for a design patent to be applicable, the new features must be for aesthetic or ornamental purposes and should not have any significant functional purpose—otherwise the PTO will reject it as nonornamental—that is, only a utility patent will be appropriate. Also, the design must be inseparable from the object and not merely surface ornamentation. In the latter case, copyright is the proper form of coverage. For example, the label design on a jar of juice cannot be protected by a design patent, but a new shape for the jar would qualify for one. If you do come up with a distinctive design, you should, of course, record it in the same manner as you recorded your invention. And as with your invention, you should build a prototype or model as soon as practicable. You should also prepare and file a design-patent application (Box 28) on the ornamental appearance (not workings) of your invention.

Unless you live near the PTO or a Patent and Trademark Resource Center, it doesn't pay to search a new design beyond the most cursory look in product catalogs. This is because the cost of the search will greatly exceed the cost and effort to prepare and file a design-patent application. A design-patent application consists simply of a drawing and a few forms that you fill out; it's very easy and economical to prepare.

4. Provide Distinctive "Trade Dress"

If you can't come up with a new design (or even if you can), you can enhance the proprietary value of your invention by providing it with a distinctive "trade dress"—distinctive shapes (the Coca-Cola bottle) or packaging (the choice of red colors on the Netflix envelope). Collectively, these types of identifying trade dress features are commonly protected under trademark law. (Note: Functional aspects of trade dress cannot be protected under trademark law.)

5. Provide Copyrightable Labeling

Look closely at some of the packaged products that you see in your home or on display in a store for a copyright notice, for example, "© 2018 S.C. Johnson & Son, Inc." This copyright is intended to cover either the wording on the label or container, the artwork, or both. While relatively easy to design around (that is—come up with a close but noninfringing alternative), unique labeling with a copyright notice nevertheless provides a measure of offensive rights that is well worth the small effort it takes to invoke. Many market researchers have shown that an attractive label can make all the difference in the success of a product. Accordingly, it can pay, if you're marketing a packaged product, to spend some effort, either on your own or in hiring a designer, to come up with an attractive, unique label, affix a copyright notice—for example, © Smith and Sons—and apply for copyright registration.

6. Consider Trade Secret Protection

A trade secret is any information that has commercial value, that has been maintained in confidence by a business, and that is not known by competitors. An inventor who owns trade secrets is entitled to court relief against those who have stolen the secrets or divulged them in violation of a legal duty—for example, after signing an agreement not to disclose (a nondisclosure agreement or NDA), or the duty of an employee to keep the secrets of his or her employer. Keep your invention secret, at least until you file. Or, if you choose not to file, and your invention is not easy to reverse engineer, consider maintaining trade secrecy as a form of invention protection.

7. Submit Your Idea to Quirky.com

In lieu of submitting your unpatentable but commercially valuable brainchild to conventional manufacturers, one online service, Quirky.com, seeks niche products to evaluate and manufacture even though the product may not be different enough to be patentable. As reported in *Parade* for 2010 Oct 24, Quirky, founded by Ben Kaufman, receives ideas from the public, submits them to its members (called "Quirks"), and designs and manufactures the product if (a) the Quirks provide a favorable opinion and (b) Quirky gets enough premanufacturing orders to cover production costs. Quirky isn't concerned with patents and relies on fast production and marketing to head off potential copiers. They charge submitters $10 to submit an idea (to make sure submitters are serious) and they pay royalties on the sales as the product is manufactured and sold.

F. Make and Sell Your Invention Yourself Without a Utility Patent Application (Chart Route 16-24-26-28-30-C)

Here we assume again that you have an unpatentable invention, but hopefully one that you can make and distribute yourself (Box 30). It's generally better to do so (Box C) than to try to sell it to a manufacturer outright. Even if you have a good trademark, a design patent application, distinctive trade dress, and/or a unique label, the absence of a utility patent application means a manufacturer does not get a privileged position, and so will generally not be as inclined to buy your invention. However, if you decide to manufacture the invention yourself, and you reach the market first, you'll have a significant marketing advantage despite the lack of a utility patent. Also, because you're the manufacturer, you'll make a much larger profit per item than if you received royalties from a manufacturer. Note: If you're not going to, or won't be able to, bring your invention to the market right away and you want to prevent anyone else from patenting it, consider making a "defensive publication" (see Chapter 14) of it to create prior art on it.

G. Manufacture and Distribute Your Invention Yourself, Keeping It as a Trade Secret (Chart Route 20-32-D)

Even though your invention may be commercially valuable and patentable, it isn't always in your best interest to patent it. The alternative, when possible, is to keep an invention a trade secret and manufacture and sell the invention yourself, for example, by direct mail marketing, broadcast or periodical advertising, possibly eventually working your way up to conventional distributors and retailers. A trade secret has numerous advantages and disadvantages. An invention can be maintained as a trade secret right up until the time a patent application is published or a patent actually issues, but after that the trade secret is lost. If you file a Nonpublication Request (NPR) at the time of filing, and you don't file for a patent outside the U.S., your application will never be published if it doesn't issue. (Your application will not issue if you can't convince the PTO to grant you a patent, or you abandon it—for example, you don't respond to an Office Action or you don't pay the issue fee.) In that case your invention will remain a trade secret as long as you continue to treat it as one and as long as the invention is not publicly disclosed by others, provided it can't be discovered from the final product (reverse engineered).

You should not consider (and you can't protect) every bit of information as a trade secret. You can only protect secret information that has commercial value because it is not known by others. Write up this important information—the crown jewels. After you write it up, take normal precautions to keep the information secret. Keep your documentation safe, don't let anyone see it (or the actual manufacture of the product) unless they have a "need to know" (for example, an employee) and have signed a nondisclosure (keep-confidential) agreement. Also, keep the trade secret information out of any service or instruction manual that goes with the product. You don't need to file any governmental forms or applications to create trade secret rights.

Remember that you can't maintain trade secret rights on an invention unless it can't be discovered from the final product—even if sophisticated reverse engineering is used. One good example of an invention that was kept as a trade secret is the formula used in the Toni home permanent wave kit. Its inventor, Richard Harris, manufactured and sold the unpatented invention through his own company for many years, making large profits, and thereafter sold his business for $20 million when he decided to retire.

Although not specifically covered on the chart, there is another possibility in the trade secret category. That is, you may sell your invention to a manufacturer who may choose to keep it as a trade secret, provided you've filed an NPR at the time of filing. This may occur with either unpatentable or patentable inventions (Chart routes 16-24-26-28-30-B or 16-18-20-22-A), but you don't have to worry about this alternative since it's the manufacturer's choice, not yours. If you've filed an NPR, the manufacturer can simply allow the patent application to go abandoned so it won't be published, thereby maintaining the trade secret.

> **CAUTION**
>
> **One disadvantage of keeping a "hardware" (as opposed to a process) invention as a trade secret is that someone else can validly patent the hardware if they invent it independently and can then sue you for patent infringement,** even if you've been using the trade secret commercially for 20 years! However, under a "prior user's rights" statute (35 USC 273), if someone has a method patent, but you've used the method commercially for over a year before the method patent application was filed, you have a complete defense to any action for patent infringement on the method.

> **TIP**
>
> **You shouldn't refer to your abandoned patent application in any other application that will issue as a patent,** since anyone can gain access to an abandoned application that's referred to in a patent.

H. File Patent Application and Manufacture and Distribute Your Invention Yourself (Trade-Secret Protectable Invention) (Chart Route 20-32-34-E)

Suppose your invention is not discoverable from your final product so that you can keep it secret for a while, but not for the life of a patent (Box 32). Or, suppose, after evaluating the advantages and disadvantages of a trade secret under the criteria above, you don't wish to choose the trade-secret route, preferring instead to patent your invention. You should then prepare and file a patent application (Box 34) and then manufacture and distribute the invention yourself with the notice "patent pending" affixed to the invention (Box E).

You may think that preparing and filing a patent application is a lot of hassle (it is), but if you have a patentable invention and a commercially viable product and you don't pay for a patent application now (by hiring an attorney or doing it yourself), you will pay for it later. If you have a successful product on the market, competitors will copy it. If you "go naked" by putting it out with no patent rights, you won't be able to stop the copiers and you'll lose far more market share than what the cost of a patent would have been.

CAUTION

Keep It Secret. While the patent application is pending, you should—provided you've filed an NPR—not publish any details of your invention. That way, if the patent application is finally rejected, you can allow it to go abandoned and still maintain your trade secret. Remember, by law, the PTO must keep your patent application secret until it's published (your non-provisional patent application will be published 18 months after filing unless an NPR was filed), or until it issues (if it was not published). In practice, the PTO is very strict in this regard. Until pending patent applications are published or they issue, outsiders have no access to them, and PTO personnel must keep patent applications in strict confidence. If you've filed a patent application without an NPR and decide to maintain your invention as a trade secret, you can still prevent the normal 18-month publication of the application by abandoning the application before it's published.

TIP

Effect of "Patent Pending" Notice. The patent-pending notice on your product does not confer any legal rights, but it is used by most manufacturers who have a patent application on file in order to deter potential competitors from copying their inventions. The notice effectively warns competitors that the manufacturer may get a patent on the product, so that if they do invest the money and effort in tooling to copy the invention, they could be enjoined from further manufacturing, with a consequent waste of their investment. However, make sure you don't use a patent-pending notice with a product that is not actually covered by a pending application: To do so is a criminal offense.

I. File Patent Application and Manufacture and Distribute Invention Yourself (Non-Trade-Secret Protectable Invention) (Chart Route 20-32-34-E)

This will be the route followed by most inventors who wish to manufacture their own invention. Assume that the essence of your invention, like most, is discoverable from the final product. You should then prepare and file a patent application (Box 34), and then manufacture and distribute the invention yourself (Box E).

Remember that under the AIA, any patent application will be invalid if the PPA or RPA is filed after marketing done by someone other than the inventor, or someone who obtained details of the invention from the inventor. In summary, test marketing before filing by anyone other than the inventor, or one who obtained details of the invention from the inventor, is now a no-no.

TIP

Don't give up your day job. While patents can sometimes be very profitable for their inventors, unfortunately great success stories are few and far between. Do not to depend on your invention or any patent to pull you out of poverty or change your lifestyle, because few patents do this and even if a patent is successful, it usually takes years to bear fruit. Keep your present vocation unless and until you attain success. If your invention does succeed, that's a great win and you should enjoy the success to the fullest. However, in case it does not, you can still continue as before and learn from the experience.

J.   Summary

After you make your patentability decision and evaluate the commercial potential of your invention, you have a number of possible routes to take. If you feel that your invention lacks commercial potential, drop it and move on to something else. If you feel that it has commercial potential, but you can't prepare a regular patent application, file a PPA or try to sell it without filing a PPA or an RPA. If your invention is patentable, file first and then try to sell it to a manufacturer. (You should file first to secure your rights, especially if you sign a manufacturer's waiver form.)

If your invention isn't patentable, you may be able to file a design patent application, or secure trademark rights, copyright, or trade dress rights before offering it to a manufacturer. You can make and sell the invention yourself with or without a patent application, and you can keep it as a trade secret after putting it on the market if it's the type of invention that can't be reverse engineered. Test marketing before filing a PPA or an RPA by anyone other than the inventor, or one who obtained details of the invention from the inventor, will defeat your patent.

How to Draft the Specification and Initial Drawings

Inventor's Commandment 10

In recent years, the Patent Court began limiting the scope of some patents by relying upon "limiting statements" that the patentees made in their specifications and remarks to the PTO. For that reason, your patent application should not contain any statements that the courts could possibly use against you to limit the claims of your invention—that is, do not indicate any field of the invention, do not mention any problems with the prior art that are not already known, or that your invention doesn't solve, do not indicate that any embodiment is preferred, do not include any specific advantage unless at least one embodiment has this advantage, indicate that "one or more aspects" have the advantages, do not include any objects, make the summary and abstract as broad and nonspecific as possible, do not refer to "the invention" but only to "this embodiment," do not state that any part is essential, and include as many embodiments as possible.

Inventor's Commandment 11

The specification and drawings of your patent application must contain a description of your invention in full, clear, concise, and exact terms so that anyone having ordinary skill in the field will be readily able to make and use it. While a statute requires you to disclose the best mode for carrying out the invention, you should disclose all possible modes (embodiments) without indicating any preference, unless the PTO requires you to do so.

Inventor's Commandment 12

In your patent application, you should "sell" your invention to the examiner or anyone else who may read the application. State all the disadvantages of the prior art factually and the advantages of one or more embodiments (not the invention per se) in a nonlimiting way.

This and the next two chapters are the heart of this book: They cover the writing and transmittal of your patent application to the Patent and Trademark Office (PTO). This chapter provides an overview of the patent application drafting process and contains specific instructions on drafting a specification and preliminary drawings. Chapter 9 explains how to draft patent claims (sentence fragments that delineate the precise scope of the patent being sought). Chapter 10 explains how to "final" the application as well as the precise steps involved in transmitting it to the PTO. In addition, Chapter 10 covers design patent applications.

Consider Drafting The Claims First

Patent attorneys almost always draft the claims before drafting the specification and drawings. Why? Because the specification must show in a figure, and describe in text, every element of every claim. If you draft the claims first, they will provide a good checklist as you draft the specification. How? Your invention disclosure (see Chapter 3) should provide enough information for you to take a first cut at the claims. Drafting the claims and the specification is an iterative process, and you will need to go back and forth between them as you draft. Though you can read chapters 8 and 9 in any order you like—you may find it helpful to draft the claims first.

Have you filed a Provisional Patent Application (PPA)? As a result of legislation enacted in 1999, you may convert the PPA to a regular patent application (RPA) even if the PPA did not include any claims. (35 USC 111.) However, converting the PPA to an RPA is not recommended because your patent will expire 20 years from the earlier date of your PPA (rather than the later date of your RPA).

If you filed a PPA and are ready to file your RPA, file a separate RPA to start the 20-year term from the date of your RPA. To file a separate RPA, follow the instructions in this chapter for preparing an RPA from scratch. You should claim the benefit of the PPA in the RPA. If the one-year anniversary of your PPA falls on a weekend or holiday, you can still get the benefit of the PPA—in the United States—by filing the RPA on the next business day. (Other countries are not so generous; see Chapter 12 for more details.) Remember that your PPA will not be read by any PTO personnel unless you need to rely on its date to predate a reference cited against your claims or in case you're unfortunate enough to get into an interference or derivation proceeding (unlikely situations in which the PTO must decide who is entitled to a patent, when two pending patent applications by different applicants claim the same invention).

A. Lay Inventors *Can* Do It!

It's a common myth that a lay inventor won't be able to prepare a patent application, or prepare it properly. Lay inventors can and have done very good jobs, sometimes better than patent attorneys, by following this book. To prepare a proper patent application, you should be mainly concerned with four basic, essential considerations:

1. The specification (description and operation of your invention and drawings) should be detailed enough so that there will be no doubt that one skilled in the art will be able to make and use the invention after reading it.
2. You should not state anything in the application that a court could use to limit your invention.
3. The main claims should be as broad as the prior art permits. (More about this in Chapter 9.)
4. You should "sell" your invention by stressing all of its advantages in a nonlimiting way.

If you satisfy these four criteria, you'll be home free. All the other matters are of lesser import and can be fixed if necessary.

B. What's Contained in a Patent Application

A regular patent application that is filed by mail or hand delivery to the PTO consists of the following parts, which are all sent together to the PTO after assembly in the below order. (Certain items that are omitted when filing by EFS-Web are indicated by the ‡ symbol.)

1. A self-addressed receipt postcard
2. A check or, if paying by credit card, a completed Form PTO-2038 for the filing fee. ‡
3. A Transmittal Letter, Form AIA/15 for utility applications, Form AIA/18 for designs, or Form AIA/19 for plants.
4. A Fee Transmittal, Form SB/17.‡
5. A Nonpublication Request (NPR), Form SB/35. Send this if you don't intend to file counterpart applications outside the U.S. and don't want the application to be published 18 months after filing (if it's still pending then), for example, if you want to keep your invention secret if it doesn't issue. ‡
6. A drawing or drawings of the invention—unless the invention is of a nature where drawings are not needed (this is rare; it is recommended that you include drawings, even if you think you don't need them).
7. A Specification containing the following sections:
   a. Title of the Invention (no more than 500 characters)
   b. Cross-Reference to Related Applications.† This is used to refer to and claim priority of any PPA or prior related applications that you've filed.
   c. Federally Sponsored Research.† This is used to indicate that the invention was made under a government contract and that the government has rights in it.
   d. Sequence Listing or Program.† This is used to indicate if the application contains a biotech sequence listing or computer program as an appendix or on CD-ROM.
   e. Background. This section should state any known problems that the invention definitely solves and discuss and criticize the relevant prior art (previous patents and other relevant developments in the same technological areas). (A Field of Invention was previously required

---

† If this section is not applicable, it can be omitted or the phrase "not applicable" should follow the heading.

but is no longer needed and should not be used because it can be used to bring in prior art that might not otherwise be relevant.)

f. Summary. This should briefly describe the invention as claimed.

g. Drawings†—Figures. This is a brief listing of the Drawing figures and may include the subsection below, Reference Numerals.

h. Reference Numerals (optional but desirable). These are the Drawing numbers that designate the respective parts of your invention, such as 10 motor, 12 shaft, etc.

i. Detailed Description—First Embodiment— Figs. 1–X. This is a narrative description of the structure of the invention's main embodiment. The Detailed Description also includes the three subsections below, Operation—First Embodiment, Description—Additional Embodiment, and Operation—Additional Embodiment.

j. Operation—First Embodiment. This portion of the Detailed Description explains how the main embodiment of the invention works or operates.

k. Description—Additional Embodiment— Figs. Y–Z. This portion of the Detailed Description describes the structure of an alternative embodiment, if you have one.

l. Operation—Additional Embodiment. This portion of the Detailed Description describes the operation of the alternative embodiment. (Repeat for all additional embodiments.)

m. Conclusion, Ramifications, and Scope. This part again summarizes the invention's advantages, the alternative physical forms or uses it can take, and a broadening paragraph to remind any judge that it shouldn't be limited to the particular form(s) shown.

n. Claims. These are precise sentence fragments that delineate the exact nature of your invention—see Chapter 9. Begin the listing of claims with: "What is claimed is:"

o. Sequence Listing.† Include this heading only if a nucleotide or amino acid sequence is part of the invention and you provide it on paper.

p. Abstract. This is a brief (150 words or less) summary of the entire technical content of the application.

Note that the Specification includes the written Description of the invention, the Claims, and the Abstract. This is according to a patent statute (35 USC 112) and usage in the PTO. However many practitioners and previous editions of this book referred to the Specification as the written Description without including the Claims. To be consistent with the statute and PTO usage, the statutory definition of Specification—that is, the written Description, Claims, and Abstract—is used.

8. A completed Patent Application Declaration (PAD) form, Form AIA/08. (Use the simpler AIA/01 if you include an Application Data Sheet—see Item 10). The PAD is a statement under penalty of perjury that you're the true inventor and that you acknowledge a duty to keep the PTO informed of all material information and prior art related to your invention.

9. An Information Disclosure Statement, List of Prior Art Cited by Applicant, Forms SB08a and 08b, and copies of such prior art, other than U.S. patent references. Technically, these aren't part of the patent application, but because they're supposed to be sent to the PTO with or soon after the application, they are included here. These inform the PTO of relevant prior art or any circumstances known to you that may potentially affect the novelty or obviousness of your invention.

10. An Application Data Sheet (ADS), Form AIA/14, to provide the bibliographic data about the application (inventors' names, addresses, etc.). This document is mandatory if filing by EFS-Web but it is recommended that you file one if you are filing by mail to reduce data-entry errors. You can use a simpler declaration, AIA/01, if you include an ADS.

Note that a printed patent contains additional data, such as references cited, field of search, and so on. You should not include this additional data in your patent application. The PTO will add this data when they print the patent.

A Provisional Patent Application (PPA) must include some, but not all, of the parts just listed for a regular patent application. The parts that must be included for a PPA are:

- items 1–4, and 6 (postcard, payment, cover sheet (Form SB/16), fee transmittal, and drawings), and
- items 7a (title), 7g (drawing figures), 7i (description —main embodiment), 7j (operation—main embodiment), and 7k and 7l (description and operation—alternative embodiments).

Note that the PPA uses a different cover sheet instead of a transmittal letter, and has a different fee.

The PTO's Rule 77 (37 CFR 1.77) states that the elements of a patent application should be arranged in the above order with the above headings in capital letters. Use this format for smoothest sailing of your application through the PTO. However, because the headings are rather broad and don't break your application into enough easily digestible parts, add the additional headings in the above list, namely the Advantages, Reference Numerals, and Description and Operation of the various embodiments. Add any further headings you think would be useful, especially if your application is long or technically complex.

C. What Happens When Your Application Is Received by the PTO

Once the PTO receives your application, it will go to an application processing branch, whose clerical personnel will deposit your check or process your credit card payment. They'll scan all of your papers sent by mail or assemble all of your "papers" filed online, assign a filing date and serial number to your application, put this information onto your postcard if you filed by mail, and return it. If you filed online, the PTO's server (computer) will provide you with an instant equivalent of the postcard receipt. Then, regardless of how you filed, if everything is not complete—for example, you didn't sign the application or pay the proper fee—they'll send you an objections sheet (called a Notice to File Missing Parts), indicating what you must do to complete the

application. Once your application is complete they'll send you an official filing receipt and forward your file to the drafting department, where your drawings will be reviewed for formal requirements. A drawing objection slip will be put in your file if your drawings have any formal errors, such as blurred lines. They may send you a notice stating that your application will not be examined until you file replacement drawings; if so, file corrected drawings in the time allotted. Once your drawings are approved, your file will be sent to an appropriate examining division.

Within a few months to a few years, your application will be reviewed by an examiner who will usually send you an "Office Action." The Office Action will do one or more of the following:

- allow your application, subject to a final fee payment (this is rare)
- object to one or more informalities of your application
- object to one or more aspects of your specification and/or drawings
- reject some or all of your claims because of imprecise language, or
- reject some or all of your claims because of lack of patentability over the prior art.

To overcome these objections and/or rejections, you'll have to submit an "Amendment" in which you:

- make changes, additions, or deletions in the drawings, specification, or claims, and/or
- convince the examiner that the Office Action was in error.

Your application will be published 18 months from your earliest claimed filing date, unless you filed an NPR at the time of filing. If you filed an NPR, the information in your patent application will become publicly available only if a patent eventually issues. If you file the NPR and later decide to foreign file, you must rescind your NPR (use Form SB/36) within 45 days from the day you file your foreign application.

If the examiner eventually decides to allow the application (either as originally presented or as amended), you'll be sent a Notice of Allowance which gives you three months to pay an issue fee, a publication fee if applicable, and fix any remaining drawing errors. Your specification and claims, along

Copyright and Patent Issues:
Using or Reproducing Prior Art in Connection With Your Patent Application

It is common for an applicant to reproduce non-patent literature (NPL) when submitting an Information Disclosure Statement (IDS) and occasionally to use text or drawings from a prior-art patent in the patent application. Occasionally there have been disputes as to whether a patent's text or drawings are protected by copyright, or alternatively whether copyrighted NPL can be reproduced to submit prior art with an IDS. With regard to using extracts from patents, it is the position of the PTO that, "Subject to limited exceptions reflected in 37 CFR 1.71(d) & (e) and 1.84(s), the text and drawings of a patent are typically not subject to copyright restrictions." (See: www.uspto.gov/news/media/ccpubguide. jsp.) With regard to copying and submitting NPL with an IDS, in January 2012, the PTO's General Counsel issued the PTO's position on fair use and NPLs and concluded, "We believe that it is fair use for an applicant to make copies of NPL and submit those copies to the PTO during examination in an IDS."

The issue regarding using extracts from patents is somewhat confusing because PTO regulations (37 CFR 1.84 (s)) permit copyright notices regarding authorship in patent text or drawings. Even if a patent does not contain a copyright notice, this does not guarantee that the author does not claim copyright in the text or drawings of the patent. The

PTO's website also states, "There are also instances where a portion of the text or drawings of a patent may be under copyright. You should consult an attorney regarding these potential trademark and copyright issues." In addition, in a 2003 case, *Rozenblat v. Sandia Corp.*, 69 USPQ2d 1474 (7th Cir. 2003), the Seventh Circuit acknowledged the copyrightability of an inventor's patent drawings (although ruling against the inventor as to the issue of infringement). Finally, Copyright Office regulations (37 CFR 202.10(a)) do not prohibit registration of patent drawings. As a general rule, the use of technical language or drawings from a prior-art patent for use in a patent application is a fair use and is not a copyright infringement unless the patent includes a copyright notice (that is, "© [or Copyright] J. Smith 2012"). However, keep in mind the problem with fair use is that there are no distinct boundaries to define it and ultimately, the issue is up to a court. In 2012, a publisher of technical and scientific journals sued a Minnesota law firm for copyright infringement claiming that the law firm made copies of articles from technical journals without permission and submitted them to the PTO. The court found that such copying was permissible under the "fair use" doctrine of copyright law.

---

with certain other information (your name, address, and a list of all prior art cited by the examiner), will then be sent to the U.S. Government Printing Office. There they'll be printed verbatim as your patent. From filing to issuance, the process usually takes somewhere between six months to three years, but sometimes longer.

TIP

Model of Invention. You never have to furnish or demonstrate a working model of your invention. However, in rare cases, if the examiner questions the operability of your invention, such as if you claim a perpetual motion or energy machine, one way for you to prove operability is by demonstrating a working model. Working models are also useful to enable the examiner to understand and appreciate the commercial or intrinsic value of your invention.

D. Do Preliminary Work Before Preparing Your Patent Application

If adequate preparations are made beforehand, the actual writing of the application will go far more smoothly and will rarely take more than several partial days. Here are the basic preparatory steps.

1. Review the Prior Art

Assemble all your prior-art references. Read each of these references carefully, noting the terms used for the parts or steps that are similar to those of your invention. Write down the terms of the more unusual parts and, if necessary, look them up in your prior-art patents, textbooks, magazine articles (see Appendix 3, Glossary of Useful Technical Terms), or a visual. In this way you'll be familiar with the term for every art and its precise meaning. Also, note the way the drawings in these prior-art references are arranged and laid out. Pay particular attention to what parts are done in detail and what parts need be shown only very roughly or generally because they are well known or are not essential to the invention.

As a general rule, if you see any prior-art patent whose specification contains words, descriptions, and/or drawing figures that you can use in your application you can copy what you need. But beware that some patent owners have begun to assert copyright claims in their drawings and text, and in nonpatent prior art materials. These assertions are most often based on copying of prior art publications, not on the copying of patents (see below). Generally, unless a patent states that it is covered by copyright, the PTO does not consider that patents are covered by copyright, and you can copy the ideas in prior art materials if you express those ideas in your own words, instead of simply copying the text and figures.

2. Review Your Disclosure

Review the description (with sketches) of your invention that you prepared in Chapter 3. Be sure you have all of the details of your invention drawn or sketched in understandable form and that the description of your invention is complete. If you haven't done this yet, do it now, referring to Chapter 3 when necessary. With that done, you should use it to make a first draft of your claims.

3. Ramifications

Write down all of the known ramifications (potentially different uses, materials, sizes, and methods of operation) and embodiments (other forms which the invention can take). That is, record all other materials that will work for each part of your invention, other possible uses your invention can be put to, and other possible modifications of your invention. Think of ways in which its size or shape can be altered, parts (or steps in its manufacture) that can be eliminated, and so on. If your invention is a process or method, other ramifications and embodiments can be different

materials that your inventive process modifies, variations of your process (e.g. optional steps; steps in a different order), and different environments in which the process can be used.

The more ramifications and embodiments you can think of, the broader your patent claims will be interpreted, and the more you'll be able to block others from obtaining patents either on devices similar to your invention or on improvements to it. Also, you'll have something to fall back on if your main or basic embodiment is "knocked out" by prior art that your search didn't uncover or that surfaced after your search.

For instance, suppose your invention is a delaying device that closes the lid of a potpourri box automatically a few moments after the lid is opened. Another embodiment that could make advantageous use of the delaying device might be in a "roly-poly man" toy to make the man stand up again automatically a few moments after he's tipped over. If you have a process invention, alternative embodiments might be the use of the process for different end purposes.

TIP

Several Related Inventions. If you have two or more related inventions, such as a car radio mount and a housing for the same radio, you may show, describe, and claim both in the same application. The examiner may allow both inventions at once and you'll save fees and effort. However, you're allowed only one invention per filing fee, so the examiner may require you to restrict your application to one invention. If so, you can easily file a divisional application on the other inventions before the original application issues and still get the benefit of your original application's filing date. However, each divisional application will require its own filing, issue, and maintenance fees (a substantial expense). Also, your original application and any divisionals you file will expire 20 years from the filing date of your original application. The advantage of filing a divisional later is that you postpone the second filing fee a year or two, and you'll avoid paying it altogether if you find the invention hasn't panned out and you decide to drop it. The advantage of filing divisionals sooner is that your patent will have more remaining term when it issues. (In any case, don't include several inventions on one application if they're from different inventors or are not related.)

4. Sources of Supply

Suppose your invention contemplates the use of an exotic or uncommon material or component, or involves unusual manufacturing steps. In this case you must obtain the names and addresses of potential suppliers and/or identify textbooks or other references outlining how one should obtain or make such unusual elements or procedures. Describe these unusual dimensions, materials, or components in detail.

For example, with an electrical circuit, you generally don't have to include the technical values or identifications of components. However, if the operation of the circuit is at all unusual, or if any component values are critical, or if it contains a possibly novel feature, write down their names or identifications. With a chemical invention, write down the source or full identification of how to make any unusual or possibly novel components or reactions. With a mechanical invention, if any unusual or possibly novel parts, assembly steps, or materials are required, be sure you provide a full description and reference as to where to obtain or how to perform them.

EXAMPLE 1: Griselda invents a new photofinishing process that requires the use of a special trade-marked developer, Hypoxx, made by the Briskin Co. of Merion, Pennsylvania. If Griselda knows the composition of the developer, she must indicate this in the specification, but if not she can simply refer to the developer as Hypoxx developer from the Briskin Co. of Merion, Pennsylvania.

EXAMPLE 2: Bruce invents a new plumbing fixture that uses a special valve that also is positioned where two parts pivot with respect to each other. No such "pivoting valve" exists. In order to fulfill the PTO's disclosure requirement, Bruce must design the pivoting valve and describe and draw it in his patent application.

The reason why you will need the full details of any special aspects of your invention is simple. Section 112 of the patent laws (35 USC 112(a)) mandates that the specification provide a "full, clear, concise, and exact" description of the invention such that anyone skilled in the art can make and use it without too much effort. In addition, if any feature is possibly novel, you may have to claim it specifically, so you will want to provide adequate terminology in the specification to support your claim language.

5. Advantages/Disadvantages

List all disadvantages of the relevant prior art that your invention overcomes, referring to the checklist (Form 4-2) in Appendix 7 to make sure your listing is complete. Then list all the advantages of your invention over the prior art.

E. Flowchart

To get you oriented, Fig. 8A below, provides a self-explanatory flowchart of the entire application preparation process. Steps A to P, V, and W are covered in Chapter 8, Steps Q to U in Chapter 9, and Steps X to Z in Chapter 10.

F. Your Written Description Must Comply With the Full Disclosure Rules

Your goal is to disclose clearly everything you can think of about your invention. In case of doubt as to whether or not to include an item of information, put it in. The statutory provision that mandates the inclusion of all this information in your patent application is Section 112(a) of the patent laws, paragraph 1, which reads as follows:

"The specification shall contain a written description of the invention, and of the manner and process of making and using it, in such full, clear, concise, and exact terms as to enable any person skilled in the art to which it pertains, or with which it is most nearly connected, to make and use the same, and shall set forth the best mode contemplated by the inventor or joint inventor of carrying out the invention."

Review
A. Review your invention disclosure and all prior art thoroughly.

Rough Sketches
B. Make rough CAD or penciled sketches of invention in separate, numbered Figs. Show every aspect of invention and ramifications, mainly in perspective views.

Name Parts
C. Pencil a suitable name or names adjacent to every part in the drawings —for example, "lever," "pivot," etc.

Title*
D. Type a meaningful title that includes some novelty of the invention—for example, "Chair With Water-Filled Seat."

Cross-Reference to Related Applications*
E. Under this heading provide a cross-reference to any parent applications and a claim to priority of any PPA that you've filed.

Federally Sponsored Research*
F. Put in the statement required by your government contract or "nonapplicable."

Sequence Listing or Program*
G. Indicate if the application contains a sequence or program or type "nonapplicable."

Background*
H. Indicate field. One sentence is adequate—for example, "This application relates to bicycles, particularly to a derailleur."

Background*—Prior Art
I. Under this heading indicate the problems of the prior art, if any, and describe and knock all prior art.

Summary*
J. Prepare a brief summary of your claimed embodiments by paraphrasing your claims.

Drawings*—Figures
K. Type a "Drawing Figures" section. Use one brief sentence to describe each Fig. without details of the invention.

Drawings*—Reference Numerals
L. While doing this step, list your reference numbers on Form 8-1 and write them at appropriate places on the drawing Figs., using lead lines. Later insert this list after Drawing Figs.

Detailed Description*— First Embodiment
M. Type a "Description—Fig(s). 1-X" section. Describe overall structure of first embodiment, then structure and function of parts and their interconnections. Number each part (10, 12, etc.).

Operation—Fig(s) 1-X
N. Write an "Operation—Fig(s). 1-X" section. Describe in detail the operation, use, and advantages of the structure in these Figs.

Repeat Steps L, M, and N
O. Repeat Steps L, M, and N as necessary for all other sets of figures and embodiments.

Conclusion, Ramification, Scope
P. Type a "Conclusion, Ramifications, and Scope" section. Repeat advantages, describe less important ramifications, and add broadening paragraph.

Claims*—What Is Claimed Is
Q. Type first independent claim: type name of invention, then describe essential parts and their interconnections. Then broaden by eliminating as many parts as possible and generalizing remaining parts.

Dependent Claims
R. Type a set of dependent claims. Each must add feature(s) ["The widget of claim 1, further including"] or recite existing features more specifically ["The widget of claim 1 wherein"].

Second Main Claim
S. Type an additional independent claim, phrased differently than the first one.

Second Set of Dependent Claims
T. Type a second set of dependent claims, if possible. These can be similar to the first set of dependent claims.

More Sets of Claims
U. Repeat Steps S and T if possible. Don't exceed three independent or 20 total claims, unless justified.

Sequence Listing*
V. If applicable, type a sequence listing, starting on a separate sheet.

Abstract
W. Type abstract: Describe essence of structure and operation of invention and ramifications. Add reference numbers in parentheses.

Final Drawing (Chapter 10)
X. On drawings, remove part names (unless unusual), combine Figs. on same sheet, as possible, and neaten and final.

Final Application
Y. Insert claims after "Conclusion..." and before Abstract. Start claims and abstract on new pages. Use consecutive numbers. Final specification and claims.

Final Check & Formal Papers
Z. Check all reference numbers and part names and proofread carefully. Do formal paper. Mail application with check and receipt postcard.

*This word or words should appear as section heading in all capitals without boldface.

Fig. 8A—Steps in Preparing a Patent Application Chart

The statute imposes three requirements on a patent specification: (1) it must provide a written description of the invention, that is, it must tell what it is, (2) it must fully, clearly, concisely, and exactly teach one skilled in the art how to make and use it, and (3) it must set forth the best mode of carrying out the invention. The reason for these requirements is based upon the "exchange theory" of patents. The government grants you a patent (that is, a monopoly on your invention) for a term of 17 to 19 years in exchange for your disclosing to the public the full details of your invention (written description, how to make and use it, and the best mode of doing so). In this way the public will get the full benefit of your creativity after your patent expires. If you describe the parts of the invention and how it operates, you will satisfy the first two requirements (written description and how to make and use).

However, under current court decisions, it's dangerous to specifically identify a "best mode" since a court may use this to limit your invention to this mode or embodiment. Under the AIA, it is no longer possible to get a patent invalidated for failure to disclose the best mode. So most practitioners now recommend that, to prevent any court from limiting your invention to one mode, you disclose all of the embodiments "fully, clearly, concisely, and exactly" without stating which one is "best." For example, in the delay device referred to above, its use to close a box lid after a few minutes might be your first embodiment, and the delayed "roly-poly man" might be an alternative embodiment.

Another reason for disclosing as much as you can about your invention is, to block others from getting a subsequent improvement patent on your invention. Suppose you invent something and disclose only one embodiment of it, or only one way to do it. If you get a patent that shows only that one embodiment, someone may later see your patent and think of another embodiment or another way to do it that may be better than yours. This person will then be able to file a new patent application on this "improvement invention" and thereby, assuming a patent is issued, obtain a monopoly on the improvement. If this occurs, you won't be able to make, use, or sell the improvement without a license from the person who owns that patent. This is so even though you have a patent on the basic invention.

"New Matter" May Not Be Added After Filing

What happens if you don't put enough information in about your invention to enable "one skilled in the art" to make and use it without undue effort? Either your entire application can be rejected under Section 112 on the grounds of "incomplete disclosure," or it may be later invalidated if an infringer challenges it when you try to enforce it. Also, if your patent application is rejected because of incomplete disclosure, usually there is nothing you can do since you aren't allowed to add any "new matter" (additional technical information) to a pending application. (See Chapter 13.) In other words, "You must get it right the first time." While many inventors object to and rail against the "no-new-matter rule" ("Why can't I add improvements to my application?"), a moment's thought will convince you that the rule has a good purpose. Without the rule, an applicant could continuously add improvements and modifications, so that you would never know exactly what their invention covers. Imagine looking at a competitor's patent and thinking you are safe, then being sued out of the blue for infringing an improvement they just added!

As mentioned earlier, you must provide enough information in your patent application to enable anyone working in the field of your invention to be able to build and use it, without undue effort. That is, anyone in the field must be able to make a working version of your invention from the information contained in your patent application. To comply with this section, you ordinarily don't have to put in dimensions, materials, and values of components, since the skilled artisan is expected to have a working knowledge of these items. However, as described above, dimensions, materials, or components that are critical to the performance of your invention, or that are at all unusual, must be included. If in doubt, include this specific information.

A common error in preparing the specification of a patent application is a failure to include enough detail about the invention, or enough ramifications. Thus, if you "sweat the details" like a good professional does, you'll seldom go wrong.

Common Misconception: A patent specification should not include details of the invention since this will limit the invention to such details.

Fact: The scope of the invention is determined by the claims; so including details in the specification will not limit its scope.

 NOTE

Software Note. If your invention includes a microprocessor and an application program for it, either in software or in firmware, you should either include a source or object code listing of the program with your patent application, or a detailed flowchart. The flowchart should be detailed enough so that a programmer having no more than ordinary skill would be able to use your chart to write the program and debug it without undue effort or significant creativity—even if the task would take several months. Applicants who file a paper application can now file program listings on a CD-ROM (in duplicate for program listings, see Rule 52(e)). When a program has 300 lines or fewer (72 characters per line), you can submit it on drawing sheets or in the specification. (If it has more than 60 lines, put it at the end of the specification.) When it has more than 300 lines, it must be on CD-ROM if you file a paper application. If you file via EFS-Web, you can file the program listing in a separate file.

 NOTE

Biotechnology Note. If your invention requires a biological material that is not widely available, you must make a deposit of your biological material in an approved depository. The Rules define "biological material" as including "material that is capable of self-replication either directly or indirectly. Representative examples include bacteria, fungi including yeast, algae, protozoa, eukaryotic cells, cell lines, hybridomas, plasmids, viruses, plant tissue cells, lichens and seeds." (See 37 CFR 1.801–1.809, and MPEP (*Manual of Patent Examining Procedure*), 608.01(p)(c), and Chapter 2400.) A list of acceptable depositories is included in Section 2405 of the MPEP.

 NOTE

Nucleotide and/or Amino Acid Sequence Note. If your application contains disclosures of nucleotide and/or amino acid sequences, it must contain, as a separate part of the disclosure, a paper copy disclosing the nucleotide and/or amino acid sequences and associated information using the symbols and format in accordance with the requirements of Sections 1.822 and 1.823. (37 CFR 1.821(c).) A copy of the sequence Listing "must also be submitted in computer readable form in accordance with the requirements of Section 1.824 (37 CFR 1.821(e))," and "a statement that the content of the paper and computer readable copies are the same must be submitted with the computer readable form,"—specifically a statement that "the information recorded in computer readable form is identical to the written sequence listing." (37 CFR 1.821(f)). (See MPEP 2420 et seq. for the rules and availability of a program called "PatentIn" (MPEP 2430) for submitting the sequence in electronic form.)

 NOTE

Formula Note. You can enter formulas in the text the same way you would do if you were writing a college paper or textbook. However, it's best to avoid formulas, Greek letters, and subscripts, if at all possible: The printer may get them wrong, and if your patent ever gets into court, they'll turn off or intimidate a lay judge.

 NOTE

Trademarked Chemical Note. If your invention uses a trademarked chemical—such as "Ajax developer"—and you don't know its composition, see if any other similar chemicals will work. If so, you can just refer to the chemical by its generic name, with a reference to a suitable manufacturer—for example, "developer, preferably Ajax brand, sold by Ajax Chemical Company, Inverness Park, California." If the trademarked chemical is critical, try your best to find its generic constituents—for example, by contacting the company or doing research. One clever inventor found the composition by calling a Poison Control Center hotline. If you can't find the constituents, you'll have to refer to the chemical by its trademark and manufacturer, but this can limit your invention.

G. Software, Computer-Related Inventions, and Business Methods

Developments in the U.S. law of subject matter eligibility have made it more difficult to procure patents on software-implemented inventions. You should understand the standards used by the PTO in examining claims for such inventions, and prepare your claims, text, and figures accordingly.

The main consideration applicable to these inventions is in meeting the full disclosure requirement, including disclosure sufficient to support claims that will pass muster under Section 101 of the U.S. patent law. (35 USC 101.)

A patent application must contain a sufficiently detailed description of the invention so that one having ordinary skill in the art to which it pertains, or to which it is most nearly connected, will be able to make and use the invention without undue effort. In practice, the PTO and courts strictly enforce this requirement when software, computer-related inventions, or business method inventions are involved, since the newness of the field makes most people less comfortable with it. So if you're preparing a patent application on a software or computer-related invention, be absolutely sure that no one will ever be able to challenge it for "incomplete disclosure." That is, make absolutely sure it contains a "full, clear, concise, and exact" description of the invention and how to make and use it.

How should you fulfill this requirement in practice with software inventions? Virtually every software invention uses a computer program of some sort, whether it's in a PROM (programmed read-only memory) or a separate program on a disk that is used with a general-purpose computer. To fulfill the complete disclosure requirement, it is essential that you disclose either a listing of the program or a detailed flowchart of the operations and steps involved with the invention that a programmer can use to create a working version.

All Process Inventions Must Now Be Hardware Based

Due to a 2010 decision of the Supreme Court, *Bilski v. Kappos*, all process claims must now recite a process that either (1) is tied in a substantial way to a particular machine or apparatus, or (2) transforms an article into a different state or thing, or (3) does not cover an "abstract" process. The former *State Street* case standard that required the claim to recite a "useful, concrete, and tangible result" is no longer applicable. Most patent attorneys and inventors disagree strongly with the *Bilski* and *Alice* decisions, but have to live with them (unless the Supreme Court reverses itself or Congress changes the law). In order to have your claims be hardware-based to better withstand challenges under *Bilski* and *Alice*, you should describe the hardware (machine or apparatus), and the relationship between the process and that hardware, in the specification. For example, if you have a financing method that involves monetary manipulations, or an Internet invention that involves transactions, you will have to describe the manipulations or transactions as hardware based—that is, by including a computer to tally and monitor the monetary amounts and transactions in its CPU and memory and possibly the display, and discussing and claiming the invention basically in terms of the computer.

The Supreme Court left the door open for additional ways to claim processes, to be determined in future cases. Unless you want your application to be a test case, follow the rules of *Bilski* and *Alice* (until and if the rules are broadened).

If you've already written the program, the easiest way to provide the necessary disclosure is to supply the listing as part of the patent application. (See "Computer Programs Note" in Subsection I2k below, for how to do this.) If you file electronically, the listing must be submitted in ASCII format per PTO Rule 52(e) (37 CFR 1.52(e)). Therefore, unless you can somehow supply the object code in ASCII, you will have to submit the source code.

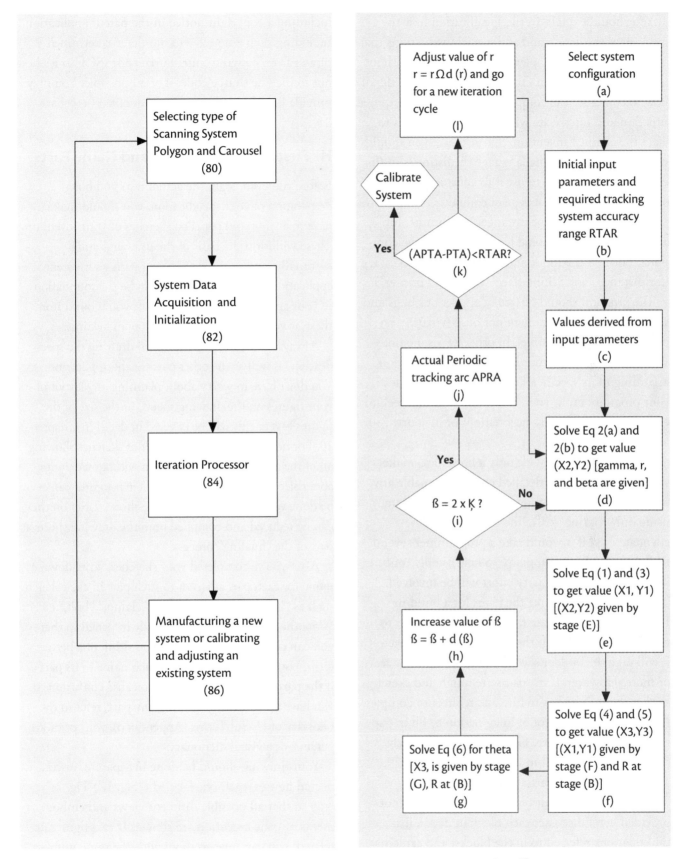

General   Specific

Fig. 8B—Software Flowcharts

You should explain in the specification how to implement the listing and any special instructions that may be necessary to implement the invention without undue experimentation. The explanation should detail how to configure the computer to perform the required function and interrelate with any other elements to yield the claimed invention. For instance, you should state what programming language the listing is in (for example, "C++"), how to use it to control the computer or microprocessor, what type of computer or microprocessor to use it with (for instance, "a Pentium chip"), and what hardware should be connected to the computer, both on the input and output sides as necessary (for instance, "a USB interface" and "a 3D printer").

The program should be free of any serious bugs and should not have too many minor bugs (virtually no program is 100% bug free). In other words, no one should be able to say your listing wouldn't function according to its specifications. (The PTO won't test your program, but if you get a patent and later seek to enforce it during license negotiations or in court, your adversary will!)

If you choose to provide only a flowchart, make sure it's complete and detailed enough to enable any reasonably skilled programmer to write a program, using only routine skills. The flowchart will be adequate even if it would take a programmer several months to write the program, so long as only routine skill and not extraordinary effort will be involved. Think of a flowchart like the plans for a building: If the plans are adequate for an ordinary builder to construct the building, they will be adequate, even if it will take the builder several months, or even a year or more. However, if the plans are rough and sketchy, so that the builder has to hire an architect to complete them, or has to use a lot of imagination to fill in gaps, then they're inadequate. Fig. 8B shows adequately detailed flowcharts (from U.S. Pat. No. 5,170,279, 1992 Dec 8) in two parts: general and specific. The associated explanation in the specification (not provided here) discusses each block in detail, lists the equations referred to in the blocks, and explains exactly how to implement the flowchart.

You may be able to deter readers of your patent from copying and using your program listing by including a copyright notice in the patent application. Including such a notice will not deter determined pirates from copying your source code (SC), so it's best not to include source code, if at all possible. You may provide just the object code or a detailed flowchart.

H. First Prepare Sketches and Name Parts

Before you even begin the actual nuts and bolts preparation of your specification, you should make (or have made for you) penciled sketches of your invention. These will form the basis of the drawings you'll eventually send to the PTO along with your patent application. Your sketches will also be the foundation of your application. In other words, you'll build from these as you write your specification and claims.

Always do your sketches prior to drafting the specification, as well as the other parts of the application. You don't have to worry about planning any layout of your figures on the drawing sheets, or the size of the figures—yet. This will be covered in detail in Chapter 10. For now, merely complete a set of sketches showing all of the aspects of your invention without worrying about size or arrangement; these sketch-figures can even be done very large and on separate sheets. Later on they can be reduced and compiled onto the drawing sheets as part of the "finaling" process.

After you've completed your sketches, write down a name for each part adjacent to such part in each sketch, such as "handlebar," "handgrip," "clamp," "bolt," etc. Write the names of the parts lightly in pencil so that you can change them readily if you think of a better term. Use lead lines to connect each name to its part if the parts are crowded enough to cause confusion. If you have any difficulty naming any part, refer to the Glossary of Useful Terms (Appendix 3), your prior-art patents, or a visual dictionary.

Your drawing should be done in separate, unconnected figures, each one labeled ("Fig. 1," "Fig. 2," etc.) so that all possible different views and embodiments of your invention are shown. If two figures are related, you can refer to them with the same number but with different suffixes or primes, for example, "Fig. 1A," "Fig. 1B." Use as many views as necessary. Look at a relevant prior-art patent to get an idea as to how it's done. The views should generally be perspective or isometric views, rather than front, side, and top, engineering-type views. If you have trouble illustrating a perspective view, take a photo of a model of your invention from the desired angle and draw the photo —perhaps by enlarging and tracing it. Alternatively you can use a "see and draw" copying device of the type employing a half-silvered mirror in a viewing head on a pedestal; these are available in art supply stores and through gadget mail-order houses. Hidden lines should be shown in broken lines, as shown in Fig. 8C. For complicated machines, exploded views are desirable as shown in Fig. 8D. The drawings must be filed as a separate document from your patent application (whether filing on paper or online). Never include your drawing sheets as part or pages of the written description.

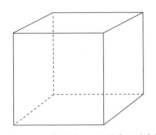

Fig. 8C—Isometric View With Hidden Lines

You can use any reasonable symbols for mechanical, electronic/electrical, and chemical parts; the PTO has no requirements in this area, except that the symbols not be outrageous. Use conventional symbols, such as those approved by the ANSI (American National Standards Institute), those used in conventional texts, or those used in your prior-art patents. In lieu of graphical symbols, labeled boxes are also acceptable, so long as the part represented by the box is standard or conventional.

If you have an electronic system, a block diagram with each block labeled (for example, "Schmitt Trigger," "flip-flop," "inverter") is fine. If any block represents a nonconventional circuit, however, be sure that you provide a schematic diagram and explain clearly what's in the block or provide a reference to a suitable publication. If any block represents a programmed microprocessor or computer, remember that you must provide a listing of the program or a software flowchart to provide a complete disclosure.

If possible, one figure of your drawing should be comprehensive enough to show the basic idea of the invention and to be suitable for inclusion in the *Official Gazette* (OG). If the PTO grants your patent, they will publish one figure, the main claim, and the bibliographic details of your patent in the OG. See Chapter 6 for more on the OG. The other figures can be fragmentary or partial views; you don't have to show the same details more than once.

Different colors and different shades of gray can be shown with different types of shading lines, but provide a suitable decoding legend in a separate figure. If your invention is related to a prior-art device, you may want to illustrate the prior-art device in the first figure of drawings so that you can explain it and its drawbacks. This Fig. must be labeled "Prior Art."

1. Machine Sketches

If your invention is a machine or an article, your sketches should contain enough views to show every novel feature of the invention in detail. However, you don't have to show every feature that's old and known in the prior art. For example, if you've invented a new type of pedal arrangement for a bicycle, one view can show your pedal arrangement in gross view without detail. Other views can show your pedal arrangement in detail, but you don't have to include any views showing the bicycle itself in detail, since it isn't part of your invention and bicycles are well known. If one figure of your drawing shows a sectional or side view of another figure, it is customary to provide cross-section lines in the latter figure; these lines should bear the number of the former figure. Look at prior-art patents to see how this is done and see the example in Fig. 8E. If your machine is complicated, you should show an exploded view of it, as in Fig. 8D. If you have a moderately healthy budget and complex machine figures, consider hiring a patent figure drafting professional. There is substantial competition in this area, so high-quality figures like Fig. 8E may be obtained for a few tens of dollars each.

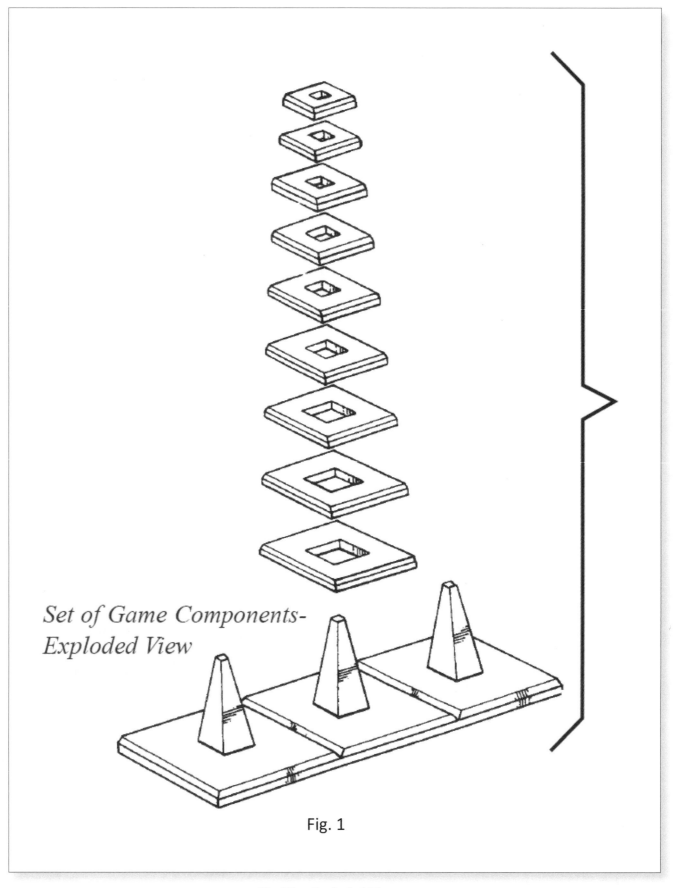

Set of Game Components-
Exploded View

Fig. 1

Fig. 8D—Exploded View

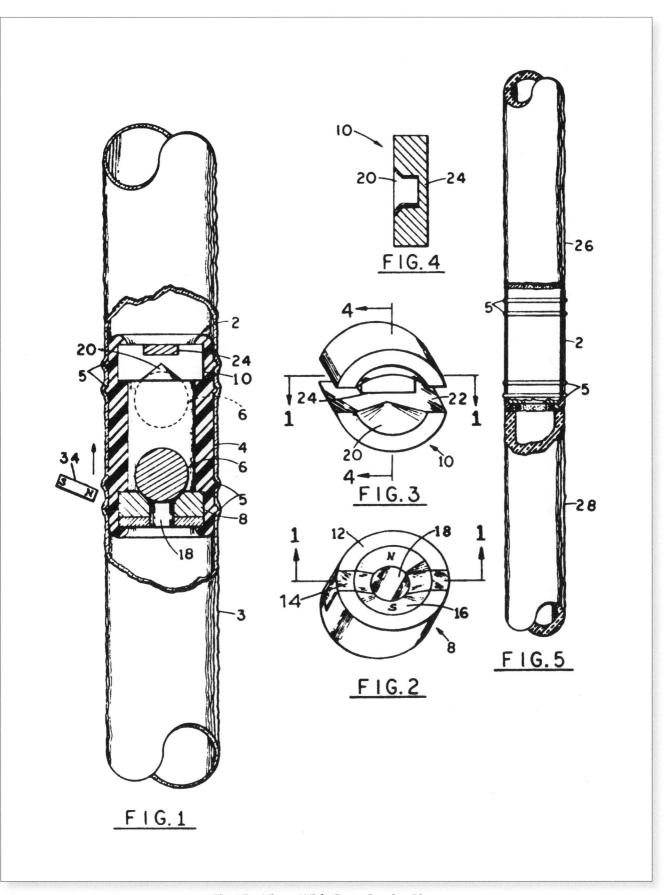

Fig. 8E—Views With Cross-Section Lines

2. Chemical Composition Sketches

If your invention is a chemical composition, the PTO won't generally require drawings unless your invention is a material that has a nonhomogeneous composition (internally differentiated through layering, for example), in which case you should show it in cross-section detail. Also, if a step-by-step process is involved, the PTO will require a flowchart, even though the process is fully described in your specification (see the next section). The reason: so examiners, judges, and future searchers will be able to understand your patent more rapidly. Benzene rings and other molecular diagrams can usually be presented in the specification.

3. Computer, Chemical, or Mechanical Process Sketches

If your invention includes a process of the electronic-computer, chemical, or mechanical type, you should provide a flowchart (or a program listing for software inventions—see above). This flowchart must show the separate steps involved, each described succinctly in a different block. If your blocks are connected, they should all be labeled as one figure; if disconnected, they should be labeled as separate figures. As before, each figure should be labeled—for example, Fig. 1, Fig. 1A, Fig. 1B, Fig. 2, Fig. 3, etc.

If you desire, you can try providing a short title after each figure, giving a general description of the part of your invention shown in the figure, just as you would do if you were writing a scientific article for an engineering magazine or textbook. However, PTO drafting personnel often object to such titles for some unknown reason. If this occurs, you'll have to delete the titles (white out the titles on the originals of your drawing or delete the titles on your computer drawings) and send in replacement figures.

If you believe it will help in understanding your invention, you may (and should) include a drawing of the prior art as one figure of your drawings. This figure must be labeled "prior art" to indicate that it isn't part of your invention.

I. Drafting the Specification

Once you've reduced your invention to sketches, it's time to begin drafting the detailed description portion of your patent application. Review the detailed descriptions of your prior-art patents—or the sample detailed description at the end of this chapter—to find out how they're written. Your detailed description should be written as one continuous document with separate sections, each with a heading, the way this book is written.

1. Drafting Tips

Here are some general rules to keep in mind when drafting your detailed description.

Consider Your Audiences

A patent specification is meant for many different audiences, beginning with you. When you have finished your specification, you should be comfortable that it communicates all of the advantages of your invention. You are also writing for an examiner at the PTO, whose job it is to make sure that your specification complies with the complete disclosure laws. Depending on how you plan to monetize your patent, you may be writing for potential investors or manufacturers, who need to know how to evaluate your invention for its profit potential. And if you ever need to enforce your offensive rights against an infringer, you are writing for the judge and the jury who will have to read your specification to understand how your invention works, so you can convince them why you should win your case.

Avoid Legalese

You'll be pleased to learn that legalese is not favored by the PTO because it makes your writing stilted, less clear, and harder to understand. The only legal requirements for a patent detailed description is that it be a full, clear, concise, and complete description of how to make and use the invention. (The claims, however, should be written with extreme clarity and precision, and to do this you may have to use a few "saids" and "wherebys," as explained in Chapter 9.)

Use Short and Simple Sentences

It's best to write your description in short, simple sentences, with short paragraphs. Each paragraph should generally be shorter than 200–250 words, or one page (double-spaced), and should relate to one part or subpart of your invention. The Cybernetics Institute has found that short sentences communicate best. Your main goal is to include all points of substance of your invention and make your description clear and understandable. There's an especially good legal reason for this: If a disclosure isn't clear, a court will interpret it narrowly. If you get stuck and don't know how to phrase a description of a part or an operation, here's a helpful trick: Simply pretend you're describing your invention aloud to a close friend. Remember what you said (or make an audio recording) and write it down. Then go back and polish the language. If you attack the job in small chunks or in piecemeal fashion, it usually will go much easier.

Write Clearly

Write clearly, not only so you can be understood, but also so that you will not be misunderstood.

Avoid Grammar and Spelling Errors

Although the PTO's examiners aren't very concerned with grammar and spelling errors, you should avoid them in your application and all of your correspondence. You will get more respect from your examiner, potential licensees, or a judge. Proofread or use a spelling and grammar checker. Here are some examples of common grammar errors in redacting patent applications:

Wrong: "lever 202's left end."

Right: "the left end of lever 202."

Wrong: "connected to switch 502 wires."

Right: "connected to the wires 503 leading to switch 502."

Most writing tends to be less formal and even sloppy now because many people do a lot of informal texting and emailing. However a patent application (and any other legal document), should be formal, perfect, and crystal-clear, because any flaw, error, solecism, ambiguity, vagueness, or unintelligibility will be attacked or looked upon with disdain by anyone who reads the application, such as an examiner, a potential licensee, a judge, or an adversary.

Use Copious Headings

If you use copious subheadings (such as "Fig. 1— Description of Handlebar Attachment"; "Fig. 2—Front Fork Detail"; "Fig. 10—Operation of Derailleur"; etc.) throughout your specification, most people will find it far easier to read. This allows them to take in the information in separate, small, inviting chunks that are easy to digest one at a time. Refer to the specification at the end of this chapter (Fig. 8G) to see examples of headings in an application.

If you have trouble getting started, don't worry; many writers have blocks from time to time, and lots of inventors initially (and erroneously) lament, "I could never write my own patent application." The words of Lao-Tse will encourage you:

"A journey of a thousand miles begins with a single step."

If you feel that you can't write adequately, give it your best shot and then have someone you trust and who will keep your draft confidential—a writer, college English major, high school English teacher, etc.—to edit your draft.

CAUTION

Avoid Negative, Restrictive, or Wishy-Washy Statements That Could Be Used Against You Later. When you write, be especially careful not to include anything that an adversary could later use against you to invalidate or narrow your patent. For example, never say that any novel part of your invention is similar to something that is already known, that the novelty of your invention is solely in a certain part, that something "might" work, that something is always better or necessary or critical, or that something is not done or constructed in a certain way. If your patent is ever involved in litigation, any adversary will use such statements against you in court.

Avoid "Patent Profanity"

Here are some words and phrases that patent attorneys avoid using, or use with caution, to avoid having a judge limit your invention; one wag has called these words "patent profanity." They include: *absolutely, always, beneficial, crucial, critical, desirable, eliminate, essential, every, hypothetical, important, invention, key, maximize, minimize, must, necessarily, necessary, never, obviously, only, peculiar, preferred, preferred embodiment, present invention, require(s)(d), special, superior, surprisingly, the invention,* and *very important.*

Common Misconception: If you put any specific feature of your invention, such as a preferred size, a preferred material, a preferred shape, etc., in your specification, the scope of your invention will be limited to this feature, so any device that lacks this specific feature will not infringe.

Fact: The scope of an invention is determined almost entirely by the claims and not by specifics that are included in the specification. If you do recite any specific feature in a claim, that claim will be limited to this specific feature, but if the specific feature is stated in the specification, it will help provide an adequate disclosure. The patent laws, rules, court decisions, and practitioners actually require and recommend that the specification include as many specifics of the invention as possible, especially in critical areas, so no one will ever be able to validly attack the adequacy of the specification for failure to teach how to make and use the invention. However when stating the specifics of an invention in the specification, it's important to (1) state that these are what you presently contemplate for this embodiment but that other values, dimensions, etc., can be used, and (2) include as many variations as you can envision. For example, "In some embodiments, the lever has a rectangular cross section 2 mm by 4 mm and is 4 cm long and made of austenitic steel. However it can have different cross sections, such as oval, triangular, circular, etc., and different sizes and materials, such as high-carbon steel, titanium, polycarbonate, etc." Never refer to "the invention"—only to this embodiment. Also never state that any embodiment is preferred; instead just list the embodiments as the first, second, third, etc.

Now let's get to the nitty-gritty of preparing the specification portion of a patent application.

Make an Outline Before Starting

Prior to starting, in order to guide your path, you will find it helpful first to make an outline, which should be the same as the headings set out below. However, you may want to make the Description and Operation headings more specific and/or break them into several more specific headings each, in accordance with your figures and specific situation. A skeleton patent application is provided in Fig. 8F, which you should copy into a word processor to get you started.

2. The Parts of the Specification

There are also some commonsense rules governing the best presentation of each of the separate parts of your specification. The sections with a "PPA" superscript, below, are needed to file a Provisional Patent Application.

a. Title PPA

Have your title reflect the essence of your invention without being too long (about 500 characters maximum) or so specific that it's narrower than your invention's full scope, including all of its embodiments. For example, if your invention is a foot pedal but the mechanism can be used as a handhold, don't call it "Foot Pedal"; call it "Hand or Foot Pedal" or the like. On the other hand, don't pick a title so broad—such as "Electrical Apparatus"—as to be essentially meaningless. A look at some recently issued patents in your field should give you a good idea of how specific to make your title.

b. Cross-Reference to Related Applications

In this section refer to any PPA that you've filed, to any parent applications (see Chapter 14), or to any technically related application and incorporate it by reference just in case you need to rely on anything in it. For example, if you've filed a PPA, type, "This application claims the benefit of provisional patent application Ser. Nr. xx/xxx,xxx, filed 20xx xxx xx by the present inventor(s), which is incorporated by reference in its entirety." If the application is a continuation-in-part of an earlier application, type, "This application is a CIP of Ser. Nr. xx/xxx,xxx, filed 20xx xxx xx by the present inventor(s), which is incorporated by reference in its entirety." If you want to refer to a technically related case, type, for example, "This application uses the frammis vane disclosed in my patent x,xxx,xxx, granted xxxx xxx xx, which is incorporated by reference in its entirety."

You can omit this part if you don't have any related applications. Also, incorporation by reference may not be accepted by foreign patent offices, so if something is important to your application—that is, it is necessary to describe your invention so that a person of ordinary skill in the art could make and use it—or if it is necessary to support your claims, be sure to put it into the application and don't incorporate it by reference.

c. Federally Sponsored Research

If your invention was made under a government contract, include the required contract clause here. You can omit this part if you don't have any Federally Sponsored Research.

d. Sequence Listing or Program

If you've included a CD-ROM (if filing on paper) or an ASCII attachment (if filing via EFS-Web) to provide a program listing, refer to it here. If your invention uses a biological sequence, refer to it here and state where it can be found. You can omit this part if you don't have any Sequence Listing or Program.

e. Technical Field

Here, describe in general terms the field of technology into which your invention fits. Describe the field at two levels—a broad, general level and a somewhat less general level, but do not drill down to a specific level of technology. Both levels should describe, in a broad sense, some preexisting area of technology. In other words, do not use this section to describe your invention—after all, your invention defines a new part of the technology, so it doesn't fully fit into a narrow preexisting field. For example, if your invention is a new sprocket for a bicycle's gear system, your Technical Field might read: "The present invention relates to bicycles, and more specifically to drive systems for bicycles."

f. Background—Discussion of Prior Art

Here, discuss the problem that your invention definitely solves, the way the problem was approached previously (if it was approached at all), and then list all the disadvantages of the old ways of doing it.

 CAUTION

Do Not Describe Your Invention in the Background Section. If you do, it will be interpreted as a confession that your invention is already known in the prior art, and can be used by the PTO to reject your claims, or later used by an infringer to attack your patent. When it comes to writing your Background section, remember the line you've heard so many times when the police arrest someone on television—anything you say can and will be used against you in a court of law—and by the PTO.

Your application will be more interesting if you can write this section as a story describing the history of the field and its sorry state up to the present. For example, you can start as follows: "Originally bicycles were made with a fixed transmission ratio. This made pedaling up hills difficult. This problem has been partially solved by the implementation of derailleur mechanisms, but these had and still have significant problems." Then list the derailleurs that were used in the past and their disadvantages. Again, look at prior-art patents to get an idea of what was done. If you can, tell why prior-art people failed to solve the problem and why a solution is needed. But be sure that every prior-art approach you discuss was definitely known, because by listing approaches in the prior art section you are making a full admission that all of such approaches are old.

Beware of admitting that any problem in the prior art was recognized. If it wasn't recognized and you state otherwise you will deprive yourself of credit for recognizing the problem and enable the examiner or an adversary to cite more prior art against you. If you do want to list a problem that you found, give yourself credit for recognizing it—for example, "I have found that derailleurs often broke down because their linkages were too flimsy." Don't say what the prior art can't do because this can make your invention or the problem that you discovered look obvious.

Cite all prior-art U.S. patents, published patent applications, foreign patent publications, and non-patent literature in a four-part table, in the same format as on the PTO's Information Disclosure Statement (IDS) form, PTO/SB/08a. Then discuss (knock) these references later in narrative paragraphs. This makes it easier for the examiner to review your prior art and for you to fill out your IDS later. (See an example in the specification of the sample application, Fig. 8G below.)

While the PTO doesn't want needlessly derogatory remarks about the inventions of others, you should, as much as possible, try to "knock the prior art" here in order to make your invention look as good as possible. Keep your statements factual (for example, "The derailleur in patent 3,456,789 to Prewitt, 1982 May 3, had a limited number of discrete gear ratios") and not opinionated (don't say, "Prewitt's derailleur was an abject failure"). If applicable, tell why prior-art people didn't think of any solution before and why a solution is needed. Do not discuss any detailed structure or operation of any prior art in this section (unless you provide a suitable figure—see next paragraph), since detailed mechanical discussions without the benefit of drawings will be incomprehensible to most people. Occasionally, you may have such a completely unique invention that there's really no prior art directly germane to your invention. If so, just state the general problem or disadvantage your invention solves.

If you've provided a prior-art figure, you can discuss (and knock!) it here. Use reference numerals to refer to the individual parts of the prior-art device. Alternatively you may discuss (and knock) your prior-art figure in the "Description of Invention" section.

You must also file an Information Disclosure Statement listing all of the prior-art publications (including U.S. patents and published patent applications) you're aware of, together with copies of any non-U.S. patent publications.

If your invention doesn't solve a specific problem—for example, it's a new game or toy—you won't be able to state any problem that your invention solves. However, you still can discuss the closest prior games or toys and mention some faults or disadvantages of them.

Since this is a discussion of the prior art, you should not discuss your invention or any of its advantages here.

g. Advantages

Although it is optional, you may list the advantages of your invention in a narrative form. If you do so, make it the first paragraph in your Detailed Description section. Include this because it helps orient your readers to your subject matter, and helps sell the invention to the examiner or a judge who may rule on your patent. The advantages may also help distinguish your invention from a "judicial exception" that is not patentable.

For example, if your invention does any of the following, explain in narrative form the shortcoming of the prior art and the advantage of your invention: improves another technology or technical field; improves the functioning of the computer itself; or includes a feature or function that is more than what is well-understood, routine, and conventional in the field. However, it's important not to use language that a court may consider limiting; don't use the words "invention" or "objects," and use weasel words so you don't paint yourself into a corner. First, state that the advantages are for "one or more aspects." Second, list the advantages that are the reverse of the disadvantages listed in the prior-art section, then any additional advantages you know, followed by a catchall sentence. Here's a condensed example incorporating all of the foregoing: "Thus some embodiments provide a computer that is lighter or faster than prior-art computers. Some embodiments provide a computer that is less expensive or more attractive than prior-art computers. These and other benefits of one or more aspects will become apparent from a consideration of the ensuing description

[Title]

Cross-Reference to Related Applications (if applicable)

[0001] The present application claims priority from _____

Federally Sponsored Research (if applicable)

[0002] _____

Incorporate by Reference CD of Sequence Listing or Program Listing (if applicable)

[0003] _____

Technical Field

[0004] The present invention relates to _____, and more particularly to _____

Background Art

[0005] It is known in the prior art to _____

Summary of the Embodiments

[0006] A first embodiment includes _____

Brief Description of the Drawings

[0007] Fig. 1 schematically illustrates _____ ;

Detailed Description of Specific Embodiments

[0008] Embodiments provide _____

[0009] Program Code Listing (if applicable and if code more than 60 lines) _____

· page break ·

What is claimed is:

1. _____

· page break ·

Sequence Listing (if applicable) _____

· page break ·

Abstract

Fig. 8F—"Skeleton" Patent Application

and accompanying drawings." Be certain that each advantage that you list is fulfilled by at least one aspect of your invention.

h. Summary

The PTO's Rules 73 and 77 (37 CFR 1.73 and 1.77) state that the specification "should" contain a summary of the claimed invention, and Rule 72 requires an abstract of the entire specification. In practice, some patent attorneys omit the summary, since the abstract, as well as the claims, already provides one. Also if the summary focuses on one embodiment, the courts may limit your invention. However, including a summary is recommended.

Your summary should include a broadly stated overview of your invention, and should also contain text that paraphrases all of your claims. You may want draft a broad overview paragraph when you begin drafting your specification, but the rest of your summary after you have finalized your claims.

PTO Rule 73 states that the summary may include the object of the invention. However, you should never refer to any object of the invention, since some courts have used a statement of an object to limit the claims. Instead you can refer to advantages, but always state that they are for one or more aspects and not for "the invention." Also make sure your advantages are not too narrow.

i. Drawings PPA

Here, provide a series of separate paragraphs, each *briefly* describing a respective figure of your drawing—for example, "Fig. 1 is a perspective (or plan, side, exploded, or rear) view of a first embodiment"; or, "Fig. 2 is a view in detail of the portion indicated by the section lines 2—2 in Fig. 1." Do not include any reference numerals, specific parts, or any other details in this section—just a brief overall description of each figure.

j. Drawings—List of Reference Numerals

Although the PTO doesn't require or even recommend a separate list of the reference numerals and the names of their respective parts in an application, it is advisable to include such a list in a separately headed section at the end of Detailed Description, since it would disrupt the flow of the specification if you put it at the beginning. Why? There are three very important reasons for providing the list:

- to help you to keep your reference numerals straight—that is, to avoid using the same number for different parts
- to help you to keep your nomenclature straight—that is, to avoid using different terms for the same part, and
- to provide a very visible and easy-to-find place where examiners, searchers, and others who read your application or patent can go to instantly identify any numbered part on your drawings.

It may be helpful to compile this list in a separate word-processing window or on a separate sheet of lined paper, and then incorporate the list in the text. Also, to keep confusion at a minimum, you use reference numbers with at least three-digits, and that you begin your numbers with a the same digit as the figure number in which it first appears. For example, if you have Figs. 1 to 12 of drawings, begin your reference numbers in Fig. 1 at 100 (e.g., bicycle 100 having seat 101 and wheels 102 and 103, etc.), and in Fig 12 as at 1200 (e.g., basket 1200 and bell 1202, etc.).

Some inventors use three-digit reference numbers throughout. The first digit represents the figure number, so that the parts of Fig. 1 would be 110, 112, etc. The parts in Fig. 2 would be 210, 212, etc. If Fig. 2 has a part that is also in Fig. 1, the reader would instantly know that this part (that is, part 110) was first introduced in Fig. 1. Also this enables any reader of the specification to go directly to the drawing figure where this part is introduced.

Lastly, use even-numbered reference numerals when you write the application. In this way, if you later have to add another reference number, you can use an odd number and put it between two logically related even numbers. (See the list in the sample specification at the end of the chapter.)

k. Detailed Description PPA—First Embodiment—Figs. 1–xx

Here you should describe in great detail the static physical structure of the first embodiment of your invention (not how it operates or what its function is). If this embodiment is a process, describe the procedures or machinery involved in it. Begin by first stating what the figure under discussion shows generally—for example, "Fig. 1 shows a perspective view of one version of a widget." Then get specific by describing the main parts and how they're connected. (These main parts can form the basis for your claims, as discussed in Chapter 9.) Then get more specific: Describe each main part in detail and all of the sub- or component parts in detail. If a detail is worth describing, it is probably worth at least one paragraph of text.

Start with the base, frame, bottom, input, or some other logical starting place of the embodiment. Then work up, out, or forward in a logical manner, numbering and naming the parts in your drawing as you proceed. Use the part names that you previously wrote on your sketches.

To number the parts, write a number near each part and extend a lead line from the reference number to the part to which it refers. Don't circle your reference numerals, since a PTO rule prohibits this. The lead lines should not have arrowheads—for example, a bicycle grip might be designated "22———." You should not use a reference numeral to designate the embodiment of a whole figure; instead just say " … the widget of Fig. 1."

Although you may think that the patent examiner won't need to have parts that are clearly shown in the drawing separately described in detail, all patent attorneys provide such a description. This is part of a repetition technique that is used to familiarize the examiner with the invention and set the stage for the operational description and the claims. When you mention each part twice, once in the description and again in the operation discussion, the first mention will initially program your reader to relate to the part so that the reader will really understand it the second time around, when it counts. This is the same technique as is used in the lyrics of blues songs, where the first two lines are always restated to enhance communication. Another reason to describe and name each part and each detail is to form a basis for the claims: All terms used in the claims are supposed to be first used in the specification.

Another good technique is to use several different equivalent names for a part the first time you refer to it in order to provide one with which your reader will be familiar—for example, "connected to base 10 is a strut, pylon, or support 12." Then pick one name and use it consistently thereafter.

Before you begin a description of any figure, refer to it by its figure number—for example, "Fig. 1 shows an overall view of the can opener of the first embodiment." Then as you come to each part or element, give it a separate reference number—for example, "The can opener comprises two handle arms 110 and 112 (Fig. 1) that are pivotally attached at a hinge 114." It is essential always to keep your reader apprised of which figure you are discussing.

Also, always try as much as possible to discuss one figure at a time. However, where several figures show different views of an embodiment, you can refer to several figures at once—such as "Figs. 1 and 2 show plan and elevational (front) views of a scissors according to one embodiment. The scissors comprises first and second legs 112 and 114, the second leg being best shown in Fig. 2." However, again don't refer to too many figures at once, and always keep your reader advised as to which figure is under discussion.

Discuss every part shown in your drawings in detail and be sure to use consistent terminology and nomenclature for the parts in the drawing. For example, if gear 844 is shown in Fig. 8 and also in Fig. 11, label it with the same reference numeral "44" in both figures. However, if the gear is even slightly different in Fig. 11, it must have a different reference numeral, such as, "844a," "844π," or "844bis." Fill out the Drawing Reference Numerals Worksheet (Form 8-1) as you write, to keep your numerals and nomenclature consistent. If you use a word processor, refer to each part by a number only and then, consistent part names—such as, you can write "844 is connected to 836" and later change "844" to "widget 844" and "836" to "base 836" throughout your specification.

Lastly, be sure to detail all the interconnections or mountings between parts—for example, "Arm 114 is joined to base 112 by a flange 116."

💡 **TIP**

Recall the childhood song that details virtually every bone-to-bone connection in the body in logical order—for example, "The knee bone's connected to the thigh bone, the thigh bone's connected to the hip bone." In a similar manner, your description should also detail every part-to-part interconnection, even if you think the reader would find it obvious from your drawing.

💡 **TIP**

Don't Be Secretive. Suppose your invention uses some special or exotic parts, techniques, or relationships, but you don't want to describe these because such information is valuable and you want to keep it as a trade secret and not give it away to potential copiers and competitors. Unfortunately, you can't be secretive. You must include complete detailed descriptions of these, including dimensions, relationships, materials, and sources of supply, as applicable, in this section in order to comply with the "full disclosure" statute (35 USC 112). Putting in such specifics will not limit your invention in any way since the claims will determine its scope. However, failing to include these specifics can render your patent application fatally flawed if they are necessary for one skilled in the art to make and use the invention.

💡 **TIP**

Write the Prior Art Section With Care. Anything you say in the PA (Background) section can be used against you. If your invention is an improvement to a prior-art (PA) device, don't describe the PA device in detail in the PA section and then state, in the description of your invention, how your invention improves upon the PA device by describing how you would change the PA device. This will isolate your changes, making it easier for an examiner or future adversary to invalidate your patent by showing a reference with just the changes. Instead describe the PA device generally in your PA section and then, in the description of your invention, describe your whole device in detail and in a manner different from the description of the PA device. This will make it much more difficult for anyone to invalidate your invention.

Including details and dimensions at crucial places can also prove vital later if you have to rely on these in order to support and distinguish your claims over a close prior-art reference cited by the examiner. Thus, it's almost axiomatic in patent law that you should make your specification as long, specific, and detailed as possible, and your main (independent) claims as short, broad, and general as possible. If you're tempted to skip the details, remember that a few strokes on a keyboard now can save you from losing many thousands of dollars later. Be especially sure to expand your discussion in the areas where you feel that your invention is novel over the prior art.

Despite my admonitions to include full details, you'll be relieved to learn that common sense prevails: you don't need to supply full blueprints or a full list of dimensions, materials, etc. for your invention. The specification need only be detailed enough for a PHOSITA to make and use it, even if some experimentation and design work is required. The standard is that a skilled artisan should be given adequate guidance so that there is no need to exercise any inventive facilities to realize the invention. (See MPEP 2164.06 for more on this subject.)

💡 **TIP**

Selecting and Arranging the Right Words Is Key to Good Writing. The following is reprinted with thanks by permission of Leslie A. Gordon, Esq., and the Bar Association of San Francisco:

The key to good writing is "variety, rhythm, and balance," according to my graduate journalism text. In addition to selecting the right words, arranging them optimally can add emphasis and improve readability.

Put the subject, verb, and object close together. The subject is the "doer" of the sentence; the verb is the main action; the object (if any) is the recipient of the action.

1. MEDIOCRE: Lisa, encouraged by her science teacher, applied to MIT. (*Subject and verb are separated.*)
   BETTER: Encouraged by her science teacher, Lisa applied to MIT.
2. MEDIOCRE: My dog walker, because he was sick Monday, could not exercise my bulldog.
   BETTER: Because my dog walker was sick Monday, he could not exercise my bulldog. (*Subject and verb are together.*)

Put modifying words near what they modify. A modifier is a word or words that explain, describe, or qualify another.

3. UNCLEAR: Concerned about the possibility of salmonella, the cutting boards were washed. (Since cutting boards don't get concerned, this sentence must be rewritten to avoid a dangling modifier.)
BETTER: Concerned about the possibility of salmonella, the chefs washed the cutting boards.

Be especially mindful of modifiers like "only" or "always" because placement can significantly change the meaning. For example:
- Only Ann called Dave a louse.
- Ann only called Dave a louse.
- Ann called only Dave a louse.

Begin and end with punch words. The beginning and end of sentences are more emphatic than the middle. So place words you want to stress—usually the subject, object, or verb—at the front or the back.

4. MEDIOCRE: The defendant died two months later while visiting New York. (Emphasizes location.)
BETTER: The defendant died while visiting New York two months later. (Emphasizes time.)
BEST: Two months later, while visiting New York, the defendant died. (Emphasizes the main point.)

If you're uncertain which words carry the most punch, read your sentences aloud.

Common Misconception: If you put a specific feature of your invention, such as a preferred size, a preferred material, a preferred shape, etc., in your specification, the scope of your invention will be limited to this feature, so any device that lacks this specific feature will not infringe.

Fact: The scope of an invention is determined mainly by the claims and far less by specifics that are included in the specification. If you do recite any specific feature in a claim, that claim will be limited to this specific feature, but if the specific feature is stated in the specification, it will help provide an adequate disclosure. The specific feature should not be stated in a limiting manner, however. Wrong: "The lever of my invention is made of nylon." Right: "The lever of this embodiment may be made of nylon, but other materials are also suitable." When describing a range, state whether the range includes its endpoints (for example: "The length may be as short as 2 centimeters, but in some embodiments may be longer, up to and including 5 centimeters"). It is to your benefit that the specification include as many specifics of the invention as possible, especially in critical areas, so no one will ever be able to validly attack the adequacy of the specification for failure to teach how to make and use the invention. However, again, when stating the specifics of an invention in the specification, it's important to (1) state that these specifics are what you presently prefer for this embodiment, and (2) include as many variations as you can envision—for example, "The embodiment of Fig. 1 may have a rectangular cross section 2 mm by 4 mm and be 4 cm long and made of austenitic steel. However it can have different cross sections, such as oval, triangular, circular, etc., and different sizes and materials, such as high-carbon steel, titanium, polycarbonate, etc."

Avoid technical language, Greek letters, and subscripts, insofar as possible, but if you use any technical terms, be sure to define them for any lay judge or young examiner who may read your application, but remember that your definition may be used to limit your claims, so craft your definition to support your disclosure, but not too narrowly. One patent litigator has suggested drafting all patent applications for a judge with a degree in political science, English, or government—that is, try to make your description as nontechnical as possible, without eliminating any crucial details. If you do have a technical invention, such as a computer, biotechnical, electronic, chemical, medical, or complex mechanical invention, start your explanation from ground zero, assuming your reader, who may be a new examiner or a judge with a degree in political science, knows nothing about the field. Then explain the field of the invention, the problem you solve, and any technical information your reader will need to understand it. You don't need to write a complete textbook, but you should provide a full guide from ground zero to the level of the invention. For any reasonably complex invention, include a glossary of technical and other terms of the invention and make the definitions as broad as possible. You can put the glossary in its own section after the Drawing Figures section.

Use of "A," "The," and "Said"

Although the articles "a" and "the" are two of the most common and elementary words in the American language, many writers often use them improperly.

The articles "a" and "an" are indefinite articles, i.e., they do not refer to any definite or already known thing. Example: "I bought a car."

The articles "the" and the legal word "said" are definite articles, i.e., they refer to a definite or already known thing. Example: "I bought the car that we saw yesterday."

When you first introduce something, your reader is not familiar with it, so always introduce it with an indefinite article. Example: "The device has a handle 110 that is connected to an ax head 112."

When your specification refers again to something that has already been introduced, your reader is familiar with it, so always use a definite article "the." For example, if the parts have already been introduced, say, "The lever 110 and the handle 112 may be made of plastic."

If you are referring to the parts by their number, or if they're plural, you often don't need to use "the." Examples: "Lever 110 and handle 112 may be made of plastic," or "Levers such as this are well known."

In claims the same rules apply, except that you should use "the" to refer to a part that has not been expressly mentioned but is implied and "said" to refer to a part by the exact name by which it has already been recited. For example, if the claim has already recited a tabletop comprising a flat sheet and four elongated legs, say, "… said legs being attached to the underside of said tabletop."

Never use "a" to refer to an already-introduced part. For example, if a lever has been introduced, do not subsequently say, "A lever is connected to the handle."

Never introduce something with "the." For example, if a lever has not been introduced, do not say, "The lever is made of plastic."

Claiming Copyright in a Program, Specification, or Drawing

If you want to put a copyright or mask work notice in the specification or drawings to provide notice that you claim copyright in the program listing, mask work, or other written material in the specification, you may do so since Rule 71(d) (37 CFR 1.71(d)) permits this. Make the notice the first paragraph of your specification; Rule 71(e) states that the notice shall read as follows:

A portion of the disclosure of this patent document contains material which is subject to (copyright or mask work) protection. The (copyright or mask work) owner has no objection to the facsimile reproduction by anyone of the patent document or the patent disclosure, as it appears in the Patent and Trademark Office patent file or records, but otherwise reserves all (copyright or mask work) rights whatsoever.

 NOTE

Computer Programs Note. If your invention involves a computer program, include a program listing in ASCII format or a detailed flowchart with a detailed explanation as to how to configure the computer to perform the required function and interrelate with any other elements to yield the claimed invention. If the listing is 300 lines or fewer (72 characters per line), it can be submitted as part of the specification, or as part of the drawings. In either case, the listing should be a very black, camera-ready copy. If the printout is to be submitted on drawing sheets, these should be of the proper size, with each sheet including a separate figure number (Fig. 1, Fig. 2, etc.; or Fig. 1-A, Fig. 1-B, etc.). If the printout is to be submitted as part of the specification, it must be on the same size sheets. The printout should be positioned just before the claims if it has more than 60 lines of code.

If your program is longer than 300 lines, and you are filing by EFS-Web (strongly recommended), you may submit it as an attachment as an ASCII text file (MPEP 502.05], with the program(s) clearly identified and referenced in the specification. Only one copy is needed.

If your program is longer than 300 lines, and you are filing your application on paper, it must be submitted on two CDs (original and duplicate), as an appendix. It will not be printed with the patent, but will be referred to in the patent. You may use CD-ROMs or CD-Rs with your files in ASCII format. Each CD should be in a hard case in an unsealed, unpadded, mailing envelope, accompanied by a transmittal letter. The letter (and a separate paragraph in the specification) must list the machine format (IBM-PC, Macintosh, etc.), the operating system compatibility (MS-DOS, MS-Windows, Macintosh, Unix, Linux, etc.), and a list of files on the CD (including their names, size in bytes, dates of creation, etc.). The discs must be labeled "Copy 1" and "Copy 2" and the letter must state that the discs are identical. The standards for CD-ROMs are contained in Rules 96 (37 CFR 1.96) and 52(e) (37 CFR 1.52e), available at all Patent and Trademark Resource Centers (or "PTRCs"; formerly known as "Patent and Trademark Depository Libraries" or "PTDLs") and over the PTO's website (see Appendix 5, Mail, Telephone, Fax, and Email Communications With the PTO) or in any law library.

Trademarks

If any material, substance, or component of your invention is a trademarked product, you should refer to it by its generic name, without using the mark—unless the mark is necessary for full identification. For example, if you have a hook-and-loop fastener, you can say, "hook-and-loop fastener 20 holds tab to base 14." It is not necessary to use either of the marks *Velcro* or *Latchlok*, since H&L fasteners are well known. The same holds true for the trademark *Teflon*—use PTFE instead. However, if the product is not common, you can use its mark, provided you use it properly. This means capitalizing the mark, identifying it as a trademark, using the mark as an adjective with a generic descriptor, and identifying the owner of the mark—such as "Ajax™ developer, manufactured by Goldberger Graphics of San Francisco." If the trademarked product is crucial and you're going to recite it in your claims, and you don't know its composition, see "Trademarked Chemical Note," above. (If you have your own (new) trademark for your invention, you should not use it in your specification.)

TIP

The terms you need to define, if any, will not come into focus for you until you write the claims. Don't write a glossary to define terms until you have written the claims. Remember that defining terms is a double-edged sword. Definitions may add clarity and precision to your claims, and may make it more difficult for an examiner to construe or interpret your claims with unreasonable breadth. However, definitions may also limit the breadth of your claims in ways difficult to foresee at the drafting stage. Even experienced patent attorneys struggle to know when to define a term, and when to leave it open to interpretation.

I. Operation PPA

After you complete the static description of your main or preferred embodiment, you should then describe in extensive detail the operation or function of the entire machine or system, and then the individual parts covered in your description. Refer to each part by its name and reference numeral, and be sure to describe the working or function of every part. Your invention may be of such a nature that it may not be possible to include a physical description and an operational description in separate sections. However, you'll find that this mode of description works generally for most inventions, and you should try to adhere to it since it will force you to be complete and comprehensive. Your operation section should not introduce any part or use any reference numeral that was not introduced in the description section. Again, always keep your reader apprised as to which figure is under discussion. At the end of or in the Operation section, stress the advantages of your invention—for example, "Thus, since the lever 341 is bent in this embodiment it avoids the jamming that some prior-art couplings experienced." Just say what your invention can do and not what it can't do because this will denigrate your invention and give your adversaries ammunition to attack it.

m. Description and Operation of Alternative Embodiments PPA

If your invention includes several embodiments and ramifications, you should first fully describe the structure of the most preferred or most basic embodiment. (However, never call it a "preferred" or "main" embodiment.) Then, describe its operation in a separate section immediately following the structural description. In this way, your reader or examiner will get a full understanding of one embodiment of the invention, including its operation.

Then describe each additional important embodiment—those embodiments that you feel have a good chance of being commercially implemented. Describe these additional embodiments in the same manner, but more briefly, since you only need detail the differences over the first embodiment. Thus, several sets of description/operation sections will result. For example, "Fig. 1—Description of Motor," "Operation of Motor," "Fig. 2—Description of Hand Version," "Operation of Hand Version." You must include a highly detailed description of each and every part of your invention, together with a highly detailed description of the operation of each part and its relation to the other parts.

You should describe, draw, and claim specifically all reasonably important embodiments and ramifications so that you'll have more support for broader claims. Also, if an infringer is making or selling a ramification, you'll be able to show the judge that you specifically showed that ramification in your application. Infringement is supposed to be determined mainly by the wording of your claims. However, as a practical matter, judges are psychologically influenced in your favor if your specification and drawings show and discuss the very embodiment that is being infringed.

If you are aware of less important embodiments and ramifications, you can describe these in the Ramifications section, discussed below, without drawing or claiming them specifically.

TIP

Medical Devices and Drugs. If your invention is a medical device or drug, you don't need to supply proof of efficacy if it's obvious that it will work and be safe. For instance, if your invention is a drug that is close or analogous to an existing drug that is already recognized as safe and efficacious, you don't need further proof. But if your invention is a drug that is substantially different from anything on the market, and it's not apparent that the drug will be safe and efficacious, you must be prepared to prove those things. Applications for patents on drugs often are referred to the FDA, which has its own requirements, but in cases where the drug or device isn't radically different, declarations by experts regarding safety and efficacy will usually be accepted by the PTO.

n. Conclusion, Ramifications, and Scope

After you finish your detailed description of the invention's operation, add a "Conclusion, Ramifications, and Scope" section to sum things up and to remind the judge who sees your patent that the claims control. Here's an example:

"Thus the reader will see that at least one embodiment of the can opener provides a more reliable, lightweight, yet economical device that can be used by persons of almost any age …. [Keep selling it!]"

Some inventors have provided arguments for unobviousness here, but it's advisable to just state the advantages without discussing unobviousness.

"While my above description contains many specificities, these should not be construed as limitations on the scope, but rather as an exemplification of one [or several] embodiment(s) thereof. Many other variations are possible. For example [then continue with brief description of possible variations that aren't important enough to show as ramifications in the drawing].

"Accordingly, the scope should be determined not by the embodiment(s) illustrated, but by the appended claims and their legal equivalents."

In the first paragraph quoted above, the advantages of the invention are restated and summarized to hammer home the great value of your invention. But don't refer to "the invention" here—just the embodiments—and avoid absolute terms, for example, state that you have found that it is "more reliable" rather than that you have found it "completely or highly reliable." In the "for example" portion of the second quoted paragraph, include a brief description of any alternative embodiments you can think of and that you didn't consider important enough to show in the drawing and describe in detail in your description. Put exotic, untested embodiments, as well as minor variations in color, size, and materials in the broadening paragraph. It's very desirable to include as many ramifications as possible in order to get your claims, especially "means" clauses, interpreted as broadly as possible. The courts will interpret a patent in a narrower manner if it describes a single embodiment only. (See Chapter 9 on drafting claims for a discussion of "means" clauses and their relationship to the specification.)

Thus you should go through the entire application and, for each element of the inventive device or method, state in the ramifications paragraph whether that element can be:

- eliminated or duplicated
- changed in size (made smaller or larger)
- made of a different material
- made in a different shape
- made of a different color
- connected or associated with its adjacent elements in a different manner
- given a different mode or function of operation— for example, suction rather than blowing, or
- made integrally or separately (modular or in sections).

It's very important to be as comprehensive as possible when describing ramifications because the recent decisions of the court have tended to interpret claims narrowly, unless the infringed device is described or mentioned in the specification.

Look at the sample specification at the end of this chapter to see how this is done.

That's just about all there is to drafting the specification portion of your application. What's left, you ask? The small matter of "Claims," that's what. We'll tell you how to write these in the next chapter.

o. Sequence Listing PPA

If you provide a sequence listing of a nucleotide or amino acid sequence on paper, you should include this heading and the listing on a separate sheet after your claims and before your abstract. If you have no sequence listing, don't include the sheet or this heading.

p. Abstract

Your abstract should be drafted on a separate sheet, after the claims. However, it will be printed on the first page of your patent and appears right after the sample specification of Fig. 8G, since the claims have been saved for the next chapter. The abstract is relatively easy to do once you've done the specification, and since it's very closely related to the specification, we'll cover it here.

The abstract should be put on a new page with the heading "Abstract." To do the actual abstract, write one paragraph providing a concise summary of the specification in no more than 150 words. Spend enough time writing the abstract to make it concise, complete, clear, and as broad (nonlimiting) as possible. This is because the abstract is usually the part of an application that's read first and most frequently consulted. Look at the abstracts of several of your prior-art patents to get an idea of what's involved. To be concise, your abstract should not include throat-clearing phrases like "This invention relates to," but rather, should get right into it and state—for example, "An improved bicycle pedal mechanism having…, etc." Also don't limit your abstract to the invention or one embodiment; rather refer to other embodiments and never "the invention." If you think you may file the application in other countries, you should include reference and figure numbers in the abstract (with each one in parentheses) to comply with the international rules. It's also desirable to include some advantages of one or more embodiments in the abstract.

J. Review Your Specification and Abstract Carefully

After you've completed your draft, review it carefully to be sure you've included everything about your invention you can think of. Also, be sure that there is no possible ground for anyone to say that you haven't included enough to teach one skilled in the art how to make and use your invention or that there's anything in the specification that a court can use against you to limit your invention. Also make sure whatever you write is clear and unambiguous because if it's possible to do so, some reader will always interpret anything you write to mean something other than what you intended. You may have to go through two, three, or more drafts to get it right. Be sure to compare your specification with those of other recent patents in the field so that yours is at least as complete as theirs. Allow yourself plenty of time—for example, a few days to do the drawings, a few days to write the introductory parts of your specification, and a few days to do the static description. In this way you won't feel pressured and thus you'll be able to do a better, more readable, more legally adequate job. Because the drafting of an excellent patent application is admittedly a difficult and tiring task, you may be tempted, after finishing the draft, to file it right away and not to check it carefully. It's better to wait a day or two and check it carefully; you'll be grateful that you waited.

> *"Don't do your work in haste. Later on, the public won't ask whether it was completed in three days, but whether it's accurate and complete."*
>
> —*Anonymous*

CAUTION

Many prior-art patents are not properly described under today's demanding standards, so don't absolutely rely on them as a standard. Instead, follow the guidelines of this chapter. After you complete the draft of your specification, show it to a coworker, relative, or friend—someone you can trust to keep your application confidential. Have them double-check that: It clearly teaches how to make and use the invention, it sells your invention and states all of its advantages, it is logical, free of errors (grammatical and technical), it is clearly written, and it doesn't tend to limit your invention.

If You Use an Attorney

If you're fortunate enough to be able to hire an attorney (or agent) to prepare your patent application, don't blindly accept whatever the attorney gives you to sign, since even the best attorneys make mistakes and omit important things at one time or another. All attorneys do better work when they have a critical client. Carefully review the attorney's work in detail, making sure the application is well and clearly written, clearly teaches how to make and use the invention, discloses all possible ramifications, isn't limiting, contains broad main claims, and has a spectrum of claims. You're paying the attorney a lot of money, so you deserve a high-quality product. You should get another attorney if your attorney won't listen to your suggestions or does less than high-quality work.

K. Checklist for Your Patent Application Draft

In the following sections are three lists of the most common errors and areas generally needing improvement. The first list (in two parts) follows; it covers the preliminary drawings and draft specification. Before you go on to the claims or to the finaling process, check this list carefully and make any needed corrections in your work. The specification checklist includes many grammar and punctuation rules that inventors violate frequently.

L. Specification of Sample Patent Application

The application shown below is reproduced in final form, ready for filing in the PTO. However, your application will be in draft form after completing this chapter.

M. Summary

The specification must describe how to make and use the invention in full, clear, concise, and exact terms. The patent application should also "sell" the embodiments of the invention by stressing their advantages in the Operation and Conclusion sections. But don't include anything that could be used to limit your invention or that could be used against you.

Any layperson who can write a detailed description in conjunction with drawings will be able to write a competent patent application. A patent application should contain certain prescribed headings and additional informative headings.

When your application is received in the PTO it will be processed and put in a file by clerical personnel and later reviewed by drawing reviewers and then an examiner.

Prior to doing your drawings and writing the application you should review your papers and make full preparations. For inventions that use software, the application should have a detailed flowchart or a listing. Do rough drawings first and provide a name for every part. Then draft the specification according to an outline and without legal terms, using short, simple sentences.

Provide a static description of each embodiment before describing its operation and sell the invention throughout. Follow the checklists for the preliminary drawings and specification draft.

Checklist for Preliminary Drawings

☐ Every significant part in the drawings has its own reference numeral.

☐ Every unique part has a different reference numeral—that is, the same reference numeral is never used to indicate different parts. (Suffixed numbers (10, 10'; 10A, 10B, etc.) can be used for different parts.)

☐ The same reference numeral is always used to indicate the same part when such part is shown in different Figs.; that is, two different numerals are never used to indicate the same part.

☐ Arrowheads are not used on any lead line, unless it refers to an entire assembly of elements.

☐ The drawings show enough details of your invention to enable it to be fully and readily understood by a lay judge.

☐ The reference numerals start with a number higher than your highest Fig. number.

☐ Even reference numerals (10, 12, etc.) are used so you can add more numerals in sequence later, if needed.

☐ The Fig. details and reference numerals are large enough to be easily read.

☐ Separated parts of any figure are joined by projection lines (see Fig. 8D) or a large bracket (unless there is only one figure on the sheet).

☐ A descriptive label is placed on or near each component whose function is not apparent. (If the component's function is understandable as shown, you aren't allowed to label it.)

☐ The drawings show every part and modification that you intend to include in your claims. (See Chapter 9.)

☐ No dimensions are used on drawings (unless essential for the invention).

☐ Each figure has a separate number. Suffixed figure numbers (Fig. 1-A, Fig. 1-b; Fig. 1, Fig. 1') are okay.

☐ Separate figures are not connected by any line.

☐ Exotic or special parts are labeled—for example, "saturated transistor"; "gray water"; "electric conduit."

☐ Perspective (isometric) views, rather than engineering (top, side, bottom) views, are used wherever possible.

☐ Any figures that show a prior-art device are so labeled.

☐ A reference number is not used for an entire figure.

☐ A sectional view is indicated by two arrows with crossbars on the main view, numbered with the number of the sectional view. If, within a subsidiary figure, you show an enlarged view of an area of a main figure, draw a circle around the area in the main figure and label the circle with the figure number of the subsidiary figure.

Checklist for Draft of Specification—Writing in General

☐ No sentence is over about 13 words (unless really necessary or unless two independent clauses are used).

☐ No paragraph is longer than about 150–200 words or about half a page.

☐ A heading is supplied for approximately every two pages of discussion.

☐ Each discussion relates to and explains only its heading.

☐ Adjacent paragraphs are connected by transitions, and no paragraph is longer than about one page, double-spaced.

☐ Every sophisticated term is defined clearly.

☐ The description is written in simple, nontechnical terms, insofar as possible, so that a lay judge can understand it.

☐ All writing is clear, reads smoothly, and is logical.

☐ Unisex personal pronouns (he, his, hers, etc.) aren't used exclusively; your examiner may be of the opposite sex.

☐ No sentence is started with a number.

☐ Every reference numeral is preceded by a noun ("lever 21").

☐ A comma isn't used between subject and verb. (Wrong: "Lever 24, is connected to brace 26.")

☐ A comma is used at all natural pauses.

☐ Don't omit "Oxford" comma: "He ate bread, ham, and eggs." (Comma indicates the ham and eggs aren't mixed.)

☐ All possessives are apostrophized, except "its."

☐ Loose, informal writing isn't used.

☐ The Specification has been carefully checked for spelling and grammar errors.

☐ A descriptive noun ("lever") rather than a general term ("part") is used for every element.

☐ A group of words serving as a single adjective is hyphenated—for example, "impact-resistant glass."

☐ No sentence fragments are used. (Wrong: "Because the gear is made of nylon.")

☐ Writing is proofread carefully.

☐ The indefinite article "a" (rather than "the") is used to introduce parts in the specification.

☐ The definite article "the" isn't used to refer to a part by its name and reference numeral.

☐ Already introduced parts are not referred to with the article "a."

☐ Every part is referred to by a consistent name throughout. (Multiple alternative names should be used to introduce the part.)

☐ Your writing does not contain "flab" phrases such as "It will be noted that." (Flab slows reader's pace and detracts from drama and strength of work.)

☐ The writing doesn't change voices (active to passive, or vice versa) in a paragraph, and you use the active voice as much as possible. (*Wrong:* "The second gear is turned by the first gear." *Right:* "The first gear turns the second gear.")

☐ The discussion discusses one Fig. at a time, insofar as possible, and doesn't jump from figure to figure too much.

☐ Your reader is always kept clearly advised which figure is under discussion.

☐ "Fig." (rather than figure) is used throughout to speed reading.

Checklist for Draft of Specification—Specification

☐ The title indicates the essence of your invention without being longer than 500 characters.

☐ The Background—Prior Art section does not mention your invention.

☐ All detailed technical discussions refer to a drawing Fig. (most humans can't comprehend abstract technical discussions).

☐ Each prior-art approach you discuss is knocked.

☐ When any patent or prior-art reference is referred to, the inventor's or author's name(s), the patent number, or publication and page, and its issue date are included.

☐ The Drawing Description section has just one short sentence for each Fig.

☐ A List of Reference Numerals section is included.

☐ Every reference numeral on the drawings is used in the specification and every reference numeral in the specification is on the drawings.

☐ The same reference numeral is not used for two different parts. (Suffixed numerals—10, 10A, 10' for different parts—are okay.)

☐ The description and the operation of the invention are discussed in separate sections.

☐ Overall or main parts and overall operation are described before describing details of parts and operation.

☐ If any part mentioned in the specification isn't shown in the drawings (for example, because it's conventional), state this. (For example, "Output 24 of generator 22 is connected to a conventional storage battery (not shown).")

☐ You don't refer to your device as "the invention"; you're specific. (Wrong: "My invention thus …" Right: "The embodiment of my can opener thus…")

☐ Ramifications are discussed after the first embodiment and its operation is explained.

☐ A separate "Summary" section is provided (optional) in general terms.

☐ Wishy-washy descriptions ("a plastic brace might work here") are eliminated; all descriptions are firm, sure, and positive.

☐ The specification doesn't contain any "Patent Profanity" (see Section I.1. above).

☐ The dimensions, exemplary materials, relationships, and/or sources of supply are stated for all exotic or critical parts in a nonlimiting manner—for example, "at present I contemplate the use of nylon for the bevel gear, but other materials are suitable."

☐ For ease of reading, a shorter term is used when you refer again to a part with a long name. For example, First time: "A liquid-overflow check valve 12." Second time: "Valve 12."

☐ Generic terms, rather than trademarks, are used if possible. Each trademark used is identified as such, typed in caps, used with a generic noun, and its owner is indicated.

☐ No legal words, such as "said" or "means," are used in the specification or abstract.

☐ Metric (or metric followed by British) dimensions are used.

☐ All possible novel features of each embodiment are discussed in great detail with dimensions, materials, shapes, interconnections, etc. in a nonlimiting manner, so as to provide language to support any claims that might be directed to this feature.

☐ The Description and Operation sections contain enough detail to enable your invention readily to be built, understood, and used. Every part of each embodiment is discussed, its purpose is stated, and the overall operation of the invention is explained.

☐ If a best mode is indicated, it is done in a nonlimiting manner. The application does not contain any statements that could be used against you to narrow or invalidate your invention.

☐ The Operation section does not introduce any part.

☐ A Conclusion, Ramifications, and Scope section is provided at the end of the specification to repeat the advantages, discuss all possible alternatives (less important embodiments and ramifications), and to indicate that the claims control.

☐ The Abstract is broad and nonlimiting, without listing too many advantages.

☐ The Abstract has a reference numeral in parentheses "(12)," after each named part, for possible foreign filing.

☐ You have had another person check the draft for completeness, accuracy, and clarity.

☐ Include a glossary with broad definitions of the terms used in your specification if it's at all complex.

A2-KoppeLam.SB   your disc and file # (optional)

Note: Dimensions and layout are indicated for typing or printing on letter-size paper (8.5" x 11") so that, if foreign filing is later desired (see Chapter 12), photocopies made directly on A4 paper will have the proper format for foreign filing. If foreign filing is not likely to be desired, legal or letter-size paper with the usual margins (always provide at least a 1" top margin for hole punching), 1.5 or double line spacing, and page numbers at bottom or top can be used.

8-9 cm top margin on p. 1

2.5 cm
left margin

Printout should have minimum 1.5 line spacing (4 lines/inch) but is shown with denser spacing since this example is shown on a reduced scale.

Patent Application of

Lou W. Koppe

for

PAPER-LAMINATED PLIABLE CLOSURE FOR FLEXIBLE BAGS

Cross-Reference to Related Applications

This application claims the benefit of provisional patent application Ser. No. 60/123,456, filed 2003 Aug 9 by the present inventor.

Background—Prior Art

description of
and knocking
of prior art

2.8–3.8 cm
right margin on
8.5" x 11" paper

The following is a tabulation of some prior art that presently appears relevant:

U. S. Patents

Patent Number	Kind Code	Issue Date	Patentee
4292714	B1	1981-08—9	Walker
2981990	B1	1961-05-22	Balderree

U. S. Patent Application Publications

Publication Nr.	Kind Code	Publ. Date	Applicant
200712345678	A1	2007-07-21	Paxton

Foreign Patent Documents

Foreign Doc. Nr.	Cntry Code	Kind Code	Pub. Dt	App or Patentee
883771	GB	B2	1961-12-24	Britt et al.

Nonpatent Literature Documents

Himmelfarb, L. W., *Bread Baker* magazine, "Clips for bread bags come in various colors" (May 2009)

Fig. 8G—Specification of Sample Patent Application

2.5 cm top margin

Patent Application of Lou W. Koppe for "Paper-Laminated
Pliable Closure for Flexible Bags" continued
Page 2

continue
knocking the
prior art

Grocery stores and supermarkets commonly supply consumers with polyethylene bags for holding produce. Such bags are also used by suppliers to provide a resealable container for other items, both edible and inedible.

Originally these bags were sealed by the supplier with staples or by heat. However, consumers objected since these were of a rather permanent nature: the bags could be opened only by tearing, thereby damaging them and rendering them impossible to reseal.

Thereafter, several types of closures were designed to seal plastic bags in such a way as to leave them undamaged after they were opened. Walker discloses a complex clamp which can close the necks of bags without causing damage upon opening; however, these clamps are prohibitively expensive to manufacture. Balderree shows a closure which is of expensive construction, being made of PTFE, and which is not effective unless the bag has a relatively long "neck."

Thus if the bag has been filled almost completely and consequently has a short neck, this closure is useless. Also, being relatively narrow and clumsy, Balderree's closure cannot be easily bent by hand along its longitudinal axis. Finally, his closure does not hold well onto the bag, but has a tendency to snap off.

Although twist closures with a wire core are easy to use and inexpensive to manufacture, do not damage the bag upon being removed, and can be used repeatedly, nevertheless they simply do not possess the neat and uniform appearance of a tab closure, they become tattered and unsightly after repeated use, and they do not offer suitable surfaces for the reception of print or labeling. These ties also require much more manipulation to apply and remove.

Several types of thin, flat closures have been proposed—for example, in U.K. patent 883,771 to Britt et al. (1961) and U.S. patents 3,164,250 (1965), 3,417,912 (1968), 3,822,441 (1974), 4,361,935 (1982), and 4,509,231 (1985), all to Paxton. Although inexpensive to manufacture, capable of use with bags having a short neck, and producible in break-off strips, such closures can be used only once if they are made of frangible plastic since they must be bent or twisted when being removed and consequently will fracture upon removal. Thus, to reseal a bag originally sealed with a frangible closure, one must either close its neck with another closure or else close it in makeshift fashion by folding or tying it. My own patent 4,694,542 (1987) describes a closure which is made of flexible plastic and is therefore capable of repeated use without damage to the bag, but nevertheless all the plastic closures heretofore known suffer from a number of disadvantages:

Fig. 8G—Specification of Sample Patent Application (continued)

Patent Application of Lou W. Koppe for "Paper-Laminated
Pliable Closure for Flexible Bags" continued
Page 3

(a) Their manufacture in color requires the use of a compounding facility for the production of the pigmented plastic. Such a facility, which is needed to compound the primary pigments and which generally constitutes a separate production site, requires the presence of very large storage bins for the pigmented raw granules. Also, it presents great difficulties with regard to the elimination of the airborne powder which results from the mixing of the primary granules.

(b) If one uses an extruder in the production of a pigmented plastic—especially if one uses only a single extruder—a change from one color to a second requires purging the extruder of the granules having the first color by introducing those of the second color. This process inevitably produces, in sizable volume, an intermediate product of an undesired color which must be discarded as scrap, thereby resulting in waste of material and time.

(c) The colors of the closures in present use are rather unsaturated. If greater concentrations of pigment were used in order to make the colors more intense, the plastic would become more brittle and the cost of the final product would increase.

(d) The use of pigmented plastic closures does not lend itself to the production of multicolored designs, and it would be very expensive to produce plastic closures in which the plastic is multicolored—for example, in which the plastic has stripes of several colors, or in which the plastic exhibits multicolored designs.

(e) Closures made solely of plastic generally offer poor surfaces for labeling or printing, and the label or print is often easily smudged.

(f) The printing on a plastic surface is often easily erased, thereby allowing the alteration of prices by dishonest consumers.

(g) The plastic closures in present use are slippery when handled with wet or greasy fingers.

(h) A closure of the type in present use can be very carefully pried off a bag by a dishonest consumer and then attached to another item without giving any evidence of such removal.

summary paraphrases main claim

Summary

In accordance with one embodiment a bag closure comprises a flat body having a notch, a gripping aperture adjacent the notch and a layer of paper laminated on its side.

Fig. 8G—Specification of Sample Patent Application (continued)

Patent Application of Lou W. Koppe for "Paper-Laminated
Pliable Closure for Flexible Bags" continued
Page 4

Advantages

Accordingly several advantages of one or more aspects are as follows: to provide
bag seals that are not permanent and that can be resealed, that do not damage bags,
that are relatively inexpensive, that can be used on bags with a relatively short neck,
that can be bent without breaking, that are neat and have a uniform appearance,
that can be easily manufactured in color with designs, that will accept printing and
hold it well against smudging, that do not slip in one's fingers, and that give evidence
when removed. Other advantages of one or more aspects will be apparent from a
consideration of the drawings and ensuing description.

Drawings—Figures

In the drawings, closely related figures have the same number but different
alphabetic suffixes.

one short
sentence for
each figure

Figs 1A to 1D show various aspects of a closure supplied with a longitudinal groove
and laminated on one side with paper in accordance with one embodiment.

Fig 2 shows a closure with no longitudinal groove and with a paper lamination on
one side only in accordance with another embodiment.

Fig 3 shows a similar closure with one longitudinal groove in accordance with
another embodiment.

Fig 4 shows a similar closure with a paper lamination on both sides in accordance
with another embodiment.

Fig 5 shows a similar closure with a paper lamination on one side only, the groove
having been formed into the paper as well as into the body of the closure in accordance
with another embodiment.

Figs 6A to 6K show end views of closures having various combinations of paper
laminations, longitudinal grooves, and through-holes in accordance with other
embodiments.

Figs 7A to 7C show a laminated closure with groove after being bent and after
being straightened again.

Figs 8A to 8C show a laminated closure without a groove after being bent and after
being straightened again.

Fig. 8G—Specification of Sample Patent Application (continued)

Patent Application of Lou W. Koppe for "Paper-Laminated
Pliable Closure for Flexible Bags" continued
Page 5

Drawings—Reference Numerals

10	base of closure	12	lead-in notch
14	hole	16	gripping points
18	groove	20	paper lamination
22	tear of paper lamination	24	corner
26	longitudinal through-hole	28	neck-down
30	side of base opposite to bend	32	crease

DETAILED DESCRIPTION—FIGS. 1A AND 1B—FIRST EMBODIMENT

One embodiment of the closure is illustrated in Fig 1A (top view) and Fig 1B (end view). The closure has a thin base **10** of uniform cross section consisting of a flexible sheet of material which can be repeatedly bent and straightened out without fracturing. A layer of paper **20** (Fig 1B) is laminated on one side of base **10**. In one embodiment, the base is a flexible plastic, such as poly-ethylene-tere-phthalate (PET— hyphens here supplied to facilitate pronunciation)—available from Eastman Chemical Co. of Kingsport, TN. However, the base can consist of any other material that can be repeatedly bent without fracturing, such as polyethylene, polypropylene, vinyl, nylon, rubber, leather, various impregnated or laminated fibrous materials, various plasticized materials, cardboard, paper, etc.

At one end of the closure is a lead-in notch **12** which terminates in gripping points **16** and leads to a hole **14**. Paper layer **20** adheres to base **10** by virtue either of the extrusion of liquid plastic (which will form the body of the closure) directly onto the paper or the application of heat or adhesive upon the entirety of one side of base **10**. The paper-laminated closure is then punched out. Thus the lamination will have the same shape as the side of the base **10** to which it adheres.

The base of the closure is typically 0.8 mm to 1.2 mm in thickness, and has overall dimensions roughly from 20 mm x 20 mm (square shape) to 40 mm x 70 mm (oblong shape). The outer four corners **24** of the closure are typically beveled or rounded to avoid snagging and personal injury. Also, when closure tabs are connected side-to-side in a long roll, these bevels or roundings give the roll a series of notches which act as detents or indices for the positioning and conveying of the tabs in a dispensing machine.

Fig. 8G—Specification of Sample Patent Application (continued)

Patent Application of Lou W. Koppe for "Paper-Laminated
Pliable Closure for Flexible Bags" continued
Page 6

A longitudinal groove **18** is formed on one side of base **10** in Fig 1. In other embodiments, there may be two longitudinal grooves—one on each side of the base—or there may be no longitudinal groove at all. Groove **18** may be formed by machining, scoring, rolling, or extruding. In the absence of a groove, there may be a longitudinal through-hole **26** (Fig 6L). This through-hole may be formed by placing, in the extrusion path of the closure, a hollow pin for the outlet of air.

Operation—Figs 1, 6, 7, 8

operational description of figures

The manner of using the paper-laminated closure to seal a plastic bag is identical to that for closures in present use. Namely, one first twists the neck of a bag (not shown here but shown in Fig 12 of my above patent) into a narrow, cylindrical configuration. Next, holding the closure so that the plane of its base is generally perpendicular to the axis of the neck and so that lead-in notch **12** is adjacent to the neck, one inserts the twisted neck into the lead-in notch until it is forced past gripping points **16** at the base of the notch and into hole **14**.

To remove the closure, one first bends it along its horizontal axis (Fig 1C—an end view—and Figs 7 and 8) so that the closure is still in contact with the neck of the bag and so that gripping points **16** roughly point in parallel directions. Then one pulls the closure up or down and away from the neck in a direction generally opposite to that in which the gripping points now point, thus freeing the closure from the bag without damaging the latter. The presence of one or two grooves **18** or a longitudinal through-hole **26** (Fig 6L), either of which acts as a hinge, facilitates this process of bending.

The closure can be used to reseal the original bag or to seal another bag many times; one simply bends it flat again prior to reuse.

As shown in Figs 1C, 7B, and 8B (all end views), when the closure is bent along its longitudinal axis, region **30** of the base will stretch somewhat along the direction perpendicular to the longitudinal axis. (Region 30 is the region which is parallel to this axis and is on the side of the base opposite to the bend.) Therefore, when the closure is flattened again, the base will have elongated in the direction perpendicular to the longitudinal axis. This will cause a necking down **28** (Figs 1D, 7C, and 8C) of the base, as well as either a telltale tear **22**, or at least a crease **32** (Figs 7A and 8A) along the axis of bending. Therefore, if the closure is attached to a sales item and has print upon its paper lamination, the fact that the closure has been transferred by a dishonest

Fig. 8G—Specification of Sample Patent Application (continued)

Patent Application of Lou W. Koppe for "Paper-Laminated
Pliable Closure for Flexible Bags" continued
Page 7

consumer from the first item to another will be made evident by the tear or crease.

Figs 7A and 8A show bent closures with and without grooves, respectively. Figs 7C and 8C show the same closures, respectively, after being flattened out, along their longitudinal axes, paper tear **22** being visible.

Figs 2-5—Additional Embodiments

Additional embodiments are shown in Figs 2, 3, 4, and 5; in each case the paper lamination is shown partially peeled back. In Fig 2 the closure has only one lamination and no groove; in Fig 3 it has only one lamination and only one groove; in Fig 4 it has two laminations and only one groove; in Fig 5 it has two laminations and one groove, the latter having been rolled into one lamination as well as into the body of the closure.

Figs 6A-6B—Alternative Embodiments

There are various possibilities with regard to the relative disposition of the sides which are grooved and the sides which are laminated, as illustrated in Fig 6, which presents end views along the longitudinal axis. Fig 6A shows a closure with lamination on one side only and with no groove; Fig 6B shows a closure with laminations on both sides and with no groove; Fig 6C shows a closure with only one lamination and only one groove, both being on the same side; Fig 6D shows a closure with only one lamination and only one groove, both being on the same side and the groove having been rolled into the lamination as well as into the body of the closure; Fig 6E shows a closure with only one lamination and only one groove, the two being on opposite sides; Fig 6F shows a closure with two laminations and only one groove; Fig 6G shows a closure with two laminations and only one groove, the groove having been rolled into one lamination as well as into the body of the closure; Fig 6H shows a closure with only one lamination and with two grooves; Fig 6I shows a closure with only one lamination and with two grooves, one of the grooves having been rolled into the lamination as well as into the body of the closure; Fig 6J shows a closure with two laminations and with two grooves; Fig 6K shows a closure with two laminations and with two grooves, the grooves having been rolled into the laminations as well as into the body of the closure; and Fig 6L shows a closure with two laminations and a longitudinal through-hole.

Fig. 8G—Specification of Sample Patent Application (continued)

Patent Application of Lou W. Koppe for "Paper-Laminated
Pliable Closure for Flexible Bags" continued
Page 8

Advantages

From the description above, a number of advantages of some embodiments of my paper-laminated closures become evident:

(a) A few rolls of colored paper will contain thousands of square yards of a variety of colors, will obviate the need for liquid pigments or a pigment-compounding plant, and will permit the manufacturer to produce colored closures with transparent, off-color, or leftover plastic, all of which are cheaper than first quality pigmented plastic.

(b) With the use of rolls of colored paper to laminate the closures, one can change colors by simply changing rolls, thus avoiding the need to purge the extruder used to produce the closures.

(c) The use of paper laminate upon an unpigmented, flexible plastic base can provide a bright color without requiring the introduction of pigment into the base and the consequent sacrifice of pliability.

(d) The presence of a paper lamination will permit the display of multicolored designs.

(e) The paper lamination will provide a superior surface for labeling or printing, either by hand or by machine.

(f) Any erasure or alteration of prices by dishonest consumers on the paper-laminated closure will leave a highly visible and permanent mark.

(g) Although closures made solely of plastic are slippery when handled with wet or greasy fingers, the paper laminate on my closures will provide a nonslip surface.

Figs 7A and 8A show bent closures with and without grooves, respectively. Figs 7C and 8C show the same closures, respectively, after being flattened out, along their longitudinal axes, paper tear 22 being visible.

Conclusion, Ramifications, and Scope

Accordingly, the reader will see that the paper-laminated closures of the various **repeat advantages— keep selling it!** embodiments can be used to seal a plastic bag easily and conveniently, can be removed just as easily and without damage to the bag, and can be used to reseal the bag without requiring a new closure. In addition, when a closure has been used to seal a bag and is later bent and removed from the bag so as not to damage the latter, the paper lamination will tear or crease and thus give visible evidence of tampering,

Fig. 8G—Specification of Sample Patent Application (continued)

Patent Application of Lou W. Koppe for "Paper-Laminated
Pliable Closure for Flexible Bags" continued
Page 9

without impairing the ability of the closure to reseal the original bag or any other bag. Furthermore, the paper lamination has the additional advantages in that:

additional ramifications

• it permits the production of closures in a variety of colors without requiring the manufacturer to use a separate facility for the compounding of the powdered or liquid pigments needed in the production of colored closures;

• it permits an immediate change in the color of the closure being produced without the need for purging the extruder of old resin;

• it allows the closure to be brightly colored without the need to pigment the base itself and consequently sacrifice the flexibility of the closure; it allows the closure to be multicolored since the paper lamination offers a perfect surface upon which can be printed multicolored designs;

• it provides a closure with a superior surface upon which one can label or print;

• it provides a closure whose labeling cannot be altered or erased without resulting in tell-tale damage to the paper lamination; and

• it provides a closure which will not be slippery when handled with wet or greasy fingers, the paper itself providing a nonslip surface.

broadening paragraph

Although the description above contains many specificities, these should not be construed as limiting the scope of the embodiments but as merely providing illustrations of some of several embodiments. For example, the closure can have other shapes, such as circular, oval, trapezoidal, triangular, etc.; the lead-in notch can have other shapes; the groove can be replaced by a hinge which connects two otherwise unconnected halves, etc.

Thus the scope of the embodiments should be determined by the appended claims and their legal equivalents, rather than by the examples given.

[CLAIMS FOLLOW, STARTING ON A NEW PAGE, BUT ARE
PRINTED IN THE NEXT CHAPTER]

Fig. 8G—Specification of Sample Patent Application (continued)

start abstract on new page, after claims and
sequence listing, if supplied

Patent Application of Lou W. Koppe for "Paper-Laminated
Pliable Closure for Flexible Bags" continued
Page 13

Abstract: One embodiment of a thin, flat closure for plastic bags and of the type having at one edge a V-shaped notch (**12**) which communicates at its base with a gripping aperture (**14**). The base (**10**) of the closure is made of a flexible material so that it can be repeatedly bent, without fracturing, along an axis aligned with said notch and aperture. In addition, a layer of paper (**20**) is laminated on one or both sides of the closure. The axis of the base may contain one or two grooves (**18**) or a through-hole (**26**), either of which acts as a hinge to facilitate bending. Other embodiments are described and shown.

insert reference numerals in parentheses for
possible foreign filing

if there is sequence listing, then insert it on a
separate page titled, "SEQUENCE LISTING"

Fig. 8G—Specification of Sample Patent Application (continued)

see Fig. 10B for permitted drawing sizes

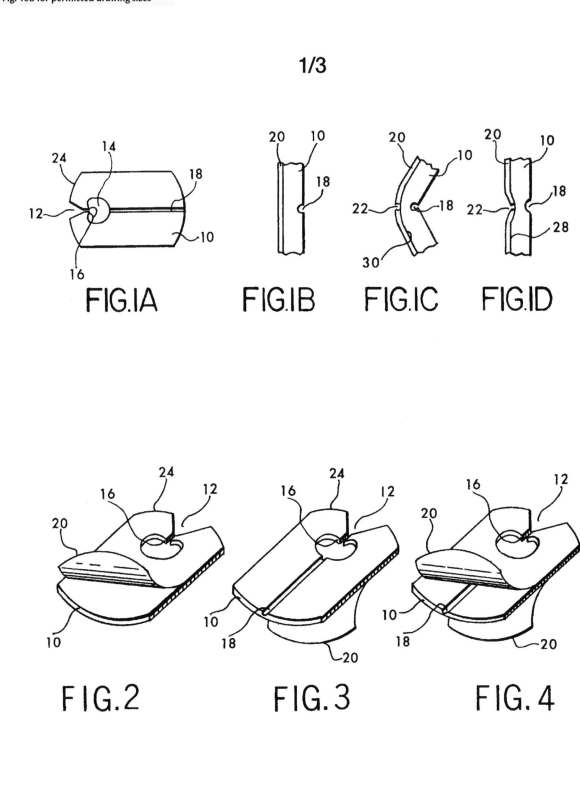

1/3

FIG.IA

FIG.IB

FIG.IC

FIG.ID

FIG.2

FIG.3

FIG.4

Fig. 8G—Specification of Sample Patent Application (continued)

2/3

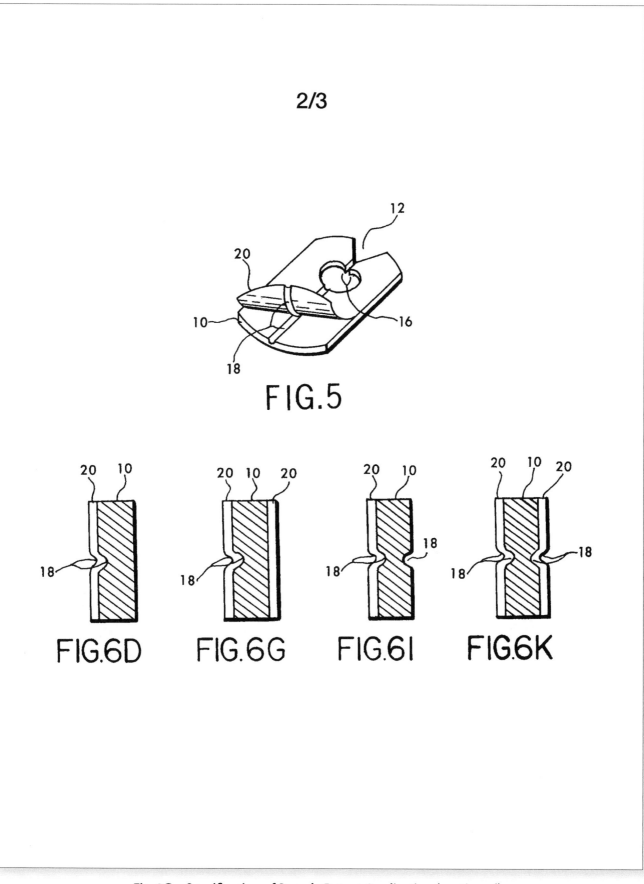

FIG.5

FIG.6D   FIG.6G   FIG.6I   FIG.6K

Fig. 8G—Specification of Sample Patent Application (continued)

3/3

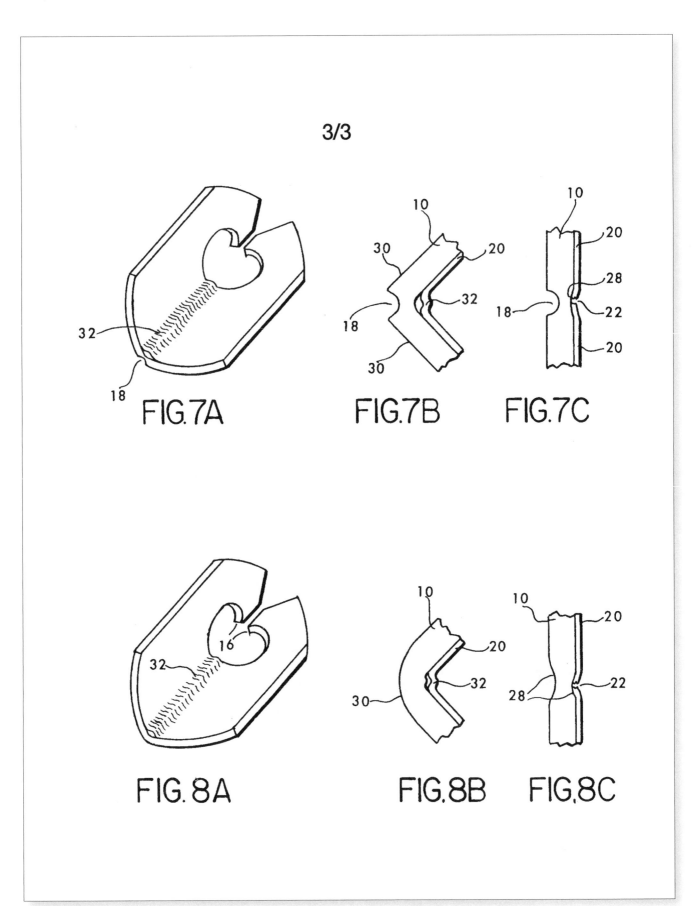

FIG.7A

FIG.7B

FIG.7C

FIG.8A

FIG.8B

FIG.8C

Fig. 8G—Specification of Sample Patent Application (continued)

Now for the Legalese—The Claims

Inventor's Commandment 13

In your patent application, write at least one main (independent) claim. Make this claim as broad as the prior art permits by (1) reciting as few elements as you can, and (2) using the broadest possible terms for such elements, to make it as difficult as possible for others to avoid infringing such claim.

Inventor's Commandment 14

In your patent application, write (1) one or two alternative independent claims, making these as broad as possible, and different from your first independent claim so that you have apparatus, means, and method independent claims, where possible, and (2) follow each independent claim with as many dependent claims as necessary to recite all of the significant additional features of your invention, thereby providing backup for each independent claim and a range of coverage.

Inventor's Commandment 15

Every term used in the claims should have an antecedent basis—that is, a previous reference—in the description, preferably by being defined broadly. Every feature recited in the claims must be shown in the drawings and discussed in the description. The claims must be clearly written and without ambiguity. Every term must be clear, and, if a term is recited more than once, it should be preceded by "said" (or "the"), followed by the same term used the first time.

A. What Are Claims?

If you don't yet know what patent claims are, or have never read any, you're in for a surprise. The word "claim" in the patent context is definitely a term of art.

A patent's claims define the scope of the patent owner's rights. A "claim," in the arcane world of patents, is a very formally worded sentence fragment contained in a patent application or patent. Claims recite and define the structure, or acts, of an invention in very precise, logical, and exact terms. They serve as tools to determine whether an invention is patentable over the prior art and whether a patent is infringed. Just as a deed recites the boundary of a real estate parcel, and a criminal statute defines what acts are punishable by fine or imprisonment, patent claims recite the "bounds" or scope of an invention for the purposes of dealing with the PTO and possible infringers. In other words, claims are the nitty-gritty of patents. While the specification must teach how to make and use the invention, the claims must define its scope.

While claims are literally sentence fragments, they are supposed to be the object of the words "I [or We] claim." They are actually interpreted, when in a patent application, as saying to the examiner, "Here is my definition of my invention. Please search to see whether my invention, as here defined, is novel and unobvious over the prior art and whether I have defined it clearly." In a patent, claims are interpreted as your own little statutes that say to the public, "The following is a precise description of the elements of this invention; if you make, use, or sell anything that has all of these elements, or all of these elements plus additional elements, or that closely fits this description, you can be legally held liable for the consequences of patent infringement."

Since there are only five statutory classes of inventions, every claim must define something that is classifiable into one of these five classes. Thus there are: (1) process or method claims; (2) machine claims; (3) article or article of manufacture claims; (4) composition of matter claims; and (5) claims reciting a new use of any of the previous four statutory classes. Again, the line between (2) and (3) is blurred. Fortunately, as mentioned in Chapter 5, you don't have to do the classifying unless the PTO decides that your invention doesn't fit within any class at all.

If all of this sounds a bit formidable, don't let it throw you; it will become quite clear as we progress, after you see some examples. What's more, when it comes to claims, every layperson who "prosecutes" (handles or controls) a patent application has a safety net: So long as you can convince the patent examiner that you have a patentable invention, the examiner should write at least one claim for you, for free. We discuss this, along with several aids to claim drafting.

But a word of caution. You must provide at least one claim in your application to obtain a filing date. In addition (and even if you use a patent attorney), familiarity with the information we provide here is essential to securing the strongest and broadest possible patent on your invention. So we urge you to approach this chapter as if there were no safety net. Take this chapter as we present it, in small, easy-to-digest chunks, and you'll have no trouble. If you don't understand something the first time, go back again so you'll be further down on the learning curve where you'll see things much more clearly.

Common Misconception: If the devices described in the prior art have disadvantages, and a patent application describes an invention that overcomes such disadvantages, the applicant will automatically be entitled to a patent.

Fact: In addition to describing an invention that is different and superior to the prior art, the application must contain claims that define the invention in a proper way (a) so that it is novel over the prior art, and (b) so that such novelty is also unobvious over the prior art—that is, it produces new and unexpected results.

B. The Law Regarding Claims

The law (statutes and PTO rules) concerning claims is written in only the most general and vague terms. Let's take a brief look at the statutes and rules.

1. Legal Requirements for Patent Claims

The only pertinent statute comprises the last five paragraphs of our old friend, Section 112 of the patent laws (35 USC 112), which states:

a. *IN GENERAL—The specification shall contain a written description of the invention, and of the manner and process of making and using it, in such full, clear, concise, and exact terms as to enable any person skilled in the art to which it pertains, or with which it is most nearly connected, to make and use the same, and shall set forth the best mode contemplated by the inventor or joint inventor of carrying out the invention.*

b. *CONCLUSION—The specification shall conclude with one or more claims particularly pointing out and distinctly claiming the subject matter which the inventor or a joint inventor regards as the invention.*

c. *FORM—A claim may be written in independent or, if the nature of the case admits, in dependent or multiple dependent form.*

d. *REFERENCE IN DEPENDENT FORMS—Subject to subsection (e), a claim in dependent form shall contain a reference to a claim previously set forth and then specify a further limitation of the subject matter claimed. A claim in dependent form shall be construed to incorporate by reference all the limitations of the claim to which it refers.*

e. *REFERENCE IN MULTIPLE DEPENDENT FORM—A claim in multiple dependent form shall contain a reference, in the alternative only, to more than one claim previously set forth and then specify a further limitation of the subject matter claimed. A multiple dependent claim shall not serve as a basis for any other multiple dependent claim. A multiple dependent claim shall be construed to incorporate by reference all the limitations of the particular claim in relation to which it is being considered.*

f. *ELEMENT IN CLAIM FOR A COMBINATION—An element in a claim for a combination may be expressed as a means or step for performing a specified function without the recital of structure, material, or acts in support thereof, and such claim shall be construed to cover the corresponding structure, material, or acts described in the specification and equivalents thereof.*

Paragraph (b) is the one that mandates the use of claims in patents. It also means that the claims must be specific enough to define the invention over the prior art ("particularly pointing out") and also should be clear, logical, and precise ("distinctly claiming"). This sentence is the most important part of Section 112 and is cited by patent examiners almost daily because of the frequency with which they reject claims for lack of clarity or for some other similar reason.

Paragraphs (c) to (e) define independent and dependent claims (more on this later) and make it clear that a dependent claim incorporates all the limitations of the claim to which it refers. Paragraph (e) refers to multiple dependent claims, but since they require a stiff surcharge and since examiners don't like them, we recommend that you don't use them.

Paragraph (f) was enacted to overrule two famous Supreme Court decisions (*G.E. v. Wabash*, 304 U.S. 371 (1938) and *Halliburton v. Walker*, 329 U.S. 1 (1946)). These decisions held certain claims invalid on technical grounds, specifically for "functionality at the point of novelty" because they expressed the essence of an invention in terms of its novel function, rather than reciting the specific structure that performed the novel function. In other words, they contained a broad expression such as "means for hardening latex" rather than a specific expression like "a sulfur additive." Congress enacted this paragraph to enable patent applicants to continue to claim their inventions more broadly. Under paragraph (f), if a claim uses the word "means" for performing a function, it must be construed to cover the structure, material, or acts described in the specification, and their equivalents. That is, if a claim recites "means for conveying rotational energy from said pedals to said rear wheels" and the specification describes a link chain for performing this function, the "means" claim will be construed by the PTO and the courts to cover the link chain and any equivalents, such as a driveshaft, a gear train, etc. (*In re Donaldson Co., Inc.*, 29 USPQ 2d 1845 (CAFC 1994).)

TIP

Many of the examples in this book are means-plus-function claims (sometimes known simply as "means" claims). Means claims are a good way to capture the embodiments of your invention disclosed in your application, but they are not a panacea. The scope of a means-plus-function claim is limited to the structure disclosed in your application for performing the function, and the equivalents of that structure. Consequently, a means claim may not encompass the full range of alternatives to that structure. If you use means claims, you should also include claims that are not means claims. You should write claims using a variety of approaches, including machine claims, method claims, system claims, and means claims, etc.

2. Legal Requirements for Patentable Subject Matter

Not every invention is eligible to be patented, even if it is novel and unobvious.

If your patent claims are directed to a judicial exception (laws of nature, natural phenomena, and abstract ideas are not patentable according to the U.S. Supreme Court) the PTO will reject them as being ineligible (or "non-statutory") subject matter under Section 101 of the U.S. patent statutes (35 USC 101). These are "the basic tools of scientific and technological work" and the courts are concerned about preemption—the "danger that the grant of patents that tie up their use will inhibit future innovation premised upon them." (*Mayo v. Prometheus*, 2012). Of course, at some level, every invention and every claim involves one of these judicial exceptions. Fortunately, the *application* of a law of nature, natural phenomenon, or abstract idea to a new and useful end is patentable subject matter.

The key to claiming patentable ("statutory") subject matter is avoiding claims that are "directed to" a judicial exception, and/or including in your claims additional elements that amount to "significantly more" than the judicial exception. In other words, your claims must include an inventive concept beyond the judicial exception. The PTO's approach to examining claims involves a search for such an inventive concept.

The law in this area has been reinvigorated by a series of U.S. Supreme Court decisions, yet important aspects of the law remain ambiguous. For example, the Supreme Court has not defined the terms "directed to"; "significantly more"; or even "abstract idea." Instead, the courts are slowly developing a body of case law to distinguish claims that are "directed to" a judicial exception from those that integrate a law of nature, natural phenomenon, or abstract idea into something more, by including elements that transform such claims into significantly more than the judicial exception.

Examples of features that amount to "significantly more" than a judicial exception include (but are not necessarily limited to): improvements to another technology or technical field; improvements to the functioning of the computer itself; applying the judicial exception with, or by use of, a particular machine; effecting a transformation or reduction of a particular article to a different state or thing; adding a specific limitation other than what is well-understood, routine, and conventional in the field, or adding unconventional steps that confine the claim to a particular useful application; or other meaningful limitations beyond generally linking the use of the judicial exception to a particular technological environment.

We provide some examples in this book, but since this area of law is still evolving, we recommend that you learn from the mistakes and successes of others by studying the most recent PTO guidance to examiners on subject matter eligibility. That guidance, which the PTO updates from time to time, appears in the Manual of Patent Examining Procedure (MPEP) in section 2106. (The MPEP may be found online easily using a search engine.) The guidance includes examples of successful and unsuccessful claims (sections 2106.04(a)(1) and (2), respectively), as well as the materials the PTO uses to train its examiners. You should study successful claims to understand why they succeed; what features allowed them to avoid a non-statutory subject matter rejection, and how they were drafted to leverage those features. You should study unsuccessful claims to understand why they fell into the section 101 quicksand, and how your claims can avoid that fate.

3. Rules of Practice

In addition to Section 112, claims are governed by the PTO's "Rules of Practice." PTO Rule 75

(37 CFR 1.75), parts b, d.1, and e to i add these additional requirements:

b. *More than one claim may be presented provided they differ substantially from each other and are not unduly multiplied.*

d.1 *The claim or claims must conform to the invention as set forth in the remainder of the specification and the terms and phrases used in the claims must find clear support or antecedent basis in the description so that the meaning of the terms in the claims may be ascertainable by reference to the description.*

e. *Where the nature of the case admits, as in the case of an improvement, any independent claim should contain in the following order: (1) A preamble comprising a general description of all the elements or steps of the claimed combination which are conventional or known, (2) A phrase such as "wherein the improvement comprises," and (3) Those elements, steps, and/or relationships which constitute that portion of the claimed combination which the applicant considers as the new or improved portion.*

f. *If there are several claims, they shall be numbered consecutively in Arabic numerals.*

g. *The least restrictive claim should be presented as claim number 1, and all dependent claims should be grouped together with the claim or claims to which they refer to the extent practicable.*

h. *The claim or claims must commence on a separate physical sheet or electronic page. Any sheet including a claim or portion of a claim may not contain any other parts of the application or other material.*

i. *Where a claim sets forth a plurality of elements or steps, each element or step of the claim should be separated by a line indentation.*

Part b requires that the claims differ substantially from each other and not be too numerous. In practice, minimal differences will suffice. The rule prohibiting numerous claims is more strictly enforced. If more than about 20 claims are presented, there should be some justification, such as a very complex invention or numerous embodiments. Also, there are substantial charges for each independent claim over three and each claim (independent or dependent) over 20 (see Appendix 4, Fee Schedule).

Part d.1, enforced only sporadically, requires that the terms in the claims should correspond to those used in the specification. It has often been said that the specification should serve as a dictionary for the claims. While U.S. examiners don't often enforce this rule, examiners in other countries can be very strict on this point, and most attorneys believe it is very important to follow in view of recent court decisions that tend to narrow the scope of claims.

Part e was introduced to require that claims be drafted, insofar as practicable, in the German or "*Jepson*" style (from a famous decision of that name). The *Jepson*-type claim is very easy for examiners to read and understand. It puts the essence of the invention into sharp focus by providing in the first part of the claim an introduction that sets forth the environment of the invention—that is, what is already known, and in the second part, or body of the claim, the essence of the invention—that is, the improvement of the current invention. In practice, this part of Rule 75 (37 CFR 1.75) is rarely enforced. Most patent attorneys recommend that you avoid use of the *Jepson*-type claim since, by isolating the novel part of the invention, it's easier to invalidate.

Parts f, h, and i are self-explanatory and part g means that the broadest claims should be number 1, all dependent claims should be together and under their independent claim, and the elements or steps of a claim should be listed individually on separate lines (which are sometimes referred to as "subparagraphs," although they're certainly not paragraphs in the traditional sense). More information is provided in Section J of this chapter.

C. Some Sample Claims

As mentioned, claims boil the invention down to its essence. In their broadest sense, they eliminate everything nonessential to the invention. In fact, many inventors first realize what their invention truly is when they write or see a claim to it, especially after the claim has been rejected in the patent prosecution process. Conversely, you won't be able to draft an adequate claim unless you have a clear understanding of your invention.

Although not a patent attorney, the great theatrical producer David Belasco showed that he understood the principle behind claims well when he said, "If you can't write your idea on the back of my calling card, you don't have a clear conception of your idea."

And claims are difficult to write just because they are so short. Blaise Pascal once concluded a letter to a friend as follows: "I have made this letter a little longer than usual because I lack the time to make it shorter." Nevertheless, don't get discouraged; if you follow the step-by-step, four-part procedure we give later, you'll find that writing claims is not too much more difficult than writing the specification.

In the following sections, we provide some hypothetical simple claims and some actual ones. Any patent applications containing these hypothetical claims would now be rejected since the "inventions" they define are obviously old and in the public domain. A few of the claims—the "method of putting" and the "new use" claim—are from patents.

1. Process or Method Claims: Conventional Process, Software Process, Business Method, and Manual Method

In this section, you'll see examples of various method claims—one to a conventional process, one to a software-based process, and one to a manual method. We also include an example of a business method claim, although business methods are difficult (if not impossible) to patent under the current state of the law. Note that these claims recite a series of steps (or individual operations), rather than a series of hardware (physical) elements as in an article claim—although claims do bring hardware in via those method steps. Note also that the software and manual method claims are similar in construction, which shows you that these processes are generally claimed the same way as any other process.

Process or "method" claims are facing increased scrutiny by the courts and PTO. If your patent claim is "directed to" a law of nature, a natural phenomenon, or an abstract idea, the PTO will reject it as "non-statutory" (ineligible) subject matter under

Section 101 of U.S. patent statute (35 USC 101) unless the claim includes "additional elements that amount to significantly more than the judicial exception."

Because the Supreme Court has provided only limited guidance on what it means for a claim to be "directed to" a judicial exception, what constitutes "significantly more," and what constitutes an "abstract idea," courts are tackling these issues by analogizing new cases to prior cases. Some of our examples below are claims that have survived court challenges, or that the PTO has provided as examples of successful claims.

a. Conventional Process

For the conventional process, assume that you just invented sewing and want to claim the process. Here's how you'd do it.

A method for joining two pieces of cloth together at their edges, comprising:

    a. providing said two pieces of cloth and positioning them together so that an edge portion of one piece overlaps an adjacent edge portion of the other piece, and

    b. passing a thread repeatedly through and along the length of the overlapping portions in sequentially opposite directions and through sequentially spaced holes in said overlapping adjacent portions, whereby said two pieces of cloth will be attached along said edge portions.

Note that the first part of this claim contains a title, preamble, or genus, which states the purpose of the method but doesn't use the term "sewing," because sewing is the invention and is assumed to be new at the time the claim is drafted. The claim contains two steps, a and b, that state in sequence the acts one would perform in sewing two pieces of cloth. Note that each clause begins with an "—ing" word (gerund). The claim also contains an optional "whereby" clause at the end to point out to the examiner or a judge the advantage of the process. Finally, note that the claim is single-spaced and is formatted in paragraphs with a hanging indent so that the second and subsequent lines are indented. This is

the way claims are printed in patents, but when you type them in your patent application you should use the hanging indent with 1.5 line spacing. You can "hang" a paragraph in Microsoft *Word* by placing your cursor in the paragraph and pressing Control-T.

b. Software Process

Computer-implemented inventions, including "software" processes, are very challenging to patent because PTO examiners find them easy to reject as being directed to an "abstract idea." Nevertheless, some computer-implemented inventions have been patented or upheld as patentable.

While this area of the law is still evolving, some patterns are emerging that indicate how courts (and by extension, the PTO) reason when it comes to computer and software inventions. The most common tactic is to first determine an abstract idea by notionally removing the computer or software entirely from the claim, then reverse course and argue that the computer is simply an efficient (but wholly conventional) tool for implementing the abstract idea that you found. This "trick" explains the large majority of outcomes, even if the courts don't expressly articulate it as the basis for their analyses, and one early post-*Alice* case mentioned its usefulness. (*DDR Holdings*, 773 F.3d 1245, 1256 (Fed. Cir. 2014) ("In some instances, patent-ineligible abstract ideas are plainly identifiable and divisible from the generic computer limitations recited by the remainder of the claim.").)

The first step often isolates a business method produced by the claim, or an algorithm that may be formulated in terms of operating on pure data: collecting, storing, computing, or displaying it. And while it might be obvious that computers require data, a little thought shows that the converse is not true. For example, it is entirely possible to write down a valid XML document and then convert it, by hand on paper with ink, to SGML or some other data format—entirely without a computer.

Armed with this logic, the computer-less business method claim becomes "just" a fundamental economic practice, and the computer-less data conversion claim is "just" an algorithm; by themselves, these are unpatentable abstract ideas. The courts and PTO then "reverse course" and argue that the software claim "is directed to" a conventional means for applying the abstract idea.

As an example of when this "trick" didn't work, the patent appeals court held that the following claim 17 from U.S. Patent 6,151,604 was patentable in the 2016 *Enfish* case:

A data storage and retrieval system for a computer memory, comprising:
  a. *means for configuring said memory according to a logical table, said logical table including:*
  b. *a plurality of logical rows, each said logical row including an object identification number (OID) to identify each said logical row, each said logical row corresponding to a record of information;*
  c. *a plurality of logical columns intersecting said plurality of logical rows to define a plurality of logical cells, each said logical column including an OID to identify each said logical column; and*
  d. *means for indexing data stored in said table.*

The court indicated that this claim was patentable because it improved an existing technology, namely computer databases. It found evidence for its conclusion in the specification, which stated "benefits over conventional databases, such as increased flexibility, faster search times, and smaller memory requirements."

The court reasoned that the claim's ability to run on a GPC was not fatal, because the claim was directed to improving the functioning of the GPC itself. This distinguished the claim from other claims using a GPC merely as a means to an end; that is, to implement "well-known business practices" or compute math formulas. In other words, when the court tried to remove the computer from the claim, no abstract idea remained for it to consider.

In addition, the court reasoned that the claim's lack of explicit physical structure also was not fatal, because having such a requirement would risk resurrecting a bright-line "machine-or-transformation test" that the Supreme Court expressly prohibited in the 2010 *Bilski*

case. The "means" for configuring and for indexing could very well be pure software, and the *Enfish* court stated: "Much of the advancement made in computer technology consists of improvements to software that, by their very nature, may not be defined by particular physical features but rather by logical structures and processes. We do not see in *Bilski* or *Alice* an exclusion to patenting this large field of technological progress."

c. Business Method

The claim below would almost certainly be rejected as drawn to a judicial exception (nonstatutory subject matter) under the *Alice* decision (see Section G13, below) since it is directed to an abstract idea—the age-old concept of assessing creditworthiness, and its steps are well-understood, routine and conventional. However, we provide it here to illustrate a true business method claim in case *Alice* is legislatively overruled or broadened.

For the business method, assume that you've just invented a procedure for checking the "creditworthiness" of a customer. Now you want to write a claim to this as a business method. Here's how you might write a suitable claim for a credit-checking process.

A method of passing on the creditworthiness of a customer comprising:
  a. *providing a form for said customer to complete, said form having spaces in which said customer must indicate a plurality of credit accounts and a plurality of credit references,*
  b. *investigating each of said credit accounts and credit references and compiling a score from 1 to 100, for each account and reference, with 1 indicating a minimal credit rating and 100 indicating a maximal or excellent credit rating,*
  c. *averaging all of said scores to compile an overall average,*
  d. *rejecting said customer if said overall average is below a predetermined value and accepting said customer if said overall average is above said predetermined value.*

d. Manual Methods

A golfer invented a new way of putting that emphasizes the golfer's dominant hand and claimed this as a manual process (U.S. Pat. No. 5,616,089). Here's how he did it.

A method of gripping a putter comprising the steps:
  a. gripping a putter grip with a dominant hand;
  b. placing a non-dominant hand over an interior wrist portion of the dominant hand behind a thumb of the dominant hand;
  c. resting a middle finger of the non-dominant hand on the styloid process of the dominant hand;
  d. pressing a ring finger and a little finger of the non-dominant hand against the back of the dominant hand;
  e. pressing the palm of the non-dominant hand against a forward surface of the putter grip as the non-dominant hand squeezes the dominant hand.

A cat owner invented a new way of exercising a cat using a laser. Some opined that this invention is ridiculous and obvious. Evidently the examiner didn't think so (U.S. Pat. No. 5,443,036). Here's the main claim.

A method of inducing aerobic exercise in an unrestrained cat, comprising:
  a. directing an intense coherent beam of invisible light produced by a hand-held laser apparatus to produce a bright, highly focused pattern of light at the intersection of the beam and an opaque surface, said pattern being of visual interest to a cat; and
  b. selectively redirecting said beam out of said cat's immediate reach to induce said cat to run and chase said beam and pattern of light around an exercise area.

2. Machine Claims

Here are examples of two machine claims, one to a conventional machine and one to a software-based machine. Note that both claims recite a series of hardware elements, rather than a series of steps as in the process claims. Note also that both claims are similar in con-struction, indicating again that a software machine is generally claimed the same way as any other machine.

a. Conventional Machine

For the conventional machine, assume now that you've just invented the automobile. Here's how to claim it.

A self-propelled vehicle, comprising:
  a. a body carriage having rotatable wheels mounted thereunder for enabling said body carriage to roll along a surface,
  b. an engine mounted in said carriage for producing rotational energy, and
  c. means for controllably coupling rotational energy from said engine to at least one of said wheels, whereby said carriage will be self-propelled along said surface.

This claim again contains a title in the first part. The second part or body contains three elements, the carriage, the engine, and the transmission. These elements are defined as connected or interrelated by the statement that the engine is mounted in the carriage and the transmission (defined broadly as "means for controllably coupling …") couples the engine to at least one wheel of the carriage. Again, the "whereby" clause recites the advantage of the hardware elements of the preamble and clauses a, b, and c.

b. Software Machine

As mentioned, courts use a "trick" to determine software patentability, namely removing the computer from the claim to find the abstract idea, then adding back the computer as a conventional, non-inventive implementation. However, even when the "trick" produces an abstract idea, it can still fail during "course reversal" if the claimed implementation is non-conventional. This was the case for claim 1 of U.S. Patent 5,987,606:

A content filtering system for filtering content retrieved from an Internet computer network by individual controlled access network accounts, said filtering system comprising:

a. *a local client computer generating network access requests for said individual controlled access network accounts;*

b. *at least one filtering scheme;*

c. *a plurality of sets of logical filtering elements; and*

d. *a remote ISP server coupled to said client computer and said Internet computer network, said ISP server associating each said network account to at least one filtering scheme and at least one set of filtering elements, said ISP server further receiving said network access requests from said client computer and executing said associated filtering scheme utilizing said associated set of logical filtering elements.*

This system claim, at issue in the 2016 BASCOM case, was ruled patentable because, even though it was directed to the abstract idea of "filtering content," and even though it recited generic computer, network, and Internet components, the "ordered combination" of these elements was non-conventional and provided an improved process for filtering content itself. The components were not merely invoked as a means to an end; rather, their mutual relationships were unusually altered, with advantageous results.

3. Article-of-Manufacture Claim

You've done it again! Here's a claim to the pencil you've just invented.

A hand-held writing instrument comprising:

a. *elongated core-element means that will leave a marking line if moved across paper or other similar surface, and*

b. *an elongated holder surrounding and encasing said elongated core-element means, one portion of said holder being removable from an end thereof to expose an end of said core-element means so as to enable said core-element means to be exposed for writing,*

whereby said holder protects said core-element means from breakage and provides an enlarged means for holding said core-element means conveniently.

This claim, like the machine claim, contains a preamble and a body with two elements: (a) the "lead" and (b) the wood. As before, the elements of the body are associated; here the wood ("elongated holder") is said to surround and encase the lead ("elongated core"). The "whereby" clause at the end of the claim states the purpose and advantage of the lead and its holder.

4. Composition-of-Matter Claim

Now, great inventor that you are, you've come up with concrete. Here's your claim.

A rigid building and paving material comprising a mixture of sand and stones, and a hardened cement binder filling interstices between and adhering to sand and stones, whereby a hardened, rigid, and strong matrix for building and paving will be provided.

This claim, although not in subparagraph form, still contains a preamble and a body containing a recitation of the elements of the composition (sand, stones, and cement binder), plus an association of the elements (sand and stones are mixed and binder fills volume between and adheres to sand and stones). Again, the whereby clause drives home the advantages of the components.

The height of claim brevity was reached (and will never be exceeded) in two composition-of-matter patents in 1964 when the PTO issued patents 3,156,523 and 3,161,462 to the late Dr. Glenn T. Seaborg, on two new elements, americium and curium. The claim for U.S. Patent No. 3,156,523 (americium) read simply,

1. *Element 95.*

The claim for U.S. Patent No. 3,161,462 (curium) read,

2. *Element 96.*

5. New Use Claim

Someone discovered that pigs put on weight faster if aspirin is added to their diet. Here's how to claim it.

A method for stimulating the growth of swine comprising feeding such swine aspirin in an amount of at least 500 milligrams per day.

This claim recites the newly discovered use of aspirin and the purpose of the new use in a manner that defines over and avoids the known, old use of aspirin (analgesic). Note that it is a method claim (as all new-use claims must be). This is because aspirin per se is old and thus must be claimed more narrowly, as a new use.

Now that you've read a few claims, I suggest you try writing a practice claim or two of your own to become more familiar with the process. Try a simple article or machine with which you are very familiar, such as a table, chair, pen, etc. Write the preamble and then the body. To write the body, first list the elements or parts of the article or machine, and then associate or interconnect them. Don't worry too much about grammar or style, but try to make the claim clear and understandable.

D. Common Misconceptions Regarding Claims

Inventors' misconceptions about claims are more widespread than in any other area of the patent law, except possibly for the misconception regarding the "Post Office Patent" explained in Chapter 3. Consider some of the following.

Common Misconception: The more claims that the PTO (Patent and Trademark Office) allows in your patent application, the broader your scope of coverage.

Fact: The scope of your monopoly is determined by the wording of your claims, not their number. One broad claim can be far more powerful than 50 narrow claims.

Common Misconception: If you want to get broad coverage on a specific feature of your invention, you should recite that specific feature in your claims.

Fact: If you recite a specific feature of your invention in a claim, that claim will be limited to that feature as recited, and variations may not be covered—for example, if you have a two-inch nylon gear in your apparatus and you recite it as such in a claim, the claim may not cover an apparatus that uses a one-inch

gear, or a steel gear. The best way to cover all possible variations of your gear is to recite it simply as a "gear," or better yet, "rotary transmission means."

Common Misconception: To cover a specific feature of your invention per se, you need merely recite it in a dependent claim.

Fact: As stated in the statute quoted in Section B, above (35 USC 112(d)), a dependent claim is construed (and reads) as if it incorporated all of the limitations of the claim to which it refers. Thus if your independent claim (#1) recites a telephone having a connecting cord and your dependent claim reads, "The telephone of Claim 1 wherein said connecting cord is coiled," the dependent claim doesn't monopolize the coiled cord per se, but rather the coiled cord in *combination with the telephone*. More on this later in Section J, below.

Common Misconception: If a claim doesn't recite a specific feature of your invention, then this feature is necessarily not covered. For example, if your invention includes a two-inch nylon gear and you fail to recite it specifically in a claim, then anyone who makes your invention with this gear can't infringe your patent.

Fact: The fact that a feature isn't recited doesn't mean that it isn't covered. An absurd example will make this clear. Suppose your invention is a bicycle and you show and describe it with a front wheel having 60 spokes. You don't mention the spokes at all in a claim; you simply recite a "front wheel." Any bike that has all of the limitations of the claim will infringe it. Thus a bike that has any "front wheel" will infringe, whether it has zero or 600 spokes.

As I'll explain from time to time, to infringe a claim, an accused apparatus must have at least all of the elements of the claim; if it has more elements than recited in the claim, it still infringes, but if it has fewer, then it doesn't infringe. Claim limitations are thus interpreted using Boolean logic, similar to computer search terms (as explained in Chapter 6, Section H).

Common Misconception: The more features of your invention you recite in a claim, the broader that claim will be. (Stated differently, the longer a claim is, the broader it is.)

Fact: As will be apparent from the previous misconceptions, the less you recite in a claim—that is, *the fewer the elements you recite—the broader the claim will be.* This seeming paradox exists because an accused infringing device must have all the elements of a claim to infringe. Thus, the fewer the elements specified in a claim, the fewer the elements an accused infringing device needs to have to infringe. Put differently, infringement is generally easier to prove if a claim is made shorter or has fewer elements. "To claim more, you should recite less" is a Boolean concept that is difficult for most inventors to absorb, but that you should learn well if you want to secure the broadest possible coverage. (Again, see "Computer Searching" in Chapter 6, Section H, for further clarification of this point.)

E. One Claim Should Be as Broad as Possible

There are two ways to make a claim broader: (1) *minimize* the number of elements; and (2) *maximize* the scope of these elements. Let's see how this works.

1. Minimize the Number of Elements

Take our automobile claim, above, which recites three elements, a, b, and c—that is, the wheeled carriage, the engine, and the transmission. If an accused machine contains just these three elements, it will, of course, infringe.

If the accused machine has these three plus a fourth, such as a radio, which we'll label d, it will still infringe.

But if our accused machine contains only elements a and b, the carriage and engine, it won't infringe, since it simply doesn't contain all of the claimed elements, a, b, and c.

If a claim contains many, many elements, say a to m, only devices with all 13 elements, a to m, will infringe. If the maker of the device eliminates just one of the 13 elements, say g, the device will *not* infringe. Thus, it's relatively easy to avoid infringing a claim with many elements.

If a claim contains only two elements, a and b, any device with these two elements will infringe, no matter how many other elements the device has. The only way to have the device avoid infringement is to eliminate either element a or element b, a relatively difficult task.

Thus, *the fewer the elements in a claim, the harder the claim will be to avoid*, that is, the broader it will be and the more devices it will cover. Therefore, when drafting a main or independent claim to your invention, it will behoove you to put in as few elements of your invention as possible. (You do have to include sufficient elements so that the claim recites an operative, complete assemblage that is novel and unobvious over the prior art. More on this in Sections F and G, below.)

2. Recite Each Element as Broadly as Possible

With regard to the second way of broadening a claim, that is, reciting existing elements more broadly, consider a few examples. Suppose an invention involves a chair. The chair can be drafted broadly as "a seat" or narrowly as a four-legged maple chair with a vinyl-covered padded seat and a curved plywood back. Obviously, a three-legged plastic stool would be "a seat," and it would infringe the broadly recited element, but would miss the narrowly recited maple chair by a country mile. In electronics, "controllable electron valve" is broader than "vacuum tube" or "transistor." In machinery, "rotational energy connecting element" is broader than "helically cut gear" or "V-belt."

Another way to broaden your claim is to try to anticipate what an infringer or a competitor might do to attack your patent; then cover this in the claims by eliminating it or broadening it. For example, suppose you invented a furnace that uses a blower to force air into the combustion chamber and your claim recites, "a blower for forcing air from outside said furnace into said combustion chamber." But you realize that a competitor may use a blower to draw air from the combustion chamber and thereby cause the combustion chamber to draw outside air in. Since your claim would not cover this variation, you should broaden the limitation in question to, "a blower for causing outside air to enter said combustion chamber" and also amend the specification (for example, in the ramifications section) to state that the blower may alternatively be arranged to draw air from the combustion chamber and thereby cause the combustion chamber to draw outside air in.

One way of reciting elements broadly is to take advantage of paragraph 6 of Section 112 by reciting an element, wherever possible, as "means" plus a specific function. In this way, any device or means that performs the function and is the equivalent of the supporting structure in the specification would infringe. For example, "means for conveying rotational energy" is broader than a drive belt and covers gears, pulleys, and drive shafts if these are the equivalent of a belt, which they will be determined to be if you've mentioned them in the specification. "Amplifying means" is broader than and covers such items as transistor amplifiers, tube amplifiers, and masers.

If you do use the word "means" in a claim, Section 112 requires that the claim recite a "combination"—that is, two or more elements or parts. Claims that recite a single element are not supposed to use the word "means" to describe the single element, since this is considered too broad—for example, "17. Means for providing a continuously variable speed/power drive for a bicycle" would be an example of a prohibited "single means" claim. However, you can effectively obtain practically the same breadth of coverage by adding an immaterial second element to the claim to make it a combination claim. Thus, "17. In combination, a bicycle having a pedal mechanism and means for providing a continuously variable speed/power drive for coupling rotational energy from said pedal mechanism to a wheel of said bicycle" would satisfy Section 112.

Courts have recently been construing "means" clauses narrowly, so you should also include claims with "structural" (nonmeans) clauses; these clauses can be expanded under the "doctrine of equivalents" (Chapter 15, Section J).

To sum up, while you should write your specification as specifically and with as much detail as possible (Chapter 8), you should make the substance of your main claims as general (broad) as possible by (1) eliminating as many elements as is feasible and (2) describing (reciting) the remaining elements as broadly as possible. In other words, make your specification specific and long and your main claims general and short.

An augmented quote from the French aviator and poet Antoine de Saint-Exupéry (1900–1944) will remind you of the two ways to broaden a claim:

> *"Perfection is achieved, not when there is nothing more to add, but when there is nothing left to take away [and nothing left to broaden]."*

F. The Effect of Prior Art on Your Claim

Now that you've learned how to make your claims as broad as possible, it's time for the bad news. What is "possible" has generally much less breadth than you'd like. This is because each claim must define an invention that is patentable over the prior art. Remember the issues of novelty and unobviousness? Well, they (especially unobviousness) are an ever-present factor always to be considered in claim drafting.

1. Novelty

A claim must define an invention that is novel over the prior art. It must recite something that no single reference in the prior art shows—that is, it must contain something new or novel. Your claim must recite novel hardware (or a novel process step) in a positive, structurally supported, unequivocal manner. For example, reciting "a wheel for providing lateral stabilization" won't adequately define over a prior-art wheel that doesn't provide lateral stabilization, since the function isn't supported by novel structure. The remedy: Recite the novel structure that does provide the stabilization—such as a guide for the wheel, or a "means" for providing stabilization.

Just as a claim can be made broader by eliminating elements and reciting the existing elements more broadly, it can be made narrower in order to define novel structure (1) by adding elements, or (2) by reciting the existing elements more narrowly.

For an example of adding elements, suppose a prior-art reference shows a machine having three elements—A, B, and C, and your claim recites these three elements A, B, and C. Your claim would be said to lack novelty over the prior art and would be rejected or held invalid under Section 102. But if you added a fourth element, D, to the claim, it would clear the prior art and would recite a novel invention (but not necessarily a patentable one, because of the unobviousness requirement). (If the prior art were an in-force patent that *claimed* elements A, B, and C, and your *device* had elements A, B, C, and D, it *would* infringe for reasons given in Section E1, above. However, the PTO is never concerned with infringements, so you don't need to worry about this issue in a patent application.)

For an example of reciting existing elements more narrowly, suppose the prior art shows a machine having the same three elements—A, B, and C. You could also clear this prior art and claim a novel invention by reciting in your claim elements A, B, and C′, where C′ would be the prior-art element C with any change that isn't shown in the prior art. For example, if the prior art shows element C as a steam engine, and you recite a gasoline engine (C′), you've obviated any question of lack of novelty (though probably not obviousness).

In sum, although you'd like to be able to eliminate as many elements as possible and recite all of your elements as broadly as possible, you will usually have to settle for less because there will always be prior art there to make you toe the line of novelty.

2. Unobviousness

Under Section 103 the claims must define an invention that in addition to being novel, must also be unobvious to one having ordinary skill in the art. When you have to narrow a claim to define over the prior art, you must do so by adding one or more elements or by reciting existing elements

more narrowly, and you must be sure that the added or narrowed elements define a structure or step that is sufficiently different from the prior art to be considered unobvious. Of course, your amendment must also be supported by the text and figures of your application.

For the last bit of bad news, note that if the wording of a claim has several possible interpretations, the examiner is entitled to use any one, including the one least favorable to you, in determining whether the claim clears the prior art.

You should try to write your main claim(s) as broadly as possible while keeping in mind the prior art that you've uncovered. In case of doubt, you should err on the side of too much breadth, since you can always narrow your claims later if your examiner thinks they're too broad. Conversely, if your examiner allows your narrow claims on your first office action (rare), you'll find it very difficult to broaden them later.

G. Technical Requirements of Claims

In addition to defining adequately over the prior art, each claim must also be worded in a clear, concise, precise, and rational way. If the wording of a claim is poor, the examiner will make a "technical" (non–prior-art) rejection under Section 112. It is this technical aspect of drafting claims that most often serves as a stumbling block to the layperson. To put it candidly, claims, like laws, are not written to be easily understood; they should be written so they cannot be misunderstood. Yet claim drafting really won't be that hard if you:

- study the sample claims listed later in this chapter, plus those of a few patents, to get the basic idea
- use the four-step method (preamble-element-interconnections-broaden) set out in Section H, below, and
- are conversant with the appropriate terminology associated with your invention's elements.

Remember also that you needn't write perfect claims when you file the application. Why? Because if you have a patentable invention, the examiner should draft at least one claim for you. A provision of the *Manual of Patent Examining Procedure*, Section 707.07(j), states:

> *When, during the examination of a pro se [no attorney] application it becomes apparent to the examiner that there is patentable subject matter disclosed in the application, the examiner should draft one or more claims for the applicant and indicate in his or her action that such claims would be allowed if incorporated in the application by amendment.*
>
> *This practice will expedite prosecution and offer a service to individual inventors not represented by a registered patent attorney or agent. Although this practice may be desirable and is permissible in any case deemed appropriate by the examiner, it will be expected to be applied in all cases where it is apparent that the applicant is unfamiliar with the proper preparation and prosecution of patent applications.*

You do have to at least give it a try, since you must file at least one claim with your application to get a filing date. But, as indicated, this claim need not be well written or narrow enough for patent coverage. Instead, during the ensuing prosecution stage, you can ask the examiner to write claims for you pursuant to this section if you feel yours aren't adequate. The examiner is bound to do so if your invention is patentable.

If you do choose this option, be sure the examiner's claims are broad enough, since it isn't in the examiner's own interest to write broad claims for you. As with any other claim, ask yourself if any elements of the examiner's claim can be eliminated or recited more broadly and still distinguish adequately over the prior art. If so, amend it as suggested in Chapter 13.

Also remember that many patent attorneys and agents will be willing to review your specification and drawings or draft your claims at their regular hourly rates. But use this as a last alternative, since most patent attorneys in private practice charge $200 to $500 per hour. If possible, you should choose a company-employed patent attorney or a retired patent attorney who works at home, since such attorneys'

rates will usually be one-half to one-third of those charged by their downtown counterparts.

Let's look at some of the basic rules covering the drafting of claims.

1. Use Proper Antecedents and Be Precise

Your claims must be precise, logical, and determinate. One of the most common reasons for claim rejections is the improper use of articles, such as "a," "the," and "said." Generally, the first time you recite an element, use the indefinite article "a," just as you would if you were speaking to someone who is not familiar with your device—for example, "I just bought a car." If you refer to the same element again using exactly the same words to describe it, use the extremely definite article "said"—for example, "… said car has a burglar alarm." "Said" actually means, in patent law, "the following part, which in this claim (or its parent claim) is previously recited in exactly the following word(s):" If you refer to an aspect of an element by using different, but implicitly clear words, use the definite article "the" just as you would do in ordinary speech—for example, "The auto was expensive." Here's an example showing how "a," "said," and "the" are properly used in a claim to a table.

> *An article of furniture for holding objects for a sitting human, comprising:*
>
> a. *__a__ sheet of rigid material having sufficient size to accommodate use by a human being for writing and working,*
>
> b. *__a__ plurality of elongated support members of equal length,*
>
> c. *__said__ support members being joined perpendicularly to __the__ undersurface of __said__ sheet of rigid material at spaced locations so as to be able to support __said__ sheet of rigid material in __a__ horizontal orientation.*

Note that the first time any element is mentioned, the article "a" is used, but when it's referred to again by its original designation, "said" is used. When another aspect of it is referred to with a different (but clear) designation—that is, the undersurface of the table—"the" is used.

In addition to being precise in the use of articles, you should avoid ambiguous or missing references. For example, if "said elongated lever" is used in a claim and no "elongated lever" has previously been recited in these exact words, a non sequitur has occurred and the PTO will reject the claim for indefiniteness due to a "missing antecedent." The solution is to recite the elongated lever earlier in the claim or to change "said elongated lever" to "an elongated lever." Or, if the same element is positively recited twice, such as "a lever" … "a lever," the claim is unclear. The solution is to change the second "a lever" to "said lever." On the other hand, if the two levers are actually different, call them by different names, for example "a first lever" and "a second lever." You may then refer to "said first lever" and "said second lever," but now "said lever" is ambiguous and unclear.

In a dependent claim, the antecedent can be provided in the dependent claim itself, the referent claim from which the dependent claim depends (whether independent or dependent), or any lower-numbered referent claim which the first referent claim depends from. Thus, if claim 3 is dependent on claim 2, which is in turn dependent on claim 1, an antecedent for "said lever" in claim 3 can be provided in either claims 1 or 2.

Vagueness and indefiniteness can also occur if you use abbreviations—such as, "d.c." (say "direct current"); relative terms without any reference—such as, "large" (say "larger than…" or "large enough to support three adults"), or vague, casual language, such as "strong," "suitable," "standard," "sufficient," etc.

2. Use Only One Capital, One Period, and No Dashes, Quotes, Parentheses, Trademarks, or Abbreviations

Amateurs violate this rule often. While it may be hard for you to accept, and while it may seem silly, the rules are that the only capital letter in a claim should be the first letter of the first word, the claim should contain a period only at its end, and there should be no dashes, quotes, or parentheses, trademarks, or abbreviations. (You may use capitals, periods, and parentheses for the lettered subparagraphs of a claim, for instance, "A." or "(A)"; also, hyphens ("hand-held") are okay, but dashes ("—" or "--") are not. (The PTO will allow a second capital in a dependent claim when the word "Claim" is capitalized.))

3. Use Means Clause to Avoid Functionality of Claim

The technical error of "functionality" occurs when elements of the claim are recited in terms of their advantage, function, or result rather than in terms of their structure. The remedy is to recite the elements of the claim as "means" or a "device" for performing the function or achieving the result.

For example, here are some typical improper functional claims actually written by a layperson.

7. *An additive for paints that makes the paint dry faster.*

8. *A belt buckle that does not tend to snag as much.*

Both of these claims would be rejected under Section 112 because they don't particularly point out and distinctly claim the invention since they recite what the invention does rather than what it is.

The remedy: Use "means" or "device" clauses and also recite the general composition or structure of the additive or buckle. But remember that the claim must be to a combination; a single "means" claim won't pass muster. Thus, even if Claim 7 were written as follows, it would violate Section 112.

7. *Additive means for paints for making them dry faster.*

Here's how the above two claims can be properly rewritten to pass muster under Section 112.

7A. *paint composition comprising:*
    a. *a paint compound comprising an oil-based paint vehicle and a suspended pigment in said vehicle, and*
    b. *additive means admixed with said vehicle for decreasing the drying time of said paint compound and*
    b'. *a volatile solvent admixed [etc.].*

8A. belt buckle comprising:

    a. a catch comprising two interlocking rigid parts that can be attached to opposite ends of a belt, and

    b. anti-snag means for preventing said interlocking parts from snagging on cloth when placed adjacent said interlocking parts and

    b'. a shield for preventing [etc.].

A moment's reflection will show you that claiming your invention in terms of its unique structure, rather than its results, effects, or functions, makes logical sense. This is because a monopoly, to be precise and to have reasonable limits, must be defined in terms of its structure, rather than the result such structure produces. In other words, if you recited "a belt buckle that doesn't snag" you would be claiming a result only, so that any belt buckle that fulfilled this result would infringe, regardless of its structure. This "functional" type of claim would accordingly be considered unreasonably broad or directed to an abstract idea, and therefore would have to be narrowed and made more explicit by the addition of some additional structure or a means clause in order to make it more commensurate with the invention.

However, there's now a downside to using "means plus function" clauses: Under the pertinent statute (35 USC 112(f)) and court decisions, a means plus function clause is supposed to be interpreted according to the corresponding structure or material described in the specification and the equivalents of such structure or material. Thus, a means plus function clause is not supposed to be interpreted literally to cover every possible means that fulfills the function of the means, but only according to the corresponding structure or material in the specification and its equivalents. Thus, in addition to a means plus function claim, it's best to include one or more independent nonmeans claims which are as broad as possible without using means plus function language.

Of course, while both of the above claims (as we revised them) would pass Section 112, they would not be novel or patentable under Sections 102 or 103, since they recite nothing new according to our present state of knowledge.

Means Must Be Supported

Court decisions (for example, *Biomedino, LLC v. Waters Technologies Corp.*, 490 F.3d 946, 950 (Fed. Cir. 2007)) have emphasized the importance that every means and even every nonmeans component in the claims, whether for software or hardware inventions, is clearly described and identifiable in the specification. If any component isn't clearly identifiable, we would add a sentence at the appropriate part of the specification, such as follows:

"Thus units xxx and yyy constitute a means for ...."

If the means is part of a software program, identify the part or object of the listing and state that it constitutes a means for ....

---

4. Be Complete

Each claim must stand on its own—that is, it must recite enough elements to make a working, complete device in accordance with its recognized status in its art. For example, you can recite a lightbulb per se (without reciting the entire lamp) since lightbulbs are a well-known item of commerce. But a claim to just the glass envelope of a lightbulb would probably be rejected as incomplete, since it won't do anything on its own and isn't a recognized item of commerce. The remedy for failing to include enough elements is simply to add the needed elements. Examiners and attorneys frequently disagree as to whether a claim is incomplete, the examiner wanting the claim narrowed by the addition of elements and the attorney wanting it to remain broad, that is, not to add any more elements.

5. Keep Language Straightforward and Simple

Properly drafted claims use a minimum number of words to delineate the essence of the invention. Excess wordiness of a claim, termed "prolixity" by the PTO, is a frequent error committed by beginners. The remedy is to reword the claim in more compact language.

6. All Elements of Invention Must Logically Interrelate and Interconnect

Each of the elements in a claim must be logically related and connected to the other elements. When the elements of an invention don't appear to cooperate and to be connected in a logical or functional sense, the PTO will reject the claim. Think of a do-it-yourself kit that comes with all the parts, but no assembly instructions. This is a more substantive type of rejection, since it's often directed at the underlying invention rather than simply the way the claim is drafted. For example, if you claim the combination of a waffle iron and tape recorder, these elements don't cooperate and hence your claim would be rejected as failing to point out and distinctly claim the invention. But the elements don't have to work at the same time to cooperate; in a typewriter, for example, the parts work at different times but cooperate toward a unitary result.

Wrong: A foot pedal device, comprising: an elongated element, a spring, and a hinge. [Elements aren't connected together.]

Right: A foot pedal device, comprising: an elongated element, a spring, and a hinge having a pair of leaves, said elongated element being connected to one of said leaves, said spring being mounted on said hinge so that it urges said leaves to be folded adjacent each other. [Elements are connected together.]

7. Aggregation

Claims drafted to a combination of elements that don't cooperate toward a common end, such as a washing machine and a telephone, can be rejected on the ground of aggregation. But the elements do not have to function simultaneously to cooperate: A typewriter is a good example of elements (keys) that don't function simultaneously but do cooperate.

8. Use Only Positive Limitations

Positive limitations recite what your invention is ("a box"). Negative limitations recite what your invention is not ("a box not used for shipping").

Negative limitations cannot be used when they make the claim unclear or awkward. However, because many examiners still wince when they see negative limitations in claims, it's best to avoid them by reciting what the invention is, rather than what it isn't. For instance, instead of saying, "said engine connected to said wheels without any transmission," say "said engine connected directly to said wheels." You are permitted to recite holes, recesses, etc. in a recited structure; see "Voids" in the Glossary of Useful Technical Terms for a list of "hole-y" words.

Markush Group Claims

Another, sophisticated way to write a claim for an invention with two or more elements is to recite the disjunctive elements by using a *Markush* group. A *Markush* group (from a decision with that name) is a series of related elements joined by "and," which follows these magic words: *"Selected from the group consisting of."* Thus, a tube or a transistor could be recited in one claim as follows: "Said amplifying circuit containing a device *selected from the group consisting of* tubes and transistors."

---

9. Use Proper Connective Expressions

Be careful when using "and" and "or." As an example of how esoteric claim interpretation can be, in 2008 the patent appeals court interpreted the word "and" to mean "or" in a drug case including a claim with a complex chemical formula, because treating "and" as meaning "both" in one claim made some other claims meaningless. (*Ortho-McNeil Pharm. v. Mylan Labs.*, 520 F.3d 1358 (Fed. Cir. 2008).) Try to separate occurrences of "and" from "or." One way is to limit the use of "and" to necessary structure, and use "or" for optional structure or variations on the main theme. If possible, consider claiming alternative structures or functions using a common name or label in one claim, and reciting the alternatives in a dependent claim. So, for example, claim 1 might say "a magnetic fastener" and claim 2 might say "wherein the magnetic material of the fastener includes iron or steel."

10. Avoid Too Many Claims

If you've put in too many similar claims, even though you've paid for them, you'll have to eliminate some to make the examiner's job easier. If you ever have more than 20 claims, the invention should be complex enough or have enough ramifications to justify them and the claims should differ substantially. This point counterbalances the previous point, which tends to produce more claims.

11. Make Sure Claims Correspond With Disclosure

First, the literal terms or words of the claim must be present somewhere in the specification. For this reason, all patent attorneys we know write the claims first, and then write the specification. If some claim terms are not in the specification, the remedy is to revise the specification by adding the exact terms used in your claims, or to revise the claims by replacing those terms that aren't literally in the specification with terms that are in the specification. This requirement is especially important in view of patent court decisions that have narrowly interpreted terms not defined or described in the specification. As stated, it's useful to provide a glossary in the specification that broadly defines all important terms. Second, any operation, structure, or result recited in a claim must be clearly and completely described in the "spec."

12. Make Sure Claims Are Supported in Drawing

Under Rule 83 (37 CFR 1.83), the drawings must show every feature recited in the claims. If they don't, revise either the drawing or the claims. A broad recitation in a claim, such as "fuel atomizing means," can be supported by specific hardware, such as a carburetor, in the drawings. But remember that you can't add any new matter to an application once it's on file. So be sure to include all possibly relevant details of your invention in your drawings and spec. before you file. For example, if an examiner rejects a claim that recites "fuel atomizing means" for lack of support in the drawings, you can overcome this rejection by adding a box labeled "fuel atomizing means" to the drawings. You can't add a carburetor unless your spec. mentions a carburetor, since this would be prohibited new matter.

13. Avoid the Software-As-Means Trap

If your invention uses computers, software, or the Internet, then your claims must do more than broadly recite an algorithm or other abstract idea. The claims must be directed to an application of the abstract idea to a new and useful end, and include additional elements that amount to significantly more than an abstract idea. (*Bilski v. Kappos*, 561 U.S. 593 (2010); *Alice Corp. v. CLS Bank Int' l*, 134 S. Ct. 2347 (2014)).

To prevent your claims from being rejected as being "directed to" an abstract idea, don your patent examiner's hat and apply the "trick" discussed above. Try claiming your invention without any software, computers, networks, or even physical hardware. Can you do it? If it's completely impossible (for example, because your invention changes the way a computer program accesses its memory), then you're in luck: your invention is "necessarily rooted in computer technology in order to overcome a problem specifically arising in the realm of computer[s]" (*DDR Holdings*), and should be patentable.

However, if it's at all possible to practice your invention without a computer—no matter how inefficiently—then you may have an abstract idea on your hands. In this case, your goal is to avoid the trap of using software or a computer merely as a means to implement that idea.

You may claim an improvement to the underlying idea itself; for example, the Supreme Court held in *Diamond v. Diehr* that a rubber molding process was improved by using a computer to calculate when to open the mold. Or, you may claim unconventional or unusual hardware, and tie your invention to the specific operation of that hardware that distinguishes it from a general purpose computer. Or, you may claim an unconventional "ordered combination" of conventional elements—a collection of relationships between these elements that is unusual and provides "something more" than just a straightforward implementation of the idea.

If you find the state of the law difficult to understand, you're not alone! Most attorneys and legal scholars are befuddled too. Perhaps Congress will cut the Gordian knot and clarify the law someday.

Being in a Statutory Class Is Not Enough

Even though a claim recites statutory subject matter, it still must pass the other tests to be patentable. That is, claims still have to particularly point out and distinctly claim the invention, be supported by the specification, and define novel and unobvious subject matter. Also, all "means plus function" language still must have clear supporting structure in the specification.

14. Recite Each Element Affirmatively as Subject of Its Clause

For maximum clarity, the elements of your invention should be affirmatively and directly recited; don't bring them in by inference or incidentally—for example, say "A transmission comprising: (a) a gear, (b) a shaft, (c) said gear being mounted on said shaft" [etc.], and not "A transmission whose gear is mounted on its shaft." In other words, each significant element of the claim should be recited for the first time (introduced) in a positive, affirmative manner, preferably with the word "a," so it's the subject of its clause, and not with wording that makes it part of the object or assumes that the reader already knows that it's there. This rule is especially important for do-it-yourselfers to follow in order to write clear and understandable claims.

15. Include Structural Support in Recitation of Operation

Assume a claim recites "a lever connected to move said pendulum to and fro at the same rate as said lights flash." The movement of the pendulum at this special rate is too much for the lever to do all by itself. In other words, there's not enough structural support for the operation recited. The remedy? Recite either (a) enough structure to do the job or (b) use a "means" clause. Here are examples of both methods.

a. *a photoresponsive electromechanical circuit terminating in a lever that is connected to said pendulum and is arranged to move said pendulum at the same rate as said lights flash.*

b. *means, including a lever connected to said pendulum, for moving said pendulum at the same rate as said lights flash.*

16. Recite Each Element Affirmatively, Followed by Its Shape or Function

Do not follow any element with the function of any other element.

Right:

> *a container for holding said beans*

Right:

> *a container having a cylindrical shape*

Wrong:

> *a container which receives said beans individually at a speed of 40 cm/second or greater.*

Right:

> *a container having a cylindrical shape, means for shooting said beans individually at a speed of 40 cm/second or greater into said container.*

17. Format

As stated in PTO Rule 75(i) (37 CFR 1.75(i), quoted above), if the claim has several elements or steps, each should be in a separate paragraph with the first line of the paragraph hanging out to the left for maximum clarity, as is done in printed patents and in the claims in Section 13 above.

18. Precede Every Function by an Affirmative Recitation of the Element That Performs That Function

Don't recite any function without preceding the function with an affirmative recitation of the element that performs the function.

Wrong:

> *said beans being shot individually at a speed of 40 cm/second or greater into said container.*

Right:

> *means for shooting said beans individually at a speed of 40 cm/second or greater into said container.*

or

> *a gun for shooting said beans individually at a speed of 40 cm/second or greater into said container.*

19. Make Sure Relative Terms Are Not Ambiguous

Generally the PTO will hold that a claim with a relative term, such as "small," "large," "close," etc., is indefinite—that is, it fails to particularly point out and distinctly claim the invention under Section 112(b). However if the relative term is such that it would normally be understood by a person having ordinary skill in the art (PHOSITA), the Patent Court has held that the PTO should accept it. *Power-One v. Artesyn Tech* (CAFC 2010 Mar 31). In this case a claim that stated that a regulator was "near" a load was held to be unambiguous to a PHOSITA because the description stated that the regulator was to be placed close enough to the load so that the system will operate properly and thus no specific distance was needed.

H. Drafting Your Main (Independent) Claim

There are two basic types of claims: "independent" and "dependent." "Independent claims" are those that don't refer to any preceding claim; they stand alone. Examples of independent claims are all of those given in the preceding sections of this chapter. Note that these claims don't refer back to any preceding claim and each defines a complete, operative invention by itself.

"Dependent claims," which will be covered in the next section, refer back to a preceding or "parent" claim (this preceding claim can either be independent or dependent). A dependent claim recites narrower subject matter than its preceding claim in either of the two standard ways—that is, either by adding an additional element(s) or defining one or more elements of the preceding claim more narrowly.

The reasons for providing dependent claims will be covered in the next section also; the main point to remember here is that your independent claims are the important ones, since they're the basic and broadest definitions of your invention. If a dependent claim is infringed, its independent or parent claim(s) must also be infringed. If an independent claim is infringed, however, that's enough to win the case. You don't have to worry about your dependent claims.

To draft an independent claim, the easiest and most direct way to do it is to follow these four basic steps:

1. Write a preamble giving the name or title of the invention, or the problem which it solves.
2. List the elements (or steps) of the claim.
3. Interconnect the elements or steps.
4. Broaden the claim as much as possible but not so much that it reads on the prior art.

The claim can be structured so that the elements of the claim appear together, followed by the interconnections. Or, each element can appear in conjunction with its interconnection(s) to adjacent elements. Most patent attorneys use the latter method —see Claims 2, 3, and 4 in Section C, above, for examples—but you may find it easier to recite the interconnections separately. An exception is process claims, where you'll find it easier to directly associate each step with its predecessor.

Start by writing your first claim without regard to breadth—that is, just get a preamble written, set down the elements of the invention, and interconnect them, paying no attention to how broadly you can recite the invention. In other words, just define your invention as you believe necessary to "get it all down" in a complete manner.

Then, see how many elements (or steps) you can eliminate and how many remaining elements you can broaden so that the result maintains sufficient structure and yet does not tread on the prior art too much. Remember that the broadest way of defining any element is by using "means-plus-a-function" language. Don't forget to refer to your prior-art patents for examples. And when you are finished, try to make the claim even broader by thinking of ways that an infringer might change your invention while still using your inventive concepts and see if you can broaden the claim to cover these changes, while still defining an invention that is patentable over the prior art.

To provide a real example that everyone can understand, let's assume you've just invented a table. Since you've already written your specification, you have a name for each part of your invention, so that chore is already behind you. If you believe your part names leave something to be desired, you can get additional part names from your prior-art search patents, the Glossary of Useful Technical Terms at the end of this book, or any visual dictionary (see Appendix 2, Resources: Government Publications, Patent Websites, and Books of Use and Interest), or in a thesaurus (in a book or computer). All that remains now is to provide a title or preamble. List the parts, interconnect them, and then broaden your claims.

1.   The Preamble

To write the preamble, you can name the statutory class of the claim (recommended in view of recent court decisions) or pick a name or title for the whole unit or the problem that it solves, remembering that you can't use the word "table" since it hasn't been invented until now. To have the preamble recite just a statutory class, it should simply read, "A machine, comprising:"; "An article, comprising:"; "A method, comprising:"; "A composition, comprising:"; or "A new use, comprising:." To have the preamble recite a title for the whole unit, you can say, "An article of furniture, comprising:" or "A work station device, comprising:." To have the claim recite a function, you can recite, "A support for holding objects to be handled by a sitting human." We've used "an article of furniture" in the sample claim since it would be hard to construe this too narrowly.

2.   The Elements

Next, to list the parts of the table, we'll start with the largest, most visible part, the top, and then add the smaller, less apparent parts, the legs. Since the table's just been invented, we'll assume that the words "top" and "legs" are still unknown, but even if they were known, it's not wise to use "top" anyway, since it's a notoriously vague homonym (it can mean anything from a hat to a bottle cap to a toy). To define the top, then, we need a more meaningful term or phrase. Let's suppose we've made a model of our invention and have used a large sheet of chipboard for the top. All we need to do at this stage is to say so; thus our first and most basic element becomes "(a) a large sheet of chipboard."

Suppose our model table has four legs and we've made them of six-cm diameter circular oak dowels, each 65 cm long. Then our legs would be recited simply as "(b) four oak dowels, each having a circular cross section 6 cm in diameter and each 65 cm long." Our elements are now all recited—wasn't that easy!

3.   Interconnections

Lastly, we have to interconnect the legs to the top, an easy task. Suppose our legs are joined at the underside of the top using four metal flanges, attached at the four corners of the top with each having a cylindrical portion with female threads, and with the top sections of the legs having mating male threads that are screwed into the respective flanges so that the legs extend at right angles to the top. Merely recite the flanges positively and add an interconnection clause as follows.

c. *four flanges, each having means for attachment to one side of said sheet of chipboard and each having a cylindrical portion with female threads, and*

d. *said four flanges being attached to one side of said sheet of chipboard at four respective corners thereof and said four oak dowels having male threads on a top section thereof and being screwed into the cylindrical portions of said respective flangesso that said dowels extend from said sheet of chipboard at right angles.*

Eureka! It's done. You've written a complete independent claim.

Here's how it looks.

11. *An article of furniture, comprising:*
   a. *a large sheet of chipboard,*
   b. *four oak dowels, each having a circular cross section 6 cm in diameter and each 65 cm long, and*
   c. *four flanges, each having means for attachment to one side of said sheet of chipboard and each having a cylindrical portion with female threads, and*
   d. *said four flanges [etc.].*

Note, always recite the elements and their interconnections in lettered subparagraphs. Also, we format paragraphs with a hanging indent style, just as the claims are printed in patents.

Is there anything wrong with this claim? Yes! As you probably will have realized by now, this claim is far too narrow—that is, it has many elements and each of these is recited too specifically. In fact it even recites specific dimensions, which you don't generally even need in the specification. Thus the claim as written would be easy to avoid infringing: all that an infringer would have to do is to use plywood instead of chipboard, use four pine dowels instead of oak, etc. Let's broaden it, then.

Remember, you broaden a claim by (1) eliminating elements where possible, and (2) reciting the remaining elements as broadly as possible.

Going through the claim to eliminate elements, we see that the top can't be eliminated since it's an essential part. However, we don't need to recite four legs—we can eliminate one of these since three legs will support the top. But better yet, we can even use the word "plurality" since this covers two or more legs. (The term "plurality" means more than one). Used here, it is an example of how you'll sometimes need to search for a word or phrase that most broadly describes a particular element. Even though two may not be sufficient to support a top, the PTO will usually not object to this word in this context. We could even go further and eliminate the recitation of legs entirely by reciting "support means," but this would include solid supports, such as in a chest or bureau, which would not be suitable for table-type uses. Lastly, we can eliminate the flanges, since these aren't essential to the invention and

since there are many other possible ways of attaching legs to a tabletop.

Next, let's go through the claim to see which elements can be recited more broadly. First, the top. Obviously "a large sheet of chipboard" is a very narrow recitation since plywood, solid wood, metal, and plastic tops would avoid infringement. A broad recitation would be "a large sheet of rigid material," but, as stated above, the word "large" is frowned upon by the PTO as too vague to satisfy Section 112. So let's make the top's size more specific. Since we're interested in providing a working surface for humans, let's merely specify that the top is "a sheet of rigid material of sufficient size to accommodate use by a human being for writing and working."

Next, the legs. Obviously, the recitation of four circular oak dowels with specific dimensions is very limiting. Let's eliminate the material, shape, and dimensions and recite the legs as merely "a plurality of elongated support members of substantially equal length." This covers square, round, triangular, and oval legs, regardless of their length or material.

Lastly, instead of the flanges (that we've eliminated as unnecessary) to join the legs to the top, let's use "means" (to make it as broad as possible) as follows: "means for joining said elongated support members at right angles to the underside of said top at spaced locations so as to be able to support said top horizontally."

The result would look like this.

11. *An article of furniture, comprising:*
   a. *a sheet of rigid material of sufficient size to accommodate use by a human being for writing and working*
   b. *a plurality of elongated support members of equal length, and*
   c. *means for joining said elongated support members at right angles to the underside of said sheet at spaced locations so as to be able to support said sheet horizontally.*

Obviously, Claim 11 is now far broader than our first effort. Your first independent claim should be as broad as possible, but of course, you can't make it so

Beware of Divided Infringement

Sometimes the most natural way to write a method claim produces a claim that is difficult to enforce. For example, drafting a method claim by simply listing the steps in order, without considering who performs those steps, may lead to "divided" infringement.

Direct infringement of a method claim requires that a single actor perform all of the claim's steps. Ideally, you should craft your claims to focus the action on a single actor. A claim that divides the steps among two or more actors is more difficult and expensive to enforce, and may render your patent less valuable.

The case of *Akamai v. Limelight* involved a patented content delivery service by which a service provider improves delivery of a customer's webpage to a client Web browser by maintaining some of the webpage content on a network of "ghost" servers. When the client requests the customer's webpage, the webpage directs the client to retrieve the content from one of the ghost servers, rather than from the customer's webpage server. However, the customer must "tag," on its webpage, the portions of the webpage content to be delivered in this way, so that webpage can redirect requests for that content to a ghost server. Claim 34 is paraphrased below, along with an indication of which actor performs each step:

- **distributing** a set of page content across a network of ghost servers (performed by the content delivery service);
- **tagging**, on a customer's webpage, page content to be delivered by the ghost servers (performed by the customer);
- **sending**, to a client in response to a request for the tagged content, an IP address of the ghost server from which the client may retrieve the content (performed by the customer via the customer's webpage).

Akamai accused Limelight of infringing the patent by providing such a content delivery service. The problem, as Akamai found out, is that no single actor performs all of the steps, since Limelight performs the "distributing" step, but Limelight's customers perform the remaining steps. This left Akamai with a very difficult case of "divided infringement."

The claim might have been improved by focusing the action on the customer. For example, remove the "distributing" step and rework the claim so that all steps are performed by the customer:

34. *A content delivery method, comprising:*
    a. *tagging, on a customer's webpage, page content to be delivered by a ghost server;*
    b. *sending, to a ghost server having an IP address, the set of page content that has been tagged;*
    c. *receiving, at the customer's webpage, a request from a client for the page content;*
    d. *sending, to the client in response to the request for the page content, the IP address of the ghost server from which the client may retrieve the page content.*

Better yet, focus the claim entirely on the service provider, since it may be more efficient to sue the service provider than its customers:

34. *A content delivery method, comprising:*
    e. *receiving, from a customer, a set of page content that has been tagged on a customer webpage;*
    f. *storing the set of page content on a ghost server, the ghost server having an IP address;*
    g. *providing, to the customer webpage, the IP address of the ghost server; and after the customer webpage provides the IP address to a client web browser;*
    h. *delivering, from the ghost server to the client web browser, the set of page content in response to a request sent to the IP address from the client Web browser.*

Even better, include both such claims in your patent application, to cover the actions of the content service provider, as well as the actions of its customer.

Note: In 2015, the Court of Appeals for the Federal Circuit held that a claim can be infringed by an entity (i) if the entity directs or controls the actions of other actors, (ii) where the entity and one or more other actors form a joint enterprise, or (iii) if the entity "conditions participation in an activity or receipt of a benefit upon performance of a step or steps of a patented method and establishes the manner or timing of that performance." Limelight has appealed that ruling to the Supreme Court. Stay tuned.

broad that it lacks novelty or unobviousness. Thus, when you eliminate as many elements as possible, and when you broaden the remaining elements in the manner just described, keep in mind that you must leave enough structure or acts to define your invention in a novel manner over the prior art so that the novelty is unobvious.

Put differently, writing claims is like walking on a fence: You can't sway too far on the side of specificity or you'll fall onto the side of worthlessness and you can't sway too far onto the side of breadth or you'll fall onto the prior art. To obtain the broadest possible coverage, you should not draft your main claim primarily to cover your invention; rather draft it as broadly as possible with at least some thought of clearing the prior art, then go back and make sure that it at least covers your invention.

Some patent attorneys compare the writing of their first claim to passing through a wall of fire. However, we have found that if we follow the above four steps—(1) write a preamble, (2) recite the elements, (3) interconnect them, and (4) broaden the claims—the going is relatively painless. In case of doubt, err on the side of breadth at this stage, since you can always narrow your claims later, but you may not be able to make them broader if the application's allowed on the first Office Action.

I. Other Techniques in Claim Writing

Now that you understand the basics, here are some other tricks you may want to use when writing your claims. Obviously, not all apply all of the time, but you will probably find that at least several can be used to improve your claim writing.

- **Weasel Words.** Use "weasel" words like "substantially," "about," or "approximately" whenever possible—that is, whenever you specify a dimension or any other specific parameter—to avoid limiting your claim to the specific dimension specified. The renowned judge, Learned Hand, who wrote many famous patent decisions, once opined that judges should read the modifier "substantially" into every claim, even if it's not already cited. However, we strongly recommend that you don't rely on a judge

to broaden your claim for you, but rather do it yourself when you first write the claim.

- **Antecedents.** Provide a proper antecedent in the beginning of your claim for every term you use in the latter part of the claim. For example, in Claim 11 in the preceding part, the clause "the underside of said sheet" near the end of the claim has no clear antecedent in the beginning of the claim and thus might be objected to by some examiners. The claim would be better if clause a were amended by adding, "said sheet having an underside" to provide unequivocal support for the underside phase later. Conversely, if you recite an element and recite the same element again, you must use the article "said" (some attorneys now use "the") before the second occurrence. If you want to recite two similar elements in different parts of the claim, you should use the article "a" or "an" to introduce both elements, but you must use different adjectives to clearly differentiate the levers—for example, "a *prying lever* connected to…; and a *force-transmitting* lever positioned on…."

- **"Whereby" Clause.** At the end of your claim, we recommend adding a "whereby" clause to specify the advantage or use of the invention to hammer home to the examiner, or anyone else who reads your claim, the value of your invention. Thus in Claim 11, above, you should add at the end of this claim, "whereby a human can work, eat, and write in a convenient seated position." "Whereby" clauses don't help to define over the prior art, but they do force the examiner to consider the advantages (Section 103 features) of your invention and thus help to get the claims allowed. However, don't make the whereby clause too narrow or a court may construe it against you.

- **Reference Numbers.** You may put the drawing's reference numerals in your claims after the appropriate elements. Although this is required in some foreign jurisdictions, practitioners in the U.S. seldom do it unless the elements of the claim aren't clear. Including reference numbers in your draft claims, but removing them before filing the application, is a good way to test whether your drawings show all of the claim elements.

- **Recesses.** If your invention has an opening, hole, or recess in its structure, you may, as stated, recite the hole directly as such, even though it isn't tangible. For example, the recitation "said member having a hole near its upper end" is permissible. (See Appendix 3 (Glossary of Useful Technical Terms) for a list of recesses.)

- *Jepson* **Claims.** With regard to the rarely enforced Rule 75(e) (quoted in Section B2, above) requiring the use of the *Jepson* style (a preamble containing old elements and body of claims containing improvements of your invention), most patent attorneys recommend that claims not be cast in this style unless the examiner requests it or unless the examiner is having trouble understanding exactly what your inventive contribution is. The reason for this is that a *Jepson* claim isolates and hence minimizes your improvement, making it easier to invalidate. If you do claim in the *Jepson* format, draft your preamble so that it includes all the elements or steps and their interconnections that are already known from the prior art; then add a "cleavage" clause such as "the improvement comprising" or "characterized in that"; and then recite the elements of your invention and their interconnections.

- **Predetermined.** Examiners prefer the word "predetermined." We recommend you use it whenever possible to indicate that something has a size, thickness, length, quality, etc., without limiting the claim to any specific dimension or quality. For example, "said member having a predetermined cross-sectional shape" and "said valve arranged to open when a predetermined gas pressure is developed."

- **Consisting versus Comprising.** A claim that recites a group of elements can be made "open" or "closed." An open claim (the normal case) will cover more elements than it recites, whereas a closed claim is limited to and will cover only the elements it specifically recites. To make a claim open, use "includes" or "comprising"—for example, "said machine *comprising* A, B, and C."

In this case, a machine with four elements A, B, C, and D will infringe. To make a claim closed (rarely done), use "consist" or "having only"—for example, "Said machine *consisting* of A, B, and C." In this case, a machine with elements A, B, C, and D will not infringe, since, in patent law, the word "consist" is interpreted to mean "having only the following elements."

- **A Plurality Of.** Also, whenever you recite several units of anything, preface your recitation with "a plurality of"—such as, "a plurality of holes in said hose."

- **Less Is More.** Remember that, because of the Boolean "less is more" rule in interpreting claims, it's not necessary to recite a specific feature in your main claim in order to cover that feature in combination with the other elements of your invention. For example, once we drafted a claim for a client where one embodiment of her invention had a fingerlike support. Not seeing the finger in the main claim, she asked me, "Did you claim the finger?" We then explained to her that since the main claim didn't recite the finger, the main claim was broad enough to cover her invention with or without the finger.

- **Is It Sketchable?** After drafting your claim, you or a friend should be able to make enough sense out of it to sketch your invention. If this isn't possible, the claim is unclear and needs to be reworked.

- **Special Terms.** You can use any technical or descriptive terms that you feel are reasonably necessary to define or describe your invention— the claim does not have to be limited to any special "legalese." One patent attorney we know had a devil of a time defining (to the satisfaction of the examiner) a convex transistor structure with a nubbin on top until he simply called it "mammary-shaped."

- **Method Claim.** If possible, provide a method claim to cover your invention; you usually can do this if there's any dynamic operation involved in the invention. Most machines and electrical circuits can be claimed in terms of a method. Method claims are usually broader than apparatus claims, since they're not limited to any specific hardware.

- **Gerunds in Method Claims.** Each substantive clause of a method claim must usually start with an "—ing" or gerund word, such as "attaching," "heating," "abrading," etc. If you want to recite some hardware in a method claim, use "providing"—such as, "providing a central processor." (Don't say "comprising the steps of" in a method claim since claims that recite "step" may tend to be interpreted less broadly.)

- **Label Means.** If you do recite any "means," it's desirable to label the means with a nonfunctional adjective in order to provide a mnemonic aid in case you need to refer to the means later. For example, "first means," "second means," etc. Also, the "means" must be followed by or be modified by a function or some structure. For example, "first means for printing" (means plus function); "second means comprising a doctor blade" (means plus structure).

- **Padding.** Lastly, many patent attorneys recommend that a claim not be too short. A claim that is short will be viewed adversely (as possibly overly broad) by many examiners, regardless of how much substance it contains. Thus, many patent attorneys like

---

Patent Attorney Words

If you get stuck and don't know how to phrase something, usually one of the "patent attorney words" below will help.

a (used to introduce a part)

about (used to fudge a specific quantity)

at least (used to hammer home that more elements can be used)

contiguous (used to indicate elements are touching)

device for (interpreted like "means for")

disposed (used to indicate a part is positioned in a particular place)

further comprising (used in dependent claims to add additional parts)

further including (used in dependent claims to add additional parts)

heretofore (used to refer back to something previously recited)

indicium (used to recite something that a human can recognize, such as a mark or a sound)

means for (used to claim something broadly, in terms of its function, rather than specific hardware)

member (used to recite a mechanical part when no other word is available)

multitude (used to recite a large, indefinite number)

perimeter (perimetric, perimetrical, perimetrically—refers to a border around something)

pivotally (used to indicate that a part is rotatably mounted)

plurality (used to introduce more than one of an element)

predetermined (used to state that a part has a specific parameter)

providing (used to recite a part in a method claim)

releasably (indicates something can be released from a position)

respectively (used to relate several parts to several other parts in an individual manner)

said (used to refer to a previously recited part by exactly the same word)

sandwiching (used to indicate that one part is between two other parts)

selected from the group consisting of (used in a *Markush* claim to create an artificial group)

slidably (used to indicate that two parts slide with respect to each other)

so that (used to restrict a part to a defined function)

substantially (used to fudge a specific recitation)

such that (used to restrict a part to a defined function)

surrounding (used to indicate that a part is surrounded)

the (used to refer to a previously recited part by a slightly different word)

thereby (used to specify a result or connection between an element and what it does)

thereof (used as a pronoun to avoid repeating a part name)

urging (used to indicate that force is exacted upon a part)

whereby (used to introduce a function or result at the end of a claim)

wherein (used in a dependent claim to recite an element (part) more specifically)

(For names of components, see Glossary of Useful Technical Terms in Appendix 3.)

to "pad" short claims by adding "whereby" clauses, providing long preambles, adding long functional descriptions to their means clauses, etc. The trick here, of course, is to pad the claim while avoiding a charge of undue prolixity under Section 112, and without adding unnecessary limitations.

You'll find that a well-written claim is like a well-written poem. Each has a beautiful symmetry, order, and logic.

J. Drafting Dependent Claims

In Section H, we pointed out that there are two basic types of claims—independent claims (these stand on their own) and dependent claims (these incorporate an entire preceding claim, which can be an independent or dependent claim). A dependent claim is simply a shorthand way of writing a narrower claim—that is, a claim that includes all the elements of a preceding claim, and/or recites one or more additional elements or recites one or more elements of the preceding claim more specifically.

1. Reasons for Writing Dependent Claims

If an independent claim is broader, you may wonder why you need dependent (narrower) claims—especially since the independent claim must be infringed if its dependent claim is infringed. Below are eight good answers to that question:

1. **Backup.** Dependent claims are by definition always narrower than the claims on which they depend. You may accordingly be wondering, "If my broad independent claim covers my invention, why do I need any more claims of narrower scope?" True, if all goes well, your broad claim will be all you'll need. However, suppose you sue an infringer who finds an appropriate prior-art reference that neither you nor the PTO examiner found and that adversely affects the validity of ("knocks out") your broad claim. If you've written a narrower claim you can then disclaim the broad claim and fall back on the narrower claim. If the narrower claim is patentable over the prior art, your patent will still prevail. Thus the dependent claims are

insurance in case of broad claim invalidity. Each claim, whether independent or dependent, is interpreted independently for examination and infringement purposes. If the claim is dependent, it's interpreted as if it included all the wording of its parent (incorporated) claim or claims, even if the incorporated claim is held invalid. Dependent claims are crucial in order to recite all of the significant subsidiary elements of your invention. A feature that doesn't seem significant now can prove to be crucial later. One inventor we know (Morrie) submitted a large set of dependent claims to recite every less-important feature of his invention that he could think of, including one that recited that a certain flap was bendable. He got a patent and was involved in a licensing negotiation where the infringer found an earlier patent that showed his complete invention, except for the bendable flap. While the earlier patent invalidated most of Morrie's claims, fortunately he was able to rely on the still-valid dependent claims that recited the bendable flap to conclude a licensing deal, albeit at a lower rate than he originally wanted.

2. **Reification and Differentiation of Broad Claims.** Dependent claims are useful to explain, reify (make real), and differentiate (broaden) some of the broad, abstract terms in your independent claims. For instance, if you recite in a claim "additive means," many judges may not be able to understand what the "additive means" actually covers, but if you add several dependent claims that state, respectively, that the additive means is benzene and toluene, they'll get a very good idea of what types of substances the "additive means" embraces. If your main claim recites a new parlor game, adding a dependent claim that recites that the game is simulated on a computer will make it clear that the main claim covers more than computer simulations, that is, it covers board versions too. (Don't forget to show the computer version in your drawings and discuss it in your specification.) This independent-claim broadening function of dependent claims is called "differentiation" and is most effective if you recite just one element in the dependent claim.

3. **Provide Spectrum of Coverage.** Narrower claims can be used to provide a range, spectrum, or menu of proposed coverage from very broad to very narrow so that your examiner can, by allowing some narrower claims and rejecting the broader ones, indicate the scope of coverage the examiner's willing to allow.

4. **Prevent Premature Final Action.** Providing dependent claims of varying scope and approaches forces the examiner to make a wider search of your invention on the first examination. This will prevent the examiner from citing new prior art against your application on the second Office Action, which usually must be made "final." Thus, you should include every possibly novel feature (or novel combination of features) of your invention in your dependent claims.

5. **Provide Broader Base for Infringement Damages.** By providing dependent claims that add more elements, you define your invention (in these claims) as a more comprehensive structure, thereby providing a broader base upon which a judge can calculate infringement damages.

6. **Provide a Specific, Descriptive Recitation.** This reason is slightly different than Item 2 above. If the recitation in the independent claim is broad and abstract, such as, "urging means for …," we strongly recommend that you provide dependent claims with a descriptive, definite recitation (for example, "wherein said urging means is a coil spring") to hit the nail on the head, or provide a specific hardware recitation so a judge won't have to use his or her imagination.

7. **Preserve Right to Rely Upon Doctrine of Equivalents.** Traditionally patent owners have been able to rely on a "Doctrine of Equivalents" (DoE) to effectively expand a claim beyond its literal wording if it didn't cover an infringing device. However, the U.S. Supreme Court in *Festo v. Shoketsu* (122 S.Ct. 1831 (2002)), held that a patentee who amended (narrowed) a claim when it was before the PTO may no longer be able to rely on the DoE. To preserve your right to rely

on the DoE, draft as many dependent claims as possible to cover all aspects of your invention. In this way you'll have some claims that won't have to be amended (narrowed) if the PTO cites relevant prior art against these claims, and thus you'll preserve your right to use the DoE to expand these claims if necessary.

8. **Litigators Prefer Them.** Litigators prefer narrower and more specific claims (provided they cover the infringing device) because they provide a broader base for infringement damages and are more difficult to invalidate since they read on less prior art. Furthermore, it's easier for a litigator to prove infringement since the claim is less abstract and recited the specific structure that is infringed.

2. The Drafting

For the reasons above, when you're satisfied with your first, basic, and broadest independent claim, you should write as many dependent claims as you can think of, keeping in mind that the PTO charges extra if the total number of claims exceeds 20. Each dependent claim should begin by referring to your basic claim, or a previous dependent claim, using its exact title.

EXAMPLE:

Independent claim:

1. *A cellular telephone having a hinged body and a coiled antenna.*

Improper dependent claim:

2. *The hinged body of claim 1 wherein said hinge has five knuckles.* [The preamble or beginning of the claim does not correspond with claim 1 and there's no antecedent for "said hinge."]

Proper dependent claim:

2. *The cellular telephone of claim 1 wherein said hinged body includes a hinge with five knuckles.*

If the dependent claim recites one or more elements of the independent claim more narrowly, it should use the word "wherein"—for example, "The bicycle of Claim 1 wherein"—and then continue by reciting one or more elements of the independent claim.

Note that a dependent claim does not narrow the scope of any previous claim from which it depends; it merely provides an alternative, narrower recitation in a shorthand manner.

If the dependent claim recites additional elements, it should use the words, "further including" or "further comprising"—for example, "The bicycle of Claim 1, further including ..."—then continue by reciting the additional feature(s) of your invention. The additional features can be those you eliminated in broadening your basic claims and all other subsidiary features, including all combinations and permutations of such features of your invention you can think of. The features recited more narrowly or the additional elements recited by the dependent claims can be specific parameters (such as materials and temperatures) or other specifics of your invention (such as specific shapes, additional elements, or specific modes of operation). Refer to your prior art patents for guidance on how to draft these.

Note that a dependent claim must either recite the elements of its parent claim more specifically, or recite additional elements. It may not change any element to a different type or kind. Thus if the parent claim is an apparatus claim, each of its dependent claims must recite additional structure or recite some previously recited structure more specifically. For example, if your parent claim recites "1. A house made of red bricks," its dependent claim can say "2. The house of Claim 1 wherein said bricks are made of clay" (recites bricks more specifically) or "2. The house of Claim 1, further including a layer of paint over said bricks" (recites additional structure). The dependent claim can't say "2. The house of Claim 1 wherein said bricks are yellow." A method claim may not be made dependent upon an apparatus claim and vice versa, but most examiners will allow an apparatus claim that is dependent upon a method claim.

If the parent claim is a method claim, each of its dependent claims must recite an additional step, or recite a previously recited step (or structure in such a step) more specifically. For example, suppose your parent, independent claim recites:

> *1. A method of heating comprising irradiating a foodstuff in a chamber with microwaves.*

You can provide a dependent claim that recites one element of claim 1 (the microwaves) more specifically as follows:

> *2. The method of Claim 1 wherein said microwaves have a frequency of 2250 megahertz.*

Alternatively (or in addition), you can provide a dependent claim that recites an additional step as follows:

> *2A. The method of Claim 1, further including freezing said foodstuff after it is irradiated.*

Or as another alternative (or in addition), you can combine both dependent claims to provide a narrower dependent claim as follows:

> *2B. The method of claim 1 wherein said microwaves have a frequency of 2250 megahertz and further including freezing said foodstuff after it is irradiated.*

You can see that many variations and permutations are possible. Although we used letter suffixes to distinguish the above claims, you must use numbers for each set of your claims (an independent and its dependents). An independent apparatus claim (means or structural) requires that you recite a part or a series of parts. In a claim that is dependent upon an apparatus claim you must recite an additional part or modify a previously recited part. In an independent method claim you must recite a step or a series of steps. In a claim that is dependent upon a method claim you must recite an additional step or modify a previously recited step or part.

Here are some dependent claims for Claim 11 (set out in Section H, above). Note that each dependent claim either recites an additional element or recites an already recited element more specifically.

> *11. An article of furniture (etc.).*
>> *12. The article of furniture of Claim 11 wherein said sheet of rigid material is made of wood.*
>>> *13. The article of furniture of Claim 12 wherein said sheet of rigid material of wood is made of chipboard.*

14. The article of furniture of Claim 13 wherein said sheet of chipboard has a rectangular shape.

15. The article of furniture of Claim 11 wherein said means for joining comprises a set of flanges, each of which joins a respective one of said support members to the underside of said sheet of rigid material.

16. The article of furniture of Claim 15 wherein each of said flanges is made of iron and includes a cylinder with female threads and wherein one end of each of said elongated members has male threads and is threadedly mated with the female threads of a respective one of said flanges.

17. The article of furniture of Claim 11, further including a layer of a rigid plastic laminate bonded to a top side of said sheet of rigid material.

Note that a dependent claim may be dependent upon the parent claim or another dependent claim. We advise making almost all dependent claims directly dependent upon an independent claim, (rather than another dependent claim), since this will make the dependent claims broader: a dependent claim that depends from another dependent claim incorporates the other dependent claim and the independent claim from which the other dependent claim depends. A dependent claim should be numbered as closely as possible to the number of its parent claim (independent or dependent). Note also how we've made a physical indication of claim dependency by indenting (nesting) each dependent claim under its parent claim(s) as shown above. This is optional, but makes things clearer for you and the examiner. Also, you should always skip a line between claims (we didn't do it here in order to conserve space).

A dependent claim will be read and interpreted by examiners and judges as if it incorporated all the limitations of its parent claim(s). Thus suppose your independent and dependent claims read, respectively, as follows:

18. A rifle having an upwardly curved barrel.

19. The rifle of Claim 18 wherein said barrel is made of austenitic steel.

The dependent claim (19) will be treated independently, but with Claim 18 incorporated, so that it effectively reads as follows:

19. A rifle having an upwardly curved barrel, said barrel being made of austenitic steel.

Multiple Dependent Claims

A dependent claim may be made directly dependent upon several previous claims. This is called "multiple dependent claiming" (MDC) and is common in Europe. Example: "3. The widget of claims 1 or 2 wherein …". However we recommend that you do not use MDC since the PTO's examiners dislike the practice, there's a stiff surcharge for the privilege, and for fee purposes each MDC counts as the number of claims to which it refers.

💡 TIP

Use Only Significant Limitations. You can make your dependent claims as specific as you want, even to reciting the dimensions of the tabletop, its color, etc. However, extremely specific limitations like this, while possibly defining an invention that is novel over the prior art (Section 102), do not recite unobvious subject matter (Section 103), so they'll be of little use to fall back on if you lose your independent claim. Thus, you should mainly try to use *significant* limitations in your dependent claims—that is, limitations that an infringer might use if he or she made your invention.

You should draft dependent claims to cover all possible permutations of the subsidiary features of your invention. For example, suppose you've invented a telephone and some of the dependent features are that it has (a) a musical ringer, (b) a coiled cord, and (c) a stand. You can provide three dependent claims with features a, b, and c, respectively. Then write four more dependent claims with features a and b, a and c, b and c, and a, b, and c, if you think these combinations are feasible.

Although most of your dependent claims should have just a single element (to obtain maximum claim differentiation), you should try to draft at least one dependent claim with as many parts as possible so as to provide as broad a base as possible for maximizing infringement damages. Also try, insofar as possible, to draft at least one claim to cover parts of the invention whose infringement would be publicly verifiable, rather than a nonverifiable factory process or machine.

As with independent claims, you should not make your dependent claims purely "functional"—that is, each dependent claim should contain enough physical structure to support its operational or functional language. Here are some examples.

Wrong:

17. *The bicycle of Claim 16 wherein said derailleur operates with continuously variable speed-to-power ratios.* [This claim has no structure to support its operational limitation.]

Right:

17. *The bicycle of Claim 16 wherein said derailleur contains means for causing it to operate with continuously variable speed-to-power ratios.* [The "means" limitation is a recitation of structure that supports the operational limitation.]

Right:

17. *The bicycle of Claim 16 wherein said derailleur contains a cone-shaped pulley and a belt pusher for causing it to operate with continuously variable speed-to-power ratios.* [The pulley and pusher constitute structure that supports the operational limitation.]

If your independent claim recites a means plus a function, your dependent claim should modify the means and not the function. For example, assume an independent Claim 20 recites, "variable means for causing said transmission to have a continuously variable gear ratio." Here are the right and wrong ways to further limit this "means" in a dependent claim.

Claims of Different Scope

The concept of claims of different scope (independent and dependent) is confusing to most inventors. Here's another way of explaining it, if you still don't understand.

An *independent claim* (IC) is one that *doesn't* refer back to any previous claim. For example, "*1. A telephone comprising (a) a base, (b) a handset, and (c) a rotary dial,*" is an example of an IC.

To write another independent claim like Claim 1 (C1), but that is narrower than C1 by reciting a base of black plastic, simply repeat all of Claim 1 and add that the base is black plastic. For example, "*2. A telephone comprising (a) a base of black plastic, (b) a handset, and (c) a rotary dial,*" is an example of a second IC that is narrower than C1.

However, there's an easier, shorter, and cheaper way to avoid repeating all of C1 each time: Simply write a claim that refers to the IC 1 so as to incorporate all of it by reference, and then state one or more additional elements, and/or recite one or more elements of the incorporated claim more specifically. Such a shorthand claim is called a *dependent claim* (DC). A DC is thus one that refers back to and incorporates all of a preceding claim and adds or modifies one or more limitations to recite the invention more narrowly. For example, "*2′. The telephone of Claim 1 wherein said base is made of black plastic,*" is a dependent claim that has the same scope as C2. C2′ will be interpreted as if it included *all* of the subject matter of C1, *together with the additional subject matter in C2′.*

It follows that to infringe a DC, a device must have all of the elements of the DC, *plus all of the elements of the incorporated claim.*

Thus, adding a DC to recite a specific feature of your invention won't broaden or narrow your coverage; it will just provide another, yet more precise, missile. The eight reasons for including DCs are in Section J.

Also note that a DC can refer back to a preceding claim, and the preceding claim can in turn refer back to a further preceding claim. To infringe such a *third-level DC*, the device must have all of the elements of *all three claims* in the chain.

Wrong:

> 21. *The transmission of Claim 20 wherein said continuously variable gear ratio ranges from 5 to 10.*

Right:

> 21. *The transmission of Claim 20 wherein said variable means is arranged to provide ratios from 5 to 10.*

Common Misconception: If a dependent claim recites a specific feature of your invention, say a two-inch nylon gear, your invention will be limited to this gear, so that if any copy of the invention uses a one-inch gear, or a steel gear, it won't infringe on your patent.

Fact: Although the copy won't infringe the dependent claim, it will infringe the independent claim so long as it isn't limited to this specific feature. And as long as even one claim of a patent is infringed, the patent is infringed and you can recover as much damages (money) as if 50 claims were infringed.

Common Misconception: If a dependent claim recites a feature or element of the invention, it will protect this feature per se.

Fact: A dependent claim must be read to include all of the features of its referent claim (preceding or independent claim to which it refers). Thus it will not cover the feature it recites per se, but rather will cover that feature in combination with all of the elements of its referent claim.

Common Misconception: The limitations in a dependent claim will narrow its independent claim.

Fact: The independent claim is interpreted independently of its dependent claims and the latter never narrow the former although they can make the independent claim broader by claim differentiation.

If you still don't get the principle of broad and narrow claims, here are three simple claims that everyone can understand:

> *1. A house that has a sloping roof with a gable.*
> 2. *The house of Claim 1 wherein said gable has a dormer.*
> 3. *The house of Claim 2 wherein said dormer has eight panes of glass.*

Claim 1 is very broad: It will cover any house that has a sloping roof with a gable. Thus it may cover, say, 30 million houses in the United States. Claim 2 is of narrower scope because it incorporates all of Claim 1 and has additional verbiage (houses with sloping roofs that have a gable with a dormer), making it longer than Claim 1. Thus it will cover fewer houses, say, ten million in the U.S. Claim 3 is still longer and is far narrower than Claim 2 since it is limited to houses with sloping roofs that have a gable with a dormer with eight panes of glass. Thus it will cover fewer houses still, say one million houses in the United States.

Note that we made the number of the independent claim (#1) bold and we indented the dependent claims to indicate the dependency so that each dependent claim is nested under its referent claim. This is optional but desirable since it makes the claims clearer. As indicated above in Section G1, if you're working on a computer, use its "windows" function (if available) to keep your independent claim displayed while you write your dependent claims.

K. Drafting Additional Sets of Claims

After you've written your first independent claim (IC) and all the dependent claims you can reasonably think of (all numbered sequentially), consider writing another set of claims (an IC and a set of dependent claims) if you can think of a substantially different way to claim your invention. See the prior-art patents and the sample set of claims at the end of this chapter (Fig. 9A) for examples of different independent claims on the same invention. Your second set of dependent claims can be similar to your first set; a word processor with a block copy function will be of great aid here. Writing more sets of claims will not always give your invention broader coverage, but will provide alternative weapons to use against an infringer. That is, writing a second set of claims is like going into battle with a sword as well as a gun. Also, writing more sets of claims will give your examiner additional perspectives on your invention. That is, your chances of getting your examiner to bite will be increased if you present many flavors to choose from.

In the example above (Claim 11), you might start the second IC with the legs instead of the top and you might try to define the top and legs differently—for example, instead of "elongated members," you might call the legs "independent support means." Instead of calling the top a "sheet of rigid material," you might call it a "planar member having paralleled, opposed major faces."

Here are still other ways to write a different IC: (1) Rewrite one of the dependent claims from your first set in independent form; (2) wait a few days and write an IC again, with independent thought; (3) write the IC by reciting the elements of the first IC in reverse or inverse order; and (4) if your first IC has any "means" clauses, make your next IC a structure (apparatus) claim (no means clauses), or vice versa; (5) if your invention uses any unique supplies, blanks, or starting elements, or accessories, it is wise to provide claims to these also. For example, if you've invented a unique paper cup that is made from a unique starting blank, provide independent claims to both the cup and the blank.

Another valuable way to write a different IC is to provide a method (process) claim if your first IC is an apparatus claim, or vice versa; you're usually allowed to have both method and apparatus claims in the same case. You should always include an independent method claim if possible, since a method claim is usually not limited to specific hardware and thus affords broader coverage. Every step of each independent method claim must be an action step, for instance, "providing…." or "heating…." If your invention is a product and the process of making it is novel, or if it uses an intermediate construction in the process, you should claim the process and the intermediate construction.

Another valuable way to write a different IC occurs if your invention involves software: add a claim to cover any manufacture or machine that might contain your software. This can include a computer memory, a hard drive, a CD-ROM, a DVD, or any other medium. Such a claim gives you offensive rights against those who would distribute your software without permission, and you probably would rather assert your rights against an illegal distributor with deep pockets than against your own software users.

A software medium claim might begin as follows:

A tangible, computer-readable medium in which is non-transitorily stored computer program code that, when executed by a computer processor, causes performance of a method for …, the method comprising: …

This phrasing offers the advantage that you can simply copy your method claims, both independent and dependent, after this preamble, and you will only have to renumber the dependent claims and change their preambles to read "The medium of claim X" rather than "The method of claim X." (The "tangible" and "non-transitory" limitations ensure that the claim does not run afoul of any judicial exceptions to patentable subject matter, such as transitory electrical signals, which are unpatentable.)

Note that each independent claim must stand by itself: It may not refer to, incorporate, be based in any way on, or use referents from any previous claim. Even if claim 1 recites "a first lever" you may not recite, in a second independent claim, say claim 10, "a second lever" unless a first lever has already been recited earlier in claim 10. Similarly even if claim 1 recites "a wheel," claim 10 may not recite "said wheel" unless "a wheel" has been recited earlier in claim 10. The basic filing fee entitles you to up to three ICs and 20 total claims. We generally try to use up my allotment by writing three ICs and three sets of five to seven dependent claims each. However, if we feel that we can write a fourth, substantially different IC and the cost can be borne by my client, we will add it, plus more dependent claims. The PTO now charges a substantial additional fee for each IC over three, and for each claim (independent or dependent) over 20.

On the other hand, for relatively simple inventions, we may not be able to think of any substantially different ways to write an IC, so we may submit only one, plus a few dependent claims. We advise you generally not to submit more than the number of claims permitted for your basic filing fee—that is, three ICs and 20 total claims—unless the complexity of your invention justifies it, or you have some other good reason. Don't make your case like one published application (U.S. Pub. Pat. Appn. 20030100451): It has 7,215 claims!

L. Checklist for Drafting Claims

Below is the second part of the application checklist that we started in Chapter 8.

M. Summary

Claims define the invention in logical and precise terms. They are sentence fragments beginning with the words "I claim" and are provided at the end of a patent application.

The patent statute and rules regarding claims require that they (a) be clear and unambiguous, (b) be independent or dependent, (c) must use terms from the specification, and (d) should be phrased in a two-part form (prior art plus improvement). Claims can also have elements expressed in "means-plus-function" form.

Every claim should be classifiable into one of the five statutory classes of invention: machine, article, composition, process (method), or new use. Software or business claims are usually process claims, but can be machine claims. The number of claims is not as important as their breadth and the specific features of the invention need not be recited in a claim to be covered.

For a device to infringe a claim, it must meet all of the elements of the claim. Claims can be made broader by eliminating elements or broadening existing elements, but each claim should define a novel and unobvious invention over the prior art. When an element is first introduced in a claim, the article "a" should be used, but when the element is referred to again the article "the" or "said" should be used.

A "means clause" in a claim covers the hardware in the specification and its equivalents. A patent application should have means, nonmeans (apparatus), and method independent claims, if possible.

Each independent claim should be followed by a set of dependent claims. Each dependent claim must recite additional element(s) or recite the existing elements more narrowly (specifically). Claims must be logical, complete, unambiguous, and every element in every claim must be shown in the drawings. All method claims must (1) be tied in a substantial way to a particular machine or apparatus, or (2) recite the transformation of an article into a different state or thing.

Checklist for Draft Claims

☐ Grammatical articles are used properly in the claims: "a" or "an" to introduce any singular part, "the" to refer to a part a second time when using a different (but clearly implied) term as before, and "said" only to refer to a part using the IDENTICAL term as before.

☐ Two articles together, such as "the said," aren't used.

☐ Every part and feature in every claim is shown in the drawings and discussed in the specification.

☐ No claim uses any disjunctive ("or") expression (except to recite two equivalent parts or a disjunctive function of a machine).

☐ No claim uses any naked functional clause; all claims contain a structural recitation or "means" to support every functional recitation.

☐ A memory aid is recited adjacent each "means," for example, "first means"; also, each "means" is followed by "for ..." plus some function or structure.

☐ For each unique "means" followed by a function in the claims, the specification describes some hardware or an element which implements or provides the function for such means, using the same words as used in the claim to describe the function.

☐ "Consisting" isn't used in any claim (except if you want to say "having only").

☐ No claim uses any abbreviation, dash, parentheses, or quote.

☐ No term is used for the first time in any claim.

☐ The subparagraph form is used in long claims for ease of reading.

☐ Each claim has just one capital letter (two if "claim" is capitalized in a dependent claim) and one period (except lettered paragraphs), and no parentheses (except lettered paragraphs, quotes, or abbreviations).

☐ All significant parts are affirmatively recited in the claims as the subject and not the object of a clause.

☐ The main (independent) claim is made as broad as possible by reciting minimum number of elements and by general-izing existing elements (without reading on prior art).

☐ No vague, loose, or casual language is used in any claim.

☐ Space between adjacent claims is greater than space between adjacent lines of a claim.

☐ No dependent claim recites an additional function unless "means" or structure is specified to support such structure.

☐ All parts recited in claims are connected.

☐ All claims recite enough parts to provide a complete assemblage.

☐ You haven't submitted over 20 total or over three independent claims unless the case is very complex or extra claims are justified.

☐ No independent claim refers to any other claim and all dependent claims refer to a previous claim in line 1 or line 2.

☐ You've filed enough dependent claims to cover all features and permutations and you've filed second and third sets of claims (with differently phrased independent claims) if possible.

☐ You've included an independent method claim and a set of dependent method claims, if possible.

☐ Every dependent claim starts with either:
"The _____ of Claim x wherein ..." (to provide a separate recitation of an element(s) of the parent claim in a narrower fashion), or,
"The _____ of Claim x further including ..." (to provide a separate recitation of the element(s) of the parent claim, plus a recitation of one or more element(s)).

☐ No dependent claim is used to substitute a different part for any part recited in the parent claim. Each dependent claim recites an element(s) of the parent claim in a narrower fashion, and/or recites one or more element(s), in addition to those recited in the parent claim.

☐ No dependent claim recites a method limitation if its parent claim is an apparatus claim.

☐ In order to comply with the *Bilski* decision, all process claims recite a process centered on hardware—that is, the process either (1) is tied in a substantial way to a particular machine or apparatus, or (2) transforms an article into a different state or thing.

☐ The same element isn't recited more than once in any claim unless the second and later recitations use "said" before the element.

☐ You've included a set of claims (one independent and several dependent) with means plus function clauses and a set without means plus function clauses.

☐ Each independent claim has a set of several dependent claims to provide backup.

☐ Every possible novel or significant feature of the invention is recited in the claims to (hopefully) provide some claims that will not have to be canceled or narrowed.

☐ At least one dependent claim has as many elements or parts of the inventive apparatus as possible, providing a larger base for infringement claims and greater damages.

☐ Method limitations and apparatus limitations aren't used together in any single claim or in any *Markush* group.

start claims on new page

Patent Application of Lou W. Koppe for "Paper-Laminated
Pliable Closure for Flexible Bags" continued
Page 10

Printout should have
minimum 1.5 line
spacing (4 lines/inch)
but is shown with
denser spacing since
this example is shown
on a reduced scale.

**first
independent
claim**

**Number of each
independent
claim is bold**

CLAIMS: I claim:

1. In a bag closure of the type comprising a flat body of material having a lead-in notch on one edge thereof and a gripping aperture adjacent to and communicating with said notch, the improvement wherein said bag closure has a layer of paper laminated on one of its sides.

**Skip a line
between
claims—
omitted here to
conserve space.**

2. The bag closure of claim 1 wherein said body of material is composed of polyethyleneterephthalate.

3. The bag closure of claim 1 wherein said body is elongated and has a longitudinal groove which is on said one side of said body and extends the full length of said one side, from said gripping aperture to the opposite edge.

**optional indent
for dependent
claims**

4. The bag closure of claim 3 wherein said groove is formed into and along the full length of said lamination.

5. The bag closure of claim 1 wherein said body is elongated and has a longitudinal groove which is on the side of said body opposite to said one side thereof and extends the full length of said one side, from said gripping aperture to the opposite edge.

6. The bag closure of claim 1 wherein said body is elongated and has two longitudinal grooves which are on opposite sides of said body and extend the full lengths of said sides, from said gripping aperture to the opposite edge.

7. The bag closure of claim 6 wherein the groove on said one side of said body is formed into and along the full length of said lamination.

8. The bag closure of claim 1 wherein said body has a paper lamination on both of said sides.

9. The bag closure of claim 8 wherein a groove is on one side of said body and extends the full length of said one side, from said gripping aperture to the opposite edge.

10. The bag closure of claim 8 wherein two grooves, on opposite sides of said body, extend the full lengths of said sides, from said gripping aperture to the opposite edge.

Fig. 9A—Specification of Sample Patent Application

Patent Application of Lou W. Koppe for "Paper-Laminated
Pliable Closure for Flexible Bags" continued
Page 11

11. The bag closure of claim 10 wherein said grooves are rolled into and along the full lengths of said laminations, respectively.

12. The bag closure of claim 1 wherein said paper lamination is colored.

13. The bag closure of claim 1 wherein said body is elongated and has a longitudinal through-hole.

14. A bag closure of the type comprising a flat body of material having a lead-in notch on one edge thereof, a gripping aperture adjacent to and communicating with said notch, characterized in that one of its sides has a layer of paper laminated thereon.

15. The bag closure of claim 14 wherein said body of material is composed of polyethyleneterephthalate.

16. The bag closure of claim 14 wherein said body is elongated and has a longitudinal groove on said one side of said body and which extends the full length of said one side, from said gripping aperture to the opposite edge.

17. The bag closure of claim 14 wherein said body is elongated and has a longitudinal groove which is on the side of said body opposite to said one side thereof and extends the full length of said one side, from said gripping aperture to the opposite edge.

18. The bag closure of claim 14 wherein said body is elongated and has two longitudinal grooves which are on opposite sides of said body and extend the full lengths of said sides, from said gripping aperture to the opposite edge.

19. The bag closure of claim 14 wherein said body has a paper lamination on both of said sides.

20. The bag closure of claim 19 wherein a groove is on one side of said body and extends the full length of said one side, from said gripping aperture to the opposite edge.

21. The bag closure of claim 19 wherein two grooves, on opposite sides of said body, extend the full lengths of said sides, from said gripping aperture to the opposite edge.

Fig. 9A—Specification of Sample Patent Application (continued)

Patent Application of Lou W. Koppe for "Paper-Laminated
Pliable Closure for Flexible Bags" continued
Page 12

22. The bag closure of claim 14 wherein said paper lamination is colored.

23. The bag closure of claim 14 wherein said body is elongated and has a longitudinal through-hole.

24. A method of closing a plastic bag, comprising:

(a) providing a bag closure of the type comprising a flat body of material having a lead-in notch on one edge thereof, a gripping aperture adjacent to and communicating with said notch, and a layer of paper laminated on one of its sides,

(b) providing a plastic bag and inserting contents into said plastic bag,

(c) twisting said plastic bag so that it forms a neck portion to hold said contents from falling out of said plastic bag,

(d) inserting said bag closure onto said neck portion of said plastic bag so that said neck portion of said plastic bag passes said lead-in notch and into said gripping aperture,

   whereby said bag closure can be easily marked to identify and/or price said contents in said plastic bag.

25. The method of claim 24 wherein said flat body of material is composed of polyethyleneterephthalate.

26. The method of claim 24 wherein said layer of paper is colored.

Fig. 9A—Specification of Sample Patent Application (continued)

Finaling and Filing Your Application

Inventor's Commandment 16

Before signing any document, whether in the patent field or elsewhere, read it carefully and be sure that you understand and agree to it fully. After signing, obtain and be sure to save an identical copy of what you signed.

Inventor's Commandment 17

Avoid Fraud on the PTO: In addition to making a full disclosure of your invention in your patent application, promptly tell the PTO, in an Information Disclosure Statement, about any pertinent "prior art" or other material facts concerning your invention of which you are aware or of which you become aware.

Inventor's Commandment 18

Except for the actual application (which the PTO does not accept by fax), you can and should Web-file or fax all papers to the PTO to avoid loss in the mail. When you Web-file or fax to the PTO, be sure all blanks on all forms are completed, all forms and documents are signed, a Credit Card Payment Form is completed or included, if needed, all pages are present, and the document is timely sent. If you do mail any papers, follow the admonitions for Web-filing or faxing (you may mail a check or a credit card payment form) and always include a receipt postcard addressed to you with all of the paper(s) listed on the back of the card.

Inventor's Commandment 19

Orderly File: Prepare and maintain file folders for (1) Official Papers and (2) Correspondence. Include a copy of every paper you send to or receive from the PTO in the Official Papers file. Include a copy of every paper you send to or receive from anyone other than the PTO in the Correspondence file. Write the date received on every incoming paper, and date and make sure your name, signature, address, and phone number is on every outgoing paper.

Now that you've drafted your patent application, it's time to put it in final form. Since the PTO places great emphasis on thoroughness, this chapter is, accordingly, filled with many picky details. In the event you want to rebel and simply pass over those requirements that are inconvenient, remember that the PTO has many rules with which you must comply. In addition, your patent examiner has discretion to approve or reject your application. An application that fully meets the requirements and standards of the PTO will have much smoother sailing than one that doesn't. If you fail to comply with certain rules—for example, you forget to enclose a check—the PTO will impose substantial monetary penalties.

Fortunately, while you must pay attention to detail, meeting the PTO's requirements and standards is relatively easy if you've followed my suggestions in the previous chapters. Because you've reviewed a number of patents in the same field as your own, you'll be familiar with the standards for writing the specification and claims. Because you've prepared preliminary drawings in basic conformance with the rules for final drawings, putting them in final form will not involve great difficulty. Because you've analyzed all relevant prior art known to you and can distinguish it from your invention, you are in a good position to follow through with your application to a successful completion.

Electronic Filing Note: The PTO has an electronic filing system called EFS-Web that enables electronic patent application filing. Since 2011, the PTO has charged a $200 filing fee for utility application filings by a "small entity" unless the filing is made using EFS-Web. It may take you several extra hours to learn and use the EFS-Web system. You must prepare the application as if you were going to file by mail (except that you can eliminate a few forms), convert all papers into PDF files, and fill out various forms online. However, it may be worth your time to become a registered eFiler with the PTO, which will require additional work and red tape. Since you already have to do a lot of learning to file a patent application, the extra time to learn and use EFS-Web may discourage you. Nevertheless, because of the lower cost and numerous advantages of electronic filing, first-time filers will benefit from EFS-Web.

A. The Drawings

When you file your application, the PTO's Office of Patent Application Processing ("OPAP") will review your drawings to determine whether they are "readable and reproducible for publication purposes" (the PTO no longer classifies drawings as "formal" and "informal"). If your drawings are not acceptable, the OPAP will send you a Notice specifying the deficiencies and setting a deadline by which you must submit replacement drawings. If the OPAP accepts your drawings, your Examiner may still raise objections in an Office Action, and require that you submit replacement drawings with your response to the Office Action. You cannot put off responding to the requirement for replacement figures.

You should avoid these pitfalls if you prepare your drawings correctly in the first instance.

Drawings can be filed in either:

- the U.S. letter size (8½" x 11"), or
- the A4 international size (210 mm x 297 mm or 8¼" x 11^1/$_{16}$").

If you want to file abroad, you'll have to prepare formal drawings on A4 size paper approximately 11 months after filing.

As far as the choice of the U.S. or international sizes is concerned, if you have ink drawings and have any serious thoughts about filing abroad, it's better to use the international (A4) size, since you can make good photocopies, file these for your U.S. application, and later use the originals (or another good set of copies) for the international application. (We discuss foreign filing in Chapter 12.) If you do make paper drawings in the U.S. size and later decide to foreign file, you can still make A4 copies by using a scanner, photocopier, or a patent drawing service in the Arlington, or Alexandria, Virginia, area (about $20 a sheet).

If color is an essential part of the invention, color photos or color drawings may also be used. However, be aware that color drawings are not acceptable when filing an "international application" under the Patent Cooperation Treaty, or PCT. (More on the PCT in Chapter 12.) File three sets of color photos or drawings in one of the two permitted sizes with:

1. a petition explaining why color is necessary; use the format of the petition of Fig. 10U (Form 10-9 in Appendix 7) but change the title. For example, write "Petition Explaining Why Color Is Necessary" and change the body of the form to provide an explanation

2. the petition fee, and

3. a statement in the specification as the first paragraph of the brief description of the drawings reading as follows: "The patent or application contains at least one drawing executed in color. Copies of the patent or patent application publication with color drawing(s) will be provided by the Office upon request and payment of necessary fee."

If filing by EFS-Web, only one set of color photos or drawings is required. However, the set must be uploaded as file type "Drawings – other than black and white line drawings" with document code "DRW.NONBW."

Black and white photos may no longer be used for patent drawings, unless necessary to illustrate the invention, for example, to show a photomicrograph of a composite material. File one set of black and white photos in one of the two permitted sizes on double-weight photographic paper or mounted on Bristol board. You must also file a petition explaining why black and white photos are necessary. No fee is needed.

All photos must be of sufficient quality that all details can be reproduced in the printed patent and the photos must illustrate all features of the invention, just as ink or CAD drawings must do.

B. PTO Rules for Drawings

The PTO has a number of rules for preparing drawings. For step-by-step instructions and examples on how to implement these rules, see *How to Make Patent Drawings*, by Jack Lo and David Pressman (Nolo). When your drawings arrive at the PTO, whether with your application or after allowance, your drawings are inspected by the PTO's drawing inspectors. If they find that any of your drawings are informal or in violation of any of the above rules, they will fill out and insert

UNITED STATES PATENT AND TRADEMARK OFFICE

UNITED STATES DEPARTMENT OF COMMERCE
United States Patent and Trademark Office
Address: COMMISSIONER FOR PATENTS
P.O. Box 1450
Alexandria, Virginia 22313-1450
www.uspto.gov

APPLICATION NUMBER	FILING OR 371(C) DATE	FIRST NAMED APPLICANT	ATTY. DOCKET NO./TITLE
09/123,456	02/29/2010	Ann Inventor	7890/1001

CONFIRMATION NO. 2714

FORMALITIES LETTER

Ann Inventor
128 Innovation Road
Washington, MA 09999

Date Mailed:

03/19/2010

NOTICE TO FILE CORRECTED APPLICATION PAPERS

Filing Date Granted

An application number and filing date have been accorded to this application. The application is informal since it does not comply with the regulations for the reason(s) indicated below. Applicant is given TWO MONTHS from the date of this Notice within which to correct the informalities indicated below. Extensions of time may be obtained by filing a petition accompanied by the extension fee under the provisions of 37 CFR 1.136(a).

The required item(s) identified below must be timely submitted to avoid abandonment:

- Replacement drawings in compliance with 37 CFR 1.84 and 37 CFR 1.121(d) are required. The drawings submitted are not acceptable because:
    - Numbers, letters, and reference characters on the drawings must measure at least 0.32 cm (1/8 inch) in height. See Figure(s) all.

Applicant is cautioned that correction of the above items may cause the specification and drawings page count to exceed 100 pages. If the specification and drawings exceed 100 pages, applicant will need to submit the required application size fee.

Fig. 10A—Draftsperson's Drawing Objection Sheet

a drawing objection sheet in your file. A copy of this (shown in Fig. 10A) will be sent to you before or with your first Office Action or after allowance. The OPAP will require corrected drawings if: the lines are too light to be adequately reproduced; the drawings contain illegible text, excessive text, or text not in English; the drawings are missing a lead line between a reference number and the feature indicated by that reference number; the pages are not on the correct size of paper or have incorrect margins, have more than one figure and are not distinguished with proper labeling; include a photograph where another figure would suffice, or contain color drawings or photographs without the required petition.

Other frequently encountered defects are:

- Lines are pale.
- Paper is poor.
- Numerals are poor.
- Lines are rough, blurred, or matrixy (zig-zag).
- Copier marks are on the drawing.
- Shade lines are required.
- Figures must be numbered.
- Heading space is required.
- Figures must not be connected.
- Crisscross or double line-hatching is objectionable.
- Arrowheads are used on lead lines for individual parts.
- Parts in section must be hatched.
- Solid black is objectionable (in design patent applications).
- Figure legends are placed incorrectly (for example, inside figure or vertically when drawing is horizontal).
- Drawing has mounted photographs.
- Drawing contains extraneous matter.
- Paper is undersized or oversized.
- Margins are too small.
- Lettering is too small.
- The sheets contain wrinkles, tears, or folds.
- Both sides of the sheet are used.
- Sheets contain broken lines to illustrate regular parts of the invention.
- Sheets contain alterations, interlineations, or overwritings.
- Sheets contain unclear representations.
- Sheets contain figures on separate sheets that can't be assembled without concealing parts.
- Sheets contain reference numerals that aren't mentioned in the specification.
- Sheets contain the same reference numeral to designate different parts.
- Figures aren't separately numbered.

C. Doing Your Own Drawings

Many inventors choose to prepare their own patent applications instead of hiring a patent attorney or agent to do it for them. However, these same inventors frequently conclude that preparing the drawings is beyond their ability and turn the job over to a professional draftsperson. This can be costly. The typical draftsperson charges $75 to $150 per sheet of patent drawings (each sheet may contain several figures or separate drawings). Since most patent applications have between two to ten sheets of drawings, an inventor can sometimes pay up to $1,500 for drawings.

Fortunately, patent drawings, like the application itself, are frequently susceptible to a self-help approach. To be sure, you'll need to learn some PTO rules and a certain learning curve is involved. However, the result will not only save you a lot of money over many patent applications, but also:

- You will be able to prepare promotional brochures for marketing your invention to prospective manufacturers or customers.
- You will be able to render your invention more accurately than a hired professional, because you know your invention best. By doing your own drawings, you do not have to take the time to make someone else understand your invention, or have to send the drawings back and forth for corrections.
- You will have the satisfaction of properly completing the entire patent application by yourself—an impressive accomplishment for an inventor.

How to Make Patent Drawings, also published by Nolo, provides detailed guidance on making the drawings yourself. There are two methods for making patent drawings: pen and ruler, and computer-aided drafting (CAD). (You may not use photos unless necessary to illustrate an invention that involves fine details.)

You can file your application with either informal or formal drawings. If you are submitting "informal" drawings, the copies need not be perfectly clean and neat, but if you choose the formal route, the copies must be very clean and neat, and all lines must be sharp and black. You don't have to notify the PTO which type of drawing you're filing; they'll notify you if the drawings are inadequate. (The typed specification sheets must have different margins—see below.)

Even if you file informal drawings, you must include everything necessary in your drawings, since you won't be able to add any "new matter" (any new technical information that is not present in your original sketches) after you file. Be sure to study the drawings of the patents uncovered in your patentability search to get an idea of what's customarily done for your type of invention, and to better understand the PTO rules.

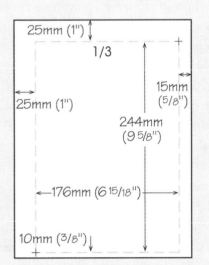

U.S. Letter Size
(8.5" x 11" or 216mm x 279mm)

Notes:

Metric-to-inch conversion numbers are not exact but are copied from Rule 84(f)&(g). In case of doubt, always use a wider margin (smaller sight).

Margin lines should not be used but are shown as broken lines to indicate the margin and "sight" sizes. Visible crosshairs (targets) should be put in either pair of opposite corners and should be about 1.5 cm (0.5") long. (The crosshairs are shown on these two sheets in the lower left and upper right corners.)

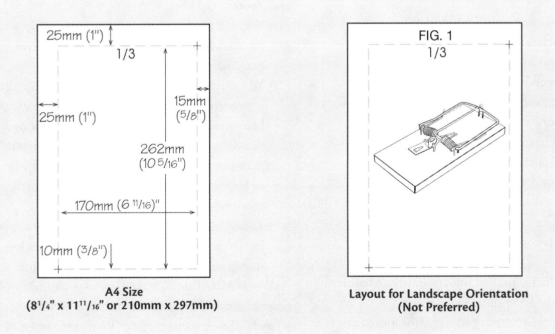

A4 Size
(8¼" x 11¹¹⁄₁₆" or 210mm x 297mm)

Layout for Landscape Orientation
(Not Preferred)

Fig. 10B—The Two Permitted Drawing Sizes

Summary of PTO Drawing Rules

The PTO's rules for drawings are found in rules 81 and 85 (37 CFR 1.81–1.85).

1. **Need for Drawings:** One or more drawings must be filed whenever necessary to understand the invention.

2. **Flowcharts:** Flowcharts should also be included whenever useful for an understanding of the invention.

3. **Must Show Features Claimed:** The drawings must show every feature recited in the claims.

4. **Conventional Features:** Conventional features that are not essential for an understanding of the invention, but are mentioned in the description and claims, can be shown by a graphical drawing symbol or a labeled rectangular box. For example, a motor can be shown by an encircled "M," and a CPU in a computer can be shown by a rectangle labeled "CPU."

5. **Improvements:** When your invention consists of an improvement in an old machine, the drawing should show the improved portion disconnected from the old structure with only so much of the old structure as is necessary to show how your improvement fits in. For example, if you've invented a new taillight for a bicycle, show the bicycle itself without the new taillight (without detail) in one figure labeled as "prior art." Then show just the portion of the bike where the taillight is mounted in detail in another figure, together with details of the mounting hardware.

6. **Paper:** The filed drawings (xerographic copies if filing in paper) should be on paper that is flexible, strong, white, smooth, nonshiny, and durable. Ordinary 20-pound bond is acceptable but a heavier weight paper is more desirable. You should do the originals on Mylar film, vellum, or hard, rather than soft, Bristol board; this is available in most good art supply stores. Strathmore Paper Co. makes excellent patent drawing boards in both U.S. and A4 sizes (about $1 per sheet), but you can get your sheets more economically by buying larger sheets of hard Bristol board and cutting them to the proper size. If you're using CAD but not filing by EFS-Web, do the originals on regular bond and, since additional originals are so easy to make, send the originals to the PTO. (Keep your disk copy and a backup of your drawing file!) If filing by EFS-Web and you've made the drawings on paper, scan the drawings to PDF. If you've made the drawings in the computer, convert the computer files to PDF directly and file the PDFs online, via EFS-Web.

7. **Lines:** The main requirement for all drawings is that all lines must be crisp and perfectly black. For paper copies, a good photocopy on good quality bond paper is usually used and the lines should be crisp and sharp. A good xerographic copy from a dark-penciled original will be accepted. Jagged slant lines from a dot matrix printer or bitmapped drawing program are forbidden for formal drawings. For EFS-Web filers, the same sharp, black lines are required on PDF versions.

Lines the PTO Recognizes on Drawings:

Normal Lines: Use a solid thin line (_____) to show regular parts and a thick solid line (▬▬▬) to show a shadowed edge—see Rule 14—or hatching a cross-section.

Hidden Lines: This is a dashed line (– – – –) to show a part behind another part—see Fig. 8C.

Projection Lines: This is composed of alternating long dashes and dots (— • — • —) and is used to connect exploded parts—see Fig. 8D.

Phantom Lines: Similar to a projection line, but that uses two dots instead of one (— • • — • •); this is used to show an alternate position of a movable part, or on an adjacent structure that is not part of the invention.

8. **White Pigment:** Some use of white pigment (for example, White Out™, Liquid Paper™) to cover lines is acceptable, provided all lines are sharp and black.

9. **Uniform Size:** All drawing sheets in an application must be exactly sized in the same U.S. letter or A4 size. Fig. 10B shows these two sizes.

10. **Invisible Margins:** The margins must not contain any lines or writing; all writing and lines must be in the remaining "sight" (drawing area) on the sheet. Margin border lines are forbidden, but crosshairs (about 1 cm long) should be drawn over two opposite (catercorner) margin corners.

11. **No Holes:** The drawing sheets should not contain any holes.

12. **Instrument Work:** All lines must be made with drafting tools or a CAD computer program. Copies made by a laser printer must be very dense, sharp, uniformly thick, and black. Fine or crowded lines must be avoided. Solid black areas are not permitted. Freehand work must be avoided unless unavoidable.

Summary of PTO Drawing Rules (continued)

13. **Hatching:** Parts in section must be filled with slanted parallel lines (hatching) that are spaced apart sufficiently so that they can be distinguished without difficulty.

14. **Shading:** Objects can be shaded with surface and edge shadings so that the light appears to come from the upper left at a 45-degree angle. Thus the shade sides of all objects (the right and bottom) should be done with heavier lines. Surface shading should be open. On perspective views, the closest edges should be made heavier. Edge and surface shading is mandatory in design patent applications, and optional in utility patents.

15. **Scale:** The scale should be large enough to show the mechanism without crowding when the drawing is reduced to two-thirds of its original size for reproduction. Detailed parts should be shown on a larger scale, and spread out over two or more sheets if necessary, to accomplish this, but the number of sheets should not be more than necessary.

16. **Figures:** The different views should be consecutively numbered figures, for example, "Fig. 1A," "Fig. 1B," "Fig. 2," etc. Each figure should be separate and unconnected with any other figure. If possible, you should number the figures consecutively on consecutive sheets. However, if you want to arrange the figures in nonconsecutive order to use space efficiently, that's okay, albeit less desirable.

17. **Reference Numerals and Lead Lines:** Numbers must be plain, legible, carefully formed, and not encircled. They should be at least ⅛" high (12-point font should suffice). When parts are complex, they should not be placed so close that comprehension suffers. They should not cross or mingle with other lines. When grouped around a part, they should be placed around the part and connected by lead lines to the elements to which they refer. They should not be placed on hatched or shaded surfaces unless absolutely necessary; if then, they should be underlined and placed in a blank space in the hatching or shading. (Numerals are preferred to letters.) Arrowheads should not be used on lead lines, but if a numeral refers to an entire assembly or group of connected elements, its lead line can have an arrowhead, or it can be underlined to distinguish it from the lead lines of numerals that refer to a single part.

18. **No Duplication of Reference Numerals:** The same part in different figures must always be designated by the same reference numeral. Conversely, the same reference numeral must never be used to designate different parts. Numbers with primes and letter suffixes are considered different numbers.

19. **Graphic Symbols:** These can be used for conventional parts, but must be defined in the specification. For instance, if you use an encircled "M" for a motor, the specification should say, for example, "A motor, represented in Fig. 2 by an encircled 'M.'" Conventional symbols, such as those approved by the IEEE, ASA, etc., or from any standards or symbols book, can be used. Arrows should be used to show direction of movement, where necessary.

20. **Descriptive Matter:** The rules state that descriptive matter on the drawings is not permitted. We vehemently oppose this rule, since the use of descriptive matter on drawings makes them far more meaningful, and since textbooks, magazine articles, etc., all use drawings with ample descriptive matter. Just put the figure number and nothing else under each figure—for example, "Fig. 1," and not "Fig. 1—Apparatus in Ready State." If a drawing depicts prior art, the figure number should include the words "prior art" in parenthesis [i.e., "Fig. 1 (prior art)"].

    The Rules permit legends to be used within rectangular boxes, on flowcharts, piping (plumbing) lines, or wherever else additional clarity is highly desirable. If used, the descriptive matter lettering should be as large as, or larger than, the reference numerals.

21. **Views:** The drawings should have as many views (figures) as are necessary to show the invention. The views may be plan, sectional, exploded, elevational, or perspective; detailed larger-scale views of specific elements should be employed. Engineering views (such as front, side, bottom, or back) should not normally be used if perspective views can adequately illustrate the invention. If exploded views are used, the separated parts of the same figure must be embraced by a bracket. (See Fig. 8D.)

    A large machine or schematic or flowchart can be extended over several sheets, but the views should be arranged to be easily understandable and so that the

Summary of PTO Drawing Rules (continued)

sheets can be assembled adjacent each other to show the entire machine. Never place one figure within another unless the view is the only one on the sheet.

22. **Sectional and Enlarged Views:** The plane upon which a sectional view is taken should be illustrated in the general view by a broken line, the ends of which should be designated by numerals corresponding to the figure number of the sectional view with arrows indicating the direction in which the sectional view is taken. For example, suppose your Fig. 1 shows a left-side front view of your carburetor and Fig. 2 shows a cross-sectional front of the back half of the carburetor on a plane vertically bisecting the carburetor into front and back halves. In this case, Fig. 1 should contain a broken vertical line spaced halfway from left to right with arrows pointing to the right at the top and bottom of this line; the arrows should each be labeled "2" to indicate the section is shown in Fig. 2. To show an area of a main figure in an enlarged view, encircle the area in the main figure and indicate the circled area with the number of the figure of the enlarged view—that is, if your main figure is Fig. 1 and the enlarged view is to be Fig. 1A, designate the circled area of Fig. 1 with a lead line numbered "1A."

23. **Moving Parts:** To show two positions of a movable part, show its main position in full lines and its secondary position in phantom lines, provided this can be done clearly. If not, use a separate view for the secondary position.

24. **Modifications:** Show modifications in separate figures, not in broken lines.

25. **No Construction Lines:** Construction lines, center lines, and projection lines connecting separate figures are forbidden.

26. **Position of Sheet:** All views (figures) on a sheet must have the same orientation, preferably so that they can be read with the sheet upright (that is, in portrait orientation with its short side at the top) so the examiner won't have to turn the sheets or the file to read the drawing. However, if views longer than the width of the sheet are necessary for the clearest illustration of the invention, the views may be drawn with the sheet in the landscape orientation, with the top margin on the right-hand side. The orientation

of any lettering on a sheet must conform with the orientation of the sheet, except that the sheet number and number of sheets separated by a slash (1/2) must always be at the top. (See Fig. 10B.)

27. **OG Figure:** One figure should be a comprehensive view of the invention for inclusion in the *Official Gazette*, a weekly publication of the PTO that shows the main claim and drawing figure of every patent issued that week.

28. **No Extraneous Matter:** No extraneous matter—that is, matter that is not part of the claimed invention or its supporting or related structures—is permitted on the drawings. However, you can (and should) place additional matter, such as a hand on a special pistol grip, if necessary to show use or an advantage of the invention. Also, you should put the sheet number and total number of sheets ("1/4, 2/4," etc.) below the top margin, in centered numerals that are larger than the regular reference numerals. If the center space is occupied, the sheet number should be placed to the right.

29. **No Wrinkled Sheets:** If you're filing by mail, the sheets should be sent to the PTO with adequate protection so that they will arrive without wrinkles or tears. You should send the sheets flat, between two pieces of corrugated cardboard within a large envelope, but they can also be rolled and sent in a mailing tube, provided they don't wrinkle. Never fold patent drawing sheets or typed sheets of the specification.

30. **Phantom Lines:** Parts that are hidden, but that you want to show, for example, the inside of a computer, should be shown in phantom lines—that is, broken lines. Reference numeral lead lines that refer to phantom parts should also be broken, in accordance with standard drafting practice. Broken lines must never be used to designate a part of the actual invention, unless to illustrate a phantom part or a moved position of a part.

31. **Identification on Back:** So that the PTO can identify and utilize the drawings in case they get separated from the file, you should include the title of the invention, and the first inventor's name and telephone number on the back of each sheet, at least 1 cm down from the top. Use a label or sticker if necessary to prevent this information from showing through to the front.

Make your drawings as comprehensive and meaningful as possible, almost to the point that most people can fully understand the invention by looking at the drawings alone. Most people can understand an invention far more readily from drawings because they are a lower level of abstraction than text.

For example, in electronic schematics, try to arrange the parts so that:

- the signal progresses from left to right
- the input sources and output loads are clearly indicated
- transistor states are indicated (that is, NNC = normally nonconductive; NC = normally conductive)
- signal waveforms are shown, and
- circuits are labeled by function (for example, "Schmitt Trigger").

In chemical and computer cases, we suggest you use a flowchart, if possible. In mechanical cases, we suggest you use exploded views, perspective views from several directions, and simplified perspective "action" views, showing the apparatus in operation and clearly illustrating its function. In other words, do the drawings so completely that they "speak" to their reader.

1. Making Drawings Manually

The oldest way of making patent drawings is manually, with pen, ruler, and other instruments. Pen and ruler allow little room for mistakes, because, except for very small marks, it is very difficult to correct misplaced ink lines. Few professional patent draftspersons still make drawings this way.

The necessary tools include pencils for preliminary sketches, ink drafting pens (also known as technical pens) for drawing ink lines, straight rules for drawing straight lines, triangles for drawing angled lines, templates for drawing certain standard shapes, French curves for drawing curves, an optional drafting table, and Mylar (best) or Vellum film or Bristol board. Pen and ruler may be used to make patent drawings in the following ways:

a. Drawing From Scratch

You can draw an object by visualizing in detail what it should look like, carefully sketching that image on the film or board with a pencil, correcting it until it looks about right, and finally inking over the pencil lines. The sketch of a telephone is illustrated in Fig. 10C. You must have some basic drawing skills to draw from scratch.

b. Tracing

Tracing is much easier than drawing from scratch. An obvious method is to trace a photograph of an object that you wish to draw, as shown in Fig. 10D. You can also trace an actual, three-dimensional object by positioning a transparent drawing sheet on a transparent sheet of glass or acrylic, as shown in Fig. 10E, looking at the object through the glass, tracing the lines of the object on the film, and photocopying the tracing onto a sheet of paper. Tracing requires very little skill other than a steady hand.

c. Drawing to Scale

You can also draw by scaling—that is, measuring and then reducing or enlarging—the dimensions of an actual object to fit on a sheet of paper, and drawing all the lines with the scaled dimensions. For example, if an object has a height of 50 cm and a width of 30 cm, you can reduce those dimensions by 50%, so that you would draw it with a height of 25 cm and a width of 15 cm to fit on the paper, as shown in Fig. 10F. All other dimensions of the object are scaled accordingly for the drawing. Making a drawing that looks right is easier by drawing to scale than by drawing based on only a mental image.

After making your ink drawings on film or Bristol board, make good photocopies on good-quality 20- or 24-pound bond paper for submission to the PTO. Keep the originals in case you have to make changes later.

2. Drawing With a Computer

CAD (computer-aided drafting or design) allows you to produce accurate drawings even if you consider yourself to have little or no artistic ability. In fact, no drawing skills in the traditional sense are needed at all. Furthermore, CAD enables you to correct mistakes as easily as a word processor enables you to edit words in a document. Even if you discover a mistake after you've printed a drawing, you can easily correct the mistake and print a new copy.

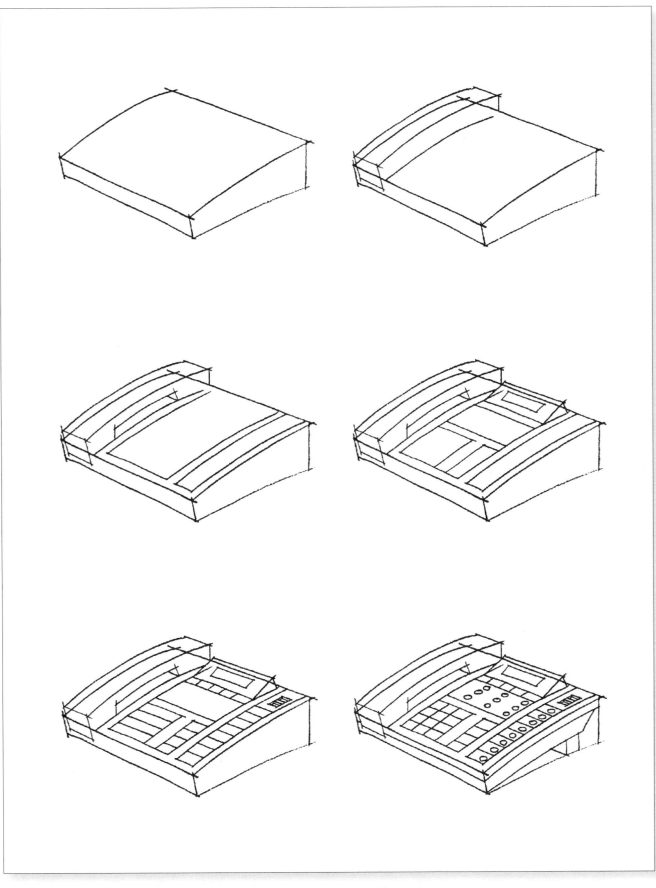

Fig. 10C—Sketching Techniques

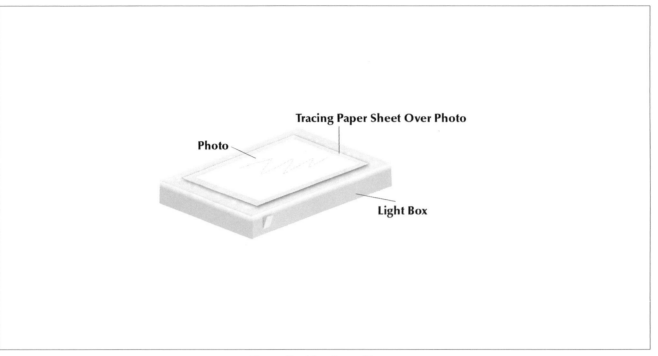

Photo

Tracing Paper Sheet Over Photo

Light Box

Fig. 10D—Tracing a Photo

Fig. 10E—Tracing Large Object on Long Table

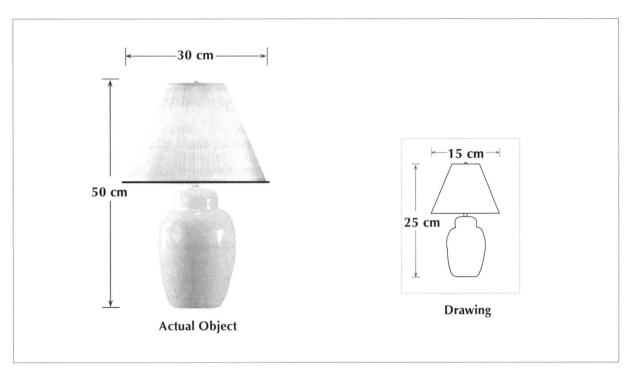

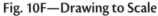

Fig. 10F—Drawing to Scale

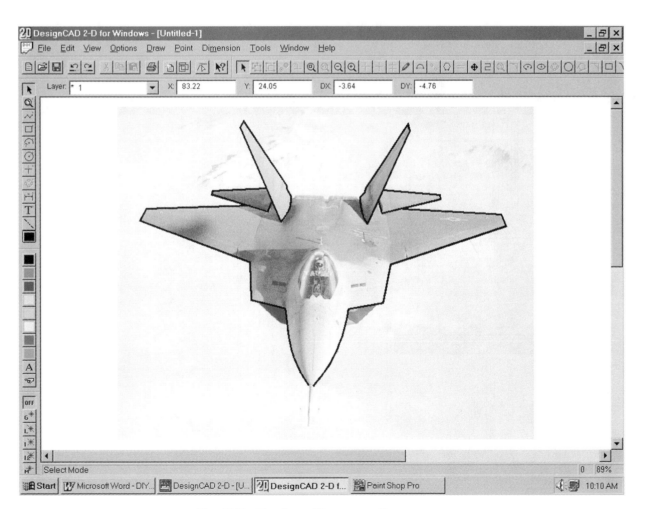

Fig. 10G—Tracing a Photo on a Computer

A variety of free CAD programs are available on the Internet. For example, the Draw utility in the LibreOffice suite (www.libreoffice.org) is useful for simple drawings, can export your drawings directly to a PDF document, and even has some 3D capabilities.

a. Tracing

Using a scanner, you can scan a photograph of an object, import the scanned image into a CAD program, and trace it easily, as shown in Fig. 10G, a traced photo of an aircraft (the black outlines are the tracing lines, which are difficult to see in a black-and-white book). If you have a digital camera, you can take a photograph of the object and download the image directly into your computer without having to print and scan the photograph. Once it is in your computer, tracing the image is very easy, since you use

a mouse or stylus and tablet. Available photo editing software may also be able to trace a photograph.

b. Drawing From Scratch

A 3D (three-dimensional) CAD program enables you to construct an accurate, 3D representation of your invention within the computer, such as the pipe fitting shown in Fig. 10H. A 3D model is typically built by using and modifying basic geometric building blocks, such as boxes, cylinders, planes, and custom-defined shapes. You may create each part with specific dimensions, or you may simply draw a shape that looks about right. You can easily rotate the finished model to see it from any angle. You can also easily zoom in or out to adjust the viewing distance. Once you are satisfied with the view, you can print it as a line drawing (a drawing of dark lines on a light background).

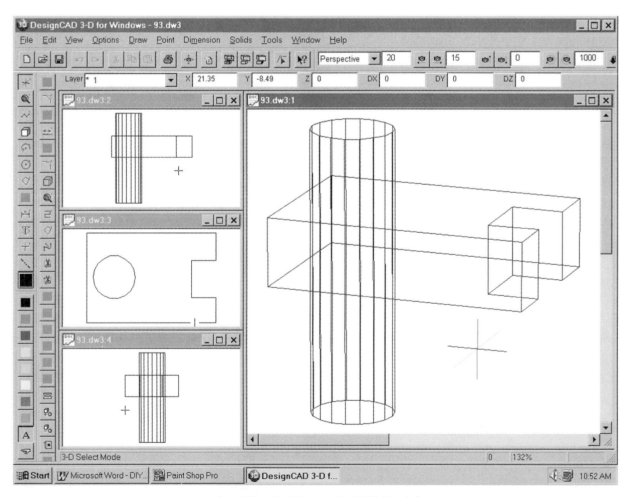

Fig. 10H—Building a 3D CAD Model

3. Photography

While photographs may no longer be submitted as patent drawings (except in rare cases), they may be converted into acceptable line drawings by tracing them, by scanning them, or with a digital camera. Their images may be copied directly into and manipulated and cleaned up with a CAD program. Although photography spares you from having any drawing skills, you must have some photographic skills to take clear pictures, including a basic understanding of lighting and exposure. To take an accurate photograph, you will need a high-resolution camera with a selectable aperture, zoom and macro (close-up) lenses, and a tripod.

> ⚠ CAUTION
>
> **Although the PTO has not published anything official, current practice indicates that the PTO may not be rigidly enforcing its drawing rules.** As a result some patents are issuing with sloppy drawings. Still, you should file well-executed drawings and avoid making a negative impression on your examiner or on any judge who may have to rule on your patent.

D. Consider Using a Professional Patent Draftsperson

If you don't feel competent to do your own drawings, you'll want to hire someone to do them for you. You can locate people who specialize in preparing patent drawings by searching the Internet. While expensive (about $30 to $50 per hour, or $75 to $150 per sheet), these people should do the job correctly the first time with CAD. Also, you can use a "starving artist" who's proficient in the medium to be used (CAD or India ink), and reads and understands the rules thoroughly.

If you use a professional, take care to avoid inadvertently making a public disclosure of your drawings—have the draftsperson sign a Consultant's Work Agreement—Form 4-3 in Appendix 7. A competent patent draftsperson should understand the public disclosure rule and be willing to sign this Agreement (or a standard one of their own). Under no circumstances should you hire any drafter who will not sign a confidentiality agreement to protect your trade secrets.

You should consider including a copy of your specification under the NDA, to assist the drafter's understanding of your invention. Doing so may speed up the drafting process by reducing back-and-forth communication.

E. Finaling Your Specification for Paper Filing

Even though filing by EFS-Web requires some learning, the advantages of online filing outweigh the learning task. Briefly the advantages of filing via EFS-Web are: the ability to file from anywhere in the world that has Web access, a substantially cheaper filing fee, no need to print out the specification and make file copies, no need to go to the post office to send the application via Priority Mail Express (and pay the Priority Mail Express fee), no need to include a receipt postcard, no need for a transmittal letter, fee transmittal, credit card payment form or check, no need to wait several weeks to get a receipt postcard back to learn whether the application was filed okay, no risk of loss in the mails, etc. Note that if you file your application on paper, the PTO will still convert it to electronic format in its data processing system anyway because they are virtually a no-paper office now. In any case, read the following sections on paper filing because these contain certain requirements and will give you more background and a willingness to tackle electronic filing.

Before putting them in final form, you (and perhaps a trusted acquaintance of yours sworn to secrecy) should reread your specification, claims, and abstract, to make sure your writing is clear, complete, understandable, and free of grammatical and spelling errors. Another alternative is to prepare the application, put it down for the day, and review the application the following day for mistakes. Make sure that the main substantive requirements (as discussed in Chapters 8 and 9) are satisfied.

Try to do a perfect job with your patent application, because doing so will make a better impression on the examiner and anyone else, such as a judge or potential licensee, who reads it. Remember that the examiner's job is to seize upon any flaws or faults in the application. The less excuse you give your examiner to find objections, the smoother will be the sailing of your application in the PTO. And keep in mind the words of Pearl S. Buck: "The secret of joy in work is contained in one word—excellence. To know how to do something well is to enjoy it."

As with your drawings, you must format your specification, claims, and abstract on either U.S. or A4-size paper. All sheets (whether filing on paper or by EFS-Web) must be of the same size, free of holes, and have 2.5 cm (1") top, bottom, right, and left margins. Use 1.5 or double spacing and number the sheets at the top or bottom, in the center, and inside the margin. (All correspondence that you send to the PTO at any time should always be 1.5 or double-spaced; never use single spacing and never type on both sides of a sheet.)

If you think you may later want to file corresponding foreign applications, one way to minimize work is to type your application on U.S. letter-size paper with proper margins, so that if photocopied onto A4 size paper it will have the proper A4 margins. To do this print out or type the application on letter-size or computer paper (8.5" x 11"). Use a 1" left margin, 6.2" line width, 1" top margin, and a bottom margin of 0.3", so that the last line is almost at the bottom of the page. Save the original for possible later use in making an A4 version for an international application. Alternatively, since modern word processing programs enable easy reformatting, it's easy to reformat a file for an A4 printout. Use a conventional, sans-serif typeface (such as Arial, Calibri, Helvetica, Lucida Sans or the like, but not Garamond, Palatino, or Times New Roman) in at least 12-point type. You should not justify (line up the right margin of) your typing, since unjustified printing (as in this book) is much easier to follow.

You must start your claims and abstract on new pages, with the abstract on the last sheet, *after* the claims. The title should go on the first page. Don't submit an application on easily erasable paper, or on paper that has white pigment covering any typewritten lines, since these are not considered permanent, unaltered records. If you're not a good typist, and you don't have a word processor, one solution is to type your application

on easily erasable paper or regular paper, cover the errors with white pigment, or erase them, type in the corrections, and then make bond paper photocopies of your typewritten original for submission to the PTO.

If, after putting your specification in final form, you find you must make a few minor changes (one or two words in a few places), it's okay to do so, provided you make these changes neatly in ink—in handwriting— and date and initial the margin adjacent to each change *before* you sign the Patent Application Declaration.

1. Typing and Filing Application on A4 Paper

Alternatively, you can type and file your U.S. application on A4 paper (or in an A4-formatted PDF), following the proper requirements for such matters as margins and line spacing (the abstract page). A4 paper can be obtained from a printer's supply house. Also, you can cut it yourself or have it cut for you. If you cut it yourself, the sheets should be 210 by 297 mm ($11^{11}/_{16}$" x 8¼") in size, with top margins 2 to 4 cm, left margins of 2.5 to 4 cm, and bottom and right margins of 2 to 3 cm, with sheets numbered consecutively at the top and typed with 1.5 line spacing—that is, four lines per inch or per 2.5 cm. Keep the originals and file an A4 xerographic copy. As stated, the PTO isn't very strict about format, but if you later file a PCT application, these measurements must be followed to comply with WIPO (and EPO) requirements.

You don't have to file your drawings and your typewritten papers on the same size sheets; the drawings can be on A4 paper and the typewritten pages on U.S.-size paper, or vice versa. However, all drawing sheets must be the same size, as must all typed sheets. Never use both sides of a sheet, either for drawings or for the specification. A neatly typed specification will certainly make a very favorable impression on your examiner. If you can do your application with a laser printer with larger heading fonts, the result will be most impressive. As mentioned earlier, if you don't own a laser printer, consider using one at a copy center.

Some inventors have prepared their applications to look like patents, complete with narrow, single-spaced columns and cited references. Don't do this; your application should look like the sample in Chapter 8. When it issues the patent, the PTO will print it in

PTO/AIA/01 (06-12)
Approved for use through 11/30/2020. OMB 0651-0032
U.S. Patent and Trademark Office; U.S. DEPARTMENT OF COMMERCE
Under the Paperwork Reduction Act of 1995, no persons are required to respond to a collection of information unless it displays a valid OMB control number.

DECLARATION (37 CFR 1.63) FOR UTILITY OR DESIGN APPLICATION USING AN APPLICATION DATA SHEET (37 CFR 1.76)

Title of Invention	Food Chopper with Convoluted Blade

As the below named inventor, I hereby declare that:

This declaration is directed to:

[✓] The attached application, or

[ ] United States application or PCT international application number _____

filed on _____.

The above-identified application was made or authorized to be made by me.

I believe that I am the original inventor or an original joint inventor of a claimed invention in the application.

I hereby acknowledge that any willful false statement made in this declaration is punishable under 18 U.S.C. 1001 by fine or imprisonment of not more than five (5) years, or both.

WARNING:

Petitioner/applicant is cautioned to avoid submitting personal information in documents filed in a patent application that may contribute to identity theft. Personal information such as social security numbers, bank account numbers, or credit card numbers (other than a check or credit card authorization form PTO-2038 submitted for payment purposes) is never required by the USPTO to support a petition or an application. If this type of personal information is included in documents submitted to the USPTO, petitioners/applicants should consider redacting such personal information from the documents before submitting them to the USPTO. Petitioner/applicant is advised that the record of a patent application is available to the public after publication of the application (unless a non-publication request in compliance with 37 CFR 1.213(a) is made in the application) or issuance of a patent. Furthermore, the record from an abandoned application may also be available to the public if the application is referenced in a published application or an issued patent (see 37 CFR 1.14). Checks and credit card authorization forms PTO-2038 submitted for payment purposes are not retained in the application file and therefore are not publicly available.

LEGAL NAME OF INVENTOR

Inventor: M. Goldberger _____   Date (Optional): Feb. 28, 2016 _____

Signature: Mildred Goldberger _____

Note: An application data sheet (PTO/SB/14 or equivalent), including naming the entire inventive entity, must accompany this form or must have been previously filed. Use an additional PTO/AIA/01 form for each additional inventor.

This collection of information is required by 35 U.S.C. 115 and 37 CFR 1.63. The information is required to obtain or retain a benefit by the public which is to file (and by the USPTO to process) an application. Confidentiality is governed by 35 U.S.C. 122 and 37 CFR 1.11 and 1.14. This collection is estimated to take 1 minute to complete, including gathering, preparing, and submitting the completed application form to the USPTO. Time will vary depending upon the individual case. Any comments on the amount of time you require to complete this form and/or suggestions for reducing this burden, should be sent to the Chief Information Officer, U.S. Patent and Trademark Office, U.S. Department of Commerce, P.O. Box 1450, Alexandria, VA 22313-1450. DO NOT SEND FEES OR COMPLETED FORMS TO THIS ADDRESS. **SEND TO: Commissioner for Patents, P.O. Box 1450, Alexandria, VA 22313-1450.**

Fig. 10IA—Completed Declaration for Patent Application Using an Application Data Sheet (Form 10-1A in Appendix 7)

Doc Code: Oath
Document Description: Oath or declaration filed

PTO/AIA/08 (11-15)
Approved for use through 11/30/2020. OMB 0651-0032
U.S. Patent and Trademark Office; U.S. DEPARTMENT OF COMMERCE
Under the Paperwork Reduction Act of 1995, no persons are required to respond to a collection of information unless it contains a valid OMB control number.

DECLARATION FOR UTILITY OR DESIGN PATENT APPLICATION (37 CFR 1.63)	Attorney Docket Number	Goldberger-Briskin
	First Named Inventor	M. Goldberger
	COMPLETE IF KNOWN	
	Application Number	
	Filing Date	
	Art Unit	
	Examiner Name	

[✓] Declaration Submitted With Initial Filing   OR   [ ] Declaration Submitted After Initial Filing (surcharge (37 CFR 1.16(f)) required)

(Title of the Invention)

As a below named inventor, I hereby declare that:

This declaration is directed to:

[✓] The attached application,

OR

[ ] United States Application Number or PCT International application number _____

filed on_____.

The above-identified application was made or authorized to be made by me.

I believe I am the original inventor or an original joint inventor of a claimed invention in the application.

I hereby acknowledge that any willful false statement made in this declaration is punishable under 18 U.S.C. 1001 by fine or imprisonment of not more than five (5) years, or both.

| Direct all correspondence to: | [ ] The address associated with Customer Number: | | OR | [ ] Correspondence address below |

Name	
Address	
City	State	Zip
Country	Telephone	Email

[Page 1 of 2]

Fig. 10IB—Completed Declaration for Patent Application (Form 10-1A(2) in Appendix 7)

PTO/AIA/08 (11-15)
Approved for use through 11/30/2020. OMB 0651-0032
U.S. Patent and Trademark Office; U.S. DEPARTMENT OF COMMERCE
Under the Paperwork Reduction Act of 1995, no persons are required to respond to a collection of information unless it contains a valid OMB control number.

DECLARATION — Utility or Design Patent Application

WARNING:

Petitioner/applicant is cautioned to avoid submitting personal information in documents filed in a patent application that may contribute to identity theft. Personal information such as social security numbers, bank account numbers, or credit card numbers (other than a check or credit card authorization form PTO-2038 submitted for payment purposes) is never required by the USPTO to support a petition or an application. If this type of personal information is included in documents submitted to the USPTO, petitioners/applicants should consider redacting such personal information from the documents before submitting them to the USPTO. Petitioner/applicant is advised that the record of a patent application is available to the public after publication of the application (unless a non-publication request in compliance with 37 CFR 1.213(a) is made in the application) or issuance of a patent. Furthermore, the record from an abandoned application may also be available to the public if the application is referenced in a published application or an issued patent (see 37 CFR 1.14). Checks and credit card authorization forms PTO-2038 submitted for payment purposes are not retained in the application file and therefore are not publicly available. Petitioner/applicant is advised that documents which form the record of a patent application (such as the PTO/SB/01) are placed into the Privacy Act system of records DEPARTMENT OF COMMERCE, COMMERCE-PAT-7, System name: *Patent Application Files* . Documents not retained in an application file (such as the PTO-2038) are placed into the Privacy Act system of COMMERCE/PAT-TM-10, System name: *Deposit Accounts and Electronic Funds Transfer Profiles.*

LEGAL NAME OF SOLE OR FIRST INVENTOR:

(*E.g.,* Given Name (first and middle if any) and Family Name or Surname)

mildred Goldberger

Inventor's Signature		Date (Optional)
Mildred Goldberger		2/28/2016

Residence: City	State	Country	
Philadelphia	PA	U.S.	

Mailing Address

1901 Kennedy Blvd.

City	State	Zip	Country
Philadelphia	PA	10103	U.S.

☐ Additional inventors are being named on the _____ Supplemental sheet(s) PTO/AIA/10 attached hereto

[Page 2 of 2]

Fig. 10IC—Completed Declaration for Patent Application (Form 10-1A(2) in Appendix 7)

PTO/AIA/10 (06-12)
Approved for use through 01/31/2014. OMB 0651-0032
U.S. Patent and Trademark Office; U.S. DEPARTMENT OF COMMERCE
Under the Paperwork Reduction Act of 1995, no persons are required to respond to a collection of information unless it contains a valid OMB control number.

SUPPLEMENTAL SHEET FOR DECLARATION	ADDITIONAL INVENTOR(S)
	Supplemental Sheet (for PTO/AIA/08,09)
	Page _____ of _____

Legal Name of Additional Joint Inventor, if any:

(*E.g.,* Given Name (first and middle (if any)) and Family Name or Surname)

Nathan F. Briskin

Inventor's Signature	*Nathan F. Briskin*	Date (Optional)

Residence: City	Philadelphia	State	PA	Country	U.S.

Mailing Address   1919 Chestnut Street

City	Philadelphia	State	PA	Zip	10103	Country	U.S.

Legal Name of Additional Joint Inventor, if any:

(*E.g.,* Given Name (first and middle (if any)) and Family Name or Surname)

Inventor's Signature		Date (Optional)

Residence: City		State		Country	

Mailing Address

City		State		Zip		Country	

Legal Name of Additional Joint Inventor, if any:

(*E.g.,* Given Name (first and middle (if any)) and Family Name or Surname)

Inventor's Signature		Date (Optional)

Residence: City		State		Country	

Mailing Address

City		State		Zip		Country	

This collection of information is required by 35 U.S.C. 115 and 37 CFR 1.63. The information is required to obtain or retain a benefit by the public which is to file (and by the USPTO to process) an application. Confidentiality is governed by 35 U.S.C. 122 and 37 CFR 1.11 and 1.14. This collection is estimated to take 21 minutes to complete, including gathering, preparing, and submitting the completed application form to the USPTO. Time will vary depending upon the individual case. Any comments on the amount of time you require to complete this form and/or suggestions for reducing this burden, should be sent to the Chief Information Officer, U.S. Patent and Trademark Office, U.S. Department of Commerce, P.O. Box 1450, Alexandria, VA 22313-1450. DO NOT SEND FEES OR COMPLETED FORMS TO THIS ADDRESS. **SEND TO: Commissioner for Patents. P.O. Box 1450. Alexandria. VA 22313-1450.**

Fig. 10ID—Completed Supplemental Sheet for Declaration (Form 10-1B in Appendix 7)

two-column format with a list of references cited, your name, and all other data that normally goes on the abstract page.

The PTO suggests that you number all paragraphs (not including headings) of your application as follows: [0001], [0002], etc. (Include the brackets; don't use parentheses.) Since any changes must now be done by replacing entire paragraphs, such numbering will facilitate amendments. Fortunately, this is optional.

2. Name All True Inventors and Only True Inventors

In the application and several of its forms, you're required to name the applicants or inventors. For example, the first page of the application lists the names, and Form 10-1 (Patent Application Declaration) must be signed by the inventors (see Figs. 10I (A and B) discussed below).

While anyone can apply for a patent, the named applicant(s) must be the true inventor(s) of the invention. So, if you discover an invention abroad or that your deceased uncle invented, you aren't allowed to apply to patent it in your name. If you've conceived the invention (as defined by the claims) entirely on your own, there are no coinventors. If you've invented it with someone else, both of you should be named as "joint inventors." But be sure that both of you actually are joint inventors. If somebody other than you played a significant role in conceiving the invention, review Chapter 16 for a more detailed discussion on inventorship.

PTO Rule 45 states that each joint inventor must have contributed something to at least one claim of the application. However, joint inventors need not have worked together or at the same time, their contributions need not be equal, and each need not have contributed to every claim of the application. Under no circumstances should you name your financier, your boss, or anyone else who was not an actual inventor. If you are not a U.S. citizen or are living outside the U.S., your rights are as good as a U.S. citizen-resident. The PTO will correspond with you in any country. If you're filing from abroad, you may bypass U.S. mail delays by filing from and using a U.S. correspondence address or by filing via EFS-Web.

3. The Essential and Optional Parts of Your Application

A basic patent application filed by mail consists of a set of minimal but necessary parts. (The elements marked with an asterisk are not required when using the EFS-Web filing system.) However, for the reasons indicated below, you may wish to file additional or optional parts with your application. The following is a list of the minimal and necessary parts and also the additional and optional parts to get you familiar with them before we discuss them in detail later.

a. Minimal and Necessary Parts

- **Receipt Postcard.*** This is stamped by the PTO and returned to you to let you know when your application was filed and its serial number.
- **Patent Application Transmittal Letter.*** This tells the PTO what parts you're sending for your patent application.
- **Fee Transmittal.*** This makes it easy for the PTO to compute and verify your filing fee.
- **Credit Card Payment Form, Check, or Money Order.*** This pays your fees to the PTO.
- **Drawings.** These are required if the invention can be illustrated with a drawing.
- **Specification, Including Claims, and Abstract.** These parts are discussed in detail in Chapters 8 and 9.
- **Patent Application Declaration.** This states who the inventors are, that they've read the application, that they will disclose all material information, and that they understand that they can be charged with perjury if they lie on this form. The PTO no longer requires that the Patent Application Declaration (PAD) be filed simultaneously with the application, but we recommend that you submit the PAD at this stage as long as doing so does not delay the filing of the application.

b. Additional and Optional Parts

- **Request for Claim Drafting by Examiner Under MPEP 707.07(j).** This asks the examiner to draft claims for you if your application contains allowable subject matter.

- **Nonpublication Request (NPR).** This instructs the PTO not to publish your application to preserve your trade secret rights. All applications are normally published 18 months after filing unless they're issued before then. By filing the NPR, you are certifying that the invention disclosed in the application has not been—and will not be—the subject of an application filed in another country, or under a multilateral international agreement, that requires publication of applications 18 months after filing. If you are not sure whether you will file a corresponding application in another country, do not make a Nonpublication Request. If you do make an NPR, and later change your mind and decide to foreign-file the application, you must file a revocation of the NPR within 45 days after the date you foreign-file. A "Request Not to Publish" check box is included on the Application Data Sheet (ADS).
- **Assignment and Transmittal.** This transfers ownership of your application to another individual or company.
- **Information Disclosure Statement, PTO Forms PTO/SB/08 (A and B), and Copies of Any Non-U.S. Patent References.** This cites any prior art of which you are aware, usually from any search that you made. PTO rules require that you supply a list of such prior art within three months after filing or before the first Office Action.
- **Application Data Sheet, PTO Form PTO/AIA/14.** This provides data about the application and the inventors. Whether you file on paper or by EFS-Web the PTO can extract your data from this form, thereby obviating errors.

This book provides copies of actual PTO forms, most of which are now available in editable PDF format and can be completed and printed on your computer. (The PTO prefers that inventors use PTO forms.) The most up-to-date forms may be obtained at www.uspto.gov/patent/patents-forms.

⃝! CAUTION

Print out any PDF forms you have prepared, since the information you enter on the forms will be lost once you turn off your computer. Alternatively you can save a computer file of a completed PDF form. The latest PDF software will allow you to save a copy with the information filled in, or you can "print" a filled-out form to a new PDF using any program that converts files to PDF, such as CutePDF (free), and printing out the new PDF. However the new PDF will no longer be fillable with your computer.

4. Completing the Patent Application Declaration

Each patent application must include a patent application declaration (PAD), which is a written statement under oath. Although the PTO no longer requires that the PAD be filed simultaneously with the patent application, you must file the PAD before the PTO issues the patent. We strongly recommend that you file the PAD with the application, but only if it is possible to do so without delaying the filing of the application (since, under the FTF system, such delay could be fatal to your claim), or as soon as possible after you have filed the application. Since the PAD is essential, we'll discuss it first. A PAD form is provided as Form 10-1A, and a completed example is provided above in Fig. 10I (A, B, and C).

While completing the PAD is a straightforward process, you should not treat it lightly. Rather, you should read and review it very carefully before you sign. If anyone can prove that you signed the declaration knowing that any of its statements were false, your patent can be held invalid. In fact, we've seen so many inventors sign PADs without reading or keeping a copy that we've provided Inventor's Commandment 16 at the beginning of this chapter to advise you to read, understand, make sure you agree with, and keep a copy of all documents you sign.

You should file a PAD signed by each inventor along with your application, although you can file it later, for a fee.

You can view and complete the PAD on your computer, a typewriter, or with a pen (do it neatly). If you want to use the computer, go to the PTO's forms website listed above, open the editable version of the appropriate form, as described below, and refer to Fig. 10I (A, B and C).

If you can file the PAD with an Application Data Sheet (ADS) when you file your application, use one form PTO/AIA/01 for each inventor. Complete the form PTO/AIA/01 as follows, as shown in Fig. 10IA:

Title of Invention: make sure to use the same title here as in your Application Data Sheet;

This declaration is directed to: check the box for "The attached application" (unless you are entering the U.S. from a PCT international application, in which case this book is not for you);

Fill in the full name of the inventor on the "Inventor" line, being sure that it is the same here as on the Application Data Sheet;

Have that inventor sign and date the Declaration.

Finally, note the statement in the middle of the PAD. This states that everything on the form is true and that you are liable for perjury, and the patent application and any resulting patent may be held invalid, if you knowingly lie.

In all other cases (e.g., if you cannot file the PAD simultaneously with your application), use form PTO/AIA/08, and additional sheets for additional inventors on form PTO/AIA/10 as necessary. Complete the form PTO/AIA/08 as follows:

Attorney Docket Number. No entry is needed, but if you prefer you may use any reference characters or names you wish to help you locate your patent application file. The PTO will include this docket number on all correspondence it sends to you.

First Named Inventor. Type the name of the sole inventor or the first inventor if there's more than one. The PTO will put this inventor's name on all correspondence that it sends to you. (This name will hold a prominent place on the patent, if and when it issues.)

Leave the Application Number, Filing Date, Art Unit, and Examiner Name blank, unless the application has already been filed and you have this information.

Declaration Submitted With Initial Filing. Check this box, if accurate, otherwise check the other box and fill-in the application number and the date on which the application was filed.

Title of the Invention. Type the title in this large box.

Under "This declaration is directed to," check the box before "The attached application" if you are filing the Declaration at the same time as the application, otherwise check the box for "Declaration Submitted After Initial Filing" and fill in the blanks with the

application number and the date on which the application was filed.

If there is any chance that you will file corresponding patent applications in other countries, check the box for "Authorization To Permit Access To Application by Participating Office," and otherwise leave that box blank.

Complete the second page of Form 10-1A(2) (Fig. 10IB) as follows:

If you want the PTO to correspond with someone other than an inventor, check the box after "direct all correspondence to" and the box before "Correspondence address below." In the next four lines, complete the name, address, phone, and fax (if any) of any noninventor who is to receive correspondence. (If you have several applications on file at the PTO, you may want to get a Customer Number, which enables you to use a number instead of your address. You can apply for a Customer Number using PTO Form SB/125.)

If you want the PTO to correspond with an inventor, check the box by "Correspondence address below" and the PTO will send all correspondence to Sole or First Inventor.

While every joint inventor must sign most papers that are sent to the PTO, the PTO will correspond with one inventor only. Therefore you should list the inventor who is most available (or who has best access to a photocopier or scanner) in the top section of part two of the form.

In the bottom section of the form, complete the given name, family name, city (or county), state, and country of legal residence, and mailing address of the sole or first inventor. Leave the date blank (unless you know the date it will be signed). Non-U.S. citizens have the same rights as U.S. citizens. The PTO will correspond with them no matter where they are and they don't have to be represented by an attorney in the U.S.

If there is more than one inventor, open and complete an additional sheet—Form PTO/AIA/08 (see Fig. 10IC).

If you are not the person who wrote the specification and claims, you should carefully read and understand them. Failure to do this can cause you embarrassment and may even result in fines for perjury.

Finally, note the statement in the middle of page 1 of the PAD. This states that everything on the form is true and that you are liable for perjury, and the patent application and any resulting patent may be held invalid, if you knowingly lie. Each inventor should then sign and date the appropriate "Inventor's Signature" spaces in the middle and bottom sections of page 2 of the PAD.

> ⓘ **CAUTION**
>
> **The PTO rules are very strict in requiring that you should not sign the PAD until the entire application is completed.** If the PTO finds out that you signed it before it was completed, or if you made any changes to the application after you signed the PAD, your application can be stricken or rejected entirely. If you need to make any changes to the application after it's finaled, you can do so neatly in ink, provided you date and initial each change and you do this before you sign the PAD. You can also make changes by amendment(s) after the application is filed (see Chapter 13), provided you don't add new matter to the application.

Claiming the Benefit of a PPA

If you have filed a Provisional Patent Application (PPA) and wish to claim the benefit of its filing date, you should do so in the "CROSS REFERENCE TO RELATED APPLICATIONS" section of your specification—as we have done in the sample specification included in Chapter 8, and must do so in your Application Data Sheet.

---

5. Complete the Transmittal Letter and Fee Transmittal, Payment, and Postcard

Now it's time to prepare the routine paperwork necessary to actually send your patent application to the PTO. Here's how to do it.

a. Prepare the Transmittal Letter

The transmittal letter (Form 10-2; PTO/AIA/15) should be completed as follows (see Fig. 10J for an example of a completed form):

Attorney Docket No. and **First Inventor:** Complete as you did with the PAD (see above).

Title: Complete as you did with the PAD (see above).

Express Mail Label: If you use Priority Mail Express (recommended) to mail your application, type or write the Priority Mail Express number from the post office's Priority Mail Express Label here.

Box 1: Check Fee Transmittal Form and complete this form (Form 10-3) as explained below.

Box 2: Check this Small Entity Box if you qualify for a Small Entity (SE) fee. An individual or individuals qualify for SE fees if they haven't assigned (transferred) or licensed the invention (and they have no obligation to assign or license the invention) to a for-profit company with over 500 employees.

Box 3: Check this Micro Entity Box if you qualify for a Micro-Entity (ME) status. A micro entity is anyone who is either (1) an independent inventor (a) who has not been named as an inventor in more than four nonassigned patent applications in their lifetime, and (b) whose gross income in the preceding calendar year is less than three times the median U.S. income, and (c) who has no obligation to assign and who has not assigned their application to a non-micro-entity, or (2) an employee of a college and who is obligated to assign their invention to the college.

Box 4: "Specification" is used here in the statutory sense, meaning the specification (written description), including the claims and abstract. Check this box and type the total pages of all of these parts of your application.

Box 5: Check this box (unless your application has no drawings) and indicate the total number of drawing sheets.

Box 6: Oath or Declaration. Type the number of pages of your declaration. Your declaration should be two pages unless you have additional sheets for more than two inventors. Check Box A, since you're submitting a new application.

Box 7: Application Data Sheet. The PTO's fillable Application Data Sheet form (PTO/AIA/14) can be saved to your computer. In case you don't have Internet access we provide Form 3-4 in Appendix 7. Filing this form is optional but it helps the PTO's clerical personnel maintain all the data about your application in one place.

PTO/AIA/15 (10-17)
Approved for use through 11/30/2020. OMB 0651-0032
U.S. Patent and Trademark Office; U.S. DEPARTMENT OF COMMERCE
Under the Paperwork Reduction Act of 1995 no persons are required to respond to a collection of information unless it displays a valid OMB control number.

UTILITY PATENT APPLICATION TRANSMITTAL

(Only for new nonprovisional applications under 37 CFR 1.53(b))

Attorney Docket No.	Goldberger-Briskin
First Named Inventor	M. Goldberger
Title	Food Chopper with Convoluted Blade
Priority Mail Express® Label No.	DP123456789USIUS

ADDRESS TO:

**Commissioner for Patents
P.O. Box 1450
Alexandria, VA 22313-1450**

APPLICATION ELEMENTS
See MPEP chapter 600 concerning utility patent application contents.

1. ✓ **Fee Transmittal Form**
(PTO/SB/17 or equivalent)

2. ✓ **Applicant asserts small entity status.**
See 37 CFR 1.27

3. ✓ **Applicant certifies micro entity status.** See 37 CFR 1.29.
Applicant must attach form PTO/SB/15A or B or equivalent.

4. ✓ **Specification** [Total Pages __12__]
Both the claims and abstract must start on a new page.
(See MPEP § 608.01(a) for information on the preferred arrangement)

5. ✓ **Drawing(s)** (35 U.S.C. 113) [Total Sheets __2__]

6. **Inventor's Oath or Declaration** [Total Pages _____]
(including substitute statements under 37 CFR 1.64 and assignments serving as an oath or declaration under 37 CFR 1.63(e))

  a. ✓ Newly executed (original or copy)

  b. ☐ A copy from a prior application (37 CFR 1.63(d))

7. ☐ **Application Data Sheet** *See note below.*
See 37 CFR 1.76 (PTO/AIA/14 or equivalent)

8. ☐ **CD-ROM or CD-R**
in duplicate, large table, or Computer Program (*Appendix*)
  ☐ Landscape Table on CD

9. **Nucleotide and/or Amino Acid Sequence Submission**
(if applicable, items a. – c. are required)

  a. ☐ Computer Readable Form (CRF)

  b. ☐ Specification Sequence Listing on:

    i. ☐ CD-ROM or CD-R (2 copies); or

    ii. ☐ Paper

  c. ☐ Statements verifying identity of above copies

ACCOMPANYING APPLICATION PAPERS

10. ☐ **Assignment Papers**
(cover sheet & document(s))
Name of Assignee _____

11. ☐ **37 CFR 3.73(c) Statement**   ☐ **Power of Attorney**
(when there is an assignee)

12. ☐ **English Translation Document**
(if applicable)

13. ✓ **Information Disclosure Statement**
(PTO/SB/08 or PTO-1449)
  ☐ Copies of citations attached

14. ☐ **Preliminary Amendment**

15. ✓ **Return Receipt Postcard**
(MPEP § 503) (Should be specifically itemized)

16. ☐ **Certified Copy of Priority Document(s)**
(if foreign priority is claimed)

17. ✓ **Nonpublication Request**
Under 35 U.S.C. 122(b)(2)(B)(i). Applicant must attach form PTO/SB/35 or equivalent.

18. ☐ **Other:** _____
_____
_____
_____
_____

*Note: (1) Benefit claims under 37 CFR 1.78 and foreign priority claims under 1.55 **must** be included in an Application Data Sheet (ADS).
(2) For applications filed under 35 U.S.C. 111, the application must contain an ADS specifying the applicant if the applicant is an assignee, person to whom the inventor is under an obligation to assign, or person who otherwise shows sufficient proprietary interest in the matter. See 37 CFR 1.46(b).

19. CORRESPONDENCE ADDRESS

☐ The address associated with Customer Number: _____ **OR** ✓ Correspondence address below

Name	Goldberger-Briskin
Address	1901 Kennedy Blvd
City	Philadelphia
State	PA
Zip Code	10193
Country	
Telephone	
Email	

Signature	Mildred Goldberger	Date 2/28/2015
Name (Print/Type)	*Mildred Goldberger*	Registration No. (Attorney/Agent)

This collection of information is required by 37 CFR 1.53(b). The information is required to obtain or retain a benefit by the public which is to file (and by the USPTO to process) an application. Confidentiality is governed by 35 U.S.C. 122 and 37 CFR 1.11 and 1.14. This collection is estimated to take 12 minutes to complete, including gathering, preparing, and submitting the completed application form to the USPTO. Time will vary depending upon the individual case. Any comments on the amount of time you require to complete this form and/or suggestions for reducing this burden, should be sent to the Chief Information Officer, U.S. Patent and Trademark Office, U.S. Department of Commerce, P.O. Box 1450, Alexandria, VA 22313-1450. DO NOT SEND FEES OR COMPLETED FORMS TO THIS ADDRESS. **SEND TO: Commissioner for Patents, P.O. Box 1450, Alexandria, VA 22313-1450.**

Fig. 10J—Utility Patent Application Transmittal (Form 10-2 in Appendix 7)
*Use latest fees—See Appendix 4, Fee Schedule.

Boxes 8, 9, 11, 12, 14, 16, and 18: Leave these blocks blank unless you're providing a computer program on a CD, a biosequence, a translation, a preliminary amendment, a certified copy based on a foreign filed application, or a continuing application.

Box 10: If you're filing an assignment with the application check this box.

Box 13: If you're supplying an Information Disclosure Statement with the application, check this box. Otherwise you must file your IDS within three months. If your IDS cites any foreign or nonpatent references, check the "Copies of citations attached" box. You don't have to send U.S. patent references to the PTO.

Box 15: Check this box and don't forget to complete and include a return receipt postcard.

Box 17: Nonpublication Request (NPR). We recommend that you file an NPR (Form 10-7; PTO/SB/35) and check this box. (If you file an ADS, you don't need to file a separate NPR if you check the "Request Not to Publish" on page two of the ADS form.) Don't file an NPR if you definitely will be foreign filing, or unless you want an early publication of your application to be able to use against infringers. If you check this box but later decide to foreign-file, be sure to revoke your NPR within 45 days—use Form PTO/SB/36. If you don't file an NPR, your application will be published electronically 18 months after filing (if it hasn't issued by then), or sooner if you request it, and you will have to pay a stiff publication fee when you pay the issue fee. The fee can be particularly unfair if, as sometimes happens, the patent issues within a few weeks of publication. Another reason for filing an NPR is that when your application is published, your application and its history will be open to the public on the PTO's public PAIR site. You may find this undesirable since it will give competitors and potential infringers a peek at your prosecution strategy and arguments before your patent issues. If you check the NPR box and later file abroad and you don't revoke your NPR and notify the PTO of such foreign filing within 45 days (use Form PTO/SB/36), your application will be regarded as abandoned unless you pay a stiff fee and declare that delay was unintentional. To fill out the NPR, merely fill in the name of the first inventor, the title, the docket number, and the date. The first inventor should sign it and print

their name under the signature. You must file the NPR with the application; if you file it later it will be in vain.

Common Misconception: If the PTO publishes your patent application, this indicates that it believes your invention is patentable.

Fact: If you don't file an NPR at the time of filing the application, the PTO will publish your application 18 months later, regardless of its patentability.

Box 18: Other: If you attach any other documents, check this box.

If you're not sure your claims are entirely proper and would like the examiner to write claims for you if they find allowable subject matter, type "Request Under MPEP Section 707.07(j)" and file the Request (Form 10-8). (We recommend this.)

Box 19: Check the box before "Correspondence address below" and complete the next four lines as you did with the PAD (see Section E, above).

In the next-to-last line type the name of the inventor who is to receive correspondence from the PTO. This inventor should sign and date the bottom lines.

PPA: The form does not contain any box to refer to any PPA that you've filed. (Do not use Box 18 to refer to a PPA.) You should claim the benefit of any PPA that you've filed in the "CROSS REFERENCE TO RELATED APPLICATIONS" section of the specification, as explained in Chapter 8, Section I. Be sure to include the serial number and filing date of your PPA. You must file your regular patent application (RPA) within one year of your PPA's filing date if you want to claim the benefit of your PPA. If the last day of the one-year period falls on a weekend or holiday, you may file your Regular Patent Application (RPA) on the next business day after the weekend or holiday.

However, if you have any desire to seek foreign protection, do not wait for the next business day to file your RPA, as other countries may not recognize the delay as permissible.

The RPA must name at least one inventor who has been named in the PPA. If you file the application without a PPA claim in your specification, you must amend the specification within four months from your RPA's filing date or 16 months from your PPA's filing date.

PTO/SB/17 (01-18)
Approved for use through 11/30/2020. OMB 0651-0032
U.S. Patent and Trademark Office; U.S. DEPARTMENT OF COMMERCE
Under the Paperwork Reduction Act of 1995 no persons are required to respond to a collection of information unless it displays a valid OMB control number

FEE TRANSMITTAL

	Complete if known
Application Number	
Filing Date	
First Named Inventor	M. Goldberger
Examiner Name	
Art Unit	
Practitioner Docket No.	Goldberger-Briskin

☐ Applicant asserts small entity status. See 37 CFR 1.27.

☑ Applicant certifies micro entity status. See 37 CFR 1.29.
Form PTO/SB/15A or B or equivalent must either be enclosed or have been submitted previously.

TOTAL AMOUNT OF PAYMENT	($)	

METHOD OF PAYMENT (check all that apply)

☐ Check ☑ Credit Card ☐ Money Order ☐ None ☐ Other (please identify): _____

☐ Deposit Account Deposit Account Number: _____ Deposit Account Name: _____

For the above-identified deposit account, the Director is hereby authorized to (check all that apply):

☐ Charge fee(s) indicated below   ☐ Charge fee(s) indicated below, **except for the filing fee**

☐ Charge any additional fee(s) or underpayment of fee(s)   ☐ Credit any overpayment of fee(s)
under 37 CFR 1.16 and 1.17

WARNING: Information on this form may become public. Credit card information should not be included on this form. Provide credit card information and authorization on PTO-2038.

FEE CALCULATION

1. BASIC FILING, SEARCH, AND EXAMINATION FEES (U = undiscounted fee; S = small entity fee; M = micro entity fee)

	FILING FEES			SEARCH FEES			EXAMINATION FEES			
Application Type	**U ($)**	**S ($)**	**M ($)**	**U ($)**	**S ($)**	**M ($)**	**U ($)**	**S ($)**	**M ($)**	**Fees Paid ($)**
Utility	300	150*	75	660	330	165	760	380	190	585
Design	200	100	50	160	80	40	600	300	150	_____
Plant	200	100	50	420	210	105	620	310	155	_____
Reissue	300	150	75	660	330	165	2,200	1,100	550	_____
Provisional	280	140	70	0	0	0	0	0	0	_____

* The $150 small entity status filing fee for a utility application is further reduced to $75 for a small entity status applicant who files the application via EFS-Web.

2. EXCESS CLAIM FEES

Fee Description	**Undiscounted Fee ($)**	**Small Entity Fee ($)**	**Micro Entity Fee ($)**
Each claim over 20 (including Reissues)	100	50	25
Each independent claim over 3 (including Reissues)	460	230	115
Multiple dependent claims	820	410	205

Total Claims		**Extra Claims**	**Fee ($)**		**Fee Paid ($)**	
24	-20 or HP =	4	x	20	=	80

HP = highest number of total claims paid for, if greater than 20.

	Multiple Dependent Claims	
	Fee ($)	**Fee Paid ($)**
	_____	_____

Indep. Claims		**Extra Claims**	**Fee ($)**		**Fee Paid ($)**	
4	-3 or HP =	1	x	105	=	105

HP = highest number of independent claims paid for, if greater than 3.

3. APPLICATION SIZE FEE

If the specification and drawings exceed 100 sheets of paper (excluding electronically filed sequence or computer listings under 37 CFR 1.52(e)), the application size fee due is $400 ($200 for small entity) ($100 for micro entity) for each additional 50 sheets or fraction thereof. See 35 U.S.C. 41(a)(1)(G) and 37 CFR 1.16(s).

Total Sheets		**Extra Sheets**		**Number of each additional 50 or fraction thereof**		**Fee ($)**		**Fee Paid ($)**
_____	- 100 =	_____	/ 50 =	_____ (round **up** to a whole number)	x	_____	=	_____

4. OTHER FEE(S)   **Fees Paid ($)**

Non-English specification, $130 fee (no small or micro entity discount)   _____

Non-electronic filing fee under 37 CFR 1.16(t) for a utility application, $400 fee ($200 small or micro entity)   _____

Other (e.g., late filing surcharge): _____   _____

SUBMITTED BY

Signature		Registration No. (Attorney/Agent)		Telephone 215-555-0362
Name (Print/Type)	M. Goldberger		Date 11/11/2014	

This collection of information is required by 37 CFR 1.136. The information is required to obtain or retain a benefit by the public which is to file (and by the USPTO to process) an application. Confidentiality is governed by 35 U.S.C. 122 and 37 CFR 1.14. This collection is estimated to take 30 minutes to complete, including gathering, preparing, and submitting the completed application form to the USPTO. Time will vary depending upon the individual case. Any comments on the amount of time you require to complete this form and/or suggestions for reducing this burden, should be sent to the Chief Information Officer, U.S. Patent and Trademark Office, U.S. Department of Commerce, P.O. Box 1450, Alexandria, VA 22313-1450. DO NOT SEND FEES OR COMPLETED FORMS TO THIS ADDRESS. **SEND TO: Commissioner for Patents, P.O. Box 1450, Alexandria, VA 22313-1450.**

If you need assistance in completing the form, call 1-800-PTO-9199 and select option 2.

Fig. 10K—Fee Transmittal (Form 10-3 in Appendix 7)

PTO-2038 (02-2015)
Approved for use through 01/31/2018. OMB 0651-0043
United States Patent and Trademark Office; U.S. DEPARTMENT OF COMMERCE
Under the Paperwork Reduction Act of 1995, no persons are required to respond to a collection of information unless it
displays a valid OMB control number.

Credit Card Payment Form
(Do not submit this form electronically via EFS-Web)
Please Read Instructions before Completing this Form

Credit Card Information

Credit Card Type: ☑ Visa   ☐ MasterCard   ☐ American Express   ☐ Discover

Credit Card Account #: 2175-3210-1497-3218

Credit Card Expiration Date (mm/yyyy): 05/2017

Name as it Appears on Credit Card: Mildred Goldberger

Payment Amount (US Dollars): $ 585

Cardholder Signature: | Date (mm/dd/yyyy): 11/11/2016

The USPTO does not accept an s-signature (37 CFR 1.4(e)) on credit card payment forms.
Refund Policy: The USPTO may refund a fee paid by mistake or in excess of that required. A change of purpose after the payment of a fee will not entitle a party to a refund of such fee. The USPTO will not refund amounts of $25.00 or less unless a refund is specifically requested and will not notify the payor of such amounts (37 CFR 1.26). Refund of a fee paid by credit card will be issued as a credit to the credit card account to which the fee was charged.
Maximum Daily Limit: There is a $24,999.99 daily limit per credit card account effective June 1, 2015. There is no daily limit for debit cards.

Credit Card Billing Address

Street Address 1:   1901 Kennedy Blvd.

Street Address 2:

City: Philadelphia

State/Province: PA | Zip/Postal Code: 19103

Country: US

Daytime Phone #: | Fax #: 215-555-0362

Request and Payment Information

Description of Request and Payment Information:

☑ Patent Fee	☐ Patent Maintenance Fee	☐ Trademark Fee	☐ Other Fee
Application No.	Application No.	Application No.	IDON Customer No.
Patent No.	Patent No.	Registration No.	
Attorney Docket No. Goldberger-Briskin		Identify or Describe Mark	

If the cardholder includes a credit card number on any form or document other than the Credit Card Payment Form or submits this form electronically via EFS-Web, the United States Patent and Trademark Office will not be liable in the event that the credit card number becomes public knowledge.

Fig. 10L—PTO's Credit Card Payment Form (Form 10-4 in Appendix 7)

b. Fill Out Fee Transmittal and Pay by Credit Card or Check

Fill out the Fee Transmittal (Form 10-3 or PTO/SB/17) by completing the name of the first (or only) inventor and docket number at the top right. Form 10-3 includes the fees as of this edition. Note, that the PTO usually raises its fees on October 1 of each year, so if you're filing after October 1, check for current fees at the PTO website. The PTO also frequently changes its form PTO/SB/17, so you can download the most current version of that, as well. (See Fig. 10K for an example of a completed Fee Transmittal.)

A. Fill out the First Named Inventor and Attorney Docket No. boxes in the upper right corner as before.

B. Check "Applicant asserts small entity status. See 37 CFR 1.27" box if you qualify. You qualify for small entity status if you haven't assigned or licensed (or are not obligated to assign or license) the invention to a for-profit company with over 500 employees. (See PTO Rule 27 (37 CFR 1.27).) Check "Applicant certifies micro entity status. See 37 CFR 1.29" if you qualify. Otherwise do not check either of these boxes.

C. Fill in the "Total Amount of Payment" box. (Do this last after you calculate the total.)

D. Check the appropriate Check, Credit Card, or Money Order box.

1. Basic Filing, Search, and Examination Fees: Add the Small Entity fees in the "Utility" line and type the total ($1,370 in our example in Fig. 10K) in the rightmost column. You must pay all three fees together.

2. Excess Claim Fees: The Basic Filing Fee entitles you to file up to three independent claims and 20 total claims, assuming that each dependent claim refers back to only one preceding claim (independent or dependent). If you don't have more than 20 total and three independent claims, you can leave this section blank.

If you're filing over 20 total claims, three independent, or a multiple dependent claim

(not recommended) fill out these blanks. Enter the total number of claims (independent and dependent) in the blank under "Total Claims." Subtract 20 from this figure, enter the difference under "Extra Claims," and type the fee for each extra total claim over 20 (Large, Small, or Micro-Entity) from the list in the upper right of this section under "Fee ($)," and type the product under the "Fee Paid ($)." If you have more than three independent claims, enter the total number of independent claims under "Indep. Claims," subtract 3 from this figure, enter the difference under "Extra Claims," type the fee for each extra independent claim over three (Large, Small, or Micro-Entity) from the list in upper right part of this section under "Fee ($)," and type the product under the "Fee Paid ($)."

It's best not to file any Multiple Dependent Claims (MDCs) because the fee is high and examiners don't like them. However, if you do file any MDCs, enter the fee from the right side of this section in the MDC boxes. The fee is also in Appendix 4 and at the PTO's website.

3. Application Size Fee: If your specification and drawings exceed 100 pages, fill in the boxes in this section.

Note that the fees for extra claims and MDCs are very high now.

4. Don't forget to add the Non-electronic filing fee under 37 CFR 1.16(t), under "Other Fee(s)," if you are not filing electronically.

5. Other Fee(s): Normally you won't have any additional fees at this stage, so you won't have to enter anything in the Other Fees section. However, if you want to obtain a somewhat speedier processing of your application, file a "Petition to Make Special" (see Section I below). If your petition requires a fee, type "Pet. Special"

after "Other Fee" and include the amount in the "Other" box. If you're enclosing an assignment (see Section H below), type "Asgt. Recordal." on the blank line.

Total the amounts in Sections 1 to 4 and enter the sum in the "Total Amount of Payment" box at the top left of the form.

Finally, sign and print the corresponding inventor's name and phone number in the next-to-last line of the form and enter your phone number and sign and type the date on the last line.

The PTO accepts payment by credit card, check, or money order. If you pay by credit card, use the PTO's Credit Card Payment Form (CCPF—Form 10-4 in Appendix 7 or PTO Form 2038) in conjunction with the Fee Transmittal. The PTO will not accept debit cards or check cards that require the use of a personal identification number as a method of payment.

Complete the CCPF as in Fig. 10L. Fill in all credit card information, including the amount to be charged to your credit card and your signature. Complete the Credit Card Billing Address. That information is required for verification of your credit card account. Under "Request and Payment Information," complete the "Description of Request and Payment Information" with a short statement of what you are paying for. In the present case, since you're paying a patent filing fee, write "Patent Application Filing Fee." Circle "Patent Fee" and write your docket number.

If paying by check or money order, make payment to Commissioner for Patents for the total amount, and attach it to the transmittal letter.

CAUTION

Be sure you have enough credit reserve in your credit card account or money in your checking account to cover the charge. If your payment bounces, you'll have to pay a stiff surcharge. (Note that if the PTO makes any fee errors, they are never penalized.)

Unfortunately, the PTO does not discount its fees for the needy, handicapped, or aged, or allow such individuals to postpone their fees. However, the AIA has a Micro Entity fee provision, under which Micro Entities will be able to get a 75% reduction on most fees (see above for the qualifications).

CAUTION

Be sure to make every payment as appropriate for your entity size. The rules for paying discounted fees are different for small entities than they are for micro entities. According to the PTO rules; for small entities, "Once status as a small entity has been established in an application or patent, fees as a small entity may thereafter be paid in that application or patent without regard to a change in status until the issue fee is due or any maintenance fee is due" (37 CFR 1.27(g)(1)). When you pay the issue fee, or any maintenance fee, you must determine whether your eligibility for small entity status has changed, and if so you must notify the PTO and pay the undiscounted fees (37 CFR 1.27(g)(2)). Unfortunately for micro entities, every time you pay a fee to the PTO you must determine whether your eligibility for small micro status has changed ("a fee may be paid in the micro entity amount only if status as a micro entity as defined in paragraph (a) or (d) of this section is appropriate on the date the fee is being paid," (37 CFR 1.29(g)). If you are no longer entitled to micro entity status, you must notify the PTO and pay the fee as a small entity, or pay the full, undiscounted fee, as appropriate.

a. Postcard

As stated in Inventor's Commandment 18 at the beginning of this chapter, you should enclose a self-addressed, postage paid receipt postcard with every paper you mail to the PTO. Those few attorneys who still file by mail use receipt postcards because the PTO receives many thousands of pieces of mail each day and occasionally loses some. It may be months before you receive any reply to a paper you've sent to the PTO, so you'll want to be assured it arrived safely.

Fig. 10M indicates how an application receipt postcard should be completed. Note that the back of the card contains the inventors' names, title of invention, the number of sheets of drawing, the number of pages of specification, claims, and abstract, the Patent Application Declaration (if you are filing it with the application), including the number of pages and date it was signed, the Patent Application Transmittal, the Fee Transmittal, CCPF or the check number and amount, and the NPR. Leave space at the bottom of the back of the card for the PTO to affix its date and Serial Number sticker. Occasionally, receipt postcards get lost because of their size and inconspicuous color. We have had better results by using colored (bright red) postcards.

Patent application of Mildred Goldberger and Nathan Briskin for "Food Chopper With Convolute Blade" consisting of two sheets of drawing, 12 pages of specification, claims, and abstract, Patent Application Declaration (2 pp., signed 2014 Nov 11), Patent Application Transmittal, Fee Transmittal, Credit Card Payment Form, Nonpublication Request, and Information Disclosure Statement received for filing today:

Fig. 10M—Completed Back of Receipt Postcard to Accompany Patent Application

The PTO will stamp your application postcard receipt with the date your papers arrived and the serial number assigned to your application and mail it back to you as soon as they open your letter (which can take two weeks).

If you're filing from abroad, be sure that your return postcard has sufficient U.S. postage. You can confirm the postcard postage to any nation at the U.S. Postal Service website (www.usps.gov) and you can usually buy U.S. stamps abroad at a philatelic store.

6. Maintain an Orderly File

It's good practice to write the date received on every paper you receive connected with your invention and also date every outgoing paper. You should have a two-part folder or jacket for (a) your application, and (b) correspondence to and from the PTO. Keep your prior-art references in a large envelope loose inside the folder. To avoid confusion, we recommend that you keep other nonofficial papers concerning your invention in a separate folder.

7. Assembly and Mailing of Your Application—Final Checklist

Congratulations! You're now ready to mail your patent application to the PTO, unless you want to include an Information Disclosure Statement, an Assignment, and/or a Petition to Make Special. If you do want to include any of these with your application (optional), consult the indicated sections, complete your paperwork, and then come back to this point.

Assemble in the following order—and carefully check—the following items, which are the third part of the checklist we started in Chapter 8; please do this carefully and methodically, as "haste makes waste," especially when applying for a patent.

We suggest that you file a good photocopy of your signed application and keep the original of your application. In this way you can make copies later if the application is lost in the mail, or if you need to send them to manufacturers when you market your invention.

Staple the pages of the specification, claims, abstract, and declarations together. Attach the drawings with a paper clip or other temporary fastener. Only one copy need be filed.

If you mail the application by Priority Mail Express, the papers should be transmitted in a Priority Mail Express envelope. If the application doesn't have more than about eight pages, you should include one or two sheets of cardboard or internal envelopes to protect the drawing from bending.

You may send the application to the PTO by first-class mail, but if it's lost in the mail, you will lose your filing date. We strongly recommend that you use Priority Mail Express (see next section).

8. Using Priority Mail Express to Get an Instant Filing Date

We strongly recommend you send your application to the PTO by Priority Mail Express (PME). This will provide strong protection against loss of your application, secure full legal rights in case it is lost, give you an "instant" filing date (the date you actually mail your application), and will enable you to make absolutely sure your application is on file before the one-year period expires if a PPA was filed or the invention was put on sale, sold, or published. You must use "Priority Mail Express Post Office to Addressee" service and you must indicate that you're

Final Checklist for Filing a Patent Application by Mail

☐ Return Receipt Postcard addressed to you with all papers listed on back.*

☐ If you are paying the filing fee by a check or money order, make it out for the correct filing fee (basic fee plus fee for any excess claims).* Make sure you have adequate funds on deposit or available on your credit card.

☐ Transmittal Letter and Fee Transmittal properly completed and signed.*

☐ If you are paying the filing fee using a Credit Card Payment Form, be sure it is made out for the correct filing fee (basic fee plus fee for any excess claims).* Make sure your credit limit is not in jeopardy.

☐ Drawing sheets all present; drawings clear, complete, and understandable. Drawings show every feature in claims. The sheet number and total number of sheets (e.g. "1/3") is on the front (below top margin) and your name is on the top back. Originals of drawings (or disk file if CAD used) kept in safe place.

☐ Specification, Claims, and Abstract included; description of invention clear and complete, all reference numbers, dates, spelling, and grammar double-checked, and claims drafted per Chapter 9.

> ☐ Typing is clear and readable and 1.5 or double-spaced; use any normal font, 12-point minimum size.
>
> ☐ Application is prepared in form for making proper A4 copies later if foreign filing contemplated (optional).
>
> ☐ Top (above page numbers) and left margin is at least 2.5 cm on all pages.
>
> ☐ No sentence is longer than about 13 words, paragraphs are not longer than about a half a page, and a heading is supplied about every two pages.

☐ Claims are separated by an extra line.

☐ Claims and abstract start on new pages.

☐ No changes made after application signed.

☐ Patent Application Declaration (PAD) completed, signed, and dated in ink. (The PTO will accept a PAD, or virtually any other document which has a photocopy of your signature. However, you must always be able to produce the ink-signed original.)

☐ Parts are assembled in above order and copies are made for your file.

☐ Information Disclosure Statement, Forms 10-5 and 10-6 (A and B) with references attached if you're filing it with your application (see Section G below). Otherwise IDS must be sent within three months.

☐ Petition to Make Special, Form 10-9 and Supporting Declaration (optional to speed application processing; see Section I below).

☐ Assignment and transmittal letter (optional—see Section H below).

☐ Envelope addressed to:
    Mail Stop Patent Application
    P.O. Box 1450
    Alexandria, VA 22313-1450*

☐ If there are joint inventors, all should complete, sign, and date multiple copies of a Joint Owners' Agreement (Form 16-2; Chapter 16, Section C) and each inventor should keep an original. Do not file this with the PTO.

☐ Have another person check your papers for compliance with these rules.

* Not applicable for EFS-Web filings.

using this service by completing the PME section at the top of your transmittal letter (Form 10-2, Fig. 10J). Type the PME number in the box at the top right, fourth line of Form 10-2.

The PTO's Rule 10 (37 CFR 1.10) states, in effect, that mailing any paper to the PTO by PME, with the PME number on the transmittal letter, is the same as physically delivering the paper directly to the PTO. Thus you can consider and call your application "patent pending" as soon as the postal clerk hands you the PME receipt, and your filing date will be the date on this receipt, provided all papers of the application are present and are properly completed. Since postal clerks often don't press hard enough when they date the PME receipt, we recommend you ask the clerk to stamp the receipt also with their rubber date stamp. If you've followed the final checklist above, your application will now be properly on file, i.e., patent pending.

> **CAUTION**
>
> **You should NOT send your application by registered mail, fax, certified mail, or private courier (Federal Express, etc.), and you should NOT use any "Certificate of Mailing."** This is because Rule 10 does not give applicants any advantages if they use these methods of transmission. If you use any of these, your filing date will be the date the application is actually received at the PTO and you'll have no rights if your application is lost.

9. Receipt That Application Was Received in PTO

About two to four weeks after you send your application to the PTO, you'll get your postcard back, with the filing date of your application, and also with an eight digit serial number (for example, "11/123,456") that has been assigned to your application. Within about a week to a month after that (sometimes longer), you should get an official filing receipt back from the PTO indicating that your application has been officially filed. Check the information on the filing receipt carefully and let the OPAP (Office of Patent Application Processing) know if there are any errors.

If for any reason your application is incomplete or deficient, the PTO will not regard it as officially "filed" but rather as "deposited." The PTO will send you a letter stating the deficiency in your application and telling you to promptly remedy it. However, if you follow all the instructions in this chapter, including the checklist on the previous page, carefully, you'll get your filing receipt in due course.

Once you get the filing receipt, your application is officially "patent pending." Unless you want to keep your invention a trade secret in case your patent application is eventually disallowed, you may publish details of your invention or market it to whomever you choose. You will not lose any legal rights in the U.S. or Convention or treaty countries. If you manufacture anything embodying your invention, you should mark it "patent pending" and keep your application, serial number, and filing date confidential to preserve rights in non-Convention countries and prevent access by potential copiers. As stated, if you mailed your application by Priority Mail Express and you faithfully followed the checklists, you may refer to your invention as "patent pending" as soon as you get the PME receipt.

F. Finaling Your Specification for EFS-WebFiling

The PTO's Electronic Filing System using the Internet (EFS-Web) enables patent applications, amendments, and other documents to be filed electronically over the Internet. However, it requires some time to master, as well as effort to convert documents to the Portable Data Format (PDF). But its advantages are so great that even if you're filing just one application, it is worth the effort. As stated, its advantages are: You can (1) file an application anytime and from anywhere that has Internet access, (2) obtain instant confirmation of receipt of documents by the PTO, (3) send an application to the PTO without having to go to the post office to get a Priority Mail Express receipt, (4) file with confidence because you will get an instant acknowledgment without having to prepare a postcard or wait for a postcard receipt, (5) pay a substantially reduced filing fee with no paper-filing surcharge—see Fee Schedule in Appendix 4, and (6) file an application without having to prepare an application transmittal, a fee transmittal, receipt postcard, or check or Credit Card Payment Form (CCPF).

The PTO now has an optional "e-Office Action" service whereby they will send all correspondence to up to three of your email addresses in lieu of postal mail. To guard against lost emails, they will send a postcard reminder if the email is not opened within a week. This service can be useful if you're traveling, your mail is unreliable, or you want to get correspondence quickly. If you're a registered eFiler, it is easy to do from within your Private PAIR account. Details are at www.uspto.gov/patents-application-process/checking-application-status/e-office-action-program.

If you're ready to file electronically, take the following steps:

- **Prepare the Application as Usual:** Before you go online, prepare the entire application as instructed in Chapters 8 to 10, except omit the Application Transmittal form, Fee Transmittal form, Receipt Postcard, and check or CCPF. Sign the Declaration as usual. You may "sign" a downloaded declaration form (PTO/SB/01A) by typing an "/s/" signature on the form as follows: "/Sam Smith/." You don't need to print out the form and sign it in ink if you use the /s/ signature format.

Become a Registered eFiler (If Time Permits)

If you plan on filing electronically and if you can wait several weeks to file, we recommend you become a registered eFiler. You'll have to deal with red tape, including filling out a form to obtain a customer number, sending a notarized certificate to the PTO, obtaining access codes, and calling the PTO to confirm, but as a registered eFiler you'll be able to track your application's progress and file additional documents or corrections. To register go to www.uspto.gov/patents-application-process/applying-online/getting-started-new-users and follow the detailed instructions. If you can't wait several weeks, you can use EFS-Web to file an application as an unregistered eFiler and register later.

- **Convert Your Application to PDF Format:** Convert all documents of the application (Drawings, Specification, including any Claims and Abstract), to PDF documents in your computer. All PDF documents submitted via EFS-Web must have a minimum resolution of 300 DPI and a white background. Put all of the PDF application computer files into a separate PDF Application Holding Folder with a suitable name (for example, Derailleur RPA PDFs).

- **Prepare a PDF Data Sheet:** Find the fillable and savable EFS Application Data Sheet (ADS) (PTO Form AIA/14) by going to www.uspto.gov/patent/forms/forms-patent-applications-filed-or-after-september-16-2012 and downloading the form. This will enable you to fill in the form, save it with the data you filled in, and revise it later if necessary. If you fill the form in online, you won't be able to do this. We also recommend that you download the instructions for the form AIA/14, which provide greater detail. After you've saved Form AIA/14 to your desktop, check "Highlight Required Fields." The program will then automatically fill in the header blanks. Most of the fields are self-explanatory, and/or are explained in the instructions for the form AIA/14, but we draw your attention to the following issues. Leave blank the "Filing by Reference" section, which is only useful in rare circumstances that probably do not apply to you, and in any case do not apply if you submit a complete application as instructed in this book. Check "Request Not to Publish" (recommended, but only if you have decided not to file a corresponding foreign application) but remember to revoke your Nonpublication Request (NPR) within 45 days of your foreign filing, if you foreign-file later. Then, save the completed form using a suitable name, such as Data.pdf, in your PDF Application Holding Folder with your other PDF application forms. Consider carefully the "Statement under 37 CFR 1.55 or 1.78 for AIA (First Inventor to File) Transition Applications," which rarely applies. Read the text on the form carefully. If your application meets both criteria

(1) and (2), you must check the box; otherwise, leave the box unchecked. Also consider carefully the "Authorization or Opt Out of Authorization to Permit Access." The PTO will not allow others to access your application unless you give them permission, or until your application is published or issues as a patent. If you do not opt out by checking both box A and box B, you grant the PTO permission to allow other patent offices to access your application file. Note that if you do not opt out (i.e., if you leave one or both of box A and box B unchecked) your ADS may be somewhat more complicated to sign (more on this in the "Caution" section below). Follow the instructions for the "Applicant Information" section—but note that if the applicant is a juristic entity (e.g., a corporation or organization), and you name that juristic entity as an applicant, then the ADS must be signed by a patent practitioner (i.e., a registered patent attorney or patent agent) (more on this in the "Caution" section below).

CAUTION

Properly signing your Application Data Sheet requires close attention. There are three possible scenarios, each with unique requirements. The least complicated route, if no applicant is a juristic entity (e.g., a corporation or association) is to have the ADS signed by all of the applicants. **Scenario 1):** If one or more of the applicants is a juristic entity (e.g., a corporation or association), then the ADS *must* be signed by a patent practitioner (i.e., a registered patent attorney or patent agent). Otherwise (if no applicant is a juristic entity), there are two other scenarios. **Scenario 2):** If you are submitting the ADS along with your initial filing (most likely), and if you have not checked both box A and box B in the "Opt Out" section, then you are giving permission for the PTO to allow other patent offices access to your application file, in which case the ADS must be signed by (i) all of the applicants; or (ii) a patent practitioner (patent attorney or patent agent) of record; or (iii) an authorized official of an assignee of record (per 37 CFR 3.71); or (iv) a registered attorney or patent agent [see rule 1.14(c), 37 CFR 1.14(c)]. **Scenario 3):** If you have

checked both box A and box B in the "Opt Out" section, and/or you are submitting the ADS sometime after your initial filing (this is rare; for example, you are submitting a revised ADS), then the ADS must be signed by (i) a patent practitioner (i.e., a registered patent attorney or patent agent, per 37 CFR 1.32(b) or 37 CFR 1.34); or (ii) an assignee of the application (per 37 CFR 3.71(b)); or (iii) all of the applicants; or (iv) one or more joint inventor-applicants who hold a power of attorney (USPTO form AIA/81, signed by all of the applicants) (see rule 1.33(b), 37 CFR 1.33(b)). If one or more inventors refuse to sign, seek assistance from a registered patent attorney. If you are not sure you are doing this correctly, seek assistance by calling the PTO's Patent Ombudsman's office at 571-272-5555 or 855-559-8589, or the Application Assistance Unit at 571-272-4200 or 888-786-0101.

TIP

Before uploading your electronic filing documents, take a dry run using the PTO's Simulated EFS for Unregistered eFilers at www.uspto.gov/ebc/portal/sandbox/efs0-3-0.htm, or for Registered eFilers at www.uspto.gov/ebc/portal/sandbox/efs0-4-0.htm.

- **Sign On:** Go to www.uspto.gov/patents-application-process/applying-online/about-efs-web. If you haven't registered as an eFiler, click on "EFS-Web Unregistered eFilers" and fill in your name and email; then click "New application/proceeding." A series of new dialog boxes will open as you progress, in which you must select the type of application (Utility or Design) and specify a number of other options that are described in this book (e.g., for a Utility application, specify "Provisional" if you are filing a provisional application, otherwise select one of the nonprovisional options: "Nonprovisional"; "Accelerated" (not recommended); or "Track 1"), and click "Continue."

  If you have registered, click on "EFS-Web Registered eFilers." Then fill in your Digital Certificate and password. You can recover the Digital Certificate by browsing to Program Files/USPTO in your computer and opening the file with your name and a ".epf" suffix, for example, "John Smith.epf." Check the box to confirm that you are not accessing (or permitting access to) technology or software in a manner that would violate or circumvent the Export Administration Regulations, if you are certain that your technology is not export-controlled by those Regulations. Otherwise, consult an export control specialist. Click "Authenticate" and then certify your identity, select "New Application" and the type of application, and click "Continue." If you get stuck at any time, call the PTO's Electronic Business Center at 866-217-9197.

- **Application Data:** On the Application Data page fill in the title of the invention, a docket number for the application of your choosing (optional, but a suitable docket number can be something like "Krypton Derailleur"), and your name and Customer Number or address. It's best to copy this data electronically from your Data Sheet so that everything will be consistent. (Even if you're not registered you can obtain a Customer Number, which will take a few days but will save you from having to type your address each time.) Click "Continue."

Yes, There Is a Way to Save the Fillable PDF Declaration Form

Some of the forms you may use for EFS-Web filing may state, "You cannot save data typed into this form. Please print your completed form if you would like a copy for your records." How can you obtain a PDF copy of a completed form? Instead of filling it in online, install a file converter (for example, CutePDF Writer or any other PDF creation program with a print-to-PDF feature) and then, after you fill in the Declaration Form online, open the printer window and select your PDF program in the Printer Name window.

- **Attach PDF Files:** In the Attach Documents page click the "Browse" button and find your PDF Application Holding Folder that contains the PDF files of your application. Select one of your PDF application files, that is, the Data file, click open, and you should see it in the Files to Be Submitted box adjacent the Browse button. Then open the Category pull-down menu adjacent the middle window and select Application Part. Then open the rightmost pull-down menu and select Application Data Sheet. (Make sure the No button opposite "Does your PDF file contain multiple documents?" is checked because it's more difficult to work when everything is in one PDF document.) Then click the Add File button and another row of three windows will open. Repeat the above steps for each of your other PDF application files (that is, Dwgs.pdf, Spec.pdf, and Dec.pdf), selecting the Document Description in the third window for each. When you've attached all of the PDF files in your PDF Application Holding Folder, click the Upload & Validate button at the bottom.

- **Review Documents:** After a few minutes, you'll eventually get a Review Documents page, which should show all of the documents you've attached. Make sure all four parts of your entire application (drawings, specification, data sheet, and Declaration) are there and there are no errors. If any errors are indicated, you'll have to go back and fix them. Occasionally, the PTO's server may reject one or more PDF documents for technical reasons—for example, the document contains nonembedded fonts or it has been scanned in gray format. If the PTO's server rejects your PDF because of embedded fonts or another fatal error, it will post a red inverted triangle next to the name of the file. Many of these problems can be eliminated by recreating the PDF—that is, open your PDF creation program and convert the document a second time to a new "image" PDF. If you convert the PDF to an image PDF the server may object to it using a yellow inverted triangle, which indicates that the error isn't fatal, in which case you can proceed. It merely means that the PTO will have to copy your data manually into their data processing system. Sometimes the PTO's server (computer) will fatally reject a PDF because you saved it using a newer version of a PDF Reader program that the PTO's system doesn't support. In this case you will have to remove this version from your computer and download and use an earlier version. When there are no fatal errors click "Continue."

- **Calculate Fees:** On the Calculate Fees page, select your entity size, which will usually be Small Entity. Check and complete all the applicable boxes on the form (the Search, Filing, and Examination fees must all be paid simultaneously) and then click the Calculate button.

- **Submit Application:** This page will list all of your PDF files, a Fee-Info.pdf file, and the filing fee. If everything is okay, click the Submit button at the bottom to bring up a "Congratulations!" page with an assigned Application Number, Confirmation Number, and Total Fees due. Click the YES! I want to pay now button at the bottom.

- **Review Fees and Select Payment Method:** Unless you have a PTO Deposit Account or are set up for EFT, select Charge Credit Card, then the Start online payment process to bring up the payment page. Fill out the blanks and click the Confirm button at the bottom.

- **Acknowledgment Receipt:** If everything is okay you'll get an Acknowledgment Receipt, which is analogous to the receipt postcard that was used for mailed filings. The Acknowledgment Receipt will list the Application (Serial) Number, the Confirmation Number, and the application data and parts that you've filed. Congratulations! You've bypassed the post office, filed an application electronically, and have gotten an instant filing acknowledgment. Select Print This Page to print the receipt for your records. In due course you'll get an official filing receipt by mail, as usual.

- **IDS:** As stated in the next section, you must generally file an IDS (Information Disclosure Statement) within three months after filing if you know of any relevant prior art. If you're a registered eFiler you can file an IDS online. Download IDS form SB08a from the PTO site (www.uspto.gov/patent/forms/forms-patent-applications-filed-or-after-september-16-2012). Open the SB08a form and fill out the Document Number, Publication Data, Name and Relevant Information column for each U.S. patent or U.S. published patent application you disclose, and Country Code, Number and Kind Code (if you know it), Publication Data, Name and Relevant Information column for each foreign patent document you disclose. Open the SB08b and fill out the central column to describe any nonpatent documents that you disclose. Then save the completed form using a suitable name, such as IDS.pdf, and file it online in a similar manner as you filed the PDFs of the application. If you're unregistered you'll have to fax or mail the IDS. Remember that you don't have to accompany the IDS with copies of any U.S. patents or published patent applications, but you do have to accompany it with copies of any foreign patents (with an explanation of relevance) and copies of any nonpatent prior art (referred to as Non-Patent Literature (NPL)).

- **Assignments:** If you want to file an assignment, you must do this through a separate part of the PTO's website. After you complete your electronic filing and have your Acknowledgment Receipt, or after you receive your official filing receipt by mail, fill in the Serial Number of your application on the assignment, and complete and sign the rest of the assignment. Then convert the signed assignment to PDF and go to http://epas.uspto.gov and follow the instructions.

- **Designs:** To file a design application via EFS-Web, prepare it as instructed below, except omit the postcard, Design Application Transmittal, Fee Transmittal, and CCPF or check. Do prepare the drawings, preamble, specification, and claim, and prepare and sign and date the declaration as instructed above and save these documents as PDF files. Then proceed as described above.

Enhanced First Action Interview Pilot Program for Registered eFilers

If you are a registered eFiler, you may wish to avail yourself of a new program that the PTO is testing. Under the Enhanced First Action Interview Pilot Program applicants will have an opportunity to interview their examiner after the examiner makes a search. The goal of the program is to dispose of applications early without the need for Office Actions and amendments. Under the program, the examiner will send a first Office Action (examination report) and you will study it and the references cited and request an interview with the examiner and hopefully negotiate whatever claim amendments and other changes will put the application in condition for allowance. If you and the examiner cannot come to any agreement, then prosecution will revert to the normal procedure. If you feel confident enough to study the references in an Office Action, redraft your claims, and handle an interview, we recommend you enter the program. The program is on a trial basis but may be extended or implemented permanently. To enter the program you must be a registered eFiler and you must file a request on Form PTO/SB/413C.

G. File the Information Disclosure Statement Within Three Months

The PTO's rules impose on each patent applicant a "duty of candor and good faith" toward the PTO. This means that all inventors (and attorneys) have a duty to disclose to the PTO information (prior art and any other information such as relevant litigation) of which they are aware. The information must be of the type that might influence the patent examiner in deciding on the patent application. (This duty is embodied in Inventor's Commandment 17.) To comply with the "prior art" part of Inventor's Commandment 17, all applicants who are aware of any relevant prior art, that is, from a search, should submit an Information Disclosure Statement (IDS) at the time of filing the application or within the following three months. It's not enough to cite the prior-art references in the Prior

Art section of your specification. You must cite them on a SB808a or SB808b form and supply copies of non-U.S. patent references to the PTO.

Even if it weren't required, it's to your advantage to file an IDS and to list as many relevant prior-art references as possible in order to have them considered and noted by the examiner. In this way they will be listed as "References Cited" in the patent. This creates a presumption that the claims of your patent are patentable over these references—that is, you'll have put these references behind you. You may file the IDS with your application but we suggest that you file the IDS afterward; this will prevent overload while preparing your basic application.

The IDS actually consists of an IDS cover letter (Form 10-5) and the actual IDS (Form SB808a and SB808b), on which you list the prior art. A filled-in sample is provided in Figs. 10N, 10O, and 10P. (If you file via EFS-Web—discussed in Section F—you should first fill out the SB808a and SB808b forms and make PDF copies of any non-U.S. patent references (foreign patents and Non-Patent Literature or NPL). You will not need a cover letter because the EFS-Web form provides its own cover letter.)

The IDS should list all prior-art references known to the inventors (and any assignees) that are relevant to the patentability of the application. These should include all the references you discovered in your patentability search, plus any other prior art of which you're aware, including even your own papers. In addition, the inventors must include with the IDS a copy of each cited non-U.S. patent reference and a discussion of the relevance of any non–English-language references to the invention. You must cite all references even if you discussed them in the prior-art section of your patent application. (If you haven't made a search or otherwise aren't aware of any prior art, don't file an IDS.) You should remove all marks and notes from any references that you send to the PTO. If you have compiled a very large number of references, list only those that are truly relevant and don't include any cumulative (duplicative) references.

If you cite a significant number of irrelevant references, a court may hold that you tried to deceive the PTO by burying the relevant references with a large number of irrelevant references.

In the United States Patent and Trademark Office

Serial Number: __11/123 456__

Appn. Filed: __2014 Nov 12__

Applicant(s): __M. Goldberger & N. Briskin__

Appn. Title: __Food chopper with convolute Blade__

Examiner/GAU: __/ 3240__

Mailed: __2014 Dec 13, Thu__

At: __Philadelphia, PA__

Information Disclosure Statement Cover Letter

Commissioner for Patents
P.O. Box 1450
Alexandria, VA 22313-1450

Sir:

Attached is a completed Form PTO/SB/08(A&B) and copies of any non-U.S. patent references cited thereon.

Following are comments on any non-English-language references pursuant to Rule 98:

Rasmussen shows a fruit peeler with a bent guide for controlling the thickness of the fruit as it is being peeled. Gillet shows a knife mounted parallel to a space with knife that can be tilted out or in to adjust the spacing of its edge.

None of the references shows a knife for making a cut of controlled depth wherein a flat-bladed knife with an elongated sharpened edge with an outward protrusion attached to the blade that is spaced back from the edge for limiting the depth of cut that can be made by said edge when it is used to cut in a direction perpendicular to the plane of the blade, as it is recited in independent claims 1 and 17, and hence their dependent claims 2 to 11 and 18 to 20.

To the contrary, all of the references show guides that are mounted generally parallel to the blade for limiting the thickness of the peel that can be cut by the blade when it is used to peel in a direction parallel to its plane.

Also, none of the references show any blade having a substantially right-angle bend parallel to its direction of elongation, as it is recited in independent claim 12 and its dependent claims 13 to 16.

Very respectfully,

Applicant(s): _Mildred Goldberger_

Nathan Briskin

Enc.: PTO/SB/08(A&B)

c/o: __M. Goldberger, Applicant Pro Se__

__1901 Kennedy Blvd.__

__Philadelphia, PA 19103__

Telephone: __215-555-0362__

Certificate of Mailing

I certify that this correspondence will be deposited with the United States Postal Service as first class mail with proper postage affixed in an envelope addressed to: "Commissioner for Patents, P.O. Box 1450, Alexandria, VA 22313-1450" on the date below.

Date: 20__14 Dec 15__   _Mildred Goldberger_   , Applicant

Fig. 10N—Completed IDS Cover Letter (Form 10-5 in Appendix 7)

PTO/SB/08a (07-09)
Approved for use through 11/30/2020. OMB 0651-0031
U.S. Patent and Trademark Office; U.S. DEPARTMENT OF COMMERCE
Under the Paperwork Reduction Act of 1995, no persons are required to respond to a collection of information unless it contains a valid OMB control number.

Substitute for form 1449/PTO

INFORMATION DISCLOSURE STATEMENT BY APPLICANT

(Use as many sheets as necessary)

	Complete if Known
Application Number	11/123,456
Filing Date	2016 Nov 11
First Named Inventor	M. Goldberger
Art Unit	3240
Examiner Name	
Attorney Docket Number	Goldberger-Briskin

Sheet | 1 | of | 2

U. S. PATENT DOCUMENTS

Examiner Initials*	Cite No.[1]	Document Number — Number-Kind Code[2] *(if known)*	Publication Date MM-DD-YYYY	Name of Patentee or Applicant of Cited Document	Pages, Columns, Lines, Where Relevant Passages or Relevant Figures Appear
	A	US- 21,695	10-15-1858	Oot	
	B	US- 602,758	11-11-1898	Landers	p4, ll.21-22
	C	US- 2,083,368	8-9-1937	Gambino	
	D	US- 2,968,867	10-11-1961	Wolff	
		US-			
		US-			
		US-			
		US-			
		US-			
		US-			
		US-			
		US-			
		US-			
		US-			
		US-			
		US-			
		US-			
		US-			
		US-			
		US-			

FOREIGN PATENT DOCUMENTS

Examiner Initials*	Cite No.[1]	Foreign Patent Document — Country Code[3] Number[4] Kind Code[5] *(if known)*	Publication Date MM-DD-YYYY	Name of Patentee or Applicant of Cited Document	Pages, Columns, Lines, Where Relevant Passages Or Relevant Figures Appear	T[6]
	E	DK-69,640	5-22-1949	Rasmussen	p2, ll. 13-17	
	F	FR-1,029,924	3-23-1953	Gillet		

Examiner Signature		Date Considered	

*EXAMINER: Initial if reference considered, whether or not citation is in conformance with MPEP 609. Draw line through citation if not in conformance and not considered. Include copy of this form with next communication to applicant. [1] Applicant's unique citation designation number (optional). [2] See Kinds Codes of USPTO Patent Documents at www.uspto.gov or MPEP 901.04. [3] Enter Office that issued the document, by the two-letter code (WIPO Standard ST.3). [4] For Japanese patent documents, the indication of the year of the reign of the Emperor must precede the serial number of the patent document. [5] Kind of document by the appropriate symbols as indicated on the document under WIPO Standard ST.16 if possible. [6] Applicant is to place a check mark here if English language Translation is attached.

This collection of information is required by 37 CFR 1.97 and 1.98. The information is required to obtain or retain a benefit by the public which is to file (and by the USPTO to process) an application. Confidentiality is governed by 35 U.S.C. 122 and 37 CFR 1.14. This collection is estimated to take 2 hours to complete, including gathering, preparing, and submitting the completed application form to the USPTO. Time will vary depending upon the individual case. Any comments on the amount of time you require to complete this form and/or suggestions for reducing this burden, should be sent to the Chief Information Officer, U.S. Patent and Trademark Office, P.O. Box 1450, Alexandria, VA 22313-1450. DO NOT SEND FEES OR COMPLETED FORMS TO THIS ADDRESS. **SEND TO: Commissioner for Patents, P.O. Box 1450, Alexandria, VA 22313-1450.**

If you need assistance in completing the form, call 1-800-PTO-9199 (1-800-786-9199) and select option 2.

Fig. 10O—Information Disclosure Statement (Form 10-6A in Appendix 7)

Substitute for form 1449/PTO

INFORMATION DISCLOSURE STATEMENT BY APPLICANT

(Use as many sheets as necessary)

Complete if Known

Application Number	11/123,456
Filing Date	2016 Nov 11
First Named Inventor	m. Goldberger
Art Unit	3240
Examiner Name	
Attorney Docket Number	Goldberger-Briskin

Sheet 2 of 2

NON PATENT LITERATURE DOCUMENTS

Examiner Initials*	Cite No.[1]	Include name of the author (in CAPITAL LETTERS), title of the article (when appropriate), title of the item (book, magazine, journal, serial, symposium, catalog, etc.), date, page(s), volume-issue number(s), publisher, city and/or country where published.	T[2]
	G	PHILLIPS, Food Comminuting, Restaurant News, April 1959, Food Press, Willow Grove, PA	

Examiner Signature		Date Considered	

Fig. 10P—Information Disclosure Statement (Form 10-6B in Appendix 7)

As a general rule, if you are not sure whether a reference is relevant enough to cite, it's best to cite it. It doesn't cost anything to cite an additional reference and the penalty for not citing a relevant reference is severe—your patent can be held invalid. One way to determine whether a reference is relevant enough to cite as prior art in your IDS is to consider not citing it in your IDS and then assume you get a patent. Further assume that you sue an infringer and they find out through discovery that you knew about the reference. If the infringer then cites the reference to the judge and charges you with fraud on the PTO for not citing it, the reference is relevant if a reasonable judge would be likely to find that you should have cited it to avoid fraud on the PTO.

Note that the PTO's Rule 56 (37 CFR 1.56) states that applicants should examine the following to be sure that they disclose all relevant prior art:

1. Prior art cited in search reports of a foreign patent office in a counterpart application.
2. The closest information over which individuals associated with the filing or prosecution of a patent application believe any pending claim patentably defines, to make sure that any material information contained therein is disclosed to the Office.

The PTO considers that information is material to patentability when it is not cumulative to information already of record or being made of record in the application, and (a) it establishes, by itself or in combination with other information, a *prima facie* (on first sight) case of unpatentability of a claim; or (b) it refutes, or is inconsistent with, a position the applicant takes in (i) opposing an argument of unpatentability relied on by the Office, or (ii) asserting an argument of patentability.

A *prima facie* case of unpatentability is established when the information compels a conclusion that a claim is unpatentable under the preponderance of evidence burden-of-proof standard, giving each term in the claim its broadest reasonable construction consistent with the specification. This is done before any consideration is given to evidence which may be submitted in an attempt to establish a contrary conclusion of patentability.

As mentioned, you can send the IDS with your application instead of taking advantage of the three-month grace period. In this event, the names of the inventors and title of your invention are the only information you need to put at the top of Form 10-5. Don't fill out the Certificate of Mailing at the bottom of the form. If you send it after your application is filed, you'll know the serial number, filing date, and group art unit, and can insert them. Also, you should fill out the Certificate of Mailing at the bottom of the form.

The blanks in Forms 10-5 and 10-6 are self-explanatory. Information about the Art Unit (requested in the upper right-hand corner of Form 10-6) is on your filing receipt. Before each patent number in the Foreign Patent Documents section, you may use a two-letter international country code, as indicated. The most common county codes are FR (France), JP (Japan), CN (China), GB (United Kingdom), CA (Canada), EP (Europe), and DE (Germany). In the right-hand column, headed "Pages, Columns …," you can list any places in the document that you feel are particularly relevant, but this is optional since the pertinent rules (Rules 97 and 98) require that you merely cite the documents.

If you include any non–English-language reference on Form 10-6, Rule 98(a)(3) requires that you also provide a concise explanation of its relevance on a separate paper or in the specification. We recommend that you also state how your invention, as claimed, differs physically from this reference(s). State the relevance of any non-English references, and any discussion as to how your invention differs, on Form 10-5. Fig. 10N provides an example.

If you send in the IDS with the application, note this on the postcard and transmittal letter that you send with your application and don't fill out the Certificate of Mailing at the bottom of Form 10-5. If you send it in after the application is filed, send it with a separate postcard and fill out the Certificate of Mailing. Again, address the front of the card to you; the back should read as in Fig. 10Q. If you file the application by EFS-Web and include the IDS, you don't have to send the PTO a postcard. The acknowledgment receipt you receive will list the IDS. If you file by EFS-Web and you're a registered eFiler (or become one later), you can file the IDS via EFS-Web after you get your official filing receipt. If you file by EFS-Web and you're not a registered eFiler, you will have to mail the IDS and cover sheet with a receipt postcard.

If you haven't made a search and are not aware of any prior art—you don't have to file an IDS. The PTO won't deny or delay your application if you don't file an IDS. However, if they (or an infringer whom you later sue for patent infringement) discover that you knew of relevant prior art and didn't file an IDS, your patent application or patent can be held invalid for "fraud on the PTO." This is so even if the examiner discovers the reference you withheld and cites it in a regular Office Action. In one case, a Dallas patent law firm neglected to disclose some relevant prior art to the PTO in its client's patent application. The client got a patent and sued on it but because of the cloud the nondisclosed art cast on the patent, it had to settle the suit for far less than it would have gotten if the firm had disclosed the prior art to the PTO. The client then sued the firm and a jury awarded the client $72 million in damages for the firm's omission!

Suppose you are aware of information other than prior art that may be material to patentability—for example relevant litigation, an assertion by another person claiming to be an inventor, or a sale of a product embodying the invention before the filing date (but not before your date of invention). You have a duty to disclose this information also. You can do this with a narrative statement on a form such as Form 10-5. Also, be sure to state why the information does not negate the patentability of your invention.

Information Disclosure Statement, Form PTO/SB/08 (A and B), and *[insert number]* References in patent application of *[insert name(s) of inventor(s)]*, Serial No. _____ , Filed _____ received for filing today:

Fig. 10Q—Back of Postcard for Sending IDS After Filing

H. Assignments

As we mentioned, a patent application must be filed in the name or names of the true inventor or inventors of the invention claimed in the patent application. The inventors then become the applicants for the patent, and the law considers that they automatically own equal shares of the invention, the patent application, and any patents that may issue on the application (Chapter 16, Section B). However, inventorship can be different from ownership. Often all or part of the ownership of the invention and the patent application must be transferred to someone else, either an individual or a legal entity, such as a corporation, a partnership, or an individual. To make this transfer, the inventor(s) must "assign" (legally transfer) their interest. The assignment transfers ownership (or part of it) from the inventor(s) to another entity. However, inventorship remains the same after an assignment is made. (Directions and forms for completing the assignment are in Chapter 16, Section E.)

If you have assigned the application to another person or company and you want to send the assignment to the PTO for recording (highly advised), you can either send it in with the patent application or at any time afterward. We prefer to send in assignments later, after we get the postcard receipt back, when we know and can add the serial number and filing date of the application to the assignment. This will make the two documents (the assignment and the application) correspond to each other more directly. In this case, you can add the serial number and filing date to the assignment in the spaces indicated. Then prepare an Assignment "Recordation Form Cover Sheet" (Form 16-4 or PTO 1595). In space 1, the conveying parties are the inventor applicants. In space 2A, the receiving party is the assignee—the person or organization to whom you're assigning the application. The Internal Address is the mail stop or apartment number if any, in the assignee's building. In space 3, the Conveyance is an assignment and the execution date is the date you signed the assignment. In space 4, the Application Number is the Serial Number of your patent application. We recommend that you also type the filing date. If you don't know these numbers yet, just fill in the execution (signing) date of your PAD. If you're assigning

United States Patent [19]

Sarriugarte et al.

[11] **Patent Number:** Des. **404,074**

[45] **Date of Patent:** ✳✳**Jan. 12, 1999**

US00D404074S

[54] **CARD, PLACARD, OR RIGID PICTURE HOLDER**

[76] Inventors: **Jon Sarriugarte; Sina Hanson**, both of 2601 Adeline St., Oakland, Calif. 94607

[**] Term: **14 Years**

[21] Appl. No.: **69,268**

[22] Filed: **Mar. 21, 1997**

[51] **LOC (6) Cl.** **19-02**
[52] **U.S. Cl.** **D19/90**; D20/43; D19/86; D6/313
[58] **Field of Search** D6/313; D11/121; D20/43; D19/65, 75, 78, 86, 87, 90, 91, 95, 99, 100; 211/69.1–69.9, 181.1; 40/606, 659, 642.02; 248/229.26, 175, 475.1, 623; 5/246, 252, 256

[56] **References Cited**

U.S. PATENT DOCUMENTS

D. 26,320	11/1896	Arkin	D19/86
D. 27,364	7/1897	Hill et al.	D20/43
D. 32,692	5/1900	Muth	D20/43
D. 178,356	7/1956	Galef	D19/86
D. 203,185	12/1965	Leaboldi	D19/87
D. 247,265	2/1978	Ledebuhr	D20/43
3,474,555	10/1969	McCaffrey	40/659
3,721,414	3/1973	Yoder	248/175

Primary Examiner—Martie K. Holtje
Attorney, Agent, or Firm—David Pressman

[57] **CLAIM**

The ornamental design for a a card, placard, or rigid picture holder, as shown and described.

DESCRIPTION

FIG. **1** is a front elevational view of a card, placard or rigid picture holder showing our new design, the rear view being substantially a mirror image thereof;
FIG. **2** is a right side elevational view;
FIG. **3** is a left side elevational view;
FIG. **4** is a top plan view; and,
FIG. **5** is a bottom plan view thereof.

1 Claim, 3 Drawing Sheets

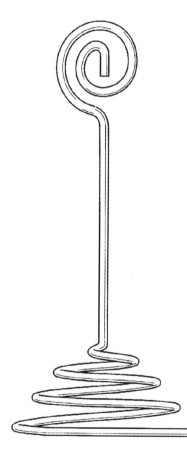

Fig. 10R—Sample of Design Patent

How to Market Your Invention

Inventor's Commandment 20

Try to market your invention as soon as you can after filing your patent application; don't wait until your patent issues. Favor successful companies that are close to you, small in size, and already make and sell items as close to yours as possible.

Inventor's Commandment 21

If you want your invention to be successful, pursue commercial exploitation with all the energy that you can devote to it, and use every avenue available.

Inventor's Commandment 22

Never pay any money to any invention developer unless the developer can prove to you that it has a successful track record—that is, most of its clients have received more income in royalties than they have paid in developer fees.

The Project Team Approach

If you already know how your invention will be marketed, or you work for a corporation that plans to handle this task, you can skip this chapter and continue reading about obtaining patent coverage. Also, if you would rather spend all your time at your workbench and not have to deal with marketing, a good way to go is to put together a team consisting of persons with diverse skills, such as an inventor, a manufacturing expert, a marketing expert, a person to handle the legwork, a model maker, etc. Chapter 12 deals with obtaining patents in other countries and Chapter 13 with getting the U.S. PTO to grant your patent.

In this chapter we make an important detour from the central task covered by this book—obtaining a valid and effective patent on your invention. The reason for this sudden turn is simple. In the usual course of events, you'll have an interval (six months to three years) after you file your patent application before you need to either consider foreign filing or reply to an Office Action from the PTO. We strongly recommend that you use this interval to get your invention out on the market.

RESOURCE

For more information on licensing your invention, consult *Profit From Your Idea: How to Make Smart Licensing Deals*, by Richard Stim (Nolo).

"Out on the market?" you ask. Shouldn't you keep your invention, and the fact that you've filed the application, secret? The answer is, "No." In fact, once you file a patent application (including a Provisional Patent Application; see Chapter 3) on your invention, you may show it to whomever you think might be interested in buying or licensing it with minimal risk of having someone scoop you on your invention.

This is because it would be very difficult for someone to steal your invention when you're the first to file a patent application on it. Any thief would have to file their patent application after yours, a useless and wasted effort since you would be the first to file, and the PTO would reject their later-filed application based on your earlier filing.

Your next question might be: Why try to sell or license your invention before a patent has been issued? While there are advantages to selling an already-patented invention, generally it's best to try to sell or license your invention as soon as possible after filing your patent application. This is because prospective corporate purchasers of your invention will want time to get a head start on the competition and to have the time the patent is in force coincide with the time the product's actually on the market. Also, you'll be able to offer the manufacturer the right to apply for foreign patents; this right will be lost once your patent issues. The lack of prestige that a pending patent has as compared to an already issued patent can be compensated for by a favorable search report showing that there's no strong prior art—that is, that a patent is likely to issue on your invention.

A. Perseverance and Patience Are Essential

Even if you get a patent, it will almost certainly be totally worthless unless it covers a commercially exploited invention. In fact, millions of patents have issued on inventions that were never successfully commercialized. None of these patents ever yielded a nickel to their owners.

To get your invention into commercial production, you'll have to persevere. There's no magic solution to the invention marketing process. As noted toy inventor Paul Brown says, "You almost have to be obsessed with your invention to get it going." Or put another way, Emerson's famous adage about building a better mousetrap would have been better written, "If you build a better mousetrap, you'll still have to beat a path to many doors to get it sold."

Even though you believe you've got the greatest thing since sliced bread, the money won't start flowing in that quickly in most cases. It takes time to develop, market, and sell a product. Consider the following quote:

> *"There is no reason anyone would want a computer in their home."*

> –Ken Olson, President, Digital Equipment Corp., 1977

Chester Carlson, a patent attorney and the inventor of xerography, may have exaggerated somewhat, but he wasn't too far off base when he said:

> *"The time scale of invention is a long one. Results do not come quickly. Inventive developments have to be measured in decades rather than years. It takes patience to stay with an idea through such a long period.*
>
> *"In my case, I am sure I would not have done so if it were not for the hope of the eventual reward through the incentives offered by the patent system."*

Unfortunately, the marketplace is not rational or linear. An inferior product can be successful and a superior product can be a failure, depending upon how it's promoted.

B. Overview of Alternative Ways to Profit From Your Invention

As you can see from the chart of Fig. 11A, there are seven main ways or routes for the independent inventor to get an invention into the marketplace and profit from it. These choices involve increasing

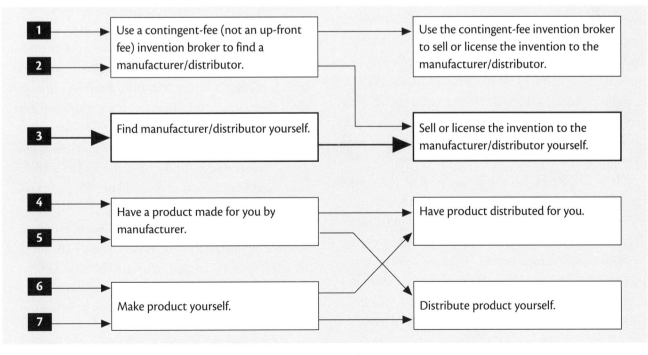

Fig. 11A—Alternative Ways to Profit From Your Invention

difficulty and work for you. We recommend that most inventors use Route 3, and have accordingly highlighted this route.

1. Route 1: Using a Contingent-Fee Intermediary

Some organizations that market or develop inventions for inventors are legitimate and honest. Many others are illegitimate and dishonest; they exist solely to exploit inventors, regardless of the harm caused. There is an easy way to tell the difference. The dishonest ones usually require up-front money before they will undertake to develop or promote your invention. The honest ones typically represent you on a contingent fee basis and do not require an up-front fee. In this section, we will discuss dealing with honest contingent-fee invention brokers (CFIBs) and will advise you regarding the up-front-fee types, which we call FBIEs (Fee-Based Inventor Exploiters).

Starting at the top, Route 1 involves getting a contingent-fee invention broker or intermediary to find a suitable manufacturer/distributor for you and then using the broker to represent you in the sale or license of your invention.

Don't confuse a CFIB with fee-based "invention developers," "invention promoters," and the like: A CFIB is a firm that will represent you and try to market your invention by selling or licensing it for a percentage of your rights, the "contingent-fee basis." Unlike the dreaded fee-based inventor-exploiters (or FBIEs; see "Don't Use a Fee-Based Inventor-Exploiter," below) CFIBs do not charge a fee for their services. They are generally considered to be reputable, honest, and provide a legitimate service for a fair form of compensation.

Obviously, Route 1 is the easiest possible path, since the CFIB will do all of the work for you. However, it's neither that difficult to find suitable manufacturer/distributors if they exist, nor to present your invention to them once you locate them. Thus, we recommend that you consider handling this task yourself. No one can sell an invention as sincerely and with as much enthusiasm and conviction as you, the true inventor.

Also, you'll get 100% of the benefits and won't have to share the fruit of your creativity with a salesperson. Finally, companies will respect you more if you approach them directly; if you approach them through an intermediary, they'll think less of you and your invention. Why? They may think that you don't have the ability or initiative to approach them yourself.

If you do use a CFIB, you should be concerned about two main possibilities for harm:

1. loss of your invention rights through theft or communication to a thief, and
2. loss of time and hence other opportunities.

The first possibility isn't great because you've already got a patent application on file. However, the second possibility is very real, and you should accordingly verify the efficacy of any CFIB beforehand. Unfortunately, about the only surefire way to do this is by word-of-mouth. Check with a patent attorney, an inventors' organization, or some of the CFIB's clients if your own associates are unable to provide you with a lead.

Once you're satisfied with the CFIB's honesty and references, you should next investigate the contract they offer you to be sure you don't lose time needlessly. Thus, the contract should specify that the CFIB will perform substantial services, such as identifying the prospective manufacturers, preparing an invention presentation or demonstration, building and testing the invention, submitting your invention to the prospects, negotiating a license or sales agreement for you, etc. And most important, the agreement should set a time limit for the CFIB to succeed—that is, get you a firm offer to buy, license, or get your invention on the market in product form. We feel that a year is reasonable; 18 months is about the maximum you should ever consider. Make sure that if the CFIB fails to succeed in the allotted time, all of your rights will be returned to you, together with all of the CFIB's research, presentation documents, models, etc.

Some organizations that claim to be CFIBs include AmericaInvents.com and InnovationVillage.com. ThinkFire.com (www.thinkfire.com) specializes in patent brokerage and licensing. However, before

Don't Use a Fee-Based Inventor-Exploiter

There are firms that we call fee-based inventor-exploiters (FBIEs), that you should avoid. Paul Turley of the FTC reported that of 30,000 people who paid such FBIEs a fee, not one ever received any payback. These companies or organizations run ads in newspapers, magazines, radio, and TV, stating something like "Inventions and Ideas Wanted!" They will commonly first send you an "inventor's kit" that includes a disclosure form similar to our Form 3-2 and that promises to "evaluate" your invention for free or for a relatively small fee (say $200 to $600). The evaluation almost always is glowingly positive. Then they'll ask for a relatively large fee—$1,000 to $5,000 and up—using very high-pressure sales tactics. They'll promise to do "market research" and try to sell your invention or have it manufactured. They sometimes also take a percentage (for example, 20%) of your invention to make you feel that they are your partner and want success as much as you do.

Generally, FBIEs will do little more than write a brief blurb describing your invention and send it to prospective manufacturers in the appropriate fields. Their efforts are virtually 100% unsuccessful, as reported in the *Wall Street Journal* and on the TV program *20/20*. In other words, FBIEs make their money from inventors, not inventions. As a result of federal legislation (35 USC 297), FBIEs must now make certain disclosures to prospective customers. If they don't, they can be sued for false statements or material omission. The invention promoter must disclose to you in writing:

- the total number of inventions evaluated by the FBIE for commercial potential in the past five years, as well as the number of those inventions that received positive evaluations; and the number of those inventions that received negative evaluations
- the total number of customers who have contracted with the FBIE in the past five years, not including customers who have purchased trade show services, research, advertising, or other nonmarketing services from the invention promoter or who have defaulted in their payment to the FBIE

- the total number of customers known by the FBIE to have received a net financial profit as a direct result of the invention promotion services provided by such invention promoter
- the total number of customers known by the FBIE to have received license agreements for their inventions as a direct result of the invention promotion services provided by such invention promoter, and
- the names and addresses of all previous FBIE companies with which the invention promoter or its officers have collectively or individually been affiliated in the previous ten years. This statute also enables defrauded customers to recover damages and sometimes triple damages against an FBIE who violates it.

Despite this strict statute and its penalties, many FBIEs still operate at full steam and still defraud inventors of millions of dollars annually. They do this in spite of the disclosures that the above statute requires them to make by telling prospective customers something like, "This means nothing—we're required to show you this. Don't worry about this but look at the bright side: We'll prepare a great color presentation and present your invention to industry and they'll be clamoring for it and you'll make a lot of royalties and will be able to retire, etc., etc."

The PTO does not investigate complaints or participate in legal proceedings against invention promoters. The PTO will accept complaints, forward these complaints to the FBIEs, and make the complaints and responses publicly available on the PTO's Independent Inventor website.

To learn what you will need to file a complaint, visit the PTO website (www.uspto.gov/patent/forms/forms-patent-applications-filed-or-after-september-16-2012) for a complaint form (PTO Form SB/2048A). Complaints should be mailed to the following address:

United States Patent and Trademark Office
Mail Stop 24, P.O. Box 1450
Alexandria, VA 22313-1452

you engage any of these companies, please be sure that they will not charge you an up-front fee and that any contract they offer you is fair. We strongly recommend that you never pay an up-front fee because any organization that charges an up-front fee is an FBIE. You can find other CFIBs through inventors' organizations. Also, when negotiating license agreements, attempt to have all of your royalties sent directly to you (and the CFIB's portion sent to the CFIB). That can head off accounting issues that sometimes result when all the payments must run through the CFIB.

In addition, many universities now have invention marketing departments that exist primarily to market the technology developed in the universities' research labs, but they also take ideas from outsiders on a contingent-fee basis.

2. Route 2: Partial Use of an Intermediary

Route 2 (a seldom-used path) is the same as Route 1, except that here you use a broker to find prospects and then you take over and do the selling. Contingent-fee brokers typically won't accept this type of arrangement, because they'll want to control the sales negotiations. However, there are many inventor assistance companies that will provide you with product evaluation, illustration, advertising, packaging design, market research, and product testing services for a fee; one such organization is Synergy Consultants (https://synergyconsulting.us). If you feel that your strong suit is in presenting and selling, and that sales research is for someone else, you can pay a broker or market researcher (either CFIB or fee-based) to research possible purchasers. Then go out and present your invention yourself.

3. Route 3: Finding a Manufacturer and Distributor Yourself

Route 3 is the path we most favor and which most independent inventors use. Here you do your own research and selling. If you succeed, you'll get 100% of the rewards and you'll control the whole process, yet you won't be bothered with manufacturing or distributing.

4. Route 4: Having Your Invention Manufactured and Distributed for You

Route 4 is a viable alternative for some relatively uncomplicated products. Here you have your invention manufactured for you—a Far Eastern manufacturer will usually be cheapest—and then use U.S. distributors to sell the product. Of course, you have the headaches of supervising a manufacturing operation, including such details as quality control and red tape associated with importing. But, if you succeed, you'll keep much of the manufacturing profit for yourself.

Some precautions to observe if you use any manufacturer is to make sure the manufacturer is honest and to have them agree:

- that you are the inventor and that they received the details and information about the invention from you
- not to sell your product to anyone else
- to return any tooling and all papers and materials to you if you terminate the relationship
- that they recognize a strict and absolute duty of fidelity and trust to you, and
- that they will not file any patent applications anywhere on the invention.

5. Route 5: You Distribute

In Route 5, you handle distribution as well as supervising manufacturing. More profit, but more headaches and work.

6. Route 6: You Manufacture

In Route 6, you really get into it; you have to do the manufacturing yourself, with all of its headaches (see Section J), but you'll get a lion's share of the profits, if there are any.

7. Route 7: You Manufacture and Distribute

Last, and most difficult, in Route 7 you do it all yourself—manufacturing and distributing. While you get all of the profits, you'll have all of the headaches. Successful inventor Robert G. Merrick advocates this route in his book, *Stand Alone, Inventor!*

Because, as we said, Route 3 makes the most sense for most independent inventors, we devote the bulk of this chapter to finding a manufacturer/distributor to build and market your patent. (If you want to pursue the possibility of manufacturing and distributing your invention, we've included an overview of potential resources, below, to help you do this.)

C. Be Ready to Demonstrate a Working Model of Your Invention to Potential Customers

Assuming that you choose Route 3, the best way to get a manufacturer or others to "buy" your invention is to demonstrate an actual working model. Pictures and diagrams may convey an idea and get a message across, but the working model is the thing that will make believers out of most people and show them that your invention is real and doable.

"Products sell; ideas don't."

–David Kewit, Patent Agent

So, if you haven't made a model before, do your best to make one now, even if it has to be made of cardboard or wood. One essential is to make your model or prototype as simple as possible. Simplicity enhances reliability, decreases cost, decreases weight, and facilitates salability, both to a manufacturer and to the public.

If you're not handy, hopefully you can afford to have a professional model maker or artisan build the model, or you may have a handy friend or relative. Where can you find model makers? Ask your local inventors' organization or if that fails, an inventor's magazine; *Inventors Digest* has ads in every issue from model makers. Another obvious place is online searching under "Model Makers." Also try "Machine Shops" and "Plastics—Fabricating, Finishing, and Decorating." One service, eMachineShop (www.emachineshop.com), will supply you with free software that you can use to draw your part and click to have them custom-make it for you.

In addition, your local college or community college may have a design and industry department that may be able to refer you to a model maker. If you live near an industrial plant that employs machinists or model makers, perhaps you can get one of these employees to moonlight and do the job for you—put a notice on the plant's bulletin board, call, or ask around.

If you do use a model maker and you disclose critical information, including dimensions, materials, suppliers, or other data you consider to be proprietary (a trade secret), it is best to have the model maker sign a Consultant's Work Agreement (Form 4-3) before you turn over your drawings or other papers. Follow the instructions in Chapter 4 to fill out this form. I also suggest that you add a confidentiality legend to any drawings or descriptions you turn over to your model maker. Such a legend can be made in rubber-stamp or sticker form or can be typed on the drawings, and should read as follows:

"This drawing or description contains proprietary information of [your name] and is loaned for use only in evaluating or building an invention of [your name] and must be returned upon demand. By acceptance hereof, recipient agrees to all of the above conditions. © [year] [your name]."

After you've made a working model, you should take at least one good photograph of it. The photograph should be of professional quality—if you are not a good photographer, have a professional do it, and order several views if necessary. Then write a descriptive blurb about your invention, stating the title or the trademark, what it is, how it works, its main advantages and selling points, plus your name, address, telephone number, and the legend "Patent Pending." Don't get too bogged down in detail, however. In other words, make your write-up snappy and convincing. You should then make copies (either print or digital depending on your method of communication).

If you can't build a real working model, you can build (or have a designer build) a "virtual prototype" (computer simulation) using computer-assisted-design (CAD) software.

D. Finding Prospective Manufacturers/Distributors

The next step is to compile an initial listing of manufacturers who you believe could manufacture and distribute your invention profitably. You should keep your marketing notes, papers, and correspondence in a separate file from your patent application (legal) file. Your initial list should comprise all the manufacturers who meet the following four criteria:

- they're geographically close to you
- they already manufacture the same or a closely related product
- they're not too large, and
- they're anxious to sell new products.

Nearby or local manufacturers who already work in your field are best. If they manufacture your invention, you can monitor their progress, consult with them frequently, and take any needed action more easily if anything goes wrong. Obviously, it's a big help to deal with a company that has experience with devices similar to yours. They already know how to sell in your field, are aware of competitive pricing policies, can make your invention part of their existing product line—which allows them to keep sales costs low—and presumably want new models related to their existing products in order to keep ahead of the competition. If the manufacturer is not in a closely allied line, both the seller and the product will be on trial, so why start with two strikes against you?

The reasons for avoiding giant manufacturers are these:

1. Smaller manufacturers are more dependent on outside designers. In other words, most don't have a strong inbred prejudice against inventions they did not invent themselves.
2. You can contact the decision makers or the owners of the company directly, or more easily.
3. Decisions are made more rapidly because the bureaucracies are smaller.
4. You are less likely to be required to sign a waiver form.
5. Giant companies have more access to patent lawyers and, hence, a greater tendency to try to "get around" your invention by investigating and trying to invalidate your patent or trying to avoid infringing it. Medium and small companies, on the other hand, will be more interested in your invention's profit potential and its effect in the marketplace.

Obviously, you shouldn't use companies that are so small that they don't have enough money to finance the manufacture of your invention or market it adequately. Companies with sales of about $10 million to $100 million are best (unless you have enormous market potential).

To find companies meeting the above criteria, start by first considering people you know. Which one of them is likely to have contacts in the field of your interest? Put them to work for you and you may be amazed that with a few phone calls you can get just the introduction you need.

If this doesn't work, try looking in your appropriate local stores for manufacturers of closely allied products that are already on the shelves. You'll know for sure that these companies have a successful distribution and sales system or operation.

Research online or at a local library checking resources such as the *Thomas Register* or *Dun's Million Dollar Directory*. In addition, check the ads at pertinent trade and hobby websites. Lastly, services that provide stock analysis, such as *Value Line Investment Survey*, *Standard & Poor's*, *Hoover's*, and *Moody's*, supply excellent information about companies. Get the names of the company presidents, vice presidents, directors of engineering, marketing, etc. Find out all you can about each company you select; know its products, sales and corporate history, profitability, and factory location(s).

If your invention is in the gadget category and you believe it would appeal to the affluent, try Hammacher Schlemmer (www.hammacher.com), Sharper Image (www.sharperimage.com), or one of the many other specialty stores that sell gadget exotica. These companies receive thousands of ideas for inventions each year, accept some of these, and arrange to have them produced by manufacturers. Also, trade fairs or shows—such as San Francisco International Gift Fair or NY Now—are good places for you to wander about, looking for prospective manufacturers. Talk to the people who run the exhibits to get a feel for the companies, whom to contact, and what their attitude toward outside inventions is.

Some suggestions: If your invention is a new automotive tool or device, Lisle Corp. (www.lislecorp.com), and Kraco (www.kraco.com) seek such inventions. Homax Products, (www.homaxproducts.com), wants home improvement inventions. Hog Wild Toys (www.hogwildtoys.com) is looking for novel toys and gifts. The toy store F.A.O. Schwartz also looks for toys and gifts, and has "toy auditions" in New York City (usually coinciding with the annual toy fair). If you have a new exercise or fitness machine, consider NordicTrack (www.nordictrack.com).

One company, quirky.com, has a unique approach. You submit a description of your idea to them with a $10 fee and drawings if you have them. If they like it they will have it made and pay you royalties—about ⅓ of sales. They have a community that assists in evaluations and design. So far they have developed and are selling many products and have paid their inventors millions in royalties. They do not deal with patents, so you're on your own here. Go to their site and listen to their video manifesto to see if it's right for you.

If you can't find any U.S. companies, try foreign ones. Sadly, many U.S. firms are complacent or tight. They've refused to undertake new ventures that foreign firms have jumped at, which can work to your advantage as an inventor.

E. The "NIH" Syndrome

Before presenting your invention to any manufacturer, two possible impediments should be kept in mind:
- the "NIH" (Not Invented Here) syndrome, and
- the common insistence that you give up many of your legal rights by signing a waiver.

Generally, the larger the manufacturer, the greater the chances of encountering one or both of these impediments.

The NIH syndrome is an unwritten attitude that handicaps inventors who submit their ideas to a company, no matter how meritorious such ideas may be. Put simply, many companies have a bias against any outsider ("the enemy") or any outside invention because it was "not invented here." This attitude prevails primarily because of jealousy. The job of the corporate engineering department is to create new and profitable products for their company. If an engineering department were to recommend an outside invention, it would almost be a tacit admission that the department had failed to do its job in solving a problem and coming up with the solution the outside inventor has found.

How can you overcome the NIH syndrome? First, realize that it's more likely to exist in larger companies, or companies with extensive engineering departments. Second, when forced to deal with engineering departments or any department in a company where the NIH syndrome may be present, always remember that the more your invention appears to be a logical extension of ideas already developed within the company, the better your chances of acceptance will be.

F. The Waiver and Precautions in Signing It

Most inventors affected with the paranoia part of the "Paranoia/Greed/Laziness Syndrome" (see Chapter 2) are afraid to show their invention to anyone, even after they've filed a patent application. The truth is, however, that most companies are far more afraid of you suing them for taking your invention than they are interested in stealing it. Most companies with access to legal advice will require you to sign their agreement (called a "waiver"), under which you give up a number of important rights that you would otherwise possess under the law. The reason for this waiver is that many companies have been sued by inventors claiming violation of an implied confidentiality agreement, or an implied agreement to pay if all or any part of the invention is used. Even though the company's own inventor may have come up with the invention independently of the outside inventor, many companies have lost these suits or were forced to compromise because of the uncertainties and expenses of litigation.

The waiver itself usually requires you to give up all your rights, except those that you may have under the patent laws. Specifically, the waiver typically asks you to agree that:

1. The company has no obligation to pay you if they use your idea.
2. The company isn't bound to keep your idea in confidence.
3. The company has no obligation to return any paper you submit.
4. The company has no obligation whatever to you, except under the patent laws.

Many companies add many other minor provisions, which are not significant enough to discuss here. The effect of the waiver is that you have no rights whatever against the company if they use your invention, except to sue them for patent infringement if and when you get a patent.

The usual procedure, if you send a letter mentioning your idea to the company, is for the company to route your letter to the patent or legal department, which will send you a form letter back stating their policy and asking you to sign the waiver before they agree to review your idea. Once you do so, the patent or legal department will approve your submission for review and send it to the appropriate engineering manager of the company.

Since you may not get a patent, since the company may use a variation of your idea that may not be covered by any patent you do get, and since you would like to have the company keep your submission in confidence, it's best to avoid signing any waiver if at all possible. For this reason, you should, at least initially, concentrate on smaller companies. The smaller the company, the less likely they are to make you sign a waiver. In fact, the best sort of relation you can have with a company to which you submit your ideas is to have them sign an agreement that you have drafted. Many small companies actually want to review outside inventions and are willing to sign a proprietary-submission agreement.

If the company is willing, or if you can swing it (say, by touting the commercial potential of your invention, being dramatic, establishing a rapport with the research people, etc.), have the company sign a Proprietary Submission Agreement such as the following:

Proprietary Submission Agreement

X Company agrees to review an invention from [*your name*] for a new and improved [*describe invention*], to keep in confidence such invention and all papers received, to return upon request all papers submitted, and to pay [*your name*] a reasonable sum and royalty to be settled by future negotiation or arbitration if X Company uses or adopts such invention.

If a company won't sign the above agreement, you can make it a bit more palatable by eliminating the last clause regarding the payment of a reasonable fee and royalty. Even with the last clause eliminated, you're in a very good position if you've gotten them to sign. If the company still refuses to sign your agreement, you can add the following clause:

The foregoing shall not obligate X Company with respect to any information which X Company can document (a) was known to it prior to receipt from me, either directly or indirectly, or (b) which is now or hereafter becomes part of the public domain from a source other than X Company.

If you can't get them to sign even this, you're still in a pretty good position legally if you can get them to review your invention without any agreement being signed by either side.

If all else fails and you do have to sign a waiver before the company will look at your invention (that's what will usually happen), it's not all that bad, since you do, at least, have a pending patent application. And most companies are far more afraid of you suing them (for taking your invention) than they are interested in stealing your invention. Now you can understand why we emphasized the need to file your patent application before submitting your invention to any company. If you sign the waiver, your position won't be seriously jeopardized if your patent issues. However, if you're submitting an invention to a company without having first filed a patent application, it's very important that you try to get the company to sign the above Proprietary Submission Agreement or, failing that, try to submit it without signing their waiver.

If you do have to sign a waiver, try to make sure the company is a reliable and fair one and read the waiver carefully, or have an attorney do so, to make sure you retain your patent rights and that it's fair. Also, it's important to insist, by means of a separate letter, that the company make its decision within a given time, say six months, or else return all of your papers to you. This is because many companies, especially large ones, can take many months or years to make a decision if you let them, which may interfere with your efforts to market the invention to others.

Note that the above choices provide a continuum of safety when presenting your invention to a company: On one end of the continuum you take a very high risk of theft of your invention if you sign a waiver without filing a patent application, while on the other end, you will be fairly well protected if you have the company sign a Proprietary Submission Agreement like the one above. However, there's no such thing as a completely safe submission, so always be prepared for some risk and minimize it as much as possible.

To the extent you are uncertain about whether signing a waiver is a good idea under the circumstances, a consultation with a patent attorney might be wise. On the other hand, don't let the waiver prevent you from showing your invention to a reputable manufacturer that promises to give you a decision in a reasonable time. As long as your patent is pending and eventually issues, you'll have reasonably strong rights.

G. The Best Way to Present Your Invention to a Manufacturer

The best and most effective way to sell your invention to a manufacturer is personally to visit the decision maker in the company you elect and demonstrate a working model or prototype of your invention (or present drawings of it if you have no working model). To accomplish this, write a brief, personal, friendly, and sincere letter to the president of the company, saying that you have a very valuable invention you believe would be profitable for the company's business and that you would like to make an appointment when convenient to provide a brief demonstration. You can disclose the general area of your idea, but don't disclose its essence until you can present it properly. Keep the initiative by stating that you will call in a few days. Follow through accordingly. Here's an example:

Mr. Orville Billyer
President, Billyer Saw Co.
[etc.]

Dear Mr. Billyer:

I'm employed as an insurance agent, but in my spare time I like to tinker. While building a gun rack, I thought of and have perfected a new type of saw fence, which I believe can be produced at 60% of the cost of your A-4 model, yet which can be adjusted in substantially less time with greater accuracy. For this reason, I believe that my fence, for which I've applied for a patent, can be a very profitable addition to your line. I'll call you in a few days to arrange a demonstration of my invention for you in your plant.

Most sincerely,

Marjorie Morgenstern
Marjorie Morgenstern

They may ask you to sign their Waiver form (described above) and submit your materials in writing, but try your best (by stressing the advantages of your invention and how much money they'll make) to bypass the Waiver and make an appointment for a personal presentation.

When you come to the demonstration, be prepared! Set up your presentation well in advance. Practice it on friends. Explain the advantages of your invention first: how it works, how it will be profitable for their business, and why it will sell. Make sure your model works. Also, prepare appropriate and attractive written materials and photos for later study by the decision maker.

In your presentation and written material, it's wise to cover the "Three Fs"—Form, Fit, and Function.

Form is the appearance of your invention. Stress how it has (or can have) an attractive, enticing appearance.

Demonstrate how your invention fits with other products, or with the environment in which it is to be used. If your invention is a highly functional device, such as a saw fence, show and tell how it fits onto a table saw. If it's a clock, show (or present attractive pictures showing) how it looks attractive on a desk or coffee table.

Function is what your invention does, how it works, what results it attains. Demonstrate and discuss its function and its advantage here. Mention all of the advantages from your Positive and Negative Factors Evaluation (Form 4-1). In addition, be prepared to discuss such items as cost of manufacture, profit, retail price, competition, possible product liability, and product life. Review all of the positive and negative factors from the list in Chapter 4 to be sure you've covered all possible considerations.

During the verbal part of your presentation, it's wise to use diagrams and charts, but keep your model, written materials, and photos hidden from view. Otherwise, the people you're trying to sell to will be looking at these instead of listening to you. Then, at a dramatic moment, bring out your model and demonstrate how it works. Don't apologize if your model is a crude or unattractive prototype, but radiate enough confidence in yourself and your invention that they will overlook any lack of "cosmetics." If you can't bring or show them your model for any reason, a video, drawing, diagram, or slide presentation that shows the three F's will be a viable, though less desirable way, to show the invention.

If possible, make them think that the invention is basically their idea. You can do this by praising their related product line and then showing how your idea compliments theirs, or by enthusiastically endorsing any reasonable suggestion they make for your idea.

At the end of your verbal presentation, produce your written materials and pictures for study (either then and there or at a later time). If they're interested in the invention, be prepared to state your terms and conditions. (See Chapter 16.) If they're really serious and ask for it, you can show them your patent application without your claims, but only with the understanding that it won't be copied and will be returned to you. You shouldn't offer the claims, prior art from your search, serial number, or filing date, unless you're asked. If you're relying on a Provisional Patent Application for your patent pending status, then you won't have drafted your claims yet, and you also may not have conducted a patentability search.

If you've done your best and still get a rejection, try to turn it into an asset for next time. Talk to the executives about it and learn exactly why they decided not to accept your idea so that in the future you'll be better prepared to answer and overcome the disadvantage that blocked your initial acceptance.

Assuming the company is interested, you shouldn't blindly or automatically accept it as your patron. Rather, you should evaluate the company to which you're demonstrating your invention just as they're evaluating you and your invention. For example, if the company seems to lack energy or vision, don't go with them. Also, you should check out the company with their local Better Business Bureau to see if they have a clean record. After all, you're risking a lot, too, when you sign up with a company. If the company doesn't promote your invention enthusiastically and correctly, it can fail in the market, even if it's the greatest thing to come down the pike in 20 years.

TIP

Don't Be Afraid of Simultaneous Submissions. If you're aware of several prospective companies that you feel might be interested, I recommend that you approach all of the companies simultaneously; otherwise, you'll waste too much time. If several companies "bite" concurrently, you'll be in the enviable position of being able to choose your licensee. (Some companies do ask that you not submit your invention to anyone else while they're looking at it; you should honor this request.)

H. Presenting Your Invention by Correspondence

Another way to present your invention is by correspondence—either online or via letters. Because a personal presentation is a thousand times more likely to make a sale, we strongly advise against submitting an invention to a manufacturer in this way if you can avoid it. Try your utmost to arrange a personal demonstration with a working model as described in the previous section. Nevertheless, if you do have to resort to correspondence, don't let your efforts slacken.

Your letter or email should always be addressed to a specific individual. If you receive an expression of interest from the company, you will probably be faced with the waiver question. My comments in the previous discussion cover how to handle this problem. Before you ship a model, get an advance written commitment from the company that they'll return it within a given time. The key is to present your message as a simple unexpected, credible, concrete, and emotional story.

I. Making an Agreement to Sell Your Invention

If you sell your invention to a manufacturer/distributor, the next step is to sign an agreement of some sort with the manufacturer. The question thus arises, what will be the terms of the agreement, exactly what will you sell them, and for how much? There are many possibilities. These are covered in Chapter 16, which deals with ownership and transfer of patents rights.

J. Manufacturing and/or Distributing the Invention Yourself

For reasons stated earlier, manufacturing and/or distributing a product embodying your invention yourself—unless you already have manufacturing experience, a plant, and/or distribution facilities—is very difficult. Besides, you can spend your time more effectively selling your invention or patent application, rather than dealing with manufacturing and product-marketing problems.

If you do plan to manufacture and/or distribute your invention yourself, we strongly suggest that you learn about the subject thoroughly beforehand so you will know what is involved and which pitfalls to avoid. The best place to obtain literature and reading material is your local SBA (Small Business Administration) office (www.sba.gov), which has literature and aids available to apprise you of the problems and pitfalls. They even have a service that allows you to obtain the advice of an experienced executive free. Nolo publishes *How to Write a Business Plan*, by Mike P. McKeever, which tells potential businesspeople how to assess the costs of a proposed business, how to draft a business plan, and how to obtain sufficient start-up money.

1. Financing the Manufacture of Your Invention

Financing any manufacturing venture of your own is a separate and formidable problem. If you have an untried and unsold product, most banks will not lend you the money to go ahead. However, if you can get orders from various local firms, the bank may lend you the money. A local test-marketing effort on a limited scale may be desirable.

Generally you'll need a money lender who's willing to take risk. Such a person is usually termed a "venture capitalist" (VC). A VC will lend you money in exchange for shares or a portion of your enterprise. *Pratt's Guide to Venture Capital Sources* (www.pehub.com/pratts) is the most popular source of VCs, however other resources are available at libraries and online. VCs won't lend you money on the same terms a bank would. Because of the higher risks they take, they demand a much larger return—namely a piece of the action. Also, they'll want to monitor your company and exercise some degree of control, usually by putting their people on your board of directors. While most VCs are companies or partnerships, sometimes wealthy individuals finance inventions, so if you have a rich uncle or know of a suitable patron, include them on your list. A recent development in the VC field is the "Incubator VC." This is a VC that provides several different inventors with offices, labs, and/or a manufacturing area in a special building, called an "innovation center."

2. Prepare a Business Plan

To obtain venture capital to start a business based on your invention, you'll have to prepare a business plan —a presentation that tells all about your invention, the market for it, and how you plan to use the money. Again, *How to Write a Business Plan* is also recommended for this purpose. Other sources for guiding your business plan writing are the SBA (www.sba.gov), Business Plan Pro (www.bplans.com), and Business Owner's Toolkit (www.bizfilings.com/toolkit).

How to Get Funding From a Venture Capitalist

Ari Zoldan, CEO of Quantum Networks, a venture capital (VC) firm, provided some tips for soliciting VCs in an issue of *Popular Science*. Among his suggestions:

- Don't send a letter and don't email. Call the CEO and pitch your invention briefly. Be sure to sell both your product and your skills and expertise.
- Look for a VC that will be actively involved.
- Review the VC's track record and funding.
- Don't be intimidated by VCs and never give the VC a majority control of your company.
- Get the VC to sign a nondisclosure agreement and always bring a business plan and prototype to your meeting.

---

3. Utilize Government Services

If your invention is or can be used in a product that the federal government might purchase, contact the General Services Administration, Federal Supply Service, (www.gsa.gov). Tell them that you're offering a product that you feel the government can use. They'll send you appropriate forms and instructions. Also, don't neglect your corresponding state and local purchasing agencies.

If you have an energy-related invention, the Department of Energy may give you a research grant if the National Bureau of Standards gives it a favorable evaluation. Contact the U.S. Department of Energy, e-center (www.energy.gov).

4. Publicity

Publicity will sometimes be of great aid to you before you get your invention into production, and is invaluable once it's on the market. Assuming it's not yet on the market and you're either looking for a manufacturer or distributor, or thinking of manufacturing or distributing it yourself, publicity can cut both ways. As stated, many manufacturers like to get a secret head start on their competition and thus won't be too interested if your invention has already been disseminated to the public.

If you're going to make and sell it yourself, we believe you should wait until you've got the product out before you try to publicize it. Why? The public's memory span is short, so they'll be likely to forget about your product by the time you get it on sale. My advice is to not seek publicity until a product with your invention is almost or actually on the market, unless you've tried unsuccessfully, after substantial efforts, to get it on the market.

Assuming you're ready for publicity, one way to get it (at a price) is to hire a public-relations or marketing research firm to promote your invention for you. There are many reputable firms that can come up with many creative and valuable ideas for a fee. However, since the cost of public-relations services is very high, I don't recommend it unless you can bear the cost without difficulty.

Many magazines will feature new ideas free if you send them a clear, understandable, professional-quality photo or drawing of your invention, plus a brief, clear, and understandable description of it. They may even write a full-length feature about your invention if they think it's interesting enough.

Other sources of publicity and possible sale or licensing opportunities are exhibits, trade fairs, and business shows. We don't recommend that you use these, since we've heard only a few success stories from exhibitors. On the other hand, we have heard of many more cases where foreign or domestic manufacturers copy good inventions and hope to make a quick killing or avoid any pertinent patents. But if you feel that you may get a bite from this type of exposure, try one—the cost is usually a few hundred dollars. You'll be given a table or booth, or equivalent space to demonstrate your invention at the fair or show. Naturally, your exhibit should be attractive and interesting, and it is preferable to have a working model or very good literature available in connection with your invention. There are exhibition-service companies that will prepare a display exhibit for you for a fee.

Don't overlook the media (radio, TV, newspapers, and magazines) as an excellent source of free publicity, which most experts say is the best kind. Many local radio and TV stations feature talk shows whose hosts are always looking for interesting guests; some stations even have shows in which new inventors can demonstrate or discuss their inventions. One popular syndicated show is Shark Tank (abc.go.com/shows/shark-tank).

One of the best ways to get media publicity (and concomitant interviews) is to dream up or pull a stunt. For example, if you've invented a new bicycle drive mechanism, you might enter and win a local bike race, or sponsor some type of contest (which you can win!).

5. The Premium Marketing Route

If you can't get a manufacturer or distributor to take your invention, try offering it as a premium to accompany a related product that is already on the market. For example, one television magazine show featured a girl, Abbey Mae Fleck, 8, of St. Paul, Minnesota, who invented a great plastic hanger to suspend bacon in a microwave oven so that the grease dripped away while it cooked. However, none of the manufacturers of plastic microwave accessories would bite (their loss!). So ingenious Abbey approached a bacon company and got them to offer her MAKIN BACON® via a discount coupon on their bacon packages. The result: An instant success! The bacon company's investment was minimal, yet it profited handsomely by providing a way to cook its bacon dryly. And Abbey got her commercial distribution. Abbey's story also shows that creativity has no age limits.

6. The Celebrity Endorsement Route

If a product bears a celebrity's name or endorsement, people will be far more likely to buy it. So, getting a celebrity to endorse it is often a key to instant success.

Consider George Foreman's Lean, Mean Fat-Reducing Grilling Machine. Without the champ's endorsement and name it might not have been a fabulous success. Celebrity endorsements are particularly useful if you have a sporting goods invention, such as a golf club. To get a celebrity endorsement, first perfect and get your product ready for market. Prepare suitable sales and promotional materials, with photos, and then approach the celebrity you feel would do your baby justice. While you'll have to share a good portion of your profits, you'll find that your chances of success will be almost assured if you have a good product and can get a famous celebrity to endorse and name it.

K. Summary

After filing a patent application, try to get your invention on the market; don't wait until your patent issues. Since it can take a long time to license an invention, perseverance and patience are essential.

There are seven routes to profit from an invention and they involve using a marketing intermediary, manufacturing and/or marketing your invention yourself, or licensing your invention to a company. Most inventors use the latter.

Don't use a fee-based intermediary (a company that wants up-front money) unless they can demonstrate that many of their clients have made more money than they paid the intermediary.

The best way to sell or license an invention is to demonstrate a working model. Find prospective manufacturers in stores, catalogs, and trade magazines. Larger companies will require that you sign a waiver (giving up all rights except patent rights) before they will look at your invention. You may have better luck with companies that are smaller and geographically close to you. These companies usually communicate in a more direct manner, avoid the NIH syndrome, and often don't require a waiver.

If you want to manufacture and/or distribute the invention yourself you may need financing and a business plan.

There are many ways to get publicity for your invention including premium marketing and celebrity endorsements.

Going Abroad

Inventor's Commandment 23

Foreign Filing: It's not wise to file in any foreign country unless you're confident your invention has very strong commercial potential there (or unless someone else will pay the costs). You can file abroad by filing a Patent Cooperation Treaty (PCT) application or filing directly in Paris Convention (major industrial) countries within one year of your earliest U.S. filing date. Don't file abroad until you receive a foreign-filing license from the PTO or until six months after your U.S. filing date.

A U.S. patent will give you a monopoly in the U.S. only. If you think your invention is important enough to be manufactured or sold in large quantities in other countries, and you want to create a monopoly there, you'll have to go through the considerable effort and expense of foreign filing in order to eventually get a patent in each desired foreign country. Otherwise, anyone in a foreign country where you have no patent will be able to make, use, and sell your invention with impunity. However, if you have a U.S. patent they won't be able to bring it into the U.S. without infringing your U.S. patent.

This chapter doesn't give you the full, detailed instructions necessary to file abroad. That would take another book. Instead, our mission is to alert you to the basic procedures for foreign filing, so that you won't lose your opportunity to do so. However, once you decide to foreign-file, you'll probably need some professional guidance.

The most important points you can learn from this chapter are:
- don't foreign-file in any foreign country unless you're confident your invention has strong commercial potential there
- don't foreign-file until you get a foreign-filing license from the PTO (the filing receipt usually, but not always, includes a foreign-filing license) or until six months has elapsed from your U.S. filing date
- you must file in non-Convention countries before you publish or sell the invention, and

- you must file a Patent Cooperation Treaty (PCT) application or file in all other countries (Convention countries) within one year of your earliest U.S. filing date (regular or Provisional Patent Application (PPA)).

A. Don't File Abroad Unless Your Invention Has Very Good Prospects in Another Country

Because patent prosecution and practice in other countries is relatively complicated and very expensive, you should not file applications abroad unless:
- a significant market for products embodying the invention is very likely to exist
- *significant* commercial production of your invention is very likely to occur, or
- you've already located a foreign licensee or there is someone else willing to pay for the foreign filing.

Far too many inventors file abroad because they're in love with their invention and feel it will capture the world. Unfortunately, this almost never happens. Almost all inventors who do file abroad never recoup their investment—that is, they usually waste tens of thousands of dollars in fees and hardly ever derive any royalties, let alone enough royalties to cover their costs. Thus, as a general rule, we suggest that you file in another country only if you feel that you're:
- very likely to sell at least $500,000 worth of products embodying your invention there, if you're selling it yourself
- very likely to earn at least $100,000 in royalties from sales of your invention there by others, or
- associated with a licensee or sales representative there who contracts to pay you royalties with a substantial advance or guarantee, or who will pay for your foreign filing in that country.

In addition to the high initial cost of foreign filing, you will have to pay substantial expenses to obtain foreign patents and maintenance fees each year to keep them in force.

Note that even if an infringement occurs in a country where you didn't file, it still is not worth paying for foreign filing there, unless the infringement is substantial enough to justify the expense of filing, getting the patent, paying the maintenance fees, and the uncertainties of licensing and litigation.

TIP

The U.S., with its approximately 325 million people, provides a huge marketplace that should be a more-than-adequate market from which to make your fortune, especially if it's your first invention. In comparison, most foreign countries are relatively insignificant. For example, Switzerland, Lebanon, and Israel are each smaller in size than San Bernardino County in California and smaller in population than Los Angeles County; Canada has fewer people than California. In other words, filing in the U.S. usually gives you ten to 50 times more bang for your buck than filing abroad, which costs ten to 50 times as much anyway.

B. Foreign Filing: The Basics

Most countries are treaty members of the "Paris Convention," which gives you the full benefit of your filing date in your home country in any foreign "Convention" country, provided you file in the foreign Convention country within one year. Also, most of the countries of Europe have joined the European Patent Convention, which has created a single patent office—the European Patent Office to grant European patents that are good in all member countries provided they're registered and translated in each country (and you pay annuities or maintenance fees there). Similarly, most African countries are members of one of two African patent organizations, the African Intellectual Property Organization (OAPI—for French-speaking countries) or the African Regional Industrial Property Organization (ARIPO—for English-speaking countries), while the Eurasian Patent Organization (EAPO) comprises the former Soviet republics. Lastly, most industrialized countries are also members of the PCT—Patent Cooperation Treaty—that enables applicants to file a relatively economical international application in the patent office of their home country within one year of their home-country filing date.

The PCT gives applicants up to a 30-month delay and enables them to have a search, and optimally an examination, performed before making an expensive filing abroad. Let's discuss these areas in detail.

U.S. patent applications are published 18 months after the earliest claimed filing date, unless the applicant files a Nonpublication Request (NPR) at the time of filing, stating that the application will not be filed abroad. If you do file an NPR and then file abroad, you must revoke the NPR and notify the PTO of the foreign filing within 45 days (use PTO Form PTO/SB/36).

C. The Paris Convention and the One-Year Foreign-Filing Rule

The most important thing to know about foreign filing is the "Paris Convention" or simply "the Convention." (The official title is International Convention for the Protection of Industrial Property.) The majority of industrialized nations of the world are parties to this international treaty, which was entered into in Paris in 1883 and has been revised many times since. Generally, the Paris Convention governs almost all reciprocal patent filing rights. Like most of these international treaties, the Paris Convention is administered by the World Intellectual Property Organization (www.wipo.int) in Geneva, Switzerland.

For the purpose of this chapter, there's one thing you need to know about the all-important Paris Convention: If you file a patent application (regular or PPA) in any one member jurisdiction of the Paris Convention (such as the U.S.), you can file a corresponding application in any other member jurisdiction (such as the U.K., Japan, the EPO, Australia, etc.), within one year of your earliest filing date (or within six months for designs). Your application in each foreign jurisdiction will be entitled to the filing date of your U.S. application (regular or PPA) for purposes of pre-dating disclosures by others that would otherwise rob your invention of novelty. ("Jurisdiction" refers to any country or group of countries that have joined under a treaty, that is, the EPO, PCT, AIPO, ARIPO, and EAPO, as listed above.)

You have to claim "priority" of your original application. "Priority" means that a later application is entitled to the benefit of the filing date of an earlier application. If you fail to file any foreign applications under the Convention within the one-year period, you can still file after the one-year period in Convention jurisdictions, provided you haven't sold, published, or patented your invention yet. However, any such late application won't get the benefit of your original U.S. filing date, so any relevant prior art that has been published in the meantime can be applied against (used to reject) your foreign applications. Put differently, once you miss the one-year deadline, your foreign application won't be entitled to the filing date of your original application. Rather, it becomes a non-Convention application, even in Convention countries. Also, once your U.S. application issues, it's too late to foreign-file anywhere (unless you file within the one-year period)—that is, if you file a Convention application.

All jurisdictions that are members of the Paris Convention are indicated in Fig. 12A, where the most popular jurisdictions for foreign filing are indicated in boldface.

D. The World Trade Organization and TRIPS

Nine non-Convention countries (Cape Verde, Fiji, Hong Kong, Macao, Maldives, Myanmar (Burma), Solomon Islands, Taiwan (Republic of China), and Vanuatu) are members of the World Trade Organization (WTO). Each WTO member is bound by the April 1994 treaty concerning Trade-Related Aspects of Intellectual Property Rights (TRIPS). Article 2 of TRIPS requires WTO members to comply with the patent provisions of the Paris Convention, including those granting the one-year right of priority. Therefore you can claim priority to your original application in these non-Convention countries as if they were Convention members.

E. European Patent Office/ Europäisches Patentamt/Office Européen des Brevets (EPO)

The European Patent Office (EPO) (www.epo.org) is a separate and vast trilingual patent office at Bob-van-Benthem-Platz 1, 80469 Munich, Germany, across the Isar River from the famous Deutsches Museum. (There is a separate website for searching the European Patent Office (www.espacenet.com).) There is also a facility in The Hague, Netherlands. The EPO grew out of the earlier formation of the European Union (EU, formerly EEC), and the economic integration that resulted. Member nations of the EEC are also members of a treaty known as the European Patent Convention (EPC). Under the EPC you can make one patent filing in the EPO. If this filing matures into a European patent, it will, when registered in whatever individual member countries you select, cover your invention in these selected countries. And since the EPC is, in turn, considered the same as a single country (a jurisdiction) under the Paris Convention and the PCT, your effective EPO filing date will be the same as your original U.S. filing date, so long as you comply with the one-year foreign-filing rule. In other words, filing in the EPO allows you to kill many birds with one stone.

Once your application is on file, the EPO subjects it to a rigorous examination, including an opposition publication 18 months after filing. (See Chapter 13.) Even though you'll have to work through a European agent, patent prosecution before the EPO is generally smoother than in the PTO, because the examiners are better trained (all speak and write three languages fluently) and because they actually take the initiative and suggest how to write your claims to get them allowed. If your application is allowed, you'll be granted a European patent that lasts for 20 years from your filing date (provided you pay maintenance fees in the member countries you've selected). Your patent will be valid automatically in each member country of the EPC that you've designated in your application, provided that you register it in and file translations in each country and appoint an agent there.

(!) CAUTION

Filing in the EPO Is Extremely Expensive for U.S. Residents, who have to pay a substantial annuity to the EPO each year an application is on file there until it issues. Thereafter, U.S. residents must pay substantial fees to register and translate the Europatent and pay annuities in

Members of Paris Convention (Total Contracting Parties: 174)

Afghanistan	Comoros	Hungary	Mongolia	Serbia
Albania	Congo	Iceland	Montenegro	Seychelles
Algeria	Costa Rica	India	Morocco	Sierra Leone
Andorra	Côte d'Ivoire	Indonesia	Mozambique	Singapore
Angola	Croatia	Iran	Namibia	Slovakia
Antigua and Barbuda	Cuba	Iraq	Nepal	Slovenia
Argentina	Cyprus	Ireland	Netherlands	South Africa
Armenia	Czech Republic	Israel	New Zealand	Spain
Australia	Dem. People's Rep. of Korea	Italy	Nicaragua	Sri Lanka
Austria		Jamaica	Niger	Sudan
Azerbaijan	Dem. Rep. of Congo	**Japan**	Nigeria	Suriname
Bahamas	Denmark	Jordan	Norway	Swaziland
Bahrain	Djibouti	Kazakhstan	Oman	Sweden
Bangladesh	Dominica	Kenya	Pakistan	Switzerland
Barbados	Dominican Republic	Kuwait	Panama	Syrian Arab Republic
Belarus	Ecuador	Kyrgyzstan	Papua New Guinea	Tajikistan
Belgium	Egypt	Lao People's Dem. Rep.	Paraguay	Thailand
Belize	El Salvador	Latvia	Peru	Togo
Benin	Equatorial Guinea	Lebanon	Philippines	Tonga
Bhutan	Estonia	Lesotho	Poland	Trinidad and Tobago
Bolivia	Finland	Liberia	Portugal	Tunisia
Bosnia and Herzegovina	**France**	Libya	Qatar	Turkey
Botswana	Gabon	Liechtenstein	Republic of Korea	Turkmenistan
Brazil	Gambia	Lithuania	Republic of Moldova	Uganda
Brunei Darusallam	Georgia	Luxembourg	Romania	Ukraine
Bulgaria	**Germany**	Macedonia (Former Yugoslav Rep. of)	Russian Federation	United Arab Emirates
Burkina Faso	Ghana		Rwanda	**United Kingdom**
Burundi	Greece	Madagascar	Saint Kitts and Nevis	United Rep. of Tanzania
Cambodia	Grenada	Malawi	Saint Lucia	**United States**
Cameroon	Guatemala	Malaysia	St. Vincent & Grenadines	Uruguay
Canada	Guinea	Mali		Uzbekistan
Central African Republic	Guinea-Bissau	Malta	Samoa	Venezuela
Chad	Guyana	Mauritania	San Marino	Vietnam
Chile	Haiti	Mauritius	Sao Tome and Principe	Yemen
China	Holy See	Mexico	Saudi Arabia	Zambia
Colombia	Honduras	Monaco	Senegal	Zimbabwe

Fig. 12A—Membership in Patent Conventions

Members of Patent Cooperation Treaty (Total Contracting Parties: 147)

Albania	Côte d'Ivoire	India	Mongolia	Serbia
Algeria	Croatia	Indonesia	Montenegro	Seychelles
Angola	Cuba	Iran	Morocco	Sierra Leone
Antigua and Barbuda	Cyprus	Ireland	Mozambique	Singapore
Armenia	Czech Republic	Israel	Namibia	Slovakia
Australia	Dem. People's Rep. of Korea	Italy	Netherlands	Slovenia
Austria	Denmark	**Japan**	New Zealand	South Africa
Azerbaijan	Djibouti	Jordan	Nicaragua	Spain
Bahrain	Dominica	Kazakhstan	Niger	Sri Lanka
Barbados	Dominican Republic	Kenya	Nigeria	Sudan
Belarus	Ecuador	Kuwait	Norway	Swaziland
Belgium	Egypt	Kyrgyzstan	Oman	Sweden
Belize	El Salvador	Lao People's Dem. Republic	Panama	Switzerland
Benin	Equatorial Guinea	Latvia	Papua New Guinea	Syrian Arab Republic
Bosnia and Herzegovina	Estonia	Lesotho	Peru	Tajikistan
Botswana	Finland	Liberia	Philippines	Thailand
Brazil	**France**	Libya	Poland	Togo
Brunei Darusallam	Gabon	Liechtenstein	Portugal	Trinidad and Tobago
Bulgaria	Gambia	Lithuania	Republic of Korea	Tunisia
Burkina Faso	Georgia	Luxembourg	Republic of Moldova	Turkey
Cambodia	**Germany**	Macedonia (Former Yugoslav Rep. of)	Romania	Turkmenistan
Cameroon	Ghana	Madagascar	Russian Federation	Uganda
Canada	Greece	Malawi	Rwanda	Ukraine
Central African Republic	Grenada	Malaysia	Saint Kitts and Nevis	United Arab Emirates
Chad	Guatemala	Mali	Saint Lucia	**United Kingdom**
Chile	Guinea	Malta	St. Vincent & Grenadines	United Rep. of Tanzania
China	Guinea-Bissau	Mauritania	San Marino	**United States**
Colombia	Honduras	Mexico	Sao Tome and Principe	Uzbekistan
Comoros	Hungary	Monaco	Saudi Arabia	Vietnam
Congo	Iceland		Senegal	Zambia
Costa Rica				Zimbabwe

Member States of the European Patent Organization

Albania	Finland	Latvia	Netherlands	Slovakia
Austria	**France**	Liechtenstein	Norway	Slovenia
Belgium	**Germany**	Lithuania	Poland	Spain
Bulgaria	Greece	Luxembourg	Portugal	Sweden
Croatia	Hungary	Macedonia (Former Yugoslav Rep. of)	Romania	Switzerland
Cyprus	Iceland	Malta	San Marino	Turkey
Czech Republic	Ireland	Monaco	Serbia	**United Kingdom**
Denmark	Italy			

Fig. 12A—Membership in Patent Conventions (continued)

each member country in which the Europatent is registered. That's why you should not file for a Europatent unless you're very confident your invention will be commercially successful there (or unless someone else, such as a European licensee, is paying the freight).

All member countries of the EPO are indicated in Fig. 12A. The member countries have agreed to establish a community patent for all of Europe at sometime in the future.

F. The Patent Cooperation Treaty (PCT)

The PCT is another important treaty to which most industrial countries are a party. Under the Patent Cooperation Treaty (PCT), which was entered into in 1978, U.S. residents can file in the U.S. and then make a single international filing in the USPTO within the one-year period. This can cover all of the PCT jurisdictions, including the European Patent Office (EPO). Eventually, you must file separate or "national" applications in each PCT jurisdiction (including the EPO) where you desire coverage. These separate filings, which must be translated for non–English-speaking jurisdictions, must be made for most countries within 30 months after your U.S. filing date.

If you file a PCT application, the USPTO (or another country's patent office, if you so choose), acting under the PCT, will make a patentability search of your invention and will give you an indication of its patentability. If you want an actual examination of your invention to see what claims are allowable or rejected and to prosecute the application and revise claims, elect Chapter II of the PCT by 19 months after your U.S. filing date. Except for the single international filing, the PCT affords you a 30-month extension in which to file in most PCT countries or the EPO.

Also, you can file your first application under the PCT and then file in any PCT jurisdiction (including the U.S.) within 30 months from your PCT filing date. You should take this route if you've filed a PPA and you've decided to foreign-file by one year after your PPA filing date. Further, if you file with the

PCT first instead of a PPA, you can file in any other country within one year from your PCT filing date under either the Convention or TRIPS (or both, in the majority of cases). As stated, after you file your PCT application, you'll receive a "search report" citing any pertinent references against your application. If you elect Chapter II of the PCT (optional) you'll receive an "examination report," which allows or rejects the claims of your application on the cited references. A list of PCT jurisdictions is indicated in Fig. 12A. All PCT jurisdictions are bound by Chapter I (searching part) and Chapter II (examination part). The PCT is administered by the World Intellectual Property Organization (WIPO), www.wipo.int.

 NOTE

Distinguishing Among PCT Member Countries. Technically, only individual countries (and not associations of countries such as the EPO) can become members of the PCT. For purposes of filing, this distinction is immaterial and when possible, associations should be designated—for example, the EPO, and not the individual member country such as Germany. For that reason, we list associations of countries as members of the PCT. Below is a list of country associations that grant regional patents and whose constituent countries are members of the PCT: ARIPO (African Regional Intellectual Property Organization), EAPO (Eurasian Patent Association), EPO, and OAPI (Organisation Africaine de la Propriété Intellectuelle).

G. Non-Convention Countries

There are several, generally nonindustrial countries (such as Bermuda, the Cook Islands, etc.) that aren't parties to any patent treaty or convention. If you do want to file in any of them, you may do so at any time, provided:

- your invention hasn't yet become publicly known, either by your publication, by patenting, by public sale, or by normal publication, in the course of prosecution in a foreign jurisdiction (the PCT and the EPO publish 18 months after filing), and

- you've been given a foreign-filing license on your U.S. filing receipt or six months has elapsed from your U.S. filing date.

I won't discuss filing in non-Convention countries in detail, except to note that if you do wish to file in any, you should do so in exactly the same manner as you would for an individual filing in a Convention country. However, you won't need a certified copy of your U.S. application since you won't be able to obtain priority (the benefit of your U.S. filing date).

Don't Wait Until the Deadline to Foreign-File

The timing of foreign filing can be confusing and you want to avoid missing a deadline.

- If you file a U.S. application, you have one year after you file, to file foreign Convention patent applications (and be entitled to your U.S. filing date) in the PCT, the EPO, or any country that's a member of the Paris Convention. You also have 30 months after you file a U.S. application to file in the individual PCT jurisdictions, including the EPO, provided you filed a PCT application.
- If you file under the PCT first, you have one year to file in non-PCT Convention countries and 30 months to file in the PCT countries, respectively.

On one hand, you should make your decision and start to take action about foreign filing two or three months before any required deadline. This is to give you and the foreign agents time to prepare the necessary correspondence and translations and to order a certified copy, if needed, of your U.S. application. So mark your calendar in advance accordingly. At the same time, there's no advantage in filing too early, unless you need an early patent—for example, because you have a foreign infringement. It's actually better to wait as long as possible before filing abroad since you may receive an Office Action from the PTO, which will indicate whether or not you're likely to get a patent.

H. The Early Foreign-Filing License or Mandatory Six-Month Delay

Normally, the official filing receipt that you get after filing your U.S. application gives you express permission from the PTO to file abroad. This permission usually will be printed on your filing receipt, as follows: "If required, Foreign Filing License Granted (DATE)." However, if your filing receipt fails to include a foreign-filing license (only inventions with possible military applications won't include the license), you aren't allowed to foreign-file on your invention until six months following your U.S. filing date.

The reason for this is to give the U.S. government a chance to review your application for possible classification on national security grounds. You probably won't be affected by any of this, as most applications get the foreign-filing license immediately and, in any case, there is usually no good reason to file before six months after your U.S. filing. If your situation is different, however, and your filing receipt doesn't include a license, see a patent lawyer. If your invention does have military applications, not only will you fail to get a foreign-filing license on your filing receipt, but after you receive the receipt, you may receive a Secrecy Order from the PTO. This will order you to keep your invention secret until it's declassified, which often takes 12 years. (The government kept Dr. William Friedman's application, filed in 1933 on a cryptographic system, secret until 2000 August 1, when it issued as patent 6,097,812—67 years later! Dr. Friedman is regarded as the father of American cryptography.) Your patent can't issue while it's under a secrecy order, but the government may compensate you if they use your invention in the meantime. You can foreign-file an application that is under a secrecy order, but it's complicated; see a patent lawyer who has experience in this area.

I. The Patent Laws of Other Countries Are Different

Despite the Paris Convention and other treaties covering patent applications, and except for Canada,

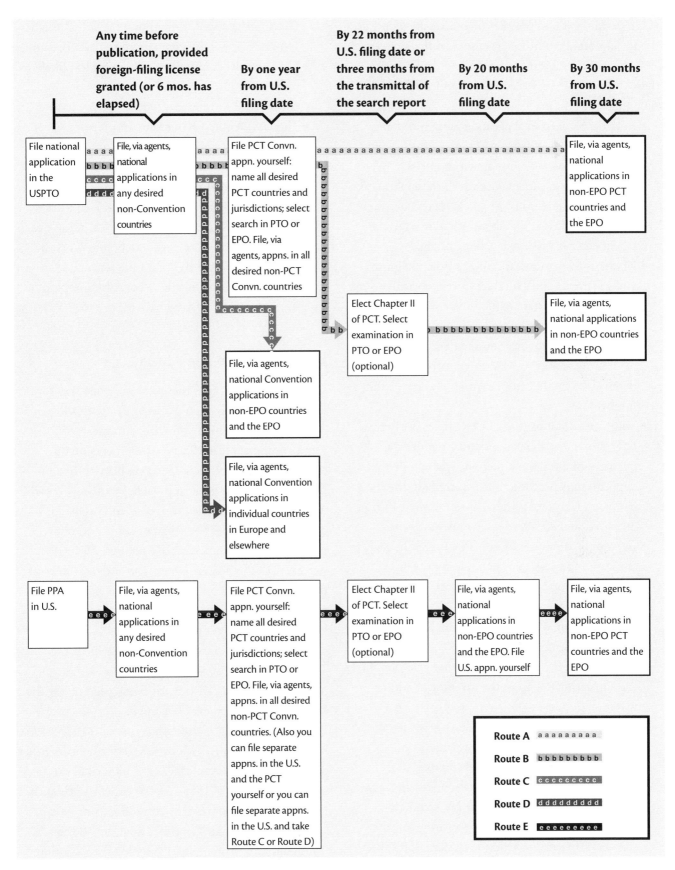

Fig. 12B—Foreign-Filing Routes (After Filing Basic U.S. Application)

whose patent laws and practice are practically identical to ours, almost all countries have some differences from the U.S. in their substantive patent laws and practices. These differences have been reduced under TRIPS, but some that still exist are as follows:

- In the U.S., once an application is examined and allowed, the patent issues without any further proceedings. However, most foreign countries have an opposition proceeding under which the application is published and anyone who believes the invention isn't patentable can cite additional prior art to the patent office in order to block the patent.

- Many smaller countries (for example, Belgium and Portugal) don't conduct novelty examinations on applications that are filed there directly (not through the EPO), but instead simply issue a patent on every application filed and leave it up to the courts (in the event of an infringement) to determine whether the invention was novel and unobvious.

- Some jurisdictions (the EPO, France, Germany, Italy, Australia, the Netherlands) require the payment of annual maintenance fees while the application is pending. But if you file in these countries (except Australia) through the EPO, no individual country fees are due until the European patent issues and is registered in each country. However, substantial annual EPO fees plus European agent fees are due until the Europatent issues.

- Any disclosure of your invention before filing will be fatal to the application, unless the disclosure was made by the inventor or another who obtained the subject matter from the inventor or a joint inventor.

- Some countries such as Italy don't grant patents on drugs and some don't grant patents on computer programs or business methods.

- In Japan, the filing and translation fees are very high. Then, examination must be separately requested within seven years, requiring another stiff fee. After examination is requested, it takes about three years before the Japanese Patent Office, which is understaffed, gets around to it.

Getting the application allowed is very difficult. However, it will be given more respect than in the U.S. That is, competitors will be far less likely to infringe or challenge it. Nevertheless, Japanese courts tend to interpret patents narrowly.

- The U.S., United Kingdom, and Japan use "peripheral claiming": each word in a claim shrinks a notional fence that surrounds and defines the legal right. So, fewer words mean broader U.S. claims. However some countries, especially in Europe, use "central claiming": each word in a claim more accurately pinpoints the center of the legal right and the fence is as large as the nature of the inventive contribution permits, so more words actually may mean broader claims.

J. The Ways to File Abroad

Until several years ago, there was only one way to foreign-file, namely, to file a separate application in each country in which you wished to file. As this was a cumbersome and expensive process, many of the countries got together to simplify things. Now there are five basic approaches to filing abroad in Convention countries. You may end up using different approaches for different countries, or the same approach for all. The chart above, Fig. 12B, summarizes these alternatives. The lettered routes in the explanation below are keyed to the paths in the chart (see the legend at the bottom right of the chart). In essence, the routes are:

Route A: This is the most common. File in U.S. Then file in non-Convention countries before publication or sale. Then, within one year, under the Paris Convention, file a PCT application to cover the PCT countries and jurisdictions (including the EPO). Select the PTO or EPO for the search (there are other countries whose patent offices are allowed to do the search, and many of them are less expensive than the PTO and EPO, but they often produce prior art in languages other than English). Then, by 30 months from your U.S. filing date, file national applications (you'll have to hire agents and spend big bucks) in the EPO and non-EPO PCT countries.

Route B: This is the same as Route A, except that within 19 months from your U.S. filing date, or three months from the transmittal of the search report, you have the option to elect Chapter II of the PCT to get the application examined, either in the PTO or EPO. Finally, file in the EPO and non-EPO countries within 30 months from your U.S. filing date.

Route C: This is the same as Route A, except that the PCT is eliminated entirely and you file Convention applications in the EPO and non-EPO countries within 12 months from your U.S. filing date.

Route D: This is the same as Route C, except that you file directly in the individual EPO countries (rather than the EPO). Caution: this route is not available for France, which requires that an application go through the EPO, as described in Route A.

Route E: In addition, if you've filed a Provisional Patent Application (PPA), and by the time almost one year elapses from your PPA's filing date you want to file in the U.S. and abroad, you can do so in three basic ways: (1) File a PCT application yourself, naming the U.S. and all other desired PCT countries. File in non-PCT Convention countries using agents. By 22 months from your PPA filing date or three months from the transmittal of the search report, you may elect Chapter II of the PCT and select examination in the PTO or EPO. By 30 months from your PPA filing date, file, via agents, national applications in the EPO and non-EPO countries and file yourself in the U.S., claiming priority of your PCT application. (2) File separate applications in the U.S. and PCT yourself. Continue as in Route A for your PCT application. (3) File separate applications in the U.S. and either (a) use agents to file in non-EPO countries and the EPO (Route C), or (b) use agents to file national Convention applications in individual countries in Europe and elsewhere (Route D).

Let's discuss each of these alternatives in more detail.

1. Route A: Non-Convention/Convention (PCT and Non-PCT/Chapter II/National)

Route A is the most popular way to go. Not surprisingly, it's also the cheapest way to go in the short run, since you won't have to file national applications (with foreign patent agents and the huge expense they entail—indicated by boxes with bold lines on the chart) until 30 months from your U.S. filing date. Under Route A, you file in the U.S. first and then go abroad through the PCT, insofar as possible. Here's how it works for U.S. inventors:

- First file in the U.S. in the usual manner.
- Next, file directly in any non-Convention countries you desire, before your application or invention is published, but after you get your foreign-filing license or six months has elapsed from your U.S. filing date.
- Then, before one year from your U.S. filing date, file a PCT request form and a separate "international application" under the PCT with the USPTO within 12 months from your filing date. The application designates the PCT member countries or jurisdictions (such as the EPO) in which you desire coverage.
- The request and application are forwarded to the "International Searching Authority" (a branch of the PTO or the EPO if you've elected to have your search made there) where an "international search report" is prepared. If you select the PTO, the examination will generally be done by the same examiner who handles your U.S. application.
- Copies of the search report and application are then forwarded to the countries designated in the application. Cite any new references to the PTO on your basic U.S. case through another Information Disclosure Statement.
- Within 30 months from your U.S. filing date, you must hire agents and prosecute the application in the individual countries. You must also provide a translation (except in the EPO) and must pay any fees that are required. While separate prosecution is required in each country, it's commonly made easier by the fact that the PCT member countries generally rely on the international search and examination. It is no longer necessary to elect Chapter II to obtain the 30-month delay, except for certain individual country filings.

a. How to Prepare a PCT (International) Application

To prepare an international application under the PCT, first prepare your original U.S. application and drawings in the A4 international format. The main differences between the PCT and U.S. national formats (both of which are acceptable for U.S. applications) are the paper and drawing size and margins. (These differences are detailed in Chapter 10.)

The World Intellectual Property Organization has software ("PCT-SAFE") that enables you to pay somewhat reduced fees and automates the process of completing the PCT filing forms. You can download PCT-SAFE from the WIPO's website (www.wipo.int/pct-safe/en/download/download_client.html).

You can file a PCT application on EFS-Web or by mail. We strongly recommend that you use the EFS-Web since the paper size restrictions will be looser and you don't have to fuss with making file copies and using Priority Mail Express. If you want to file by mail, obtain and complete a multipage "Request" (Form PCT/RO/101) including the Fee Calculation Sheet and the Transmittal Letter (Form PTO 1390) from the PTO's website (www.uspto.gov). The form can also be obtained from Mail Stop PCT, Commissioner for Patents, P.O. Box 1450, Alexandria, VA 22313-1450, Phone 571-272-4300 or Fax 571-273-0419. Ask for the latest fees when you call, or you can find these in the latest *Official Gazette* on the PTO's website. Complete the forms (full instructions and examples are attached), requesting the PTO to prepare a certified copy of your U.S. application for use with your PCT application, and attach a copy of your application in PCT (A4) format (with drawings) and a credit card payment form or check (payable to "Commissioner for Patents") for the international application filing fees as computed on the Fee Calculation Sheet—the last page of the Request form. To file a PCT application by EFS-Web, first prepare a PDF copy of your application and drawings in A4 size. Then complete the "Request" (Form PCT/RO/101) including the Fee Calculation Sheet and Transmittal Letter (Form PTO 1390) from the PTO's website (www.uspto.gov). Full instructions are on the forms. Then file the forms (all must be in PDF format) on the

PTO's site (www.uspto.gov/learning-and-resources/support-centers/electronic-business-center/patent-online-services). You will be able to pay the fees by credit card as part of the process. Call the PTO's PCT Help Desk at 571-272-4300 if you have any questions.

b. PCT Fees

The PCT fees frequently vary due to exchange rate fluctuations. They're composed of several parts as follows:

- Transmittal Fee
- Search Fee: (a) if you haven't already filed in the U.S. (that is, you filed your first application in the PCT, rather than the U.S.—very rare); (b) if you've already filed in the U.S. (the usual case); and (c) if you want to use the EPO as your searching authority (recommended), and
- International Filing Fee

You should designate the EPO as your searching authority if you intend to file there since they generally do a better search than the USPTO and you'll save money and time in the EPO later. But be warned: Sometimes the EPO does such a good search that you might have to abandon both your U.S. and EPO applications. If any foreign patent office cites a new reference against your application, be sure to cite it in your U.S. application by filing it with a supplemental IDS and PTO-1449. (See Chapter 10.)

c. How to File PCT and Non-PCT Convention Applications

To file a paper PCT application by mail, mail the Transmittal Letter, Request (including the Fee Calculation Sheet), a copy of your application and drawings (both on A4 size), and CCPF or check, and a receipt postcard to: Mail Stop PCT, Commissioner for Patents, P.O. Box 1450, Alexandria, VA 22313-1450, which, as mentioned, is a designated receiving office for the International Bureau. Like Convention applications, the international (PCT) application should be filed within one year of your U.S. filing date, also known as the priority date.

We advise filing the PCT application at least a month before the anniversary of your U.S. filing date, so you'll have time to correct any serious deficiencies. But you can mail the PCT application as late as the last day of the one-year period from your U.S. filing date if you use Priority Mail Express and complete the PME on page 1 of the Transmittal Letter. (Never use a plain Certificate of Mailing for any PCT correspondence.)

To electronically file a PCT application using EFS-Web, complete the Transmittal Letter online and save a PDF copy. Complete the Request online, print it, sign it in Box X, and convert it back to PDF by scanning. Prepare a copy of your application and drawings and convert them to PDF. Then, file online at the PTO's EFS site (in the same manner as instructed for your U.S. application in Chapter 10). You will get an instant acknowledgment and PCT Serial Number.

To file any non-PCT Convention applications, use a foreign patent agent in each country you select to prepare an appropriate application. The easiest way to do this is to send the agent a copy of your U.S. application and ask what else is needed. The requirements vary from country to country, but special drawings in each country's format will always be needed. You can have your foreign agent prepare these, or you can have these prepared yourself at lesser cost by the same companies that make drawings for U.S. divisional applications. Also, the agent will send you a power of attorney form that you'll have to sign. Further, you'll generally need a certified copy of your U.S. application; this can be obtained from the PTO for a fee. (See Appendix 4, Fee Schedule.) The cost for filing a foreign application in each individual country is about $1,000 to $5,000, depending on the country, the length of your application, and whether a translation is required.

If you wish to correspond directly with the foreign patent agents yourself, you'll first have to get the name of a patent agent in each country.

d. What Happens to Your International Application?

You'll receive a (PCT) filing receipt and separate serial number for your international application, and the application will eventually be transmitted for filing to the countries (including the EPO) you've designated on your request form. If you make any minor errors in your PCT application, the PCT Department of the USPTO will give you a month to correct them.

e. Search Report

When you receive your PCT search report (either from the PTO or EPO and usually after several months), it will include a written opinion on patentability. You can comment on it and amend your claims if necessary, but no extended prosecution or negotiation is permitted. If you enter Chapter II of the PCT (optional), you will receive a more formal examination of your application, but it will be similar to the written opinion on patentability of Chapter I. The WIPO will publish your PCT application 18 months from your priority date. Your priority date is the date you filed a PPA or an RPA if you didn't file a PPA.

> **CAUTION**
>
> **If the search report cites any new references,** be sure to cite these to the PTO by way of a supplemental IDS (see Chapters 10 and 13).

f. National Stage

Within 30 months from your U.S. filing date, whether or not you elect Chapter II, if filing in Europe you must hire an agent there (get one in London, if you are seeking one who is fluent in English, or Munich, if seeking an agent close to the EPO offices) and file an EPO application based on your PCT application. Also, you must have an agent in each non-EPO PCT country (such as Japan or Australia) in which you wish to file and get national applications on file in these countries. Expect to pay very stiff fees to file and a high maintenance fee each year that the EPO application is pending.

As mentioned, each of the separate countries and the EPO will rely to a great extent on the international examination they'll receive from the International Bureau. (In most cases this will be the EPO search or an adoption of the U.S. search.) Thus, one advantage of the PCT approach is that you'll save much of what used to be the agonizing, extremely expensive job of separately and fully prosecuting an application in each country in which you elected to file.

> ⓘ **CAUTION**
>
> **You will not receive a reminder to enter the national stage by 30 months from your priority (U.S. filing) date.** You are solely responsible for meeting the deadline. We suggest setting your own calendar reminders in the weeks leading up to the 30-month deadline.

2. Route B: Elect Chapter II of PCT If You Want an International Examination

Route B is the same as Route A, except that instead you elect Chapter II of the PCT before filing your national applications. You have, as indicated, 22 months from your U.S. filing date or three months from the transmittal of the search report, to do this.

Get the forms (PCT/IPEA/401) from the PTO's site or the PCT department of the PTO, and also get the latest fees for Chapter II. If you select the EPO to do the examination, you must file the papers with the EPO in Munich and pay the fee in Euros. You'll get an examination report where claims will actually be allowed or rejected. You can amend your application once and even interview your examiner.

You file your EPO and non-EPO applications in the same way you did under Route A—that is, you elect agents, send them copies of all of your papers, and tell them you want to file national applications in their countries based upon your U.S. and PCT applications. Route B will cost more than Route A since you incur the expense of Chapter II of the PCT.

3. Route C: Convention Applications in EPO and Non-EPO Countries

Under Route C, you bypass the PCT entirely and file, through agents, national convention applications in the EPO and non-EPO countries within 12 months of your U.S. filing date. This is the cheapest way to go in the long run if you wish to file in several European

countries. An EPO filing, while expensive, is generally considered cheaper than separate filings if:

1. Two or more non–English-speaking countries are involved (for example, it's cheaper to file in the EPO than to file separate applications in Italy and Germany), or
2. The U.K. and more than one non-English country are involved. Conversely, it's cheaper to file separate applications in the U.K. and Germany, for instance, than to go through the EPO.

As mentioned, to file a Convention application in the EPO you'll have to go through a European patent agent, unless you have an address in one of the EPO countries, in which case you can do it yourself. Correspondence with the EPO must be in English if your application is based on your U.S. case.

Including the agent's fee, expect to spend a stiff fee to get your application on file and examined in about six countries. (See Appendix 4, Fee Schedule.) Additional large fees will be incurred for prosecution (getting your application approved once it's filed) and issuance. Then you'll have to arrange to get translations and individual agents for the respective countries you designate. For more information, write to the EPO for a copy of *How to Get a European Patent*.

4. Route D: Convention Applications in Individual Countries

Here you bypass both the PCT and the EPO. It's not a wise idea to bypass the EPO unless you want to file in just two countries in Europe—in which case it's usually cheaper to make individual filings rather than go through the EPO. This is the simplest way to go, on the charts, although it can get very complex and involve a lot of parallel correspondence and paperwork, since you'll have to make simultaneous prosecutions in each country. Filing is accomplished by sending a certified copy of your U.S. application to a patent agent in each country and instructing the agent to file a Convention application based upon your U.S. application. The agent will tell you what else is needed.

5. Route E: PPA Filed

If you've filed a PPA (see Chapter 3), your choices and procedures are the same as Routes A to D, except that at each stage there's another national country in which you can file: the United States. If you've filed a PPA, I recommend you file in the U.S., separately, by one year after you file your PPA, because it's simpler and somewhat cheaper. However, if you want to delay your U.S. filing, you can name the U.S. in your PCT application when you file your PCT application within one year after your PPA's filing date. You can then file your U.S. national application by 30 months after your PPA date. Your U.S. application should be identical to a "regular" U.S. application, except that you should add the following sentence to the PAD (Form 10-2) to get the benefit of your PCT filing date: "I hereby claim foreign priority benefits under 35 USC 119 of PCT patent application, Ser. No. _____, Filed 20___; which in turn claims priority of provisional patent application Ser. Nr. _____ filed _____."

6. File the PCT Application First

Although not listed on the chart because it's not a very popular method, if you haven't filed a PPA you can file a PCT application first (before you file anything) and then file in the U.S. and PCT countries (including the EPO) through the PCT. File in the non-PCT countries through the Convention or TRIPS. You can use this method to postpone the examination of your U.S. application until 30 months after your PCT filing date.

If you haven't filed a PPA and you know for certain, before you file anywhere, that you'll want to file in the U.S. and at least one foreign PCT country, then you can save some fees and effort by filing the PCT application first, before you file in the U.S. Then, within one year of your PCT filing date, you should file Convention or TRIPS applications, based upon your PCT application, in any non-PCT country.

Within 30 months of your PCT filing date, file separately (claiming priority of your PCT application) in each country or jurisdiction you've designated in your PCT application, including the U.S. and the EPO. Then order (from the PTO) a certified copy of your PCT application and file this within a few months after your U.S. filing date.

Whether you're filing in a PCT or non-PCT jurisdiction based upon a PCT filing, your foreign patent agents will tell you what you'll need to file PCT-based applications in their countries; allow at least two months before the 20- or 30-month deadline to give them (and you) time to prepare the applications and translations, if necessary.

> ### Patent Prosecution Highway—Expedited Examination of Applications Filed Abroad
>
> Your application is examined ahead of turn in almost all major foreign patent offices if you first filed your application in the U.S. and then filed a foreign application claiming priority of your earlier-filed U.S. application. In order to enter this program in the foreign patent office, the USPTO must have officially allowed at least one claim in the first-filed U.S. application. If you want to enter this program you must have your foreign agent file a request in the foreign patent office.

K. Rescind Any Nonpublication Request

When you filed your U.S. application, you had the opportunity to file a Nonpublication Request (NPR) (see Form 10-7). If you filed an NPR, you must file a rescission of this Request with the PTO within 45 days after filing your foreign application. You must file the rescission regardless of whether you are filing directly in a foreign country or using a PCT application. If you do not file the rescission, the PTO will cancel your U.S. application.

To make the rescission, complete and file Form PTO/SB/36, available on the PTO's website. If you don't have Internet access, you can use Form 13-1, but title it "Request to Rescind Previous Nonpublication

Request." Remove the sentence stating "In response to Office Letter …" and substitute the following statement: "Applicant has foreign filed the above application on or about [date] and therefore hereby rescinds the previously filed Nonpublication Request under 35 USC 122(b)." Remember to complete or include a Certificate of Mailing at the end of the rescission as in Form 13-2. (If you forget to rescind the NPR within 45 days of your foreign filing your application is technically abandoned but you may revive it by a petition under Rule 136(6), accompanied by a stiff fee.)

After notification, the PTO will schedule publication of your application 18 months after your U.S. filing date (or as soon as possible after the 18-month period).

Beware of Scams

Unfortunately the scammers have even invaded the world of the PCT and foreign patent filings. Once your application is published, you may get offers from scammers seeking to lighten your wallet. For example, after filing a PCT application for a client and revoking the Nonpublication Request that I had originally filed, the PTO published his application about 18 months after filing. Shortly thereafter he got a letter from a "Patent Registry" in Washington, DC, offering to register his patent in their private "American Patent and Trademark Register"—an apparently worthless endeavor—for only $2,489.46! WIPO "names and shames" these scammers at www.wipo.int/pct/en/warning/pct_warning.html.

L. Foreign-Filing Resources

There are a number of resources to assist you in foreign filing your patent application. Let's look at them separately.

- **U.S. Patent Practitioners.** Most U.S. patent attorneys and agents have experience in foreign filing and will handle the PCT filing and national stage filings for you for a fee, in addition to the filing fees.
- **Foreign-Filing Firms.** At least one firm, Inovia, specializes in foreign patent filing (https://.inovia.com).
- **Foreign Patent Agents.** You'll almost certainly need to find a foreign patent agent who's familiar with patent prosecution in the countries where you desire protection. (In most countries, patent professionals are called "agents" rather than attorneys.) Your best bet is to find one through a U.S. patent attorney, as most are associated with one or more patent agents in other major countries. If you don't know a U.S. patent attorney, use an Internet search engine, for example, by entering "patent agent [name of country]" or look in the telephone directory of the city where the patent office of the foreign country is located. Foreign consulates also often have a list of patent agents. *Martindale-Hubbell Law Directory* (www.martindale.com), also lists some foreign patent agents in each country. Finally, you can hire a British firm of patent agents to do all your foreign filing. The reason for this is that they speak English and they're familiar with foreign filing. This would be especially appropriate if you're filing with the EPO (although most German agents in Munich, though not as fluent in English, have the compensating advantage of their physical proximity to the EPO). Whichever way you find your foreign patent agent, be careful, since many foreign agents are bound by a minimum fee schedule, which is sometimes exorbitant. Also, keep in mind that some foreign patent agents—like their U.S. counterparts—are incompetent or inclined to overcharge.
- **Written Materials.** Read *Patents Throughout the World*, by Henry Teegarden (Clark Boardman Callaghan). This book is revised annually, so be sure you have the most recent version. For more information on how to utilize the PCT, "The PCT Applicant's Guide," "Basic Facts," and other instructive materials and forms are available online at www.wipo.int and from the PCT Department of the USPTO.

M. Summary

A U.S. patent provides a monopoly in the United States only, so it is necessary to file for corresponding foreign patents in any other countries in which you want offensive rights. Foreign filing is very expensive and few inventors who foreign-file ever recoup their investment, so an inventor should foreign-file the application in a country only if the invention has extremely strong commercial potential there or if someone is paying the freight.

Various conventions govern foreign filing. The Paris Convention grants anyone who files a basic application in any member country the benefit of the basic filing date in any other country where a corresponding application is filed within one year. TRIPS provides the same benefit from World Trade Organization (WTO) countries.

The European Patent Office enables one to file a single patent application and get a European patent that is valid in any European country, provided the Europatent is registered in and translated for each country.

The Patent Cooperation Treaty (PCT) enables a U.S.-resident inventor who has filed a patent application in the PTO to file a PCT application in the USPTO within one year and have it searched and examined to determine patentability and delay filing of national stage applications in foreign jurisdictions for 30 months from the U.S. filing date.

An inventor who files a U.S. application must wait six months before foreign filing, unless the PTO grants a foreign filing license, which it usually grants on the filing receipt. The laws of other countries are different from the U.S. in certain respects—for example, some countries have no interferences, no one-year grace period, and no patents on drugs. Some countries have maintenance fees during pendency, hold opposition proceedings, and companies can apply for patents in the name of the company or an assignee.

There are several routes for filing abroad, but most inventors file in the U.S. first, then file a PCT application within a year, and then file national-stage applications within 30 months of the U.S. filing date. An inventor can file a PCT application in the USPTO by completing the PCT forms and filing an A4 copy of the application with the appropriate fees. You can file a PCT application on paper or via EFS-Web.

If an inventor files a U.S. application with a Nonpublication Request, the inventor must revoke this within 45 days after any foreign filing. It is necessary to hire a foreign patent agent in any jurisdiction where a national-stage application (in an individual country or in a regional office like the EPO) is to be filed.

Getting the PTO to Deliver

Inventor's Commandment 24

Never admit or state anything negative or limiting about your invention on the record (in writing), since anything negative you admit will be used against you later by an adversary or construed against you in a judicial proceeding.

Inventor's Commandment 25

Your application will go abandoned if you don't file a timely response to any PTO communication. Whenever you have a patent application pending, you must be available to receive Office Actions (letters) from the PTO and you must respond to every OA within the time allotted or within the time period of any extension you buy (when possible).

Inventor's Commandment 26

You may not add any "new matter" (technical information not in the application as filed) to any patent application. If you want to add any new matter you must file a continuation-in-part application as explained in Chapter 14.

Inventor's Commandment 27

In order to answer an Office Action from the PTO, you must respond to each and every point (objection or rejection) in the OA, either by suitable argument or by complying as required.

Inventor's Commandment 28

When drafting an amendment in response to the first Office Action, do your very best job. Include a complete response, all available arguments for patentability, and the narrowest and most comprehensive claims possible, since the next OA will almost certainly be made final, foreclosing any future substantive changes unless you pay another filing or continued examination fee.

You can file a lawsuit against anyone for anything. Whether you can prove your case and win is, of course, a very different matter.

Similarly, anyone can file a patent application on anything. But getting the Patent and Trademark Office (PTO) to issue you a patent is, of course, a very different matter.

This chapter tells you how to get the PTO to deliver, assuming your invention meets the standards of patentability. This material is sure to seem confusing the first time you read it. A little familiarity with the process, however, should do a world of good when it comes to your understanding.

A. What Happens After Your Patent Application Is Filed

It will be helpful to review exactly what will occur after your patent application is filed.

1. Receipt Postcard

If you filed by mail, you'll receive your receipt postcard back in about two to four weeks. If you filed electronically, you'll receive your filing acknowledgment immediately, and you should print it for your files immediately. The postcard or acknowledgment will have an eight-digit number—for example, "U.S. Patent & TM Office, 22 August 2012; 12/123,456" The date is the "deposit" date (date of receipt), and the number is the serial number (sometimes called "application number") of your application. Your electronic acknowledgment will also contain another four-digit number, called a confirmation number, which you will need to file amendments via EFS-Web if you're a registered eFiler. Keep your serial number and filing date confidential unless a prospective manufacturer has shown serious interest and asks for this information—for example, because you're about to enter into a license or sale agreement.

2. Official Filing Receipt

About one to three months later you should receive an official filing receipt by mail. This is a sheet containing the following:

- the name(s) of the inventor(s)
- the title of your patent application
- the examining group to which your application has been assigned
- the filing date and serial number of your application and the confirmation number
- the number of claims (total and independent)
- the filing fee you paid
- your name and address
- the words "Small Entity" if you filed as a small entity, and
- the words "Foreign Filing License Granted [date]" if the invention hasn't been militarily classified (most won't be).

Check all of this information carefully; it's what's entered into the PTO's data-processing system about your application. If the filing receipt has any errors, indicate the error on the filing receipt and send a copy or fax it to the Office of Patent Application Processing (OPAP) whose numbers will be on the filing receipt. Request a new filing receipt.

Assuming you've done everything properly, your patent application is technically pending once you receive your Priority Mail Express receipt from the Post Office clerk or electronic acknowledgment. However, the actual filing receipt makes it official and shows that it's actually recorded in the PTO.

If You Receive a Foreign Filing License

The words "Foreign Filing License Granted," along with a date, on your filing receipt mean that you can foreign file at any time, rather than waiting six months. However, you still should wait until approximately nine months have passed before considering filing abroad in Convention countries. There is a slim chance you will receive an Office Action during that time, and if you do, you'll have better information about patentability and to accumulate additional commercial information on your invention. You should file abroad in non-Convention countries before you sell or publish details of the invention.

You may continue to label your invention and any descriptive literature "Patent Pending," or "Patent Applied For." They have the same meaning. Note that it's a criminal offense to use the words "patent applied for" or "patent pending" in any advertising when there's no active, applicable Regular or Provisional Patent Application on file.

If for any reason, your application hasn't been filed properly (for example, your check bounced, or you didn't pay enough for the filing fee), you won't get the filing receipt. Instead, the PTO will send you a deficiency notice telling you what's needed and what surcharge (fine) you'll have to pay for the error of your ways. Once you comply with the deficiency notice (they usually give you a month), you'll get your filing receipt a few weeks later.

3. Patent Pending Status

The patent pending period begins when your Regular Patent Application or Provisional Patent Application is filed and lasts until the RPA issues as a patent or the PPA expires after 12 months. During the patent pending period, your rights depend upon whether you have filed a Nonpublication Request (NPR). If you have not filed an NPR, the PTO will publish your regular patent application 18 months after the filing date. Once it is published, you obtain provisional rights that allow you to obtain royalties from an infringer for activities that occurred from the date the infringer gets actual notice of the published application, if your patent issues with claims that are substantially identical to the claims in the published application (35 USC 154(d)). (You can provide actual notice to the infringer by sending a copy of the published application by certified mail, return receipt requested.) You must wait until after the patent issues to request (and sue if necessary for) these "patent pending" royalties. If the patent does not issue, you cannot obtain any royalties.

If, at the time of filing your application, you filed an NPR, your application will not be published prior to issuance and no provisional remedies will accrue during the patent pending period. In other words, if it is not published prior to issuance, anyone can freely make, use, sell, and offer your invention for sale during the entire pendency period.

In general, a potential infringer won't copy a device that it knows is patent pending. This is because the infringer would have to take the chance that a patent will later be issued and you'll use your patent to enforce your monopoly—that is, stop any further production and marketing. In this case, the money the infringer would have to spend on expensive tooling, product development and marketing will have been wasted. (If you're willing to license the infringer under your patent, the infringer's tooling outlay will be worthwhile, but few infringers will be willing to take this chance.) Another reason for marking a device "patent pending" is to show that you have given notice to potential infringers, which gives a court discretion to assess treble damages and attorneys' fees (after your patent issues) if the court finds that the infringement was willful.

After your application is filed, you may publish articles on your invention without loss of any legal rights in the U.S. or foreign Convention countries, but you'll lose rights in non-Convention countries. However, it's not desirable to reveal details of your invention to potential competitors at this early stage, especially since your application may not become a patent.

4. Send in Your Information Disclosure Statement (IDS)

If you haven't done so already, after receiving your official filing receipt send in your Information Disclosure Statement as discussed in Chapter 10. If you filed your application by mail send in the IDS by filling out a Transmittal Form (SB/21 or Form 10-05). Accompany it with the SB08a and SB08b or 10-6A and 10-6B forms as necessary, and copies of any non-U.S. patent references you listed on the form. If you filed electronically, and you're a registered eFiler, you won't need a transmittal form. Instead get the electronic SB08a EFS-Web form by going to www.uspto.gov/patent/forms/forms-patent-applications-filed-or-after-september-16-2012. Open the SB08a EFS-Web form, fill the blanks, and save the form as a PDF file, (for example, IDS.pdf) as you did with the Data Sheet when you filed, and make a PDF of any non-U.S. patent references (known as Non-Patent Literature or "NPL"), and file all of these using the PTO's electronic business site. Remember that the PTO wants the IDS to be filed within three months of the application's filing date. Don't forget to fill in all the blanks that identify your application.

If you don't file the IDS within three months of your filing date, or before your first Office Action, or within three months after entry into the "national" stage for references cited in foreign applications, the PTO will still consider it. However, you must file it before a final action or a notice of allowance is sent, and (1) pay a "Late IDS Fee" (see Appendix 4, Fee Schedule), or (2) include a certificate as follows.

"(A) Each item of information contained in this Information Disclosure Statement (IDS) was cited in a communication from a foreign patent office in a counterpart foreign patent application not more than three months prior to the filing of such IDS, or (B) no item of information contained in this IDS was cited in a communication from a foreign patent office in a counterpart foreign patent application, or, to my knowledge after making reasonable inquiry, was known to any individual designated in 37 CFR 1.56(c) (inventor, attorney, assignee, etc.) more than three months prior to the filing of such IDS."

You can even file the IDS after a final action or notice of allowance is sent, but before you pay the issue fee. However, you must include the above certificate, a petition requesting consideration of the IDS, and a petition fee (see Appendix 4, Fee Schedule).

If you send an IDS and later discover any additional references—for example, in the course of foreign prosecution—you must bring these to the attention of the PTO through a supplemental IDS. (Don't send an IDS for any references the examiner cites in your U.S. case; these will automatically be listed, along with those which you cited, on the patent.)

5. First Office Action

About six months to three years after the filing date (patent prosecution is mostly a waiting game) you'll receive a communication from the PTO known as a "first Office Action" (OA), sometimes called an "official letter." It consists of forms and a letter from the examiner in charge of your application, describing what is wrong with your application and why it cannot yet be allowed. (Rarely will an application be allowed in the first OA.)

Specifically, the OA may:

- reject claims
- list defects in the specification and/or drawings
- cite and enclose copies of prior art that the examiner believes shows your invention is either:
  - not novel, or
  - obvious, and/or
- raise various other objections.

The PTO sends foreign patents and non-patent literature with the first OA in which they were cited. You must download the patent references from the Internet, and Google Patents is often a good source. The PTO has a batch downloading procedure under its PAIR system, but you must be a registered eFiler to use this. You can also download the patents from of the free patent copy supply sites listed in Chapter 6.

To find out approximately when you'll receive the first OA from the PTO and you are a registered e-Filer, you can access your application's file on Private PAIR and select the "First Action Prediction" link. Otherwise, go to the PTO's home page (www.uspto.gov), then click "Patents," then "Patent Statistics," and then select "First Office Action Estimator." Also, you can call the clerk of the examining group where your application has been assigned. The name of this group will be typed on your filing receipt. PTO phone numbers are listed on the PTO website, in Appendix 5, and are published irregularly in the *Official Gazette* (OG). Each issue of the OG also gives date status information for patent applications in each examining group.

We suggest that you write three date entries (as shown below) on every paper you receive from the PTO:

Received ____[date]_____
Start preparing response by ____[date]_____
Response due by ____[date]_____

6. Response to First Office Action

Every OA itself will specify a deadline, usually three months (extendable, for a fee, up to six months from the date of the OA) after the OA was mailed, by which you must file a response. Your response must take whatever action is necessary to overcome the objections and rejections listed in the OA. The response you file is technically called an "amendment" (assuming it contains any changes), or a "response" (assuming it doesn't contain any changes). The entire process of correspondence (Office Actions and amendments) to and from the PTO is known as "prosecuting" your patent application, although no one is "prosecuted" in the usual sense.

7. Second/Final Office Action

About two to six months after you file your first amendment, you'll receive a second OA from the PTO; this will usually be designated a "final" OA by the PTO. A final OA is supposed to end the prosecution stage before the examiner. However, as we'll see later, this is far from true. In other words, a "final action" is rarely final. Again, you have three months to reply, but you must reply to a final OA in a way that takes definitive action on the application, as we will see.

8. Notice of Allowance

After the first OA, if you are fortunate enough to submit an amendment or whatever is necessary to get your application in condition for allowance, you'll be sent a Notice of Allowance, indicating that all of your claims are allowed and that an issue fee is due within three months (this term is not extendable). Sometimes you'll get a "Notice of Allowability" before or with the formal allowance; this merely states that your claims are all allowed, the Notice of Allowance will be sent, and whether formal drawings are due.

9. Issue Fee and Issue Notification

Four to six weeks after you pay the issue fee and file formal drawings (if you didn't do so before), you'll receive an Issue Notification from the PTO, indicating the forthcoming issue date and number of your patent. Be sure to file any desired divisional application or continuation application by the day before the patent issues.

10. Receipt of Official Patent Deed

Shortly after the date your patent issues, you'll receive your official "Letters Patent" or deed from the PTO. If you ordered any printed copies of the patent, these will arrive in a separate envelope.

11. First Action Interview Program

The PTO's First Action Interview program provides applicants an opportunity to interview their examiner before the first Office Action but after the examiner makes a search. The goal of the program is to dispose of applications early without the need for Office Actions and amendments. If your application is eligible for the program and you feel confident enough to study the references, redraft your claims, and handle an interview, we recommend you enter the program. To see if the program is still in force, go to the PTO's home page (www.uspto.gov) and search for "First Action Interview." To enter the program you must be a registered eFiler and you must file a request on Form PTO/SB/413C.

B. General Considerations During Patent Prosecution

Patent application prosecution is generally more difficult than the preparation of the initial application. Assuming that you're going to handle the prosecution phase pretty much on your own, we recommend that you keep the following general considerations in mind.

1. The PTO Can Write Claims for You

You can ask the PTO to write one or more claims for you if the application contains allowable subject matter. Then you can either accept this claim or amend it if you think you can get it past the examiner.

You should generally have several sets of varied claims (one independent and several dependent per set) to cover your invention fully.

2. Consultation With a Patent Professional Might Be Wise

You might wish to consult with a patent expert at this point to amend your claims and argument (which is usually what's required). We particularly recommend seeking the assistance of a registered patent attorney if you run into an issue that is over your head, which may occur for example when the PTO rejects a claim for being directed to non-statutory subject matter, or if you are unable to think of a convincing way around a claim rejection.

3. Intervals Are Approximate

Except for official periods, such as the three-month period for response to an OA or to pay the issue fee, the dates and times we've given in this chapter are only approximate and are gleaned from recent experience. They can vary quite widely, depending on conditions in the PTO at the time you file your patent application. You have to be patient. If you don't receive any communication from the PTO for a long time, say over a year after you file your application, you should check the latest *Official Gazette* for the status of the cases in your group. Also, if it's over four months after you file an amendment, you should make a call, or send a letter, to the examiner or examining group to determine the status of your case. (If you are willing to submit a lot of paperwork, install software, and so forth, you can access the PTO's "Private PAIR" system, which enables you to see a docket sheet and all of the papers for your patent application on the PTO's website. To get on Private PAIR, see the instructions in Chapter 10.)

4. You'll Be Able to Correct Technical Errors

Don't worry too much about minor technical errors (except for dates—see next consideration) when dealing with the PTO. If you make one, you'll be given an opportunity to correct it. The PTO has so many rules and regulations that even patent attorneys who deal with them all the time can't remember them all. Also, the PTO is flexible in giving do-it-yourself (pro se) applicants opportunities to correct nondate errors that don't affect the substance of the application.

5. Dates Are Crucial

Every OA that you receive from the PTO will specify an interval by which you must reply to the OA. If you fail to reply in the time the PTO allots you, the penalty is draconian: Your application will go abandoned, although it can be revived at a price. (See below.) Thus, you should write the due date for response to every OA promptly on the OA and on your calendar and heed it carefully. If you're not the type who can faithfully heed due dates, you must do something about this—for example, by hiring a methodical friend to bug you. You can even turn the whole job of prosecution over to a patent attorney. If you miss a crucial date, you'll find that the PTO is a cruel and unforgiving bureaucracy.

6. Situations Not Covered

If any situation occurs that isn't covered in this book, and you can't find the answer by looking in the *Rules of Practice* or *Manual of Patent Examining Procedure*, call the PTO, consult an attorney or agent, or use common sense and do what you would expect to be the logical thing to do in such a situation.

Newly Discovered Reference: For example, suppose that after you've filed your patent application you find a prior-art reference that considerably narrows what you thought your invention to be. You should bring this to the attention of the PTO by way of another (supplemental) IDS and PTO/SB/08, and submit an amendment substituting narrower claims that avoid the reference. Remember that you have a continuing duty to disclose all material information about your invention to the PTO.

Embodiment Changes: If you discover that an embodiment of your invention doesn't work, delete it from your application. If you discover a new embodiment of your invention that supersedes the present embodiments, file a continuation-in-part application. (See Chapter 14.)

Entity Size Change: If you license or assign your application to a large entity (or such a license is terminated or your application is reassigned back to you), you should send a letter to the PTO asking that your small-entity status be canceled (or send in a letter to establish SE status).

Change of Address: If you change your address, you should send a change of address form (use Form PTO/AIA/122 on the PTO's site) or an appropriate letter (caption as in Form 13-1 but headed "Change of Applicant's Address") to the PTO.

PTO Mistakes: If the examiner cites a prior-art reference against your application that is later than your filing date, obviously the examiner made an error (this happens occasionally). You should call or write to bring it to the examiner's attention so that a new Office Action can be issued. If the PTO fails to send you a copy of a non-U.S. patent reference that it has cited against you, send an appropriate paper (captioned as in Form 13-1) headed "Request for Copy of Missing Reference" to the PTO. If a part of the OA doesn't make sense, or a part seems to have been omitted, send an immediate "Request for Clarification of Office Action."

Finally, as a wise person said, "Don't be afraid to ask dumb questions: They're easier to handle than dumb mistakes."

Bureaucratic Static: The examiner may object to something in your application if it's unusual or irregular, even if it's otherwise proper and harmless. This is the result of bureaucratic attitudes—that is, examiners like others in government sometimes have a tendency to rigidly enforce a "standard" administrative procedure. The remedy is to explain to the examiner that what you have done is proper and to respectfully challenge the examiner to provide a specific reason for the objection and a suggestion for correction. The next paragraph shows how we responded to an examiner who objected when we typed "stateless" in the citizenship blank of the declaration form, even though the applicant was stateless; the examiner did not repeat the objection again.

*"**The Objection to the Declaration:** The Office Action objected to the Declaration since it listed the citizenship of the applicant as 'stateless.' The Examiner required a new declaration. Applicant does not understand this objection, the legal basis therefor, or what remedial action the Examiner would like on any new declaration. Applicant's citizenship is indeed 'stateless.' In the past, applicant's representative has filed other patent applications for various stateless individuals. He always listed their citizenship as 'stateless' and all of these cases went on to patent without ever before encountering any objection. Therefore applicant respectfully submits that the 'stateless' entry is proper.*

"Applicant is willing to file a new declaration if the Examiner still desires, but he doesn't know what the Examiner would like applicant to enter in the Citizenship blank in lieu of 'stateless.' If the Examiner continues the objection, applicant respectfully requests that the Examiner explain what specifically he objects to about the 'stateless' entry, the legal basis for the objection, and exactly what replacement entry Examiner would like in any new declaration. Thereupon applicant will be pleased and eager to comply. Note that applicant cannot enter any specific country in the Citizenship blank since he is not a citizen of any country."

7. Standards of Patentability Vary Widely

What actually happens when your application is examined will vary, depending upon the personality, whims, training, and current emotions of the examiner assigned to handle it. Most examiners adhere to the basic standards of patentability outlined here and are competent, knowledgeable, and occasionally helpful when it comes to telling you what to do to put the case in condition for allowance. Unfortunately, due to a recent PTO hiring initiative to reduce a large backlog of pending patent applications, many examiners are very new and inexperienced, new to the U.S. and unfamiliar with English, incompetent or unable to comprehend a true advance in the art, ignorant in the field or art being examined, or lacking in the requisite sensitivity to appreciate the huge financial and work burdens their acts might impose on applicants. This can sometimes lead them to make arbitrary or irrational rulings and deny patents that should be granted or vice versa.

The solution to the problem with an unreasonably tough or inexperienced examiner is to, first, be persistent. Go to the PTO (or hire a patent attorney to go) to interview your examiner. If necessary, appeal. Appealing is a powerful weapon against a tough examiner. Examiners don't like to write answers to appeal briefs since these take a lot of time. Also, they usually must have an appeal conference with two other examiners, and it looks bad on their record if they get reversed.

The problem with an easy examiner is that your allowed application might not stand up in court (should this ever become necessary). Accordingly, if you believe that your examiner is not rigorous enough (for instance, all your claims are allowed in the first Office Action), make especially sure yourself that at least some of your claims are clearly patentable. That is, they should define a novel enough invention to withstand a court challenge. (See Chapter 15.)

It may help to know that examiners themselves have to contend with two opposing forces. On the one hand, they're expected to dispose of (allow or get the applicant to abandon) a certain number of cases. However, on the other hand, they're subject to a quality review program to make sure they're not too lenient.

Note that even if you have a great invention that is clearly patentable, but you haven't claimed it properly, most U.S. PTO examiners, unlike their counterparts in the European Patent Offices, won't volunteer help or constructive suggestions or try to assist you. They'll simply reject your claims or make a requirement and leave it to you to figure out how to do what's necessary to remedy the situation. Thus, it's up to you to claim and fight for what's rightfully yours. Never automatically accept any examiner's rejection.

8. Don't Take Rejection Personally

If the examiner rejects your claims, don't take such a rejection as a condemnation of you personally. The examiner doesn't know you and is thus merely rejecting your claims and not you. In other words, a rejection of your claims just means one examiner, at one point, feels that your claims are not different enough from the prior art or clear enough to be allowed. You still are a good and worthwhile person and your innovation may still be patentable with revised claims, or if you successfully argue over the rejection.

9. Dealing With the PTO Can Be Frustrating and Unfair

Dealing with the PTO, as with any other government agency, can sometimes be a very difficult, time-consuming, and frustrating experience. We could spend a whole chapter listing the errors and mistakes we've encountered recently, but one example will suffice. We once filed an application for an inventor whose last name was "Loe." The filing receipt came back with the name "Lee." After several letters and calls with no response, a "corrected" filing receipt arrived with the name spelled "Leo." After a few more calls and much frustration, a correct filing receipt finally arrived. Put succinctly, dealing with the PTO is not like dealing with an efficient and competitive private company. All I can tell you is to be philosophical, scrupulously check your correspondence with the PTO to make sure they get it right, and persist in correcting errors when they occur.

As far as the unfairness goes—there are many situations when you deal with the PTO where you'll find an inherent unfairness due to no reciprocity. For example, while you have to reply to an OA when the PTO tells you to, they can reply to you whenever they get around to it. Your patent term will be extended to give you a minimum of 17 years of coverage provided the delay wasn't your responsibility. While you are supposed to make your claims and specification clear, grammatical, and free of spelling errors, you'll often find that the correspondence you receive from the PTO doesn't meet these standards. While you have to pay a stiff fine if you forget to sign your check or make some other inadvertent error, the PTO never is liable, no matter how negligent they are. There's nothing you can do about this unfairness except, again, to be philosophical and resign yourself to accept the rules of the game before you play.

One inventor was so frustrated that he sued his examiner and the PTO for negligence. The judge said, "This is the sad tale of an inventor frustrated by the bureaucratic mindset and Byzantine workings of the PTO." While he won in trial court, the appellate court reversed, holding that examiners are not legally responsible for their actions.

10. PTO Reference Books

During patent prosecution, you may need to refer to the MPEP, the PTO's Rules of Practice, and/or the patent statutes. All can be viewed on or obtained from the PTO's website and the latter two can be obtained from regional government bookstores in paperbound forms. The PTO's patent rules are given the prefix number "1" to distinguish them from trademark rules "2" and copyright rules "3." For example, Patent Rule 111, referred to later in this chapter, is officially identified as Title 37 of the Code of Federal Regulations, Section 1.111, or in legal citation form, 37 CFR 1.111. *The Manual of Patent Examining Procedure* (MPEP), which is often referred to as the "examiner's bible," covers almost any situation you can encounter in patent prosecution and contains the patent rules and statutes. It's a large, loose-leaf volume with about four megabytes of text, but you can view and print any part (or all of it) from the PTO's Internet site. A complete copy of the MPEP is available on the PTO's site and it contains the PTO's Rules of Practice (37 CFR) and all of the Patent Statutes (35 USC). Unfortunately it isn't always up to date, so it's also wise to search for any update notices about your subject of interest in the search box on the PTO's home page.

11. Never Make Negative or Limiting Statements on the Record

When dealing with the PTO, always remember this "Miranda" warning: anything you say can and will be used against you in a court of law (should you ever have to enforce your patent). Never say or write anything that derogates your invention, never admit that any prior-art reference shows (includes) any feature of your invention, and never state anything that a court could use to limit your invention. For example, here are some improper statements that could be used against you:

- "While applicant's device is not as good as Smith's …"
- "It is true that Jones shows applicant's gear ratio …"
- "Applicant's device is designed for use with an electronic control."

Admittedly, this advice may be very difficult to follow in some situations, but it's important to comply with. Why? The PTO puts all correspondence into your official file (called your "file wrapper"), and if litigation arises regarding your patent, your adversary will use any negative admission or limiting statement against you.

12. Remember Your Continuing Duty to Disclose Material Information

You have a duty to disclose all material information, such as relevant prior art, known to you that bears on the patentability of your invention. This duty is normally fulfilled when you send in your IDS as discussed above. However, if you discover any additional information later, you must send in a supplemental IDS. Of course, if you find a prior-art reference that you feel is so close that you believe your invention is not patentable, you should abandon your application.

13. The PTO Can Request Search Information and Literature

In connection with your continuing duty to disclose, above, the PTO can require, under Rule 105, that any applicant supply any search information and literature which the applicant knows of, which the applicant used to draft the application, or which the examiner can use to examine the application properly. This may include a form paragraph or letter in your application requesting this. If you receive such a Request, comply with it, but don't include any information that you already included with your IDS.

14. Be Available to Answer Office Actions

As mentioned, you'll normally be required to respond to a PTO Office Action within three months. If an OA is sent while you're away or unavailable and you fail to reply to it, your application will, as stated above, be considered abandoned. Thus, we've provided Inventor's Commandment 25, at the beginning of this chapter, to give you ample warning. If you will be unavailable for an extended period while your application is pending, you should empower a patent attorney to handle it for you or arrange to have your mail forwarded by a reliable friend or relative. You can ask to have correspondence from the PTO sent to anyone you choose, but the PTO generally won't allow you to appoint a layperson to represent you, so all inventors must sign every paper that is sent to the PTO.

15. Consider Foreign Filing

About eight to ten months after you file your patent application, you should consider whether you want to file for coverage in other countries. Foreign filing is extremely expensive, time-consuming, and arduous, so do it only if you have a very important, innovative invention or a foreign licensee who will pay the freight. There are international conventions or agreements among most countries that entitle you to the benefit of your U.S. filing date on any foreign applications you file within one year after you file your U.S. regular or provisional application.

16. You Can Call and Visit Your Examiner

If you have any questions about your application, or any reference that is cited against it, you are permitted to call, and/or make an appointment with and visit, the examiner in charge of your application. Your examiner's telephone number will be listed on official letters that you receive from the PTO. (If the first action hasn't been sent yet and you're a registered eFiler you can go to the Private PAIR site and view the docket sheet for your application to obtain the

Fax and Internet Filing Available

The PTO prefers that responses, including amendments, petitions, appeals, and elections, should be filed via the Internet if you're a registered eFiler since otherwise they have to scan and upload paper responses. If you're a registered eFiler, go to the PTO's Electronic Business site and eFile the papers in PDF format as you did with the original application.

If you're not a registered eFiler, you should file responses by fax. (Do not file applications, fees, or drawings by fax.) Faxed papers should include, "I certify I have transmitted this paper by fax to the Patent and Trademark Office at [#] on [date]." The PTO will consider the paper as having been filed on the date of transmission or the next business day if you fax it on a nonbusiness day. Keep your signed original and your machine's record of successful transmission. The PTO's fax machines will now automatically fax back a "fax received" receipt. (The PTO's main fax numbers are in Appendix 5, Mail, Telephone, Fax, and Email Communications With the PTO.) If you don't have a fax machine, there are methods to fax via computer—using either fax software that is included with your computer's operating system or using an online fax service (that can also provide you with a telephone number to receive faxes). To fax a signed document, you will need to scan or convert it to PDF.

As a last alternative, you still can mail your responses; be sure to always include a receipt postcard.

Email communications may be used for minor matters, such as status requests, minor corrections in a paper, notification that a communication has been sent, etc., but not major papers, such as amendments and patent applications. However, since email is not a secure form of communication and the PTO is obligated to preserve all patent applications in secret, PTO employees are not allowed to send email containing any sensitive information unless you specifically authorize this. If you are willing to receive email from the PTO containing sensitive information about your application, you must file the following statement in your application: "Recognizing that Internet communications are not secure, I hereby authorize the PTO to communicate with me concerning any subject matter of this application by electronic mail. I understand that a copy of these communications will be made of record in the application file." Similarly, you should print out and put in your file a copy of all email communications you receive from the PTO.

name of your examiner.) However, usually only one, or at most two, applicant-initiated interviews are permitted. So save this privilege for when you really need it. If you have an interview, you must summarize its substance in the next amendment, even if the examiner sends a summary of the interview to you. An interview is often a very valuable way to get a difficult case allowed, since communication is greatly enhanced when you and the examiner can discuss your differences and reach an understanding through the give and take and multiple feedback loops an interview permits. Also, it's harder to say "no" directly to a person face-to-face. Lastly, an interview provides an excellent opportunity to bring in and demonstrate a working prototype or sample of the invention to the examiner; this is usually an excellent persuader.

However, we recommend that you try to avoid calling or interviewing any examiner on Fridays, since, like most of us, they're likely to be less attentive then. An excellent guide for negotiating with examiners is presented by Examining Group Director A.L. Smith at page 168 of the 1990 February *Journal of the Patent and Trademark Office Society*.

We cannot overstate the value of an interview. One pro se applicant that we know (Alex) had a very difficult time getting his case allowed. On our suggestion he traveled to the PTO to have an interview with his examiner. To his dismay Alex found from discussing the case that the examiner had likely never read his application and definitely did not understand the invention. Fortunately he was able to explain the invention on the spot and, with some claim adjustments, managed to get the case allowed. One free site (www.usptoexaminers.com), allows attorneys and applicants to post reviews of examiners anonymously. Another, albeit somewhat expensive new pay site, www.juristat.com, has statistical data on examiners, indicating types of rejections, average number of OAs sent per case, average time between filing and issuance, the percentage of cases allowed, abandoned, and appealed, the percentage of cases allowed after appeal, etc. The PTO provides some of these data for free in its Data Visualization Center (www.uspto.gov/dashboards/patents).

Sometimes your examiner will call you, offering to allow the application if some changes are made in the application. If the changes are minor you can agree to them on the spot. But if the changes are substantive and involve the claims, we suggest you tell the examiner you would like to study them for a day or two and will call back. You should study the proposed changes carefully. If they would unduly narrow the claims, try to formulate and suggest some less restrictive changes that are still allowable.

17. Working or Commercial Model

If you have a working or commercial model of your invention, it's usually desirable to show or send this (or literature on it) to your examiner. This may make the examiner a believer in your invention, its operability, its advantages, and its commercial success. If your invention is out on the market and has had commercial success, you should submit a Declaration Under Rule 132 with exhibits attesting to such success and explaining why such success is a result of the novel features of your invention. The Supreme Court has specifically stated that the PTO must consider such commercial success when deciding on patentability (see MPEP 1504.03).

18. No New Matter Can Be Added to Your Application

Once your application is filed, the statute, 35 USC 132, prohibits you from adding any "new matter" to it. (New matter consists of any technical information, including dimensions, materials, parts, values, arrangements, connections, methods, etc., that was not present in your application as originally filed.) This prohibition makes sense since, if patent applicants were permitted to add continuing improvements and changes to their applications, the date of invention, and what was invented when, would be too difficult to determine.

If you do want to add any new developments to your application, consider a special type of supplementary application (termed a "continuation-in-part application" or CIP and covered in Chapter 14). If your improvement is really significant, you should seek an independent, subsequent patent application.

New matter should be distinguished from prior art that may be discovered after an application has been filed. You are obligated to inform the PTO about any newly discovered, relevant prior art. Such prior art doesn't form part of your specification, nor does it affect the nature of your invention. Rather, it provides the PTO with more information by which to judge your invention for patentability. Also note that if you submit new claims that are broader, narrower, or different, the PTO does not consider them new matter, unless the new claims contain new information that was not originally present in the application.

19. Official Dates Are When the PTO Receives Your Submission

Every paper that you send to or receive from the PTO has an official date. This is the date on which it was mailed from or received by the PTO. You should put your actual date of mailing on anything you send to the PTO, but the date of the PTO's "Received" stamp on your paper will be the "official" date of the paper. If you send in your application by Priority Mail Express with PME Certification (see Chapter 10), the PTO will stamp it as of the date you express mailed it, even though they receive it one to three days later. This is because, under PTO Rule 10, they consider your local post office their agent to receive your correspondence, provided you use PME.

20. Know Who Has the Ball

To use an analogy drawn from the game of football, during patent prosecution the "ball" (burden of action) will always be either on your side or the PTO's. If you just sent in your case, the ball will be with the PTO until they return your postcard, send you an official filing receipt, and send you a first Office Action. It doesn't go back to your side until that first OA. Once they send the first OA, you have the ball and must usually take action within three months. Once you file an amendment, the PTO has the ball again, and so on.

21. Reread Appropriate Chapters

When you respond to an OA, you should go back and reread the chapter that covers the issue you need to address. For example, if a claim is rejected for prolixity, reread Chapter 9.

22. Respond to Each and Every Point in the Office Action

A typical OA will contain several criticisms (termed "objections" and/or "rejections"), such as drawing objections, specification objections, claim rejections for indefiniteness, and claim rejections based upon prior art. You must respond to each and every criticism in your next amendment or your amendment will be considered nonresponsive, in which case you'll usually be given two weeks to complete the amendment. Suitable responses can be an argument against the criticism or some action to eliminate the criticism— for example, by canceling claims, amending the specification, supplying new drawings, or substituting different claims and arguing that the substituted claims are patentable over the prior art cited.

23. Form Paragraphs

Your actual Office Action, unlike the sample below, will usually include several form paragraphs that quote statutes or rules. Examiners love to use such form paragraphs. Therefore, don't assume, if you receive an Office Action with numerous form paragraphs that quote basic statutes and rules, that you've been singled out or that your application is substandard: All attorneys get OAs with these form paragraphs as well. Also, the form paragraphs that the examiner chose may sometimes be inapplicable or only partially applicable. If so, courteously point this out in your response.

24. Preliminary and Supplemental Voluntary Amendments

In addition to the "regular" amendments discussed in this chapter (sent in response to an OA), you can also file a voluntary Preliminary Amendment before your first OA to correct any errors in the specification or claims, or narrow or broaden the claims. Also, you may file a Supplemental Amendment (after you file a regular amendment, but before the next OA) to correct any errors or omissions in your Amendment. However, under Rule 111(a)(2) you don't have the right to file a Supplemental Amendment unless it is clearly limited to (a) canceling claims, (b) adopting an examiner's suggestions, (c) placing the application in condition for allowance, (d) replying to an Office requirement made after the first reply was filed, (e) correcting informalities, such as typographical errors, or (f) simplifying issues for appeal. The best way to avoid the need for a Supplemental Reply is to do the first amendment well in advance of the due date, wait a day or two, and then review it again and polish and correct it as necessary. Also remember the rule against adding any new matter to your patent application. Finally, you aren't allowed to amend your application after allowance or after a final action, unless the examiner authorizes it.

The patent term for any invention will be extended in the event of certain delays caused by the PTO in the course of the patent prosecution process. Every patent is guaranteed an in-force period of at least 17 years provided you did not delay unduly on your side.

25. Double Patenting Obviousness Rejections

If the PTO rejects a claim of your application under Section 103 for obvious-type double patenting on an earlier patent or application that you own and it is not early enough to be prior art against your application, you can disqualify the earlier patent as prior art. You should submit a terminal disclaimer (Rule 321(c), 37 CFR 321(c)) with a fee and a declaration stating that the patent is owned by you and has the same inventor (Rule 131, 37 CFR 131).

26. Eighteen-Month Publication

If you haven't filed a Nonpublication Request, your application will be published on the PTO's website 18 months after filing (if it's still pending) and anyone can view and download and print out a copy of your application and prosecution history. Anyone will then be able to cite prior art against your application if they think your claims are not patentable. (PTO Rule 290.) We advise you of this so that you will be aware of the fact that, even if the PTO allows your application, they can change their mind and still reject it if someone cites better prior art than your examiner found. Publication by the PTO after 18 months does not confer patent rights and does not mean that the application has been allowed.

27. *Festo* Considerations

You should have drafted a full spectrum of claims (from broad to specific) which cover every aspect of your invention and all possible permutations. The reason for this is the Supreme Court's decision in *Festo v. Shoketsu* (535 U.S. 722), which holds essentially that the Doctrine of Equivalents (DoE) can be used to broaden any claim that was amended during prosecution provided (a) the equivalent was unforeseeable at the time the application was filed, or (b) the equivalent is not related to the way the claim is amended. However, if the claim was amended to overcome prior art, or if the court cannot determine the reason for the amendment, the DoE cannot be used. By submitting a full spectrum of claims, at least some of them will stand a good chance of being allowed in the prosecution stage without amendment, thereby preserving your full DoE rights for those claims. During the prosecution stage, you should try, if at all possible, not to amend any claims, or to amend as few as possible. If you have to amend any claims, state the reason for the amendment.

28. Rejection v. Objection

Office actions may contain (either or both of) two types of disapproval or criticism of various parts of your application. It's useful to know the difference so that you can use these terms correctly in writing your amendment and in case you have to appeal.

A *rejection* is made by an examiner to a substantive claim deficiency, such as a lack of patentability of a claim over a prior-art reference or indefiniteness in the claim. An *objection* is made to a nonclaim defect, such as an unclear drawing or a misspelling in the specification, or to a non-substantive claim matter, such as a dependent claim that is allowable in substance, but that can't be allowed because it's dependent upon a rejected independent claim. You have to fix or successfully argue over both types of disapproval (rejection or objection) to get the application allowed; the only practical difference is that a rejection that can't be overcome must be appealed, while an objection that can't be overcome must be petitioned (unless it's associated with a rejection).

29. When Submitting Arguments, Rely on Statutes, Rules, and the MPEP, Rather Than Case Law

When drafting the remarks portion of an amendment, it's helpful to cite authority for any rule of law or requirement that you rely upon. We've tried to provide most of the rules and main arguments in this chapter, but there are many more that we do not have room to include. If you need to find an authority for your position, look in the MPEP, which is available online at the PTO's site. The MPEP has a full online index and its Chapter 2100 on patentability is very helpful. If and when you do cite any authority, keep in mind that examiners consider the patent statutes (35 USC), the *Rules of Practice* (37 CFR), and the MPEP to be the most meaningful authorities. Examiners are strictly bound to follow these authorities. There are thousands of patent cases available also, but examiners find these far less persuasive and less useful. (One reason is that it's difficult and time-consuming for an examiner to look up and analyze a case.) In fact, when we were employed as examiners, our supervisors told us never to cite a case since the attorney for the applicant could always rebut us by citing a *different* case with a contrary holding!

30. Don't Wait Until the Last Minute

We find that most inventors who receive an Office Action tend to wait until near the end of the three-month period, or even later, to draft their response. The reason for this procrastination is usually due to fear of tackling a new task. However we strongly advise you grit your teeth and do the job as soon as possible so that you will have enough time, you won't be rushed, you can ramp up to the nuances and intricacies of the process, and you'll have time to review and polish your work.

31. Patents and Published Patent Applications Are Prior Art as of Their Filing Date as Well as Their Publication Date

As discussed in Chapter 5, patents and published patent applications (PubPAs), unlike other publications, are effective as of their filing date, in addition to their publication date. So if the examiner rejects your claims on a patent or PubPA, you may have to consider both dates when formulating your response. Prior to the First-To-File changes in 2013, if the patent or PubPA was published over a year before your filing date, it's a statutory bar (Section 102(b)) so you can't swear behind it (see Section D3 below) and thus only the publication date is relevant. If the patent or PubPA was published less than a year before your filing date, it is considered as prior art as of its publication date (Section 102(a)) and as of its filing date (Section 102(e)). For applications filed prior to FTF, you can swear behind the earlier (filing) date by proving an earlier date of invention. If you are able to prove an earlier date of invention, the patent or PubPA cannot be used as prior art against your application, as explained further below. Check the date of all prior

art cited against your application, since examiners sometimes make mistakes—for example, after the PTO published an application of Nokia's, an examiner examined the application and mistakenly cited the published patent application against itself!

Any U.S. patent or U.S. PubPA is prior art as of its filing date. Such patent or PubPA can be used in a rejection against any patent application that was filed after such filing date; there is no longer any way to overcome the earlier-filed patent or PubPA unless the inventor in the patent application can prove, in a derivation proceeding, that the inventor on the patent or PubPA derived it from such inventor.

If the patent or PubPA claims priority (the benefit of the filing date) of an earlier-filed foreign application or PPA, the patent or PubPA is prior art as of its priority date, that is, the filing date of the foreign application or PPA.

If a pending patent application of another person claims the same invention as your application, the pending application of the other person, being prior art as of its filing date, can be used to reject your application under Section 102 (lack of novelty) and thereby prevent your application from issuing, just as if you had lost an interference with the pending application. The AIA has abolished the previous right to swear behind or get into interference with any earlier publications or patents, regardless of their publication or filing dates.

32. Patent Examiners Are Overwhelmed

The quality of patent examination has been declining and the delay in receiving an Office Action has been increasing, a situation that could be harmful to U.S. competitiveness. For this reason you may have to wait a long time before you receive a first Office Action. You can obtain an estimate of when your application will receive a first office action by using the PTO's First Office Action Estimator (www.uspto.gov/learning-and-resources/statistics/first-office-action-estimator) or if you are a registered e-filer, by clicking on the First Action Estimator tab in your application's page in Private PAIR.

33. Beware of "Whack-a-Mole" Rejections

Examiners have been increasingly making subsequent rejections on a different ground from a previously rebutted rejection, even though the subsequent rejection could have been made when the previous rejection was made. Some patent attorneys have termed this practice, "Whack-a-Mole Rejecting." (It is also called piecemeal prosecution and condemned in the MPEP.) There is no good solution except to be aware in advance that it may occur and to take it philosophically if it does occur and patiently respond to each new rejection in the usual manner. If it becomes excessive it is possible to complain to the examiner's supervisor, but frankly supervisors usually support the examiner in these situations.

34. Limitations on Number of Claims

The basic filing fee entitles an applicant to submit three independent and 20 total claims. If an application is filed with or amended to have over three independent claims or over 20 total claims, the PTO requires a large fee for each extra independent claim and a medium fee for each extra total claim. However if you file more than the basic "3/20" allotment of claims, be sure that they differ significantly because examiners don't like to examine a lot of claims, even if you pay for them. The examiner can reject excessive claims (that is, they do not differ substantially) as unduly multiplied.

35. The PTO Has Been Very Difficult on Applicants

Make sure your claims are in optimal condition and define your invention's novelty over the references taken individually or in any combination. If necessary, file a continuation to revise your claims after a final action. Don't hesitate to appeal if necessary. If you appeal, be sure to try a "Pre-Appeal Brief Request for Review" (see J4 below). Always keep your temper and don't attack your examiner personally since he or she is merely following instructions or doing the best that they can under the circumstances.

Remember to always use the two-part 102 (novelty)/103 (unobviousness) approach whenever you argue patentability (see Inventor's Commandment 7 in Chapter 5).

36. Avoid Fraud on the PTO

Be honest and forthright and don't make any statements by which you intend to deceive, mislead, or "snow" the examiner. This is because a court can hold your patent invalid if it ever discovers that any statement that you made to the PTO amounted to "fraud on the PTO" and you intended to deceive the PTO.

37. Keep Your Remarks as Short as Possible

Examiners tend to be put off and hence may not read overly long responses. So keep your remarks as short as possible, but include all the arguments that you feel are necessary. Longer arguments tend to be less persuasive than shorter arguments and more prone to error.

38. Enablement

Remember our old friend, Section 112 of the patent statutes, which reads as follows:

The specification shall contain a written description of the invention, and of the manner and process of making and using it, in such full, clear, concise, and exact terms as to enable any person skilled in the art to which it pertains, or with which it is most nearly connected, to make and use the same, and shall set forth the best mode contemplated by the inventor of carrying out his invention.

This statute contains at least three requirements: (1) The specification must have a written description of the invention, (2) It must enable a PHOSITA (person having ordinary skill in the art) to make and use it, and (3) It must set forth the best mode contemplated by the inventor. While requirements 1 and 2 appear similar, the courts have held that they are somewhat different. Part 1 requires that the specification describe the invention but not necessarily to any degree of detail. Part 2 specifies the detail: it must be sufficient for a PHOSITA to make and use it. In practice the courts have held that Part 2 means that any specific embodiments claimed must be disclosed in the description. Thus when one inventor's description described a needle holder with a pressure jacket, his claims to a needle holder with the pressure jacket complied with Part 2. However when he broadened his claims to recite a needle holder alone, the courts held that they were invalid because the description did not describe this. (*Liebel-Flarsheim Company v. Medrad, Inc.*, 358 F.3d 898 (Fed. Cir. 2004).) Thus, to avoid violating Part 2, you must be sure that every embodiment covered by your claims (originally and as amended) is described in the specification and shown in the drawings. While Section 112 still requires that you set forth the best mode, objections on this ground are rare, and under the AIA a failure to do so will not be grounds for invalidating the patent. Nevertheless, you should do your best to comply.

39. Ombudsman Pilot Program

The PTO has implemented an Ombudsman Pilot Program under which you may be able to resolve breakdowns in the normal patent prosecution process (e.g., your examiner is being extremely unreasonable) with the aid of a Technology Center Ombudsman (TCO). This program is not intended to resolve normal issues, such as good-faith differences of opinion on issues of patentability, but only applies when you have a question about a specific application in prosecution and have not been able to find the right person to assist you or when you have not been able to obtain assistance from your examiner or the Supervising Patent Examiner (SPE). To invoke the aid of a TCO, go to www.uspto.gov/patent/ombudsman-program to see if it is applicable to your situation. If so, complete and file the form in the notice. The TCO will contact you by phone to obtain the details from you orally and thereafter work to resolve the problem.

C. A Sample Office Action

Fig. 13A, below, shows a sample OA in an imaginary patent application. A study of this example will enable you to deal with your first OA far more effectively. It has been purposely written to include the common objections and rejections; an actual OA is usually not this complicated and quotes applicable statutes.

First let's look at Fig. 13A/1 (page 1 of the OA). At the top of the OA, the examiner's name and his examining section (Art Unit 2540) are given. Art Unit 2540 is part of Examining Group 2500. Before that, in the large brackets, are the serial number, filing date, and inventor's name. To the right is the date the OA was mailed; this is its official date.

Below the address of the attorney, the first box that is checked indicates: "This application has been examined," denoting that this is the first OA in this application. If it had been a second and nonfinal OA, the second box, "Responsive to communication filed on [date]," would have been checked; had it been a final OA, the third box, "This action is made final," would have been checked.

The next paragraph indicates that the period for response will expire in three months and that failure to respond will cause the application to be abandoned. Since the OA was mailed 1998 Oct 9, the period for response expires 1999 Jan 9. If the last date of the period falls on a Saturday, Sunday, or holiday, the period for response expires on the next business day. Be sure to calculate the period for response from the date the OA was mailed, not the date you received it.

Under "Part I," the checked boxes indicate that two attachments, a "Notice of References Cited" and a "Notice re Patent Drawing," are part of the OA. A typical Notice of References Cited is shown in Fig. 13A/3, below, and the drawing notice is shown in Fig. 13A/4. Be sure to calculate the period for response from the date the OA was mailed, not the date you received it.

Under "Part II—Summary of Action," the examiner has checked various boxes to indicate what action he has taken with the application. He has rejected all seven claims pending. He has also acknowledged that informal drawings were filed and has indicated that these will be acceptable until allowable subject matter is indicated.

Now it's time to look at Figs. 13A/2 and 13A/3 (pages 2 and 3 of the OA).

UNITED STATES DEPARTMENT OF COMMERCE
Patent and Trademark Office

Address: COMMISSIONER OF PATENTS AND TRADEMARKS
Washington, D.C. 20231

SERIAL NUMBER	FILING DATE	FIRST NAMED APPLICANT	ATTORNEY DOCKET NO.
07/345,678	1998 Aug 9	LeRoy Inventor	

Portia Barrister
1237 Chancery Lane
Puyallup, WA 98371-3841

*Received
1998 Oct 14
P. B.*

EXAMINER	
HEYMAN, J	
ART UNIT	PAPER NUMBER
2540	3

DATE MAILED: 1998 Oct 9

This is a communication from the examiner in charge of your application.

COMMISSIONER OF PATENTS AND TRADEMARKS

Response Due 1999 Jan 9 P.B.

☑ This application has been examined   ☐ Responsive to communication filed on _____   ☐ This action is made final.

A shortened statutory period for response to this action is set to expire _3_ month(s), _0_ days from the date of this letter.
Failure to respond within the period for response will cause the application to become abandoned.   35 U.S.C. 133

Part I   THE FOLLOWING ATTACHMENT(S) ARE PART OF THIS ACTION:

1. ☑ Notice of References Cited by Examiner, PTO-892.   2. ☑ Notice re Patent Drawing, PTO-948.
3. ☐ Notice of Art Cited by Applicant, PTO-1449   4. ☐ Notice of Informal Patent Application, Form PTO-152
5. ☐ Information on How to Effect Drawing Changes, PTO-1474   6. ☐ _____

Part II   SUMMARY OF ACTION

1. ☑ Claims _1-7_ are pending in the application.

   Of the above, claims _____ are withdrawn from consideration.

2. ☐ Claims _____ have been cancelled.

3. ☐ Claims _____ are allowed.

4. ☑ Claims _1-7_ are rejected.

5. ☐ Claims _____ are objected to.

6. ☐ Claims _____ are subject to restriction or election requirement.

7. ☑ This application has been filed with informal drawings which are acceptable for examination purposes until such time as allowable subject matter is indicated.

8. ☐ Allowable subject matter having been indicated, formal drawings are required in response to this Office action.

9. ☐ The corrected or substitute drawings have been received on _____. These drawings are ☐ acceptable; ☐ not acceptable (see explanation).

10. ☐ The ☐ proposed drawing correction and/or the ☐ proposed additional or substitute sheet(s) of drawings, filed on _____ has (have) been ☐ approved by the examiner. ☐ disapproved by the examiner (see explanation).

11. ☐ The proposed drawing correction, filed _____, has been ☐ approved. ☐ disapproved (see explanation). However, the Patent and Trademark Office no longer makes drawing changes. It is now applicant's responsibility to ensure that the drawings are corrected. Corrections **MUST** be effected in accordance with the instructions set forth on the attached letter "INFORMATION ON HOW TO EFFECT DRAWING CHANGES", PTO-1474.

12. ☐ Acknowledgment is made of the claim for priority under 35 U.S.C. 119. The certified copy has ☐ been received ☐ not been received ☐ been filed in parent application, serial no. _____; filed on _____.

13. ☐ Since this application appears to be in condition for allowance except for formal matters, prosecution as to the merits is closed in accordance with the practice under Ex parte Quayle, 1935 C.D. 11; 453 O.G. 213.

14. ☐ Other

PTOL-326 (Rev. 7-82)   **EXAMINER'S ACTION**

Fig. 13A/1—Sample Office Action

Serial No. 07/345,678   -2-

Art Unit 254

The drawing is objected to under Rule 1.83(a) in that all the features recited in the claims are not shown. See Claims 1 and 2 regarding the "electronic counter means" and "first and second solid state counters."

The specification is objected to under Rule 1.71(b) as inadequate. In particular, there is insufficient information regarding the "counter," "counter memory," and how the counter controls the illumination of the lights. Applicant is required to amplify the disclosure in this regard without the introduction of new matter, 608.04 MPEP.

Claims 1-7 are rejected under 35 U.S.C. § 112, 1st. paragraph, as based on an insufficient disclosure. See above.

Insofar as adequate, Claims 1-6 are rejected under 35 U.S.C. § 102(b) as fully anticipated by Ohman. Ohman shows an electronic cribbage board counter that fully meets these claims. See Fig. 1. The microprocessor 300 shown in Fig. 3 inherently includes the counter means of Claims 1 and 2.

Claim 7 is rejected under 35 U.S.C. § 112, ¶ 2. The term "said LCD readout" lacks proper antecedent basis in parent independent claim 1 as claim 1 recites only an "LCD monitor."

Claim 7 is rejected under 35 U.S.C. § 103 as unpatentable over Ohman in view of Morin. Ohman shows an electronic cribbage board counter, as stated. Morin shows an LCD tally monitor. It would be obvious to substitute Morin's LCD tally monitor for Ohman's mechanical readout, since the substitution of LCD readouts for mechanical readouts is an expedient well known to those skilled in the art. See column 13, lines 34-41 of Morin, which indicate that in lieu of the LCD readout shown, other types of readouts may be used.

No claim is allowed.

The remaining art cited shows other electronic board games containing the claimed structure. Note Morin, which shows the details of a computer as containing first and second counter means.

Any inquiry concerning this communication should be directed to Examiner Heyman at telephone number 703-557-4777, Fax number 703-872-9314.

Heyman/EW

    98/10/09

                                                John S. Heyman

                                                Examiner

                                                Group Art Unit 254

Fig. 13A/2—Sample Office Action

FORM PTO-892	U.S. DEPARTMENT OF COMMERCE PATENT AND TRADEMARK OFFICE	SERIAL NO. 07/345,678	GROUP ART UNIT 254	ATTACHMENT TO PAPER NUMBER 3
NOTICE OF REFERENCES CITED		APPLICANT(S) LeRoy Inventor		

U.S. PATENT DOCUMENTS

*		DOCUMENT NO.	DATE	NAME	CLASS	SUBCLASS	FILING DATE IF APPROPRIATE
	A	4 3 6 8 5 1 6	1/1983	Morin	377	5	
	B						
	C						
	D						
	E						
	F						
	G						
	H						
	I						
	J						
	K						

FOREIGN PATENT DOCUMENTS

		DOCUMENT NO.	DATE	COUNTRY	NAME	CLASS	SUB-CLASS	PERTINENT SHTS. DWGS	PP. SPEC.
	L	8 1 0 1 7 6 6	6/1981	International P.U.B. (ACT)	Ohman	273	148R	5	21
	M	1 1 9 5 0 0 1	10/1985	Canada	Mah	273	148R	3	14
	N	2 1 7 3 4 0 6	10/1986	Gr. Britain	Armstrong	273	148R	3	6
	O								
	P								
	Q								

OTHER PRIOR ART (Including Author, Title, Date, Pertinent Pages, Etc.)

R	
S	
T	
U	

EXAMINER J.S. Heyman	DATE 4/1/20xx	

*A Copy of this reference is not being furnished with this office action.
(See Manual of patent Examining Procedure, section 707.05(a).)

Fig. 13A/3—Notice of References Cited

UNITED STATES PATENT AND TRADEMARK OFFICE

UNITED STATES DEPARTMENT OF COMMERCE
United States Patent and Trademark Office
Address: COMMISSIONER FOR PATENTS
P.O. Box 1450
Alexandria, Virginia 22313-1450
www.uspto.gov

APPLICATION NUMBER	FILING OR 371(C) DATE	FIRST NAMED APPLICANT	ATTY. DOCKET NO./TITLE
09/123,456	02/29/2010	Ann Inventor	7890/1001

CONFIRMATION NO. 2714

FORMALITIES LETTER

Ann Inventor
128 Innovation Road
Washington, MA 09999

Date Mailed:

03/19/2010

NOTICE TO FILE CORRECTED APPLICATION PAPERS

Filing Date Granted

An application number and filing date have been accorded to this application. The application is informal since it does not comply with the regulations for the reason(s) indicated below. Applicant is given TWO MONTHS from the date of this Notice within which to correct the informalities indicated below. Extensions of time may be obtained by filing a petition accompanied by the extension fee under the provisions of 37 CFR 1.136(a).

The required item(s) identified below must be timely submitted to avoid abandonment:

- Replacement drawings in compliance with 37 CFR 1.84 and 37 CFR 1.121(d) are required. The drawings submitted are not acceptable because:
  - Numbers, letters, and reference characters on the drawings must measure at least 0.32 cm (1/8 inch) in height. See Figure(s) all.

Applicant is cautioned that correction of the above items may cause the specification and drawings page count to exceed 100 pages. If the specification and drawings exceed 100 pages, applicant will need to submit the required application size fee.

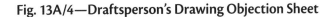

Fig. 13A/4—Draftsperson's Drawing Objection Sheet

On page 2 of the Office Action, the examiner gives his specific reasons for rejecting or objecting to the claims.

The first paragraph of page 2 of the OA objects to the drawings because they fail to show certain features recited in the claims. Remember (Chapter 10) that the drawings must show every feature recited in the claims.

The second paragraph objects to the specification as inadequate. The specification must teach, in full, clear, and exact detail, how one skilled in the art would make and use the invention. This is a potentially serious and fatal flaw, since it is not permissible to add new matter to supply the missing description.

In the third paragraph, the examiner rejects all of the claims under Section 112, since they are based on an inadequate specification for reasons stated in the second paragraph.

The fourth paragraph rejects Claims 1 to 6 on the Ohman reference (see Fig. 13A/3—page 3 of the OA), under Section 102. This means that the examiner feels that these claims contain no novelty over Ohman. The requirement that the claims contain novel physical features was discussed in Chapters 5 and 9.

At the bottom of page 2 of the OA, the examiner has rejected Claim 7 under Section 112 since a "said" clause in Claim 7 has no proper antecedent in parent, independent Claim 1 from which Claim 7 depends. Remember (Chapter 9) that every "said" clause must contain an identical antecedent earlier in the claim or in a parent claim. Many examiners, especially young ones, lean heavily on any Section 112 defects.

In the last paragraph of page 2 of the OA (Fig. 13A/2), the examiner has rejected Claim 7, under our old and troublesome friend Section 103, as unpatentable over two references. Note that the examiner states what each reference shows and why it would be obvious to combine the teachings of these references. Also note that by using two references, or by relying on Section 103, the examiner has tacitly admitted that this claim has satisfied the novelty (Section 102) requirement.

The examiner next summarizes by stating that no claim is allowed.

Finally he refers to certain other prior art, which he cites but does not apply, to provide background and to put on the record in case he wants to use it later.

The examiner will sign the Office Action at the bottom and list his telephone number and fax above his official name stamp.

Next, we turn to Fig. 13A/3 (the Notice of References Cited). It lists one U.S. and three foreign patents. All of the foreign references will be attached to the OA, except any checked in the column marked with the asterisk (*), which were furnished in a prior Office Action, a prior related application, or were furnished by you in your Information Disclosure Statement. The "Document Number" column generally lists patent numbers. Because the PTO no longer includes copies of patent documents with OAs, you will have to download them from the Internet.

The date column indicates the date the patent issued, or the document was published. If this date is later than your filing date, the reference is not a good reference against your application, unless it is a U.S. patent filed before your application. In the latter instance, the examiner is supposed to indicate the filing date of the patent reference in the last column.

Finally, if the OA objects to the drawings (see Fig. 13A/4), be sure to file replacement figures with your response to the OA.

If you've sent in your IDS and PTO-1449, the OA will also include a copy of your PTO-1449, and a list of your references will be included under "References Cited" in the printed patent.

When the PTO cites patents as prior-art references, some inventors react in various illogical ways, as indicated by the following Common Misconceptions:

Common Misconception: The PTO can't cite foreign or non-English patents or other publications against a U.S. patent application.

Fact: Any publication, including a patent from anywhere in the world, in any language, is valid prior art against your patent application, provided it was published before your filing date. In applications with a priority date prior to the date FTF took effect, if your earliest provable date of invention is earlier than the publication date, you can swear back of (or "swear behind") the publication date by proving an earlier date of invention, so long as the publication date occurred less than one year before your filing date. If the publication is a U.S. patent or published U.S. patent application, its filing date, or the filing date of any U.S. or foreign application from which it claims priority, is treated the same as a publication date. After FTF takes effect, you will not be allowed to swear back of any publication with an earlier effective date, unless the publication came from you and is not over one year old.

Common Misconception: An in-force foreign patent that shows or claims your invention will prevent you from making the invention in the U.S.

Fact: A patent of any country is enforceable only within the geographical area of that country and has no enforceability elsewhere. Thus, for example, a French patent is enforceable only in France and has no enforceability or effect in the U.S. However, it is a good prior-art reference in the U.S.

Common Misconception: If an examiner cites an in-force U.S. patent as a prior-art reference against your application, this means that your invention, if manufactured, sold, or used, would infringe this patent.

Fact: The only way you can tell if your invention would infringe any patent is to compare the patent's claims against your invention. Most cited in-force patents would not be infringed by your invention, since their claims are directed to a different invention. Again, examiners hardly ever read claims of patents they cite and the PTO is never concerned with infringements.

Common Misconception: If an examiner cites a very old prior-art reference against your application, it is not as good a reference as an in-force patent or a very recent reference.

Fact: The age of a reference is totally irrelevant, so long as its date is earlier than your filing date or your earliest provable date of invention. (See Chapter 5.)

D. What to Do When You Receive an Office Action

When you receive an OA, don't panic or be intimidated or take it personally. It's common for some examiners to reject all claims, even if the rejections are not valid. This type of rejection is termed a "shotgun" or "shoot-from-the-hip" rejection. Although they shouldn't do so, examiners sometimes do this because of the pressure of work, and sometimes to force you to state more clearly the essence of your invention and its true distinguishing features. You'll find that even if your examiner rejects all of your claims, if you approach your OA in a calm, rational, and methodical manner, as outlined below, you shouldn't have too much difficulty in ultimately getting your patent if your invention meets the legal tests for patentability.

If the PTO Suggests You Get an Attorney

Some examiners insert a form paragraph in an OA, suggesting that you hire a patent attorney, regardless of how well the application is prepared, if there is no attorney of record. This has been done even in cases where attorneys prepared applications, but where they did not appear as the attorney of record. You can safely ignore this form paragraph, unless you feel uncomfortable without an attorney.

1. Record Due Date on Your Calendar and OA, and Mount OA in Your File

After you get your Office Action, write the date you received the OA and the due date of your response right on it (as is done in Fig. 13A/1), and also on your calendar so you don't forget it. You should actually write the date thrice on your calendar: once on the date it's actually due, once two weeks before it's due, and once one month before it's due. If the due date falls on a weekend or holiday, your due date is the next business day.

2. Check the References and Review Your Application

Your OA will usually cite prior-art references. Some will be applied against your claims and some will be cited as background as a matter of interest. In either case, the PTO does not send copies of any cited U.S. patent and published patent application references with OAs. They do send copies of cited foreign patents and nonpatent references. If you receive an OA that cites U.S. patent references, you must obtain copies of the cited references yourself. You have several ways to do this: (1) Download them from the PTO's website, (2) Download complete patents for free from one of the free patent sites, (3) Obtain access to the PTO's Private PAIR (Patent Application Information Retrieval) system and download complete U.S. patents cited against your patent application. At present we don't see any significant advantage of getting copies via Private PAIR over the private services, but PAIR can also be used to file patent applications electronically and Private PAIR can be used to view the status of your applications and file amendments. (Since it is somewhat inconvenient to obtain references, you may wish to obtain and print paper copies of only those that the PTO has actually applied against your claims and merely review on the monitor those that were cited as being of interest.)

To obtain access to Private PAIR, you must: (1) Obtain a PKI (Public Key Infrastructure) Digital Certificate by completing and mailing to the PTO a notarized application; (2) Obtain a Customer Number by sending or faxing an application to the PTO; (3) Associate your Customer Number with your patent application(s) by completing an Excel spreadsheet and mailing it on a CD or USB memory stick to the PTO; (4) Obtain and save the PTO's digital certificate on your computer. The full instructions can be found at the PTO website (www.uspto.gov/ebc).

After you obtain copies of the cited references, check all of them carefully to make sure you've received all the correct references listed in the Notice of References Cited. If there's any discrepancy, or if any seem irrelevant, call or write the examiner at once. This call will not count as an interview. (You are usually limited to two interviews.)

If you sent in an IDS and PTO/SB/08, the examiner will send, with your first OA, a copy of your PTO/SB/08, with the blank adjacent each reference initialed to show that the examiner has considered it. If you don't get the PTO/SB/08 back with every reference initialed, check with your examiner. Otherwise, the references you cited on your PTO/SB/08 won't be listed on your patent when it's printed.

Next, read the OA carefully and make a detailed written summary of it so that you'll have it impressed in your mind. After that, reread your application, noting all grammatical and other errors in the specification, claims, and drawings that you would like to correct or improve. Remember, however, that you can't add any "new matter" to your application.

3. Read and Analyze Each Cited Reference, Except Patent Claims

Next, read every applied prior-art reference (except the claims of patent references) completely and carefully. (You don't have to read the nonapplied references carefully, but you should review them to be sure none is more relevant than an applied reference.) Make sure that you take enough time to understand each reference completely, including all of the structure involved and how it works. Write a brief summary of each reference, preferably on the reference itself, even if it has an adequate abstract, in order to familiarize yourself with it in your own words.

CAUTION

Don't Fall Into a Claims Trap. Don't read the claims of any patent cited as a reference. Why not? Because the patent has not been cited for what it claims, but rather for what it shows about the prior art. The claims generally only repeat parts of the specification and are not directly relevant to the patent prosecution process, since they are only used to determine whether infringement exists. If you think of cited patents as magazine articles, you'll avoid this "claims trap" that most laypersons fall into.

"Swearing Behind" References: If your application was filed prior to March 15, 2013, and the PTO cites a reference against your application that has an effective date later than your date of invention, and you can prove your date of invention, you're in luck: You can "swear behind" this reference and thereby completely eliminate it from consideration. Typical references that you can swear behind are U.S. patents with filing dates, and other publications with publication dates earlier than your filing date but later than your date of invention.

To swear behind such a reference, you must submit a declaration containing facts with attached copies of documents showing that you built and tested the invention, or conceived the invention and were thereafter diligent in building and testing it, or filing the patent application before the effective date of the reference. (See MPEP 715 for details.) If you've filed a PPA and need to rely on its filing date, you may do so before and after FTF. Merely refer to it by its Serial Number and Filing Date and point out to the examiner that a reference that the examiner cited is ineffective because you have an earlier effective filing date due to your PPA. For applications filed after March 15, 2013, you can no longer swear behind any reference.

One-Year Rule and Interference Limitations: Prior to FTF (March 15, 2013), two important limitations exist on your right to swear behind: (1) Because of the "one-year rule," you can't swear behind any reference (U.S. patent or otherwise) with a publication date over one year before your filing date. (There's no limitation as to how far you can swear back if the reference is a U.S. patent that issued less than one year before your filing date.) (2) You can't swear behind a U.S. patent, which claims the same invention as yours; the only way you can overcome such a patent is to get into interference with it and win "priority." Again, for applications subject to FTF, there is no right to swear behind and there will no longer be any interferences.

4. Make a Comparison Chart

You'll find it helpful to make a comparison chart showing every feature of your invention across the top of the chart and listing the references down the left-hand side of the chart, as in Fig. 13B:

Features of My Invention

References	Pivot arm	Bracket at end of arm	Bracket has screw tightener
A	X	X	
B	X		X

Fig. 13B—Comparison Chart

Be sure to break up your invention so that all possible features of it, even those not already claimed, are covered and listed across the top of the chart. Remember that a feature can be the combination of two known separate features or a new use of an old device. Then indicate, by checking the appropriate boxes, those features of your invention that are not shown by each reference. This chart, if done correctly and completely, will be of tremendous aid in drafting your response to the first OA.

5. Follow the Flowchart

Fig. 13C provides a comprehensive, self-explanatory flowchart for dealing with all prior-art (Sections 102 and 103) rejections. Fig. 13D provides a list of all possible arguments we've found against obviousness rejections. For each claim (or set of claims) rejected, follow the chart and list carefully.

6. Compare Your Broadest Claim With the Cited References for Novelty

If the examiner applies any prior-art references under Section 102, you'll need to deal with the novelty question. However, if the reference is said to apply under Section 103 (obviousness), the examiner is tacitly admitting that you've made it past Section 102 —that is, your claimed structure is novel. Therefore, you won't have to go through the full analysis in this section. Instead, review the section briefly, and then concentrate on Section 7.

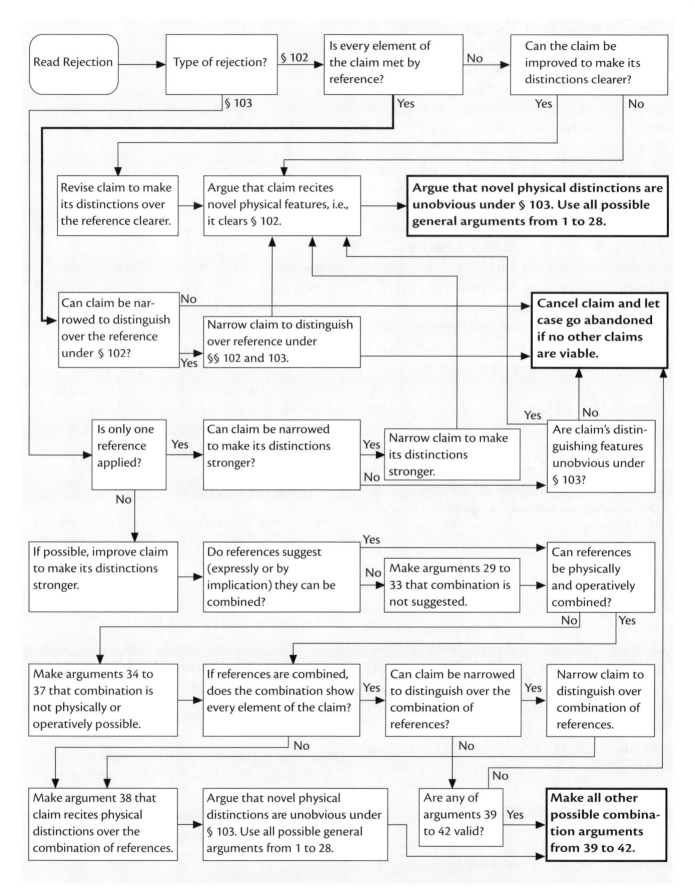

Fig. 13C—Flowchart for Handling Prior-Art Rejections

First, reread your broadest claim to see which features it recites. Remember, only positively recited physical structure or acts (steps in a method claim) count. Then consider whether these features distinguish your invention from each reference cited against this claim. Don't pay any attention to the advantages of your invention, your statements of function, or your "whereby" clauses. Only focus on the novel features (physical, structural, or method steps), including those that are in the form of a means clause followed by a function.

EXAMPLE: "A lever having a threaded end with a counterbalance thereon" is a proper physical recitation that can distinguish your invention from the prior art. The phrase "means for counterbalancing" is a means clause followed by a function and is equivalent to a physical recitation. But "said lever counterbalancing said arm" is a mere statement of result or function and can't be used to distinguish the prior art.

If only one reference has been cited against your broadest claim, consider whether your claim distinguishes over this reference under Section 102 (that is—whether your claimed structure is novel; see Chapter 5, Section E). In other words, are there any features recited in the claim that are not shown in the reference being cited against it? If not, the claim is "fully met" or anticipated by this reference and will have to be narrowed or canceled.

Remember that the examiner is entitled to interpret any claim in any reasonable way against you. That is, if your claims, or any word in one of your claims, has two reasonable interpretations, the examiner is entitled to take the one least favorable to you when determining if your claim has novel physical structure or method steps under Section 102. For example, suppose your invention uses a clamp that is halfway between two ends of a rod and a reference shows a clamp near one end of a rod. If your claim recites that the clamp is "intermediate" the ends of the rod, this won't distinguish over the reference since "intermediate" means "between" as well as "in the middle." The remedy? Recite that your claim is

"substantially in the middle" of the rod in order to distinguish over the reference under Section 102 (but not necessarily under Section 103).

Suppose the physical features of your claim are all shown in a prior-art reference, but the features are used for a different purpose than yours. For example, you claim "a depression in a wall plate for holding a clock" and the prior art shows a large oil drip pan under a milling machine; this pan literally constitutes "a plate with a depression." Thus your claim literally "reads on" the prior art, but your claimed elements are directed to a different purpose than the elements of the prior-art reference. Unfortunately, the rejection is valid: You'll have to narrow the claim, or consider claiming your structure as a "new use" invention.

Sometimes, even though a claim recites a limitation that is novel, the examiner will overlook the limitation. In order to force the examiner to consider the limitation, it will help to rewrite the limitation in a stronger, separate, more prominent clause in its own paragraph—that is, change "a series of beads" to two paragraphs reading "a plurality of beads, said plurality of beads being connected in series to form a chain of said plurality of beads."

7. Analyze Novel Features for Unobviousness

If the claim recites (or has been amended to recite) novel features, consider whether these are unobvious over the reference cited against it. All possible reasons for arguing unobviousness are listed in Fig. 13D (Part I). When you use any reasons from this chart, you should not merely copy the reason, as we've seen some inventors do. Rather, you must state facts in support of each reason you use. For example, if you select Reason 1 (Unexpected Results) after stating that your novel claimed structure produces new and unexpected results, state precisely what they are—such as that it does a job faster or more reliably.

If you consider the features of your invention obvious, you'll have to narrow the claim, either by adding more features from your specification or from narrower (dependent) claims (refer to Fig. 13C, above) or by reciting the existing features more narrowly.

Part I—General Arguments Against Obviousness

Below are arguments you may be able to make in response to a charge that your invention is obvious. You will have to go into more detail than to simply recite the argument. For example, if you are responding that the invention achieves unexpected results, you will have to list those unexpected results. For arguments 16 through 20, you may also need—in addition to a detailed explanation—a suitable declaration (Rule 132, 37 CFR 1.132) with attached exhibits. In addition, some arguments contain references to the MPEP. Check these sections before responding to make sure they have not been amended and that they are still relevant.

1. **Unexpected Results:** The results achieved by the invention are new, unexpected, superior, disproportionate, unsuggested, unusual, critical, and/or surprising.

2. **Assumed Unworkability:** Up to now those skilled in the art thought or were skeptical that the techniques used in the invention were unworkable or presented an insuperable barrier.

3. **Assumed Insolubility:** Up to now those skilled in the art thought or found the problem solved by the invention to be insoluble—that is, the invention converts failure into success. The failures of prior-art workers indicate that a solution was not obvious.

4. **Commercial Success:** The invention has attained commercial success. (Prove this by a declaration with supporting documents showing that the commercial success of your invention is due to its novel features that you are claiming.)

5. **Unrecognized Problem:** The problem solved by the invention was never before even recognized, much less solved. The recognition and solution of an unrecognized problem militates in favor of patentability.

6. **Crowded Art:** The invention is classified in a crowded art; therefore, a small step forward should be regarded as significant.

7. **Omission of Element:** An element of a prior-art device has been omitted or a prior-art version has been made simpler without loss of capability.

8. **Unsuggested Modification:** The prior art lacks any suggestion that the reference should be modified in a manner required to meet the claims.

9. **Unappreciated Advantage:** Up to now those skilled in the art never appreciated the advantage of the invention, although it is inherent.

10. **Inoperative References:** The prior-art references that were relied upon are inoperative.

11. **Poor References:** The prior-art references are vague, foreign, conflicting, or very old, and, therefore, are weak and should be construed narrowly.

12. **Ancient Suggestion:** Although the invention may possibly have been suggested by the prior art, the suggestion is many years old, was never implemented, and produced greatly inferior results.

13. **Lack of Implementation:** If the invention was in fact obvious, because of its advantages, those skilled in the art surely would have implemented it by now. That is—the fact that those skilled in the art have not implemented the invention, despite its great advantages, indicates that it is not obvious.

14. **Misunderstood Reference:** The reference does not teach what the examiner relies upon it as supposedly teaching.

15. **Solution of Long-Felt and Unsolved Need:** The invention solves a long-felt, long-existing, but unsolved need.

16. **Commercial Acquiescence:** The invention has been licensed, especially to a competitor.

17. **Professional Recognition:** The invention has been given an award or recognized in a professional publication.

18. **Purchase Offers:** Others, especially accused infringers, have tried to purchase or take a license under the invention.

19. **Copying by Others:** Others have chosen to copy and implement the invention, rather than using the techniques of the prior art.

20. **Competitive Recognition:** The invention has been copied by an infringer; moreover, the infringer has made laudatory statements about it, or has admitted it is unobvious.

21. **Contrarian Invention:** The invention is contrary to the teachings of the prior art—that is, the invention goes against the grain of what the prior art teaches.

22. **Strained Interpretation:** The examiner has made a strained interpretation of the reference that could be made only by hindsight.

Fig. 13D—Arguments Against Obviousness Rejections (Part I)

Part I—General Arguments Against Obviousness (continued)

23. **Paper Patent:** The reference is a "paper patent"—that is, it was never implemented or commercialized and therefore should be construed narrowly. (Don't use if reference completely anticipates your invention.)

24. **New Principle of Operation:** The invention utilizes a new principle of operation. Applicant has blazed a trail, rather than followed one.

25. **Inability of Competitors:** Competitors were unable to copy the invention until they were able to learn its details through a publication or reverse engineering a commercial model; this indicates unobviousness.

26. **Nonanalogous Art:** The reference is from so different a field that it would not have commended itself to an inventor's attention when considering the invention as a whole. (MPEP 2141.01.)

27. **No Convincing Reasoning:** The examiner has not presented a convincing line of reasoning as to why the claimed subject matter as a whole, including its differences over the prior art, would have been obvious.

28. **Reference Is Nonanalogous Art or Isn't Pertinent to the Problem Applicant Has Solved:** If a cited reference is nonanalogous or is directed to a different problem, this weighs against its use in a rejection.

Part II—Arguments Also Used When Combination of References Applied

29. **Unsuggested Combination:** The prior-art references do not contain any suggestion (express or implied) that they be combined, or that they be combined in the manner suggested. In 2007 the U.S. Supreme Court held that that an invention should not be held obvious over several prior-art references unless there is a suggestion, motivation, or teaching that the references can or should be combined. (MPEP 2143.)

30. **References Are Individually Complete:** Each reference is complete and functional in itself, so there would be no reason to use parts from or add or substitute parts to any reference.

31. **References Take Different Approaches:** The references take mutually exclusive paths and reach different solutions to a similar problem. Since they teach away from each other, it would not be logical to combine them.

32. **References Teach Away:** The references themselves teach away (expressly or by implication) from the suggested combination.

33. **Reference Is From Different Field:** One reference is from a very different technical field than that of the invention—that is, it's "nonanalogous art." (MPEP 707.07(f).)

34. **Impossible to Combine:** Those skilled in the art would find it physically impossible to combine the references in the manner suggested.

35. **Inoperative Combination:** If they could be combined, the references would produce an inoperative combination, or render the reference being modified unsuitable for its intended purpose.

36. **Modifications Necessary:** It would be necessary to make modifications, not taught in the prior art, in order to combine the references in the manner suggested.

37. **Mutually Exclusive Paths:** The references can't be legally combined because they take mutually exclusive paths to reach different solutions to a problem, and, therefore, by implication each teaches away from combining itself with the other.

38. **Claimed Features Lacking:** Even if combined, the references would not meet the claims.

39. **Synergism:** The whole (that is—the result achieved by the invention) is greater than the sum of its parts (that is—the respective results of the individual references).

40. **Multiplicity of Steps Required:** The combination suggested requires a series of separate, awkward combinative steps that are too involved to be considered obvious.

41. **Multiplicity of References:** The fact that a large number of references (over three) must be combined to meet the invention is evidence of unobviousness.

42. **Intended Function Destroyed:** The references are not legally combinable since doing so will destroy the intended function(s) of at least one of the references.

Fig. 13D—Arguments Against Obviousness Rejections (Part II)

8. If References Are Cited in Combination Against Your Broadest Claim

If two or more references have been cited in combination against your broadest claim, refer to Fig. 13D (Part II) to see whether the examiner has a point.

TIP

You should especially consider reasons 29 to 33—that is, ask yourself whether it is proper to combine these references in the manner that the examiner has done. Also note that when you use any of the reasons of Fig. 13D, you should not merely state the applicable reason, but also supporting facts that pertain to your invention.

9. Does the Combination Disclose Subject Matter of Your Broadest Claim?

Assuming that the references are combined (whether or not they can be), ask yourself if the combination discloses the subject matter of your claim (Reason 37). If not, are the distinctions in your claim patentable under Section 103 (Reasons 1–28 and 39–41)? Also ask yourself whether there are any other errors in the examiner's logic or reasoning.

10. If Your Claims Are Rejected Under Section 112 of the Patent Laws

If your claim has been rejected under Section 112—a very common occurrence, even for patent attorneys—the examiner feels that the language of your claim is not clear or proper. For example, a very common rejection is for failure to supply an antecedent for a "said xxxx" phrase. This is easy to fix. Either positively recite the missing antecedent earlier in the claim or in a referent claim which the claim depends from, or rewrite the phrase to eliminate the "said." If you accept an examiner's rejection that the claim has vague or unclear language, you'll have to substitute a more specific recitation. Try not to limit your invention too much. For example, if you recite that a sheet is "flexible" and the examiner objects to this word as too vague, try substituting a recitation such as, "flexible enough so that it can be repeatedly folded

and opened without tearing." You may benefit by calling the examiner to seek suggestions or approval for new proposed language. If the examiner makes any other type of Section 112 rejection, try to work out alternative language that will obviate this rejection. Alternatively, you can ask the examiner to write clear claims for you.

11. If Your Claims Are Rejected Under Section 101 of the Patent Laws

If your claim has been rejected under section 101 for being directed to a "judicial exception" (a law of nature, natural phenomenon, or an abstract idea), begin by reviewing the rejection to determine whether the examiner has faithfully followed the required process, and note any shortcomings in the analysis.

To reject a claim under section 101, the examiner must conclude either that the claim does not fall within one of the four statutory categories of patentable subject matter (process, machine, manufacture, or composition of matter), or that it does fall into a judicial exception (laws of nature, natural phenomena, abstract ideas). The examiner is not allowed to simply jump to such a conclusion. Rather, the examiner must support the rejection by performing a thorough analysis to establish *a prima facie* (at first sight) case that the claim fails to define patentable subject matter under section 101, and then by clearly explaining the rejection in writing.

The PTO rarely rejects a claim for falling outside of the four statutory categories of patentable subject matter. The Manual of Patent Examining Procedure (MPEP) lists the following examples of claims rejected for this reason: "transitory forms of signal transmission (for example, a propagating electrical or electromagnetic signal *per se*); human *per se*; a legal contractual agreement between two parties; a computer program *per se*; a company; a mere arrangement of printed matter; and data *per se*. Because we are confident that you will be able to avoid such rejections by thoughtful claim drafting, or to amend your claims to overcome such objections without much difficulty, we focus on the judicial exceptions.

To establish a *prima facie* rejection based on a judicial exception, the examiner's analysis must follow a two-step process (known as the "Mayo test," which was applied to method claims in the *Alice v. CLS Bank* case in 2014) described by the U.S. Supreme Court: (A) first determine whether the claim is "directed to" a judicial exception, and if so, then (B) determine whether the elements of the claim transform the claim into something significantly more than the judicial exception itself. This second step has been called a search for an inventive concept.

In step (A), the examiner must distinguish claims that are "directed to" a judicial exception from those that merely involve a law of nature, natural phenomenon, or abstract idea. The PTO instructs examiners to proceed cautiously, because the Supreme Court has cautioned that "all inventions at some level embody, use, reflect, rest upon, or apply laws of nature, natural phenomenon, or abstract ideas." The PTO's guidance confirms that "an invention is not considered to be ineligible for patent simply because it involves a judicial exception." However, the December 16, 2014 PTO guidance set a very low bar for finding that a claim is "directed to" a judicial exception: a claim is "directed to" a judicial exception if a judicial exception is "set forth or described" in a claim.

Examiners typically will not identify a claimed concept as an abstract idea unless it is similar to at least one concept that the courts have identified as an abstract idea, such as "fundamental economic practices," "certain methods of organizing human activities," "an idea of itself," and "mathematical relationships/formulas." Here are a few concepts that are not abstract ideas:

- a method isolating malicious code from email messages, because that invention is "inextricably tied to computer technology and distinct from the types of concepts found by the courts to be abstract" (January 2015 PTO Examples: Abstract Ideas); and

- a system that implements a method of manipulating webpages to convince a shopper that he or she remains on a host website when viewing information from a merchant's website, because the invention does not merely recite a process "known from the pre-Internet world" with instructions to apply the known process using the Internet, but instead claims a solution that is "necessarily rooted in computer technology in order to overcome a problem specifically arising the realm of computer networks." (January 2015 PTO Examples: Abstract Ideas, based on *DDR Holdings, LLC v. Hotels.com*).

In practice, because it is easy to identify an abstract idea within a method claim, examiners find it easy to conclude that a claim is "directed to" an abstract idea. Note that the examiner's standard here is low: the examiner must only conclude that it is more likely than not that your claim is "directed to" a judicial exception. As discussed below, in making rejections of this type, examiners often rely heavily on examples drawn from post-*Alice* court cases by arguing that your claims are like one of the examples.

If you receive such a rejection, we recommend reviewing the discussion in Chapter 5, and assessing the PTO's rejection of your claim accordingly. For example, does the alleged abstract idea fall within one of the four categories listed above ("fundamental economic practices," "certain methods of organizing human activities," "an idea of itself," and "mathematical relationships/formulas")? Is the claim directed to something that is "inextricably tied to computer technology and distinct from the types of concepts found by the courts to be abstract," or "necessarily rooted in computer technology in order to overcome a problem specifically arising the realm of computer networks?" Conversely, is it possible to perform the processes of the claim to achieve its intended result using an arbitrary mechanism, however inefficiently?

If you agree that the Office Action's analysis meets its low (and subjective) standard, then move on to step (B) of the analysis. Otherwise, develop an argument as to how and why the analysis fails—and then move on to step (B) of the Mayo test for good measure. For example, you may argue that your claims are analogous to claims that are allowable under the most recent PTO guidance, and/or that your claims are different from the kinds of claims that are not allowable under the most recent PTO guidance. Amend the claims if doing so makes your argument stronger.

In step (B) of the Mayo test (as applied to abstract ideas in the Supreme Court's 2014 *Alice v. CLS Bank* decision), the examiner must study the claim again and determine whether the claim's elements limit the claim to an application of the abstract idea to a new and useful end. This has been called the "search for an inventive concept," and it requires that the claim do more than recite an abstract idea, along with a general instruction to "apply it." Since such an instruction implies a conventional application, you may think of step (B) as a hunt for unconventionality. For example, if you have invented a new way of converting a number expressed in one format into a different format, that method will be deemed to be an abstract idea, and your claim will be rejected if it is directed to that method, even if the claim requires that the method be performed via computer because a conventional computer is designed to perform arbitrary computations, including format conversions.

Step (B) of the Mayo test requires the examiner to consider the elements of your claim both individually and as an "ordered combination," to assess whether the claim amounts to significantly more than the exception itself. In practice, when considering the claim elements individually, it is often easy for the examiner to conclude that the elements fail to amount to significantly more than the exception itself by observing that each of the elements is well-understood, routine, and conventional in the field (in other words, none of the elements, considered individually, introduces an "inventive concept").

You should confirm that the Office Action includes some reasoning for a conclusion, rather than simply jumping to one. However, the examiner may be correct; after all, most inventions involve the use of previously known elements, even when those elements are arranged to describe a novel invention. If you agree that each of the elements is well-understood, routine, and conventional, and their combination as you have described it is either known or would produce a predictably conventional result, then arguing with the examiner on this point is unlikely to be fruitful.

Otherwise, be prepared to argue why at least one of the elements is not well-understood, routine, and conventional in the field, or why the particular combination yields unknown or unconventional functions or results.

Examples of features that amount to "significantly more" than a judicial exception include (but are not necessarily limited to): improvements to another technology or technical field; improvements to the functioning of the computer itself; applying the judicial exception with, or by use of, a particular machine; effecting a transformation or reduction of a particular article to a different state or thing; specific limitations other than what is well-understood, routine, and conventional in the field, or adding unconventional steps that confine the claim to a particular useful application; and other meaningful limitations beyond generally linking the use of the judicial exception to a particular technological environment.

In responding to rejections of this type, try to find one or more examples in the guidance that are determined to be patent-eligible, and show the examiner why those examples should apply to your situation.

Here are a few examples drawn from that guidance, in which claims were found to be "significantly more" than a judicial exception:

- A method for processing a digital image in a computer, which involves executing a mathematical operation (the claim is thus "directed to" an abstract idea, so the analysis continues to step (B) of the Mayo test). When considered individually, some elements of the claim require using a computer processor to manipulate the image data into a "halftoned" image. The PTO guidance concludes that these steps "tie the mathematical operation to the processor's ability to process digital images"; and "add meaningful limitation to the abstract idea ... more ... than mere computer implementation." When considered in an "ordered combination," the claim steps "improve the functioning of the computer itself" because the process "allows the computer to use less memory than required" in the prior art, "results in faster computation without sacrificing the quality of the resulting image," and "produces an improved digital image." (January 2015 PTO Examples: Abstract Ideas, hypothetical based on *Research Corporation Technologies, Inc. v. Microsoft Corp.*)

- A method for calculating an absolute position of a GPS receiver and an absolute time of reception of satellite signals, which involves executing algorithms on a mobile GPS processor, and a number of other related steps (the claim is thus "directed to" an abstract idea—mathematical operations—so the analysis continues to step (B) of the Mayo test). When "taking all the additional claim elements individually, and in combination, the claim as a whole amounts to significantly more than the mathematical operations by themselves." In the PTO's analysis of a corresponding system claim (a system for implementing the method), the PTO concluded that the "claim is not directed to performing mathematic operation on a computer alone" because "the elements impose meaningful limits in that the mathematical operation are applied to improve an existing technology (global positioning) by improving the signal-acquisition sensitivity of the receiver...." (January 2015 PTO Examples: Abstract Ideas, hypothetical based on *SiRF Technology v. ITC.*)

Based on your study of part (B) of the Office Action's analysis, develop arguments as to how and why your claims amount to substantially more than an abstract idea. For example, you may argue that your claims are analogous to those that are allowable under the most recent PTO guidance, and/or that your claims are different from the kinds of claims that are not allowable under the most recent PTO guidance. You may also argue that your claims amount to more than a judicial exception, according to the list above. Amend the claims if doing so makes your argument stronger.

Before you file your response to the Office Action, we advise that you have a telephonic interview with the examiner (or even meet with the examiner in person) to discuss the rejections, and options for responding. Throughout this process, bear in mind that the PTO examiner is not your adversary. Most examiners are just trying to do their jobs, and are suffering with the same vague standards that plague inventors and patent attorneys. At the same time, you must hold the examiner to those standards as best you can, but remember to always be professional and courteous.

In the interview, politely remind the examiner that you are working *pro se* (i.e., without the assistance of a patent attorney), and ask the examiner to walk you through any part of the rejections that you don't understand, or with which you don't agree. You can politely press the examiner on any weak points of the Office Action's analysis by asking the examiner to elaborate on the reasons for each such point (or at least the weakest points), but your effectiveness will depend on your understanding of the law (e.g., the Mayo test) and your ability to express similarities and distinctions between your claims and the examples in the most recent PTO guidelines.

You should not expect the examiner to change his or her mind during the interview, or even admit a fatal flaw in the Office Action analysis—examiners are human, too, and don't like to be told (or to admit that) they are wrong. Also, remember that as a *pro se* applicant, you can ask the examiner to suggest ways to amend your claims in order to overcome the rejection. In any case, an examiner interview will allow you to test the rejection and your own analysis, and better understand the examiner's point of view, and thereby strengthen your response strategy.

Finally, we suggest that you seek assistance from a patent attorney with experience in your area of technology, and with experience addressing subject matter eligibility issues for patent applications in your area of technology. Even skilled professionals are struggling with these issues, and you might benefit from an attorney's experience and insight.

Provide 1" top margin (omitted here) to allow for mounting hole punching.

In The United States Patent and Trademark Office

Applicant: R. Wood

Appl Ser No: 07/910,721   Art Unit: 2872

Filed: 3/20/2017   Examiner: Yon J. Couso

Title: Pathway Lamp with Adjustable Illumination Pattern   Date: July 4, 2018

Confirmation No: 1961

Mail Stop AMENDMENT
Commissioner for Patents
P.O. Box 1450
Alexandria, VA 22313-1450

$$\boxed{\text{AMENDMENT A}}$$

Dear Sir:

In response to the Office Action of March 22, 2018, please amend the above-identified application as follows:

Amendments to the Description begin on page 2 of this paper.

Amendments to the Claims are reflected in the listing of claims which begins on page 3 of this paper.

Amendments to the Drawings begin on page 5 of this paper and include both an attached replacement sheet and an annotated sheet showing changes.

Remarks begin on page 6 of this paper.

An Appendix including amended drawing figures is attached following page 8 of this paper.

Fig. 13E/1—Sample "Regular" Amendment

Amendments to the Description:

Please replace the second paragraph on page of the application as filed with the following new paragraph:

The lamp housing 200 also contains a rotatable reflector 208, as schematically illustrated in Fig. 2A and Fig. 2B. The rotatable reflector 208 includes a concave reflecting surface 209 that reflects light from the light source 204 so that the reflected light 206 exits the lamp housing 200 <u>through</u> the translucent bell 203. The reflected light 206 exits the translucent bell 203 in a direction substantially perpendicular to the post axis 110. The rotatable reflector 208 is movably coupled to the lamp housing 200 by bearing 221 so as to be controllably rotatable around the post axis 110.

Fig. 13E/2—Sample "Regular" Amendment

Amendments to the Claims:

This listing of claims will replace all prior versions, and listings, of claims in the application:

Listing of Claims:

1. (currently amended) A pathway light with adjustable illumination pattern for illuminating the ground near a pathway, comprising:
   a post having a first end and a second end, and defining a post axis extending through the first end and the second end;
   <u>a spike coupled to the first end of the post, the spike configured to engage the ground and support the post in a vertical position relative to the ground;</u>
   a lamp housing coupled to the second end of the post, the lamp housing comprising a translucent bell;
   a light source disposed within the lamp housing; and
   a concave reflector movably disposed within the housing between the light source and the translucent bell, the concave reflector configured to controllably rotate around the post axis so as to controllably reflect light from the light source through the translucent bell.

2. (original) A pathway light according to claim 1, wherein the translucent bell comprises a transparent glass hemisphere.

3. (original) A pathway light according to claim 1, wherein the translucent bell comprises a diffusive plastic hemisphere.

4. (original) A pathway light according to claim 1, wherein the light source is a halogen lamp.

5. (original) A pathway light according to claim 1, wherein the light source is an incandescent lamp.

6. (original) A pathway light according to claim 1, wherein the light source is an LED light, and the pathway light further comprises a rechargeable battery, and solar cell electrically coupled to the battery and disposed to capture sunlight to recharge the battery.

7. (original) A pathway light according to claim 1, wherein the post comprises a hollow tube.

8. (original) A pathway light according to claim 7, wherein the post comprises an aluminum tube.

Fig. 13E/3—Sample "Regular" Amendment

9. (original) A pathway light according to claim 7, wherein the post comprises a plastic tube.

10. (canceled)

11. (original) A pathway light according to 7, further comprising a battery compartment configured to hold batteries for powering the light source.

12. (new) A pathway light according to claim 7, further comprising electrical wires extending through the tube from the first end to the lamp housing and electrically coupled to the light source.

Fig. 13E/4—Sample "Regular" Amendment

Amendments to the Drawings:

- The attached sheet of drawings includes changes to Fig. 1, Fig. 2A and Fig. 2B.

- The attached sheet, which includes Fig. 1, Fig. 2A and Fig. 2B, replaces the original sheet including Fig. 1, Fig. 2A and Fig. 2B.

Attachments: One Replacement Sheet

Fig. 13E/5—Sample "Regular" Amendment

REMARKS

Claims 1-11 were pending. Claim 1 has been amended. Claim 10 has been canceled. New claim 12 has been added. Therefore, claims 1-9, 11 and 12 are pending. The Applicants respectfully requests reconsideration of the claims in view of the above amendments and the following remarks.

The office action of March 22, 2018 (herein, the "Office Action") objected to the figures, and rejected the claims under 35 U.S.C. 103 as obvious over US patent 6,874,905 to Beadle (herein "Beadle") in view of US patent 2,569,069 to Maxwell (herein "Maxwell"). The Applicant provides the following response.

I. Amendments to the Specification

The Applicant has amended the second paragraph on page 4 of the application as filed to correct a typographical error.

II. Amendments to the Drawings

The Office Action objected to Fig. 1, Fig. 2A and Fig. 2B for being too light. In response, the Applicant has darkened the lines of the figures.

III. Response to Rejection Under 35 U.S.C. 112

The Office Action rejected claim 1 under 35 U.S.C. 112(a) as failing to point out and distinctly claim the subject matter that the Applicant regards as the invention. In particular, the Office Action alleges that the claim must include some structure for supporting the pathway lamp relative to the ground. In response, the Applicant has amended claim 1 to include the spike, as originally included in claim 10. The Applicant has therefore canceled claim 10.

IV. Beadle in View of Maxwell Does Not Render the Claims Obvious Under 35 U.S.C. 103

The Office Action rejected independent claim 1 over Beadle in view of Maxwell. However, the Office Action fails to establish a prima facie case of obviousness under 35 U.S.C. 103 as explained below.

A. The Office Action Fails to Establish a Prima Facie Case of Obviousness Because Beadle May Not Be Modified By Maxwell as Alleged in the Office Action

Claim 1 requires, among other things, "a concave reflector movably disposed within the housing between the light source and the translucent bell, the concave reflector configured to controllably rotate around the post axis . . ."

The Office Action cited Beadle and Maxwell, and concluded that claim 1 was obvious over Beadle in view of Maxwell.

As set forth in section 2143.01 of the Manual of Patent Examining Procedure ("MPEP"), a "proposed modification cannot render the prior art unsatisfactory for its intended purpose"

Fig. 13E/6—Sample "Regular" Amendment

("If proposed modification would render the prior art invention being modified unsatisfactory for its intended purpose, then there is no suggestion or motivation to make the proposed modification.").

The proposed modification of Beadle by Maxwell would render Beadle unsatisfactory for its intended purpose, with the result that there is no motivation to modify Beadle with Maxwell.

In short, the purpose of the invention in Beadle is to produce a "uniform dispersion of light" (Beadle, column 5, line 36-42). In contrast, the purpose of the reflector 10 in Maxwell is to reflect light emitted by a lamp bulb, while the reflector is supported so that the reflector does not move during use (Maxwell, column 1, lines 1-16). The reflector in Maxwell prevents light from scattering in a uniform direction, since some of the light from the lamp bulb is reflected by the reflector.

As such, while Beadle teaches the production of a uniform dispersion of light, Maxwell teaches the non-uniform dispersion of light. Therefore, modifying Beadle with the reflector of Maxwell, as proposed by the Office Action, would render Beadle unsatisfactory for its intended purpose.

Consequently, there is no motivation to modify Beadle in view of Maxwell, and for at least this reason, the Office Action has failed to establish a prima facie case of obviousness for claim 1 over Beadle in view of Maxwell under 35 U.S.C. 103. Therefore, claim 2 and all claims that depend from claim 1 are also not rendered obvious over Beadle in view of Maxwell under 35 U.S.C. 103.

B. Beadle in View of Maxwell Fails to Teach All of the Elements of Claim 1

Claim 1 requires, among other things, "a concave reflector movably disposed within the housing between the light source and the translucent bell, the concave reflector configured to controllably rotate around the post axis . . . ."

Neither Beadle nor Maxwell teaches such a rotatable reflector, and therefore Beadle in view of Maxwell fails to teach all of the elements of claim 1.

Beadle does not teach a reflector at all. Maxwell teaches a reflector, but does not teach a reflector that is movable around an axis with respect to a lamp housing. Rather, Maxwell's reflector is a fixed part of the lamp.

Consequently, the combination of Beadle and Maxwell as proposed by the Office Action fails to teach all of the elements of claim 1.

For at least this reason, the Office Action has failed to establish a prima facie case of obviousness for claim 1 over Beadle in view of Maxwell under 35 U.S.C. 103. Therefore, claim 1 and all claims that depend from claim 1 are also not rendered obvious over Beadle in view of Maxwell under 35 U.S.C. 103.

For all of the foregoing reasons, the applicant submits that all pending claims are in condition for allowance. The applicant respectfully requests early allowance of the application.

Fig. 13E/7—Sample "Regular" Amendment

V. New Claim 12

The Applicant has added a new claim 12, directed to electrical wires extending through the tube from the first end to the lamp housing and electrically coupled to the light source. This claim is supported at least by Fig. 4 and the text at page 7 of the application as filed.

Conditional Request for Constructive Assistance

Applicants have amended the specification and claims of this application so that they are proper, definite, and define novel structure which is also unobvious. If, for any reason this application is not believed to be in full condition for allowance, applicants respectfully request the constructive assistance and suggestions of the Examiner pursuant to MPEP 707.07(j) in order that the undersigned can place this application in allowable condition as soon as possible and without the need for further proceedings.

The Applicants petition for a one (1) month extension of time. In the event that a further extension is needed, this conditional petition of extension is hereby submitted.

Date: July 4, 2018

Respectfully submitted,

Richard Wood

Richard Wood, Inventor

Fig. 13E/8—Sample "Regular" Amendment

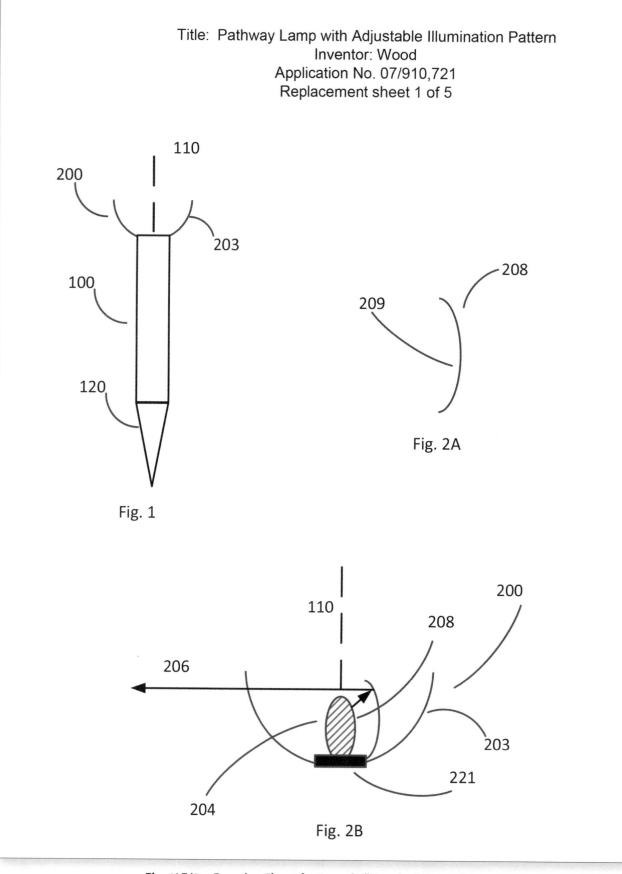

Title: Pathway Lamp with Adjustable Illumination Pattern
Inventor: Wood
Application No. 07/910,721
Replacement sheet 1 of 5

110

200

203

100

120

Fig. 1

209

208

Fig. 2A

110

206

208

200

204

203

221

Fig. 2B

Fig. 13E/9—Drawing Sheet for Sample "Regular" Amendment

12. What to Do If You Disagree With the Examiner

If you believe your broadest claim is patentable over the prior art and that there is a serious flaw in the examiner's logic, it is theoretically permissible to "stand pat"—that is, leave the claim as it is and argue its patentability in your response. It can be desirable to do this to emphasize the rightness of your position if the examiner is very wrong. If you do file a reply to an OA without changing the specification or claims, your reply is technically not an "amendment," so call it a "response."

In most situations, it is advisable not to stand pat, because it's difficult psychologically for the examiner to back down. In other words, it's easier to get the examiner to change directions slightly than to make an about turn. Thus, to save the examiner's ego, it may be best to try to make some amendment to the claim, even if it's insignificant.

"Treat all persons you deal with as if they had a sign around their neck reading, 'Make Me Feel Important.'"

—*Mary Kay Ash*

13. Making Amendments Without Narrowing Scope of Claim

It's usually possible to make amendments to a claim that don't narrow its scope. For example, you can recite that a member, which of necessity must be elongated, *is* elongated. By doing this, you have amended the claim without narrowing your scope of coverage. Also, in the electronic field, you can state that a circuit is energized by a direct-current source. For almost any claim you can add a "whereby" clause to the claim stating the function of the mechanism of the claim, and you can add a longer preamble stating in more detail (but not in narrower language) the environment of your invention. The important thing is to add some words to the claim(s), even if you already believe they distinguish over the prior art under Sections 102 and 103, in order to show that you're meeting the examiner partway.

14. Amending Your Claim When You Agree With the Examiner

If you believe your broadest claim isn't patentable as written, and you agree with all or part of the examiner's rejection, you'll have to narrow the claim by adding physical or structural limitations, or by narrowing the limitations already present, in the manner outlined in Chapter 9, or by canceling the broadest claim(s) and making a dependent claim the new independent claim.

Here are some suggestions on how to approach the amendment of your claims:

1. Look for the physical feature(s) in Fig. 13B that constitute the essence of why your invention can be distinguished from the prior art. Then try to put this essence into your claim. Note that you should amend the main claim so as to distinguish physically over the references under Section 102. The physical distinctions should also be significant enough to define structure that is unobvious under Section 103. Merely reciting a single descriptive word will usually not be enough. For example, "Manifold" may not distinguish over a single pipe (even though it should), but reciting "a pipe with a plurality of outlets" will be explicit enough to do the trick. In addition to putting the reasons as to why the physical distinctions are unobvious in your remarks or in a "whereby" clause at the end of the claim, you can also put them in the body of the claim right after the novel physical distinction. That is, "said bolt having a triangular cross-section [novel feature] so that only wrenches with triangular openings will fit it to increase security [reason for unobviousness]."

2. "Whereby" clauses can state the advantages of the invention in a relatively informal manner, without as much concern for antecedents, etc. Keep in mind that the examiner doesn't have to give a "whereby" clause any weight in defining your invention over the prior art.

3. Don't make your main claim narrower than necessary. Often you can find the limitation you are looking for in one or more dependent claims.

4. Show your invention and the cited references to friends or associates; often they can readily spot the distinguishing essence of your invention. (Remember to use the Nondisclosure Agreement (Form 3-1) if you are maintaining the invention as a trade secret in the patent prosecution phase.)

5. After you've narrowed your main independent claim so that it distinguishes over the prior art cited by the patent examiner, and you feel the distinguishing features are patentable under Section 103 (that is, they're unobvious), do the same for all your other independent claims.

6. If you've changed any independent claims, change your dependent claims so that they completely and correctly correspond in language and numbering with your main claim. If you incorporate a limitation from a dependent claim into your main claim, cancel the dependent claim. This is because the dependent claim will no longer be able to add anything to narrow the independent claim. You may also think of other, narrower dependent claims to replace those that you've canceled; refer to the comparison chart to be sure you've claimed every feature.

7. You should write the narrowest possible claims you're willing to accept, since it will be difficult to amend again if your amended claims are rejected next time around.

Changing Claim Language or Invention

If you have to amend your claims to define over the prior art, you should, of course, try to keep them as broad as possible and worded appropriately to cover your invention in its latest and most likely commercial embodiment. If you change the design of your invention from that shown and described in your application, this will not prejudice you so long as your claims are still broad enough to cover the new design. Judges recognize that designs frequently change as inventions mature. If your design changes by a great amount, consider filing a CIP or a new application.

---

8. Be sure all of the less-important specific features of your invention are recited in your amended dependent claims.

9. Try to distinguish by adding quantitative or relative, rather than qualitative, recitations to your claims, since these carry far more weight. For example, say "a rod at least one meter long" or "a rod that is longer than said post" not "a rod of great length" (or "strength").

15. Plan an Outline of Your Response

Indicate in pencil on a copy of your application, or on separate sheets, the amendments you intend to make to your specification, your claims, your drawing, and your remarks. The "remarks" section of your amendment (as shown in Fig. 13E, below) should consist of:

1. a positive statement indicating that you have amended the application to place it in condition for allowance

2. a brief summary of all your amendments

3. a discussion of any technical (Section 112) rejections and that the new claims overcome them or how you overcame them

4. a review of the first prior-art rejection made by the examiner, containing

   4a. review of the rejection

   4b. review of your invention, emphasizing its novelty

   4c. review of the reference(s) cited by the examiner

   4d. summary of how you changed the independent claims of this rejection, quoting your changes, and a request for reconsideration of the examiner's position

   4e. statement as to how your independent claims under this rejection recite novel subject matter over the reference under Section 102 if one reference was cited; be sure to quote the novel limitations from the claim

   4f. statement of why the references can't legally be combined, if more than one reference was cited

4g. statement that even if the references were to be combined, the claims would still recite novel subject matter over the combination, if more than one reference was cited; be sure to quote the novel limitations from the claim

4h. statement that the novel features of the claim are unobvious, using all possible arguments from Fig. 13D; be sure to elaborate on each argument and not merely state the argument from the chart

4i. discussion of dependent claims under this rejection, indicating that they incorporate all of the features of their referent (independent) claims and add additional limitations and thus are a fortiori (by stronger reason) patentable

4j. discussion of any independent claims that are independently patentable

5. repeat steps 4a through 4h for each additional prior-art rejection, but don't repeat any text, just refer to it above

6. any request for aid you may wish to make under MPEP 707.07(j) requesting the examiner to write claims, and

7. a conclusion restating your main arguments briefly.

(See below, for specifics on drafting your remarks. At this point, read Fig. 13E.)

E. Format for Amending the Specification and Claims

Form 13-1 in Appendix 7 provides the initial part of your amendment. Copy the text from this form into a new file on your word processor.

Fill in the serial number, filing date, your name, title of your application, and the examiner's name and examining unit or group art unit. The date on which you actually mail the amendment goes after "date," and the date of the office letter goes at the space indicated in the first paragraph. Put an appropriate letter (A, B, etc.) after "Amendment" or "Response" to indicate which response it is (your first, second, etc.). Then immediately after the "In response to …" sentence, list the sections of your application (Drawings, Specification, and/or Claims,

and Remarks) and their page numbers in the manner indicated below. (You should refer to yourself and the examiner in the third person as we have done in the sample amendment and never format your amendment in the form of a personal letter to the examiner, as we have seen some inventors do. That is, do not say anything like, "Dear Mr. Examiner: I have revised my claims and I hope you will now find them allowable.")

1. Changes to Specification

If you're going to make any changes to the specification, provide the heading "SPECIFICATION:" on a new page after the sentence printed on Form 13-1. Then indicate the specific paragraphs (or sections) in your application that you want to replace and provide replacement paragraphs marked to indicate deletions by strikethroughs and additions by underlining. If you are deleting five characters or fewer, you may indicate the deletion by double brackets (e.g., "[[claim]]") instead of strikethroughs. If you are deleting a short item, such as a number or punctuation mark, it's better to delete and replace extra portions of the text for clarity (e.g., "[[lever 4 and bracket 5]] lever 6 and bracket 5"). See the second page of the sample amendment below. (You may refer to paragraphs to be replaced by number, e.g., "Paragraph [0005]," if you numbered the paragraphs when you filed the application.)

When your amendment is received, the clerk of the examining group will make each change on the official copy of your application in the manner you direct. Thus, you should ensure that there is no ambiguity in your amendments.

Be sure that your amendments to the specification don't contain any "new matter."

If you want to make a large number of amendments to the specification, it's better to submit an entirely retyped specification, called a "substitute specification." To file a substitute specification you must submit an entirely new specification with the changes made in clean copy form, plus a comparison specification with each change highlighted so the examiner can verify that you haven't added any new matter. Many word processing programs will compare the original and revised specifications and generate a suitable comparison specification easily.

Also, you must certify that the substitute specification doesn't contain any new matter (see MPEP 608.01(q) for instructions.)

2. Amendments to Claims

If you want to amend your claims, start on a new page with the following heading and text:

CLAIMS: Please amend the claims according to the status designations in the following list, which contains all claims that were ever in the application, with the text of all active claims.

The number and status of each claim that is now or was ever in the application must be indicated by providing one of the seven parenthetical expressions, below, after the claim number. (We've indicated the meaning of each parenthetical expression.)

A. (ORIGINAL) The claim has the same number and content as originally filed.

B. (CURRENTLY AMENDED) The claim has the same number as originally or later filed, but is marked up to make amendments (additions and deletions) to it.

C. (PREVIOUSLY PRESENTED) The claim was previously amended in marked-up form. It is now typed in clean copy form with the same number as before.

D. (CANCELED) The claim has been or is currently being canceled. Its text is not typed here.

E. (WITHDRAWN) The claim is directed to a nonelected invention, so it is no longer active but since it is still pending it must be typed. (It may be submitted in a divisional application.)

F. (NEW) The claim is new and is typed with a new number.

G. (NOT ENTERED) The claim was previously submitted but the examiner refused to enter it.

You must list all claims in numerical order, regardless of what action you're taking with them; you may not group all deleted claims together unless they're consecutive. (See the example below.)

For canceled and not entered claims, you should provide only the number and status, but not the claim's text. You should provide the number, status, and claim text for every active (currently under examination) claim. (Fortunately word processors with a copy function allow rapid entry.)

You must present the text of all active claims in clean copy form, except for claims that are being currently amended; use the CURRENTLY AMENDED format for the latter.

Which format should you use to amend claims—CURRENTLY AMENDED or NEW?

I recommend that you use the CURRENTLY AMENDED (marked-up) format if you are making minor changes only to the claim, and/or if you want to point out to the examiner just how you're amending the claim. Use ~~strikethroughs~~ to show deletions and <u>underlining</u> to show additions—the same as for specification amendments. As with specification amendments, if you are deleting five characters or fewer, you may indicate the deletion by double brackets (e.g., "[[lever]]") instead of strikethroughs. If you are deleting a short item, such as a number or punctuation mark, it's better to delete and replace extra portions of the text for clarity (e.g., "[lever 4 and bracket 5] <u>lever 6 and bracket 5</u>").

If you are making any major changes to the claim or prefer to present it in clean copy form, as we usually do and as is done in all foreign countries, we recommend that you use the NEW format: Type the status expression (CANCELED) after the number of the old claim or claims that you're replacing and retype the claim with a new number (use the next highest number) followed by the status expression (NEW), followed in turn by the text of the claim in clean copy form. Include all the changes that you care to make.

Don't forget to re-present all other active claims (those that you're not currently amending) in clean copy form with their statuses indicated. If you cancel a claim that has dependent claims, be sure to change the dependency of the dependent claims so that they don't refer to the canceled claim.

Here's an example of a claim listing for an amendment.

CLAIMS: Please amend the claims according to the status designations in the following list, which contains all claims that were ever in the application, with the text of all active claims.

1–5 (CANCELED)

6. (ORIGINAL) A bucket made of nylon.

7. (WITHDRAWN) A bucket with a carrying strap.

8. (PREVIOUSLY PRESENTED) A bucket with a handle.

9. (CANCELED)

10. (CURRENTLY AMENDED) A bucket with a blue ~~green~~ handle and a round and oval bottom.

11. (WITHDRAWN) A bucket with a bottom hole.

12. (CANCELED)

13. (NEW) A bucket with sides and a bottom that are both made of plastic.

F. Drafting the Remarks

Next, add the "remarks" portion of your amendment starting on a new page. Some general rules for drafting remarks that we'll state first may seem strange, but they're the customary practice, and to deviate substantially may make the examiner feel uncomfortable and take a negative attitude toward your invention.

1. General Rules for Drafting Remarks

Rule 1: Never admit that any prior art anticipates or renders any part of your invention obvious. Similarly, never derogate your invention or any part of it. Also, never state that your invention is limited in any way— that is, don't state anything that an adversary could use against you in a legal dispute.

Rule 2: Never get personal with the examiner. If you must refer to the examiner, always use the third person. For example, never state "You rejected…"; instead, state "The Examiner [note the capitalization] has rejected…." Better yet, state "The Office Action rejects…" or "Claim 1 was rejected…." Never, never address the examiner by name (do list the examiner's name the caption), and never make your amendment a "Dear Mr. [Examiner's Name]" letter. (See the sample amendment of Fig. 13E, above, for how it's done.)

Rule 3: If there's an error in the OA, refer to the error in the OA, and don't state that the examiner made the error. Even if you find the examiner made a completely stupid error, just deal with it in a very formal way, keep emotions and personalities out of

your response, and don't invalidate the examiner. Remember, you've probably made some stupid errors in your life also, and you wouldn't want your nose rubbed in them. It is okay to respectfully challenge an examiner who you feel is wrong. For example, "If this rejection is repeated, applicant respectfully requests that the examiner explain where, in the references themselves, or in the art, there is a suggestion that they be combined."

Rule 4: When referring to yourself, always refer to yourself in the third person as "Applicant" and never as "I."

Rule 5: Stick to the issues in your remarks. Be relevant and to the point and don't discuss personalities or irrelevant issues. Never antagonize the examiner, no matter how much you'd like to. It's improper, and, if you turn the examiner against you, it can considerably narrow the scope of claims that are ultimately allowed.

Rule 6: Use only the legally relevant, logical arguments that are listed in Fig. 13D. Don't use arguments that, although plausible, aren't legally relevant or logical. Among these are: (1) stating that your invention is superior to a prior patented device (§ 103) without first stating that your claims recite novel hardware (or method steps) over the prior patent (§ 102); (2) that a cited patent shouldn't have been granted or has less novelty than yours (the PTO isn't bound to repeat its past mistakes); (3) that you have a Ph.D. and spent a lot of ingenuity to come up with the invention (the qualifications of the inventor and the amount of time it took to come up with an invention are irrelevant), (4) that you put your heart and soul and years of effort into the invention (again irrelevant), (5) that the apparatus of the reference as shown in its drawings or claims is different from yours (only the differences of your claims over the reference's specification and drawings are relevant). Also, some inventors have actually telephoned the patentee-inventor of a cited patent. This is a futile exercise, since there's nothing a patentee can do to help you; a patent speaks for itself. As a further example, if the examiner says pages 11 and 12 of your specification don't provide a clear description of the invention, tell why these pages do the job; don't simply explain how it works without reference to these pages.

Rule 7: Whenever you write any new claims or make any additions to a present claim, you must tell why the claim was amended and how the amendments distinguish over the prior art the examiner has cited under Sections 102 and 103. Follow Inventor's Commandment 7 from Chapter 5, repeated below, and Patent Rule 111(b) and (c):

Inventor's Commandment 7

To evaluate or argue the patentability of any invention, use a two-step process. First determine what novel features (§ 102) the invention has over the closest prior-art reference(s). Novelty can be a new physical (hardware) feature, a new combination or rearrangement of two separate old features, or a new use of an old feature. Second, determine if the novelty produces any new and unexpected results or otherwise indicates unobviousness (§ 103).

---

1. *(b) In order to be entitled to reconsideration or further examination, the applicant or patent owner must reply to the Office Action. The reply by the applicant or patent owner must be reduced to a writing which distinctly and specifically points out the supposed errors in the examiner's action and must reply to every ground of objection and rejection in the prior Office Action. The reply must present arguments pointing out the specific distinctions believed to render the claims, including any newly presented claims, patentable over any applied references. If the reply is with respect to an application, a request may be made that objections or requirements as to form not necessary to further consideration of the claims be held in abeyance until allowable subject matter is indicated. The applicant's or patent owner's reply must appear throughout to be a bona fide attempt to advance the application or the reexamination proceeding to final action. A general allegation that the claims define a patentable invention without specifically pointing out how the language of the claims patentably distinguishes them from the references does not comply with the requirements of this section.*

2. *(c) In amending in reply to a rejection of claims in an application or patent under reexamination, the applicant or patent owner must clearly point out the patentable novelty which he or she thinks the claims present in view of the state of the art disclosed by the references cited or the objections made. The applicant or patent owner must also show how the amendments avoid such references or objections.*

Rule 8: If you do disagree and think the OA was wrong, you must state exactly why you disagree. If you agree that a claim is obvious over the prior art, don't admit this in your response; simply cancel the claim and don't give any reason for it, or if you must comment, state merely that it has been canceled in view of the coverage afforded by the remaining claims. However, if you amend any claim be sure to state why you are amending it to preserve your rights to use the DoE later.

Rule 9: Make a careful, complete, and convincing presentation, but you don't have to overly agonize about words or minutiae. The reality is that many examiners don't read your remarks or else skim through them very rapidly. This is because they're generally working under a quota system, which means they have to dispose of (finally reject or allow) a certain number of cases in each fiscal quarter. Thus, the examiners are under time pressure and it takes a lot of time to read remarks. It's important to cover all the substantive points in the Office Action and to deal with every objection and rejection. If you do make an error, as stated, the PTO will almost always give you an opportunity to correct it, rather than forcing you to abandon your application.

Two good ways to make sure your examiner reads and (hopefully) understands your points and reasons are to liberally sprinkle your amendment with boldfaced "arguing" headings that themselves tell your whole story (as is done in the sample amendment of Fig. 13E), and to keep your paragraphs short and inviting. For example, some arguing headings might be, "Briskin Does Not Show Any Elongated Lever," "Claim 1 Clearly Defines Over Warner Under Section 102," "Ihara Could Not Be Operatively Combined With Harolde," and "Applicant's Rasterizer Produces New and Unexpected Results Over Hearsh."

Rule 10: If possible, thank or praise the examiner if you can find a reason to do so with sincerity—for example, "Applicant thanks the Examiner for the clear and understandable Office Action." Examiners get criticized and told they're all wet so often that they'll welcome any genuine, deserved praise.

Rule 11: Don't emphasize your beliefs; they're considered irrelevant. For example, don't say "Applicant *believes* this invention is patentable." Rather say, "Since the claims define novel structure that produces new and unexpected results as described above, Applicant *submits* that such claims are clearly patentable."

Rule 12: Although it's okay to state *briefly* why your invention is superior to that of the reference(s), the main thrust of your argument should be a two-part legal argument that tells (a) how your invention, as claimed, differs from the reference(s), and (b) why these differences are important. Again, see Inventor's Commandment 7 above.

TIP

You may wonder whether it makes sense to put much effort into your remarks even though the chances are great they won't be carefully read. Our opinion is that it does, because you never know. Think of your effort as a kind of insurance against being the one in five (or whatever) whose remarks are in fact subjected to close scrutiny.

Although it's difficult, we recommend that you do the best job you possibly can in your first response (which you might call Response A), since it will probably be the last chance you get to amend your claims in this application. This is so important and is violated so often, that we've made it Inventor's Commandment 28, at the beginning of this chapter. After you draft your response, we suggest that you wait a few days and come back and review it again, pretending that you're the examiner. This will probably give you important insights and enable you to improve it further.

2. How to Draft Your Remarks

Your remarks should first provide a brief positive summary of what you've done to the specification

and claims. For example, you can start off with a summary as follows: "Applicant has amended the specification and claims to put this application in full and clear condition for allowance. She has amended the specification editorially and to correct those errors noted by the Examiner. Also she has rewritten claims 1 to 5 as new Claims 13 to 18 to more particularly define the invention in a patentable manner over the cited prior art." Then briefly summarize what each claim recites, as is done in Fig. 13E, above. If the drawing has been objected to, you must submit corrected drawing, because objections to drawings will not normally be held in abeyance. If you want to make a voluntary amendment to the drawing, refer to the drawing amendment explanation on page one of the amendment, include a drawing amendment on a separate drawing amendment page, and attached replacement sheets and a red-marked sheet indicating the changes, if necessary. Then include a separate section for each rejection in the amendment.

a. Restate First Rejection

After providing a positive heading for the first rejection of the OA (for example, "The New Claims Overcome the Rejection on Jones and Smith"), restate this rejection. For example, "The Office Action rejected Claims 1 to 5 as unpatentable over Jones in view of Smith." The examiner, thus oriented, saves the time it would take to reread the OA.

b. Review Each Reference Relied on in the Rejection

One or two sentences for each is sufficient. For example: "Reference A (Smith patent 1,234,567) shows a … [and so forth]."

c. Specifically Describe Any Claim Changes and Argue Section 102 and Then Section 103

Discuss specifically how and why the claim in question has been amended and how it recites structure that physically distinguishes over each reference under Section 102. The flowchart of Fig. 13C gives the specifics as to how to do that. For example, "Claim 1, now rewritten as new Claim 5, recites…." "This language distinguishes over Smith and Jones under Section 102 because Smith does not show [etc.] and Jones does not show [etc].”

If the examiner rejected a claim on one or more references individually under Section 102, the examiner is stating that the claim doesn't recite any novel feature(s) over any of these references. If the examiner rejected a claim on one reference under Section 103, the examiner is stating that the claim recites a novel feature(s) over the reference but the examiner doesn't consider the novel feature(s) significant enough to be patentable. If the examiner rejected a claim on a combination of two or more references under Section 103, the examiner is stating neither reference shows all of the features of the claim but the combination of references does. To argue against such a combination, state—if accurate—that (1) the references can't be legally combined because (a) there is no reason in the references themselves or in the art to combine them, and that (b) the combination would not be operable, and (2) even if they were to be combined the claim would recite novel features over the combination and these are unobvious. Don't state that the novel features of the claims define over the combination under Section 102 since Section 102 only applies to a rejection on a single reference.

Then, once you've established the novelty of your claim(s), show why the novel features are unobvious and patentable—for example, “These distinctions are submitted to be of patentable merit under Section 103 because [discuss new results that flow from your novel structure, giving as many reasons as you can from Fig. 13D, Part I, and your completed Form 4-2].”

Note that even if an independent claim was rejected under Section 102 (lack of novelty) over a single reference, you should consider whether the examiner might consider the claim to be obvious over the same art under Section 103, and if so, address that as well as Section 102, as follows: (1) rebut the Section 102 rejection by showing that the claim contains novelty over the single reference, and (2) cover Section 103 (obviousness) by describing how the novel feature(s) are also unobvious (produce new and unexpected results) over the single reference.

Moreover, even if you show that that the independent claim is novel and unobvious over the single reference, you should also be aware that the independent claim may also be unpatentable over a combination of the single (main) reference with any pertinent secondary references. This is because, even though the independent claim is novel and unobvious over a single reference, it might be obvious to combine the main reference with a pertinent secondary reference. So you should review all of the other cited references to be sure that no valid combination of the main reference and a pertinent secondary reference shows all the features of the independent claim. If you do find a pertinent secondary reference, you should also argue patentability over the combination of references (if warranted) to head off any future rejection on such combination. You may want to add a new dependent claim, to bolster your chances of getting a claim allowed over the secondary reference.

Once you argue the patentability of the independent claim over the single reference and any combination of the single reference with any pertinent secondary reference(s), you don't need to argue the patentability of any claims that are dependent on this independent claim because they are narrower than the independent claim and thus are a fortiori (by stronger reason) patentable. You need merely state that dependent claims y-z are dependent upon claim x and thus incorporate all the limitations of claim x and include further limitations and thus are a fortiori patentable. However, if any dependent claim contains a significant additional limitation, you can state that it is independently patentable and state the reasons.

Use a 102/103 Approach

You must use a 102/103 approach even if your claim was rejected on Section 102 alone. This 102/103 approach is useful if you don't understand the examiner's reasoning. That is, rather than try to figure out what the examiner was trying to say, or questioning the examiner, simply put forth a detailed, cogent 102/103 argument. This will usually win the day, or at worst, reframe the issues in your favor.

You should discuss how your invention, as claimed, distinguishes over—that is, has novel physical features not shown in—the reference, not how the reference differs from your invention, and not, at this stage, why your invention is better than the reference. Remember that under Section 112, a means plus a function is considered a physical recitation.

The following jingle may help you remember this important rule:

*"Never argue what's not in your claim
You'll miss the mark and may lose the game."*

Also be logical in your arguments. For example, if you're claiming B and a reference shows A and B, don't argue that A is no good. Also, don't argue that a reference should be taken lightly—that is, it's a "paper patent," because its invention was never put into commercial use—unless you're absolutely sure of your facts and the reference isn't a dead ringer for your invention.

d. Refute Any Improper Combination of References

If a combination of several references has been cited against your claim, first state why the combination cannot properly be made and then discuss your distinctions under Section 103. MPEP Sections 2142 and 2143 require that, in order for two references to be combined in a rejection, the examiner must establish a prima facie (at first sight) case for obviousness. Below are relevant excerpts from MPEP 2142:

The legal concept of prima facie obviousness is a procedural tool of examination which applies broadly to all arts. It allocates who has the burden of going forward with production of evidence in each step of the examination process.

To reach a proper determination under 35 USC Section 103, the examiner must step backward in time and into the shoes worn by the hypothetical "person of ordinary skill in the art" when the invention was unknown and just before it was made. In view of all factual information, the examiner must then make a determination whether the claimed invention "as a whole" would have been obvious at that time to that person. Knowledge of applicant's disclosure must be

put aside in reaching this determination, yet kept in mind in order to determine the "differences," conduct the search, and evaluate the "subject matter as a whole" of the invention. The tendency to resort to "hindsight" based upon applicant's disclosure is often difficult to avoid due to the very nature of the examination process. However, impermissible hindsight must be avoided and the legal conclusion must be reached on the basis of the facts gleaned from the prior art.

The key to supporting any rejection under 35 U.S.C. 103 is the clear articulation of the reason(s) why the claimed invention would have been obvious. The Supreme Court in KSR International Co. v. Teleflex Inc., *550 U.S. 39, 82USPQ2d 1385, 1396 (2007) noted that the analysis supporting a rejection under 35 U.S.C. 103 should be made explicit. The Federal Circuit has stated that 'rejections on obviousness cannot be sustained with mere conclusory statements; instead, there must be some articulated reasoning with some rational underpinning to support the legal conclusion of obviousness.'*

If you feel that the examiner has not set forth a prima facie case, make your case tactfully. For example, "Applicant submits that the rejection of claim 1 on Jones and Smith does not set forth a prima facie case of obviousness, as required by MPEP 2142. This section requires that *there must be a clear articulation of the reason(s) why the claimed invention would have been obvious. Applicant submits that the rejection does not meet this requirement because the rejection gives a mere conclusory statement that the combination would be obvious. Note that neither Smith nor Jones suggests such a combination, and one skilled in the art would have no reason to make such a combination. That is, the fact that Smith shows a specific lever does not suggest that his lever can be used with Jones's pedal mechanism, especially since Jones shows his own workable lever. Further the references are from a different field than that of applicant's invention* [explain why] *and/or they are not directed to solving the same problem as applicant's invention solves* [explain why].

Moreover, applicant submits that the rejection is improper because the combination could not be made physically since the lever of the Smith type would not fit in or work with Jones's pedal mechanism because…. Also the references are not combinable because their intended function would be destroyed if one attempted to combine them [explain why].

Finally applicant submits that the rejection is improper because, even if the combination could be legally made, the combination does not show [here quote novel language of claim]. *Applicant submits that these distinctions are patentable under Section 103 because* [discuss new results and give as many reasons as you can from Fig. 13D and Form 4-2]."

If the references themselves don't suggest that they should be combined (Reasons 29–33 in Fig. 13D), and there is no reason in the art to combine them, you can use the arguments in MPEP 2142 and 2143. In our experience most rejections do not articulate any clear reasons to support a combination rejection and these MPEP sections provide powerful arguments.

e. Note Secondary Factors of Unobviousness

If your invention has achieved any commercial success or has won any praise, this is relevant, and you should mention it here. If possible, submit copies of advertisements for your invention, copies of industry or trade praise, sales figures, a commercially sold sample, etc. These things reify the invention (that is, make it a "fait accompli") and impress most examiners. If you are submitting any evidence of commercial success, you should do it with a declaration with attached exhibits stating how the invention has achieved commercial success and how such success is related to the novel features of the invention. (See the next section for the format (not the substance) of such a declaration.)

f. Draft Any Needed Declaration Under Rule 132 to Refute Technical Points Raised by Examiner

If you want to challenge any technical points raised by the examiner, such as proving that your invention works in a superior manner to a reference, that two references can't be combined, or that a cited reference works in a far inferior way to yours, you or an expert in the field should do the necessary research and make

the necessary tests (including building and testing a model of the cited reference) and then submit a "Declaration Under Rule 132." The Declaration should have a caption as in Form 13-1 and an appropriate heading, such as "Rule 132 Declaration Regarding Inferior Performance of Elias Patent." The body of the Declaration should start,

Jane Inventor declares as follows:

I am the inventor [or I am a mechanical engineer (state education, experience, and awards)] in the above patent application.

Then, in numbered paragraphs, detail your technical facts and/or reasons, including tests you made, etc., but state facts, not conclusions or arguments. Whenever you make any legal declaration or affidavit (as opposed to a brief or remarks), heed the words of the immortal Joe Friday, of television's *Dragnet* fame: "Just the facts, ma'am." You can attach and refer to "exhibits"—that is, documents in support of your arguments.

Then conclude with a "declaration paragraph," as in the last paragraph of Form 10-1 (that states "I hereby declare…") and sign and date the declaration.

Similarly, if you want to mention any additional factors relating to your invention, such as commercial success or copying by an infringer, which are relevant to patentability, you can submit a similar Rule 132 declaration. You can attach relevant "Exhibits," such as a prototype, a commercial sample, advertising, or sales reports. As stated, working models usually make believers out of negative examiners.

g. Request Reconsideration

Request reconsideration of the rejection(s) and allowance of the claim: "Therefore applicant submits that Claim 5 is allowable over the cited references and solicits reconsideration and allowance."

If you have dependent claims that were rejected, treat these in the same manner. Since a dependent claim incorporates all the limitations of the parent claim, you can state that the dependent claim is patentable for the same reasons given with respect to the parent claim, and then state that it is even more

Checklist for Sending In a Regular Amendment

Before you mail your amendment, please check the following list carefully to be sure that the amendment is complete and properly done.

☐ You have responded to each point in the OA.

☐ You have responded to any needed drawing objection.

☐ You have re-proofed the specification and have made any needed corrections.

☐ You have amended the prior-art portion of the specification to account for any significant new prior art (optional).

☐ You have not included any new matter in any amendments to the specification.

☐ You have checked all new claims against the checklist in Chapter 9.

☐ All claims recite structure that is physically different from every cited reference (Section 102).

☐ You have presented the amendment in the prescribed format: (a) a list of contents is on page 1, (b) the Specification and Drawing Amendments (if any) start on respective new pages, (c) the Claim Amendments (if any) start on a new page, (d) the Remarks start on a new page, (e) the specification is amended by replacing whole paragraphs with words to be deleted struck through and words to be added underlined, (f) all claims that were ever in the application are listed in numerical order, (g) the number of every claim is followed by one of the seven required parenthetical expressions (Original, Currently Amended, Previously Presented, Canceled, Withdrawn, New, and Not Entered), (h) for Canceled and Withdrawn claims, only the claim number without the text is provided, and (i) for claims in the Currently Amended format, words to be deleted are struck through and words to be added are underlined.

☐ The physically different structure in every claim is sufficiently different to produce new and unexpected results or otherwise be considered unobvious (Section 103).

☐ The application includes several very narrow dependent claims with a variety of phraseologies so that you won't have to present them for the first time if the next action is made final.

☐ The wording in the remarks is clear, grammatically correct, and understandable.

☐ The remarks are written in short paragraphs with ample "arguing" headings.

☐ Every embodiment covered in your claims (originally and as amended) is described in the specification and shown in the drawings.

☐ The patentability of all new claims is argued with respect to the references, using a two-part approach: (a) The claim has physical distinctions over the references under Section 102; (b) The claimed physical distinctions produce new and unexpected results or are otherwise unobvious under Section 103.

☐ You have included all possible arguments for unobviousness (Fig. 13D).

☐ A request for claim-drafting assistance under MPEP 707.07(j) has been made, if desirable.

☐ The amendment is 1.5- or double-line-spaced with an ample top margin for punching mounting holes.

☐ The last page of the amendment includes your name, address, and phone number.

☐ If the amendment will cause the case to have over 20 total or over three independent claims, the proper additional fee is included (if not previously paid).

☐ The amendment is signed and dated (no pencil) by all applicants.

☐ An identical file copy of the amendment has been made if you are mailing the amendment.

☐ The amendment is being transmitted on time or includes a properly completed Petition to Extend with the proper fee included.

☐ A Certificate of Faxing or Mailing is typed in the amendment unless it's being filed electronically.

☐ All pages are complete and present.

☐ A receipt postcard is attached to the amendment, if you are mailing it.

☐ If mailing, the envelope is properly stamped and addressed to "Mail Stop Non-Fee Amendments, Commissioner for Patents, P.O. Box 1450, Alexandria, VA 22313-1450." If you are sending any money with your amendment, omit "Box Non-Fee Amendments." If you're faxing the amendment, make sure you feed your pages carefully.

patentable because it adds additional limitations, which you should discuss briefly. If a dependent claim is independently patentable—that is, its added limitations are independently patentable—state this and explain why.

h. Respond to Rejections Under Section 112 for Lack of Clarity or Conciseness

If a technical rejection has been made (under Section 112), discuss how you've amended your claim and why your new claim is clear and understandable. Often an examiner will reject, for indefiniteness, a claim that you feel is clear and unambiguous. Even if we disagree with the examiner we always try to fix the claim in a way that will overcome the examiner's rejection because this is always easier than arguing with the examiner and risking the uncertainty of another rejection. If you can't figure out how to fix the claim you can call the examiner and ask for a suggestion. Nevertheless sometimes a claim may seem perfectly clear and not amenable to any improvement. In this case you can point out to the examiner that the Court of Appeals for the Federal Circuit has stated that the definiteness requirement of Section 112 "is satisfied if a person skilled in the field of the invention would reasonably understand the claim when read in the context of the specification." (*Marley Mouldings, Ltd. v. Mikron Industries, Inc.*, 417 F.3d 1356 (Fed. Cir. 2005).)

i. Request Claim-Drafting Assistance From PTO

Once again, we emphasize that if you feel you have patentable subject matter in your application but have difficulty in writing new claims, you can request that the examiner write new claims for you pursuant to MPEP Section 707.07(j). Your remarks are the place to do this. For example, state, "Therefore Applicant submits that patentable subject matter is clearly present. If the Examiner agrees but does not feel that the present claims are technically adequate, applicant respectfully requests that the examiner write acceptable claims pursuant to MPEP 707.07(j)." If the examiner writes any claims for you, don't rest on them unless you're sure that the broadest one is as broad as the prior art permits, or at least broad enough to prevent competitors from copying your product, using the criteria above and in Chapter 5. Remember, if you are dissatisfied with the examiner's claims, you can once again submit your own claims, you can submit the examiner's claims with whatever amendments you choose, or you can interview the examiner to discuss the matter. You should request claim drafting assistance when you file, or after the first OA, not after a final OA.

j. Repeat the Above for Any Other Rejections in the Office Action

After you've covered and hopefully decimated the first rejection in the manner discussed in Subsections a to i, above, then do the same for each additional rejection—that is, provide a separate heading for the rejection, review the rejection, review the reference(s), review your new claims, discuss why they distinguish under Section 102, then why the novel features are patentable under Section 103, and request reconsideration and allowance.

k. Discuss Nonapplied References

If any references of interest have been cited but not applied against any claim, you should read these to be sure they are less relevant than the applied references. If they are less relevant, state that you've reviewed them but that they don't show your invention or render it obvious. If any reference is more relevant or you think it might be used against you later, be sure your claims define your invention in a patentable manner over it and lightly explain the differences between that art and your claims.

l. Acknowledge Allowed or Allowable Claims

Often the examiner will allow some claims, or indicate that certain claims would be allowed if amended in a certain way or rewritten in independent form. You should acknowledge this statement and if necessary, tell how you handled it—for example, "Applicant acknowledges the allowance of Claims 1 to 7 with appreciation," or "Applicant has rewritten Claim 13 (indicated to contain allowable subject matter) in independent form as new Claim 26."

m. Conclusion

Last, provide a conclusion that should repeat and summarize—for example, *"For all the reasons given above, applicant respectfully submits that the errors in the specification are corrected, the claims comply with Section 112, the claims define over the prior art under Section 102 [briefly repeat why], and the claimed distinctions are of patentable merit under Section 103 because of the new results provided [repeat them briefly again]. Accordingly, applicant submits that this application is now in full condition for allowance, which action applicant respectfully solicits."* Then add the closing, "Very respectfully," followed by your signature, typewritten name, your address, and telephone number on the left-hand side. If you have a coinventor(s), all of you must sign the amendment.

n. Do Your Very Best Job

It's important to do your very best job in your first amendment, since it's the only full opportunity you'll get to answer the examiner's position. We suggest that after writing the amendment, you have a friend read it or you come back to it after a few days and read it from the viewpoint of your examiner. Make sure your amendment in response to the first OA is complete, carefully crafted, and includes all arguments and the narrowest claims possible, since the next OA will be final.

G. Drawing Amendments

If your Office Action includes any objections to the drawing(s), you must correct these in your response. The replacement sheet should include a notation in the top margin reading, "Replacement Sheet, Ser. Nr. __/ _____." Fill in your Ser. Nr. and be sure that the replacement sheet includes the correct sheet number below the top margin, that is, "1/2." A replacement sheet must include all of the figures that were on the sheet that it is replacing. In other words, if you are replacing a sheet that originally included Fig. 1 and Fig. 2, the replacement sheet must also include Fig. 1 and Fig. 2, even if only one of those figures is being amended.

A common drawing objection, made under Rule 83(a), is that the drawing doesn't show every feature recited in the claims. For example, suppose your original claim was directed to a hose having an atomizer head and your drawing shows only a hose with a sprinkler head. How can you add an atomizer head to the drawing to remedy this objection without showing details of the atomizer, which would violate the rule against adding new matter to your application? Easy: just add a legend or label adjacent the end of the plain hose reading, "Can be atomizer." This will not add any new matter since it's no more specific than the claim, which already recites an atomizer.

To deal with any drawing objections by the examiner or the OPAP, first include or check the listing paragraph on page 1 (contents page) of your amendment as follows:

"DRAWINGS: A statement explaining the drawing amendments made by this amendment begins on page *[state page]* of this amendment; or text to that effect."

Then, on the appropriate DRAWINGS page of the amendment, state that you have attached a replacement sheet with the drawing objections corrected. Although not necessary, we prefer to refer briefly to the corrected sheets at the beginning of the Remarks. To make the corrections correct your Bristol board or Mylar film originals, or make new CAD originals, and file new, good xerographic (or CAD output) copies. All lines must be crisp, black, and sharp, and all objections on the drawing objection sheet must be corrected.

List the sheets as an enclosure at the end of the amendment and attach new (corrected) sheets to the amendment for substitution for your original drawings. (If filing by mail, attach the new drawing sheets with a paper clip—do not staple them.) In the top margin of each replacement sheet, write "Replacement Sheet" and add your name, Serial Number, and Examination Group.

If *you* find any errors in your drawings, you should voluntarily make any necessary (nonrequired) amendments or corrections. Formerly the PTO required that you obtain approval in advance, but now you may go right ahead and file replacement sheets. If the examiner or the PTO's drawing checkers disapprove of the changes they will notify you.

Make the changes and attach new, good copies of the changes sheets. List the sheets as an enclosure at the end of the amendment and attach red-marked sheets and new (corrected) sheets to the amendment for substitution for your original drawings.

If you want to send any replacement drawing sheets separately from an amendment, or with your issue fee transmittal, use Form 13-1. Check the box on this form if you are also including a copy of any sheets marked in red to indicate any changes.

Remember that the PTO prohibits the addition of any new matter to the drawings. However, you may correct obvious errors, such as a reversed diode, a missing reference numeral, or a missing line. We recommend that you keep a file copy of every version of every drawing sheet in case you ever have to refer to any sheet before changes.

H. Typing and Filing the Amendment

The amendment should be typed with 1.5- or double-line-spacing on letter-size or A4 paper with 1-inch top and 1-inch left, right, and bottom margins. The PTO prefers that you file the amendment by EFS-Web (so it won't have to scan it into its computers). Less preferred is that you fax the amendment, and last, you may mail the amendment. In the last two cases—fax and mail—don't forget to keep an identical copy of your amendment in your file. If you mail the amendment, be sure to attach a receipt postcard addressed to you (postage paid) with a full identification of the amendment on the back. The PTO won't return any paper you send them, although they will make a copy of any paper or record for the per-sheet photocopy charge in the Fee Schedule. If you mail it, don't forget the postcard. The signatures of all inventors must be on the copy you send to the PTO.

If you file the amendment by EFS-Web, the online forms will provide a transmittal for the amendment. However if you file the amendment on paper (by fax or by mail) no transmittal letter is needed. If your amendment increases the number of claims above what you originally paid for when you filed the application, you have to pay for the extra claims. It's helpful (but not necessary) to attach a completed form PTO/SB/06 to calculate the extra fee.

Documents With Copies of Signatures Now Okay

The PTO now accepts documents that contain a copy of any required signature, provided you retain a copy of the document with an original signature, in case it's ever needed. (Original signatures are required only on (a) documents involving the registration of an attorney or agent and (b) certified copies.)

If you intend to mail or fax your amendment, after your signature add a "Certificate of Facsimile Transmission" (preferable) or a "Certificate of Mailing" as required by Rule 8 (don't use Priority Mail Express as it isn't necessary and the cost is high) as follows.

Certificate of Facsimile Transmission

I certify that on the date below I will fax this communication, and attachments if any, to Group _____ of the Patent and Trademark Office at the following number: 571-273-8300.

Date: _____

Inventor's Signature: _____

Certificate of Mailing

I hereby certify that this correspondence, and attachments, if any, will be deposited with the United States Postal Service by First Class Mail, postage prepaid, in an envelope addressed to "Box Non-Fee Amendments, Commissioner for Patents, P.O. Box 1450, Alexandria, VA 22313-1450" on the date below.

Date: _____

Inventor's Signature: _____

While all inventors must sign the amendment, only one inventor need sign this certification. If you include this certificate, you can fax or mail your amendment even at 23:59 on the last day of your response period. Even if you're mailing the amendment two months ahead of time you should use the Certificate anyway, since if the amendment is lost in the mail, causing your application technically to go abandoned, you can get it revived easily by filing a declaration stating the full facts and enclosing a photocopy of the amendment with the Certificate of Mailing—see PTO Rule 8(b). If you use mail, don't forget to attach a postcard to your amendment reading as in Fig. 13F. If you fax the amendment, and your fax machine is programmed to transmit your fax number, the PTO will send an immediate faxback receipt.

Amendment A (5 pages) plus amended and red-marked copies of sheet 2/4 of drawings in Application of John A. Novel, Ser. Nr. 999,999, filed 20xx Jan. 9, received today:

Fig. 13F—Back of Receipt Postcard for Amendment

Draft Amendments May Be Faxed for Discussion

Applicants may now send a proposed amendment for discussion to "sound out" and negotiate with the examiner. Mark the amendment "DRAFT" or "PROPOSED AMENDMENT," do not sign it, and fax it to the examiner. Then call the examiner in a few days to discuss the amendment by phone or visit the examiner personally. You still must file a regular, signed amendment by the due date to avoid abandonment.

Make sure your amendment won't cause the total number of claims of your application to exceed 20, or the number of independent claims to exceed three (unless you've paid for excess claims when you filed the application). Otherwise, you'll have to pay an additional claims fee (expensive and usually not advisable, since three independent and 20 total claims should be more than adequate).

I. If Your Application Is Allowable

Hopefully, your first amendment will do the trick and the examiner will decide to allow the case. If so, you'll often be sent a Notice of Allowability and/or a formal Notice of Allowance (N/A), the latter accompanied by an Issue Fee transmittal form. You have a statutory period of three months to pay the issue fee; the three-month period is not extendable and forms are self-explanatory. You can fax or electronically transmit the Issue Fee Transmittal, but if you mail it, be sure to include a receipt postcard. You can also place an advance order for printed copies of your patent (a space is provided on the Issue Fee Transmittal form); the minimum order is ten. However, printed copies aren't necessary as you can make photocopies from your patent deed, or download copies from the PTO or any of the free private websites. Also, be sure to fill in the Certificate of Mailing or Faxing on the Issue Fee Transmittal, unless you file this electronically as an eFiler. If your application was published 18 months after filing you will also have to pay the PTO publication fee, although in 2014 the PTO reduced the publication fee to $0. The fee is included on your Issue Fee Transmittal form. The PTO no longer sends a "Notice of Patent Term Adjustment" with your N/A, but now sends it with the notice of the issue date. Usually the patent term will not be extended, but if the PTO delayed in responding to an amendment or you had to appeal, you will get a commensurate adjustment.

When you receive your N/A, make any needed drawing corrections at once and review the application and drawings once again very carefully to make sure everything is correct, logical, grammatical, and so on. If you want to make any amendments at this time, you can still do so, provided they don't affect the substance of the application. Generally, only grammatical changes are permitted after the N/A. The format of the amendment should be similar to that of Fig. 13E, except that the first sentence should read, "Pursuant to Rule 312, applicant respectfully requests that the above application be amended as follows:"

Then make any amendments to your specification and claims in the previously used format. Under "Remarks," discuss the amendments, stating that they are not matters of substance and noting that they will require very little consideration by the examiner.

Checklist for Paying an Issue Fee

☐ You made all needed drawing corrections and enclosed any needed formal drawings.

☐ You have made any needed specification or claim amendments (PTO Rule 312).

☐ You have properly completed and signed the Issue Fee Transmittal Form.

☐ You have filed a completed Supplemental Declaration if you have made any significant claim changes during prosecution.

☐ If transmitting by mail, you have enclosed a check or a completed credit card Form PTO-2038 for the issue fee. If transmitting by fax, you used Form PTO-2038.

☐ If you are mailing the issue fee, you have attached a receipt postcard, properly stamped and addressed.

☐ If transmitting by mail you have completed a certificate of mailing or faxing on the Notice of Allowance.

☐ You are transmitting the issue fee papers by the due date (no extensions allowed).

☐ If you are mailing the papers you have made a file copy of all issue fee transmittal papers.

If you've amended your claims in any substantial way during prosecution, after the Notice of Allowance is received you should also file a Supplemental Declaration (Form 13-3) to indicate that you've invented the subject matter of the claims as amended and that you know of no prior art that would anticipate these claims. Sometimes when a case is allowed the examiner will include a "Reasons for Allowance" section. You should review this carefully to be sure the reasons aren't too narrow, since this may adversely affect the scope of your patent. If the reasons are too narrow, you should submit a rebuttal statement to neutralize the examiner's statement.

Prior to sending in the issue fee, you should go through the checklist shown above.

Once your issue fee is received, your application goes to the Government Printing Office and no further changes are permitted.

Four to six weeks after the issue fee is paid, you may receive an Issue Notification Form, which will indicate the number of your patent and the date it will issue, usually a week or so after you receive the receipt. A few days after your patent issues, you'll receive the deed, or letters patent, and, separately, any additional printed copies you've ordered.

J. If Your First Amendment Doesn't Result in Allowance

If your first amendment doesn't place the application in condition for allowance, the examiner will usually make the next OA final. However, if the second OA cites any new references, it won't be made final unless the examiner had to dig out the new references to meet some new limitations in your amended claims. If your second OA isn't made final, you should respond to it in the same manner as you responded to the first OA. However, if the second OA is made final—and it usually will be—note the provisions of Rules 113 and 116, which govern what happens after a final action is sent:

Rule 113—Final Rejection or Action

(a) *On the second or any subsequent examination or consideration by the examiner the rejection or other action may be made final, whereupon applicant's … reply is limited to appeal in the case of rejection of any claim (§ 41.31 of this title), or to amendment as specified in § 1.114 or § 1.116. Petition may be taken to the Director in the case of objections or requirements not involved in the rejection of any claim (§ 1.181). Reply to a final rejection or action must comply with § 1.114 or paragraph (c) of this section. …*

(b) In making such final rejection, the examiner shall repeat or state all grounds of rejection then considered applicable to the claims in the application, clearly stating the reasons in support thereof.

(c) Reply to a final rejection or action must include cancellation of, or appeal from the rejection of, each rejected claim. If any claim stands allowed, the reply to a final rejection or action must comply with any requirements or objections as to form.

Rule 116—Amendments After Final Action

(b) After a final … action … in an application …

(1) An amendment may be made canceling claims or complying with any requirement of form expressly set forth in a previous Office Action;

(2) An amendment presenting rejected claims in better form for consideration on appeal may be admitted; or

(3) An amendment touching the merits of the application or patent under reexamination may be admitted upon a showing of good and sufficient reasons why the amendment is necessary and was not earlier presented.

(c) The admission of, or refusal to admit, any amendment after a final … action, … will not operate to relieve the application or reexamination proceeding from its condition as subject to appeal or to save the application from abandonment….

These rules mean, in effect, that "final" isn't final after all. It's just that the rules shift a bit. If you want to continue prosecuting your patent application after a final OA, you must take one of the following actions:

1. Narrow, cancel, or fix the claims *as specified by the examiner.*
2. Argue with and convince the examiner to change position.
3. Try a further amendment narrowing the claims. Such a further amendment should not raise any new issues.
4. Appeal to the Patent Trial and Appeal Board (PTAB), together with an optional Pre-Appeal Request for Review.
5. File a continuation application or an RCE (Request for Continuing Examination) (see Chapter 14).
6. Petition the PTO Commissioner.
7. Abandon the application.

Let's examine these options in more detail.

1. Comply With Examiner's Requirements

If the examiner indicates that the case will be allowed if you amend the claims in a certain way, for example, if you cancel certain claims or add certain limitations to the claim, and you agree with the examiner's position, you should submit a complying amendment similar to the previously discussed amendment. However, instead of stating, "Please amend the above application as follows:" (Form 13-1), state "Applicant requests that the above application be amended as follows:" This is because the clerk won't enter any amendments after a final OA unless the examiner authorizes it.

Generally, no other amendments after a final OA are permitted unless you can show very good reasons why they weren't presented earlier. If your amendment changes the claims in the manner required by the examiner to get them allowed, this will clearly entitle it to entry. You should file your complying amendment as soon as possible, since you have to get the case in full condition for allowance within the three-month period, plus any extensions you've bought. If you file an after-final amendment near the end of the three-month period and the examiner agrees that it places the application in condition for allowance, but the period has expired, you'll have to buy an appropriate extension (Form 13-4): A case can't be allowed when it's technically abandoned. If you file an amendment or argument and it doesn't convince the examiner to allow your case, the examiner will send you an "advisory action," telling you why, and the three-month period will continue to run.

2. Convince the Examiner

You can try to convince the examiner to change position, either by written argument, by phone, or in person. Phone and personal interviews are especially effective because of the multiple feedback loops and give-and-take they provide in a short period. Also, it's more difficult to say no when facing someone, as any salesperson will tell you. Try to come to some agreement to get the case allowed. This is often an excellent, effective choice, especially if you have a friendly examiner and you're willing to compromise. Do this as soon as possible so you'll have time to appeal or file a continuation application, if necessary.

3. Amendment After Final Rejection

You can try a further amendment, narrowing your claims, or submitting other claims, provided you raise no new issues. If the examiner agrees that the amendment narrows or changes the claims sufficiently to place the case in condition for allowance, the examiner will authorize its entry and allow the case. Otherwise, the examiner will send you an "advisory action," reiterating the examiner's former position, and you'll still have the opportunity to exercise the other choices. Even if the examiner doesn't want to enter the amendment because it raises new issues, the advisory action will state whether the amendment will be entered for purposes of appeal. The examiner will enter it for appeal if it places the case in better condition for appeal and neither raises any new issues nor requires further search or consideration.

You should provide your amendment after final as soon as possible. eFiling is preferable. Fax or/and mail can also be used. One reason for the rush: it may save you some money. Ordinarily, you will have three months to respond to the final OA. If you respond later, you will have to buy an extension. However, if you file a response within two months of the final OA, then the extension period starts the *later* of the three-month date and the date the examiner sends the advisory action. (MPEP 710.02(e)(I).) The PTO will try to reply to After-Final amendments within 45 days, so try to file your response within one month of the final OA to save some of the original three months in case the examiner quickly turns around an advisory action. (In all cases you must respond within six months of the final OA, even if your initial quick turnaround lets you buy a shorter extension.)

If you file by mail, do the following with a red marker on paper or faxed filings: (1) mark the upper right of page 1 of your amendment "RESPONSE UNDER 37 CFR 1.116—EXPEDITED PROCEDURE—EXAMINING GROUP NUMBER [insert number]," (2) address the envelope and the amendment "Box AF, Commr. of Pats... [etc.]," and (3) write "BOX AF" in the lower left of the envelope.

If you do file an amendment after a final OA, you should head it "Amendment Under Rule 116," and request (not direct) that the case be amended as follows to place it in condition for allowance. Also comply with the checklist below.

Checklist for Sending an After-Final Amendment

☐ You have completed all points on the checklist for "regular" amendments.

☐ The amendment requests (rather than directs) entry of the amendment.

☐ The claim changes or cancellations either comply with the examiner's requirements or otherwise narrow or revise the claims to obviate the outstanding rejections.

☐ The remarks state and justify why the claim changes, if any, were not presented before.

☐ The claims don't contain any new limitations or radical changes that would raise new issues.

☐ The amendment is being filed as soon as possible after final action.

☐ The first page of the amendment and the envelope (if the amendment is being mailed) are marked in red as indicated above.

---

4. Appeal and Pre-Appeal Request for Review

If you don't see any further way to improve the claims, and if you believe the examiner's position is wrong, you can appeal a final or secondary rejection (not objection) to the PTAB (Patent Trial and Appeal Board), a tribunal of senior examiners (administrative law judges) in the PTO. If the issues are clear, prior to the appeal you can request an appeal conference of senior examiners in your examining division to review the case, hopefully to avoid filing a full brief and sending the case up to the Board.

To appeal, you must file a Notice of Appeal stating that you appeal to the PTAB from the examiner's final action There is no fee for filing an appeal, but there is a fee for forwarding the appeal to the Board, triggered when the examiner files a response to your brief. If you also want an appeal conference (strongly recommended) the Notice of Appeal should be accompanied with a "Pre-Appeal Brief Request for Review" (PTO/AIA/33—no extra fee), plus a "succinct, concise, and focused set of arguments" (no more than five pages at 1.5-line spacing) in support of your position. A copy of a PTO/AIA/33 is provided as Form 13-5 in Appendix 7. When providing the five pages of argument, you can condense your last amendment. You do not have to include the claims. The Notice of Appeal, Pre-Appeal Request for Review, and Focused Set of Arguments may be mailed, but the PTO prefers that you eFile them. The PTO prefers that you use this process only where there are clear errors in fact or law and not where the issues are in gray areas, such as interpretations of the prior art or claim scope. A panel of three examiners, including a supervisor and the examiner of record, will review your arguments and issue a decision to either (1) continue the appeal because they agree with the examiner of record, (2) reopen prosecution and propose changes that will place the application in condition for allowance or advise that a further communication from the examiner will follow, (3) allow the application, or (4) dismiss your request because it fails to comply with the submission requirements. If the panel's decision is alternative 1 or alternative 4, you must file the usual brief and fee within one month from the decision or within two months from the date you filed the Notice of Appeal, whichever is longer.

If you made a pre-appeal request for review and the decision was negative, or if you didn't request an appeal conference, file an appeal brief in triplicate if by mail, or a single copy if by fax or electronically, describing your invention and claims in issue and arguing the patentability of your claims. This brief is due within two months after you file your Notice of Appeal (or as stated above if you requested an appeal conference) and must be in a specific format specified by the Rules. Enclose an Appeal Brief fee.

If you desire it, request an oral hearing and enclose a further hearing fee (see Appendix 4, Fee Schedule). If you want an oral hearing, you'll have to travel to the PTO in Alexandria, Virginia, or ask for a telephone hearing. As always, include a Certificate of Mailing and postcard or Certificate of Faxing with all correspondence that is mailed or faxed.

For information on how to comply with the appeal procedure and write the brief, see Part 41 of the PTO *Rules of Practice* (37 CFR 41).

Appealing to Extend Your Patent's Term

If you want to obtain the maximum term possible for your patent, and three years have elapsed since the filing date of your application (or the filing date of any parent applications if it's a divisional or continuation—see Chapter 14), we recommend that you appeal after the second Office Action if the case is still under rejection, even if your second Action is not a final Action. Why? As stated, under the new laws, your patent will expire 20 years from your first filing date, regardless of when your patent issues. However, the PTO must extend this 20-year term (for up to five more years) from the date you file an appeal until the date of a final decision on appeal, except that if any portion of the appeal period occurs within three years of your filing date, this will not be counted in extending the expiration date (Rule 701).

Thus any time you take to negotiate with the examiner or file another amendment will shorten your patent's term. However, if three years have elapsed after your first filing date, you can avoid this shortening and actually extend your patent's term by filing an appeal and doing any negotiation or filing any amendments while your appeal is pending. If you can't get the examiner to allow the case, just follow through with the appeal by filing a brief and fee within two months after the date you file the notice of appeal. If you do get the examiner to allow the case while it's on appeal, just file a notice withdrawing the appeal; your patent's term will be extended for the time your appeal was active.

After you file an appeal brief, the examiner must file a responsive brief (termed an "Examiner's Answer") to maintain the rejection, and at that point, you will have to pay an appeal fee. To do this, the examiner (and usually two other examiners) must take another good, hard look at your case. Often this review will result in changing the examiner's mind. More commonly, the examiner will maintain the rejection and file an Examiner's Answer. You may then file a reply brief to respond to the Examiner's Answer. You should then file a reply brief within two months of the Examiner's Answer to respond to the Answer.

If you do have a hearing, you will be allowed 20 minutes for oral argument. Sometimes the examiner attends; if so, 15 minutes will be allowed for the examiner's presentation.

If the Board disagrees with the examiner, it will issue a written decision, generally sending the case back with instructions to allow the case. If it agrees with the examiner, its decision will state why it believes your invention to be unpatentable. The Board upholds the examiner in about 65% of the appeals.

If the Board upholds the examiner and you still believe your invention is patentable, you can take a further appeal within 60 days of the date of the PTAB's decision to the Court of Appeals for the Federal Circuit (CAFC) or file a civil lawsuit against the Director of the PTO in the U.S. District Court for the Eastern District of Virginia. The CAFC is located in Washington, but sometimes sits in local areas. The Virginia District Court is in Alexandria, near the PTO. If the CAFC upholds the PTO, you can even request the United States Supreme Court to hear your case, although the Supreme Court rarely hears patent appeals.

Under TRIPS, patents expire 20 years from the filing date of the patent application, but the PTO will extend this term up to five years if delay occurs due to an appeal to the PTAB, the CAFC, or because of an interference. (35 USC 154.)

Appeal briefs aren't easy to write, so we suggest you consult professional help if you want to appeal.

If the examiner has issued a ruling on a matter other than the patentability of your claims—for example, has refused to enter an amendment or has required the case to be restricted to one of several inventions—you have another option. Although you can't appeal from this type of decision you can petition the Commissioner of Patents and Trademarks to overrule the examiner. (See Section 6, "Petitions to the Commissioner for Nonsubstantive Matters," below.)

5. File a Continuation Application or Request Continued Examination

If you have received a final action and you want to have your claims (or new claims) reviewed further in another new round with the examiner, you can file a new "continuation application" or request continued examination in the same application.

Filing a continuation application is a relatively simple procedure involving writing new claims, paying a new filing fee, and sending in a special form requesting that a continuation application examination be prepared. (See Chapter 14 for how to do this.) As explained in Chapter 14, if you file a "regular" continuation application with a new copy of the specification, drawings, and formal papers (Rule 53(b)), you'll receive a new serial number and filing date for the purpose of your patent's duration, but you'll be entitled to the benefit of the filing date of your original application for the purpose of determining the relevancy of prior art. Your application will be examined all over again with the new claims.

An easier approach is to file a Request for Continued Examination (RCE) under Rule 114 (preferable). By filing an RCE you won't have to file a new copy of the specification or drawings and you won't receive a new serial number or filing date. You simply file an RCE form, pay an RCE fee (this is slightly less than a new filing fee), and submit another amendment including an RCE. (See Chapter 14 and form PTO/SB/30.)

If you're filing a continuation, you must actually get it on file before the end of the three-month period or any extensions you buy. You should not use a Certificate of Mailing (CM) with a continuation since, according to the PTO's Rules, a CM isn't effective when an application is being filed; you must actually get it physically on file before the other case is abandoned. The best way to do this is to use Priority Mail Express with a Priority Mail Express certificate or an electronic transmission if you're a registered eFiler. However if you file an RCE, you can fax this or use a CM (which is included on the RCE form).

6. Petitions to the Commissioner for Nonsubstantive Matters

The Commissioner of Patents and Trademarks has power to overrule almost anyone in the PTO or any objection made by an examiner. (The PTAB has jurisdiction over rejections and objections if they're associated with a rejection. See Rules 181–183.) Thus, if the examiner has made an objection that you think is wrong or if you think you've been treated unfairly or illegally, you can petition the Commissioner to overrule a subordinate. For example, if the PTO's application branch (OPAP) has made a ruling regarding your patent application, such as that it's not entitled to the filing date you think you're entitled to (but not a rejection of your claims), you can petition the Commissioner to overrule this ruling.

If you petition the Commissioner for any reason, you must do so promptly after the occurrence of the event forming the subject matter of the petition, and you must make your grounds as strong and as complete as possible. Generally, most petitions must be accompanied by a verified showing and fee. A verified showing is a statement signed by you and either notarized or containing a declaration such as that in the paragraph of Form 10-1 (that starts "I hereby declare ….."). (The petition fee is indicated in Appendix 4, Fee Schedule.)

7. Abandon Your Application

You must take any action in response to a final OA within the three-month period for response or any time extensions you buy (see below); otherwise the application will go abandoned. That is, you must either appeal, file a continuation application, or get the examiner to allow your application within the period for response. However, if you're going to file an amendment or an argument, you should do it as soon as possible, preferably within one month, so the examiner's reply will reach you in time for you to take any further needed action within the three-month period.

If all claims of your application are rejected in the final OA, and you agree with the examiner and can't find anything else patentable in your application, you'll have to allow the application to become abandoned, but don't give up without a fight or without thoroughly considering all factors involved.

If you do decide to allow your application to go abandoned, it will go abandoned automatically if you don't file a timely reply to the final action, since the ball's in your court. You'll be sent a Notice of Abandonment advising you that the case has gone abandoned because you failed to reply to an outstanding Office Action.

If you do abandon the application, that doesn't mean that you've abandoned the invention. If your invention has a unique shape and it hasn't been made available to the public, offered for sale, or sold more than a year ago, consider filing a design patent application on it. Even if a utility or design patent isn't available, it may still be commercially viable; consider trade secret or trademark protection.

K. Interferences and Derivation Proceedings

For patents filed before March 15, 2013, an interference will be instituted to determine priority of inventorship —that is, who will get the patent when two or more inventors are claiming the same invention. Interferences are abolished under the AIA for patents filed after March 15, 2013, the date FTF took effect.

Since FTF took effect, if two patent applications claim the same invention, the later-filed or junior application can be rejected as unpatentable over the earlier-filed or senior application and the inventor in the junior application has no recourse, unless he or she can prove (in a derivation proceeding) that the senior applicant derived the invention from the junior applicant. If a patent claims the same invention as a pending application, and the pending application was filed before the patent, then the claims of the patent can be canceled, unless it is proven that the applicant in the patent application derived the invention from the patentee.

If your application is subject to FTF and you find the patent, and its filing date is earlier than that of your application, you will have to abandon your application, unless you can prove that the patentee derived the invention from you, or unless you can change your claims to focus on a different aspect of your invention. If the patent has a later filing date than yours, it will not be prior art to your application, so you don't have to worry about it.

If you find a patent that is relevant prior art to your invention, but doesn't claim your invention, you should cite it via a supplemental IDS, unless your filing date is earlier than that of the patent.

L. Defensive Publication

If you want to abandon your application, but want to prevent anyone else who files after you abandon it from ever getting a valid patent on it, you can have your invention published privately, either by using a service or by yourself. (See Chapter 14 for details.)

M. If Your Application Claims More Than One Invention

Often patent applications claim several embodiments of an invention, and the PTO will regard these embodiments as separate inventions. The PTO will thus require you to "restrict" the application to just one of the inventions. The theory is that your filing fee entitles you to have only one invention examined.

Also, if two of your claims are directed to one invention, but the examiner feels that the two claims are directed to subject matter that is classified in two separate subclasses, the examiner can require you to restrict the application—that is, to elect one set of claims for prosecution.

Another situation in which restriction may be required occurs when your application contains both method and apparatus claims. Even when both sets of claims are directed to the same invention, examiners often consider them two separate inventions and require you to elect either the method or the apparatus claims.

Generally speaking, it's very difficult to successfully "traverse" (argue against) a PTO-imposed restriction. Fortunately, it's possible to file a second application (called a divisional application—see Chapter 14) if you think pursuing the nonelected claims is worth the cost (new filing fee) and if present indications are that your divisional application will comprise allowable subject matter. You can file the divisional application any time until your first (parent) application issues, and your divisional application will be entitled to the filing date of your parent application. However, you should file any divisional application(s) as soon as possible since, under TRIPS, any patent that issues on the divisional application will expire 20 years from the filing date of the original application in the chain.

One way to overcome a requirement for restriction is to add or include a "linking" claim—a claim that includes features of both inventions. If a linking claim is found allowable, the examiner will drop the restriction requirement. A linking claim is one that includes features of both inventions. For example, product and process claims can be linked by a claim to the product made by the process. While details of linking claims are found in MPEP 809.03, we recommend that you seek professional help in this area.

Another, related situation occurs when you claim several embodiments or "species" of one invention. In the first OA, the examiner may require you to elect claims to one species for purpose of examination; this is to facilitate the search. If you don't get any generic claim allowed—that is, a claim that covers all of your different species—you'll be allowed to claim only the elected species; you can file divisional applications on the nonelected species. (In this case, the PTO will consider each species to be a separate invention.) If you do get a generic claim allowed, you'll be allowed to claim a reasonable number of different species of the invention (Rule 146).

If your application contains claims to more than one invention, you may preempt the examiner by filing a Suggested Requirement for Restriction and an election of the claims that you wish to be examined (Rule 142).

N. The Public May Cite Additional Prior Art Against Your Published Patent Application

Most other countries have a practice under which they permit the public to see pending and allowed applications before they issue in order to give the public a chance to cite prior art or otherwise object to the allowance of the application. This practice has now been implemented in the U.S. by the 18-month publication system. This means, among other things, that if you allow your application to be published after 18 months from filing, you give up the confidentiality of your invention. Copies of any published application can be obtained by any member of the public who wants to download or order them; anyone can then cite prior art against your application upon payment of a fee. The public may cite prior art against your application before the earlier of (1) a notice of allowance, or (2) the later of (a) six months after publication or (b) the first rejection of any claim of the application. The citation must state the relevance of the prior art and pay a fee.

Although there are disadvantages to publication of your application (the cost, the delay, the possibility of more examination, the possibility of fatally damaging prior art being cited against your application, and the loss of any trade secret rights in the application which you could otherwise maintain if the application is not allowed), an application that is published and survives the process will be a stronger patent. Also, a published patent application can be used to recover damages from infringers for infringing activity during the pendency of your application (although such recovery will not occur until after the patent issues).

How to Cite Prior Art Against a Pending Application of Another

If you know of any prior adverse information against a published patent application of another and you want to bring this to the attention of the examiner to prevent the application from issuing, you can cite the art against such application. Use the caption of Form 13-1, filling in as much information as possible, and head the paper "Citation of Prior Art." List and enclose, but do not explain the relevance of the prior art. Be sure to cite the application's Serial Number and the name of the applicant. Under the AIA, you must file the citation before the earlier of (1) six months after the application is published, or (2) the later of (a) six months after publication or (b) the first rejection of any claim of the application. You must send a copy of your citation to the applicant in the published application and pay a Prior-Art Citation Fee (see Appendix 4).

Public Citation of Prior Art

For applications in the fields of computers, software, business methods, and e-commerce, the New York School of Law, in cooperation with the PTO, currently provides a site (www.peertopatent.org) to: (a) enable the public to cite prior art against your application, or (b) cite prior art with comments and without a fee against applications of others. By enabling the public to cite prior art against your application, you will obtain a stronger patent. However, by inviting the public to examine and cite prior art against your application, you also risk losing the application since someone in the public may find and cite fatal art against you.

O. NASA Declarations

If your invention relates to aerospace, the PTO may send you a form letter (PTOL-224) with your filing receipt or after your application is allowed.

The letter will state that because your invention relates to aerospace, you'll have to file a declaration stating the "full facts" regarding the making of your invention. This is to be sure NASA has no rights in it. If you don't file the declaration, you won't get a Notice of Allowance. Fortunately, the PTO now includes a declaration form for you to fill out. Check the appropriate blanks, indicating that you made the invention on your own time, and with your own facilities and materials, and not in performance of any NASA contract, if this is the case.

P. Design Patent Application Prosecution

Design patent application prosecution is much simpler than regular patent application prosecution, and, armed with the instructions of this chapter, you'll find it to be duck soup. Design patent application prosecution will never require anything but the most elementary changes to the specification and claim; the examiner will tell you exactly what to do.

To be patentable, the *appearance* of your design, as a whole, must be unobvious to a designer of ordinary skill over the references (usually earlier design patents) that the examiner cites. If your design has significant differences over the cited prior art, it should be patentable. If not, you'll have to narrow your claim, which can be very difficult in a design application. A claim can be narrowed only by including more limitations, and because you cannot add "new matter" (i.e., brand new lines in the drawing figures) this means you will have to convert existing unclaimed (dashed) lines into claimed (solid) lines. Unless your figures already included such dashed lines upon initial filing—for example, to show portions of your article of manufacture that do not form part of the design— such an amendment will be impossible and you will have to abandon the application.

If the examiner rejects your design as obvious over one or more references, you should use the 102-then-103 attack as explained earlier in this chapter—that is, point out the differences in your design and then argue their importance and significance, albeit from a purely aesthetic viewpoint. To reject a design claim on two or more references, one must look basically like the claimed design. (*In re Harvey*, 29 USPQ2d 1206 (Fed.Cir. 1993).)

If your design case is allowed, you must pay an issue fee (see Appendix 4, Fee Schedule), which makes the design patent effective for a term of 15 years from its date of issue. There are no maintenance fees for a design patent. You can convert a design application to a utility application, or vice versa, by filing a continuing application under 35 USC 120. However a design patent application may not claim priority of a PPA.

Q. What to Do If You Miss or Want to Extend a PTO Deadline

If you miss any PTO deadline—for example, the three-month period to reply to an OA—your application technically becomes abandoned, but you have the right to buy an extension. If your application goes abandoned, or if you want more time to reply to an OA, it can be "revived" or extended in either of the following ways:

• buy an extension, or
• file a Petition to Revive if delay was unintentional.

Let's look at these separately and in more detail.

1. Buy an Extension Before the Six-Month Period Ends (Rules 136(a) and 17(a)-(d))

Most substantive OAs give you three months from their mailing date to reply. Most non-substantive OAs (e.g., a requirement for restriction to one of two inventions) allow only one month. If you don't reply within your designated period, you can send in your reply at any time up to the end of the sixth month (from the date of the OA) by buying an extension of up to five months (if it won't carry you over six months) at the prices indicated in the Fee Schedule. To buy an extension in this manner, eFile, fax, or mail your reply (amendment) by the last day of the extension month, together with a "Petition for Extension of Time under 37 CFR 1.136(a)" (PTO/AIA/22 or Form 13-4), completed as necessary, and a check or credit card charge. It is not necessary to apply in advance. If you fax or mail, make sure you include a Certificate of Faxing or Mailing on your amendment. You should calculate your total number of months from the date of the OA; don't add your extension months to your original due date. For example, assume your OA was mailed 2014 May 12 and provided a three-month period to reply. Your original period expired 2014 Aug 12. You buy a two-month extension. Now, your total period for reply is five months from May 12—that is, you have until 2014 Oct 12—not two months from Aug 12. You should mail your response, petition for extension, and petition fee (which can be quite expensive) by midnight Oct 12. It does not have to go out or be postmarked by Oct 12. Remember that by statute you can't extend any response period beyond six months. Also, you can't buy an extension to send in your issue fee; the three-month statutory period from the Notice of Allowance is not extendable.

2. Petition to Revive If Delay Was Avoidable but Unintentional (Rule 137(b))

If you failed to send in your amendment or issue fee within the three-month period and your delay was "unintentional"—such as, you merely dropped the ball, or misinterpreted the time to reply to the OA— you can still petition to revive the application, albeit at a much higher cost. (Again, this petition can be used for any delay beyond the three-month period but most applicants use it for delays beyond the six-month period because the petition for delays up to six months can be obtained at a cheaper cost using the Extension petition of Form PTO/AIA/22 above.) You should file two papers:

- your reply
- a petition to revive (use PTO/SB/66) with the fee
- if you foreign-filed your application but failed to notify the PTO within 45 days, use PTO/SB/64a to revive the application; the fee is high.

R. Summary

After your application is filed, you will receive an online acknowledgment or receipt postcard in a few weeks and an official filing receipt soon after that, usually with a foreign-filing license that permits you to file abroad before six months has elapsed.

Check the information in the filing receipt carefully and apply for any needed corrections. Your application is now "patent pending" and you can release details if necessary without undue risk. Be sure to file an IDS within three months.

When you receive a first Office Action check it carefully and be sure to respond in the time allotted or any extensions you buy. After you respond you'll receive a second and usually final Office Action or a notice of allowance.

If you didn't file an NPR when you filed the application your application will be published on the PTO's website 18 months after filing and the public can cite new prior art against your application. If the case is allowed you'll have to pay an issue fee and then will receive the patent deed.

During prosecution you can ask the examiner to write claims for you if the invention is patentable. Note that standards of patentability vary widely and the PTO can be unfair, so you should argue against and appeal any rejection you feel is improper.

It's important to avoid making any negative statements on the record, comply with your continuing duty to disclose material information about the invention, avoid amending your claims unless necessary, and consider foreign filing within one year of your filing date. It's often useful to call or visit your examiner. You are not allowed to add any new matter to your application, but you must respond to every point in any Office Action.

To respond to an Office Action first review your application, then the cited references, and then decide what is novel and unobvious about your invention and consider amending the claims to define over the prior art if necessary. When drafting your remarks in the amendment, go through the flowchart and use possible arguments for patentability. Be sure to separate your arguments into novelty and unobvious parts and distinguish between physical novelty and new results.

Your amendment should argue the patentability of your claims. It should not argue the patentability of the inventive idea generally, nor the drawings, or specification.

The PTO requires a specific format for an amendment, with each section starting on a new page and a listing of every claim that was ever in the application. Follow the specific rules for drafting remarks.

The PTO prefers that you eFile the amendment if possible. Otherwise fax your amendment rather than mail it, unless it includes new drawing sheets. If you receive a final action your only options are to appeal, amend the claims as required, interview the examiner to come to an agreement, try a further amendment without raising new issues, file a full or RCE continuation application, or abandon the application. You can petition the Commissioner for nonsubstantive matters.

Design patent application prosecution is similar to utility prosecution, except that the design must be unobvious in the aesthetic sense. If you miss a PTO deadline, you can buy an extension, or petition to revive if the delay was unintentional.

Your Application Can Have Children

Inventor's Commandment 29

Acquire some familiarity with supplemental applications (continuations, RCEs, divisions, continuations-in-part, reissues, and substitutes) if you have a patent application pending, and be aware of the double-patenting trap and the shortening of your monopoly period before filing any such extension application.

A. Available Supplemental Cases

The patent laws and PTO rules allow you to do much more than either get a patent or abandon your patent application. Perhaps a patent application can best be understood by comparing it to a family tree, as shown in Fig. 14A, which shows all of the different extensions you may file.

The Basic Application is like a parent, and just as a parent has children, the parent application can be used to produce offshoots. Depending upon the situation, the parent application is called by many names (for example, "parent," "prior," "basic," or "original" application), while the offshoot applications are referred to as "daughter," "continuation," "divisional," "reissue," "independent," or "substitute" applications.

Note that some extensions come from the bottom point of the Basic Application (BA) or the basic patent. These are "sequential" supplements or extensions since they replace the BA or its patent.

Other supplements come from the sides of the BA; these are "parallel" supplements or extensions since they can exist in addition to the BA or its patent.

The various extensions, starting from the upper left and proceeding down, then the middle and down, etc., are as follows:

- **Division or Divisional Application:** Suppose your examiner held that your BA covered two or more inventions, and required you to "restrict" it to one of these inventions. To cover the other, "nonelected" invention you'll have to file a separate application on it. You do this by filing a divisional application. Your divisional application gets the benefit of the filing date of your BA, but also expires 20 years from your BA's filing date. Your divisional patent can be in addition to your original patent.

- **Continuation Application:** Suppose your examiner sends you a Notice of Allowance (NOA) and you want to try a new and different set of claims, or the examiner sends you a final Office Action (OA), and you want to get another round with the examiner on the same claims, or to try a new and different set of claims. You can do this by filing a new application that "continues" your original application. The continuation application gets the benefit of the filing date of your original application but also expires 20 years from your BA's filing date. A continuation patent can be in addition to your original patent, but it must claim a different invention to avoid double patenting.

- **Request for Continuing Examination (RCE):** Moving down the middle column of the chart, you will see the RCE box. An RCE enables you to purchase another round with the examiner in the same application. Note from the chart that the RCE is like a detour or second chance on the path to a patent.

- **Reissue:** If you've received an original patent, but you want to revise the claims of the patent or correct significant errors in the specification for some valid reason, you should file a reissue application. As indicated, your reissue patent takes the place of your original patent.

- **Continuation-in-Part (CIP):** Moving up to the top of the right column, if you've improved or changed your basic invention in some material way during the pendency of your application, and you want to obtain specific claims to the improvement, you should file a continuation-in-part (CIP) application. As indicated, your CIP patent can exist with your original patent, or your CIP application can replace your BA.

The above four types of applications (Division, Continuation (including RCE), Reissue, and CIP) are called continuing or extension applications because

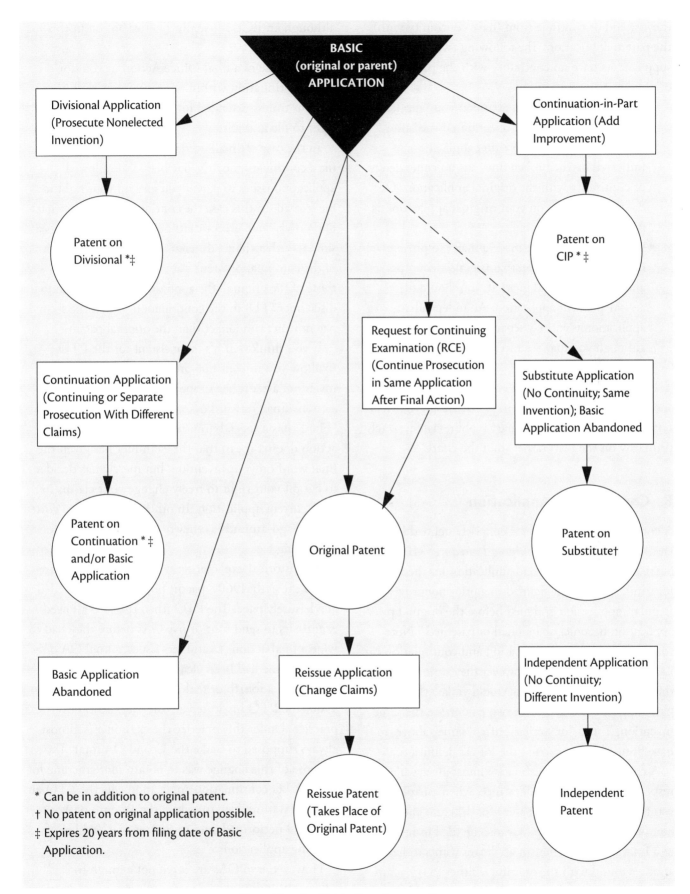

Basic (original or parent) Application

Divisional Application (Prosecute Nonelected Invention) → Patent on Divisional *‡

Continuation-in-Part Application (Add Improvement) → Patent on CIP *‡

Continuation Application (Continuing or Separate Prosecution With Different Claims) → Patent on Continuation *‡ and/or Basic Application

Request for Continuing Examination (RCE) (Continue Prosecution in Same Application After Final Action) → Original Patent

Substitute Application (No Continuity; Same Invention); Basic Application Abandoned → Patent on Substitute†

Basic Application Abandoned

Original Patent → Reissue Application (Change Claims) → Reissue Patent (Takes Place of Original Patent)

Independent Application (No Continuity; Different Invention) → Independent Patent

* Can be in addition to original patent.
† No patent on original application possible.
‡ Expires 20 years from filing date of Basic Application.

Fig. 14A—Available Supplement Cases

they extend or continue from (have continuity with) the parent application. The following two types of supplements have no continuity with the parent or original application.

- **Substitute:** Suppose you abandon your application and later refile a new application on the same invention. The new substitute application, as indicated by the broken line, has no copendency or continuity with the original application. Of course, no patent on your original application is possible.
- **Independent:** If you've made a major improvement in your basic invention that uses new concepts and can really stand by itself, you should file an independent application. An independent application is entirely separate from your BA, although you may refer to your BA in the independent.

Before you decide to file a continuation, etc., you should seriously consider seeing a patent lawyer. Also note that, of necessity, the chart is abbreviated, so rely primarily on the text, rather than the chart.

B. Continuation Application

A continuation application is concisely defined in the *Manual of Patent Examining Procedure* (MPEP), Section 201.07, as "a second application for the same [or similar] invention claimed in a prior nonprovisional [regular] application and filed before the original prior application becomes abandoned or patented." Note that both the original application and continuation can issue as separate patents. However they cannot claim the same invention since this would violate the double-patenting rule that prohibits two patents on the same invention. Thus, "[or similar]" after "same" above, to have been added to expand the PTO's definition.

A continuation application is almost always filed in response to a Notice of Allowance, when an applicant wants to pursue another patent for different claims. A continuation application may also be filed in response to a final rejection when an applicant wants to have another round with the examiner, either to try again to get the existing claims allowed or try new claims,

although an RCE is usually a better option in this circumstance.

In the case of a final Office Action, if you don't file a continuation within the response period (three months unless extended for a fee), you give up your right to file it at all.

In the case of an allowed application, if you don't file a continuation by the day before the allowed application issues to patent you give up your right to file it at all. In this case the continuation is somewhat like a divisional, except that the continuation covers a similar, rather than a different, invention. If the claims of the continuation aren't patentably different from those of the original, the applicant must file a terminal disclaimer (TD) in the continuation so that the second patent won't run longer than the original patent.

If you think that it's inconsistent for the PTO to allow you to continue prosecuting claims to an invention after it has supposedly declared an Office Action "final," a word of explanation is in order. "Final" has a special, unusual meaning. A "final" action doesn't mean that the examiner has given the final word on your invention, but merely has decided to cut off your right to freely change your claims in your current application. In other words, you've gotten as many go-arounds as they're going to give you for your filing fee.

An historical explanation will make it even clearer. Up to the early 1960s, patent prosecution proceeded at a leisurely pace. The PTO (then the PO) allowed examiners to send four or five OAs before they had to issue a final action. Examiners issued a final OA only after an issue had been clearly defined and reached, or if it was a fourth or fifth OA. However, in the late 1960s the PTO instituted a "compact prosecution" practice. Under this practice the examiner is almost always supposed to make the second OA final. The purpose of this change was to obtain more income for the PTO (a continuation application gets the PTO an additional filing fee), to reduce the amount of work the PTO performed, and to shorten the backlog of pending applications.

However, two OAs are often not enough to adequately define the invention, reach an issue with the examiner, and complete the prosecution in a proper manner. Therefore, continuation applications and RCEs are often filed, especially since the RCE process has been made very simple. Because an RCE is much simpler to prepare and costs less to file, it is recommended that you file the RCE instead of a continuation application.

You must file a continuing application like a regular application. The procedure is governed by 35 USC 120 and the PTO's Rule 53(b).

A continuation application must cover the same or a similar invention as the parent or Basic Application (BA). The BA can either be abandoned or can issue after a continuation is filed. The continuation application is entitled to the benefit of the filing date of the parent or prior application for purposes of overcoming prior art.

You can also file a continuation of a continuation. In fact, it's theoretically possible to file an unlimited sequence of continuation applications. The PTO has attempted, but so far failed, to implement rules to limit the number of continuations. Also, if an issue has been reached in a parent application, the examiner can, and often will, make the first OA final in a continuation application or will make the next OA final after a continuation is filed. In other words, a continuation application will be quickly rejected unless you truly come up with a different slant on or definition of your invention that was not previously considered by the PTO.

If you want to delete any inventors when you file a continuation, you may do so by including a simple request on a separate form. All inventors named in the prior application should sign the form.

As with a regular application, you'll receive your email acknowledgment or postcard back with the filing date of (and a new serial number for) your continuation. Thereafter, you'll receive a filing receipt and the first Office Action in due course.

Filing a continuation application is very similar to filing a regular, original application. You must prepare the continuation like an original application—that is, provide a complete new copy of the specification and claims, and drawings. You should amend the specification at the beginning (under "CROSS-

REFERENCE TO RELATED APPLICATIONS") with the following sentence:

"This is a continuation of application Ser. Nr. _____/_____ filed , with title "_____" and naming _____ as inventor(s) [or now Patent Nr. [fill in later], granted [fill in later]], the entire content of which is hereby incorporated herein by reference in its entirety."

If your continuation application claims priority through a chain of previous applications (e.g., BA, continuations, divisions, continuations-in-part), include an appropriate reference to each of those applications, such as:

"The present application is a continuation application of U.S. application serial no. _____/_____ filed, with title "_____" and naming _____ as inventor(s), which is a divisional application of U.S. application serial no._____/_____ filed with title "_____" and naming _____ as inventor(s). All of the foregoing applications are hereby incorporated herein by reference in their entirety."

Rewrite the claims as you want them and number them from number 1, and so forth. Prepare and sign a new patent application declaration (PAD—Form 10-1A), or simply re-file the declaration(s) from the parent application, and an Application Data Sheet (PTO form AIA/14). If you are going to file by mail, fill out a Patent Application Transmittal (Form 10-2) and a Fee Transmittal (Form 10-3) as before. Don't forget the return postcard. You must get the continuation application on file while the parent case is pending, so if mailing it, make sure you allow enough mailing time, or you can use Priority Mail Express with Form 10-2. (Don't use a Certificate of Mailing.) If you want to file the continuation electronically, go to the PTO's electronic filing website and fill out the forms and a new ADS (application data sheet) on your computer and file the specification, claims, drawings, declaration, and ADS in PDF format as before. In the ADS, in the "Domestic Benefit/ National Stage Information," under "Prior Application Status" select "Pending"; for "Continuity Type" select "Continuation of"; and fill in the Prior Application's

Ser. Nr. and Filing date. Your continuation will receive a new serial number and filing date, but it will be entitled to the filing date of the parent case.

You also have to file an IDS again. If you're filing by mail, prepare the cover letter (Form 10-5) and the actual IDS Forms (10-6) (use a photocopy of the IDS in your parent case but change the Serial Number and the filing Date), but you don't have to send iin copies of the references again if your IDS cover letter refers to the IDS in the prior case. Just type the following on Form 10-5:—"Pursuant to Rule 98(d), the references listed on attached Forms SB/08 (A and B) are not enclosed because these were supplied in the parent case, Ser. Nr.____/_____." If you're filing electronically follow the instructions in Chapter 13 for filing an IDS online. You may file the IDS when you file or up to three months later. Of course, you should file a supplemental IDS any time you learn of more prior art to disclose, but generally, the sooner you file the IDS, the better.

TIP

Changing Examiners. If you feel that the examiner in your parent case was unduly tough, it may be possible to get a different examiner in your continuation case by claiming your invention differently. The examining division to which a patent application is assigned is determined by the class and subclass to which the application is assigned. The class and subclass is in turn determined by the subject matter of the narrowest (longest or most specific) claim in the case.

EXAMPLE: Suppose you've invented a new gear for a bicycle and the narrowest claim of your parent case recites the fine details of the gear per se. Your case will be assigned to an examining division in the "gear" arts. If your "gear" examiner is a hardnose, you'll probably be able to get it into bicycles, a different examining division, by adding the bicycle to your narrowest claim. You can do this by providing a "bicycle" preamble for the claim or by actually reciting other parts of the bike in the body of the claim. If your narrowest claim is directed to a bike, your whole case will be classified in the bike division, and you'll have a different examiner.

Obviously, this maneuver can't be done in every instance. You should do some research on the PTO's

Examining Division art assignments (see the "Patent Examining Corps" page of any recent *Official Gazette*) to make sure your end run around a particular examiner will work. Lastly, in an effort to get a new examiner, it also helps to change the title of your invention to one that is commensurate with your revised narrowest claim. For example, change "Gear with Anti-Backlash Pawl" to "— Bicycle Pedal Drive Gear—."

SEE AN EXPERT

Changing examiners is one of several situations where a consultation with a patent attorney or agent may be called for, due to the nature of claims drafting.

CAUTION

20-Year Term. If you file an RCE or continuation application (or a continuation of a continuation) and get a patent on your RCE application or continuation, the patent will expire 20 years after the filing date of your first, original, or parent application. So it behooves you to file any RCE application or continuation as soon as possible and to prosecute it diligently if you don't want your monopoly to be shorter than the former 17-year term. Since any continuing application (continuation, division, or CIP) will expire 20 years from the filing date of its parent case, before filing any continuing application, consider whether you'll really need to rely upon the parent case's filing date. If you're certain that no adverse prior art has issued since the parent's filing date, you can have any new case expire 20 years from its filing date (rather than from the filing date of the original case) if your new case doesn't claim priority of your original case, i.e., if you file it as a regular patent application, rather than as an extension.

C. Request for Continued Examination (RCE)

Requesting a Continued Examination (RCE) of an existing application has the same effect as filing a continuation application but without going through the paperwork of filing a new application. The applicant simply sends in a form, pays an RCE fee, and continues prosecuting the same application. Prosecution continues as if the final office action had been a nonfinal action. In other words, filing an RCE is a way of buying your way out of a final action so you can continue prosecution for one or two more go-arounds, as in the old days.

In order to file an RCE, prosecution in the application must be "closed"—that is, the last OA must have been a final action, a notice of allowance, or some other action closing prosecution. Also, the application must be a regular utility application (not a PPA or design application). When a patent issues on an RCE, the heading of the patent will not indicate that it's based on the RCE.

When you file an RCE, the PTO uses your same file jacket, papers, Serial Number, and filing Date. The procedure is covered by the PTO's Rule 114 and the RCE Transmittal Form (Form 14-1/PTO SB/30).

To file an RCE, simply do the following:
- If filing by mail, complete Form 14-1.
- Prepare a check or CCPF (Form 10-4) for the RCE fee. Note that the RCE fee is less than a new filing fee and is fixed regardless of the number of claims in the application.
- Prepare an amendment containing the new claims you desire to prosecute or check the appropriate block on Form 14-1 if you want to have your Amendment under Rule 116 entered.
- If you file by mail, attach a receipt postcard.

You must send your RCE before the period for response to the final rejection expires or before any time extensions you've bought expire. (For an explanation of purchasing extensions of time, see Chapter 13.) As is the case with an amendment, you can eFile, fax, or mail your RCE request on the last day of the period for response if you complete the Certificate of Mailing section at the bottom of Form 14-1. Because you're not filing a new application, you don't have to use Priority Mail Express, but do mail the RCE with a Certificate of Mailing or Faxing before the period expires. Fax the papers to the PTO's central fax number or mail them to Mail Stop RCE, P.O. Box 1450, Alexandria, VA 22313-1450.

If you're a registered eFiler you can file the RCE electronically at the PTO's Electronic Business site. Convert the completed RCE Transmittal Form (Form 14-1/PTO SB/30), and amendment to PDF and file them as if filing an amendment. Pay the RCE fee on the PTO's site by credit card. You don't have to file a new IDS (unless you have become aware of previously undisclosed prior art) or ADS when you file an RCE.

For the Amendment, complete Form 13-1 exactly as you would do with a regular amendment. Then proceed as usual: Cancel the old claims and insert the new claims in the normal amendment manner, numbered in sequence after the highest numbered claim of the prior application. Under "Remarks," you should state, "The above new claims are submitted to be patentable over the art of record for the following reasons." Then give your reasons and arguments in the same manner as you would for a regular amendment.

Be sure to include all the claims you desire in the amendment, since the next OA after the RCE is filed may be made final if the examiner doesn't cite any new prior art. If you mailed your RCE, you'll receive your postcard back with the filing date of your RCE but no new serial numbers. After that, you'll receive the next Office Action.

Note that Divisional and CIP applications must be filed like a regular application under Rule 53(b). They cannot be filed via an RCE.

D. Divisional Applications

A divisional application or "division" is "a later application for a distinct or independent invention, carved out of a pending application and disclosing and claiming only subject matter disclosed in the earlier or parent application" (MPEP 201.06). You should file a divisional application when (1) the PTO decides that two separate or distinct inventions have been claimed in the parent application (not permitted, since your filing fee entitles you to get only one invention examined), (2) you've agreed to restrict the parent application to the set of claims to one of the inventions, and (3) you want to get a patent on the other, nonelected invention. You don't have to file a divisional application on the other invention, and should do so only if you think it's important enough to justify the expense of a separate application and patent and you think it may be patentable. Divisional applications are so called because they cover subject matter that is "divided out" of the parent case.

A divisional application is entitled to the filing date of the parent case for purposes of overcoming prior art. The parent application of a divisional application can either issue as a patent or become abandoned if you feel the parent is not patentable over the prior art. The divisional must be filed as a complete new application under Rule 53(b), and, like the Rule 53(b) continuation application, will receive its own serial number and filing date for PTO administrative purposes. A patent issuing on a divisional application will show the serial number and filing date of the divisional as well as that of the parent application; thus, the parent's filing date will be the divisional's effective filing date. But remember that the divisional application must be filed while the parent is pending. Also note that you can file a division of a continuation application, and a continuation of a divisional application. (Definitely consult an expert if you get into these murky waters.)

Whether or not you're abandoning the parent case you'll have to proceed under Rule 53(b). To file by mail, send in a complete copy of the divisional application, including an Application Transmittal (Form 10-2), Fee Transmittal (Form 10-3), filing fee, drawings, specification, claims, and abstract, PAD (Form 10-1A), postcard, and optionally an ADS. Optionally, you may also file a Preliminary Amendment. Everything should be the same as if you were filing a completely new application, with the following exceptions:

a. The claims of the divisional application should be directed solely to the invention that you are dividing out of the parent case. So replace the original claims that you filed with the parent case with claims just to the divisional invention. The divisional claims may be some of the claims that you originally included when you filed the parent case, or you may draft new claims in light of the prior art that was cited in the parent case.

b. Add the following sentence to the specification under "CROSS-REFERENCE TO RELATED APPLICATIONS":

"This is a division of application Ser. Nr. _____/_____, filed 20 _____, with title "_____" and naming _____ as inventor(s) [or now patent Nr. [fill in later], granted [fill in later] the entire content of which is hereby incorporated herein by reference."]

If your divisional application claims priority through a chain of previous applications (e.g., BA, continuations, divisions, continuations-in-part), include an appropriate reference to each of those applications, such as:

"The present application is a divisional application of U.S. application serial no. _____ /_____, filed, with title "_____" and naming _____ as inventor(s), which is a continuation application of U.S. application serial no. _____ /_____, filed with title "_____ and naming _____ as inventor(s). All of the foregoing applications are hereby incorporated herein by reference in their entirety."

Also, you should amend the specification to make any editorial amendments you desire, or which you've made in the parent case, but be careful not to add any new matter.

c. Complete the Patent Application Transmittal (Form 10-2). Fill out box 18 to refer to the parent case and to indicate you're filing a divisional.

d. You also have to file an IDS transmittal letter (Form 10-5) and the actual IDS Forms (10-6) (use a photocopy of the IDS in your parent case but change the Serial Number and the Filing Date). Do this when you file or up to three months later. You don't have to file any references again if your IDS cover letter refers to the IDS in the prior case. Just type the following on Form 10-5: "Pursuant to Rule 98(d), the references listed on attached Forms SB/08 (A and B) are not enclosed since these were supplied in the parent case, Ser. Nr. _____ /_____."

To supply drawings for a parallel divisional case (the parent case will be issuing), you have three choices:

1. If you've made formal Mylar film or Bristol board originals of your drawings, you can file very good xerographic copies of these for your divisional's formal drawings.
2. You can file rough xerographic copies as informal drawings and file formal drawings later.
3. If you've made CAD drawings, print out new copies.

If you want to delete any inventors when you file a division, you may do so by including a simple request on a separate form. All inventors named on the prior application should sign.

If you want to file the divisional electronically, prepare your specification, (including new claims directed just to the divisional invention), drawings, and signed declaration, fill out an ADS online, convert them all to PDF, and file from the PTO's Electronic Business site using similar procedures as used when filing a regular application. In the ADS, in the "Domestic Benefit/National Stage Information" portion, under "Prior Application's Status" select "Pending"; for "Continuity Type" select "Division of"; and fill in the Prior Application's Ser. Nr. and Filing date.

> **CAUTION**
>
> **Double Patent Warning.** You're not permitted to obtain two patents on the same invention. If you do, it's called "double patenting," (DP), a situation in which both patents may be held invalid. However, if in your parent case the examiner required you to restrict the application to one of several inventions, there's a special statute (35 USC 121) that helps you. This statute states that if you file your divisional(s) on the nonelected invention(s) after a requirement for restriction, you can do so with total immunity from DP. However, if the examiner didn't require you to restrict, and you're filing your divisional "voluntarily," you must be sure that it's to a clearly different invention than that claimed in the parent case. Otherwise, both patents can be held invalid for DP.
>
> Consult with a patent attorney in the event you (or the PTO) decide that a divisional application is indicated.

> **CAUTION**
>
> **20-Year Term Warning.** The 20-year term warning for continuation applications in Section B also applies to divisional applications.

E. Continuation-in-Part and Independent Applications

As defined in MPEP 201.08, "a continuation-in-part" (CIP) is an application filed during the lifetime of an earlier application by the same applicant, repeating some substantial portion or all of the earlier application and adding matter not disclosed in the earlier application. CIP applications are not common; they're used whenever you wish to cover an improvement of your basic invention, for example, if you've discovered a new material or a better design. (Remember, you can't add these to a pending application because of the proscription on "new matter" discussed in Chapter 13 and mandated by Rule 121(f).)

Generally, a CIP is filed to obtain protection of an improvement, which may be done in parallel with obtaining protection of the base invention. Thus, if you want the parent application to issue, you must be sure that the claims of the CIP application are patentably different—that is, they define subject matter, which is unobvious over that of the parent application. Otherwise the CIP and parent application patent can both be held invalid for double patenting, unless you file a terminal disclaimer.

The advantage of a CIP application over a separate application is that the CIP is entitled to the filing date of the parent application for all subject matter common to both applications. However, if any claims of the CIP cover subject matter unique to the CIP, such claims are entitled to the filing date of the CIP only.

If your "improvement" of your Basic Application is different enough to be unobvious over the basic invention, you can file an entirely separate, independent application, rather than a CIP. However, it's usually better to use a CIP application, since the common subject matter gets the filing date of the parent application.

EXAMPLE 1: Suppose you've invented a bicycle gear with a new shape. You've claimed this shape in a patent application, which we'll call the parent application. After you file the parent application, your research shows you that the gear works much more quietly if it's made of a certain vanadium alloy (VA). The VA isn't patentable over the invention of the parent case and your parent case's claims cover the gear no matter what material it's made of. However, since the VA works much better, you'd like to add a few dependent claims specifically to cover a gear made of the VA. In this way, if there's an infringer who copies your gear made of the VA, you can show the judge that the infringer is infringing your specific as well as your broad claims. Also, you will have specific claims to VA to fall back on if your broad claims are held invalid. You can't add the VA to the specification or the claims of the parent case, since it would be forbidden "new matter." The solution: File a CIP, describing the VA in the specification, keep all of the original claims, and add a few dependent claims that recite that the gear is made of VA. You may need to file a terminal disclaimer in the CIP, since the VA isn't patentable over the invention of the parent case. For purposes of clearing the prior art, your broad claims to the gear shape per se will get the benefit of the parent case's filing date. However, the claims to the gear made of the VA will be entitled only to the later filing date of the CIP.

EXAMPLE 2: On the other hand, suppose your gear shape works well, but you've come up with a related, but unobvious different shape that works better. That is, the new shape is patentable over the invention of the parent case. You should file a CIP with claims to the new shape and continue to prosecute the parent case to a patent. The CIP's claims generally will be entitled to only the CIP's filing date. However, their CIP status will entitle you to refer back to the parent's filing date to show when you came up with the underlying concept common to the parent and CIP gears. This will be useful in case the CIP is ever involved in litigation

or an interference if the CIP was filed before the First-To-File law came into effect.

EXAMPLE 3: Lastly, suppose your gear shape works well, but you come up with an unrelated, and unobvious different shape that works better. You should file a new, independent application, not related to the "parent," with claims to the new gear shape. The two applications would be entirely separate.

CAUTION

Transition Application Warning. If you file a CIP after March 15, 2013, and claim priority to an application filed before March 16, 2013, then your CIP is a "transition" application. If any claim of your transition requires support from subject matter added in the CIP, then the entire transition application will be examined under the less inventor-friendly standards of the America Invents Act (AIA). This is a one-way door: examination will not revert to the pre-AIA standards under any circumstances. Before you file such claims, consider whether the AIA's expanded definition of prior art, and its reduced grace period, will adversely impact the patentability of your claims.

CAUTION

Duty to Inform Patent Office. According to the PTO's instructions for completing the Application Data Sheet (ADS, form 3-4), when filing a transition application you must "inform the Office via a statement if the transition application contains or ever contained a claim that was not supported by the earlier filed domestic benefit or foreign priority application such that the effective filing date of the claim is the actual filing date of the nonprovisional application filed on or after March 16, 2013."

TIP

Easy Way to Inform Patent Office. Newer forms of the Application Data Sheet (ADS) include a box that you may check as a convenient way to make the statement. Be sure to check this box, as appropriate.

You can file a CIP of a continuation or divisional application or vice versa in either case. It's also theoretically possible to file an unlimited number of successive CIP applications to cover successive improvements. There have been rare cases where inventors have filed chains of CIPs with as many as eight or more applications, each of which issued into a patent.

When filing a CIP, you should amend the specification at the beginning (under "CROSS-REFERENCE TO RELATED APPLICATIONS") with the following sentence:

"This is a continuation-in-part of application Ser. Nr._____ /_____ , filed, with title "_____" and naming _____ as inventor(s) the entire content of which is hereby incorporated herein by reference."

If your CIP claims priority through a chain of previous applications (e.g., BA, continuations, divisions, continuations-in-part), include an appropriate reference to each of those applications, such as:

"The present application is a continuation-in-part of U.S. application Ser. Nr. _____/_____, filed, with title "_____" and naming _____ as inventor(s) which is a continuation application of U.S. application Ser. Nr._____/_____, filed, with title "_____" and naming _____ as inventor(s). All of the foregoing applications are hereby incorporated herein by reference in their entirety."

If you are abandoning the parent case, you may claim whatever you want in the CIP, provided that the specification supports the claims. Only those claims that are supported by the specification of the parent case will be entitled to the filing date of the parent case. If the claims of the CIP are patentably different from those of the parent case, and the parent case issues, you don't need to file a terminal disclaimer. If the claims of the CIP are not patentably different from those of the parent case, you must file a terminal disclaimer to avoid double patenting.

If you're filing the CIP by mail, you must use the same procedure (Rule 53(b)) as outlined above for filing a divisional when the parent case will issue, except substitute or check "continuation-in-part" for "divisional" in the Transmittal Letter (Form 10-2) and specification. Don't forget the filing fee and postcard.

If you're filing the CIP electronically, use the same procedure as above for filing a continuation or divisional electronically. Also use the checklist in Chapter 10. The new subject matter in the CIP and any claims directed to it will be entitled to the CIP's filing date, not the filing date of the parent case.

As with continuation and divisional applications, you also have to file an IDS cover letter (Form 10-5) and the actual IDS Forms (10-6) (use a photocopy of the IDS in your parent case but change the Serial Number and the Filing Date). File the IDS when you file the CIP or up to three months later. However, you don't have to send in copies of the references again if your IDS cover letter refers to the IDS in the prior case. Just type the following on Form 10-5:

"Pursuant to Rule 98(d), the references listed on attached Forms SB/08 (A and B) are not enclosed since these were supplied in the parent case, Ser. Nr. _____ /_____."

If you want to add or delete any inventors when you file a CIP, you may do so by including a simple request on a separate form. All inventors named on the prior applications should sign.

If you're filing an independent application (rather than a CIP), do it in the usual manner, except that you can add the following sentence to the CROSS-REFERENCE TO RELATED APPLICATION part of specification:

"This is a continuation-in-part of application Ser. Nr._____ /_____ , filed, with title "_____" and naming _____ as inventor(s), now Patent Nr. _____ , _____ , the entire content of which is hereby incorporated herein by reference."

If you want to abandon any parent case, you can do so in a separate letter or by not responding to an Office Action.

! CAUTION

20-Year Term Warning. The 20-year term warning for continuation applications in Section B also applies to CIP applications.

If You Want to Broaden the Claims by Reissue

If you wish to broaden the claims of your patent through a reissue application, you must do so within two years from the date the original patent issued. Moreover, anyone who manufactures anything between the issue dates of the original patent and the reissue patent that infringes the broadened but not the original claims is entitled to "intervening rights." These preclude a valid suit against this person for infringement of the reissue patent's broadened claims. (35 USC 251, 252.)

> EXAMPLE: Suppose you invent a new gear shape and get a patent, but unfortunately you included an unnecessary limitation in your independent claims as filed, namely they all recite that the gear is made of carbon steel. If you discover your error within a two-year period after your patent's issue date, you can file an application to reissue the patent with broader claims—that is, claims that specify only the gear's shape and not its material. Your patent will be reissued with the broader claims. However, suppose that an infringer (Peg) made gears with your inventive shape, but out of aluminum, between the date of your original and reissue patents. Peg's aluminum gears would not infringe the claims of your original patent, but they would infringe the broader claims of the reissue. Nevertheless, Peg can continue to make her aluminum gears with impunity since she has "intervening rights" by virtue of her manufacture of the aluminum gears in the interim.

Note that a reissue can't be filed to "recapture" subject matter you deliberately gave up in the original case. In the example above, suppose that in your original case you simply recited "a gear" in the claims, but during prosecution you added that the gear was made of nylon to define over the prior art. Since this was a deliberate, conscious act, you aren't permitted to eliminate the "nylon" limitation (and thus "recapture" your broader claims) in a reissue.

F. Reissue Applications

As stated in MPEP 201.05, "A reissue application is an application for a patent to take the place of an unexpired patent that is defective as a result of an error in the patent which was made without deceptive intention." Parts 1400 to 1401.12 of the MPEP discuss reissue applications extensively. Suppose you've received a patent and believe that the claims are not broad enough, that they're too broad (you've discovered a new reference), or that there are some significant errors in the specification. To remedy this, you can file an application to get your original patent reissued at any time during its term. The reissue patent will take the place of your original patent and expire the same time as the original patent would have expired.

To file a reissue application you must:
- Reproduce the entire specification of the original application (a copy of the printed patent pasted one column per page is acceptable), putting brackets around matter to be canceled and underlining matter to be added. When the reissue patent issues, it will include the brackets and underlining.
- Supply a request for a title report on the original patent and offer to surrender the original patent deed.
- Provide a declaration stating you believe the original patent to be wholly or partially inoperative or invalid and referring to and discussing at least one error in the patent. (See Patent Rules 171–179.)

Reissue patents are relatively rare and are identified by the letters "RE" followed by a five-digit number, for example, "Patent RE 26,420."

Although the procedure has been somewhat simplified recently, it is still relatively complicated, so consult a patent lawyer if you are interested in filing a reissue.

> **CAUTION**
>
> **Reissue Warning.** If you file a reissue, the reissue retains the priority date of the original application, but all of the claims of your original patent will be examined and can be rejected. Thus you should consider whether you want to take this chance before filing a reissue.

G. Defensive Publications; SIR Program Abolished

If you want or have to abandon your application but want to prevent anyone else from getting a patent on your invention, you can publish details of your invention to create a prior art reference showing your invention with an effective date as of the date you publish. You can either hire a service to publish the details for you or you can create your own publication. Two services are DefensivePublications.org and IP.com. You can also publish the details of your invention on your own website or go to a fee-based publisher (vanity press) to have a book about your invention published. If you create your own website, it will be a good defense if any later-filed patents are asserted against you. However, if you use a service, the patent examiners are more likely to search it and use it to reject any such later-filed patents. While the effective date of publication will be later than your filing date, the cost is low and the later date won't make any difference unless someone has filed on the same invention before you published it.

The PTO used to have a defensive program called a "Statutory Invention Registration" (SIR) under which an inventor could abandon a patent application yet pay a fee to have the PTO publish it to create a prior-art reference as of the filing date of the application in order to preclude anyone else from obtaining a patent on the invention, provided they didn't file an application on the invention before you. However the AIA abolished the SIR program as of 2012 Sep 16.

H. Substitute Applications

The term "substitute" is defined in MPEP 201.09 as "any application which is in essence the duplicate of an application by the same applicant abandoned before the filing of the later application." A substitute (also called a "re-file") can be filed for the same purpose that you can file a continuation, division, or CIP. That is, you can file a substitute to continue prosecution that you didn't complete, to cover a different invention, or to cover an improvement invention.

A substitute application doesn't get the benefit of the filing date of the earlier case. This is because it wasn't filed while the earlier case was pending. Thus any prior art that issues after the filing date of the earlier case and before the filing date of the substitute case is good against the substitute case. Suppose, however, that you somehow abandon your application (not your invention) and you can't successfully petition the Commissioner of Patents to revive the application. You still may be able to cover your invention by filing a substitute application, assuming significant prior art hasn't been published in the meantime.

There are no special forms or procedures for filing a substitute application; just file it like you would a regular patent application, except that you can add a reference in the specification to the prior case. As stated, you won't get the benefit of your prior case's filing date. However, the date of the parent case may be useful for applications filed before FTF went into effect (March 16, 2013) in case you have to swear behind a reference or prove earlier conception and/or reduction to practice, such as in case of an interference. If your substitute application issues into a patent, the patent will expire 20 years from the filling date of the substitute.

I. Double Patenting and Terminal Disclaimers

Double patenting (DP) is a situation that exists when one person or entity obtains two patents on the same invention, or on two inventions that are not patentably distinct. It's very important to avoid DP, since both patents can be held invalid by a court. Also, if the PTO sees that you have two applications pending that aren't patentably distinct, they will reject them on the grounds of potential DP. Thus, you must always be aware of the DP trap whenever you file a second case on any invention.

There are two types of DP: statutory DP and non-statutory (or "obviousness-type") DP.

In statutory DP, the two patents cover the same invention. This situation is prohibited by 35 USC 101, which says that "Whoever discovers any new and useful [invention] … may obtain a patent therefor …." This means that an inventor may obtain only one patent for an invention, not two patents. Statutory-type double patenting is absolutely prohibited and cannot be overcome by a terminal disclaimer.

In obviousness-type DP, an inventor obtains two patents on respective inventions that are not identical, but that are also not different enough to be considered unobvious over each other. This situation is prohibited by judicial decisions, because a second patent could historically extend the inventor's monopoly beyond the expiration date of the first patent. However, obviousness-type DP can be overcome by filing a terminal disclaimer (TD) in the later application so that any patent issuing on it will not extend beyond the expiration date of the first patent. It is important to ensure that both patents will continue to be owned by the same entity. (Rules 130(b) and 321(b).) Also, obviousness-type DP can be avoided if your examiner has required restriction. As explained in Section D, above, under "Double Patent Warning," a special statute (35 USC 121) states that you have total immunity from DP if you file a divisional after the examiner required restriction.

Under a TD, you agree to give up the terminal (end) period of your second patent so that both patents will expire on the same date, and will continue to be commonly owned, thereby eliminating the harm to the public interest (extension of monopoly beyond normal term or prohibiting a second patent that is not patentably different from issuing to a different entity) of double patenting. If you feel brave enough to venture into this area alone, TD forms and the filing fees are available on the PTO's website.

J. Summary

A patent applicant can file a number of possible supplements from an original, parent, or base patent application. If the base application has two or more inventions and is restricted to only one of these inventions, a *divisional application* may be filed to cover the other invention. If you've gotten a final action in the base application and want to submit new claims and continue prosecution, you may file a *continuation application* or a *request for a continuing examination* (RCE). If you develop an improvement on the invention of the base application and want to claim it specifically and still keep the filing date of the base application for the base invention, you may file a *continuation-in-part application* (CIP). The divisional, continuation, RCE, and CIP all get the benefit of the filing date of the base application, but also expire 20 years from the base application.

If you come up with a substantially different improvement or new invention, it's best to file an *independent application*.

If you get a patent and discover an error in it, such as claims that are too narrow, you can file a *reissue application* to have the patent reissued. The reissue patent takes the place of the original patent and expires when the original patent would have expired. You cannot use a reissue patent to claim (recapture) subject matter that you voluntarily gave up in the original case; any reissue with broader claims must be filed within two years from the original patent and is subject to the intervening rights statute.

If you can't get or don't want to get a patent on an invention, but want to prevent someone else from getting a patent on it, you can defensively publish your application privately by using a service or by creating your own paper or Web-based publication. (The Statutory Invention Registration (SIR) has been abolished.)

If you abandon your application and want to file on it again, you will have to file a *substitute application*; such an application has no connection to the base application. No one may legally receive two patents for the same invention since this would constitute statutory *double patenting*. Also no one may legally receive two patents for two inventions that are not patentably different since this would constitute *obviousness-type double patenting*. However *obviousness-type double patenting* can be avoided by filing a terminal disclaimer so that the two patents will expire at the same time.

After Your Patent Issues: Use, Maintenance, and Infringement

> **Inventor's Commandment 30**
>
> Once your patent issues, check it for printing errors, consider patent marking if you manufacture a product covered by the patent, be alert for infringements, and pay three maintenance fees (3.0 to 3.5, 7.0 to 7.5, and 11.0 to 11.5 years after issue) to keep it in force. You should also monitor all products in the field of your patent to discover any possible infringements.

A. Issue Notification

Four to six weeks after you pay the issue fee, you'll usually receive an Issue Notification. This will indicate the number and issue date of your patent (commonly about two weeks after you receive the notice). On the issue date, which will usually be a Tuesday, the patent will be granted, published, and mailed to you so that several days later you'll receive your patent deed (also called "letters patent"). This consists of a copy of your patent on stiff paper, a fancy jacket with a seal, and ribbon. You'll also receive (separately) the printed copies of your patent if you ordered them when you paid your issue fee. The *Official Gazette–Patents*, which is usually published electronically on the Tuesday of grant, will list the highlights of your patent. (The PTO publishes patent applications, in which a Nonpublication Request has not been filed, online every Thursday.) Be sure to file any continuation or divisional applications before the day the patent issues, or you will lose the ability to do so.

B. Press Release and Marketing

You may wish, when you learn the number and date of your patent, to prepare a press release about it. See any book on advertising to learn how to prepare a press release; it should cover the six facets of reporting: *who* received the patent (and *who* do you contact for more information)?; *what* is the invention?; *where* is the patent owner located?; *why* is there a need for this invention?; *when* will the product or service be available?; and *how* does the invention work? Make your headline and text simple and short yet interesting

and catchy—for example, "Midgeville Inventor Gets Patent on Jam-Free Bike Mechanism." Be conversational; don't use jargon or technical language. Type on only one side of the paper, double spaced, and include your name, address, phone number, and "For Immediate Release" at the top. Type "###" at the end to signal the end of the press release. Send the PR to your local papers and trade magazines (each with a copy of your patent) on the day you get the patent.

C. Check Your Patent for Errors

After you receive your patent, proofread it carefully, preferably aloud with a friend or coworker. Carefully examine the information in the heading of the patent—serial number, filing date, title, your name, etc.—to make sure all is correct. Then read the patent word for word and compare it with the application in your file as amended during the prosecution phase. If you find errors, you have several possible courses of action.

1. If the Errors Aren't Significant

If the errors aren't significant, that is, if the meaning you intended is obvious and clear, the PTO may not issue a Certificate of Correction, but you should make the error of record in the PTO's file of your patent. To do this, simply write a "make-of-record" letter to be put in the file of your patent, listing the errors you found. This letter should be captioned similarly to Form 15-1 with the patent number, issue date, and patentee(s) name(s) and should be headed, "Make-of-Record Letter for Errors in Printed Patent." It should then list all the errors in the patent. File the letter by mail, fax, or online if you're a registered eFiler.

2. Certificate of Correction

If any of the errors you discover are significant, that is, if the meaning is unclear because of a wrong reference numeral, missing or transposed words, failure to include a significant amendment, any errors in the claims, etc., you may obtain a Certificate of Correction. If the errors are the fault of the printer, the PTO will issue the Certificate of Correction free.

If the errors are your fault, that is, they appear in your file as well as in the printed patent, you still can get a Certificate of Correction. However, the error must be of a clerical or minor nature and must have occurred in good faith. Examples are a wrong reference numeral or an omitted line or word. (The fee for a Certificate of Correction to fix your error is listed in Appendix 4, Fee Schedule.) To obtain a Certificate of Correction (printer's fault or yours), do the following:

Step 1: Fill out Forms 15-1 and PTO/SB/44 (or Form 15-2 in Appendix 7). In Form 15-1 (the request letter), insert the patent number, issue date, patentee(s), Ser. Nr., filing date, and the date you mailed the form. Check paragraph 2 if the error is the fault of the PTO; check paragraph 3 and insert the amount from the Fee Schedule if the error is your fault.

In either case (whether you checked paragraph 2 or 3), in paragraph 4 list the places in the application file where the errors occurred and explain who was at fault; for example:

"4. Specifically, on p. 4, line 12, of the specification, applicant erroneously typed '42' instead of '24' and neither applicant nor the examiner detected this error during prosecution."

or

"4. Specifically, on p. 4, line 12, of the specification, the reference numeral '24' has been erroneously printed by the GPO in the patent as '42' instead of '24.'"

Step 2: Go to the PTO Forms webpage and save the fillable version of PTO/SB/44 to your computer (or tear out Form 15-2 from Appendix 7). Fill in the patent number, issue date, and inventor(s). In the body of the form, describing each correction in a sentence beginning with the word "Column" or "Col." and use semicolons to separate corrections if more than one in a column. Indicate the necessary corrections to the actual printed patent by (a) putting quotes around existing words to be changed, deleted, or followed by

words to be added, and (b) sandwiching words to be inserted with dashes. For example:

"Col. 3, line 54, change 'the diode' to — varistor 23—."
"Col. 4, line 21, after "a" insert —red—.
"Col. 5, line 58, delete "the former."

Put your return address and the patent number on the bottom of the form.

Step 3: If you're a registered eFiler you can file the Request and the Certificate by EFS-Web, but if not, send one copy of completed Form 15-1 and two copies of completed Form 15-2 to Commissioner for Patents, Office of Data Management, ATTN: Certificate of Correction Branch, P.O. Box 1450, Alexandria, VA 22313-1450, with a receipt postcard, and a check for the correct amount if the error was your fault. You'll get an approved copy of your Certificate of Correction back in several months and the PTO will affix copies of it to the copies of your patent that it maintains in its storage facilities and will include the Certificate as the last page of the patent on its Internet site.

D. Patent Number Marking

If you already have sales blurbs promoting your invention, change them to indicate that your invention is "patented" rather than "patent pending." If you, or a licensee of yours, are manufacturing a product embodying the invention, you should consider marking your product with the patent number.

A section of the patent laws (35 USC 287) states that products embodying a patented invention may be marked with the legend "Pat." or "Patent," followed by the patent number. In addition, patent law allows patentees to simply mark the product with a reference to a website and list any applicable patent numbers on the site, that is, "Patented—see www.JonesWidgets.com for patent numbers." If you make or sell products embodying your invention that are properly marked, you can recover damages from any infringers you sue from the date you began marking, whether they see your notice or not. If you make or sell products but don't mark them with your patent number, or mark them "Patented" without the number, your rights are reduced and you can recover damages only from the date you notify the infringer of infringement, or from the date you file suit against the infringer, whichever is earlier.

You should do the actual marking on the product itself, on its package, or by means of a label affixed to the product.

Suppose you don't manufacture any product embodying the invention, or if the invention relates to a process that's not associated with a product and hence can't be marked. In these cases you can recover damages from an infringer for the entire period of infringement without marking.

The disadvantage of patent marking is that any sophisticated person who wants to copy your product can easily see the number of your patent, order the patent, read its claims, and attempt to design around the claims of your patent. If you don't mark your product, the potential infringer can still probably get this same information, but only through a lot more expense and effort. In other words, by not marking you may depend in part on human inertia to protect your invention from being copied. Many companies, therefore, favor *not* marking their patented products, or simply marking them "Patented" without including the number. They rely on their own familiarity with the field to enable them to quickly spot and promptly notify any infringer of the existence of the patent.

In the past anyone who marked a product falsely could be sued by a private party and subject to substantial damages, even if the private party was not injured by the false marking. Now, under the AIA, only the government can sue for such false marking, although private parties can still sue anyone who marks falsely to recover compensatory damages, that is, damages that the private party incurred due to the false marking. In any case, to avoid the possibility of lawsuits from the government or a private party, be sure that you don't mark any products with incorrect, inapplicable, or expired patent numbers. Of course, if your patent expires or is found invalid or unenforceable, be sure to omit that patent number from any patent marking.

E. Advertising Your Patent for Sale

If you haven't licensed or sold your invention by the time your patent issues, you can advertise the availability of your patent for license or sale on the Internet or in one or more of several publications, such as:

- *Official Gazette for Patents*, Commissioner for Patents, P.O. Box 1450, Alexandria, VA 22313-1450
- *The Wall Street Journal, U.S.A. Today*, local newspapers in large cities, etc.

Contact the publications for listing information and fees.

The Internet provides many opportunities for advertising your invention and many sites provide methods for listing inventions for sale or license including Patent Auction (www.patentauction.com). Intellectual Ventures (www.intellectualventures.com) buys patents from inventors. Keep in mind that the number of patentees who make successful contacts by advertising their patents is relatively low. Your chances of a successful nibble will be far greater if you use the targeted, individual approach described in Chapter 11.

F. What Rights Does Your Patent Give You?

Now that you've actually obtained a patent, you'll undoubtedly want to know exactly what rights you receive under it.

1. Enforceable Monopoly Against Manufacture, Use, Sale, Offer for Sale, Importing, Etc.

The grant of a patent gives you, or any person or entity to whom you "assigned" (legally transferred) your patent or patent application, a monopoly on the invention defined by the claims of the patent. The monopoly begins with the patent's date of issuance and expires 20 years (plus any extension granted by the PTO), from the date you filed your application (or the first application in the chain if your patent issued from a division, continuation, or continuation-in-part). (For applications filed before 1995 Jun 8 and issuing thereafter, the term is the greater of the 17- or 20-year term. The PTO will extend any term if you encountered a delay due to PTO delay, FDA processing of a new drug or medical device application, an appeal, an interference, or a secrecy order. (35 USC 154 and 156.)) If the PTO published your patent application—usually 18 months after filing (unless you requested earlier publication)—and you actually notified an infringer of your patent application, you can recover damages from the infringer from the actual date of notification. (35 USC 154(d).)

Your monopoly gives you the right (35 USC 271) to bring a valid suit against anyone who does any of the following during the term of your patent:

1. Makes, uses, offers to sell, sells, or imports the invention defined by the claims of your patent. (There is a DNA exemption that is too complicated to cover here. See 35 USC 271(e)(1).) Note also the medical exemption discussed below.
2. Files a new drug application on your invention in the U.S.
3. If your U.S. patent covers a process, imports a product made abroad by your patented process.
4. Induces infringement of your patent.
5. Offers to sell, sells, or imports a material component of your patented machine or process made especially for use in infringement of your patent and not a staple article of commerce with substantial noninfringing use.
6. Supplies in or from the U.S. a substantial portion of the components of your patented machine for assembly outside of the U.S.

You can use your ownership of the patent to obtain value in any of seven ways:

1. Sell the patent outright.
2. License others to make, use, and/or sell the patented invention in return for royalties under a variety of conditions, subject to the antitrust laws mentioned in the note below.
3. Create a monopoly by preventing anyone else from making, using, or selling the invention. In this case you would manufacture the invention yourself (or have it manufactured for you) and charge more than could have in a competitive situation. Xerox did this in the early days of photocopiers. In other words, a patent will give you the right (within limits) to fix the price of your product—a capitalist's dream!

4. If accused of patent infringement by the owner of another patent, you may be able to assert your patent against the other patent holder and generate a cross-licensing arrangement to avoid paying royalties or having to stop infringing.
5. You can tout your patent in advertising.
6. The patent is a publication (as of its filing date or the filing date of any PPA or foreign patent application from which the patent claims priority) that will prevent others from patenting the same thing.
7. While a patent does not give you any immunity from infringing others' patents, if you are manufacturing anything and another patent holder charges you with infringement, you can sometimes use the patent to (a) show that your products are separately patentable and thus are not direct copies, and (b) prevent the infringer from using the doctrine of equivalents.

Extending the Effectiveness of Your Patent

If you want to continue to make money from your creativity after your patent expires, you should plow back some of your royalties or proceeds from the sale of the patent for research. In this way you can invent further developments and improvements, and thereby get more and later patents so as effectively to extend your monopoly beyond its relatively short term. You can even file a new patent application on the improvements when you invent them, but withhold the introduction of products with the improvements until you've milked the market with the basic products. DuPont did this with its *Teflon* and *Teflon II*.

TIP

Antitrust Note. Occasionally, companies or individuals who own a patent or manufacture a patented invention use their patent to extend their monopoly in ways that violate the antitrust laws. For example, compulsory package licensing, compulsory price fixing, and other practices that impose undue restraints on free trade all violate the antitrust laws. This is very rarely a problem for the independent inventor but can occasionally raise problems for large corporations.

2. Property Rights

The law considers a patent to be personal property that its owner can sell, give away, or otherwise dispose of. It can even be seized by your judgment creditors, just like your car, a share of stock, or any other item of personal property. Although it's personal property, the actual patent deed you receive from the PTO has no inherent value; thus you need not put it in your safe-deposit box or take any steps to preserve it against loss. Your ownership of the patent is recorded in the PTO (just like the deed to your house is recorded by your county's Recorder of Deeds). If you lose the original deed, you can download copies, or the PTO will sell you copies of the printed patent (certified if you desire) and/or certified copies of a title report showing that you're the owner.

A Calculator That Determines Expiration Dates and Maintenance Fee Dates

If you are uncertain as to the expiration date of a patent, there's an online Patent Calculator (www.ssjr.com) that can help. Under the "Calculators" heading in the lower-right portion of the home page, enter your patent's Application File Date and Issue Date. If your patent issued from a parent application, enter the filing date of the originally filed parent application in the blank next to Earliest Effective Filing Date. Enter any Term Adjustment if an adjustment was granted by the USPTO. The calculator will then calculate the expiration date and maintenance fees for your patents.

---

3. Medical Procedure Exemption

A few years ago, one physician sued another for infringement of a patented ophthalmic surgery technique. This upset the medical establishment, which used its considerable clout to get a federal statute enacted that exempts health care providers (for instance, doctors,

nurses, and hospitals) from liability for performing medical procedures covered by in-force patents. (35 USC 287(c).) In view of this statute, it no longer makes sense to patent medical procedures, as such. However, the statute still allows patent owners to sue health care providers for any activity that infringes a patent on (a) a device, (b) a drug, (c) the use of a drug or device, or (d) a biotechnology process invention.

G. Be Wary of Offers to Provide Information About Your Patent

Soon after being awarded a patent, you may receive an offer by mail, advising that an "article" about you patent was published and offering to send you a copy of the article for a fee. What you'll probably get is a photocopy of a page from the PTO's *Official Gazette*, showing the usual main drawing figure and claim of the patent! Keep in mind that new rackets originate all the time. Another offer very frequently received by patentees, usually about a year or more after their patent issues, comes as a postcard, such as in Fig. 15A. It's an offer with marginal utility to most inventors, and at a very high cost. You can find the information by searching the USPTO patent database.

A third offer is the "Patent Certificate." This offer is sent to many patentees in an official-looking letter from Washington, marked "U.S. Patent Certificate," "For Official Use Only" (next to the postage stamp), and "Important Patent Information." In reality, it's from a private company that wants to sell you a nicely framed version of your patent. Needless to say, this product has no official value.

A fourth offer, definitely of questionable value, also comes on a postcard that states something similar to the following: "Our search of your patent has located X companies that manufacture, market, or sell products in a field allied to your invention." It offers to sell you the names of the X companies for a stiff fee.

A fifth offer is to include you in a compendium of inventors, such as a "Who's Who" of inventors, or an offer to sell you such a volume with your name included.

Be sure to investigate and think about it carefully (or ask a trusted adviser) before you follow up on any offer.

Important Notice

To: *Owners of U.S. Patent # 4688283* _____

Assignor

Our search of your U.S. patent shows the ____[#]____

most recent patents, issued after your patent, that the U.S. Patent Office has classified identically or cross-referenced in the same class and subclass as your patent.

You may want to determine if your patent dominates the later patents, the activity of competitors, and the latest state of the art.

For each of the later-issued patents we will send you the patent no., an abstract, a drawing, plus address-information on the inventor, and/or the owner or manufacturer for $1.00 each, plus a service charge of $60.00 if you return **THIS CARD** (or a copy) with your payment of $96.00. Make check or money order to

_____**(Name)**_____ payable on a **U.S. Bank.**

Or send $60.00 for a list of later patent numbers.

CD 60

1-2-3-4-1 *Providing Patent Information Since 1976* 1-2-3-4-2

Fig. 15A—Postcard Offer of Dubious Value

H. Maintenance Fees

Under the U.S. maintenance fee (MF) system, your patent, when granted, will subsist in force for 20 years from the filing date of its application, provided three maintenance fees are paid.

If you don't pay any MFs, your patent will expire four years from grant. If you pay a first MF between years 3.0 and 3.5 from grant, the PTO will extend the patent to expire eight years from grant. If you pay a second (much higher) MF between years 7.0 and 7.5, the PTO will extend the patent to expire 12 years from grant. And if you pay a third and final (much higher yet) MF between years 11.0 and 11.5, the PTO will extend the patent to expire 20 years (plus any extension the PTO has granted), from filing. This information is presented in Fig. 15B, an MF timing chart. The adjustable arrow indicates that the expiration date varies, depending upon the length of pendency of the application. The online calculator will calculate your maintenance fees for you.

To help you remember when to pay your MFs, I've provided an MF Reminder Sheet as Form 15-3; a sample is completed in Fig. 15C. You should copy this sheet and fill it out in ink—except write the year of MF I (three years after issue) in pencil on

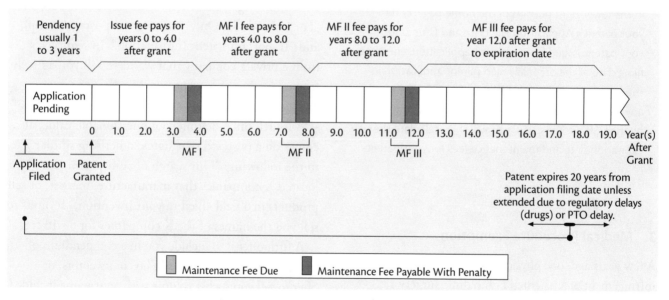

Fig. 15B—Maintenance Fee Timing Chart

Maintenance Fee Reminder

Next fee due: __2018__ / __7__ / __16__
$\qquad\qquad\qquad$ yr $\qquad$ mo $\qquad$ date

(Write year in pencil and change after each payment)

Patent Nr.: ___8,032,015___ $\qquad$ Issued: ___2007/7/16___

Application Serial Nr.: ___07/427,862___ $\qquad$ Filed: ___2005/10/27___

Title: ___"Auto mirror with valve"___

Patentee(s) (Inventor[s]/Applicant[s]): ___T.R. Jones___

Assignee(s) (if any): ___T.R. Ltd.___

Expires ___2025/10/27___ $\qquad$ (if all three maintenance fees are paid).[1]

☒ Small entity status was filed in application or patent.
$\quad$ (If not, large entity fees[2] must be paid.)

Maintenance Fee Number	Fee Due		Sent Form & Check [4]	Amount	Received Receipt Statement
	From:	To:			
I. Due 3.0 - 3.5 YAI [3]	10 / 7 / 16	11 / 1 / 16	11 / 8 / 16	$ 320	11 / 9 / 15
II. Due 7.0 - 7.5 YAI	14 / 7 / 16	15 / 1 / 16	14 / 8 / 12	$ 1,020	14 / 9 / 14
III. Due 11.0 - 11.5 YAI	18 / 7 / 16	19 / 1 / 16	/ /	$	/ /

Notes: _____

_____

_____

_____

_____

_____

_____

_____

_____

_____

_____

[1] For applications filed after 1995 June 7, expiration is 20 years from filing date of application, or from any earlier domestic nonprovisional (regular) application from which it claims priority, plus any adjustment (extension) granted by the PTO.

[2] Please check all fee amounts before paying, since PTO fees change often.

[3] YAI = Years After Issue date.

[4] Send or make Internet payment at least a month before due date to allow time to take corrective action before entering grace (penalty) period in case PTO does not accept payment.

Fig. 15C—Maintenance Fee Reminder (Form 15-3 in Appendix 7)

the top line and leave the last three columns in the table blank. Put the sheet at the end of your current year's calendar. Keep moving it ahead to the end of each new year's calendar at the end of each year, until the third year after issue when the fee is due. Write that the MF is due on the appropriate date on your calendar for the third year. Fill in the last three columns in the table. When you pay the first fee and receive your receipt statement, change the year at the top of the sheet to the seventh year after issue and repeat the process.

If you forget to pay any fee during its normal six-month payment period, you can pay it in the six-month period (grace period) following its normal six-month payment period. However, as always, whenever you miss a PTO date you must pay a penalty or surcharge. If you pay a maintenance fee in the grace period, infringers do not acquire "intervening rights"—see below.

If you forgot to pay a maintenance fee in the normal and grace periods, the patent will expire at the end of the grace period. However, an expired patent can be revived on petition if you show, by declaration, that the delay was "unintentional" (Rule 378(c)).

An "unintentional" petition (PTO/SB/66 if filing by mail, or EFS-Web PTO/SB/66 if filing electronically) must merely state the nonpayment was unintentional. You must accompany the petition by the MF, the MF transmittal letter, and a very high "unintentional" fee (see Appendix 4, Fee Schedule). The form is self-explanatory; just be sure to pay the fee for appropriate entity size. If you previously claimed small-entity status, but no longer qualify as a small entity, be sure to check the appropriate box.

If any infringement occurred or was prepared for after the patent expired and before it was revived, the infringer has "intervening rights." This means that the infringer can continue any infringing activity performed in the lapse period as if the patent were not revived. (35 USC 41(c).)

The easiest way to pay an MF is with a credit card through the PTO's website. Go to the PTO website (www.uspto.gov) and click "Patents." Next, click "Fees and Payment," "Patent Maintenance Fees Storefront."

At this point you must enter the patent number and the application serial number. You can find out how much is currently due by clicking "Retrieve Fees to Pay" or you can view the payment dates by clicking "View Payment windows." After that, click "Pay Using Credit Card" and complete the form by supplying your credit card information. The PTO will present a Maintenance Fee Statement (receipt) on the website showing receipt of payment. Print out the Statement for your records.

If you don't want to pay the fee online, use Form 15-4 or PTO/SB/45 to pay the maintenance fees. Complete every blank in the form including the serial number of the application, or the PTO won't accept your fee and the delay may carry you into the grace period, costing you a surcharge. (If you've assigned or licensed your patent to a large entity, check "large entity" on Form 15-4 and pay the large-entity fee.) If the PTO accepts your maintenance fee, they'll send you a Maintenance Fee Statement to this effect.

If you use the Certificate of Mailing at the end of the form, you can send in the fee on the last day of the period. If the last day of the period falls on a Saturday, Sunday, or holiday, it's extended to the next business day. And don't forget a postcard! Of course, if you feel, at any time a maintenance fee is due, that your invention's prospects have become nil, you shouldn't pay the fee. In this case, your patent will expire as indicated above.

The PTO won't accept a maintenance fee before its due period and usually sends you an MF reminder only after the due period expires, when you're in the six-month grace (penalty) period. They also usually send you a Notice of Patent Expiration if you don't pay the fee in either the regular or grace periods. The PTO publishes the numbers of lapsed patents in the *Official Gazette* and on its website. If you move, you must notify the PTO of your new address with a separate letter or PTO/AIA/123 sent to Mail Stop Post Issue, Commissioner for Patents, P.O. Box 1450, Alexandria, VA 22313-1450; otherwise the PTO will send your MF receipt to your old address (even if you put your new address on your MF transmittal).

I. Legal Options If You Discover an Infringement of Your Patent

If you find an infringer, you may wish that the earth would shake, the skies thunder, and a mighty lightning bolt would come down and vaporize the miscreant. Failing this, you might wish that you could present details of the infringement to the PTO and they will get on a white horse, ride out to the infringer, and strike them down with the sword of justice. In fact, nothing will happen and the infringement will continue unless you affirmatively do something about it. The PTO plays no role in infringement situations. The PTO is in the business of simply issuing patents and doing whatever ancillary functions are necessary. The patent owner must assume the full burden for stopping the infringer and obtaining damages.

Here, viewed broadly, are the steps you can take to get the remuneration you deserve:

- Ask the infringer to stop infringing and pay you compensation for the past infringement (but see the warning below regarding declaratory judgment actions).
- Ask the infringer to pay you compensation for past infringement and royalties for future activity.
- Ask the infringer to buy your patent for a sum that will cover past infringement and the present value of future activity.
- If you're a manufacturer and the infringer has a patent of interest to you, exchange licenses with the infringer.
- Sue the infringer in federal court in the district where the infringer resides or has committed infringement (in the event your request is unsuccessful). If your suit is successful, you will be awarded damages and may also get an injunction, precluding the infringer from using your invention in the future, during the remaining term of the patent.

How much can you recover if you successfully sue for infringement? Section 284 of the patent statutes states that the court shall award damages adequate to compensate for the infringement, but in no event less than a reasonable royalty for the infringer's activity, plus interest and costs. Sometimes the court will award an infringee the profits that the infringer made if it's difficult to determine a reasonable royalty.

In addition to the above "regular" damages, Section 284 also states that the court may award up to triple ("treble") the damages, and Section 285 states that in exceptional cases the court may also award attorneys' fees. Recently, the Supreme Court ruled that Section 284 enhanced damages are available at the discretion of the trial judge, not for a typical infringement case but "as a 'punitive' or 'vindictive' sanction for egregious infringement behavior. The sort of conduct warranting enhanced damages has been variously described as willful, wanton, malicious, bad-faith, deliberate, consciously wrongful, flagrant, or characteristic of a pirate." (*Halo Electronics v. Pulse Electronics* (2016).) This ruling eliminated a stumbling block that patent owners had faced since 2007 to obtain enhanced damages, namely requiring them to prove that an infringement was "objectively reckless."

Patent infringement damages and fees sometimes can even exceed the infringer's gross sales. In addition to monetary damages, the court can issue an injunction—an order signed by a federal court ordering the infringer not to infringe any more. If the infringer violates the injunction, they can be subject to contempt-of-court sanctions, including imprisonment and fines.

Unfortunately our legal system, especially in the field of patent enforcement, is mainly accessible to (and manipulated primarily by) organizations and individuals with deep pockets—those companies that can afford to hire expensive patent litigators and pay the costs of litigation. However, it is often possible for little folk to obtain relief by using a contingent-fee litigator or by just implying that they will sue as described below. However, a contingent-fee litigator will not take your case unless (1) you have a fairly strong patent, (2) the infringement is relatively easy to prove or clear, (3) the damages would be substantial, and (4) the infringer has deep pockets. Nevertheless, the value of the patent system would be far more valuable if it provided a way for those with shallow pockets to enforce their patents.

J.   What to Do About Patent Infringement

Let's now take a closer look at what to do if your patent is infringed.

Step 1: Obtain Details of the Infringement

If you discover what you believe to be an infringement of your patent, obtain as many details and particulars about the infringing device or process and infringer as possible. To do this, procure service manuals, photographs, actual samples of the infringing device, advertisements, product-catalog sheets, etc., plus details of the individual or company that is committing the infringement.

Step 2: Compare Your Broadest Claim With the Infringing Device

Many inventors, who, after being awarded a patent, somehow get the notion that it covers everything in the field, no matter what the claims recite. A patent covers only what the claims recite, plus their equivalents and contributory components (see Steps 3 and 4, below). Thus you must compare your patent's claims with the physical nature of the infringing device or process.

To infringe your patent, the device in question must physically have or perform all of the elements contained in the main or broadest claims of your patent. Even if the infringing device has additional elements, it will still infringe. For example, if your claim recites three elements, A, B, and C, and the infringing device has these three elements, it will infringe. If the infringing device has four elements, A, B, C, and D, it will still infringe. But if the infringing device has only two of the three elements, A and B, it *won't* infringe. Similarly, if the supposed infringing device has three elements A, B, and C′, it won't infringe, provided element C of your claim doesn't read on element C′ of the supposed infringing device. A patent claim is, in effect, a little statute that says, "If each and every one of the following elements is met, infringement occurs. If not all of the elements are met, there is no infringement. If more than all elements claimed are present, infringement still occurs."

To analyze infringement, you should make a claim chart with two columns. Break the first independent claim into its elements, each one in a respective block in the left column. In each corresponding block in the right column write a brief narrative stating why you feel the corresponding element in the left column is met by the infringing device. Refer to an attached drawing or exhibit. You need do only one independent claim that you believe to be infringed, but if you can

Claim 1 of Smith Patent x,xxx,xxx	Peel-O-matic Device
1. A device for peeling potatoes, comprising:	The Peel-O-matic device (POMD) is designed to peel potatoes. See description on package (Exhibit A) which states, "Peels all produce faster." A potato is an item of produce.
a handle with a series of finger grips,	The POMD has a handle with a series of finger grips as can be seen in the lower part of the photo on the package (Exhibit A).
a head attached to said handle,	The POMD has a head attached to its handle as shown in Exhibit A.
said head having an elongated blade,	The head includes an elongated blade as also shown in Exhibit A.
said elongated blade having a longitudinal slot,	The elongated blade of the POMD has a longitudinal slot as also shown in Exhibit A.
said longitudinal slot having a pair of elongated, sharpened edges on opposite sides of said slot, said edges facing each other,	The longitudinal slot of the POMD has a pair of elongated, sharpened edges on opposite sides of the slot and these edges face each other as clearly shown in Exhibit A.
whereby said device may be securely held in one's hands by said handle without slipping and may be used to peel potatoes using said sharpened edges of said slot.	The POMD device can be held securely by its handle due to its finger grips and the sharpened edges of its slot may be used to peel potatoes.

do all independent claims, that's best. If the other independent claims differ substantially from Claim 1, you should definitely chart them. A sample claim chart is shown above.

You don't need to do the dependent claims at this time. Remember that each dependent claim incorporates all of the limitations of its referent claim(s) (the claim it refers to and any claim(s) the referent claim(s) refer to). Also, each dependent claim is considered independently of its referent claim(s), after the limitations of the referent claim(s) are incorporated. This is so even if its referent claim(s) is held invalid.

Moreover, even if your patent has 50 claims, you need prove that only one claim is infringed to prove infringement; your damages do not depend upon the number of claims that are infringed. And even if your claims don't literally read on the infringing device, there are still two ways you may be able to bag the infringer: the "doctrine of equivalents" and the "doctrine of contributory infringement."

Step 3: Determine the Extent of the Infringement and the Ability of the Infringer to Pay Damages

In order to convince a contingent-fee litigator to represent you, you must show that (a) your patent is valid, (b) it is infringed, (c) the extent of the infringement is great enough to result in significant damages (money awarded to compensate you for the infringement), and (d) the infringer has enough resources to pay the damages. With regard to (a), since your patent was examined and issued by the PTO, it is presumed valid, but if a litigator wants to make a further validity search or investigation, they'll do it or tell you what to do, so it's not necessary to worry about this now. Your claim chart (Step 2) will show whether it is infringed. To determine the extent of the infringement and the ability of the infringer to pay, you'll have to do some research. Use an Internet search engine to find out all you can about the infringer and the infringing product. There are services that have sales figures for various products and can research them. A business school professor may be able to provide suggestions. You may have to spend several days and travel down many avenues to get enough information to present to the litigator.

Step 4: Apply the Doctrine of Equivalents If Possible

Under the doctrine of equivalents (DoE), even if each element of a patent's claim is not literally met by an element of the device, so long as the element of the device is the "equivalent" of the claimed element, the device can still infringe that element. A device element is equivalent if it performs the same function in the same way to achieve the same result as the claim element, or the role of the device element is substantially the same as that of the claim element. However, the DoE was severely limited by the U.S. Supreme Court on 2002 May 28 in *Festo v. Shoketsu*, (535 U.S. 722 (2002)). Under *Festo*, if the patentee amends a claim in any way during prosecution to make it allowable (this is almost always the case), the DoE can't be used with that claim unless the patentee can show that the narrowing amendment did not surrender the particular equivalent in question—that is, if the particular equivalent is not related to the way the claim was amended or was not foreseeable at the time. Also, if the court can't determine the reason for the amendment, the DoE will not be available.

Even without *Festo*, the DoE did not apply if "file wrapper estoppel" (also known as "prosecution history estoppel") existed—that is, the claim element was amended during prosecution to define over prior art.

EXAMPLE: Minerva Murgatroid of San Francisco has a patent on a mechanism for bunching broccoli. Its main claim recites the mechanism, including a recitation that the broccoli is banded with a wire-reinforced paper band. She didn't claim the band more broadly because she didn't think to do so, this being the only type of band that would work at the time she got the patent.

A few years later, LeRoy Phillips of Philadelphia discovers a plastic broccoli band that will work just as well as Minerva's wire-reinforced band. He makes broccoli-banding machines and sells them, with his plastic bands, to Fred Farmer, who uses them to band broccoli on his farm in Fresno. Minerva can sue either LeRoy in Philadelphia or Fred in Fresno. Even though her main claim doesn't literally read on LeRoy's machine—that is, describe all of its physical elements—

she can win the infringement suit using the DoE, provided she didn't amend her claims during prosecution so as to invoke the *Festo* doctrine. LeRoy's plastic band is equivalent in structure, function, and result to the wire and paper band, the band material being a relatively minor change that won't get LeRoy or Fred off the hook.

However, suppose during prosecution of her patent application before the PTO, Minerva originally had broad claims to any type of band but then narrowed them to the wire-reinforced paper band to avoid a prior-art reference. In this situation Minerva is subject to the doctrine of file wrapper estoppel and may not use the DoE to rebroaden her claim. Even if Minerva merely amended her claims to make them clearer, under the *Festo* doctrine, she can't use the DoE.

Thus you will see that the courts have severely limited the DoE. Nevertheless some patentees can use it in some circumstances, so if you can, do so if one or more elements of claims don't literally read on the infringing device. You can do so by typing something like the following in the right-hand block of your claim chart, adjacent each element that is not literally met by the infringing device: "This element is not literally met by the Ajax thresher, but the Ajax thresher's crossbeam B meets it under the Doctrine of Equivalents because…."

The Negative Doctrine of Equivalents

There's a rarely used converse of the doctrine of equivalents, the so-called negative doctrine of equivalents. Under this, even if your claims literally read on the infringing device, but the infringing device has a different structure, function, or result than your invention, the device may be held not to infringe.

Step 5: Consider Whether a Contributory Infringement Has Occurred

If your claims don't read on the infringing device, but the infringing device is a specially made component that's only useful in a machine covered by your patent, the infringer may be liable under the doctrine of contributory infringement.

EXAMPLE: In the example above, LeRoy makes an entire broccoli-banding machine like Minerva's, except that he doesn't sell or supply any bands. Minerva's claims don't literally read on LeRoy's machine since her claims recite the band. Nevertheless, Minerva can bag LeRoy under the doctrine of contributory infringement, since his broccoli-banding machine is useful only in the mechanism of Minerva's patent claim and since it has no other noninfringing use.

Under recent legislation, if a patent holder sues to enforce a method or process claim, a defendant can escape liability if the defendant built and commercially used the invention more than one year before the patent application filing date. (35 USC 273.)

Step 6: Find a Patent Attorney

When you first reasonably suspect that an infringement is occurring, you should consult with a patent attorney. This is because you'll need to embark on a course of action that is very difficult for the nonlawyer to perform in its entirety. Unfortunately, the cost is high, and it's difficult to get a patent attorney to take this type of case on a contingent fee (i.e., a case for which you pay them only if you win). This means you'll have to pay the attorney up front (or at least partially up front). It depends on the complexity of your case, but an initial retainer of $20,000 would be typical. However, if you've got a very strong case and if the infringer is solvent (would be good for the damages if you win), it's possible that you may find an attorney who will take your case on a contingent-fee basis. If you do get an attorney to do this, you still may have to pay the out-of-pocket costs through trial; these can run as high as $100,000, so be sure you can afford them.

If, as will usually happen, you can't get a contingent-fee arrangement, you should be prepared for a shock: patent trial attorneys generally charge about $350 to $700 per hour, and a full-blown infringement suit can run to hundreds or even thousands of hours' work, most of it before trial! While in recent years cost-conscious patent owners have tightened belt buckles in court, and challenged issued patents out of court, the American Intellectual Property Law

Association (a trade group for patent attorneys) still estimates that the median cost of patent infringement actions through trial (with between $1 million and $10 million at stake) is in the $1.7 million range. You should be sure that your damages, if you win, will make this worthwhile. Also, be sure the defendant can pay any judgment you obtain. And don't depend on getting attorneys' fees or triple damages; these are awarded only in "exceptional cases."

Of course, an infringer will usually have the same fee burden, and may be inclined to settle if he or she thinks you're serious about suing after your attorney writes a few letters. A substantial number of cases are in fact settled before suit is even brought and most are settled before trial.

Bear in mind that even though you think you have a good case and your patent is being willfully infringed, it is impossible to predict anything with certainty in the law. Factors may prevent a fair outcome so that an infringer prevails. As one cynical lawyer in San Francisco stated, "Whoever puts on the better show wins."

TIP

The material in the following steps is not intended to help you do your own patent infringement litigation. However, it will give you an overview of what's involved so that you can play an active role in deciding on your course of action and helping your attorney bring its prosecution to a successful conclusion.

Step 7: Write a Letter

The first step to follow in the event an infringement has occurred is to write a letter. This letter can:

- Ask the infringer to stop infringing your patent and to pay you royalties for past activity.
- Offer the infringer a license under your patent for future activity and again ask for a settlement for the past. Remember, any infringer is a potential licensee, so don't make war right away. Beware, however, that your offer of a license may prevent you from ever getting an injunction if a court construes it as evidence that infringement does not cause you irreparable harm.

As is often the case, the letter may go unanswered, or your demands may not be acceded to. If so, you'll have to sue for patent infringement if you want to recover damages or an injunction. Also, if your letter creates a reasonable apprehension that you will sue them, the infringer can sue you in an inconvenient location to have your patent declared invalid under what is known as a "declaratory judgment (DJ) action." To prevent this, don't threaten to sue, but instead simply notify the infringer about your patent. Previously I advised that you could offer the infringer a license, but, under recent antipatentee decisions, many litigators feel that even this may give the infringer a reasonable apprehension of suit and enable them to file a DJ action against you.

Step 8: Act Promptly

The statute of limitations for patent infringement is six years, which means you cannot recover damages that occurred more than six years back from the date you filed suit. However, despite this rather lengthy limitations period, it's important that you not wait six years, but act rapidly once you become aware of an infringement. Otherwise, the infringer may reasonably argue that it continued to infringe because you appeared not to be concerned. Your inactivity may prevent you from collecting the bulk of the damages you would otherwise be entitled to. This would occur under the legal doctrines known as estoppel and laches, which generally mean that a court won't award you damages if your action (or lack of action in this case) in some way brought them about.

If you're selling a product embodying the invention and you failed to mark it with the patent number, the six-year term of damages can be considerably shortened as a practical matter by application of the patent-marking statute (35 USC 287). On the other hand, you can bring suit even after your patent has expired and still go back six years during the time the patent was in force (again, provided that you had some valid reason for delaying your action).

Step 9: Who Should Be Sued?

Obviously, you can sue any manufacturer who makes, uses, sells, imports, or offers for sale any device or practices any process covered by the claims of your patent.

You must bring suit against the manufacturer where (1) it has a place of business, and (2) has committed an act of infringement. (If you have a patent that covers a process used abroad to make a device that is imported into the U.S., the importation, sale, offer to sell, and use of the device will be considered to infringe.)

You can also sue the retailer or ultimate purchaser of the invention (including a private individual) as well as the manufacturer. Suits against the retailer or customer are sometimes brought in order to find a court that's favorable, or at least geographically close, to the patent owner. If a suit is brought against the retailer or customer of a patented invention, under the Uniform Commercial Code the manufacturer of the patented invention must step in and defend or reimburse the customer's suit. If your infringer is an out-of-state manufacturer and you can sue its local retailer, it puts a tremendous burden on the manufacturer to defend at a distance.

If the Infringer Has a Government Contract

If the infringer of your patent is a company or individual who's making products embodying your invention under a government contract, you can sue only the government in the Court of Claims in Washington. You can't sue the company and you can't sue in your local jurisdiction. Moreover, you can't get an injunction prohibiting the company from manufacturing your invention, since the infringing device may be useful for national defense. In other words, we have compulsory licensing of any patent that covers an invention used by the government. You can, however, recover damages and interest.

Lastly, don't be afraid to take on a big company simply because they have more resources to defend a patent infringement suit than you have to prosecute it. You have the right to a jury trial (see Section N, below), which helps equalize the odds.

Note that if you assert patent rights, your opponent may cite prior art including (a) any publication, including a patent, that was published before your filing date, or (b) a U.S. patent that was filed on any date, or claims priority of any earlier application (PPA or foreign) that was filed before your filing date. If this prior art anticipates or renders your invention obvious, it will defeat your right to sue unless you can prove (1) you conceived the invention before the date of a or b and you were diligent in filing your patent application or building and testing the invention, or (2) you built and tested the invention before a or b. The law in this area is complicated and was changed by the AIA, so consult a patent litigator before relying on this abbreviated information.

Step 10: Consider Stopping Importation of the Infringing Device

If a device covered by your invention is being imported into the U.S. and the effect of such importation is to harm a domestic industry, you can bring a proceeding before the United States International Trade Commission (USITC, or simply ITC) to have the device stopped at the port of entry by U.S. Customs agents. This proceeding can be brought in addition—or as an alternative—to any other legal action. While such a proceeding is complex and expensive, the exclusion remedy is extremely powerful. The pertinent statute is 19 USC 1337(a), and more information is available at www.usitc.gov.

Design Patent Infringement

Since the claim of a design patent is general, the courts cannot rely on it to determine infringement, as they can with a utility patent. Thus the courts must compare the drawing of the design patent with the accused infringing device. Under the *Egyptian Goddess, Inc. v. Swisa, Inc.* case (CAFC, 2008 Sep 22, 498 F.3d 1354), design patent infringement is determined by the "deceived purchaser" test: The court will hold the design patent infringed if the defendant's accused design could reasonably be viewed as so similar to the patented design that a purchaser familiar with the prior art would be deceived by the similarity between the claimed and accused designs, "inducing him to purchase one supposing it to be the other." As in most evidentiary trials, both sides will call in their "hired guns" (experts) to testify for their side.

Patent Trolls and Submarine Patents

You may have heard of the terms "patent troll" and "submarine patent" recently. What do these terms mean and how do they affect inventors?

As defined by Wikipedia, "patent troll" is "a pejorative term for a person or company that enforces its patents against one or more alleged infringers in a manner considered unduly aggressive or opportunistic, often with no intention to manufacture or market the patented invention." Less pejorative synonyms are *nonpracticing entity, patent assertion company, non-manufacturing patentee, patent marketer,* and *patent dealer,* which describe a patent owner who does not manufacture or use the patented invention. Under the U.S. and most other patent systems, patentees are not required to—and feel that their rights should not be lessened if they don't—practice their inventions. Many inventors are very creative but are not business oriented and would like their creativity rewarded fully even if they don't commercialize their inventions. Thus if you have a patent but don't practice the invention, I suggest you consider yourself no less worthy than a patentee who manufactures the patented invention.

Wikipedia defines the related term "submarine patent" as "a patent first published and granted long after the initial application was filed … . [I]t stays under water … for long periods, then emerges … and surprises the relevant market."

I prefer to call them "delayed-issue" patents. However under present U.S. law, where supplemental cases (divisions, continuations, and CIPs) expire 20 years from the date of the original application, any patent that is significantly delayed by being a supplemental case will have a much shorter in-force period. If you obtain a patent after delay due to one or more supplemental cases, I similarly suggest you consider your patent no less worthy than a patent that issued directly from the first filing.

Remember that each type of patent (from non-practicing entities and delayed-issue), already covers a significant advance in the art since it issued only after the PTO found that the claims defined an invention that was in a statutory class and a useful, novel, and unobvious invention.

If You Discover an Infringement During Pendency

You may recover a reasonable royalty for an infringement that occurs during the pendency of your application, but you must wait until the patent issues to sue for such royalties and the royalty will only be applicable to infringements that occur after the publication of the application. You must also notify the infringer of the published patent application (PubPA) and the infringing device or process must be substantially identical to the invention as claimed in the PubPA. (35 USC 154(d).) The royalty you receive will be applicable to any infringements that occur after the publication of the application.

If you filed a Nonpublication Request, and you want to take advantage of this "royalties before issuance" provision, you should rescind the NPR in order to have your application published so that you can rely on the statute. If you discover the infringement well before the normal 18-month-after-filing publication date, you may request that the application be published earlier than 18 months by requesting same and paying the publication fee. (Rule 219 (37 CFR 01.219).)

K. Product Clearance (Can I Legally Copy or Make That?)

This is the other side of the coin: Here I'll assume that, instead of having your own invention, you're interested in copying the invention or product of someone else or making a new product that you feel may be covered by someone else's patent. What can you legally do and how do you find out?

1. Common Misconceptions

Before giving you the applicable rules and information, first I want to dispel some widespread misconceptions so you'll start from neutral territory.

Common Misconception: If you make an identical copy of a device or circuit, you can be validly sued for infringement, even if the copied device is not patented.

Fact: You are free to copy any device or circuit, even to the minutest detail, so long as you (1) do not infringe any applicable in-force patent, trademark, or copyright, and (2) don't copy any features that have a "secondary meaning."

Common Misconception: If a product is not marked "Patented" and it does not have a patent number, you are free to copy the product, since the law requires patented products to be marked with the legend "Patented" and the patent number.

Fact: Patented products don't have to be marked as such: (See "Patent Number Marking" in Section D.)

Common Misconception: If a product that you intend to make is shown in the drawing of another's patent, you would be an infringer of that patent if you made the product.

Fact: The claims of a patent essentially determine infringement, but the courts are often allowed to interpret the claims in accordance with the description of the patent.

Common Misconception: That which you do in your own home or for your own personal use or for charity will not infringe a patent that is otherwise applicable.

Fact: While "home, personal, or charity infringement" may be difficult to detect, nevertheless these are forms of infringement that are legally actionable and can subject the infringer to paying damages and/or an injunction prohibiting further infringement.

Common Misconception: If you change a patented product a fixed percentage, say 20%, you won't be an infringer.

Fact: The amount you'll have to change a patented product to avoid infringement is not subject to quantitative analysis, but rather is determined by the breadth of the patent's claims. (See Section J, above.)

2. Find Out If There's an Applicable Patent and Whether You Will Infringe It

Suppose you do want to manufacture a specific product or perform a specific process commercially, and you have some reason to believe it may be covered by an in-force patent or pending application. Under the law, you have a duty of due care to determine whether or not you infringe any in-force patents. *Knorr-Bremse v. Dana Corp*, (383 F.3d 1337 (Fed. Cir. 2004)). How can you fulfill this duty and determine whether you can proceed without infringing any existing or future patent?

Unfortunately, there is no way to be 100% sure, because no search can cover unpublished pending patent applications. However we can give you some pretty specific instructions and guidelines.

If the process or product you wish to duplicate is already manufactured or used, look at the product, the literature accompanying it, and the packing material, to see if any patent number is given. If you can get the patent number, download it from the PTO website or order the patent from the PTO or a private service. If the patent issued from an application filed before 1995 Jun 8, it expired (or expires) on the later of 17 years from issue or 20 years from its filing date. If the patent issued from an application filed on or after 1995 Jun 8, it expires 20 years from its filing date, or the filing date of any parent cases from which it originated, whichever is sooner. A patent will expire earlier than its full term if its owner fails to pay the required maintenance fees, so if you are concerned about a patent, check to see if it has expired in this way.

If the patent is in force, things usually aren't as bad as they seem. Often a patent that supposedly covers a product in reality may cover only a minor aspect of the product (such as the housing) that is easy to design around. Sometimes the patent doesn't cover the product at all. How can you be sure? The only way is to read its claims carefully, diagramming them and preparing a claim chart, if necessary, to know exactly what they cover. (See Section J, above.) If what you want to manufacture is not covered by the claims, and if you feel there is no other patent on the item you wish to manufacture, you are free to do so.

If the product or process you wish to manufacture is simply marked "Patented" and carries no number, your task is more difficult. You can write to the company, asking for the number and date of their patent, or whether their patent is in force, but they're not bound to answer, and you'll have tipped your hand by communicating with them.

You can perform a (relatively cheap) search made in the PTO or on its website of all of the patents issued to the company in question. But there is no guarantee that this will uncover the manufacturer, since the patent may not be owned by the company in question; the manufacturer may simply be a licensee. The best way to determine whether an in-force patent is applicable is to make a search in the relevant classes and subclasses of the PTO, have someone make the search for you, or search on the Google or PTO sites. The search should seek to find any patent on the invention in question. This will involve a greater expenditure of time or money, but at least you will be fairly certain of your position. If, however, there is a patent pending on the product or process, there is no way to obtain any details, even if the manufacturer marks the product "patent pending"; thus, not all risks can be eliminated.

If the product or process you wish to manufacture has been known or used in the marketplace for over 17 years, you can be pretty sure that no in-force patent will be applicable, or that even if one is applicable, it is just about to expire anyway.

If you can't find any U.S. patents and the product or process is relatively new, you shouldn't feel free to copy it because it may be the subject of a pending patent application. It's not possible to search pending U.S. patent applications, since they're kept secret unless they are published 18 months after filing. You can search published U.S. applications and you can often find some pending U.S. applications by searching for published corresponding foreign applications, which are all published 18 months after filing. (Also, if the probable owner of a patent

application you want to research has been selling the product under a trademark, such as "the Zorch widget," investigate the item in the PTO (trademark applications are not kept secret) to obtain the date of first use of the trademark in the United States. It's likely that the filing date of any patent application is just before the date of first trademark use.

If you find an applicable in-force patent or patent application, and you don't think you can break it, avoid it, or get a license at a reasonable royalty, consider designing around the patent or using older (nonpatented) technology.

3. What to Do If an In-Force Patent Is Applicable

If there is an in-force patent applicable, and you still wish to manufacture the product, you have several alternatives:

- Your first instinct should be to review the claims of the patent and then try to design around them. Often you will find that the claims of a patent, upon analysis, have one or more limitations that can be eliminated in your product or process so that you can make the patented invention even cheaper than the patentee. Alternatively, you can design around one of the elements of the patent, make an improved device, and get your own patent on it. Remember, if you don't infringe the independent claims, you won't have to worry about the dependent claims.

- Although we don't advise it, some companies manufacture or use the product or process and hope that the patentee won't catch them. When they do this, they usually follow a good accounting practice, by keeping reasonable royalty reserves (see Chapter 16 for what is a reasonable royalty) in case they're ever caught. Also, they usually analyze the patent, or have a patent attorney do so, to see if there are any good defenses to show that they were not a "willful" infringer, since willful infringers may be subject to triple damages or attorneys' fees in a lawsuit. They must always be aware that the patent owner may discover the infringement, and sue them, and get an injunction prohibiting further manufacturing. Although the idea of manufacturing without a license may seem deceitful, risky, and inadvisable, it is done frequently in the U.S. (but not commonly in Japan). The infringer simply takes the full-speed-ahead-and-damn-the-torpedoes attitude and hopes to be able to negotiate a favorable settlement or break the patent if caught.

• You can ask the patent owner for a license to manufacture under the in-force patent. However, here you take the risk, if you aren't familiar with the patent owner's practices, of being refused a license. Moreover, you'll have shown your hand, so that if you do manufacture, the patent owner will be looking out for you and will certainly sue or accuse you of willful infringement in short order.

• You can make an extended validity search to try to "break" (or "invalidate") the patent. You should use a professional, experienced searcher to do this and should expect to spend several thousand dollars in order to make the widest and most complete search possible. Also, you should obtain a copy of the PTO's file of the patent to see if there are any weaknesses or flaws in the patent that are not apparent from the printed patent itself. The PTO's Public PAIR site makes the files for most recent patents available for free download; otherwise you will have to order it from the PTO (see Appendix 4, Fee Schedule for cost) or a private service. Again, the services of an experienced attorney should be employed here, because breaking patents requires a highly skilled practitioner. If the attorney feels that the patent can be invalidated or is not infringed, you can have them write a "green-light letter" to you, explaining in detail why it would not be likely that you would be liable for infringing the patent. Such a letter can show you are not a willful infringer and thus avoid triple ("treble" in legalese) damages or attorneys' fees if you are sued.

• If you find highly relevant prior art, you can bring it to the attention of the patent owner and ask it to disclaim or dedicate the patent to the public, or ask the PTO to review the patent in view of that prior art.

Defending Against Method (Process) Claims

If you are commercially using a method or process that has been patented by someone else and your use preceded the patent's filing date by more than one year, you have an absolute defense against an infringement charge. However, this defense is personal to you and will generally not invalidate the patent. (35 USC 273.)

4. If No In-Force Patent Is Applicable

Unless there is an in-force patent covering an item, anyone is free to make and manufacture identical copies of it, provided:

• one doesn't copy the trademark of the product
• the shape of the product itself is not considered a trademark (such as the shape of the world-famous Coca-Cola bottle), and
• you don't copy "secondary meaning" features.

If you buy a product from another in the course of business, your vendor is obligated to indemnify you for any such infringement under the Uniform Commercial Code. However, you can be sued for infringement and be liable for damages. (Hopefully, your vendor will be around to reimburse you.) You can also be subject to an injunction ordering you not to infringe anymore.

One manufacturer's effort to copy a small hardware item by having it manufactured cheaply in Asia backfired. He sent the item overseas with instructions to make several thousand identical copies of the item. Since he didn't give any further instructions, the Asian manufacturer did as instructed, manufacturing and shipping back several thousand copies of the item, including a faithful copy of the embossed trademark of the manufacturer's competitor. The manufacturer then had to spend significant money obliterating the trademark, thereby losing his entire profit in the process.

L. How to Cite Prior Art and Other Information in Patent Applications and Patents

Suppose you're aware of prior art that would affect a patent or patent application and you want to make the PTO or the public aware. Perhaps you want to get the art in the file of your own patent or application to get it behind you and show your good faith and put forth your arguments as to why it doesn't invalidate your claims. Or maybe you are manufacturing (or contemplating manufacturing) something based on the invention and you don't want someone to get a patent on it. Or possibly you just want to do it as a public service to prevent an improper patent from issuing or cast a cloud on a patent you know was improperly issued. There are eight ways to cite prior art and other relevant information in order to invalidate or validate patents and patent applications:

- File a passive citation against your own patent application (Rule 97).
- Request supplemental examination of your patent.
- File a passive citation against any patent application.
- File for a post-grant review of patent.
- File for review of a business method patent.
- File a passive citation against a patent (Rule 501).
- Request *ex parte* reexamination of a patent.
- Request *inter partes* review of a patent.

Let's examine each of these in more detail.

1. File a Passive Citation Against Your Own Patent Application (Rule 97)

As part of your "duty of disclosure" under Rule 97 you are required to provide an Information Disclosure Statement (IDS) in which you cite prior art that you are (or become) aware of, against your own application. Once your patent issues, this obligation ends, although it would be considered highly improper and subject you to sanctions to sue on a patent that you know is invalid.

2. Request Supplemental Examination of Your Patent

Section 12 of the AIA establishes a new procedure, called Supplemental Examination, by which a patent owner may request reexamination of the patent in order to have the PTO consider, reconsider, or correct any information relevant to the patent. In addition to prior art, the information can even be inequitable conduct, which the patent holder may correct. If you're aware of any defects in your patent or in your past conduct that may cast a cloud on your patent, request Supplemental Examination.

3. File a Passive Citation Against Any Patent Application

Under Rule 291 (37 CFR 1.291), a third party (i.e., anyone but the patent applicant) can cite prior art against a patent application. The PTO will consider the citation if it includes a fee (see Appendix 4, Fee Schedule), an identification of the citation(s), a copy of each citation, and its relevance. Also the relevant portions of non-English citations must be translated. A copy of the citation must be sent to (served upon) the applicant. The citation must be filed before the earlier of (a) a notice of allowance, or (b) the later of six months after the application is published or the date of rejection of any claim in the application. If you are aware of another's application that you feel is not patentable, submit a timely citation.

Under Rule 291 (37 CFR 1.291), any member of the public can file a protest against a pending application before the earlier of the publication of the application, or its notice of allowance. The protest may cite prior art and even raise issues of inequitable conduct, but the rules are complex, and warrant the assistance of a patent attorney.

4. File for a Post-Grant Review of Patent

Under the AIA, a new Post-Grant Review (PGR) procedure allows anyone to challenge a patent on any invalidity ground for nine months after the patent issues. However the standard is high: the challenge must initially show that it is likely that at least one claim of the patent is unpatentable or a novel and unsettled legal question is involved. If a party initiates a post-grant or *inter partes* review (see below), the party cannot use this as the basis or grounds for the review in a later declaratory judgment or infringement civil action. If you're aware of another's patent that you feel should not have issued, and your evidence meets the criteria, file for a post-grant review within nine months after issuance. If the post-grant review is not successful, you may institute an *inter partes* review—see below.

5. File for a Review of a Business Method Patent

In addition to the above PGR procedure, the AIA provides a transitional eight-year period (expiring 2020) whereby anyone can have the PTO review the validity of any business method patent (excluding those that are for technological inventions). The review must be based on prior art only. Details on this program (called the "Transitional Program for Covered Business Method Patents") are at www.uspto.gov/patents-application-process/appealing-patent-decisions/trials/transitional-program-covered-business.

6. File a Passive Citation Against a Patent (Rule 501)

Under Rule 501, anyone can cite prior art in the file of a patent. (If the patentee makes the citation, it must include an explanation of the pertinence of the art and how the claims differ from the art.) The person making the citation may make it anonymously and should send copies to the PTO (no fee required) and the patentee, or should file it in duplicate with the PTO. No fee is required.

7. Request Ex Parte Reexamination of a Patent

Anyone can cite newly discovered prior art against a patent and have it reexamined at any time during the pendency of the patent. If you're aware of another's patent that you feel should not have issued, your evidence meets the criteria, and you're willing to go through the expense of filing, you may institute an Ex

Parte Reexamination. As the Ex Parte Reexamination procedure is somewhat complicated and the PTO fee is expensive, we suggest you consult an attorney if you want to institute an Ex Parte Reexamination.

8. Request *Inter Partes* Review of a Patent

The standard for review in an *Inter Partes* Review is the higher standard of the Post-Grant Review (above), and is limited to patents and other publications. An *Inter Partes* Review must be initiated after nine months after grant or after termination of post-grant review proceedings. If you're aware of another's patent that you feel should not have issued, your evidence meets the criteria, and you're willing to go through the expense of filing and litigating an adversary proceeding, you may institute an *Inter Partes* Review within nine months after issuance. Again, the procedure is complicated, the PTO fee is expensive, and attorney fees will be high, so we suggest you consult an attorney if you want to institute an *Inter Partes* Review.

M. The Court of Appeals for the Federal Circuit (CAFC)

Litigation favors wealthy or large corporations, which are far better equipped to defend and maintain patent infringement suits than a single individual. Nevertheless, for the patent owner a successful suit holds the promise of monetary damages for past infringement, and the potential for a court-ordered injunction forbidding the infringer from continuing the infringement.

In *eBay v. MercExchange* (547 U.S. 388 (2006)), however, the U.S. Supreme Court held that even if a court finds that a patent is valid and infringed, the patent owner is not automatically entitled to a court order enjoining further infringement. Under the Supreme Court's ruling, a trial court shouldn't issue an injunction unless the patent owner shows a balance of equity in its favor—for example, the patent owner is selling products employing the invention and would be damaged by letting the defendant continue to infringe. Before this ruling a company would be more inclined to cave in to the demands of a patent holder because of fears that an injunction would be granted automatically.

An accused infringer of a patent can avoid liability (that is—defend against the infringement action) in three different ways:

- by showing that the claims of the patent aren't infringed (discussed above)
- by showing that the patent is invalid (discussed below), or
- by showing that the patent isn't enforceable (discussed below).

With regard to the second, the validity of the patent being sued on can be challenged by:

- prior-art references that the PTO didn't discover or use properly
- proof that the specific machine covered by the patent is inoperable
- a showing that disclosure of the patent is incomplete, that is, it doesn't teach one skilled in the art to make and use the patented invention
- a showing that the claims are too vague and indefinite under Section 112, or
- a showing that the patent was issued to the wrong inventor, etc.

After trial, either party to a suit may appeal the case to the Court of Appeal for the Federal Circuit (CAFC) if they believe the law was erroneously applied in at trial. A decision from the CAFC could affirm that outcome at trial, or could reverse that outcome, or could send the suit back to the trial court for further proceedings.

N. Jury Trials

Most juries love individual patent holders and have awarded very large damages in patent infringement actions, especially where an individual patent holder has sued a large corporation. Thus, if you sue on a patent, always demand a jury trial: most juries usually award more than a judge will. Be aware, however, that the Supreme Court in *Markman v. Westview Instruments, Inc.* (116 S.Ct. 1384 (1996)), has removed juries' powers to interpret claims and hence reduced their power to decide the issue of infringement.

O. Arbitration

Instead of a lawsuit, if both parties agree, the entire infringement dispute can now be submitted to arbitration. In this case, an arbitrator, usually a patent attorney or retired judge, will hear from both sides in a relatively informal proceeding. The arbitrator will adjudicate the patent's validity, infringement, etc. The arbitrator's fee (about $10,000 to $50,000 and up) is far cheaper than the cost of a regular lawsuit complete with depositions, formal interrogatories, and other formal proceedings. In addition, it's much faster. The arbitrator must file the award with the PTO. The American Arbitration Association is frequently used and has rules for arbitration of patent disputes, but the parties can use any arbitrator(s) they choose. Note, however, that the results of an arbitration cannot be appealed, as can the results of a trial.

P. How Patent Rights Can Be Forfeited

Patents and their claims can be and often are retroactively declared invalid or unenforceable by the PTO or the courts for various reasons, such as:

- relevant prior art that wasn't previously uncovered
- public use or sale of the invention prior to the filing date of the patent application
- misuse of the patent by its owner—for example, by committing antitrust violations, or
- fraud on the PTO committed by the inventor— for example, by failing to reveal relevant facts about the invention and the prior art.

Your airtight infringement action goes down the drain when the PTO or the judge declares your patent invalid or unenforceable. Still, about 50% of patents that get to court are upheld. In addition, the percentage of patents that are treated as valid is higher than the court statistics indicate, since they don't count the many patents that don't get to court because the infringers saw the impossibility of invalidating them or didn't want to spend the $250,000 or more necessary to fight the patent.

In addition to showing that the patent is invalid or not infringed, an accused infringer of a patent can avoid liability by convincing a court that the patent should be declared nonenforceable by showing that the owner of the patent has misused the patent in some way or has engaged in some illegal conduct that makes it inequitable for the owner to enforce the patent. Some examples of conduct that will preclude enforceability of a patent are:

- false marking (marking products with patent numbers that don't cover the product marked)
- illegal licensing practices, such as false threats of infringement
- various antitrust violations, such as package licensing
- extended delay in bringing suit, which works to the prejudice of the accused infringer
- fraud on the PTO, such as withholding a valuable reference from your Information Disclosure Statement, or failing to disclose the full and truthful information about your invention in your patent application, and
- expiration of the patent due to failure to pay a maintenance fee, or acquisition of intervening rights by a defendant who engaged in activity that would have infringed during a period when a maintenance fee was not paid (see Section H above).

Q. Tax Deductions and Income

Unfortunately, most inventors give no thought whatever to taxes, either with regard to the money they spend to get their patents, or to the money they make when they sell or license their patents. We say "unfortunately" because the government may effectively subsidize your patent expenses by allowing you to deduct them. Because of space limitations, here are the basics. You should consult a tax professional or the IRS for the final word:

1. You may be able to legally deduct your patent and invention expenses (i.e., the cost of this book, patent searches, drafting and attorney fees, PTO fees, technical research, models, experimentation and testing, up to $25,000 of depreciable property, etc.) if the IRS considers that your inventing constitutes a trade or business.

2. If you license your invention on a nonexclusive basis, you haven't given away all of your rights, so your royalties are considered ordinary income.

3. If you sell all of your patent rights, or grant a full exclusive license, the IRS considers that you've sold it all; your receipts or royalties, even though received over a long number of years, are considered capital gains.

R. Patent Litigation Financing

Because of the high cost of litigation, cost assistance (at a price) is now available from several companies. Lloyd's of London (www.lloyds.com) and Intellectual Property Insurance Services Corp. (www.patentinsuranceonline.com) write policies directly. These companies will, in return for an annual premium, reimburse part or all of the cost of patent enforcement litigation, up to the policy limit. You can even begin coverage while your patent application is pending. However, some companies may have a less-than-optimum rating and some may require you to jump through difficult hoops, such as getting an infringement and validity opinion from an independent attorney, before they will reimburse your expenses.

Below are some companies and firms that finance contingent-fee patent litigation. Carefully investigate any company before engaging them. Also, as stated, most litigating attorneys will take on contingent-fee litigation if the damages are substantial, the defendant has a deep pocket, and the patent is strong and clearly infringed. Below are just a few of the many litigating patent attorneys and services who have handled contingent-fee litigation. These listings do not imply any form of endorsement or recommendation of these attorneys or their services.

- General Patent Corporation, (www.generalpatent.com)
- Costello, John P., Esq. (www.sacramentopatentattorney.com)

RESOURCE

Nolo.com. Nolo (publisher of this book) maintains a lawyer directory with links to many patent and intellectual property attorneys.

If you want to sell your patent, Ocean Tomo (www. oceantomo.com) holds auctions of patents and also provides other patent fiscal services.

S. Summary

After you pay the issue fee, the PTO will print your patent and send you an Issue Notification and then the deed in a few months. It may be helpful to prepare a press release or advertise your patent for sale at this time. Check your patent for printing or other errors and obtain a Certificate of Correction if necessary. If the error is yours, the PTO charges a fee for issuing a Certificate. If you or a licensee is manufacturing a product under the patent, consider marking the product with the patent number. If you mark you can recover damages from infringers from the date you started marking, but they will have easy access to your patent number and may be more inclined to break your patent or design around it. A patent is intangible personal property that gives you a monopoly on the invention covered by the claims (so long as maintenance fees are paid), against anyone who makes, uses, sells, imports, etc., the invention. You can profit from a patent by selling or licensing it or using it to exclude others to create a monopoly (with higher prices) for yourself. However patents on medical procedures are no longer enforceable against health care providers. Patentees often get offers for goods or services, but most are of no value.

Be sure to pay the three maintenance fees to keep your patent in force: The first is due 3.0 to 3.5 years after issue (YAI), the second 7.0 to 7.5 YAI, and the third 11.0 to 11.5 YAI. If you neglect to pay any fee in the due period you may pay it in a grace period (next six months) with a surcharge and thereafter if the delay was unintentional (two-year limit). However if you pay it after the grace period any infringer will acquire intervening rights.

If you discover an infringer the PTO will not help you; you must contact and sue the infringer. First get details of the infringing product, the company that makes it, including the amount of product sales, and the financial resources of the company. Then, compare your claims to verify infringement (be aware of the doctrine of equivalents and contributory infringement), write a letter, and sue in court or with the ITC if necessary.

To determine if you can make a product it is usually necessary to make a subject-matter search for applicable in-force patents. If an in-force patent is applicable you can design around the patent, ask for a license, or try to break the patent.

There are eight ways to cite prior art and other relevant information in order to invalidate or validate patents and patent applications:

- File a passive citation against your own patent application (Rule 97).
- Request supplemental examination of your patent.
- File a passive citation against any patent application (Rule 290 and 291).
- File for a post-grant review of patent.
- File for review of a business method patent.
- File a passive citation against a patent (Rule 501).
- Request *ex parte* reexamination of a patent.
- Request *inter partes* review of a patent.

All patent appeals must go to the Court of Appeals for the Federal Circuit. Juries no longer have the power to interpret patent claims, but they are usually otherwise pro-patentee. Arbitration is an alternative to patent infringement lawsuits. Patent rights can be forfeited in various ways, that is, if relevant prior art or a prior public use or sale is discovered, the patent is misused, or the patentee committed fraud on the PTO by not citing prior art that it knew of.

Patent expenses can be deducted from ordinary income if you're a serious inventor, or otherwise just against royalties. Insurance is available to finance patent litigation and companies and attorneys are available to finance patent infringement litigation on a contingency basis.

Ownership, Assignment, and Licensing of Inventions

Inventor's Commandment 31

The inventor(s) named in a patent application will be considered the owner(s) of the application and patent, unless they assign their ownership to another person or legal entity. To transfer part or the entire ownership of an application or patent, the inventor-applicant(s) must sign an assignment, and to give permission to practice a claimed invention (usually in return for royalties), they must use a license agreement.

Inventor's Commandment 32

If a patent has several owners, absent any agreement to the contrary the law permits any owner to practice the invention without accounting to any other owners. All joint owners should thus consider signing a Joint Owners' Agreement requiring cooperation and sharing of any profits from the patent.

In the simplest possible situation, a single inventor invents something, obtains a patent on it, manufactures it, and markets it directly to the public for the full period that the patent remains in force. In most instances, things are not that simple. Two or more people may be involved in the conception of the invention, and many more in its development and marketing. A business may want to use the invention and be willing to pay large royalties for the privilege. Employees and employers may disagree over who owns a particular invention that was developed at least partially on company time or with company materials or facilities. Thus, the entire question of invention ownership and use can become complex.

This chapter outlines some of the ways to deal with these various ownership questions and the common agreements that are used in the process. However, because the subject of invention ownership, licensing, and transfer is complicated, you'll probably want to retain a lawyer, if only to review your plans and paperwork.

TIP

Licensing Resource. For detailed assistance with the licensing process, consult *Profit From Your Idea: How to Make Smart Licensing Deals* (Nolo) by attorney Richard Stim. This guide helps to understand the licensing process, determine ownership rights, work with agents effectively, find potential licensees, publicly show inventions without risk, and draft a comprehensive licensing agreement.

A. Inventor, Applicant, Owner

The process of monetizing an idea as a patent involves people fulfilling a number of different roles at different times, each role having different duties and privileges. Sometimes, a single person involved with different stages of the process may fulfill several roles, "wearing many hats" at once, and to this person the lines between these roles may blur. However, it is important to keep in mind these distinctions, and which "hat" you are wearing at what times.

"Inventor" is a term reserved for those involved in the creative side of the process. The U.S. patent laws define an inventor as "the individual or, if a joint invention, the individuals collectively who invented or discovered the subject matter of the invention." (35 USC 100(f).)

"Applicant" is used for any person (natural or corporate) who is applying for a patent to seek protection for an invention. In many cases, the patent applicant will be the inventor. However, as discussed below, the applicant commonly is an inventor's employer. While the applicant may change over time, the inventor of a particular claimed invention does not.

An "owner" is someone who has the ability to direct how an invention may be exploited. When a patent application is filed it creates new property that is owned initially by the applicant. But like any other property, it may be transferred ("assigned") to others, whether sold or gifted. It may be carved up for sale like plots of land within a subdivision. And once it issues as a patent, the nature of the property changes, with its owner or owners taking on new responsibilities (such as the obligation to pay maintenance fees).

B. The Property Nature of Patents

Think of a patent as a valuable property right, although the "property" is essentially intangible and the type where physical possession doesn't count. The patent property right gives you the right to exclude others from manufacturing, using, selling, and importing your invention. This means that society has given you, in effect, an enforceable legal monopoly on the invention for the in-force period of the patent. If you do grant a company permission to use your invention, the law terms this permission a "license." As with most other intangible economic rights—such as the right to operate a business, the right to withdraw money from a bank account, and the right to vote stock in a corporation—patent rights, or a portion of them, can be sold to others, or licensed for a particular use over a particular period of time.

An invention has virtually no economic value to its inventor unless it is patented, sold, licensed, or used as a trade secret, or it has some other protection under intellectual property laws. Most inventors find it difficult to make sales of nonpatented inventions.

C. Who Can Apply for a Patent?

Until September 2012, only inventor(s) could apply for patents in the U.S. The inventor was considered the owner of rights in the invention unless the inventor assigned those rights to someone else. After passage of the America Invents Act (AIA) either the inventor or the inventor's assignee (person or entity to whom the patent is assigned) is allowed to file as a patent applicant. However, even though an assignee can file and prosecute a patent application, each inventor must still execute an oath or declaration. Further, the PTO has indicated that it will continue to use the inventor's name for application and patent identification purposes.

Only the true inventor(s) can be named in the patent application. The status of the applicant(s)-inventor(s) makes no difference, so long as each is a true inventor. That is, an inventor/applicant can be of any nationality, sex, age, or even incarcerated, insane, or deceased. (Insane and deceased people can apply for patents through a legal representative.)

What happens to patent ownership if more than one person is involved in a particular invention? If other people are involved in the inventing stage, they're considered joint or coinventors. Most often, the challenge is to determine what type of activity constitutes invention. For instance, suppose one person came up with the concept of the invention, while the other merely built and tested it—that is, did not contribute any inventive concepts but merely did what any skilled artisan or model maker could do. In this situation the PTO does not consider the second person to be a coinventor. Similarly, financiers, or others who provided business advice, but not technical input, should not be listed as coinventors.

On the other hand, suppose one person came up with the idea for an invention and a model maker then came up with valuable suggestions and contributions that went beyond the skill of an ordinary model maker or machinist and made the invention work far better. In this situation both people should be named as coinventors on the patent application, provided the model maker's contribution is present in at least one claim.

The PTO and the courts don't recognize degrees of inventorship. Thus, the order in which the inventors are named on a patent application is legally irrelevant, although the first-named inventor will be more prominent in the printed patent.

If the joint applicants invented different parts of the claimed invention, they should keep accurate records as to what part each invented. That way, if one inventor's part is dropped later during the prosecution, they can change the named inventors. For this purpose Form 16-1, Joint Applicants—Statement of Respective Contributions, is provided. See Appendix 7.

Completing this form is straightforward: Enter the title of the application or invention, then fill out each inventor's contribution. Have each inventor sign and date in the column adjacent to their contribution. Each inventor should keep a copy of the form (don't file it with the PTO) and refer to it later—for example, if the claims are changed in any way so that one inventor's contribution is no longer claimed, the inventors should remove that inventor from the application. (For more information, see Patent Rules 48 and 324.)

Joint inventors need not have worked together either physically or at the same time, and each need not have made the same type or amount of contribution. To qualify as a coinventor, an inventor need merely have contributed something to at least one claim of the application, even if it's a dependent claim.

Another problem sometimes arises when two or more persons work on an invention, but not all of them are named in the patent application. Disputes regarding inventorship with the omitted inventor(s) sometimes arise later. For example, a model builder may later come back, after an application is filed, and claim to have been wrongfully excluded. One way to avoid such problems is for all inventors to keep a lab notebook—that is, a technical diary, which faithfully records all developments and is frequently signed by the inventor(s) and witnesses. In that way the complaining model builder can be answered by positive proof from the true inventor(s). Also using the Consultant's Work Agreement (Form 4-3) will eliminate many potential disputes since it requires the consultant to assign (legally transfer ownership of) all inventions that they make to the inventor who hires the consultant. Absent such documentation, or agreement, expensive disputes can arise, with only vague memories to deal with.

It's important to include in your application all the inventors who are true inventors and to exclude those who aren't inventors. If it is discovered later that your inventorship is incorrect, and that the mistake resulted from bad faith, your patent can be held invalid, although this rarely happens. (If you do discover that the wrong inventor(s) is (are) named on a patent or patent application, this can be corrected under Patent Rules 48 or 324.)

Common Misconception: If you came up with a bare concept for a valuable invention and your associate "took your ball and ran with it"—that is, built and tested the invention after hundreds of hours of work leading to final success, then your associate must be named as a coinventor with you.

Fact: As stated above, only the true inventor(s)—that is, the one(s) who came up with at least one inventive concept recited in at least one claim—should be named as applicant(s). An associate who did only what any model maker would have done should not legally be named as coinventor, no matter how much work was involved. On the other hand, if your associate contributed at least one inventive concept that made the invention work better, and that is recited in at least one claim, then the associate should be named as a joint inventor with you.

Changing Inventorship

If you find that the incorrect inventors are named in a patent application or patent, for example, due to a change in the subject matter claimed (that is, cancellation of a claim that recited one inventor's contribution), or discovery of an earlier error, you can correct inventorship by following the procedures under PTO Rule 48 (patent applications) or Rule 324 (patent). At least one original inventor must always be retained, that is, it is not possible to change inventorship so that none of the inventors named in the application as originally filed remain.

D. Joint Owners' Agreement

Problems commonly arise in situations where there are two or more inventors or owners of a patent application or patent. These include questions as to who is entitled to commercially exploit the invention, who is entitled to any financial shares, what type of accounting must be performed on partnership books, etc. Fortunately, most of these predictable problems can be ameliorated, if not completely prevented from arising, by the use of a Joint Owners' Agreement (JOA).

The JOA is also desirable because a federal statute (35 USC 262) provides that either of the joint owners of a patent may make, use, or sell the patented invention without the consent of and without accounting to (paying) the other joint owner(s). This statute seems unfair, since it can work a severe hardship on one joint owner in either of two ways:

1. If one joint owner exploits and derives income from the patent while pushing the other aside, the passive joint owner (PJO) will not be rewarded for any inventive contribution (if the PJO is an inventor) or any capital contribution (if the PJO is an investor—that is, someone who has bought part of the patent).

2. If one joint owner works hard to engineer and develop a market for the patented product, the other joint owner can step in as a competitor without compensating the engineer or marketing pathmaker for the efforts accomplished.

Form 16-2 prevents these results from occurring and also accomplishes the following:

- Prohibits any joint owner from exploiting the patent without everyone's consent, except that if there is a dissenter, a majority can act if consultation is unsuccessful.
- Provides that in case of an equally divided vote, the parties will select an arbiter, whose decision shall control.
- Provides that disputes are to be resolved by mediation or binding arbitration if mediation fails.
- Provides that the parties shall share profits proportionately, according to their interests in expenditures and income, except that if one party does not agree to an expenditure, the other(s) can advance the amount in question, subject to double reimbursement from any income.
- Provides that if an owner desires to manufacture or sell the patented invention, that owner must pay a reasonable royalty to all other owners, including the manufacturing owner.

You should regard this agreement as one solution to an unfair statute. You may ignore, modify, add to, or replace this agreement with any understanding you wish, so long as you're aware of the problems of Section 262, as paraphrased above. As with any contract, you should consider seeking advice from an attorney before signing.

The manner of completing the JOA of Form 16-2 is straightforward. Fill it in after or concurrently with an assignment or a joint patent application. Fill in the names and respective percentages owned by each at the top of the form, identify the patent application

(or patent) next, and have each joint owner sign and date the end of the form. As with all agreements, each signer (joint owner) should get and preserve an original signed copy. The JOA should not be filed in the PTO.

CAUTION

If you want to be sure that your joint owners' agreement accurately reflects your needs, consult a patent attorney.

E. Special Issues Faced by the Employed Inventor

Many inventors are employed in industries that are at least somewhat related to the inventing they do on their own time. Such inventors naturally have a strong desire to learn what rights, if any, they have on inventions that they make during their employment, both on their own time and when they are on the job. This complex subject is covered in detail in *Profit From Your Idea: How to Make Smart Licensing Deals* (Nolo), by attorney Richard Stim. We'll just cover the high points here.

Generally, the rights and obligations of employed inventors are covered by the Employment Agreement (EA) they sign with their employer—that is, the EA prevails—unless it conflicts with state law. Below is an example (Fig. 16A) of a typical EA.

If you have *no* EA, it is possible that an employer may own rights to your employee-created invention under the "employed to invent" doctrine. How does this rule apply? If you are employed—even without a written employment agreement—to accomplish a defined task, or are hired or directed to create an invention, your employer will own all rights to the subsequent invention. This doctrine is derived from a Supreme Court ruling that stated, "One employed to make an invention, who succeeds, during his term of service, in accomplishing that task, is bound to assign to his employer any patent obtained." (*Standard Parts Co. v. Peck*, 264 U.S. 52 (1924).) Generally, most companies prefer to use an EA because it is more reliable and easier to enforce than this judicially created obligation.

Agreement

varian

IN CONSIDERATION of my employment or the continuance of my employment by VARIAN ASSOCIATES, I agree as follows:

For the purpose of this Agreement the term "the Company" shall include VARIAN ASSOCIATES, its subsidiaries and, or its affiliates in which VARIAN ASSOCIATES now or hereafter during the term of this Agreement owns more than twenty percent of the stock eligible to vote for directors and the assignees and licensees of VARIAN ASSOCIATES, its subsidiaries and affiliates.

I agree that all information and know-how, whether or not in writing, of a private, secret or confidential nature concerning the Company's business affairs, including its inventions, products, processes, projects, developments, and plans are and shall be the property of the Company, and I will not disclose the same to unauthorized persons or use the same for any unauthorized purposes without written approval by an officer of the Company, either during or after the term of my employment, until such time as such information has become public knowledge. I also agree to treat all U. S. Government classified information and material in the manner specified by applicable Government regulations.

I agree that all files, letters, memos, reports, sketches, drawings, laboratory notebooks or other written material containing matter of the type set forth in paragraph 2 above which shall come into my custody or possession shall be and are the exclusive property of the Company to be used by me only in the performance of Company duties and that all such records or copies thereof in my custody or possession shall be delivered to the Company upon termination of my employment.

I agree that my obligation not to disclose or to use proprietary or confidential information of the types set forth in paragraphs 2 and 3 above also extends to such types of information of customers of the Company or suppliers to the Company, who may have disclosed or entrusted such information to the Company or me in the course of business.

I hereby assign and agree to assign to the Company or its designee all my right, title and interest in and to all inventions, improvements, discoveries or technical developments, whether or not patentable which I, solely or jointly with others, may conceive or reduce to practice during the term of my employment and which are conceived or first actually reduced to practice (a) in the utilization by the Company of my services in a technical or professional capacity in the areas of research, development, marketing, management, engineering or manufacturing, or (b) pursuant to any project of which I am a participant or member and that is either financed or directed by the Company, or (c) at the Company's expense, in whole or in part. All other inventions, improvements, discoveries or technical developments shall remain my property.

I agree to promptly disclose to and to cooperate with the Company or its designee, both during and after employment, with respect to the procurement of patents for the establishment and maintenance of the Company's or its designee's rights and interests in said inventions, improvements, discoveries or developments, and to sign all papers which the Company may deem necessary or desirable for the purpose of vesting the Company or its designee with such rights, the expense thereof to be borne by the Company.

Since I am to assign to the Company certain inventions which I may conceive or first actually reduce to practice after I enter the employ of the Company, I have listed below all those inventions which I own at this time and which I believe should be brought to the attention of the Company to avoid future misunderstandings as to ownership.

I agree that I will make no claim for pecuniary award or compensation under the provisions of the Atomic Energy Act of 1954, as amended, with respect to any invention or discovery made or conceived by me, solely or jointly with others, in the course of or under any contracts that the Company now has or may have pertaining to work for the Atomic Energy Commission during the term of my employment.

DATE _____   EMPLOYEE _____

DATE _____   WITNESS _____

PRIOR INVENTIONS OWNED BY EMPLOYEE
(PLEASE USE REVERSE SIDE IF MORE SPACE IS REQUIRED)

_____

_____

_____

_____

Fig. 16A—Typical Employment Agreement

If you have no EA and are not employed to invent, you'll own all your inventions, subject to the employer's extensive "shop rights" (that is, a right to use the invention solely for the employer's business, without paying the employee) on inventions made using company time, facilities, or materials.

If you *have* an EA, it will almost certainly require that you assign (legally transfer) to your employer all inventions, that are:

1. made during the term of employment (note that Form 16A asks you to list all inventions you owned prior to employment—those are excluded from the agreement)
2. related to the employer's existing or contemplated business
3. made by using the employer's time (that is, the time for which the employee is paid), facilities, or materials, or
4. made as a result of activity within the scope of the employee's duties.

Note that under items 1, 2, and 4, even if an employee makes an invention at home, on the employee's own time, the employer still can be entitled to ownership.

Also, you'll usually be bound to disclose *all* inventions to the employer (so the employer can determine if they're assignable). Lastly, most EAs will require you to keep your employer's trade secrets confidential during and after your employment. Some states, such as California, have enacted statutes (Calif. Lab. Code, Sections 2870 et seq. and 2860) prohibiting the employer from requiring the employee to sign any EA that is broader than the foregoing. For example, under such statutes the employee can't be made to turn over all inventions, no matter where and when made, to the employer. Similarly, the employer is prohibited from providing an EA that states that everything an employee acquires from the employer (except salary) belongs to the employer.

EXAMPLE: Griselda is an engineer employed by Silicon Valley Chips (SVC) to design integrated circuits. Griselda's EA requires her to disclose to SVC all inventions made during the term of her employment at SVC and to assign to SVC all inventions which relate to integrated circuits or SVC's business, or which she makes using SVC's time, facilities, or materials. While employed, Griselda invents a new toilet valve at home in her workshop. The toilet valve is clearly outside the scope of SVC's business and therefore, Griselda owns it totally. However, she should make a signed and dated and witnessed and dated written record of the valve and disclose it to SVC (regardless of whose time it was invented on). Later, Griselda, while still employed but on vacation, is cogitating about an integrated circuit design problem she had last week at work. She comes up with a valuable, less-expensive integrated circuit passivation technique. Since this invention relates to SVC's business, SVC owns it and Griselda must disclose it to SVC and sign any patent application and assignment on it that SVC requests.

If the invention is clearly within the scope of the EA, or is in a gray area, it is wise to first disclose it to the employer. If the employer isn't interested in the invention after reviewing it, the employee can apply for a release, a document under which the employer reassigns or returns the invention to the employee. (The employer may retain a "shop right" under the release—that is, a nontransferable right to use the invention for its own purposes and business only.)

If the invention is in the gray area and the employer wants to exploit the invention, the employee can then try to negotiate some rights, such as a small royalty, or offer to have the matter decided by arbitration. Failing this, a lawsuit may be necessary.

Most EAs also require the invention-assigning employee to keep good records of inventions made and to cooperate in signing patent applications, giving testimony when needed, even after termination of employment. Most companies give the employee a small cash bonus, usually from one hundred to several thousand dollars or more, when the employee signs a company patent application. This bonus is not in payment for the signing (the employee's wages are supposed to cover that) but to encourage employees to invent and turn in invention disclosures on their inventions. Some employers, such as Lockheed, give their inventor-employees a generous cut of the royalties from their invention, and some will even set up a subsidiary entity (partly owned by the employee-inventor) to exploit the invention. Most, however, prefer to reward highly creative employees via the salary route.

F. Assignment of Invention and Patent Rights

In the arcane patent world, to make a transfer of ownership of an intangible thing like an invention or a patent application, you must sign an "assignment"—a legal document that the law will recognize as effective to make the transfer of ownership. An assignment for transferring ownership of an invention and its patent application is provided as Form 16-3. (The PTO does not provide an assignment form.) The assignment should be recorded in the PTO to be fully effective.

As indicated, employed inventors ("assignors") usually make full assignments—transfer of 100% of the invention and its patent application—to their employers ("assignees"). They do this because they have agreed, in their EA, to assign all inventions they make within the scope of their employment to their employer. In these cases the assignee is usually a corporation.

A partial assignment (transfer of less than 100%) is usually made where the assignee (the person getting the transferred interest) has financed all or part of the patent application.

The assignment document presented here, like the Joint Owners' Agreement, is but one of many possible alternatives. If you use it, you may want to change a number of provisions to fit your situation. Also, a consultation with a patent attorney is advisable if you wish to fully understand how this agreement will affect your rights. For example, where there will be many owners of the patent application, the percentage interest of each should be specifically listed in the last sentence of paragraph 1.

The assignment can also be used to convey title to provisional applications, as well as title or ownership of any reissues or continuing cases (see Chapter 14) of the basic application referred to in part (B) of the assignment, as well as any provisional

applications that the basic application claims priority of, and any regular (nonprovisional) applications which claim priority of the basic application, if the basic application is a provisional. A regular patent application can claim priority of a provisional application even if the regular and provisional are not commonly owned, so long as they both have a common inventor and the regular is filed within a year of the provisional. (This is one example where it is important to understand the difference between an inventor and an owner.)

To complete the assignment do the following:

Lines 1-3: Insert the names of the assignors (the inventor patent applicants) on lines 1 and 2 of the first paragraph after "received," and insert their cities and states of residence after "of" on line 3.

Lines 4-6: Do the same for the assignee on line 4.

Line 7: Put the percentage of the patent rights being assigned (normally 100%).

Lines 8-9: Put the title of the invention on line 7.

Lines 10-12: Put the date the patent application was signed (sometimes termed "executed" in the law) on line 11. If the application has already been filed, also put the serial number of the patent application on line 11 and put the filing date on line 12. Put the percentages owned by the assignor and assignee in the penultimate line of this paragraph.

Each assignor should sign and date the assignment. If the assignment is to be used abroad, have two witnesses sign and date the bottom two lines to make it recordable abroad. The PTO no longer requires notarization. A completed assignment is shown in Fig. 16B.

G. Record Your Assignment With the PTO

To be fully effective, the assignment must be recorded in the PTO (just as the deed to your house must be recorded with your county clerk). If the assignment is not recorded, and the assignors make a subsequent (fraudulent) assignment to a different assignee, unaware of the first assignment, the second assignee's rights will prevail over those of the first assignee if the second assignee records the assignment first. (Lawyers call this situation a "race arrangement" since the

Assignment of Invention and Patent Application

For value received, ___Roberta Ann Briskin___ ,

of ___Merion Station, PA___

(hereinafter ASSIGNOR), hereby sells, assigns, transfers, and sets over unto ___Rotten Kid Enterprises, Inc.___

of ___Marcus Hook, PA___

and her or his successors or assigns (hereinafter ASSIGNEE) __100__ % of the following: (A) ASSIGNOR's right, title, and interest in and to the invention entitled " ___Poetry Therapy Systems___
"

invented by ASSIGNOR; (B) the application for United States patent therefor, signed by ASSIGNOR on ___2018 Jan 11___ , U.S. Patent and Trademark Office Serial Number ___10/123,456___ , filed ___2018 Jan 5___ ; (C) any patent or reissues of any patent that may be granted thereon; and (D) any applications which are provisional patent applications which said application claims priority of, or nonprovisional applications which claim priority of said application, or continuations, continuations-in-part, substitutes, or divisions of said application. ASSIGNOR authorizes ASSIGNEE to enter the date of signature and/or Serial Number and Filing Date in the spaces above. ASSIGNOR also authorizes and requests the Commissioner for Patents to issue any resulting patent(s) as follows: __0__ % to ASSIGNOR and __100__ % to ASSIGNEE. (The singular shall include the plural and vice versa herein.)

ASSIGNOR hereby further sells, assigns, transfers, and sets over unto ASSIGNEE, the above percentage of ASSIGNOR's entire right, title, and interest in and to said invention in each and every country foreign to the United States; and ASSIGNOR further conveys to ASSIGNEE the above percentage of all priority rights resulting from the above-identified application for United States patent. ASSIGNOR agrees to execute all papers, give any required testimony, and perform other lawful acts, at ASSIGNEE's expense, as ASSIGNEE may require to enable ASSIGNEE to perfect ASSIGNEE's interest in any resulting patent of the United States and countries foreign thereto, and to acquire, hold, enforce, convey, and uphold the validity of said patent and reissues and extensions thereof, and ASSIGNEE's interest therein.

In testimony whereof ASSIGNOR has hereunto set its hand and seal on the date below.

Signature ___Roberta Ann Briskin___   Date ___2018 Jan 11___

Signature _____   Date _____

Witnessed by:

Signature ___Maxwell Spillane___   Date ___2018 Jan 11___

Signature ___Michael Barre___   Date ___2018 Jan 11___

Fig. 16B—Completed Assignment Form (Form 16-3 in Appendix 7)

assignee who prevails is the one who wins the race to the PTO.) This means any assignee should record the assignment as soon as possible after it's signed.

The easiest way to record an assignment in the PTO is to do so online. Make a PDF copy of the signed assignment with a scanner, then go to https://epas.uspto.gov, and follow the instructions: Fill out the recordation form online, attach the assignment, pay by credit card, and submit the forms for recording. If you don't have a scanner and Internet access, you can record the assignment by mail or fax. First fill out a cover sheet (Form 16-4 or PTO-1595) and note the PTO's recordation fee, which is listed in Appendix 4, Fee Schedule. Then send or fax the assignment and cover sheet to the PTO with the recording fee. You can pay the recording fee by a credit card payment form or check. The mail address and the fax number are listed at the bottom of the cover sheet form. The PTO will record the assignment by making a copy of it and the cover sheet, and return the cover sheet and a record sheet listing the assignment data to the person requesting recording.

If an assignment has been signed before the patent application is filed, it is permissible to send the assignment in with the application and have it recorded at that time (see Chapter 10). However, you must fill in the date the application was signed (executed) on the assignment and cover sheet. (You won't be able to insert the application serial number or filing date since you don't know those yet.) However, even if the assignment is signed before filing, you may prefer to wait until you can add the filing date and application (serial) number to it before sending it in for recording. This will connect it to the application in an unequivocal way. If you want to file the assignment after you file the application, you can file it online, or you can fax the assignment, the cover sheet, a CCPF or check (mail only) for the fee to Fax: 703-306-5995, or mail to "Mail Stop Assignment, Commissioner for Patents, P.O. Box 1450, Alexandria, VA 22313-1450." If you mail the papers, don't forget the usual receipt postcard.

H. Licensing of Inventions—An Overview

When a patent owner, sometimes called a "patentee," gives another permission to manufacture and market an invention in exchange for compensation (such as a royalty or flat payment), it is done with a document termed a "license." It is essential that a license agreement be written and signed by the inventor or owner of the patent or patent application (the licensor) and the manufacturer (the licensee). Here are just a few major considerations and terms that can be written into a license agreement:

1. The proposed licensee can buy an option from you (the licensor) under which you give it the exclusive (or nonexclusive) right to obtain a license under your patent application or patent within a fixed time, say two years. The payment for this option can be merely the company's agreement to research and develop your invention (this is a typical arrangement), or it can involve a cash payment. The general rule is that the more you receive up front, the more seriously the licensee will view and promote your invention.

2. As noted, if you grant the company a license, the license can be exclusive, under which you agree to license only the company and no one else. Alternatively, it can be nonexclusive, under which you license them but also have the right to license others. Exclusive licenses are more common, since manufacturers want to have a monopoly. Nonexclusive licenses are usually used for valuable inventions where several manufacturers want licenses to get into the business. For example, Pilkington Brothers, the great British glass company, granted many nonexclusive licenses under its float glass patents.

3. The license, if granted, can be for the life of the patent, or just for a limited term, say five years, with an option to renew for succeeding five-year terms.

4. The license can require the payment of an advance that may be recoverable against

royalties, or it may be in addition to royalties. You, of course, want to get as much money at the beginning as possible under the old "bird-in-the-hand" theory.

5. The license can require the payment of minimum annual royalty payments during each year of its existence. This is usually done when an exclusive license is granted.

6. The license rights can be transferred ("assigned") by your licensee to another manufacturer, or any such assignment can be prohibited. From your point of view, it's a good idea to try to get a provision included in the agreement prohibiting assignment without your approval.

On the other hand, there are a few traps in license agreements that you should avoid.

1. Expiration: You cannot demand perpetual royalties for a patented product, because patents expire. The implicit "bargain" struck between the inventor and the government is 17 years (or so) of exclusive rights in the invention, in exchange for the public's ability to make and use the invention afterward. Courts look unfavorably at attempts to extend the lifespan of a patent, because doing so goes against the public's interest in this bargain, and they have the power to rule a patent unenforceable based on its owner's bad behavior. (However, you can require ongoing payment for product support, the continued use of trade secrets and other know-how, and other non-patent services—if your license agreement clearly separates the value of these services from that of the patent itself.)

2. Illegal tying arrangements: A tying arrangement is one where you sell or lease one product or service only on the condition that the buyer also take a second product or service. Tying by itself is not always illegal, but if the first product is patented and a license agreement requires purchase of the second service based on that patent, that leverage disappears when the patent expires. If the license agreement requires purchase of the second product or service past the patent's expiration, a court may rule that the tying is illegal and you will lose the right to enforce your patent.

3. Sale versus License: Once your product is sold, your right to demand ongoing royalties or condition use of the product is destroyed. (*Impression Products, Inc. v. Lexmark Int'l, Inc.* (581 U.S. 1523 (2017)) This rule prevents you from "double dipping": obtaining payments both from a manufacturer for making your product, and from the wholesaler, retailer, or end purchaser of your product for owning or using it.

There are hundreds of other, less important, considerations in licensing. Licensing, as you may have gathered by now, is a difficult, complex subject, and one that requires knowledge as well as negotiation skill. Unfortunately, most invention licensing agreements tend to be tailor-made by large corporations to protect their interests. Again, for a detailed discussion about the licensing process, consult *Profit From Your Idea: How to Make Smart Licensing Deals* (Nolo), by attorney Richard Stim.

It's important to realize that even though you can make a great invention, prepare a patent application on it, and sell it to a manufacturer, you may not be able to represent yourself adequately in negotiating a license agreement unless you're familiar with licensing and adept at business. It's therefore often wise to hire a patent lawyer to review any contract that is offered to you. You'll find this will probably cost several hundred dollars or more, but the money will be well spent, especially if you have a potentially good deal in the offing.

In fact, most reputable companies would prefer that you be represented by an attorney when you negotiate a license agreement and often give you money to pay an attorney. The reason for this is that an agreement between an unrepresented inventor and a much larger company is likely to be interpreted against the company by the courts. If the inventor is represented by an experienced lawyer, the courts will tend to treat the parties equally if a dispute later arises.

Universal License Agreement

1. Parties and Summary of Terms:

Parties: This agreement is between:

Licensor: Henry Beresofsky

of Chernegov, Ukraine

Licensee: Chernobyl Reactor Works, Inc.

of Russian Hill, CA

Summary: Type of License: ☑ Exclusive ☐ Nonexclusive

Invention Title: Perpetual Energy machine

Patent Application Ser. Nr.: 07/123,456 , Filing Date: 2018 Aug 9

If Exclusive License, minimum number of units to be sold to compute Minimum Annual Royalty (MAR):

MARs start first quarter of 20xx .

☑ Option Granted: Premium $ 5,000 For term of: 18 months

Patent Royalty Rate 2.00 % ☑ Know-How Licensed: Know-How Royalty Rate: 3.00 %

Total Royalty Rate (Patent Royalty Rate plus Know-How Royalty, if applicable): 5.00 %.

Estimated 1st year's sales (units): 200 x Estimated Unit Price $ 1,000.00

x Total Royalty Rate 5.00 % = Licensing Fee $ 10,000.00

2. Effective Date:
This agreement shall be effective as of the latter of the signature dates below written and shall be referred to as the Agreement of such date.

3. Recitals:

A. LICENSOR has developed an invention having the above title and warrants that LICENSOR has filed a patent application on such invention in the U.S. Patent and Trademark Office, which patent application is identified by the above title, Serial Number, and Filing Date. LICENSOR warrants that LICENSOR has full and exclusive right to grant this license on this invention and LICENSOR's patent application. If the "Know-How Licensed" box above is checked, LICENSOR has also developed know-how in connection with said invention and warrants that LICENSOR owns and has the right to license said know-how.

B. LICENSEE desires, if the "Option Granted" box above is checked, to exclusively investigate LICENSOR's above invention for the term indicated. If said "Option Granted" box is not checked, or if said box is checked and LICENSEE investigates LICENSOR's invention for the term indicated and such investigation is favorable, LICENSEE desires to make, use, and sell the products embodying such invention and covered by the claims of LICENSOR's patent application and any patent(s) issuing thereon (hereinafter "Licensed Product").

4. If Option Granted:
If the "Option Granted" box above is checked, then (A) the patent license grant of Part 5 below shall not take effect except as defined in this part, and (B) LICENSOR hereby grants LICENSEE, for the option premium stated above, an exclusive option to investigate LICENSOR's invention for the term indicated above, such term to commence from the date of this Agreement. LICENSOR will furnish LICENSEE with all information and know-how (if any) concerning LICENSOR's invention in LICENSOR's possession. LICENSEE will investigate LICENSOR's invention for operability, costing, marketing, etc. LICENSEE shall report the results of its investigation to LICENSOR at any time before the end of the option term. If LICENSEE's determination is favorable, it may thereupon exercise this option and the patent license grant of Part 5 below shall become effective. If LICENSEE's determination is unfavorable, then said option shall not be exercised and no patent license grant shall take effect, all rights hereunder shall revert to LICENSOR, LICENSEE shall deliver to LICENSOR all results of its investigations for LICENSOR's benefit, and LICENSEE shall promptly return to LICENSOR all know-how (papers and things) received from LICENSOR or generated by LICENSEE in its investigations.

Fig. 16C—Completed First Page of Universal License Agreement (Form 16-5 in Appendix 7)

What Is Know-How?

Know-how usually refers to a particular kind of technical knowledge that is needed to accomplish some task. For example, your know-how may be necessary to train the licensee's employees how to make or use your invention. Think of know-how as a combination of secret and nonsecret information that has value because it is needed to commercialize your invention.

I. Universal License Agreement

If you do feel confident enough to represent yourself, and you're the type of person who can go through a long license agreement with nitpicking skill and then competently negotiate with corporate pros, more power to you. Start your quest by referring to the Universal License Agreement in Appendix 7 (Form 16-5). This agreement can be used to exclusively or nonexclusively license your invention as well as to license know-how. It can also be used to grant a potential licensee an option to evaluate your invention for a given period in return for a payment. As we've said, most companies will either prefer their own license agreement or make one up from scratch, but you can use the Universal License Agreement for purposes of comparison.

The sample shown (Fig. 16C) is for the first page of an exclusive license with an option grant and a know-how license.

Part 1: Parties and Summary of Terms. The licensor is the party, usually the inventor, who does the licensing, while the licensee is the party who licenses—that is, is given permission to make, use, and sell the invention, patent, know-how, etc.

The Patent Royalty rate is the percentage rate the licensee pays for use of the patent. This rate is set low (2%) purposely, since a know-how license has been granted at a rate of 3% for an overall (total) royalty of 5%. It's usually to an inventor's advantage to license know-how, as well as patent rights, and to make the know-how rate as high a proportion of the total rate as possible. This is because patents can be

held invalid and can only be licensed for a limited term (the duration of the patent application plus the approximately 18-year term of the patent), usually a total of about 19 years; whereas a know-how license can extend indefinitely. In order for know-how to be licensed, the inventor must actually transfer (or be able to transfer) some actual know-how to the licensee.

A licensing fee (advance) is customarily paid to the licensor upon signing the agreement as a reward for past work. In the agreement, the licensing fee is computed as an estimate of the first year's sales by multiplying (a) the Patent Royalty Rate by (b) the Estimated First Year's Sales in Units by (c) the Estimated Unit Price in dollars. Again, it's usually in the inventor's interest to get as large a signing bonus as possible, and not to have this money be set off against later royalty payments.

The "Exclusive" box is checked, indicating that only the licensee will be entitled to make, use, or sell the invention. If the "Nonexclusive" box is checked, the licensor will be able to license others, and the licensee and the licensor will be able to make, use, and sell the invention. The title, serial number, and filing date of the patent application are identified next.

The "Minimum Number of Units to Be Sold to Compute Minimum Annual Royalty" (whether or not they are actually sold) is provided to ensure that the licensor receives an adequate income from the licensee inasmuch as he can't, under an exclusive license, license others to derive more income. This minimum annual royalty has been computed on the basis of a minimum annual number of units to be sold (rather than a fixed dollar amount) to give the licensor the benefit of inflation in unit price. While the manufacturer can cut the price of the licensed product and thereby reduce its royalty payments to you, it's generally not in its interest to do this, since it will be reducing its profits as well. However, if you want protection against this possibility, you can substitute a fixed dollar amount for the minimum annual royalty.

For the privilege of obtaining an option to exclusively evaluate the invention for the Option Term, an Option Premium (a one-time cash payment) has been paid to the licensor.

The Know-How Royalty Rate is stated and is added to the Patent Royalty Rate to get the total, or Running Royalty Rate.

Part 2: Effective Date. The effective date of the agreement is the date when the last signature is made.

Part 3: Recitals. Here the Recitals provide the background reasons or premises for the agreement to aid in interpreting it. The recitals simply state that the licensor has an invention, a patent application, and possibly know-how, and the licensee desires to evaluate licensor's invention (if an option has been granted) and to make, use, and sell the licensed invention.

Part 4: Option Granted. This covers the parties' rights if an option has been granted. In this case, the regular license grant doesn't take effect yet, but the licensee has the exclusive right to investigate the invention for the option term indicated in Part 1. If the investigation is favorable, the licensee will exercise its option and the patent license grant of Part 5 will take effect. If not, the option will not be exercised and all rights will revert to the licensor and the licensor will get the results of the licensee's investigation of the invention.

Part 5: License Grant. This contains the actual license grant. This comes into play immediately if the invention is licensed or if an option is granted or if the option is granted and exercised. Remember, if an option is granted, the actual license isn't granted until the option is exercised. The license granted (exclusive or nonexclusive) gives the licensee the right to make, use, and sell the licensed product in the U.S., and it includes any derivative applications and patents (see Chapter 14). If the "know-how" box of Part 1 has been checked, then know-how is also licensed.

Part 6: Know-How. If know-how is licensed, then the licensor is obligated to communicate all of its know-how to the licensee within one month, plus provide up to 80 hours of consultation to the licensee, with travel and other expenses paid by licensee. The licensor disclaims any guarantee that the know-how is workable. The know-how royalty is to be paid for three years and thereafter for so long as the licensee enjoys a U.S. competitive market share of at least 15%. This means that the licensor can enjoy know-how

royalty payments indefinitely, provided its know-how was valuable enough to give the licensee a market share of over 15% after three years have passed.

Part 7: Royalties. This concerns royalties and is the heart of the agreement.

Subpart A: If a Licensing Fee is paid; it's an advance against future royalties. If the estimated Licensing Fee has been computed inaccurately (Part 1) then an adjustment is made when royalties are paid. (Note: It is permissible to draft an agreement whereby the licensing fee is a one-time payment and not an advance against royalties.)

Subpart B: The running royalty is covered and is paid quarterly, within one month after the end of each quarter, together with a report of the sales made in the quarter.

Subpart C: The minimum annual royalty (MAR) is to be paid if an exclusive license has been granted. The MAR payment is computed using the royalty rate times the minimum number of units of Part 1. Minimum annual royalties start as also stated in Part 1. If the minimum number of units is not sold in any year, the licensee must pay the appropriate makeup difference to the licensor with its payment for the fourth quarter.

Subpart D: If the minimum is not paid by licensee, either due to lack of sufficient sales or licensee's choice, then the license grant will be converted to a nonexclusive one, and the licensor can immediately license others.

Subpart E: If the license is or becomes nonexclusive, then the licensor may not grant more favorable terms to any other licensee.

Subpart F: Patent royalties are not due after the patent expires, or if it is declared invalid, or if no patent is granted.

Subpart G: Late payments earn interest at 10%.

Subpart H: The "Net Factory Sales Price," on which royalties are based, is the factory selling price, less shipping, insurance, taxes, etc., if billed separately. If the units are imported, then the importer's gross selling price is the basis for royalties. The royalty paid on returns is deductible against future royalties.

Part 8: Records. This requires the licensee to keep full records for at least two years after each payment, so that the licensor can verify the royalty payments.

Part 9: Sublicensees. Here the licensee's sublicensees are bound by all of the terms of the agreement and the licensee must notify the licensor if it grants sublicenses. A licensee will usually grant a sublicense when it has the licensed product made for it by a contracting company.

Part 10: Patent Prosecution. This simply states the parties' responsibilities for patent prosecution.

Subpart A: Requires the licensor to pay for prosecution of the U.S. patent application, together with the patent maintenance fees that are payable after the patent issues. If the licensor intends to abandon the patent application, it must notify the licensee at least two months in advance to give it the opportunity to take over.

Subpart B: The licensor may file for patent coverage abroad, but if it doesn't do so, then the licensee may do so. If licensor wants to license any foreign licensees, it has to give the licensee the opportunity of first refusal.

Subpart C: If the licensee takes over the U.S. patent prosecution, and is successful, then it can reduce its royalties by 25%, and can deduct its patent prosecution expenses. If the licensee elects to file abroad, then the royalty rate on foreign sales is 50% of the U.S. rate, less foreign prosecution expenses.

Part 11: Patent Marking. This requires the licensee to mark products sold with the legend "patent pending" while the patent application is pending and with the patent number (see Chapter 15) after the patent issues.

Part 12: Infringements. This states that if the patent is infringed, the licensor can sue to enforce its patent rights. If it doesn't choose to do so, the licensee may do so. If the licensee sues, it can keep 75% of this recovery, less costs of the suit.

Part 13-A: No Validity Guarantee. This clause states that licensor doesn't guarantee that its patent is valid or that it has any particular scope (breadth).

Part 13-B: Liability. This clause states, in effect, that if someone is injured by the patented product, the licensor is not liable.

Part 14: Term. This clause states that the term or maximum duration of the agreement shall be until the last patent of licensor expires, unless know-how is licensed, in which case Part 6 governs the term.

Part 15: Termination. This clause covers the situations when the parties may terminate the agreement before the term expires. Under Subparts A and B, the licensor may terminate the agreement if the licensee defaults in making royalty payments, or if it ever declares bankruptcy. Subpart C, the antishelving clause, is very important. This protects the licensor in case the licensee stops production for 1.5 years, or doesn't start production within 1.5 years from the date the license agreement is signed. In these cases, the licensor can terminate the agreement.

Clauses like this one (and others) are designed to put teeth into the agreement to deter the licensee from defaulting: it is not enough to make a fair agreement; all agreements should also be structured to ensure the other party's performance by giving an incentive for performance, or a penalty for nonperformance.

Part 16: Notices. This clause states how and where notices under the agreement are to be sent.

Part 17: Mediation and Arbitration. This clause provides that if the parties have any dispute, they shall submit the matter to mediation. If mediation can't resolve the dispute, the parties must submit the dispute to binding and final arbitration. In no case will the dispute go to a court for resolution, since litigation is extremely expensive and thus works to the detriment of the independent inventor.

Part 18: Transfer of Rights. This clause allows the licensor to assign (legally transfer) its rights to anyone without permission, but the licensee needs advance permission of licensor to assign the licensee's rights unless it makes an assignment to its successor in business.

Part 19: Controlling Law. This clause specifies that the laws of licensor's state shall govern interpretation of the agreement. Normally, state law on the interpretation of contracts doesn't vary much, but since a licensor is usually at an economic disadvantage, we've given it the benefit here. Also, it specifies that any lawsuit on the agreement shall be brought in licensor's county.

Lump-Sum Payment

If you're offered a single lump-sum payment for all your rights (this is rare), should you take it, and if so, how much should you get? To answer the first question, only you can decide if a relatively large bird in the hand is worth more than a potential (but by no means assured) stream of smaller, but aggregately heavier, birds in the bush over the years. To grapple with the second question, estimate the potential sales of your invention for the life of your patent application (one to three years), plus the term of the patent (approximately 18 years), then apply your royalty to this figure. Be willing to take half of this as a single-payment lump sum for a fully paid-up license.

For example, suppose you expect your widget to be sold for the next 20 years (two years during patent pendency, and 18 years during life of patent), for an average factory price of 50 cents and an average yearly quantity of 150,000 units, and that a patent royalty

of 5% is fair. Applying the formula, the substitute lump-sum payment for your royalty would be ½ x 20 years x 50¢ unit price x 150,000 units x 5% rate, or $37,500. If you are offered much less than this, it may be unwise to sell.

Don't make Mary Jacobs's mistake. She invented the bra (out of two hankies and a ribbon) and was able to sell her patent for $15,000 in 1914. Although this was a princely sum then, she practically gave it away since (as you know) her invention soon took hold and her patent eventually was worth $15 *million*!

The disadvantage with the alternative lump-sum calculation is that it's very hard to estimate anything about what will happen in the next 20 years. Will sales go up or down? Will the product become obsolete or even more popular? Will competition affect its price, etc.? These are just some of the imponderables and unknowables, so, as stated, be extremely careful before selling your rights for a single lump-sum payment.

Part 20: Good Faith. This states that neither party shall take any action that hampers the rights of the other and that both parties shall engage in good faith and fair dealing. This clause is supposed to be read into any agreement, but we've expressly stated it in order to increase cooperation and reduce disputes.

Part 21: Rectification of Mistakes. This states that in case of any mistake in the agreement, it shall be rectified to conform to the parties' intentions. The clause is designed to save a misdrafted agreement that otherwise might be thrown out.

Part 22: Supersession. This makes it clear the agreement supersedes prior or concurrent oral, or prior written, understandings.

Part 23: Counsel Consulted. This one states that the parties have carefully read the agreement and have consulted, or have been given an opportunity to consult, counsel and that each has received a signed original. This makes a challenge to the agreement more difficult.

Other terms that can be added to the Agreement, if necessary, are Definitions of Terms (use if any unusual terms are present in the Agreement), Other Obligations of Licensee (e.g., Licensor has the right to approve the quality of Licensee's product, Licensee will spend certain

efforts to commercialize product, etc.), Improvements (if Licensee or Licensor make improvements, who owns these and is royalty adjusted?).

All that remains is to sign and date the agreement. Each party should get an original, ink-signed copy.

TIP

While the Universal License Agreement incorporates most of the customary terms and covers many common licensing situations, it probably won't be appropriate for your situation without modification. Obviously, if your arrangement won't fit within the terms of this agreement, or if you don't like any of the "fixed" terms, such as the 80 hours of consultation, the 15% market share, compulsory arbitration, etc., you should propose changes, or hire an expert to help you.

J. How Much Should You Get for Your Invention?

Many inventors seem to believe that patents are almost always licensed at a royalty rate of 5%. The 5% royalty generally means that you get 5% of the money received by the factory for its sales of the item embodying your invention. This is sometimes termed 5% of the "ex-factory" price. This assumption is simply not true. While 5% is often used as a starting point in many license negotiations, very few licenses are granted at this rate. We've seen them run from 0.1% to 15% of the factory price of licensed hardware items (as high as 30% of the retail price for software).

As you've guessed, many factors affect the royalty rate. Obviously, the more desirable your invention is to the licensee, the better royalty you'll get, subject to industry norms. Here's a list of some factors that militate in favor of increasing the royalty rate. Use as many of these as possible in your negotiations:

- the product has a potential for large sales volume
- the product can be offered at a low selling price
- the product will not have much competition
- the product will have a high profit margin
- the product is ingenious and novel
- the product required a lot of development
- the invention substantially pervades the product
- the licensed territory is a large, significant, or important market
- the inventor will furnish considerable services, materials, parts, and/or tooling
- there is no competition between licensee and licensor
- this industry respects patents
- it would be difficult to avoid the patent—that is, the patent is strong
- negotiating the license agreement was difficult—for example, you expended considerable time or attorneys' fees
- the licensee will save money on costs
- the inventor has a strong reputation in the field
- the product will have a long life
- the start-up costs to produce the invention are low
- the inventor has a number of patents or patent applications
- consumers will pay a premium price for the product
- the product can be sold at lower cost than its competition, and
- a higher up-front payment will reduce the rate and vice versa.

Of course, your bargaining skill will transcend all of these considerations. As business negotiating seminar leader C.L. Karrass says: "In business, you don't get what you deserve—you get what you negotiate." Also, the custom of the industry will dominate—for example, toys usually get an exclusive royalty rate of 2.5% to 4%, medical products 6% to 7%, and software inventions up to 10% and sometimes more. An exclusive license will entitle you to about 50% more than a nonexclusive license.

In some industries the royalty rate may be a fixed (or per-unit) amount. For example, a patent owner may grant a license to a television manufacturer for a payment of 50¢ for each patented and manufactured LCD screen, 25¢ for each patented chrominance demodulation circuit used, etc.

If your licensee doesn't want to pay the rate you ask, a good technique is to accept the lower rate they're willing to pay. However, add a proviso stating that the rate will be increased to the rate you want if "x" number of units are sold.

Instead of a negotiated percentage, some experts advocate getting a royalty equivalent to "one-third of the manufacturer's profit." This means that the company will take its selling price for your invention, say $10, subtract its cost of manufacture, including overhead, say $7, and give you one-third of the difference—that is, $1 = ⅓ of its $3 profit. This type of royalty is often enticing to a manufacturer since the company only contemplates parting with a portion of its profit, not paying a fixed sum per item, whether the particular product turns out to be profitable or not. If your licensee is willing to accept this type of royalty, you can substitute this language in the Universal Agreement. But, if you do so, be sure you include an auditing right (such as Clause 8) to ensure that you can verify its cost of manufacture.

K. Summary

When dealing with a patent application or patent, always distinguish between inventorship and ownership. All actual inventors must be named in the patent application, provided each contributed something to at least one claim. Financiers, advisers, model makers, or others that did not contribute any inventive concepts should not be named as inventors, but can be made owners. If the claims of a patent application are changed, inventorship should be reviewed and changed if necessary. Use Form 16-1 to preserve each inventor's contribution.

Under patent law statute, any joint owner of a patent can practice the invention without paying any other inventor. To guarantee that all inventors receive compensation if the invention is commercialized, use the Joint Owners' Agreement—Form 16-2.

An employed inventor's rights are usually governed by an Employment Agreement, which mainly requires the employee to assign to the employer all inventions that are made in the course of the employer's business, use the employer's time, facilities, or materials, or are within the scope of the employee's duties. Employees who are hired to invent have a common law obligation to assign inventions made in the scope of their duties. Other inventions are the property of the employee, but the employment agreement may require the employee to notify the employer about them.

A patent application and a patent are intangible personal property and part or full ownership must be transferred by an assignment, which should be recorded in the PTO to prevent a subsequent, fraudulent assignment.

To collect royalties for use of an invention, an inventor (licensor) should make a licensing agreement with the manufacturer (licensee). The main considerations are the amount of any up-front payment, whether the license is exclusive or nonexclusive, and the royalty rate. It's advantageous to license know-how as well as patent rights. The Universal License Agreement (Form 16-5) covers most situations, but the terms must be negotiated. Factors affecting the royalty rate are the strength of the patent, the amount of design work already done, the anticipated sales volume, the profit margin, the field of the invention, etc. Never assign a patent or application for a series of payments; always get full payment at the time of assignment.

Abbreviations Used in *Patent It Yourself*

Throughout *Patent It Yourself* we've used many abbreviations to save space and to spare you the tedium of repeatedly reading long phrases like "Manual of Patent Examining Procedure." We've tried to define each abbreviation the first time we've used it and again if we've used it at a location remote from the first usage. However, in case we've failed to define any abbreviation adequately, here's a list of (hopefully) all the abbreviations we've used:

A&ARTP	Attorneys and Agents Registered to Practice
ADS	Application Data Sheet (PTO Form SB/14)
AF	After Final
AIA	America Invents Act; Approved 2011 Sep 16
AIPO	African Intellectual Property Organization
BA	Basic Application
BAPI	Board of Appeals & Patent Interferences
BBS	Bulletin Board System
BNA	Bureau of National Affairs
BRS	Bibliographic Research Services
CAD	Computer-Aided Drafting
CAFC	Court of Appeals for the Federal Circuit
CASSIS	Classification And Search Support Information System
CCPF	Credit Card Payment Form
CFIM	Contingent-Fee Invention Marketer
CFR	Code of Federal Regulations
CIP	Continuation-in-Part
CM	Common Misconception; Certificate of Mailing
CRTP	Constructive Reduction to Practice
D	Design Patent
DDP	Disclosure Document Program (discontinued)
DJ	Declaratory Judgment
DOE	Department of Energy; Doctrine of Equivalents
DP	Double Patenting
DPED	Domestic Priority Establishing Document
EA	Employment Agreement
EAST	Examiner Assisted Search Tool
EEC	European Economic Community
EFS	Electronic Filing System
EPC	European Patent Convention
EPO	European Patent Office
FBIE	Fee-Based Inventor Exploiter
FDA	Food and Drug Administration
FTF	First to File
FTI	First to Invent
FWC	File-Wrapper-Continuing
GATT	General Agreement on Tariffs and Trade
GPC	General-Purpose Computer

GPO	Government Printing Office	**PGL**	Paranoia, Greed, Laziness
IC	Inventors' Commandment	**PHOSITA**	Person Having Ordinary Skill In The Art
IDS	Information Disclosure Statement	**PME**	Priority Mail Express
ITC	International Trade Commission	**PPA**	Provisional Patent Application
JOA	Joint Owners' Agreement	**Pre-Ex**	Preliminary to Examination
JPTOS	*Journal of the Patent and Trademark Office Society*	**PTDL**	Patent and Trademark Depository Libraries
KISS	Keep It Simple, Stupid	**PTMS**	Petition to Make Special
MAR	Minimum Annual Royalty	**PTMSUAEP**	Petition to Make Special Under the Accelerated Examination Program
MDC	Multiple Dependent Claim	**PTO**	Patent and Trademark Office (U.S.)
MF	Maintenance Fee	**PubPA**	Published Patent Application
MPEP	*Manual of Patent Examining Procedure*	**RCE**	Request for Continued Examination
N/A	Notice of Allowance	**RPA**	Regular Patent Application
N&UR	New and Unexpected Results	**RTP**	Reduced to Practice
NCC	Non-Convention Country	**S**	Solution
NDA	Non-Disclosure Agreement	**SBA**	Small Business Administration
NIH	Not Invented Here	**SD**	Supporting Declaration
NM	New Matter	**SE**	Small Entity
N(N)C	Normally (Non-) Conductive	**SED**	Small-Entity Declaration
NPL	Non-Patent Literature	**SIR**	Statutory Invention Registration
NPR	Nonpublication Request	**SPO**	Shadow Patent Office
OA	Office Action	**SSM**	Statutory Subject Matter
OG	*Official Gazette*	**TD**	Terminal Disclaimer
OIPE	Office of Initial Patent Examination	**TM**	Trademark
P	Problem	**TN**	Trade Name
PA	Prior Art	**TS**	Trade Secret
PAD	Patent Application Declaration	**UC**	Unfair Competition
PCT	Patent Cooperation Treaty	**UCC**	Uniform Commercial Code
PDF	Portable Document Format	**USC**	United States Code
PDL	Patent Depository Library	**VA**	Vanadium Alloy

Resources: Government Publications, Patent Websites, and Books of Use and Interest

The patent resources listed below may assist you in applying for, prosecuting, and maintaining your patent rights.

A. Government Publications

All of the resources listed below are available on the Internet (www.uspto.gov) and many are also available in print and on CD-ROMs, which are updated quarterly and which may be read on the computer in any Patent and Trademark Resource Center. (See the list of libraries in Chapter 6.)

- *Attorneys and Agents Registered to Practice Before the U.S. Patent and Trademark Office.* Annual. GPO. Contains alphabetical and geographical listings of all attorneys and agents. https://oedci.uspto.gov/OEDCI
- *Index to Classification.* Loose-leaf. Contains all subclasses and cross-references arranged alphabetically. www.uspto.gov/web/patents/classification/uspcindex/indextouspc.htm
- *Manual of Classification.* GPO. Loose-leaf. Contains 300 search classes for patents arranged numerically, together with subclasses in each class. www.uspto.gov/web/patents/classification
- *Manual of Patent Examining Procedure* (MPEP). Revisions issued several times per year. GPO. Called "the patent examiner's bible," the MPEP provides answers to most questions about patent prosecution. www.uspto.gov/web/offices/pac/mpep/index.html
- *Patent Laws* (Title 35 of U.S. Code). The federal statutes governing patents. Available at the PTO's website under MPEP
- *Rules of Practice in Patent Cases* (Title 37, Code of Federal Regulations). GPO. The PTO's Rules of Practice. Available at the PTO's website under MPEP.

B. Patent Websites

Below are three groups of patent links. The first group provides sources of information for inventors, the second group includes resources on patent law and intellectual property law, and the third provides patent searching databases. As with all Internet links, we cannot guarantee the continued accuracy of any of these sites.

1. Inventor Resources

Da Vinci Partners (www.davincipartners.com). Provides information and resources that may be helpful to the inventor in building a prototype of an invention.

Intellectual Property Owners Association (IPO) (www.ipo.org). An association that serves owners of patents, trademarks, copyrights, and trade secrets.

Invention Convention (www.inventionconvention.com). The National Congress of Inventor Organizations (NCIO) maintains this invention website.

InventNet Forum (www.inventnet.com). Provides an online forum and mailing list.

Inventors Digest Online (www.inventorsdigest.com). Publishes online information and a print publication for independent inventors.

Nolo (www.nolo.com). Patent, copyright, trade secret, and trademark resources and products and updates of *Patent It Yourself.*

United Inventors Association (UIA) (www.uiausa.org). A national inventors' organization.

2. Patent Law and Intellectual Property Law Websites

Copyright Office (www.copyright.gov). The Copyright Office has numerous circulars, kits, and other publications that can help you, including one on searching copyright records.

European Patent Office (EPO) (www.epo.org). Agency that implements the European Patent Convention.

Government Printing Office (www.gpo.gov). Searchable source for U.S. Code of Federal Regulations, *Congressional Record,* and other Government Printing Office products.

Internet Patent News Service (www.bustpatents.com). Source for patent news, information about searching, and patent documents, news about patents, and information about bad patents, software, and business methods.

Legal Information Institute (www.law.cornell.edu). Intellectual property links and downloadable copies of statutes and cases.

Patent & Trademark Office (PTO) (www.uspto.gov).

PCT Applicant's Guide (www.wipo.int). PCT information and software for facilitating completion of the PCT forms.

Trademarks (www.uspto.gov). This site includes the relevant applications and trademark office forms.

3. Patent Searching Online

Here are several organizations that offer computer searching of patent records and a description of their services. Several of the "for fee" databases also provide foreign patent information.

U.S. Patent & Trademark Office (patft.uspto.gov). Free online full-text searchable database of patents and drawings that covers the period from January 1976 to the most recent weekly issue date (usually each Tuesday).

Google Patents (https://patents.google.com) is an excellent free resource that includes U.S. patents back to the beginning.

Clarivate Analytics (www.clarivate.com). Fee-based online searchable database with full-text searching capability for patents issued from 1974 to the present.

European Patent Office (www.epo.org/searching-for-patents.html). Enables searching of text, titles, and abstracts back to the 1920s.

LexPat (www.lexisnexis.com). Commercial database of U.S. patents searchable from 1971 to the present.

Patents.com (www.patents.com) is another good free search site that goes back to 1976.

Here are some additional free sites that can be used to search patents and obtain patent copies:

- www.freepatentsonline.com, and
- https://free.patentfetcher.com.

Nolo's Legal Encyclopedia

Nolo's website (www.nolo.com) features an extensive Legal Encyclopedia that includes a section on intellectual property. You'll find answers to frequently asked questions about patents, copyrights, trademarks, and other related topics; as well as sample chapters of Nolo books and a wide range of articles. Under "Get Informed" click on "Patent & Trademark."

Nolo Books on Intellectual Property

Nolo, the publisher of this book, also publishes a number of other titles on intellectual property, including:

- *How to Make Patent Drawings*, by Jack Lo and David Pressman
- *Nolo's Patents for Beginners*, by David Pressman and Richard Stim
- *Patent Pending in 24 Hours*, by Richard Stim and David Pressman
- *Patent, Copyright & Trademark: An Intellectual Property Desk Reference*, by Richard Stim
- *Profit From Your Idea: How to Make Smart Licensing Deals*, by Richard Stim
- *The Copyright Handbook: What Every Writer Needs to Know*, by Stephen Fishman
- *The Public Domain: How to Find & Use Copyright-Free Writings, Music, Art & More*, by Stephen Fishman, and
- *Trademark: Legal Care for Your Business & Product Name*, by Stephen Fishman.

Glossaries

Section A contains a glossary of words used to describe parts and functions of inventions. Section B contains a glossary of legal terms and their definitions as used in patent law.

A. Glossary of Useful Technical Terms

This Glossary[1] provides a list of useful words to describe the hardware, parts, and functions of your invention in the specification and claims. The most esoteric of these words are briefly defined. While some definitions are similar, this is due to space limitations; all words have nuances in meanings.

If you're looking for a word to describe a certain part, look through the list for a likely prospect and then check a dictionary for its precise meaning. If you can't find the right word here, look in your search patents, in *What's What* or another visual dictionary, or in a thesaurus. If you can't find an appropriate word, you'll probably be able to get away with "member" or "means-plus-a-function" language. Also, for new fields, you may invent words, preferably using Latin or Greek roots, as Farnsworth did with "television," or by extending the meaning of words from analogous devices (e.g., "base" for a part of a transistor). Very technical or specialized fields have their own vocabulary (e.g., "catamenial" in medicine, "syzygy" in astronomy); look in appropriate tutorial texts for these. The words are grouped loosely by the following functions:

1. Structure
2. Mounting and Fastening
3. Springs
4. Numbers
5. Placement (Relation)
6. Voids
7. Shape
8. Materials and Properties
9. Optics
10. Fluid
11. Electronics
12. Movement
13. Rotation/Machine, and
14. Biology.

---

[1] Expanded and used with kind permission and thanks from a list originally prepared by Louis B. Applebaum, Esq., of Newport, Rhode Island.

1. Structure

annulus (ring)
apron
apse (semicircular recess)
arbor (shaft)
arm
bail (arch wire)
band
barrel
bascale (seesaw)
base
batten (support strip)
beam
—cantilever
—simple
belt
bib
billet (ingot or bar)
blade
blower
board
bob (hanging weight)
bodkin (stiletto)
body
bollard (thick post)
boom
boss (projection)
bougie (body-insertion member)
boule (pear-shaped)
branch
breech (back part)
bunker
caisson
canard (front wing)
carriage
case
channel
charger (shallow dish)
chase
chord
cincture (encircling band)
clew (sail part)
column
configuration
container
conveyor

cornice (horiz. top of structure)
cover
crenation (rounded edge)
cupola (projection)
cylinder
dasher (plunger, churn)
derrick
detent
device
dibble (pointed tool)
die
disparate (dissimilar)
diversion
doctor blade (scraper)
dog (holder)
drum
echelon (staggered line)
element
enclosure
fence (stop on tool)
felly (rim of spoked wheel)
fillet (narrow strip)
fin
finger
finial (ornament)
flabellate (fan-shaped)
flange
fluke (triangular part)
flute (groove on shaft)
frame
fret
frit (vitreous substance)
frustrum (cut-off area)
furcate (branch)
futtock (curved ship timber)
gabion (support cylinder)
gaff (hook, spar)
gauge
generatrix (path traced)
gnomon (sundial upright)
graticulate (squares)
grommet
groove
gusset (triangular insert)
handle
head
header (base, support conduit)

homologous
horn
housing
hub
jacket
jaw
jib (crane arm)
knocker (clapper)
lagging (support)
ledger (horizonal support)
leg
lip
list (margin strip)
lobe
magazine
mandrel (tapered axle)
manifold
marge (edge)
marginate (w/margin)
medium
member
mullion (dividing strip)
nacelle (pod)
napiform (turnip-shaped)
neck
obcordate (heart-shaped)
object
outcrop
panel
parietal (wall)
particle
partition
piece
piston
placket (slit in garment)
platform
plug
plunger
pontoon
portion
post
pounce (fine powder)
projection
purlin (horiz. rafter support)
putlog (horiz. support above ledger)
race
raceway
rank (row, series, range)

reticulum (netlike)
rib
riddle (sieve)
riffles (obstructions)
ring
rod
sash (frame)
score (notch, scratch)
screed (guide strip)
scroll
sear (catch)
shell
shoe
shoulder
skeleton
sleeve
sluice (channel)
snare
snorkel
spandrel (area adjacent arch)
spar (pole, support)
spline (projection on shaft)
spoke
sponsor (projection)
sprag (spoke stop)
spur
stanchion
station
stay
stem
stent (stretcher)
step
stepped
stile (dividing strip)
stop
strake (band around ship's hull)
strip
strut
stylet
tang (shank, tool)
tare (net weight)
tendril (long, slender curl)
tine
tip
tittle (a tiny bit)
tongue
trace (pivoted rod)
tracery (scrolling)

track
trave (crossbar)
truss
tuft
turret
tuyere (air pipe)
upright
vang (guy)
volar (palm, sole)
wall
ward (ridge or notch)
warp
woof (weft)
ziggurat (pyramid with
  terraces)

2. Mounting and Fastening

attach
belay
billet (tip of belt)
bolt
bonnet
braze
busing
cable
camber
caster
clamp
cleat (reinforcer)
clevis (U-shaped pin)
colligate (bound together)
connection
corbel (cornice support)
couple
coupling
cribbing (support)
demountably
dentil (block under cornice)
docking
dowel
engage
fay (join tightly)
ferrule (barrel)
ferruminate (attach, solder)
fix
funicular (ropelike)

gib (holding member)
gland (sliding holder)
gunnel/gunwale (vessel's
  upper edge)
guy wire
harp (lampshade support)
hold
holder
hook
imbricate (regular overlap)
joint
—universal
keeper
key
latch
lock
lug
matrix
mount
nail
nut
pin
plinth (base)
pricket (holding spike)
pylon (support)
restraint
ribband (holds ribs)
rivet
scarf (notched joint)
screw
seam
seat
secure
set
sheathed
sliding
snare/loop
solder
spike
spline (projection or
  groove on a shaft)
springably
support
toe-in
thill (horse joinder stake)
thrust
trammel (restraint)
weld

3. Springs

air
bias
—element
coil
compressed
elastic
expanded
helical
—compression
—tension
leaf
press
relaxed
resilient
torsional
urge

4. Numbers

argument
caboodle (collection,
  bunch)
compound
congeries (collection,
  aggregation)
difference
dividend
divisor
equation
formula
index
lemma
minuend
modulo
multiplicand
multiplicity
multiplier
plurality
power
product
quotient
remainder
sheaf
subtrahend
variable

5. Placement (Relation)

adjacent
aft
aligned
angle
aposition (facing)
array
attached
axial
bottom
close
complementary
concentric
contiguous
contracted
course
crest
disposed
distal
divided
edge
engaged
equitant (overlap in two
  ranks)
evert (inside out)
extended
external
face
fiducial (reference)
film
fore
horizontal
imbricate (overlapping series)
incline
integral
intermediate
internal
interposed
juxtaposed
layer
located
lower
mating
meshing
mesial (between)
normal

oblique
obtuse
offset
open
opposed
overlapping
parallel
perpendicular
pitched
positioned
projecting
prolapsed (out of place)
proximal
proximate
raked (pitched)
reference
removable
resting
rim
row
sandwich
section
slant
spacer
staggered
superimposed
supported
surface
surrounding
symmetrical
tilt
top
ubiety (located in a place)
vernier (9:10 gauge)
vertical

6. Voids

aperture
bore
cavity
chamber
concavity
cutout
dimple
duct
embrasure (slant opening)
engraved

erose (irregular notch)
filister (groove)
foramen (opening)
fossa (depression)
furrow (groove)
gain (notch)
gap
groove
hole
hollow
infold
intaglinated (engraved)
invaginate (enclosed,
   turned in)
lumen (bore of tube)
lunette (crescent opening)
mortise (cutout)
nock (notch on arrow)
notch
opening
orifice
passage
placket (garment slit)
polled (dehorned)
rabbet (groove)
raceway
recess
rifling (spiral groove)
separation
slit
slot
spandrel (triangular gap
   above arch side)
sulcus (groove)
ullage (lost liquid)
via (path)
void
wicket (small door or gate)

7. Shape

acclivity (slope)
acicular (needle-shaped)
agonic (no angle)
annular
anticline (peak)
applanation
arch

arcuate
bandy (bowed out)
barrel
bevel
bifurcated (2 branches)
bight (bend)
botryoidal (like a bunch of
   grapes)
bucket
buckled
catenary (curve of hanging
   cable)
chamfer (beveled)
channel
circular
coin
concave
congruent (same shape)
conical
convex
convoluted (curled in)
corner (inside, outside)
corrugated
crest
crimp
crispate (curled)
cup
cusp (projection)
cylinder
depression
dihedral (two-faced)
direction
disc
dome
draw (depression)
drawing (pulling out)
elliptical
fairing (streamlined)
fin
flange
fold
fork
fossa (groove)
fundus (base)
furcate (branched)
goffer (ridges or pleats)
helical
hook

incurvate (curved in)
infundibuliform (funnel
   shaped)
invaginate (sheathed,
   folded in)
line
lobe
lozenge (diamond-shaped)
lune (crescent)
mammilated (nipple-shaped)
navicular (boat-shaped)
notch
oblate (flattened)
oblong
ogive (pointed arch)
orb (globe)
oval
parabolic
parallelogram
plane
plicate (pleated)
prolate (cigar-shaped)
rectangular
reticulated (gridlike)
rhomboid (nonequal
   adjacent sides)
rhombus (equal adjacent
   sides)
rick-rock
rill (long narrow valley)
round
salient (standing out)
serrated
setaceous (bristlelike)
sheet
shelf
sinusoidal
skive (shaven)
slab
spall (broken chips)
spherical
spica (overlapping reverse
   spirals)
square
stamped
striated (grooved or
   ridged)
swaged (flattened)

swale (depression)
syncline (V-shaped)
taper terminus (end)
tesselated (tiled)
topology (unchangeable
   geometry)
tortuous (twisting)
tram (on wheels)
trefoil (three-leaved)
triangular
trihedral (3-sided)
trough
tubular
tumescence
   (detumescence)
turbinate (top/spiral
   shaped)
twist
upset (distorted)
vermiculate (worm-eaten)
volute (spiral)
wafer
web
wedge
whorl (spiral)
xyresic (razor-sharp)

8. Materials and Properties

adhesive
alluvial (sand or clay
   deposited by water)
concrete
cork
dappled (spotted)
denier (gauge)
dense
elastic
enlarged
fabric
fiber
flexible
foraminous
frigorific (chilling)
frit (fused glass)
frosting (dull finish)
gloss

haptic (sense of touch)
humectant (moistener)
insulation
intenerate (soften)
liquid
material
metal
nappy
opaque
passivation (inert coating)
pied (splotched)
placer (glacial deposit)
plastic
porous
prill
refractory
resilient
rigid
rubber
sand
screen
shirred (gathered)
smectic (cleaning)
stratified (layered)
strong
sturdy
translucent
transparent
wood
xerotic (dry)

9. Optics

aniseikonic (unequal sizes)
astigmatic
bezel
bulb
—fluorescent
—incandescent
fresnel
lamp
light
—beam
—ray
opaque
parallax (change in
   direction)
pellicle

pellucid (clear)
reflection
refraction
schlieren (streaks)
translucent
transmission
transparent
window

10. Fluid

accumulator
afferent (to center)
aspirator
bellows
bibb (valve)
bung (hole or stopper)
cock (valve)
conduit
confluent (flow together)
connector
convection
cylinder
—piston
—rod
dashpot
diaphragm
discharge
dispenser
efferent (away from center)
filter
fitting
flue
gasket
hermetic
hose
hydraulic
medium
navicular (like boat)
nozzle
obturator (blocker)
outlet
pipe
plunger
poppet (axial valve)
port
—inlet
—outlet

pump
—centrifugal
—gear
—piston
—reservoir
—seal
—siphon
—tank
—vane
sluice (water channel with
   gate)
sparge (spray)
spud (short connecting
   pipe)
sprue (vent tube)
suctorial (sucking)
sufflate (inflate)
swash (channel barrier)
trompe (water-pipe blower)
tube
valve
—ball
—check
—control
—gate
—shutoff
wattle (intertwined wall)
weir (dam)
wicket (gate or door)

11. Electronics

adder
amplifier
astable
capacitance
clipping
conductor
contact
control element
demodulator
diode
electrode
electromagnet
filament
flip flop
gate (AND, OR, etc.)
impedance

inductance
insulator
integrated circuit
laser
lead
light emitting diode
line cord
liquid crystal
maser
memory
motor
multiplier
multivibrator
oscillator
pixel (CRT spot)
power supply
raster
read-and-write memory
read-only memory
resistance
sampling
Schmitt trigger
shift register
Schottky diode
socket
solenoid
switch
terminal
thermistor
transformer
transistor
triode
valve
varistor
wire
Zener diode

12. Movement

alternate
articulate (jointed)
avulsion (tear away)
cadent (rhythmic)
cam
compression
cyclic
detent (click)
downward

draft (pull)
drag
drift pin
drill
eccentric
emergent
epicyclic (on circle)
equilibrate (bring into
    equilibrium)
escapement
extensible
extrude
grinding
impact
inclined plane
inertia
interval
lag
lead
lever
linkage
—parallel
longitudinal
machine
meeting
nutate (to and fro)
pressing
propelling
pulverize
sagging
sequacious (regular)
severing
shuttle (to & fro member)
skive (peel)
slidable
snub (stop)
straight line
—motion
terminating
toggle
torque
traction
transverse
traversing
triturate (grind to powder)
trochoid (roll on circle)
urging

vibrating
wedge

13. Rotation/Machine

antifriction
—ball
—needle
—roller
—tapered
arbor (shaft)
bell crank
bobbin (spool)
brake
—band
—disk
—shoe
bushing
cam
chain
clevis (circular holder)
clutch
—centrifugal
—one-way
—sprag (stop)
—toothed
cog (tooth)
comminute (pulverize)
connecting rod
crank arm
drive
—belt
—pulley
—sheave
—toothed
flexible coupling
friction
fulcrum
gear
—bevel
—crown
—internal
—noncircular
—pinion
—right-angle
—spur
—wheel
—worm

gimbal (double pivot)
gin (hoist, pile driver, pump)
guide
gudgeon (axle)
hinge
intermittent
—escapement
—geneva
—pawl
—pendulum
—ratchet
jack
journal
mandrel
orbit
pinion (small wheel)
pintle (axle)
pivot
pulley
radial
radius bar
score (thinned strip)
screw
seal
sheave (pulley)
spindle
sprocket
swash (wobble) plate
tappet (valve cam)
trunnion
variable speed
vertiginous (turning)
ward (ridge or notch)
winch
yoke

14. Biology

anastomosis (connection
    of tubes)
atrium (cavity)
brady (slow)
catamenial (menstrual)
explant (transplant living
    tissue)
fibrillation (twitching)
tachy (rapid)
ventricle (chamber)

B. Glossary of Legal Terms

abandonment (1) allowing a pending, active patent application to be removed from the PTO's active files and treated as if the inventor has given up all claims to a patent on the invention. An inventor can expressly abandon an application by letter or allow an application to go abandoned by not timely replying to an office action. (2) treating an invention as if the inventor has lost all interest in exploiting it, usually by not developing it or by not filing a patent application on it for a very long time.

abstract a concise, one-paragraph summary of the patent. It details the structure, nature, and purpose of the invention. The abstract is used by the PTO and the public to quickly determine the gist of what is being disclosed.

actual damages (also known as compensatory damages) in a lawsuit, money awarded to one party to cover actual injury or economic loss. Actual damages are intended to put the injured party in the position he was in prior to the injury.

agent (patent) a person licensed by the PTO to represent others in handling patents and patent applications before the PTO. Patent agents are required to have a technical degree or technical knowledge in a specific field.

answer a written response to a complaint (the opening papers in a lawsuit) in which the defendant admits or denies the allegations and may provide a list of defenses.

assignee a person or legal entity to which an assignment is made.

assignment a document transferring ownership of an invention and/or a patent application or patent.

assignor one who makes an assignment.

attorney (patent) a person licensed by the PTO to represent others in handling patents and patent applications before the PTO and who is also licensed to practice law. Patent attorneys are required to have a technical degree or technical knowledge in a specific field.

best mode a term indicating that a patent application should disclose the way the inventor presently prefers to make the invention. The best mode requirement is a safeguard against the desire on the part of some people to obtain patent protection without making a full disclosure as required by the statute.

cease and desist letter correspondence from the owner of a proprietary work that requests the cessation of all infringing activity.

clear and convincing proof evidence that is highly probable and free from serious doubt.

complaint papers filed with a court clerk by the plaintiff to initiate a lawsuit by setting out facts and legal claims (usually called causes of action).

compositions of matter items such as chemical compositions, conglomerates, aggregates, or other chemically significant substances that are usually supplied in bulk (solid or particulate), liquid, or gaseous form.

conception the mental part of inventing, including how an invention is formulated or how a problem is solved.

confidentiality agreement (also known as a nondisclosure agreement) a contract in which one or both parties agree not to disclose certain information.

continuation application a new patent application that allows the applicant to re-present an invention and get a second or third bite at the apple. The applicant can file a new application (known as a "continuation") while the original (or "parent") application is still pending. A continuation application consists of the same invention, cross-referenced to the parent application, and a new set of claims. The applicant retains the filing date of the parent application for purposes of determining the relevancy of prior art.

Continuation-in-Part (CIP) less common than a continuation application, this form of extension application is used when a portion or all of an earlier patent application is continued and new matter (not disclosed in the earlier application) is included. CIP applications are used when an applicant wants to present an improvement but is prevented from adding a pending application to it because of the prohibition against adding "new matter."

Continuing Prosecution Application (CPA) a patent application that is like a continuation application in effect, but no new application need be filed. The applicant merely pays another filing fee, submits new claims, and files a CPA request form. CPAs can only be used for applications filed prior to 2000 May 29. Applications after that date must use the Request for Continued Examination.

contributory infringement occurs when a material component of a patented invention is sold with knowledge that the component is designed for an unauthorized use. This type of infringement cannot occur unless there is a direct infringement. In other words, it is not enough to sell infringing parts; those parts must be used in an infringing invention.

copyright the legal right to exclude others, for a limited time, from copying, selling, performing, displaying, or making derivative versions of a work of authorship such as a writing, music, or artwork.

counterclaim a legal claim usually asserted by the defendant against an opposing party, usually the plaintiff.

Court of Appeals for the Federal Circuit (CAFC) the federal appeals court that specializes in patent appeals. If the Board of Appeals and Patent Interferences rejects an application appeal, an applicant can further appeal to the CAFC within 60 days of the decision. If the CAFC upholds the PTO, the applicant can request the United States Supreme Court hear the case (although the Supreme Court rarely hears patent appeals).

date of invention the earliest of the following dates: (a) the date an inventor filed the patent application (provisional or regular), (b) the date an inventor can prove that the invention was built and tested in the U.S. or a country that is a member of the North American Free Trade Association (NAFTA) or the World Trade Organization (WTO), or (c) the date an inventor can prove that the invention was conceived in a NAFTA or WTO country, provided the inventor can also prove diligence in building and testing it or filing a patent application on it. Note: Though once a crucial concern for inventors (prior to adoption of the America Invents Act) the date of invention is of little importance under first-to-file rules (that is, after 2013 Mar 16).

declaratory action a request that the court sort out the rights and legal obligations of the parties in the midst of an actual controversy.

deed (patent) a document under seal or certificate issued by the PTO containing a printed copy of a patent and granting a patent monopoly to the patentee and the patentee's assignee.

deposit date the date the PTO receives a patent application.

deposition oral or written testimony of a party or witness and given under oath.

derivation hearing a PTO hearing brought by an applicant against a patent owner claiming to have the same invention and who has an earlier effective filing date. The derivation hearing must be filed within a 1-year period beginning on the date of the first publication of a claim in the earlier filed application. The procedure, implemented under the America Invents Act, replaces interference proceedings.

design patent covers the unique, ornamental, or visible shape or design of a nonnatural object.

divisional application a patent application used when an applicant wants to protect several inventions claimed in the original application. The official definition is "a later application for a distinct or independent invention, carved out of a pending application and disclosing and claiming only subject matter disclosed in the earlier or parent application" (MPEP 201.06). A divisional application is entitled to the filing date of the parent case for purposes of overcoming prior art. The divisional application must be filed while the parent is pending. A divisional application can be filed as a CPA.

Doctrine of Equivalents (DoE) a form of patent infringement that occurs when an invention performs substantially the same function in substantially the same manner and obtains the same result as the patented invention. A court analyzes each element of the patented invention separately. Under a recent Supreme Court decision, the DoE must be applied on an element-by-element basis to the claims.

double patenting when an applicant has obtained a patent and has filed a second application containing the same invention, the second application will be rejected. If the second application resulted in a patent, that patent will be invalidated. Two applications contain the same invention when the two inventions are literally the same or the second invention is an obvious modification of the first invention.

embodiment a physical version of an invention as described in a patent application; a patent application may describe several embodiments of an invention, but is supposed to state the one that the inventor considers the **best mode** as of the filing date; see **ramification**.

enhanced damages (triple or "treble" damages) in exceptional infringement cases, financial damages may be increased, at the discretion of the court, up to triple the award for actual damages (known as "enhanced damages").

examiner's answer a brief submitted by a patent examiner in response to an applicant's brief in an appeal to the PTO's Board of Appeals and Patent Interferences.

exclusive jurisdiction the sole authority of a court to hear a certain type of case.

exhaustion (see "first sale doctrine").

ex parte (Latin: one party only) refers to legal proceedings where only one party is present or represented.

experimental use doctrine a rule excusing an inventor from the one-year bar provided that the alleged sale or public use was primarily for the purpose of perfecting or testing the invention.

file wrapper estoppel (or prosecution history estoppel) affirmative defense used in patent infringement litigation that precludes the patent owner from asserting rights that were disclaimed during the patent application process. The term is derived from the fact that the official file in which a patent is contained at the Patent and Trademark Office is known as a "file wrapper." All statements, admissions, correspondence, or documentation relating to the invention are placed in the file wrapper. Estoppel means that a party is prevented from acting contrary to a former statement or action when someone else has relied to his detriment on the prior statement or action.

final Office Action the examiner's response to the applicant's first amendment. The final Office Action is supposed to end the prosecution stage but a "final action" is rarely final.

first Office Action (sometimes called an "official letter" or "OA") response from the patent examiner after the initial examination of the application. It is very rare that an application is allowed in the first Office Action. More often, the examiner rejects some or all of the claims.

first sale doctrine (also known as the exhaustion doctrine) once a patented product (or product resulting from a patented process) is sold, the patent owner's rights are exhausted and the owner has no further rights as to the resale of that particular article.

generic (genus) an entire group or class, or a group of related items or species.

grace period a period in which an action may be taken even though the normal period for taking action has passed.

indirect infringement occurs either when someone is persuaded to make, use, or sell a patented invention without authorization (inducing infringement); or when a material component of a patented invention is sold with knowledge that the component is designed for an unauthorized use (contributory infringement). An indirect infringement cannot occur unless there is a direct infringement. In other words, it is not enough to sell infringing parts; those parts must be used in an infringing invention.

infringement a product or service is infringing if it is a literal copy of a patented invention or if it performs substantially the same function in substantially the same manner and obtains the same result as the patented invention (see "Doctrine of Equivalents (DOE)").

injunction a court order requiring that a party halt a particular activity. In the case of patent infringement, a court can order all infringing activity be halted at the end of a trial (a permanent injunction) or the patent owner can attempt to halt the infringing activity immediately, rather than wait for a trial (a preliminary injunction). A court uses two factors to determine whether to grant a preliminary injunction: (1) Is the plaintiff likely to succeed in the lawsuit? (2) Will the plaintiff suffer irreparable harm if the injunction is not granted? The patent owner may seek relief for a very short injunction known as a temporary restraining order or TRO, which usually only lasts a few days or weeks. A temporary restraining order may be granted without notice to the infringer if it appears that immediate damage will result—for example, that evidence will be destroyed.

intellectual property (IP) the law dealing with works that are produced by mental activity, including ideas, inventions, patents, trademarks, trade secrets, copyrightable material, and unfair competition.

intellectual property attorney a person licensed to practice law by one or more states and who specializes in intellectual property. There are two types of IP attorneys: those who are licensed by the PTO (and can handle invention and patent matters before the PTO); and those who are not.

interference a costly, complex PTO proceeding that determines who will get a patent when two or more applicants are claiming the same invention. It is basically a method of sorting out priority of inventorship. Occasionally an interference may involve a patent that has been in force for less than one year.

inter partes (Latin: between parties) refers to legal proceedings where all parties to the action are represented.

interrogatories written questions that must be answered under oath.

invention any new article, machine, composition, or process or new use developed by a human.

jury instructions explanations of the legal rules that the jury must use in reaching a verdict.

lab notebook a system of documenting an invention that usually includes descriptions of the invention and novel features; procedures used in the building and testing of the invention; drawings, photos, or sketches of the invention; test results and conclusions; discussions of any known prior-art references; and additional documentation such as correspondence and purchase receipts.

literal infringement occurs if a defendant makes, sells, or uses the invention defined in the plaintiff's patent claim. In other words, the infringing product includes each and every component, part, or step in the patented invention. It is a literal infringement because the defendant's device is actually the *same* invention in the patent claim.

machine a device or things used for accomplishing a task; usually involves some activity or motion performed by working parts.

magistrate an officer of the court, who may exercise some of the authority of a federal district court judge, including the authority to conduct a jury or nonjury trial.

manufactures (sometimes termed "articles of manufacture") items that have been made by human hands or by machines; may have working or moving parts as prime features.

means-plus-function clause (or means-for clause) a provision in a patent claim in which the applicant does not specifically describe the structure of one of the items in the patent and instead describes the function of the item. Term is derived from the fact that the clause usually starts with the word "means."

micro entity a patent applicant status that enables qualifying applicants to pay the lowest USPTO fees (approximately one-quarter of regular fees, and one-half of small entity fees).

new matter any technical information, including dimensions, materials, etc., that was not present in the patent application as originally filed. An applicant can never add new matter to an application (PTO Rule 118).

new-use invention a new and unobvious process or method for using an old and known invention.

nonobviousness or unobviousness a standard of patentability that requires that an invention produce "unusual and surprising results." In 1966, the U.S. Supreme Court established the steps for determining unobviousness in the case of *Graham v. John Deere*, (383 U.S. 1 (1966)).

Notice of Allowance a document issued when the examiner is convinced that the application meets the requirements of patentability. An issue fee is due within three months.

objection a disapproval made by an examiner to a nonsubstantive matter, such as an unclear drawing or dependent claim having a rejected claim.

objects and advantages a phrase used to explain "what the invention accomplishes." Usually, the objects are also the invention's advantages, since those aspects are intended to be superior over prior art.

Office Action (OA, also known as Official Letter or Examiner's Action) correspondence (usually including forms and a letter) from a patent examiner that describes what is wrong with the application and why it cannot be allowed. Generally, an OA will reject claims, list defects in the specifications or drawings, raise objections, or cite and enclose copies of relevant prior art demonstrating a lack of novelty or nonobviousness.

one-year rule a pre-AIA rule that permitted an inventor one year to file a patent application after the invention was made public—either through publication, public use, or sale. After 2013 Mar 16, the "one-year rule" disappeared with one exception: if the inventor (or someone who obtained the details of the invention from the inventor) disclosed the invention, the applicant still has one year to file a provisional patent application (PPA) or regular patent application (RPA). If that deadline is missed, then the disclosure will be considered as prior art (and a bar) to the patent application.

patent a grant from a government that confers upon an inventor the right to exclude others from making, using, selling, importing, or offering an invention for sale for a fixed period of time.

patent application a set of papers that describe an invention and that are suitable for filing in a patent office in order to apply for a patent on the invention.

Patent Application Declaration (PAD) a declaration that identifies the inventor or joint inventors and provides an attestation by the applicant that the inventor understands the contents of the claims and specification and has fully disclosed all material information. The PTO provides a form for the PAD.

patent misuse a defense in patent infringement that prevents a patent owner who has abused patent law from enforcing patent rights. Common examples of misuse are violation of the antitrust laws or unethical business practices.

patent pending (also known as the "pendency period") time between filing a patent application (or PPA) and issuance of the patent. The inventor has no patent rights during this period. However, when and if the patent later issues, the inventor will obtain the right to prevent the continuation of any infringing activity that started during the pendency period. If the application has been published by the PTO during the pendency period and the infringer had notice, the applicant may later seek royalties for these infringements during the pendency period. It's a criminal offense to use the words "patent applied for" or "patent pending" (they mean the same thing) in any advertising if there's no active, applicable regular or provisional patent application on file.

patent prosecution the process of shepherding a patent application through the Patent and Trademark Office.

Patent Rules of Practice administrative regulations located in Volume 37 of the Code of Federal Regulations (37 CFR 1).

Patent Trial and Appeal Board (PTAB) a tribunal of judges at the PTO that hears appeals from final Office Actions and conducts derivation proceedings. Formerly called the Board of Patent Appeals and Interferences.

pendency period (see "patent pending").

permanent injunction a durable injunction issued after a final judgment on the merits of the case; permanently restrains the defendant from engaging in the infringing activity.

Petition to Make Special an applicant can, under certain circumstances, have an application examined sooner than the normal course of PTO examination (one to three years). This is accomplished by filing a "Petition to Make Special" (PTMS), together with a Supporting Declaration.

plant patent covers plants that can be reproduced through the use of grafts and cuttings (asexual reproduction).

power of attorney a document that gives another person legal authority to act on your behalf. If an attorney is preparing an application on behalf of an inventor, a power of attorney should be executed to authorize the patent attorney or agent to act on behalf of the inventor. The power of attorney form may be combined with the PAD.

prima facie (Latin: on its face) at first sight, obvious.

prior art the state of knowledge existing or publicly available either before the date of an invention or more than one year prior to the patent application date.

priority the benefit of the filing date of an earlier patent application accorded to a later-filed patent application.

process (sometimes referred to as a "method") a way of doing or making things that involves more than purely mental manipulations.

Provisional Patent Application (PPA) an interim document that clearly explains how to make and use the invention. The PPA is equivalent to a reduction to practice (see below). If a regular patent application is filed within one year of filing the PPA, the inventor can use the PPA's filing date for the purpose of deciding whether a reference is prior art. In addition to an early filing date, an inventor may claim patent pending status for the one-year period following the filing of the PPA.

ramification a version or variation of an invention that is different from a main version or **best mode**.

reduction to practice the point at which the inventor can demonstrate that the invention works for its intended purpose. Reduction to practice can be accomplished by building and testing the invention (actual reduction to practice) or by preparing a patent application or provisional patent application that shows how to make and use the invention and that it works (constructive reduction to practice).

reissue application an application used to correct information in a patent. It is usually filed when a patent owner believes the claims are not broad enough, the claims are too broad (the applicant discovered a new reference), or there are significant errors in the specification. In these cases, the applicant seeks to correct the patent by filing an application to get the applicant's original patent reissued at any time during its term. The reissue patent will take the place of the applicant's original patent and expire the same time as the original patent would have expired. If the applicant wants to broaden the claims of the patent through a reissue application, the applicant must do so within two years from the date the original patent issued. There is a risk in filing a reissue application because all of the claims of the original patent will be examined and can be rejected.

rejection a disapproval made by an examiner to a substantive matter such as a claim which is deemed obvious over the prior art.

repair doctrine affirmative defense based on the right of an authorized licensor of a patented device to repair and replace unpatented components. It also includes the right to sell materials used to repair or replace a patented invention The defense does not apply for completely rebuilt inventions, unauthorized inventions, or items that are made or sold without authorization of the patent owner.

reply a brief submitted by a patent applicant in response to an examiner's answer.

request for admission request for a party to the lawsuit to admit the truthfulness of a statement.

Request for Continued Examination (RCE) a paper filed when a patent applicant wishes to continue prosecuting an application that has received a final **Office Action**. Filing the RCE with another filing fee effectively removes the final action so that the applicant can submit further amendments, for example, new claims, new arguments, a new declaration, or new references.

request for production of documents the way a party to a lawsuit obtains documents or other physical evidence from the other side.

reverse doctrine of equivalents (or negative doctrine of equivalents) a rarely used affirmative defense to patent infringement in which, even if there is a literal infringement, the court will excuse the defendant's conduct if the infringing device has a different function or result than the patented invention. The doctrine is applied when the allegedly infringing device performs the same function in a substantially different way.

sequence listing an attachment to a patent application used if a biotech invention includes a sequence listing of a nucleotide or amino acid sequence. The applicant attaches this information on separate sheets of paper and refers to the sequence listing in the application (see PTO Rule 77). If there is no sequence listing, the applicant states "Nonapplicable."

small entity a status that enables small businesses and nonprofit companies to pay a reduced application fee.

species one of a group of related individual items collectively subordinate to a genus.

specification a patent application disclosure made by the inventor and drafted so that an individual skilled in the art to which the invention pertains could, when reading the patent, make and use the invention without needing further experiment.

A **specification** is constructed of several sections. Collectively, these sections form a narrative that describes and distinguishes the invention. If it can later be proved that the inventor knew of a better way (or "best mode") and failed to disclose it, that failure could result in the loss of patent rights.

statute of limitations the legally prescribed time limit in which a lawsuit must be filed. In patent law there is no time limit (statute of limitations) for filing a patent infringement lawsuit, but monetary damages can only be recovered for infringements committed during the six years prior to the filing the lawsuit. For example, if a patent owner sues after ten years of infringement, the owner cannot recover monetary damages for the first four years of infringement. Despite the fact that there is no law setting a time limit, courts will not permit a patent owner to sue for infringement if the owner has waited an unreasonable time to file the lawsuit ("laches").

statutory subject matter an invention that falls into one of the five statutory classes: process (method), machine, article of manufacture, composition, or a "new use" of one of the first four.

substitute application essentially a duplicate of an abandoned patent application. (See MPEP 201.09.) The disadvantage of a substitute application is that the applicant doesn't get the benefit of the filing date of the previously abandoned patent application, which could be useful, because any prior art occurring after the filing date of the earlier case can be used against the substitute case. If the applicant's substitute application issues into a patent, the patent will expire 20 years from the filing date of the substitute.

successor liability responsibility for infringement that is borne by a company that has purchased another company that is liable for infringements. In order for successor liability to occur, there must be an agreement between the companies to assume liability, a merger between the companies, or the purchaser must be a "continuation" of the purchased business. If the sale is made to escape liability and lacks any of the foregoing characteristics, liability will still attach.

summons a document served with the complaint that tells the defendant he has been sued, has a certain time limit in which to respond, and must appear in court on a stated date.

temporary restraining order (TRO) a court order that tells one party to do or stop doing something—for example to stop infringing. A TRO is issued after the aggrieved party appears before a judge. Once the TRO is issued, the court holds a second hearing where the other side can tell its story and the court can decide whether to make the TRO permanent by issuing an injunction. The TRO is often granted *ex parte* (without allowing the other side to respond), and for that reason is short in duration and only remains in effect until the court has an opportunity to schedule a hearing for the preliminary injunction.

traverse to argue against.

tying a form of patent misuse in which, as a condition of a transaction, the buyer of a patented device must also purchase an additional product in an anti-competitive manner. For example, in one case a company had a patent on a machine that deposited salt tablets in canned food. Purchasers of the machine were also required to buy salt tablets from the patent owner, even though salt is a commodity that was sold by many others. A party that commits patent misuse may have its patent invalidated, may have to pay monetary damages, or both.

utility patent the main type of patent, which covers inventions that function in a unique manner to produce a utilitarian result.

verified statement a statement made under oath or a declaration. A false verified statement is punishable as perjury.

vicarious liability legal responsibility that results when a business such as a corporation or partnership is liable for infringements committed by employees or agents. This liability attaches when the agent acts under the authority or direction of the business, an employee acts within the scope of employment, or the business benefits from, or adopts or approves the infringing activity.

voir dire *("speak the truth")* process by which attorneys and judges question potential jurors in order to determine whether they may be fair and impartial.

Fee Schedule

⚠ CAUTION

The following table provides some relevant patent-related PTO fees as of the date of publication of this edition. As fees may have changed since publication, visit the PTO website (www.uspto.gov), then click "Fees and payment." The PTO usually raises its fees every October 1. If you underpay any fee, the PTO imposes a stiff surcharge.

37 CFR	Description	Large-Entity Fee	Small Entity Fee	Micro Entity Fee
Patent Application Filing Fees				
1.16(a)	Basic filing fee—Utility (paper filing—also requires nonelectronic filing fee under 1.16(t))	300	150	75
1.16(a)	Basic filing fee—Utility (electronic filing for small entities)	n/a	75	n/a
1.16(b)	Basic filing fee—Design	200	100	50
1.16(b)	Basic filing fee—Design (CPA)	200	100	50
1.16(c)	Basic filing fee—Plant	200	100	50
1.16(d)	Provisional application filing fee	280	140	70
1.16(e)	Basic filing fee—Reissue	300	150	75
1.16(e)	Basic filing fee—Reissue (Design CPA)	300	150	75
1.16(f)	Surcharge—Late filing fee, search fee, examination fee or oath or declaration, or application filed without at least one claim or by reference	160	80	40
1.16(g)	Surcharge—Late provisional filing fee or cover sheet	60	30	15
1.16(h)	Independent claims in excess of three	460	230	115
1.16(h)	Reissue independent claims in excess of three	460	230	115
1.16(i)	Claims in excess of 20	100	50	25
1.16(i)	Reissue claims in excess of 20	100	50	25
1.16(j)	Multiple dependent claim	820	410	205
1.16(s)	Utility Application Size Fee—for each additional 50 sheets that exceeds 100 sheets	400	200	100
1.16(s)	Design Application Size Fee—for each additional 50 sheets that exceeds 100 sheets	400	200	100
1.16(s)	Plant Application Size Fee—for each additional 50 sheets that exceeds 100 sheets	400	200	100

37 CFR	Description	Large-Entity Fee	Small Entity Fee	Micro Entity Fee
Patent Application Filing Fees (continued)				
1.16(s)	Reissue Application Size Fee—for each additional 50 sheets that exceed 100 sheets	400	200	100
1.16(s)	Provisional Application Size Fee—for each additional 50 sheets that exceed 100 sheets	400	200	100
1.16(t)	Nonelectronic filing fee—Utility (additional fee for applications filed in paper)	400	200	200
1.17(i)(1)	Non-English translation	140	70	35
Patent Search Fees				
1.16(k)	Utility Search Fee	660	330	165
1.16(l)	Design Search Fee	160	80	40
1.16(m)	Plant Search Fee	420	210	105
1.16(n)	Reissue Search Fee	660	330	165
Patent Examination Fees				
1.16(o)	Utility Examination Fee	760	380	190
1.16(p)	Design Examination Fee	600	300	150
1.16(q)	Plant Examination Fee	620	310	155
1.16(r)	Reissue Examination Fee	2,200	1,100	550
Patent Post-Allowance Fees				
1.18(a)(1)	Utility issue fee	1000	500	250
1.18(a)(1)	Reissue issue fee	1000	500	250
1.18(b)(1)	Design issue fee	700	350	175
1.18(c)(1)	Plant issue fee	800	400	200
1.18(d)(1)	Publication fee for early, voluntary, or normal publication	0	0	0
1.18(d)(3)	Publication fee for republication	300	300	300
1.17(a)(1)	Extension for response within first month	200	100	50
1.17(a)(2)	Extension for response within second month	600	300	150
1.17(a)(3)	Extension for response within third month	1,400	700	350
1.17(a)(4)	Extension for response within fourth month	2,200	1,100	550
1.17(a)(5)	Extension for response within fifth month	3,000	1,500	750
Patent Maintenance Fees				
1.20(e)	Due at 3.5 years	1,600	800	400
1.20(f)	Due at 7.5 years	3,600	1,800	900
1.20(g)	Due at 11.5 years	7,400	3,700	1,850
1.20(h)	Surcharge—3.5 year—Late payment within 6 months	160	80	40
1.20(h)	Surcharge—7.5 year—Late payment within 6 months	160	80	40
1.20(h)	Surcharge—11.5 year—Late payment within 6 months	160	80	40

Mail, Telephone, Fax, and Email Communications With the PTO

A. Patent and Trademark Office Mail Addresses

Special Boxes for Patent Mail

If you are sending mail in any of the "Type of Mail" categories below to the PTO, add the appropriate Mail Stop below as the first line of your address as indicated. If your mail does not fall into one of these categories, e.g., an amendment with a fee for extra claims, simply address it using just the last three lines of the address below.

Mail Stop _____
Commissioner for Patents
P.O. Box 1450
Alexandria, VA 22313-1450

For the most current listing of PTO mail stops, visit: www.uspto.gov/patent/contact-patents/mailing-and-hand-carry-addresses-united-states-patent-and-trademark-office.

Mail Stop	Type of Mail
Mail Stop AF	Amendments and other responses after final rejection, other than an appeal brief.
Mail Stop Amendment	Information Disclosure Statements, drawings, Notices of Appeal, and replies to Office Actions in patent applications.
Mail Stop Appeal Brief—Patents	Appeal briefs.
Mail Stop Assignment Recordation Services	Assignments (with cover sheets).
Mail Stop Post Issue	Requests for Certificates of Correction and changes in patent files.
Mail Stop EBC	Mail for the Electronic Business Center.

Mail Stop	Type of Mail
Mail Stop Expedited Design	Initial filing of design applications accompanied by a request for expedited examination ("Rocket Docket").
Mail Stop Express Abandonment	Requests for abandonment of a patent application.
Mail Stop Issue Fee	All communications following the receipt of a Notice of Allowance and Fee(s) Due, and prior to the issuance of a patent.
Mail Stop PCT	Mail related to international applications filed under the Patent Cooperation Treaty.
Mail Stop Petition	Petitions to be decided by the Office of Petitions including petitions to revive and petitions to accept late payment of issue or maintenance fees.
Mail Stop PGPUB	Correspondence regarding publication of patent applications, including request for early publication and rescission of nonpublication request.
Mail Stop RCE	Requests for continued examination under 37 CFR 1.114.
Mail Stop Ex Parte Reexam	Requests for Reexamination for original request papers only.
Mail Stop Inter Partes Reexam	Requests for Inter Partes Reexamination.
Mail Stop Reissue	All new and continuing reissue application filings.
Mail Stop Sequence	Submission of computer-readable form (CRF) for applications with sequence listings, when the CRF is not being filed with the application.

Maintenance Fee Payments. Maintenance fee payments should preferably be submitted online: go to www.uspto.gov/patents-maintaining-patent/maintain-your-patent.

If paying by mail with a credit card or deposit account, or by hand-delivery, mail to:

Director of the U.S. Patent and Trademark Office
Attn.: Maintenance Fees
2051 Jamieson Avenue, Suite 300
Alexandria, VA 22314

PTO Is Closed for Ten Holidays. The PTO is closed on weekends and the following holidays: New Year's Day, Martin Luther King, Jr. Day, Presidents' Day, Memorial Day, Independence Day, Labor Day, Columbus Day, Veterans' Day, Thanksgiving, and Christmas. If any action falls due on a holiday or weekend, it is due on the next open-for-business day. If there is a disaster or service interruption or a mail strike, the PTO will publish a notice postponing the due dates for everyone (or just those in a particular geographical area if applicable).

B. Patent and Trademark Office Telephones and Faxes

PTO phones and fax numbers change frequently. For that reason we have not provided a complete listing. Generally, PTO telephone numbers can be located by the following methods:

- A complete current listing of all PTO phones and faxes can be found by going to www.uspto.gov and searching for "telephone directory" in the search box and then clicking "Alphabetical List of PTO Organizations."
- Alternatively, to reach a specific person or department, call the PTO's main number, 800-786-9199.
- If you have received an Office Action, the examiner's phone number will be listed at the end.
- To send a fax to the PTO, all faxed communications should be sent to the PTO's central fax number, 571-273-8300, except for (a) corrected filing receipt papers, (b) responses to a requirement to file missing parts of a patent application, (c) PCT papers, (d) issue fee transmittals, (e) express abandonments, (f) electronic business center communications, (g) assignments, (h) reexamination and interference papers, (i) communications to the PTO's general counsel and solicitor, (j) communications to Licensing and Review, and (k) Petitions to withdraw an application from issue.
- If you need help with electronic filing, call the PTO's Electronic Business Center at 866-217-9197 from 6 a.m. to midnight Eastern time.
- If you need help and don't know where else to call, call the Patents Ombudsman's office at 571-272-5555 or 855-559-8589.

Quick-Reference Timing Chart

The following is a summary of some of the more important timing intervals that apply in intangible property law. This list is not intended to be comprehensive, and certain exceptions may be applicable, so check the pertinent parts of this book, or with a patent attorney, if you have a special situation or need more precise advice.

Prior to 2014 Mar 16 (FTF), from the date of first publication, offer of sale, sale, or public or commercial use (excluding experimental use) of anything embodying an invention, one must file a U.S. utility, design, or plant patent application within **1 year.**

After 2014 Mar 16 (FTF), a patent application must be filed before any public disclosure of the invention, unless the disclosure was made by the inventor or another who obtained the subject matter directly or indirectly from the inventor.

From the date of filing a PPA, to get the benefit of its filing date, one must file a utility patent application and corresponding foreign applications within **1 year.**

To preserve foreign-filing rights in Convention Countries, one must not sell or publicly disclose details of an invention until **after U.S. filing date.**

To preserve foreign-filing rights in Non-Convention Countries (NCCs), one must not publicly disclose or sell invention until **after filing date in NCC.**

From the PTO's mailing date, unless an extension is purchased, or unless a shorter date is set, one must file a response to most Office Actions within **3 months.**

From the PTO's mailing date of a Notice of Allowance, one must pay the issue fee within a nonextendable period of **3 months.**

The maximum statutory time to reply to an Office Action, provided extensions are bought, is **6 months.**

Unless a Nonpublication Request has been filed, or unless it has issued or is abandoned, every patent application is published **18 months after filing.**

The full term of a utility or plant patent is measured from the filing date of its patent application, or from any earlier domestic nonprovisional (regular) application from which it claims priority, and is **20 years, plus any adjustment (extension) granted by the PTO.**

The full term of a design patent is measured from the issue date and is **15 years.**

From the date of issue (grant) the issue fee will keep a utility patent in force for the first **4 years.**

From the issue date of a patent, the patentee must file a reissue application that attempts to broaden the claims within **2 years.**

From the issue date of a patent, an applicant in a pending application who wants to get into interference with the patent must copy the patent's claims in their application within **1 year.**

Timely payment of Maintenance Fee I (between year 3.0 and 3.5, or 3.5 and 4.0 with late charge) will keep a utility patent in force for another **4 years.**

Timely payment of Maintenance Fee II (between year 7.0 and 7.5, or 7.5 and 8.0 with late charge) will keep a utility patent in force for another **4 years.**

Timely payment of Maintenance Fee III (between year 11.0 and 11.5, or 11.5 and 12.0 with late charge) will keep a utility patent in force until expiration, which occurs **20 years after filing.**

Unless a foreign-filing license has been granted on your filing receipt, after filing a U.S. patent application, before foreign-filing a patent application, you must wait **6 months.**

From the U.S. filing date (priority date), to obtain priority of a utility patent application, one must file a foreign Convention application (PCT, EPO, or industrial countries) within **1 year.**

From the U.S. filing date (priority date), to obtain priority of a design patent application, one must file a foreign Convention application (PCT, EPO, or industrial countries) within **6 months.**

One must file a foreign Non-Convention application (most nonindustrial countries) **before invention becomes publicly known.**

From the U.S. filing date, after filing a PCT application, if a patent in a foreign jurisdiction is desired, one must file abroad within **30 months.**

From the U.S. filing date, after filing a PCT application, if examination in the USPTO or the European Patent Office is desired (Chapter II), one must file a request within **22 months or 3 months from search report.**

Forms

Get Forms, Updates, and More at *Patent It Yourself*'s Companion Page

You can download all of the forms in this Appendix 7 at the *Patent It Yourself* companion page at Nolo.com located at:

www.nolo.com/back-of-book/PAT.html

See Appendix 8 for more details.

In addition, when there are important changes to the information in this book, we'll post updates at the companion page.

CAUTION

Some forms used for filing with the PTO have an expiration at the top of the form—for example, it may state, "Approved for use through 11/30/2019." If the date you intend to use the form is after the form's expiration date, and if there is a new form available, don't use the old form. The PTO will not accept it. Instead, download and use the latest form from www.uspto.gov/patent/patents-forms#business. There, you will find two options: forms for applications filed before September 16, 2012, and forms for applications filed on or after September 16, 2012. Locate and use the forms according to your application's filing date. The forms in this book are for applications filed on or after September 16, 2012.

TIP

Form numbers indicate the chapters in which the forms are discussed; for example, Form 10-7 is discussed in Chapter 10. Some of these forms differ from the corresponding PTO versions due to the fact that I have simplified them and added warnings. However, both versions are perfectly acceptable. The PTO forms also have a Burden-Hour Statement, which you need not include on any forms you send to the PTO. The tear-out versions of these forms are 8" wide but may be used for PTO purposes if you copy them on to 8.5"-wide paper. (Place a white backing over the form to avoid a black edge on the side.) All papers submitted to the PTO should have writing on one side of the sheet only.

Nondisclosure Agreement

1. **Parties.** This Disclosure Agreement (the "Agreement") is entered into by and between _____ _____ ("Disclosing Party"), and _____ ("Receiving Party"), for the purpose of preventing the unauthorized disclosure of Confidential Information (as defined below). The parties agree to enter into a confidential relationship with respect to the disclosure of certain proprietary and confidential information ("Confidential Information").

2. **Definition of Confidential Information.** For purposes of this Agreement, "Confidential Information" shall include the following: _____

   _____

   _____

   _____

   _____

   _____

   _____

   "Confidential Information" shall also include all information or material, written or oral, that has or could have commercial value or other utility in the business in which Disclosing Party is engaged.

   [*Receiving Party should check the box and initial the appropriate choice, below.*]

   Receiving Party:

   ☐ has received the above Confidential Information from Disclosing Party (_____).

   ☐ understands that Disclosing Party will immediately send the above Confidential Information to Receiving Party upon Disclosing Party's receipt, from Receiving Party, of a signed copy of this Agreement (_____).

   ☐ will show the above materials to Receiving Party on _____ (date) but will keep such Confidential Information in Disclosing Party's possession (_____).

3. **Loan of Tangible Copies of Confidential Information.** In the event that Disclosing Party furnishes physical or tangible copies of any of the Confidential Information to Receiving Party, Receiving Party acknowledges and agrees that these materials are furnished under the following conditions: (a) these materials are loaned to Receiving Party solely for purposes of evaluation and review; (b) these materials shall be treated consistent with the Receiving Party's obligation for Confidential Information under this Agreement; (c) Receiving Party may not copy or otherwise duplicate these materials; and (d) Receiving Party shall return to Disclosing Party any and all such material (including but not limited to records, notes, and other written, printed, or tangible materials) in its possession pertaining to Confidential Information immediately if Disclosing Party requests it in writing.

4. **Exclusions From Confidential Information.** Receiving Party's obligations under this Agreement do not extend to information that Receiving Party can show was: (a) publicly known at the time of disclosure or subsequently becomes publicly known through no fault of the Receiving Party; (b) discovered or created by the Receiving Party before disclosure by Disclosing Party; (c) learned by the Receiving Party through legitimate means other than from the Disclosing Party or Disclosing Party's representatives; or (d) disclosed by Receiving Party with Disclosing Party's prior written approval.

5. **Obligations of Receiving Party.** Receiving Party shall hold and maintain the Confidential Information in strictest confidence for the sole and exclusive benefit of the Disclosing Party. Receiving Party shall carefully restrict access to Confidential Information to employees, contractors, and third parties as is reasonably required and shall require those persons to sign nondisclosure restrictions at least as protective as those in this Agreement. Receiving Party shall not, without prior written approval of Disclosing Party, use for

Receiving Party's own benefit, publish, copy, or otherwise disclose to others, or permit the use by others for their benefit or to the detriment of Disclosing Party, any Confidential Information.

6. **Time Periods.** The nondisclosure provisions of this Agreement shall survive the termination of this Agreement and Receiving Party's duty to hold Confidential Information in confidence shall remain in effect until the Confidential Information no longer qualifies as a trade secret or until Disclosing Party sends Receiving Party written notice releasing Receiving Party from this Agreement, whichever occurs first.

7. **Miscellaneous.** Nothing contained in this Agreement shall be deemed to constitute either party a partner, joint venturer, or employee of the other party for any purpose. If a court finds any provision of this Agreement invalid or unenforceable, the remainder of this Agreement shall be interpreted so as best to effect the intent of the parties. This Agreement expresses the complete understanding of the parties with respect to the subject matter and supersedes all prior proposals, agreements, representations, and understandings. This Agreement may not be amended except in a writing signed by both parties. The failure to exercise any right provided in this Agreement shall not be a waiver of prior or subsequent rights. This Agreement and each party's obligations shall be binding on the representatives, assigns, and successors of such party. Each party has signed this Agreement through its authorized representative.

Receiving Party: _____
(Print Name of Organization or Individual)

By: _____ Date: _____/_____/_____
(Signature)

_____
(Print Name and Title, if any)

Disclosing Party: _____
(Print Name of Organization or Individual)

By: _____ Date: _____/_____/_____
(Signature)

_____
(Print Name and Title, if any)

OTHER PERSONS WITHIN RECEIVING PARTY'S ORGANIZATION OBTAINING ACCESS TO CONFIDENTIAL INFORMATION:

Signature: _____ Date: _____/_____/_____

Print Name: _____

Signature: _____ Date: _____/_____/_____

Print Name: _____

Signature: _____ Date: _____/_____/_____

Print Name: _____

Invention Disclosure

Inventor(s): _____

Address(es): _____

Title of Invention: _____

To record **Conception**, describe: 1. Circumstances of conception, 2. Purposes and advantages of invention, 3. Description, 4. Sketches, 5. Operation, 6. Ramifications, 7. Possible novel features, and 8. Closest known prior art. To record **Building and Testing**, describe: 1. Any previous disclosure of conception, 2. Construction, 3. Ramifications, 4. Operation and Tests, and 5. Test results. Include sketches and photos, where possible. Continue on additional identical copies of this sheet if necessary; inventors and witnesses should sign all sheets.

Inventor(s): _____ Date: _____ / _____ / _____

_____ Date: _____ / _____ / _____

The following understand, have witnessed, and agree not to disclose the above confidential information:

_____ Date: _____ / _____ / _____

_____ Date: _____ / _____ / _____

In the United States Patent and Trademark Office

Mail Stop Provisional Patent Application   Mailed 20_____

Commissioner for Patents

P.O. Box 1450

Alexandria, VA 22313-1450

Sir:

Please file the enclosed Provisional Patent Application (PPA) papers listed below under 37 C.F.R. § 1.53(b)(2).

Each of the undersigned understands:

A. This PPA is not a substitute for a Regular Patent Application (RPA), cannot get into interference with an RPA of another person, cannot be amended, will not be published, cannot claim any foreign priority, and will not mature into a patent.

B. If an RPA referring to this PPA is not filed within one year of the filing date of this PPA, this PPA will be worthless and will be destroyed.

C. Any desired foreign Convention applications (including PCT applications) based upon this PPA *must* be filed within one year of the filing date of this PPA in order to obtain benefit of the filing date of such PPA.

D. This PPA *must* contain a written description of the invention, and of the manner and process of making and using it, in such full, clear, concise, and exact terms as to enable any person skilled in the art to which it pertains, or with which it is most nearly connected, to make and use the same, and shall set forth the best mode contemplated by the inventor of carrying out his invention. 35 U.S.C. § 112, ¶ 1. Otherwise this PPA will be worthless.

E. Any RPA will be entitled to claim the benefit of this PPA only if such RPA names at least one inventor of this PPA and this PPA discloses such inventor's invention, as claimed in at least one claim of the RPA, in the matter provided in Item D above.

Inventor # 1, Name: _____

Legal Residence: _____

Inventor # 2, Name: _____

Legal Residence: _____

Title of Invention: _____

☐ Specification, sheets: _____   ☐ Drawing(s), sheets:_____

☐ Check or Credit Card Payment (use PTO-2038) for $_____ for

    ☐ small entity   ☐ large entity filing fee

☐ Return Receipt Postcard Addressed to Inventor # 1

☐ Return Receipt Postcard Addressed to Inventor # 2

☐ Application Data Sheet (optional).

Very respectfully,

_____   _____
Signature of Inventor # 1   Signature of Inventor # 2

_____   _____
Print Name of Inventor # 1   Print Name of Inventor # 2

_____   _____
Telephone Number of Inventor # 1   Telephone Number of Inventor # 2

_____   _____
Address (Send Correspondence Here)   Address

_____   _____

Express Mail Label # _____ ; Date of Deposit 20_____

PTO/AIA/14 (02-18)
Approved for use through 11/30/2020. OMB 0651-0032
U.S. Patent and Trademark Office; U.S. DEPARTMENT OF COMMERCE
Under the Paperwork Reduction Act of 1995, no persons are required to respond to a collection of information unless it contains a valid OMB control number.

Application Data Sheet 37 CFR 1.76	Attorney Docket Number	
	Application Number	
Title of Invention		

The application data sheet is part of the provisional or nonprovisional application for which it is being submitted. The following form contains the bibliographic data arranged in a format specified by the United States Patent and Trademark Office as outlined in 37 CFR 1.76.
This document may be completed electronically and submitted to the Office in electronic format using the Electronic Filing System (EFS) or the document may be printed and included in a paper filed application.

Secrecy Order 37 CFR 5.2:

☐ Portions or all of the application associated with this Application Data Sheet may fall under a Secrecy Order pursuant to 37 CFR 5.2 (Paper filers only. Applications that fall under Secrecy Order may not be filed electronically.)

Inventor Information:

Inventor   1   [Remove]

Legal Name

Prefix	Given Name	Middle Name	Family Name	Suffix

Residence Information (Select One)   ● US Residency   ○ Non US Residency   ○ Active US Military Service

City		State/Province		Country of Residence	

Mailing Address of Inventor:

Address 1	
Address 2	

City		State/Province	
Postal Code		Country i	

All Inventors Must Be Listed - Additional Inventor Information blocks may be generated within this form by selecting the **Add** button.   [Add]

Correspondence Information:

Enter either Customer Number or complete the Correspondence Information section below.
For further information see 37 CFR 1.33(a).

☐ **An Address is being provided for the correspondence Information of this application.**

Customer Number	
Email Address		[Add Email] [Remove Email]

Application Information:

Title of the Invention			
Attorney Docket Number		Small Entity Status Claimed	☐
Application Type			
Subject Matter			
Total Number of Drawing Sheets (if any)		Suggested Figure for Publication (if any)	

PTO/AIA/14 (02-18)
Approved for use through 11/30/2020. OMB 0651-0032
U.S. Patent and Trademark Office; U.S. DEPARTMENT OF COMMERCE
Under the Paperwork Reduction Act of 1995, no persons are required to respond to a collection of information unless it contains a valid OMB control number.

| **Application Data Sheet 37 CFR 1.76** | Attorney Docket Number | |
| | Application Number | |

| Title of Invention | |

Filing By Reference:

Only complete this section when filing an application by reference under 35 U.S.C. 111(c) and 37 CFR 1.57(a). Do not complete this section if application papers including a specification and any drawings are being filed. Any domestic benefit or foreign priority information must be provided in the appropriate section(s) below (i.e., "Domestic Benefit/National Stage Information" and "Foreign Priority Information").

For the purposes of a filing date under 37 CFR 1.53(b), the description and any drawings of the present application are replaced by this reference to the previously filed application, subject to conditions and requirements of 37 CFR 1.57(a).

| Application number of the previously filed application | Filing date (YYYY-MM-DD) | Intellectual Property Authority or Country |
| | | |

Publication Information:

☐ Request Early Publication (Fee required at time of Request 37 CFR 1.219)

☐ **Request Not to Publish.** I hereby request that the attached application not be published under 35 U.S.C. 122(b) and certify that the invention disclosed in the attached application **has not and will not** be the subject of an application filed in another country, or under a multilateral international agreement, that requires publication at eighteen months after filing.

Representative Information:

Representative information should be provided for all practitioners having a power of attorney in the application. Providing this information in the Application Data Sheet does not constitute a power of attorney in the application (see 37 CFR 1.32). Either enter Customer Number or complete the Representative Name section below. If both sections are completed the customer Number will be used for the Representative Information during processing.

| Please Select One: | ◉ Customer Number | ○ US Patent Practitioner | ○ Limited Recognition (37 CFR 11.9) |
| Customer Number | | | |

Domestic Benefit/National Stage Information:

This section allows for the applicant to either claim benefit under 35 U.S.C. 119(e), 120, 121, 365(c), or 386(c) or indicate National Stage entry from a PCT application. Providing benefit claim information in the Application Data Sheet constitutes the specific reference required by 35 U.S.C. 119(e) or 120, and 37 CFR 1.78.
When referring to the current application, please leave the "Application Number" field blank.

Prior Application Status			Remove
Application Number	Continuity Type	Prior Application Number	Filing or 371(c) Date (YYYY-MM-DD)

Additional Domestic Benefit/National Stage Data may be generated within this form by selecting the **Add** button.

PTO/AIA/14 (02-18)
Approved for use through 11/30/2020. OMB 0651-0032
U.S. Patent and Trademark Office; U.S. DEPARTMENT OF COMMERCE
Under the Paperwork Reduction Act of 1995, no persons are required to respond to a collection of information unless it contains a valid OMB control number.

| **Application Data Sheet 37 CFR 1.76** | Attorney Docket Number | |
| | Application Number | |

| Title of Invention | |

Foreign Priority Information:

This section allows for the applicant to claim priority to a foreign application. Providing this information in the application data sheet constitutes the claim for priority as required by 35 U.S.C. 119(b) and 37 CFR 1.55. When priority is claimed to a foreign application that is eligible for retrieval under the priority document exchange program (PDX)[i] the information will be used by the Office to automatically attempt retrieval pursuant to 37 CFR 1.55(i)(1) and (2). Under the PDX program, applicant bears the ultimate responsibility for ensuring that a copy of the foreign application is received by the Office from the participating foreign intellectual property office, or a certified copy of the foreign priority application is filed, within the time period specified in 37 CFR 1.55(g)(1).

Remove

Application Number	Country[i]	Filing Date (YYYY-MM-DD)	Access Code[i] (if applicable)

Additional Foreign Priority Data may be generated within this form by selecting the
Add button.

Statement under 37 CFR 1.55 or 1.78 for AIA (First Inventor to File) Transition Applications

☐ This application (1) claims priority to or the benefit of an application filed before March 16, 2013 and (2) also contains, or contained at any time, a claim to a claimed invention that has an effective filing date on or after March 16, 2013.
NOTE: By providing this statement under 37 CFR 1.55 or 1.78, this application, with a filing date on or after March 16, 2013, will be examined under the first inventor to file provisions of the AIA.

PTO/AIA/14 (02-18)
Approved for use through 11/30/2020. OMB 0651-0032
U.S. Patent and Trademark Office; U.S. DEPARTMENT OF COMMERCE
Under the Paperwork Reduction Act of 1995, no persons are required to respond to a collection of information unless it contains a valid OMB control number.

| **Application Data Sheet 37 CFR 1.76** | Attorney Docket Number | |
| | Application Number | |

| Title of Invention | |

Authorization or Opt-Out of Authorization to Permit Access:

When this Application Data Sheet is properly signed and filed with the application, applicant has provided written authority to permit a participating foreign intellectual property (IP) office access to the instant application-as-filed (see paragraph A in subsection 1 below) and the European Patent Office (EPO) access to any search results from the instant application (see paragraph B in subsection 1 below).

Should applicant choose not to provide an authorization identified in subsection 1 below, applicant **must opt-out** of the authorization by checking the corresponding box A or B or both in subsection 2 below.

NOTE: This section of the Application Data Sheet is **ONLY** reviewed and processed with the **INITIAL** filing of an application. After the initial filing of an application, an Application Data Sheet cannot be used to provide or rescind authorization for access by a foreign IP office(s). Instead, Form PTO/SB/39 or PTO/SB/69 must be used as appropriate.

1. Authorization to Permit Access by a Foreign Intellectual Property Office(s)

A. Priority Document Exchange (PDX) - Unless box A in subsection 2 (opt-out of authorization) is checked, the undersigned hereby **grants the USPTO authority** to provide the European Patent Office (EPO), the Japan Patent Office (JPO), the Korean Intellectual Property Office (KIPO), the State Intellectual Property Office of the People's Republic of China (SIPO), the World Intellectual Property Organization (WIPO), and any other foreign intellectual property office participating with the USPTO in a bilateral or multilateral priority document exchange agreement in which a foreign application claiming priority to the instant patent application is filed, access to: (1) the instant patent application-as-filed and its related bibliographic data, (2) any foreign or domestic application to which priority or benefit is claimed by the instant application and its related bibliographic data, and (3) the date of filing of this Authorization. See 37 CFR 1.14(h)(1).

B. Search Results from U.S. Application to EPO - Unless box B in subsection 2 (opt-out of authorization) is checked, the undersigned hereby **grants the USPTO authority** to provide the EPO access to the bibliographic data and search results from the instant patent application when a European patent application claiming priority to the instant patent application is filed. See 37 CFR 1.14(h)(2).

The applicant is reminded that the EPO's Rule 141(1) EPC (European Patent Convention) requires applicants to submit a copy of search results from the instant application without delay in a European patent application that claims priority to the instant application.

2. Opt-Out of Authorizations to Permit Access by a Foreign Intellectual Property Office(s)

☐ A. Applicant **DOES NOT** authorize the USPTO to permit a participating foreign IP office access to the instant application-as-filed. If this box is checked, the USPTO will not be providing a participating foreign IP office with any documents and information identified in subsection 1A above.

☐ B. Applicant **DOES NOT** authorize the USPTO to transmit to the EPO any search results from the instant patent application. If this box is checked, the USPTO will not be providing the EPO with search results from the instant application.

NOTE: Once the application has published or is otherwise publicly available, the USPTO may provide access to the application in accordance with 37 CFR 1.14.

PTO/AIA/14 (02-18)
Approved for use through 11/30/2020. OMB 0651-0032
U.S. Patent and Trademark Office; U.S. DEPARTMENT OF COMMERCE
Under the Paperwork Reduction Act of 1995, no persons are required to respond to a collection of information unless it contains a valid OMB control number.

Application Data Sheet 37 CFR 1.76	Attorney Docket Number	
	Application Number	
Title of Invention		

Applicant Information:

Providing assignment information in this section does not substitute for compliance with any requirement of part 3 of Title 37 of CFR to have an assignment recorded by the Office.

Applicant   1

If the applicant is the inventor (or the remaining joint inventor or inventors under 37 CFR 1.45), this section should not be completed. The information to be provided in this section is the name and address of the legal representative who is the applicant under 37 CFR 1.43; or the name and address of the assignee, person to whom the inventor is under an obligation to assign the invention, or person who otherwise shows sufficient proprietary interest in the matter who is the applicant under 37 CFR 1.46. If the applicant is an applicant under 37 CFR 1.46 (assignee, person to whom the inventor is obligated to assign, or person who otherwise shows sufficient proprietary interest) together with one or more joint inventors, then the joint inventor or inventors who are also the applicant should be identified in this section.

[Clear]

○ Assignee   ○ Legal Representative under 35 U.S.C. 117   ○ Joint Inventor

○ Person to whom the inventor is obligated to assign.   ○   Person who shows sufficient proprietary interest

If applicant is the legal representative, indicate the authority to file the patent application, the inventor is:

Name of the Deceased or Legally Incapacitated Inventor:

If the Applicant is an Organization check here.   ☐

Prefix	**Given Name**	Middle Name	**Family Name**	Suffix

Mailing Address Information For Applicant:

Address 1	
Address 2	
City		**State/Province**	
Country		Postal Code	
Phone Number		Fax Number	
Email Address			

Additional Applicant Data may be generated within this form by selecting the Add button.

Assignee Information including Non-Applicant Assignee Information:

Providing assignment information in this section does not substitute for compliance with any requirement of part 3 of Title 37 of CFR to have an assignment recorded by the Office.

PTO/AIA/14 (02-18)
Approved for use through 11/30/2020. OMB 0651-0032
U.S. Patent and Trademark Office; U.S. DEPARTMENT OF COMMERCE
Under the Paperwork Reduction Act of 1995, no persons are required to respond to a collection of information unless it contains a valid OMB control number.

| **Application Data Sheet 37 CFR 1.76** | Attorney Docket Number | |
| | Application Number | |

| Title of Invention | |

Assignee 1

Complete this section if assignee information, including non-applicant assignee information, is desired to be included on the patent application publication. An assignee-applicant identified in the "Applicant Information" section will appear on the patent application publication as an applicant. For an assignee-applicant, complete this section only if identification as an assignee is also desired on the patent application publication.

| If the Assignee or Non-Applicant Assignee is an Organization check here. | ☐ |

Prefix	**Given Name**	Middle Name	**Family Name**	Suffix

Mailing Address Information For Assignee including Non-Applicant Assignee:

| **Address 1** | |
| Address 2 | |

City		**State/Province**	
Country i		Postal Code	
Phone Number		Fax Number	
Email Address	

Additional Assignee or Non-Applicant Assignee Data may be generated within this form by selecting the Add button.

Signature:

NOTE: This Application Data Sheet must be signed in accordance with 37 CFR 1.33(b). **However, if this Application Data Sheet is submitted with the INITIAL filing of the application and either box A or B is not checked in subsection 2 of the "Authorization or Opt-Out of Authorization to Permit Access" section, then this form must also be signed in accordance with 37 CFR 1.14(c).**

This Application Data Sheet **must** be signed by a patent practitioner if one or more of the applicants is a **juristic entity** (e.g., corporation or association). If the applicant is two or more joint inventors, this form must be signed by a patent practitioner, **all** joint inventors who are the applicant, or one or more joint inventor-applicants who have been given power of attorney (e.g., see USPTO Form PTO/AIA/81) on behalf of **all** joint inventor-applicants.

See 37 CFR 1.4(d) for the manner of making signatures and certifications.

| **Signature** | | | Date (YYYY-MM-DD) | |
| **First Name** | | Last Name | | Registration Number | |

Additional Signature may be generated within this form by selecting the Add button.

PTO/AIA/14 (02-18)
Approved for use through 11/30/2020. OMB 0651-0032
U.S. Patent and Trademark Office; U.S. DEPARTMENT OF COMMERCE
Under the Paperwork Reduction Act of 1995, no persons are required to respond to a collection of information unless it contains a valid OMB control number.

Application Data Sheet 37 CFR 1.76	Attorney Docket Number	
	Application Number	
Title of Invention		

This collection of information is required by 37 CFR 1.76. The information is required to obtain or retain a benefit by the public which is to file (and by the USPTO to process) an application. Confidentiality is governed by 35 U.S.C. 122 and 37 CFR 1.14. This collection is estimated to take 23 minutes to complete, including gathering, preparing, and submitting the completed application data sheet form to the USPTO. Time will vary depending upon the individual case. Any comments on the amount of time you require to complete this form and/or suggestions for reducing this burden, should be sent to the Chief Information Officer, U.S. Patent and Trademark Office, U.S. Department of Commerce, P.O. Box 1450, Alexandria, VA 22313-1450. DO NOT SEND FEES OR COMPLETED FORMS TO THIS ADDRESS. **SEND TO: Commissioner for Patents, P.O. Box 1450, Alexandria, VA 22313-1450.**

Positive and Negative Factors Evaluation

Inventor(s): _____   Invention: _____

Factor	Weight (−100 to +100)	Factor	Weight (−100 to +100)
1. Cost	_____	33. Related Product Addability	_____
2. Weight	_____	34. Satisfies Existing Need	_____
3. Size	_____	35. Legality	_____
4. Safety/Health	_____	36. Operability	_____
5. Speed	_____	37. Development	_____
6. Ease of Use	_____	38. Profitability	_____
7. Ease of Production	_____	39. Obsolescence	_____
8. Durability	_____	40. Incompatibility	_____
9. Repairability	_____	41. Product Liability Risk	_____
10. Novelty	_____	42. Market Dependence	_____
11. Convenience/Social Benefit/ Mechanization	_____	43. Difficulty of Distribution	_____
12. Reliability	_____	44. Service Requirements	_____
13. Ecology	_____	45. New Tooling Required	_____
14. Salability	_____	46. Inertia Must Be Overcome	_____
15. Appearance	_____	47. Too Advanced Technically	_____
16. Viewability	_____	48. Substantial Learning Required	_____
17. Precision	_____	49. Difficult to Promote	_____
18. Noise	_____	50. Lack of Market	_____
19. Odor	_____	51. Crowded Field	_____
20. Taste	_____	52. Commodities	_____
21. Market Size	_____	53. Combination Products	_____
22. Trend of Demand	_____	54. Entrenched Competition	_____
23. Seasonal Demand	_____	55. Instant Anachronism	_____
24. Difficulty of Market Penetration	_____	56. Prototype Availability	_____
25. Potential Competition	_____	57. Broad Patent Coverage Availability	_____
26. Quality	_____	58. High Sales Anticipated	_____
27. Excitement	_____	59. Visibility of Invention in Final Product	_____
28. Markup	_____	60. Ease of Packaging	_____
29. Inferior Performance	_____	61. Youth Market	_____
30. "Sexy" Packaging	_____	62. Part of a Current Fad	_____
31. Miscellaneous	_____	63. Will Contingent Fee Litigator Take Case?	_____
32. Long Life Cycle	_____	**Total**	_____

Signed: _____   Date: _____
Inventor(s)

Positive and Negative Factors Summary

Inventor(s): _____ Invention: _____

_____ _____

List Factors With Positive Values	**Weight**	**List Factors With Negative Values**	**Weight**
_____	_____	_____	_____
_____	_____	_____	_____
_____	_____	_____	_____
_____	_____	_____	_____
_____	_____	_____	_____
_____	_____	_____	_____
_____	_____	_____	_____
_____	_____	_____	_____
_____	_____	_____	_____
_____	_____	_____	_____
_____	_____	_____	_____
_____	_____	_____	_____
_____	_____	_____	_____
_____	_____	_____	_____
_____	_____	_____	_____
_____	_____	_____	_____
_____	_____	_____	_____
_____	_____	_____	_____
_____	_____	_____	_____
_____	_____	_____	_____
_____	_____	_____	_____
_____	_____	_____	_____
_____	_____	_____	_____

Positive Total _____ Negative Total _____

NET (Positive Total less Negative Total): _____

Signed: _____ Date: _____
Inventor(s)

Consultant's Work Agreement

1. **Parties:** This Work Agreement is made between the following parties:

   Name(s): _____

   Address(es): _____

   _____

   (hereinafter Contractor), and

   Name(s): _____

   Address(es): _____

   _____

   (hereinafter Consultant).

2. **Name of Project:** _____

   _____

   _____

3. **Work to Be Performed by Consultant:** _____

   _____

   _____

4. **Work/Payment Schedule:** _____

   _____

   _____

5. **Date:** This Agreement shall be effective as of the latter date below written.

6. **Recitals:** Contractor has one or more ideas relating to the above project and desires to have such project developed more completely, as specified in the above statement of Work. Consultant has certain skills desired by Contractor relating to performance of the above Work.

7. **Performance:** Consultant will perform the above work for Contractor, in accordance with the above-scheduled Work/Payment Schedule, and Contractor will make the above scheduled payments to Consultant. Any changes to the Work to Be Performed or the Work/Payment Schedule shall be described in a writing referring to this Agreement and signed and dated by both parties. Time is of the essence of this Agreement, and if Consultant fails to perform according to the above work schedule, Contractor may (a) void this agreement and pay Consultant 50% of what would otherwise be due, or (b) require that Consultant pay Contractor a penalty of $_____ per day.

8. **Intellectual Property:** All intellectual property, including trademarks, writings, information, trade secrets, inventions, discoveries, or improvements, whether or not registrable or patentable, which are conceived, constructed, or written by Consultant and arise out of or are related to work and services performed under this agreement, are, or shall become and remain, the sole and exclusive property of Contractor, whether or not such intellectual property is conceived during the time such work and services are performed or billed.

9A. **Protection of Intellectual Property:** Contractor and Consultant recognize that under U.S. patent laws, all patent applications must be filed in the name of the true and actual inventor(s) of the subject matter sought to be patented. Thus if Consultant makes any patentable inventions relating to the above project, Consultant agrees to be named as an applicant in any U.S. patent application(s) filed on such invention(s). Actual ownership of such patent applications shall be governed by clause 8.

9B. **Disclosure:** Consultant shall promptly disclose to Contractor in writing all information pertaining to any intellectual property generated or conceived by Consultant under this Agreement. Consultant hereby assigns and agrees to assign all of Consultant's rights to such intellectual property, including patent rights and foreign priority rights. Consultant hereby expressly agrees, without further charge for time, to do all things and sign all documents deemed by Contractor to be necessary or appropriate to invest in intellectual property, including obtaining for and vesting in Contractor all U.S. and foreign patents and patent applications that Contractor desires to obtain to cover such intellectual property, provided that Contractor shall bear all expenses relating thereto. All reasonable local travel time and expenses shall be borne by Consultant.

10. **Trade Secrets:** Consultant recognizes that all information relating to the above Project disclosed to Consultant by Contractor, and all information generated by Consultant in the performance of the above Work, is a valuable trade secret of Contractor and Consultant shall treat all such information as strictly confidential, during and after the performance of Work under this Agreement. Specifically Consultant shall not reveal, publish, or communicate any such information to anyone other than Contractor, and shall safeguard all such information from access to anyone other than Contractor, except upon the express written authorization of Contractor. This clause shall not apply to any information that Consultant can document in writing is presently in or enters the public domain from a bona fide source other than Consultant.

11. **Return of Property:** Consultant agrees to return all written materials and objects received from Contractor, to deliver to Contractor all objects and a copy (and all copies and originals if requested by Contractor) of all written materials resulting from or relating to work performed under this Agreement, and not to deliver to any person, organization, or publisher, or cause to be published, any such written material without prior written authorization.

12. **Conflicts of Interest:** Consultant recognizes a fiduciary obligation to Contractor arising out of the work and services performed under this agreement. Accordingly, Consultant will not offer services to or perform services for any competitor, potential or actual, of Contractor for the above Project. Consultant will not perform any other acts that may result in any conflict of interest by Consultant, during and after the term of this Agreement.

    [*Check one*]

    ☐ Consultant represents to Contractor that prior to this agreement, Consultant has not made and does not own any inventions relating to the above Project.

    ☐ Consultant has made or does own inventions relating to this Project and has provided a list of such inventions on a separate sheet incorporated in this Agreement by reference.

13. **Mediation and Arbitration:** If any dispute arises under this Agreement, the parties shall negotiate in good faith to settle such dispute. If the parties cannot resolve such dispute themselves, then either party may submit the dispute to mediation by a mediator approved by both parties. If the parties cannot agree to any mediator, or if either party does not wish to abide by any decision of the mediator, they shall submit the dispute to arbitration by any mutually acceptable arbitrator, or the American Arbitration Association (AAA). If the AAA is selected, the arbitration shall take place under the auspices of the nearest branch of such to both parties. The costs of the arbitration proceeding shall be borne according to the decision of the arbitrator, who may apportion costs equally, or in accordance with any finding of fault or lack of good faith of either party. The arbitrator's award shall be nonappealable and enforceable in any court of competent jurisdiction.

14. **Governing Law:** This Agreement shall be governed by and interpreted under and according to the laws of the State of _____.

15. **Signatures:** The parties have indicated their agreement to all of the above terms by signing this Agreement on the respective dates below indicated. Each party has received an original signed copy hereof.

Contractor: _____ Date: _____

Consultant: _____ Date: _____

Searcher's Worksheet

Sheet _____ of _____

Inventor(s): _____

Invention Description (use keywords and variations): _____

_____

_____

_____

_____

Selected Search Classifications

Class/Sub	Description	Checked	Comments
_____	_____	_____	_____
_____	_____	_____	_____
_____	_____	_____	_____
_____	_____	_____	_____
_____	_____	_____	_____
_____	_____	_____	_____
_____	_____	_____	_____

Patents (and Other References) Thought Relevant

Patent # or Title	Name or Country	Date	Class/Sub	Comment

Searcher: _____   Date: _____

Drawing Reference Numerals Worksheet

PART NAME

PART NAME

10	_____	84	_____
12	_____	86	_____
14	_____	88	_____
16	_____	90	_____
18	_____	92	_____
20	_____	94	_____
22	_____	96	_____
24	_____	98	_____
26	_____	100	_____
28	_____	102	_____
30	_____	104	_____
32	_____	106	_____
34	_____	108	_____
36	_____	110	_____
38	_____	112	_____
40	_____	114	_____
42	_____	116	_____
44	_____	118	_____
46	_____	120	_____
48	_____	122	_____
50	_____	124	_____
52	_____	126	_____
54	_____	128	_____
56	_____	130	_____
58	_____	132	_____
60	_____	134	_____
62	_____	136	_____
64	_____	138	_____
66	_____	140	_____
68	_____	142	_____
70	_____	144	_____
72	_____	146	_____
74	_____	148	_____
76	_____	150	_____
78	_____	152	_____
80	_____	154	_____
82	_____	156	_____

PTO/AIA/01 (06-12)
Approved for use through 11/30/2020. OMB 0651-0032
U.S. Patent and Trademark Office; U.S. DEPARTMENT OF COMMERCE
Under the Paperwork Reduction Act of 1995, no persons are required to respond to a collection of information unless it displays a valid OMB control number.

DECLARATION (37 CFR 1.63) FOR UTILITY OR DESIGN APPLICATION USING AN APPLICATION DATA SHEET (37 CFR 1.76)

Title of Invention	

As the below named inventor, I hereby declare that:

This declaration is directed to:

☐ The attached application, or

☐ United States application or PCT international application number _____

filed on _____.

The above-identified application was made or authorized to be made by me.

I believe that I am the original inventor or an original joint inventor of a claimed invention in the application.

I hereby acknowledge that any willful false statement made in this declaration is punishable under 18 U.S.C. 1001 by fine or imprisonment of not more than five (5) years, or both.

WARNING:

Petitioner/applicant is cautioned to avoid submitting personal information in documents filed in a patent application that may contribute to identity theft. Personal information such as social security numbers, bank account numbers, or credit card numbers (other than a check or credit card authorization form PTO-2038 submitted for payment purposes) is never required by the USPTO to support a petition or an application. If this type of personal information is included in documents submitted to the USPTO, petitioners/applicants should consider redacting such personal information from the documents before submitting them to the USPTO. Petitioner/applicant is advised that the record of a patent application is available to the public after publication of the application (unless a non-publication request in compliance with 37 CFR 1.213(a) is made in the application) or issuance of a patent. Furthermore, the record from an abandoned application may also be available to the public if the application is referenced in a published application or an issued patent (see 37 CFR 1.14). Checks and credit card authorization forms PTO-2038 submitted for payment purposes are not retained in the application file and therefore are not publicly available.

LEGAL NAME OF INVENTOR

Inventor: _____   Date (Optional) :_____

Signature: _____

Note: An application data sheet (PTO/SB/14 or equivalent), including naming the entire inventive entity, must accompany this form or must have been previously filed. Use an additional PTO/AIA/01 form for each additional inventor.

This collection of information is required by 35 U.S.C. 115 and 37 CFR 1.63. The information is required to obtain or retain a benefit by the public which is to file (and by the USPTO to process) an application. Confidentiality is governed by 35 U.S.C. 122 and 37 CFR 1.11 and 1.14. This collection is estimated to take 1 minute to complete, including gathering, preparing, and submitting the completed application form to the USPTO. Time will vary depending upon the individual case. Any comments on the amount of time you require to complete this form and/or suggestions for reducing this burden, should be sent to the Chief Information Officer, U.S. Patent and Trademark Office, U.S. Department of Commerce, P.O. Box 1450, Alexandria, VA 22313-1450. DO NOT SEND FEES OR COMPLETED FORMS TO THIS ADDRESS. **SEND TO: Commissioner for Patents, P.O. Box 1450, Alexandria, VA 22313-1450.**

Form 10-1A: Declaration for Utility or Design Patent Application Using an Application Data Sheet

PTO/AIA/08 (11-15)
Approved for use through 11/30/2020. OMB 0651-0032
U.S. Patent and Trademark Office; U.S. DEPARTMENT OF COMMERCE
Under the Paperwork Reduction Act of 1995, no persons are required to respond to a collection of information unless it contains a valid OMB control number.

DECLARATION FOR UTILITY OR DESIGN PATENT APPLICATION (37 CFR 1.63)

Attorney Docket Number	
First Named Inventor	
COMPLETE IF KNOWN	
Application Number	
Filing Date	
Art Unit	
Examiner Name	

☐ Declaration Submitted With Initial Filing   OR   ☐ Declaration Submitted After Initial Filing (surcharge (37 CFR 1.16(f)) required)

_____

(Title of the Invention)

As a below named inventor, I hereby declare that:

This declaration is directed to:

☐ The attached application,

OR

☐ United States Application Number or PCT International application number _____

filed on_____.

The above-identified application was made or authorized to be made by me.

I believe I am the original inventor or an original joint inventor of a claimed invention in the application.

I hereby acknowledge that any willful false statement made in this declaration is punishable under 18 U.S.C. 1001 by fine or imprisonment of not more than five (5) years, or both.

Direct all correspondence to:	☐ The address associated with Customer Number:		**OR**	☐ Correspondence address below

Name	
Address	

City	State	Zip
Country	Telephone	Email

[Page 1 of 2]

Form 10-1A(2): Declaration for Utility or Design Patent Application

PTO/AIA/08 (11-15)
Approved for use through 11/30/2020. OMB 0651-0032
U.S. Patent and Trademark Office; U.S. DEPARTMENT OF COMMERCE
Under the Paperwork Reduction Act of 1995, no persons are required to respond to a collection of information unless it contains a valid OMB control number.

DECLARATION — Utility or Design Patent Application

WARNING:

Petitioner/applicant is cautioned to avoid submitting personal information in documents filed in a patent application that may contribute to identity theft. Personal information such as social security numbers, bank account numbers, or credit card numbers (other than a check or credit card authorization form PTO-2038 submitted for payment purposes) is never required by the USPTO to support a petition or an application. If this type of personal information is included in documents submitted to the USPTO, petitioners/applicants should consider redacting such personal information from the documents before submitting them to the USPTO. Petitioner/applicant is advised that the record of a patent application is available to the public after publication of the application (unless a non-publication request in compliance with 37 CFR 1.213(a) is made in the application) or issuance of a patent. Furthermore, the record from an abandoned application may also be available to the public if the application is referenced in a published application or an issued patent (see 37 CFR 1.14). Checks and credit card authorization forms PTO-2038 submitted for payment purposes are not retained in the application file and therefore are not publicly available. Petitioner/applicant is advised that documents which form the record of a patent application (such as the PTO/SB/01) are placed into the Privacy Act system of records DEPARTMENT OF COMMERCE, COMMERCE-PAT-7, System name: *Patent Application Files*. Documents not retained in an application file (such as the PTO-2038) are placed into the Privacy Act system of COMMERCE/PAT-TM-10, System name: *Deposit Accounts and Electronic Funds Transfer Profiles.*

LEGAL NAME OF SOLE OR FIRST INVENTOR:

(*E.g.,* Given Name (first and middle if any) and Family Name or Surname)

Inventor's Signature		Date (Optional)
Residence: City	State	Country

Mailing Address

City	State	Zip	Country

☐ Additional inventors are being named on the _____ Supplemental sheet(s) PTO/AIA/10 attached hereto

[Page 2 of 2]

Form 10-1A(2): Declaration for Utility or Design Patent Application

PTO/AIA/10 (06-12)
Approved for use through 01/31/2014. OMB 0651-0032
U.S. Patent and Trademark Office; U.S. DEPARTMENT OF COMMERCE
Under the Paperwork Reduction Act of 1995, no persons are required to respond to a collection of information unless it contains a valid OMB control number.

SUPPLEMENTAL SHEET FOR DECLARATION	**ADDITIONAL INVENTOR(S)** Supplemental Sheet (for PTO/AIA/08,09) Page _____ of _____

Legal Name of Additional Joint Inventor, if any:

(*E.g.*, Given Name (first and middle (if any)) and Family Name or Surname)

Inventor's Signature   Date (Optional)

Residence: City   State   Country

Mailing Address

City   State   Zip   Country

Legal Name of Additional Joint Inventor, if any:

(*E.g.*, Given Name (first and middle (if any)) and Family Name or Surname)

Inventor's Signature   Date (Optional)

Residence: City   State   Country

Mailing Address

City   State   Zip   Country

Legal Name of Additional Joint Inventor, if any:

(*E.g.*, Given Name (first and middle (if any)) and Family Name or Surname)

Inventor's Signature   Date (Optional)

Residence: City   State   Country

Mailing Address

City   State   Zip   Country

This collection of information is required by 35 U.S.C. 115 and 37 CFR 1.63. The information is required to obtain or retain a benefit by the public which is to file (and by the USPTO to process) an application. Confidentiality is governed by 35 U.S.C. 122 and 37 CFR 1.11 and 1.14. This collection is estimated to take 21 minutes to complete, including gathering, preparing, and submitting the completed application form to the USPTO. Time will vary depending upon the individual case. Any comments on the amount of time you require to complete this form and/or suggestions for reducing this burden, should be sent to the Chief Information Officer, U.S. Patent and Trademark Office, U.S. Department of Commerce, P.O. Box 1450, Alexandria, VA 22313-1450. DO NOT SEND FEES OR COMPLETED FORMS TO THIS ADDRESS. **SEND TO: Commissioner for Patents, P.O. Box 1450, Alexandria, VA 22313-1450.**

If you need assistance in completing the form, call 1-800-PTO-9199 (1-800-786-9199) and select option 2.

Form 10-1B: Supplemental Sheet for Declaration

PTO/AIA/15 (10-17)
Approved for use through 11/30/2020. OMB 0651-0032
U.S. Patent and Trademark Office; U.S. DEPARTMENT OF COMMERCE
Under the Paperwork Reduction Act of 1995 no persons are required to respond to a collection of information unless it displays a valid OMB control number.

UTILITY
PATENT APPLICATION
TRANSMITTAL

(Only for new nonprovisional applications under 37 CFR 1.53(b))

Attorney Docket No.	
First Named Inventor	
Title	
Priority Mail Express® *Label No.*	

APPLICATION ELEMENTS
See MPEP chapter 600 concerning utility patent application contents.

ADDRESS TO:
Commissioner for Patents
P.O. Box 1450
Alexandria, VA 22313-1450

ACCOMPANYING APPLICATION PAPERS

1. ☐ **Fee Transmittal Form**
(PTO/SB/17 or equivalent)

2. ☐ **Applicant asserts small entity status.**
See 37 CFR 1.27

3. ☐ **Applicant certifies micro entity status.** See 37 CFR 1.29.
Applicant must attach form PTO/SB/15A or B or equivalent.

4. ☐ **Specification** [*Total Pages* _____]
Both the claims and abstract must start on a new page.
(See MPEP § 608.01(a) for information on the preferred arrangement)

5. ☐ **Drawing(s)** (35 U.S.C. 113) [*Total Sheets* _____]

6. **Inventor's Oath or Declaration** [*Total Pages* _____]
(including substitute statements under 37 CFR 1.64 and assignments serving as an oath or declaration under 37 CFR 1.63(e))

  a. ☐ Newly executed (original or copy)

  b. ☐ A copy from a prior application (37 CFR 1.63(d))

7. ☐ **Application Data Sheet** * See note below.
See 37 CFR 1.76 (PTO/AIA/14 or equivalent)

8. **CD-ROM or CD-R**
in duplicate, large table, or Computer Program (*Appendix*)
  ☐ Landscape Table on CD

9. **Nucleotide and/or Amino Acid Sequence Submission**
(if applicable, items a. – c. are required)

  a. ☐ Computer Readable Form (CRF)

  b. ☐ Specification Sequence Listing on:

    i. ☐ CD-ROM or CD-R (2 copies); or

    ii. ☐ Paper

  c. ☐ Statements verifying identity of above copies

10. ☐ **Assignment Papers**
(cover sheet & document(s))
Name of Assignee _____
_____

11. ☐ **37 CFR 3.73(c) Statement**   ☐ **Power of Attorney**
(*when there is an assignee*)

12. ☐ **English Translation Document**
(*if applicable*)

13. ☐ **Information Disclosure Statement**
(PTO/SB/08 or PTO-1449)
  ☐ Copies of citations attached

14. ☐ **Preliminary Amendment**

15. ☐ **Return Receipt Postcard**
(*MPEP § 503*) (*Should be specifically itemized*)

16. ☐ **Certified Copy of Priority Document(s)**
(*if foreign priority is claimed*)

17. ☐ **Nonpublication Request**
Under 35 U.S.C. 122(b)(2)(B)(i). Applicant must attach form PTO/SB/35 or equivalent.

18. ☐ **Other:** _____
_____
_____
_____
_____

*Note: (1) Benefit claims under 37 CFR 1.78 and foreign priority claims under 1.55 **must** be included in an Application Data Sheet (ADS).
(2) For applications filed under 35 U.S.C. 111, the application must contain an ADS specifying the applicant if the applicant is an assignee, person to whom the inventor is under an obligation to assign, or person who otherwise shows sufficient proprietary interest in the matter. See 37 CFR 1.46(b).

19. CORRESPONDENCE ADDRESS

☐ The address associated with Customer Number: _____ **OR** ☐ Correspondence address below

Name	
Address	

City		State		Zip Code	
Country		Telephone		Email	

Signature		Date	
Name (Print/Type)		Registration No. (Attorney/Agent)	

PTO/SB/17 (01-18)
Approved for use through 11/30/2020. OMB 0651-0032
U.S. Patent and Trademark Office; U.S. DEPARTMENT OF COMMERCE
Under the Paperwork Reduction Act of 1995 no persons are required to respond to a collection of information unless it displays a valid OMB control number

FEE TRANSMITTAL

Complete if known	
Application Number	
Filing Date	
First Named Inventor	
Examiner Name	
Art Unit	
Practitioner Docket No.	

☐ Applicant asserts small entity status. See 37 CFR 1.27.

☐ Applicant certifies micro entity status. See 37 CFR 1.29.
Form PTO/SB/15A or B or equivalent must either be enclosed or have been submitted previously.

TOTAL AMOUNT OF PAYMENT	($)

METHOD OF PAYMENT (check all that apply)

☐ Check ☐ Credit Card ☐ Money Order ☐ None ☐ Other (please identify): _____

☐ Deposit Account Deposit Account Number: _____ Deposit Account Name: _____

For the above-identified deposit account, the Director is hereby authorized to (check all that apply):

☐ Charge fee(s) indicated below

☐ Charge fee(s) indicated below, **except for the filing fee**

☐ Charge any additional fee(s) or underpayment of fee(s) under 37 CFR 1.16 and 1.17

☐ Credit any overpayment of fee(s)

WARNING: Information on this form may become public. Credit card information should not be included on this form. Provide credit card information and authorization on PTO-2038.

FEE CALCULATION

1. BASIC FILING, SEARCH, AND EXAMINATION FEES (U = undiscounted fee; S = small entity fee; M = micro entity fee)

Application Type	FILING FEES U ($)	S ($)	M ($)	SEARCH FEES U ($)	S ($)	M ($)	EXAMINATION FEES U ($)	S ($)	M ($)	Fees Paid ($)
Utility	300	150*	75	660	330	165	760	380	190	_____
Design	200	100	50	160	80	40	600	300	150	_____
Plant	200	100	50	420	210	105	620	310	155	_____
Reissue	300	150	75	660	330	165	2,200	1,100	550	_____
Provisional	280	140	70	0	0	0	0	0	0	_____

* The $150 small entity status filing fee for a utility application is further reduced to $75 for a small entity status applicant who files the application via EFS-Web.

2. EXCESS CLAIM FEES

Fee Description	Undiscounted Fee ($)	Small Entity Fee ($)	Micro Entity Fee ($)
Each claim over 20 (including Reissues)	100	50	25
Each independent claim over 3 (including Reissues)	460	230	115
Multiple dependent claims	820	410	205

Total Claims		Extra Claims	Fee ($)	Fee Paid ($)	
_____	-20 or HP =	_____ x	_____	= _____	

HP = highest number of total claims paid for, if greater than 20.

Multiple Dependent Claims
Fee ($) _____ Fee Paid ($) _____

Indep. Claims		Extra Claims	Fee ($)	Fee Paid ($)
_____	-3 or HP =	_____ x	_____	= _____

HP = highest number of independent claims paid for, if greater than 3.

3. APPLICATION SIZE FEE

If the specification and drawings exceed 100 sheets of paper (excluding electronically filed sequence or computer listings under 37 CFR 1.52(e)), the application size fee due is $400 ($200 for small entity) ($100 for micro entity) for each additional 50 sheets or fraction thereof. See 35 U.S.C. 41(a)(1)(G) and 37 CFR 1.16(s).

Total Sheets	Extra Sheets	Number of each additional 50 or fraction thereof	Fee ($)	Fee Paid ($)
_____ - 100 =	_____ / 50 =	_____ (round **up** to a whole number) x	_____	= _____

4. OTHER FEE(S) Fees Paid ($)

Non-English specification, $130 fee (no small or micro entity discount) _____

Non-electronic filing fee under 37 CFR 1.16(t) for a utility application, $400 fee ($200 small or micro entity) _____

Other (e.g., late filing surcharge): _____ _____

SUBMITTED BY

Signature		Registration No. (Attorney/Agent)		Telephone	
Name (Print/Type)				Date	

Form 10-3: Fee Transmittal

United States Patent and Trademark Office
Instructions for Completing the Credit Card Payment Form

Credit Card Information

- Enter all credit card information including the payment amount to be charged to your credit card and remember to sign the form. The United States Patent and Trademark Office (USPTO) cannot process credit card payments without an authorized signature. An s-signature on credit card payment forms is not allowed under 37 CFR 1.4(e).

- The USPTO does **not** accept a general authorization to charge any payment deficiency or any additional fees to a credit card.

- The USPTO does **not** accept debit cards or check cards that require use of a personal identification number as a method of payment.

Credit Card Billing Address

- Address information is required for credit card payment as a means of verification. Failure to complete the address information, including zip/postal code, may result in the payment not being accepted by your credit card institution.

Request and Payment Information

- Provide a description of your request based on the payment amount. For example, indicate the item as "basic filing fee" (patent) *or* "first maintenance fee" (patent maintenance fee) or "application for registration" (trademark) *or* "certified copy of a patent" (other fee).

- Indicate the nature of your request by the type of fee you wish to pay: Patent Fee, Patent Maintenance Fee, Trademark Fee or Other Fee. Complete information for each type of fee as applicable to identify the nature of your request. Indicate only one type of fee per form.

- If you are requesting and paying a fee based on a previously filed patent or trademark application, indicate the application/serial number, patent number or registration number that is associated with your request. "Other Fee" is used to request copies of patent and trademark documents, certified copies, assignments, and other information products.

- IDON numbers are assigned by the USPTO for customers ordering patent and trademark information and products specified as "Other Fee" on the order form. If you have been assigned an IDON number from a previous customer order, include it with your request.

- For more information on USPTO fees and amounts, refer to the current fee schedule at www.uspto.gov. To request a copy by mail, call the USPTO Contact Center at (800) 786-9199 or (571) 272-1000. Information on mailing addresses is also available at www.uspto.gov.

Protect Your Credit Card Information

- The USPTO strongly recommends using this form for credit card payments submitted by mail, facsimile, or by hand-delivery. To protect your credit card information use only this form and do not include credit card information on any other form or document.

- To protect your credit card information, **do not submit this form electronically** through "EFS-Web" or any other USPTO Web site. Credit card information for electronic credit card payments should be entered exclusively on the USPTO Web site providing electronic payment capability.

PTO-2038 (02-2015)
Approved for use through 01/31/2018. OMB 0651-0043
United States Patent and Trademark Office; U.S. DEPARTMENT OF COMMERCE
Under the Paperwork Reduction Act of 1995, no persons are required to respond to a collection of information unless it displays a valid OMB control number.

Credit Card Payment Form
(Do not submit this form electronically via EFS-Web)
Please Read Instructions before Completing this Form

Credit Card Information

Credit Card Type: ☐ Visa ☐ MasterCard ☐ American Express ☐ Discover

Credit Card Account #:

Credit Card Expiration Date (mm/yyyy):

Name as it Appears on Credit Card:

Payment Amount (US Dollars): $

Cardholder Signature: | Date (mm/dd/yyyy):

The USPTO does not accept an s-signature (37 CFR 1.4(e)) on credit card payment forms.
Refund Policy: The USPTO may refund a fee paid by mistake or in excess of that required. A change of purpose after the payment of a fee will not entitle a party to a refund of such fee. The USPTO will not refund amounts of $25.00 or less unless a refund is specifically requested and will not notify the payor of such amounts (37 CFR 1.26). Refund of a fee paid by credit card will be issued as a credit to the credit card account to which the fee was charged.
Maximum Daily Limit: There is a $24,999.99 daily limit per credit card account effective June 1, 2015. There is no daily limit for debit cards.

Credit Card Billing Address

Street Address 1:

Street Address 2:

City:

State/Province: | Zip/Postal Code:

Country:

Daytime Phone #: | Fax #:

Request and Payment Information

Description of Request and Payment Information:

☐ Patent Fee	☐ Patent Maintenance Fee	☐ Trademark Fee	☐ Other Fee
Application No.	Application No.	Application No.	IDON Customer No.
Patent No.	Patent No.	Registration No.	
Attorney Docket No.		Identify or Describe Mark	

If the cardholder includes a credit card number on any form or document other than the Credit Card Payment Form or submits this form electronically via EFS-Web, the United States Patent and Trademark Office will not be liable in the event that the credit card number becomes public knowledge.

In the United States Patent and Trademark Office

Serial Number: _____

Appn. Filed: _____

Applicant(s): _____

Appn. Title: _____

Examiner/GAU: _____

Mailed: _____

At: _____

Information Disclosure Statement Cover Letter

Commissioner for Patents
P.O. Box 1450
Alexandria, VA 22313-1450

Sir:

Attached is a completed Form PTO/SB/08(A&B) and copies of any non-U.S. patent references cited thereon. Following are comments on any non-English-language references pursuant to Rule 98:

Very respectfully,

Applicant(s): _____

_____

Enc.: PTO/SB/08(A&B)

c/o: _____

_____

_____

Telephone: _____

Certificate of Mailing

I certify that this correspondence will be deposited with the United States Postal Service as first class mail with proper postage affixed in an envelope addressed to: "Commissioner for Patents, P.O. Box 1450, Alexandria, VA 22313-1450" on the date below.

Date: 20_____   _____, Applicant

PTO/SB/08a (07-09)
Approved for use through 11/30/2020. OMB 0651-0031
U.S. Patent and Trademark Office; U.S. DEPARTMENT OF COMMERCE
Under the Paperwork Reduction Act of 1995, no persons are required to respond to a collection of information unless it contains a valid OMB control number.

Substitute for form 1449/PTO

INFORMATION DISCLOSURE STATEMENT BY APPLICANT

(Use as many sheets as necessary)

Sheet _____ of _____

Complete if Known	
Application Number	
Filing Date	
First Named Inventor	
Art Unit	
Examiner Name	
Attorney Docket Number	

U. S. PATENT DOCUMENTS

Examiner Initials*	Cite No.[1]	Document Number Number-Kind Code[2] *(if known)*	Publication Date MM-DD-YYYY	Name of Patentee or Applicant of Cited Document	Pages, Columns, Lines, Where Relevant Passages or Relevant Figures Appear
		US-			
		US-			
		US-			
		US-			
		US-			
		US-			
		US-			
		US-			
		US-			
		US-			
		US-			
		US-			
		US-			
		US-			
		US-			
		US-			
		US-			
		US-			
		US-			

FOREIGN PATENT DOCUMENTS

Examiner Initials*	Cite No.[1]	Foreign Patent Document Country Code[3] Number[4] Kind Code[5] *(if known)*	Publication Date MM-DD-YYYY	Name of Patentee or Applicant of Cited Document	Pages, Columns, Lines, Where Relevant Passages Or Relevant Figures Appear	T[6]

Examiner Signature		Date Considered	

*EXAMINER: Initial if reference considered, whether or not citation is in conformance with MPEP 609. Draw line through citation if not in conformance and not considered. Include copy of this form with next communication to applicant. [1] Applicant's unique citation designation number (optional). [2] See Kinds Codes of USPTO Patent Documents at www.uspto.gov or MPEP 901.04. [3] Enter Office that issued the document, by the two-letter code (WIPO Standard ST.3). [4] For Japanese patent documents, the indication of the year of the reign of the Emperor must precede the serial number of the patent document. [5] Kind of document by the appropriate symbols as indicated on the document under WIPO Standard ST.16 if possible. [6] Applicant is to place a check mark here if English language Translation is attached.

This collection of information is required by 37 CFR 1.97 and 1.98. The information is required to obtain or retain a benefit by the public which is to file (and by the USPTO to process) an application. Confidentiality is governed by 35 U.S.C. 122 and 37 CFR 1.14. This collection is estimated to take 2 hours to complete, including gathering, preparing, and submitting the completed application form to the USPTO. Time will vary depending upon the individual case. Any comments on the amount of time you require to complete this form and/or suggestions for reducing this burden, should be sent to the Chief Information Officer, U.S. Patent and Trademark Office, P.O. Box 1450, Alexandria, VA 22313-1450. DO NOT SEND FEES OR COMPLETED FORMS TO THIS ADDRESS. **SEND TO: Commissioner for Patents, P.O. Box 1450, Alexandria, VA 22313-1450.**

If you need assistance in completing the form, call 1-800-PTO-9199 (1-800-786-9199) and select option 2.

PTO/SB/08b (07-09)
Approved for use through 11/30/2020. OMB 0651-0031
U.S. Patent and Trademark Office; U.S. DEPARTMENT OF COMMERCE
Under the Paperwork Reduction Act of 1995, no persons are required to respond to a collection of information unless it contains a valid OMB control number.

Substitute for form 1449/PTO	Complete if Known	
INFORMATION DISCLOSURE STATEMENT BY APPLICANT *(Use as many sheets as necessary)*	**Application Number**	
	Filing Date	
	First Named Inventor	
	Art Unit	
	Examiner Name	
Sheet ___ of ___	Attorney Docket Number	

NON PATENT LITERATURE DOCUMENTS

Examiner Initials*	Cite No.[1]	Include name of the author (in CAPITAL LETTERS), title of the article (when appropriate), title of the item (book, magazine, journal, serial, symposium, catalog, etc.), date, page(s), volume-issue number(s), publisher, city and/or country where published.	T[2]

Examiner Signature		Date Considered	

*EXAMINER: Initial if reference considered, whether or not citation is in conformance with MEPE 609. Draw line through citation if not in conformance and not considered. Include copy of this form with next communication to applicant.

1 Applicant's unique citation designation number (optional). 2 Applicant is to place a check mark here if English language Translation is attached.

This collection of information is required by 37 CFR 1.98. The information is required to obtain or retain a benefit by the public which is to file (and by the USPTO to process) an application. Confidentiality is governed by 35 U.S.C. 122 and 37 CFR 1.14. This collection is estimated to take 2 hours to complete, including gathering, preparing, and submitting the completed application form to the USPTO. Time will vary depending upon the individual case. Any comments on the amount of time you require to complete this form and/or suggestions for reducing this burden, should be sent to the Chief Information Officer, U.S. Patent and Trademark Office, P.O. Box 1450, Alexandria, VA 22313-1450. DO NOT SEND FEES OR COMPLETED FORMS TO THIS ADDRESS. **SEND TO: Commissioner for Patents, P.O. Box 1450, Alexandria, VA 22313-1450.**

If you need assistance in completing the form, call 1-800-PTO-9199 (1-800-786-9199) and select option 2.

Form 10-6B: Information Disclosure Statement by Applicant

PTO/SB/35 (07-09)
Approved for use through 07/31/2012. OMB 0651-0031
U.S. Patent and Trademark Office; U. S. DEPARTMENT OF COMMERCE
Under the Paperwork Reduction Act of 1995, no persons are required to respond to a collection of information unless it displays a valid OMB control number.

NONPUBLICATION REQUEST UNDER 35 U.S.C. 122(b)(2)(B)(i)	First Named Inventor	
	Title	
	Attorney Docket Number	

I hereby certify that the invention disclosed in the attached application **has not and will not be** the subject of an application filed in another country, or under a multilateral international agreement, that requires publication at eighteen months after filing.

I hereby request that the attached application not be published under 35 U.S.C. 122(b).

_____   _____
Signature   Date

_____   _____
Typed or printed name   Registration Number, if applicable

_____
Telephone Number

This request must be signed in compliance with 37 CFR 1.33(b) and submitted with the application **upon filing.**

Applicant may rescind this nonpublication request at any time. If applicant rescinds a request that an application not be published under 35 U.S.C. 122(b), the application will be scheduled for publication at eighteen months from the earliest claimed filing date for which a benefit is claimed.

If applicant subsequently files an application directed to the invention disclosed in the attached application in another country, or under a multilateral international agreement, that requires publication of applications eighteen months after filing, the applicant **must** notify the United States Patent and Trademark Office of such filing within forty-five (45) days after the date of the filing of such foreign or international application. **Failure to do so will result in abandonment of this application (35 U.S.C. 122(b)(2)(B)(iii)).**

If you need assistance in completing the form, call 1-800-PTO-9199 (1-800-786-9199) and select option 2.

Form 10-7: Nonpublication Request

In the United States Patent and Trademark Office

Serial Number: _____

Appn. Filed: _____

Applicant(s): _____

Appn. Title: _____

Examiner/GAU: _____

Mailed: _____

At: _____

Request Under MPEP 707.07(j)

Mail Stop Non-Fee Amendments
Commissioner for Patents
P.O. Box 1450
Alexandria, VA 22313-1450

Sir:

The undersigned pro se applicant(s) respectfully requests that if the Examiner finds patentable subject matter disclosed in this application, but feels that Applicant's present claims are not entirely suitable, the Examiner draft one or more allowable claims for applicant, pursuant to MPEP 707.07(j).

Very respectfully,

_____
Signature of Inventor # 1

_____
Signature of Inventor # 2

_____
Address

_____
Address

_____

_____

_____
Telephone

_____
Telephone

In the United States Patent and Trademark Office

Serial Number: _____

Appn. Filed: _____

Applicant(s): _____

Appn. Title: _____

Examiner/GAU: _____

Mailed: _____

At: _____

Petition to Make Special

Commissioner for Patents
P.O. Box 1450
Alexandria, VA 22313-1450

Sir:

Applicant hereby respectfully petitions that the above application be made special under MPEP Sec. 708.02 for the following reason; attached is a declaration in support thereof:

☐ Applicant's state of health is such that he or she might not be available to assist in the prosecution of the application if it were to run its normal course

☐ Applicant's age is 65 or greater

☐ The subject matter of this application will materially enhance the quality of the environment

☐ The subject matter of this application will materially contribute to the development or conservation of energy resources

☐ The subject matter of this application will materially contribute to countering terrorism

Very respectfully,

Applicant(s): _____

_____

Attachment(s): Supporting Declaration.

Applicant(s): _____

c/o: _____

_____

_____

Telephone: _____

Certificate of Mailing

I certify that this correspondence will be deposited with the United States Postal Service as first class mail with proper postage affixed in an envelope addressed to: "Commissioner for Patents, P.O. Box 1450, Alexandria, VA 22313-1450" on the date below.

Date: 20_____   _____, Applicant

Design Patent Application—Preamble, Specification, and Claim

Mail Stop Design
Commissioner for Patents
P.O. Box 1450
Alexandria, VA 22313-1450

Sir:

PREAMBLE:

The petitioner(s) whose signature(s) appear on the declaration attached respectfully request that Letters Patent be granted to such petitioner(s) for the new and original design set forth in the following specification. The filing fee of $_____ , _____ sheets of drawings, a patent application declaration, fee transmittal, a credit card payment form or check, and a return receipt postcard are attached.

SPECIFICATION:

The undersigned has (have) invented a new, original, and ornamental design entitled "_____

_____ " of which the following is a specification. Reference is made to the accompanying drawings that form a part hereof, the figures of which are described as follows:

CROSS-REFERENCE TO RELATED APPLICATIONS:

STATEMENT REGARDING FEDERALLY SPONSORED RESEARCH:

DRAWING FIGURES:

CLAIM: I (We) Claim:

The ornamental design for a _____

_____ , as shown.

Express Mail Label # _____ ; Date of Deposit 20_____

PTO/AIA/18 (10-17)
Approved for use through 11/30/2020. OMB 0651-0032
U.S. Patent and Trademark Office; U.S. DEPARTMENT OF COMMERCE
Under the Paperwork Reduction Act of 1995 no persons are required to respond to a collection of information unless it displays a valid OMB control number.

DESIGN PATENT APPLICATION TRANSMITTAL

(Only for new nonprovisional applications under 37 CFR 1.53(b))

Attorney Docket No.	
First Named Inventor	
Title	
Priority Mail Express® *Label No.*	

ADDRESS TO:
Commissioner for Patents
P.O. Box 1450
Alexandria, VA 22313-1450

DESIGN V. UTILITY: A "design patent" protects an article's ornamental appearance (e.g., the way an article looks) (35 U.S.C. 171), while a "utility patent" protects the way an article is used and works (35 U.S.C. 101). The ornamental appearance of an article includes its shape/configuration or surface ornamentation upon the article, or both. Both a design and a utility patent may be obtained on an article if invention resides both in its ornamental appearance and its utility. For more information, see MPEP § 1502.01.

APPLICATION ELEMENTS
See MPEP chapter 1500 concerning design patent application contents.

1. ☐ **Fee Transmittal Form**
   (PTO/SB/17 or equivalent)

2. ☐ **Applicant asserts small entity status.**
   See 37 CFR 1.27

3. ☐ **Applicant certifies micro entity status.** See 37 CFR 1.29.
   Applicant must attach form PTO/SB/15A or B or equivalent.

4. ☐ **Specification**   [*Total Pages* _____]
   (preferred arrangement set forth below, MPEP § 1503.01)
   - Preamble
   - Cross References to Related Applications
   - Statement Regarding Fed sponsored R & D
   - Description of the figure(s) of the drawings
   - Feature description
   - Claim (only one (1) claim permitted, MPEP § 1503.03)

5. ☐ **Drawing(s)**   [*Total Sheets* _____]
   See 37 CFR 1.152

6. **Inventor's Oath or Declaration**   [*Total Pages* _____]
   (including substitute statements under 37 CFR 1.64 and assignments serving as an oath or declaration under 37 CFR 1.63(e))

   a. ☐ Newly executed (original or copy)

   b. ☐ A copy from a prior application (37 CFR 1.63(d))

7. ☐ **Application Data Sheet**   ** See note below.*
   See 37 CFR 1.76 (PTO/AIA/14 or equivalent)

ACCOMPANYING APPLICATION PARTS

8. ☐ **Assignment Papers**
   (cover sheet & document(s))

9. ☐ **37 CFR 3.73(c) Statement**   ☐ **Power of Attorney**
   (*when there is an assignee*)

10. ☐ **English Translation Document**
    (*if applicable*)

11. ☐ **Information Disclosure Statement (IDS)**
    (PTO/SB/08 or PTO-1449)

    ☐ Copies of foreign patent documents, publications, and other information

12. ☐ **Preliminary Amendment**

13. ☐ **Return Receipt Postcard**
    (*MPEP § 503) (Should be specifically itemized*)

14. ☐ **Certified Copy of Priority Document(s)**
    (*if foreign priority is claimed*)

15. ☐ **Request for Expedited Examination of a Design Application**
    (37 CFR 1.155) (NOTE: Use "Mail Stop Expedited Design")

16. ☐ **Other:** _____
    _____
    _____
    _____

***Note:** (1) Benefit claims under 37 CFR 1.78 and foreign priority claims under 1.55 **must** be included in an Application Data Sheet (ADS).
(2) For applications filed under 35 U.S.C. 111, the application must contain an ADS specifying the applicant if the applicant is an assignee, person to whom the inventor is under an obligation to assign, or person who otherwise shows sufficient proprietary interest in the matter. See 37 CFR 1.46(b).*

17. CORRESPONDENCE ADDRESS

☐ The address associated with Customer Number: _____   **OR**   ☐ Correspondence address below

Name	
Address	

City		State		Zip Code	
Country		Telephone		Email	

Signature		Date	
Name (Print/Type)		Registration No. (Attorney/Agent)	

Form 10-11: Design Patent Application Transmittal

PTO/SB/27 (05-15)
Approved for use through 11/30/2020. OMB 0651-0031
U.S. Patent and Trademark Office, U.S. DEPARTMENT OF COMMERCE
Under the Paperwork Reduction Act of 1995, no persons are required to respond to a collection of information unless it displays a valid OMB control number.

REQUEST FOR EXPEDITED EXAMINATION OF A DESIGN APPLICATION (37 CFR 1.155)

Application Number	
Filing Date	
First Named Inventor	
Title	
Atty Docket Number	

ADDRESS TO:

**MAIL STOP EXPEDITED DESIGN
COMMISSIONER OF PATENTS
P.O. Box 1450
Alexandria, VA 22313-1450**

This is a request for expedited examination of a design application under 37 CFR 1.155.

NOTE: If the present form (PTO/SB/27) accompanies a new nonprovisional design application under 37 CFR 1.53(b), include form PTO/SB/18 "Design Patent Application Transmittal" or its equivalent. Do not include the present form (PTO/SB/27) on the date of filing a new international design application. For an international design application to qualify for expedited examination, 37 CFR 1.155(a)(1) provides that the international design application first must have been published by WIPO pursuant to Hague Agreement Article 10(3).

A preexamination search was conducted. The field of search was:

_____

_____

_____

Related applications: _____

The following items are required under 37 CFR 1.155:

- Drawings in compliance with 37 CFR 1.84, unless the design application is an international design application that designates the United States and was published by WIPO pursuant to Hague Agreement Article 10(3).
- The fee set forth in 37 CFR 1.17(k).
- An information disclosure statement in compliance with 37 CFR 1.98.

Note: The Office will not grant a request for expedited examination if all of the requirements of 37 CFR 1.155 are not satisfied. In addition, the Office will not examine an application that is not in a condition for examination (e.g., missing basic filing fee) even if the applicant files a request for expedited examination under 37 CFR 1.155.

_____	_____
Signature	Date
_____	_____
Typed or printed name	Registration Number, if applicable
_____	
Telephone Number	

Warning: Information on this form may become public. Credit card information should not be included on this form. Provide credit card information and authorization on PTO-2038.

This collection of information is required by 37 CFR 1.48. The information is required to obtain or retain a benefit by the public which is to file (and by the USPTO to process) an application. Confidentiality is governed by 35 U.S.C. 122 and 37 CFR 1.11 and 1.14. This collection is estimated to take 1 hour to complete, including gathering, preparing, and submitting the completed application form to the USPTO. Time will vary depending upon the individual case. Any comments on the amount of time you require to complete this form and/or suggestions for reducing this burden, should be sent to the Chief Information Officer, U.S. Patent and Trademark Office, U.S. Department of Commerce, P.O. Box 1450, Alexandria, VA 22313-1450. DO NOT SEND FEES OR COMPLETED FORMS TO THIS ADDRESS. **SEND TO: Commissioner for Patents, P.O. Box 1450, Alexandria, VA 22313-1450.**

If you need assistance in completing the form, call 1-800-PTO-9199 and select option 2.

Form 10-12: Request for Expedited Examination of a Design Application

Privacy Act Statement

The **Privacy Act of 1974 (P.L. 93-579)** requires that you be given certain information in connection with your submission of the attached form related to a patent application or patent. Accordingly, pursuant to the requirements of the Act, please be advised that: (1) the general authority for the collection of this information is 35 U.S.C. 2(b)(2); (2) furnishing of the information solicited is voluntary; and (3) the principal purpose for which the information is used by the U.S. Patent and Trademark Office is to process and/or examine your submission related to a patent application or patent. If you do not furnish the requested information, the U.S. Patent and Trademark Office may not be able to process and/or examine your submission, which may result in termination of proceedings or abandonment of the application or expiration of the patent.

The information provided by you in this form will be subject to the following routine uses:

1. The information on this form will be treated confidentially to the extent allowed under the Freedom of Information Act (5 U.S.C. 552) and the Privacy Act (5 U.S.C 552a). Records from this system of records may be disclosed to the Department of Justice to determine whether disclosure of these records is required by the Freedom of Information Act.
2. A record from this system of records may be disclosed, as a routine use, in the course of presenting evidence to a court, magistrate, or administrative tribunal, including disclosures to opposing counsel in the course of settlement negotiations.
3. A record in this system of records may be disclosed, as a routine use, to a Member of Congress submitting a request involving an individual, to whom the record pertains, when the individual has requested assistance from the Member with respect to the subject matter of the record.
4. A record in this system of records may be disclosed, as a routine use, to a contractor of the Agency having need for the information in order to perform a contract. Recipients of information shall be required to comply with the requirements of the Privacy Act of 1974, as amended, pursuant to 5 U.S.C. 552a(m).
5. A record related to an International Application filed under the Patent Cooperation Treaty in this system of records may be disclosed, as a routine use, to the International Bureau of the World Intellectual Property Organization, pursuant to the Patent Cooperation Treaty.
6. A record in this system of records may be disclosed, as a routine use, to another federal agency for purposes of National Security review (35 U.S.C. 181) and for review pursuant to the Atomic Energy Act (42 U.S.C. 218(c)).
7. A record from this system of records may be disclosed, as a routine use, to the Administrator, General Services, or his/her designee, during an inspection of records conducted by GSA as part of that agency's responsibility to recommend improvements in records management practices and programs, under authority of 44 U.S.C. 2904 and 2906. Such disclosure shall be made in accordance with the GSA regulations governing inspection of records for this purpose, and any other relevant (*i.e.*, GSA or Commerce) directive. Such disclosure shall not be used to make determinations about individuals.
8. A record from this system of records may be disclosed, as a routine use, to the public after either publication of the application pursuant to 35 U.S.C. 122(b) or issuance of a patent pursuant to 35 U.S.C. 151. Further, a record may be disclosed, subject to the limitations of 37 CFR 1.14, as a routine use, to the public if the record was filed in an application which became abandoned or in which the proceedings were terminated and which application is referenced by either a published application, an application open to public inspection or an issued patent.
9. A record from this system of records may be disclosed, as a routine use, to a Federal, State, or local law enforcement agency, if the USPTO becomes aware of a violation or potential violation of law or regulation.

In the United States Patent and Trademark Office

Serial Number: _____

Appn. Filed: _____

Applicant(s): _____

Appn. Title: _____

Examiner/GAU: _____

Mailed: _____

At: _____

Amendment _____

Commissioner for Patents
P.O. Box 1450
Alexandria, VA 22313-1450

Sir:

In response to the Office Letter mailed _____, 20_____, please amend the above application as follows:

☐ SPECIFICATION: Amendments to the specification begin on page _____ of this amendment.

☐ DRAWINGS: Amendments to the drawings are discussed on page _____ of this amendment.

☐ CLAIMS: Amendments to the claims begin on page _____ of this amendment.

☐ REMARKS begin on page _____ of this amendment.

In the United States Patent and Trademark Office

Serial Number: _____

Appn. Filed: _____

Applicant(s): _____

Appn. Title: _____

Examiner/GAU: _____

Mailed: _____

At: _____

Submission of Corrected Drawings

Commissioner for Patents
P.O. Box 1450
Alexandria, VA 22313-1450
Attn: Chief Draftsperson

Sir:

New drawing sheet(s) (_____) for the above application is/are enclosed, corrected as necessary. Please substitute this/these for the corresponding sheet(s) on file.

☐ A copy of sheet(s) _____ is attached and is marked in red to indicate the changes being made.

Very respectfully,

Applicant(s):

c/o: _____

_____

_____

Telephone: _____

Certificate of Mailing

I certify that this correspondence will be deposited with the United States Postal Service as first class mail with proper postage affixed in an envelope addressed to: "Commissioner for Patents, P.O. Box 1450, Alexandria, VA 22313-1450."

Date: 20_____   _____, Applicant

In the United States Patent and Trademark Office

Serial Number: _____

Appn. Filed: _____

Applicant(s): _____

Appn. Title: _____

Examiner/GAU: _____

Mailed: _____

At: _____

Supplemental Declaration
(for Use After Close of Prosecution or With Continuation-in-Part Application)

As an applicant in the above-identified application, I declare as follows:

1. If only one inventor is named below, I am a sole inventor, and if more than one inventor is named below, I am a joint inventor with the inventor(s) named below of the subject matter of the above-identified application.

2. I have reviewed and understand the contents of the specification and claims, as originally filed, and as amended by the amendment(s) dated _____.

3. I believe that I, and the other inventor(s) named below if more than one inventor is named below, am the original and first inventor or inventors of the subject matter that is claimed and for which a patent is sought.

4. I acknowledge the duty to disclose information that is material to the examination of the application in accordance with 37 C.F.R. Section 1.56(a), and if this oath accompanies or refers to a continuation-in-part application, I acknowledge the duty to disclose material information as defined in 37 C.F.R. Section 1.56(a) that occurred between the filing date of the prior application and the national or PCT international filing date of the continuation-in-part application.

5. I hereby declare that all statements made herein of my own knowledge are true and that all statements made on information and belief are believed to be true, and further that these statements were made with the knowledge that willful false statements and the like so made are punishable by fine or imprisonment, or both, under Section 1001 of Title 18 of the United States Code, and that such willful false statements may jeopardize the validity of the application, any patent issuing thereon, or any patent to which this verified statement is directed.

_____
Signature of Inventor

_____
Printed Name of Inventor

_____
Date

_____
Signature of Joint Inventor

_____
Printed Name of Joint Inventor

_____
Date

PTO/AIA/22 (03-13)
Approved for use through 11/30/2020. OMB 0651-0031
U.S. Patent and Trademark Office; U.S. DEPARTMENT OF COMMERCE
Under the Paperwork Reduction Act of 1995, no persons are required to respond to a collection of information unless it displays a valid OMB control number.

	Docket Number (Optional)
PETITION FOR EXTENSION OF TIME UNDER 37 CFR 1.136(a)	

Application Number	Filed

For

Art Unit	Examiner

This is a request under the provisions of 37 CFR 1.136(a) to extend the period for filing a reply in the above-identified application.

The requested extension and fee are as follows (check time period desired and enter the appropriate fee below):

		Fee	Small Entity Fee	Micro Entity Fee	
☐	One month (37 CFR 1.17(a)(1))	$200	$100	$50	$ _____
☐	Two months (37 CFR 1.17(a)(2))	$600	$300	$150	$ _____
☐	Three months (37 CFR 1.17(a)(3))	$1,400	$700	$350	$ _____
☐	Four months (37 CFR 1.17(a)(4))	$2,200	$1,100	$550	$ _____
☐	Five months (37 CFR 1.17(a)(5))	$3,000	$1,500	$750	$ _____

☐ Applicant asserts small entity status. See 37 CFR 1.27.

☐ Applicant certifies micro entity status. See 37 CFR 1.29.
Form PTO/SB/15A or B or equivalent must either be enclosed or have been submitted previously.

☐ A check in the amount of the fee is enclosed.

☐ Payment by credit card. Form PTO-2038 is attached.

☐ The Director has already been authorized to charge fees in this application to a Deposit Account.

☐ The Director is hereby authorized to charge any fees which may be required, or credit any overpayment, to

Deposit Account Number _____.

☐ Payment made via EFS-Web.

WARNING: Information on this form may become public. Credit card information should not be included on this form. Provide credit card information and authorization on PTO-2038.

I am the

☐ applicant.

☐ attorney or agent of record. Registration number _____.

☐ attorney or agent acting under 37 CFR 1.34. Registration number _____.

_____	_____
Signature	Date

_____	_____
Typed or printed name	Telephone Number

NOTE: This form must be signed in accordance with 37 CFR 1.33. See 37 CFR 1.4 for signature requirements and certifications. Submit multiple forms if more than one signature is required, see below*.

☐ * Total of _____ forms are submitted.

This collection of information is required by 37 CFR 1.136(a). The information is required to obtain or retain a benefit by the public, which is to file (and by the USPTO to process) an application. Confidentiality is governed by 35 U.S.C. 122 and 37 CFR 1.11 and 1.14. This collection is estimated to take 6 minutes to complete, including gathering, preparing, and submitting the completed application form to the USPTO. Time will vary depending upon the individual case. Any comments on the amount of time you require to complete this form and/or suggestions for reducing this burden should be sent to the Chief Information Officer, U.S. Patent and Trademark Office, U.S. Department of Commerce, P.O. Box 1450, Alexandria, VA 22313-1450. DO NOT SEND FEES OR COMPLETED FORMS TO THIS ADDRESS. SEND TO: Mail Stop PCT, Commissioner for Patents, P.O. Box 1450, Alexandria, VA 22313-1450.

Form 13-4: Petition for Extension of Time

Doc Code: AP.PRE.REQ

PTO/AIA/33 (03-13)
Approved for use through 11/30/2020. OMB 0651-0031
U.S. Patent and Trademark Office; U.S. DEPARTMENT OF COMMERCE
Under the Paperwork Reduction Act of 1995, no persons are required to respond to a collection of information unless it displays a valid OMB control number.

PRE-APPEAL BRIEF REQUEST FOR REVIEW

Docket Number (Optional)

I hereby certify that this correspondence is being facsimile transmitted to the USPTO, EFS-Web transmitted to the USPTO, or deposited with the United States Postal Service with sufficient postage as first class mail in an envelope addressed to "Mail Stop AF, Commissioner for Patents, P.O. Box 1450, Alexandria, VA 22313-1450" [37 CFR 1.8(a)] on _____ Signature _____ Typed or printed name _____	**Application Number** **Filed** **First Named Inventor** **Art Unit** **Examiner**

Applicant requests review of the final rejection in the above-identified application. No amendments are being filed with this request.

This request is being filed with a notice of appeal.

The review is requested for the reason(s) stated on the attached sheet(s).
    Note: No more than five (5) pages may be provided.

I am the

                                                        Signature

☐ applicant.

                                                     Typed or printed name

☐ attorney or agent of record.
    Registration number _____.

                                                     Telephone number

☐ attorney or agent acting under 37 CFR 1.34.

    Registration number if acting under 37 CFR 1.34 _____

                                                        Date

NOTE: This form must be signed in accordance with 37 CFR 1.33. See 37 CFR 1.4 for signature requirements and certifications. Submit multiple forms if more than one signature is required, see below*.

☐   *Total of _____ forms are submitted.

Form 13-5: Pre-Appeal Brief Request for Review

PTO/SB/30 (11-17)
Approved for use through 11/30/2020. OMB 0651-0031
U.S. Patent and Trademark Office; U.S. DEPARTMENT OF COMMERCE
Under the Paperwork Reduction Act of 1995, no persons are required to respond to a collection of information unless it contains a valid OMB control number.

Request for Continued Examination (RCE) Transmittal	Application Number	
	Filing Date	
	First Named Inventor	
Address to: Mail Stop RCE Commissioner for Patents P.O. Box 1450 Alexandria, VA 22313-1450	Art Unit	
	Examiner Name	
	Attorney Docket Number	

This is a Request for Continued Examination (RCE) under 37 CFR 1.114 of the above-identified application.

Request for Continued Examination (RCE) practice under 37 CFR 1.114 does not apply to any utility or plant application filed prior to June 8, 1995, or to any design application. See Instruction Sheet for RCEs (not to be submitted to the USPTO) on page 2.

1. **Submission required under 37 CFR 1.114** Note: If the RCE is proper, any previously filed unentered amendments and amendments enclosed with the RCE will be entered in the order in which they were filed unless applicant instructs otherwise. If applicant does not wish to have any previously filed unentered amendment(s) entered, applicant must request non-entry of such amendment(s).

   a. ☐ Previously submitted. If a final Office action is outstanding, any amendments filed after the final Office action may be considered as a submission even if this box is not checked.

      i. ☐ Consider the arguments in the Appeal Brief or Reply Brief previously filed on _____

      Ii. ☐ Other _____

   b. ☐ Enclosed

      I. ☐ Amendment/Reply   iii. ☐ Information Disclosure Statement (IDS)

      ii. ☐ Affidavit(s)/ Declaration(s)   iv. ☐ Other _____

2. **Miscellaneous**

   a. ☐ Suspension of action on the above-identified application is requested under 37 CFR 1.103(c) for a period of _____ months. (Period of suspension shall not exceed 3 months; Fee under 37 CFR 1.17(i) required)

   b. ☐ Other _____

3. **Fees** The RCE fee under 37 CFR 1.17(e) is required by 37 CFR 1.114 when the RCE is filed.

   a. ☐ The Director is hereby authorized to charge the following fees, any underpayment of fees, or credit any overpayments, to Deposit Account No. _____ .

      i. ☐ RCE fee required under 37 CFR 1.17(e)

      ii. ☐ Extension of time fee (37 CFR 1.136 and 1.17)

      iii. ☐ Other _____

   b. ☐ Check in the amount of $ _____ enclosed

   c. ☐ Payment by credit card (Form PTO-2038 enclosed)   d. ☐ Payment by EFS-Web

WARNING: Information on this form may become public. Credit card information should not be included on this form. Provide credit card information and authorization on PTO-2038.

SIGNATURE OF APPLICANT, ATTORNEY, OR AGENT REQUIRED			
Signature		Date	
Name (Print/Type)		Registration No.	

CERTIFICATE OF MAILING OR TRANSMISSION

I hereby certify that this correspondence is being EFS-Web transmitted to the United States Patent and Trademark Office (USPTO), deposited with the United States Postal Service with sufficient postage as first class mail in an envelope addressed to: Mail Stop RCE, Commissioner for Patents, P. O. Box 1450, Alexandria, VA 22313-1450 or facsimile transmitted to the USPTO on the date shown below.

Signature			
Name (Print/Type)		Date	

This collection of information is required by 37 CFR 1.114. The information is required to obtain or retain a benefit by the public which is to file (and by the USPTO to process) an application. Confidentiality is governed by 35 U.S.C. 122 and 37 CFR 1.11 and 1.14. This collection is estimated to take 12 minutes to complete, including gathering, preparing, and submitting the completed application form to the USPTO. Time will vary depending upon the individual case. Any comments on the amount of time you require to complete this form and/or suggestions for reducing this burden, should be sent to the Chief Information Officer, U.S. Patent and Trademark Office, U.S. Department of Commerce, P.O. Box 1450, Alexandria, VA 22313-1450. DO NOT SEND FEES OR COMPLETED FORMS TO THIS ADDRESS. **SEND TO: Mail Stop RCE, Commissioner for Patents, P.O. Box 1450, Alexandria, VA 22313-1450.**

If you need assistance in completing the form, call 1-800-PTO-9199 and select option 2.

Form 14-1: Request for Continued Examination (RCE) Transmittal

PTO/SB/30 (07-09)
Approved for use through 11/30/2020. OMB 0651-0031
U.S. Patent and Trademark Office; U.S. DEPARTMENT OF COMMERCE
Under the Paperwork Reduction Act of 1995, no persons are required to respond to a collection of information unless it contains a valid OMB control number.

Instruction Sheet for RCEs
(not to be submitted to the USPTO)

NOTES:

An RCE is not a new application, and filing an RCE will not result in an application being accorded a new filing date.

Filing Qualifications:
The application must be a utility or plant application filed on or after June 8, 1995. The application cannot be a provisional application, a utility or plant application filed before June 8, 1995, a design application, or a patent under reexamination. See 37 CFR 1.114(e).

Filing Requirements:
Prosecution in the application must be closed. Prosecution is closed if the application is under appeal, or the last Office action is a final action, a notice of allowance, or an action that otherwise closes prosecution in the application (e.g., an Office action under *Ex parte Quayle*). See 37 CFR 1.114(b).

A submission and a fee are required at the time the RCE is filed. If reply to an Office action under 35 U.S.C. 132 is outstanding (e.g., the application is under final rejection), the submission must meet the reply requirements of 37 CFR 1.111. If there is no outstanding Office action, the submission can be an information disclosure statement, an amendment, new arguments, or new evidence. See 37 CFR 1.114(c). The submission may be a previously filed amendment (e.g., an amendment after final rejection).

WARNINGS:

Request for Suspension of Action:
All RCE filing requirements must be met before suspension of action is granted. A request for a suspension of action under 37 CFR 1.103(c) does <u>not</u> satisfy the submission requirement and does not permit the filing of the required submission to be suspended.

Improper RCE will NOT toll Any Time Period:

Before Appeal - If the RCE is improper (e.g., prosecution in the application is not closed or the submission or fee has not been filed) and the application is not under appeal, the time period set forth in the last Office action will continue to run and the application will be abandoned after the statutory time period has expired if a reply to the Office action is not timely filed. No additional time will be given to correct the improper RCE.

Under Appeal - If the RCE is improper (e.g., the submission or the fee has not been filed) and the application is under appeal, the improper RCE is effective to withdraw the appeal. Withdrawal of the appeal results in the allowance or abandonment of the application depending on the status of the claims. If there are no allowed claims, the application is abandoned. If there is at least one allowed claim, the application will be passed to issue on the allowed claim(s). See MPEP 1215.01.

See MPEP 706.07(h) for further information on the RCE practice.

Form 14-1: Request for Continued Examination (RCE) Transmittal

In the United States Patent and Trademark Office

Patent No.: _____

Issued: _____

Patentee(s): _____

Ser. Nr.: _____

Filed: _____

Request for Certificate of Correction

Date: _____

Commissioner for Patents
P.O. Box 1450
Alexandria, VA 22313-1450

Sir:

1. The above patent contains significant error, as indicated on the attached Certificate of Correction form (submitted in duplicate). These errors arose at the respective places in the application file indicated below.

☐ 2. Such error arose through the fault of the Patent and Trademark Office, therefore patentee requests that the Certificate be issued at no cost.

☐ 3. Such error arose through the fault of patentee(s). A check or CCPF for $_____ for the fee is enclosed. Such error is of a clerical or minor nature and occurred in good faith and therefore patentee requests issuance of the Certificate of Correction.

4. Specifically,

Very respectfully,

_____   _____

Patentee   Copatentee

Encs.

_____   _____

Address

_____

Phone

PTO/SB/44 (09-07)
Approved for use through 01/31/2020. OMB 0651-0033
U.S. Patent and Trademark Office; U.S. DEPARTMENT OF COMMERCE
Under the Paperwork Reduction Act of 1995, no persons are required to respond to a collection of information unless it displays a valid OMB control number.
(Also Form PTO-1050)

UNITED STATES PATENT AND TRADEMARK OFFICE
CERTIFICATE OF CORRECTION

Page _____ of _____

PATENT NO.   :

APPLICATION NO.:

ISSUE DATE   :

INVENTOR(S)   :

It is certified that an error appears or errors appear in the above-identified patent and that said Letters Patent is hereby corrected as shown below:

MAILING ADDRESS OF SENDER (Please do not use Customer Number below):

This collection of information is required by 37 CFR 1.322, 1.323, and 1.324. The information is required to obtain or retain a benefit by the public which is to file (and by the USPTO to process) an application. Confidentiality is governed by 35 U.S.C. 122 and 37 CFR 1.14. This collection is estimated to take 1.0 hour to complete, including gathering, preparing, and submitting the completed application form to the USPTO. Time will vary depending upon the individual case. Any comments on the amount of time you require to complete this form and/or suggestions for reducing this burden, should be sent to the Chief Information Officer, U.S. Patent and Trademark Office, U.S. Department of Commerce, P.O. Box 1450, Alexandria, VA 22313-1450. DO NOT SEND FEES OR COMPLETED FORMS TO THIS ADDRESS. **SEND TO: Attention Certificate of Corrections Branch, Commissioner for Patents, P.O. Box 1450, Alexandria, VA 22313-1450.**

If you need assistance in completing the form, call 1-800-PTO-9199 and select option 2.

Form 15-2: Certificate of Correction

Maintenance Fee Reminder

Next fee due: _____/_____/_____
                        yr   mo   date

(Write year in pencil and change after each payment)

Patent Nr.: _____ Issued: _____

Application Serial Nr.: _____ Filed: _____

Title: _____

Patentee(s) (Inventor[s]/Applicant[s]): _____

Assignee(s) (if any): _____

Expires _____ (if all three maintenance fees are paid).[1]

☐ Small entity status was filed in application or patent.
    (If not, large entity fees[2] must be paid.)

Maintenance Fee Number	Fee Due		Sent Form & Check[4]	Amount	Received Receipt Statement
	From:	To:			
I. Due 3.0 - 3.5 YAI[3]	/ /	/ /	/ /	$	/ /
II. Due 7.0 - 7.5 YAI	/ /	/ /	/ /	$	/ /
III. Due 11.0 - 11.5 YAI	/ /	/ /	/ /	$	/ /

Notes: _____

_____

_____

_____

_____

_____

_____

_____

_____

_____

[1] For applications filed after 1995 June 7, expiration is 20 years from filing date of application, or from any earlier domestic nonprovisional (regular) application from which it claims priority, plus any adjustment (extension) granted by the PTO.

[2] Please check all fee amounts before paying, since PTO fees change often.

[3] YAI = Years After Issue date.

[4] Send or make Internet payment at least a month before due date to allow time to take corrective action before entering grace (penalty) period in case PTO does not accept payment.

PTO/SB/45 (03-13)
Approved for use through 07/31/2018. OMB 0651-0016
U.S. Patent and Trademark Office; U.S. DEPARTMENT OF COMMERCE
Under the Paperwork Reduction Act of 1995, no persons are required to respond to a collection of information unless it displays a valid OMB control number.

MAINTENANCE FEE TRANSMITTAL FORM
(Do not submit this form electronically via EFS-Web)

Address to: **Director of the United States** **Patent and Trademark Office** **Attn: Maintenance Fee** 2051 Jamieson Avenue, Suite 300 Alexandria, VA 22314 **– OR –** **Fax to: 571-273-6500**	I hereby certify that this correspondence is being deposited with the United States Postal Service with sufficient postage as first class mail in an envelope addressed to "Director of the United States Patent and Trademark Office, Attn: Maintenance Fee, 2051 Jamieson Avenue, Suite 300, Alexandria, VA 22314" on _____ Signature _____ Typed or printed name _____

Enclosed herewith is the payment of the maintenance fee(s) for the listed patent(s).

1. ☐ A check for the amount of $ _____ for the full payment of the maintenance fee(s) and any necessary surcharge is enclosed.

2. ☐ Payment by credit card. Form PTO-2038 is enclosed.

3. ☐ The Director is hereby authorized to charge $ _____ to cover the payment of the fee(s) indicated below to

   Deposit Account No. _____.

4. ☐ The Director is hereby authorized to charge any deficiency in the payment of the required fee(s) or credit any overpayment to

   Deposit Account No. _____.

Item	Patent Number* Column 1	U.S. Application Number* [e.g., 08/555,555] Column 2	Maintenance Fee Amount (37 CFR 1.20(e)-(g)) Column 3	Surcharge Amount (37 CFR 1.20(h)) Column 4	Payment Year (select one below) Column 5		
					3.5 yrs	7.5 yrs	11.5 yrs
1							
2							
3							
4							
5							
	Subtotals: Columns 3 & 4				☐ _____ additional sheets attached for listing additional patents.		
	Total Payment						

* Information required by 37 CFR 1.366(c) (columns 1 & 2). Information requested under 37 CFR 1.366(d) (columns 3, 4, & 5).

WARNING: Information on this form may become public. Credit card information should not be included on this form. Provide credit card information and authorization on Form PTO-2038.

Respectfully submitted,**

Customer's Signature _____

Customer's Name _____   Registration Number, if applicable: _____

Telephone: _____   Fax: _____

Note: All correspondence will be forwarded to the "Fee Address" or to the "Correspondence Address" if no "Fee Address" has been provided. See 37 CFR 1.363.

Payment of small entity fee is appropriate if small entity status still exists, see 37 CFR 1.27(g). To establish small entity status or to notify of a loss of entitlement to small entity status, a written assertion is required. See 37 CFR 1.27 and 1.33(b). Payment of micro entity fee is appropriate if patent owner certifies micro entity status. Form PTO/SB/15A or B or equivalent must either be enclosed or have been submitted previously. To notify of a loss of entitlement to micro entity status, a written assertion is required. See 37 CFR 1.29 and 1.33(b).
** WHERE MAINTENANCE FEE PAYMENTS ARE TO BE MADE BY AUTHORIZATION TO CHARGE A DEPOSIT ACCOUNT, BOTH THE NAME AND SIGNATURE OF AN AUTHORIZED USER ARE REQUIRED.

This collection of information is required by 37 CFR 1.366. The information is required to obtain or retain a benefit by the public which is to file (and by the USPTO to process) an application. Confidentiality is governed by 35 U.S.C. 122 and 37 CFR 1.11, 1.14 and 41.6. This collection is estimated to take 5 minutes to complete, including gathering, preparing, and submitting the completed application form to the USPTO. Time will vary depending upon the individual case. Any comments on the amount of time you require to complete this form and/or suggestions for reducing this burden, should be sent to the Chief Information Officer, U.S. Patent and Trademark Office, U.S. Department of Commerce, P.O. Box 1450, Alexandria, VA 22313-1450. DO NOT SEND FEES OR COMPLETED FORMS TO THIS ADDRESS. **SEND TO: Director of the United States Patent and Trademark Office, Attn: Maintenance Fee, 2051 Jamieson Avenue, Suite 300, Alexandria, VA 22314.**

If you need assistance in completing the form, call 1-800-PTO-9199 and select option 2.

Form 15-4: Maintenance Fee Transmittal Form

Privacy Act Statement

The **Privacy Act of 1974 (P.L. 93-579)** requires that you be given certain information in connection with your submission of the attached form related to a patent application or patent. Accordingly, pursuant to the requirements of the Act, please be advised that: (1) the general authority for the collection of this information is 35 U.S.C. 2(b)(2); (2) furnishing of the information solicited is voluntary; and (3) the principal purpose for which the information is used by the U.S. Patent and Trademark Office is to process and/or examine your submission related to a patent application or patent. If you do not furnish the requested information, the U.S. Patent and Trademark Office may not be able to process and/or examine your submission, which may result in termination of proceedings or abandonment of the application or expiration of the patent.

The information provided by you in this form will be subject to the following routine uses:

1. The information on this form will be treated confidentially to the extent allowed under the Freedom of Information Act (5 U.S.C. 552) and the Privacy Act (5 U.S.C 552a). Records from this system of records may be disclosed to the Department of Justice to determine whether disclosure of these records is required by the Freedom of Information Act.
2. A record from this system of records may be disclosed, as a routine use, in the course of presenting evidence to a court, magistrate, or administrative tribunal, including disclosures to opposing counsel in the course of settlement negotiations.
3. A record in this system of records may be disclosed, as a routine use, to a Member of Congress submitting a request involving an individual, to whom the record pertains, when the individual has requested assistance from the Member with respect to the subject matter of the record.
4. A record in this system of records may be disclosed, as a routine use, to a contractor of the Agency having need for the information in order to perform a contract. Recipients of information shall be required to comply with the requirements of the Privacy Act of 1974, as amended, pursuant to 5 U.S.C. 552a(m).
5. A record related to an International Application filed under the Patent Cooperation Treaty in this system of records may be disclosed, as a routine use, to the International Bureau of the World Intellectual Property Organization, pursuant to the Patent Cooperation Treaty.
6. A record in this system of records may be disclosed, as a routine use, to another federal agency for purposes of National Security review (35 U.S.C. 181) and for review pursuant to the Atomic Energy Act (42 U.S.C. 218(c)).
7. A record from this system of records may be disclosed, as a routine use, to the Administrator, General Services, or his/her designee, during an inspection of records conducted by GSA as part of that agency's responsibility to recommend improvements in records management practices and programs, under authority of 44 U.S.C. 2904 and 2906. Such disclosure shall be made in accordance with the GSA regulations governing inspection of records for this purpose, and any other relevant (*i.e.*, GSA or Commerce) directive. Such disclosure shall not be used to make determinations about individuals.
8. A record from this system of records may be disclosed, as a routine use, to the public after either publication of the application pursuant to 35 U.S.C. 122(b) or issuance of a patent pursuant to 35 U.S.C. 151. Further, a record may be disclosed, subject to the limitations of 37 CFR 1.14, as a routine use, to the public if the record was filed in an application which became abandoned or in which the proceedings were terminated and which application is referenced by either a published application, an application open to public inspection or an issued patent.
9. A record from this system of records may be disclosed, as a routine use, to a Federal, State, or local law enforcement agency, if the USPTO becomes aware of a violation or potential violation of law or regulation.

Joint Applicants—Statement of Respective Contributions

The parties to this statement are Joint Applicants (JAs) to the invention or patent application entitled:

"_____."

We understand that a patent application should be filed in the names of all persons who contributed to at least one claim and that any person who did not contribute to at least one claim should not be named as a JA.

We also recognize and agree that if the patent claims in any patent application based on the invention are altered so that the listing of any JA is inappropriate, that JA should be removed from the patent application.

In order to keep the contributions of the JAs in order and preserve them, we hereby record each JA's contributions as follows:

Joint Applicants

Print Name: _____   Date: _____

Signature: _____

Contributions: _____

_____

_____

_____

_____

_____

_____

_____

_____

_____

Print Name: _____   Date: _____

Signature: _____

Contributions: _____

_____

_____

_____

_____

_____

_____

_____

_____

_____

Joint Owners' Agreement

This agreement is made by and between the following parties who, by separate assignment or as joint applicants, own the following respective shares of the invention, patent application, or patent identified below:

_____ of _____ , _____%,

_____ of _____ , _____%,

_____ of _____ , _____%.

Invention Title: _____

Patent Application Ser. Nr.: _____ , Filed: _____

Patent Nr.: _____ , Issued: _____

Applicants: _____

_____

The above patent application data is to be filled in as soon as it becomes available if the application has not yet been filed.

The parties desire to stipulate the terms under which they will exploit this invention and patent application and therefore agree as follows:

1. **No Action Without Everyone's Consent:** None of the parties to this agreement shall license, use, make, or sell the invention or application, or take any other action, other than normal prosecution, without the written consent and cooperation of the other party or parties (hereinafter "parties") to this agreement, except as provided below. Any action so taken shall be committed to a writing signed by all of the parties, or as many parties as consent, with copies to all other parties.

2. **Decisions:** In case any decision must be made in connection with the invention or the patent application, including foreign filing, appealing from an adverse decision in the Patent and Trademark Office, or any opportunity to license, sell, make, or use the invention or application, the parties shall consult on such opportunity and a majority decision shall control. In the event the parties are equally divided, the matter shall be decided in accordance with Paragraph 5 below. After a decision is so made, all parties shall abide by the decision and shall cooperate fully by whatever means are necessary to implement and give full force to such decision. However, if an offer is involved and there is time for any parties to obtain a better or different offer, they shall be entitled to do so and the decision shall be postponed for up to one month to allow such other parties to act.

3. **Proportionate Sharing:** The parties to this agreement shall share, in the percentages indicated above, in all income from, liabilities, and expenditures agreed to be made by any decision under Part 2 above in connection with the invention or patent application. In case a decision is made to make any expenditure, as for foreign patent application filing, exploitation, etc., and a minority or other parties opposes such expenditure or is unable to contribute his or her proportionate share, then the others shall advance the minority or other parties' share of the expenditure. Such others shall be reimbursed by the minority or other parties by double the amount so advanced from the minority or other parties' proportionate share of any income received, provided such income has some reasonable connection with the expenditure. No party shall be entitled to reimbursement or credit for any labor unless agreed to in advance by all of the parties hereto.

4. **If Any Parties Desire to Manufacture, Etc.:** If any parties who do not constitute all of the parties to this agreement desire to manufacture, distribute, or sell any product or service embodying the above invention,

they may do so with the written consent of the other parties under Part 1 above. The cost of the product or service shall include, in addition to normal profit, labor, commission, and/or overhead, etc., provision for a reasonable royalty that shall be paid for the term of the above patent application and any patent that may issue thereon. Such royalty shall be determined before any action is taken under this part and as if a valid patent on the invention had been licensed to an unrelated exclusive licensee (or a nonexclusive licensee if the patent is licensed to others) in an arm's-length transaction. Such royalty shall be distributed to all of the parties hereto according to their proportionate shares and on a quarterly basis, accompanied by a written royalty report and sent within one month after the close of each calendar quarter.

5. **In Case of Dispute:** In case any dispute, disagreement, or need for any decision arises out of this agreement or in connection with the invention or patent application, and the parties cannot settle the matter or come to a decision in accordance with Paragraph 2, above, the parties shall first confer as much as necessary to settle the disagreement; all parties shall act and compromise to at least the degree a reasonable person would act. If the parties cannot settle their differences or come to a decision on their own, they shall submit the dispute or matter to mediation by an impartial third party or professional mediator agreed to by all of the parties. If the parties cannot agree on a mediator, or cannot come to an agreement after mediation, then they shall submit the matter to binding arbitration with a mutually acceptable arbitrator or the American Arbitration Association. The arbitration shall take place in _____ _____ (City and State) and the law of _____ (State) shall apply. The arbitrator shall settle the dispute in whatever manner he or she feels will do substantial justice, recognizing the rights of all parties and commercial realities of the marketplace. The parties shall abide by the terms of the arbitrator's decision and shall cooperate fully and do any acts necessary to implement such decision. The costs of the arbitrator shall be advanced by all of the parties or in accordance with Part 3 above and the arbitrator may make any allocation of arbitration costs he or she feels is reasonable. The arbitrator's award may be entered as a judgment by the prevailing party in any court of record.

6. **Nonfrustration:** No party to this Agreement shall commit any act or take any action that frustrates or hampers the rights of another party under this Agreement. Each party shall act in good faith and engage in fair dealing when taking any action under or related to this Agreement.

Signature _____ Date _____

Signature _____ Date _____

Signature _____ Date _____

Assignment of Invention and Patent Application

For value received, _____ ,

_____

of _____

_____

(hereinafter ASSIGNOR), hereby sells, assigns, transfers, and sets over unto _____

_____

of _____

and her or his successors or assigns (hereinafter ASSIGNEE) _____% of the following: (A) ASSIGNOR's right,

title, and interest in and to the invention entitled " _____

_____ "

invented by ASSIGNOR; (B) the application for United States patent therefor, signed by ASSIGNOR on

_____ , U.S. Patent and Trademark Office Serial Number _____ ,

filed _____ ; (C) any patent or reissues of any patent that may be granted

thereon; and (D) any applications that are provisional patent applications that said application claims priority

of, or nonprovisional applications that claim priority of said application, or continuations, continuations-in-part,

substitutes, or divisions of said application. ASSIGNOR authorizes ASSIGNEE to enter the date of signature and/

or Serial Number and Filing Date in the spaces above. ASSIGNOR also authorizes and requests the Commissioner

for Patents to issue any resulting patent(s) as follows: _____% to ASSIGNOR and _____% to

ASSIGNEE. (The singular shall include the plural and vice versa herein.)

ASSIGNOR hereby further sells, assigns, transfers, and sets over unto ASSIGNEE, the above percentage of

ASSIGNOR's entire right, title, and interest in and to said invention in each and every country foreign to the

United States; and ASSIGNOR further conveys to ASSIGNEE the above percentage of all priority rights resulting

from the above-identified application for United States patent. ASSIGNOR agrees to execute all papers, give any

required testimony, and perform other lawful acts, at ASSIGNEE's expense, as ASSIGNEE may require to enable

ASSIGNEE to perfect ASSIGNEE's interest in any resulting patent of the United States and countries foreign

thereto, and to acquire, hold, enforce, convey, and uphold the validity of said patent and reissues and extensions

thereof, and ASSIGNEE's interest therein.

In testimony whereof ASSIGNOR has hereunto set its hand and seal on the date below.

Signature _____ Date _____

Signature _____ Date _____

Witnessed by:

Signature _____ Date _____

Signature _____ Date _____

U.S. DEPARTMENT OF COMMERCE
United States Patent and Trademark Office

RECORDATION FORM COVER SHEET
PATENTS ONLY

To the Director of the U.S. Patent and Trademark Office: Please record the attached documents or the new address(es) below.

1. Name of conveying party(ies)

Additional name(s) of conveying party(ies) attached? ☐ Yes ☐ No

2. Name and address of receiving party(ies)

Name: _____

Internal Address: _____

_____

Street Address: _____

_____

City: _____

State: _____

Country: _____ Zip: _____

Additional name(s) & address(es) attached? ☐ Yes ☐ No

3. Nature of conveyance/Execution Date(s):

Execution Date(s) _____

☐ Assignment
☐ Merger
☐ Security Agreement
☐ Change of Name
☐ Joint Research Agreement
☐ Government Interest Assignment
☐ Executive Order 9424, Confirmatory License
☐ Other _____

4. Application or patent number(s): ☐ This document serves as an Oath/Declaration (37 CFR 1.63).

A. Patent Application No.(s)

B. Patent No.(s)

Additional numbers attached? ☐ Yes ☐ No

5. Name and address to whom correspondence concerning document should be mailed:

Name: _____

Internal Address: _____

_____

Street Address: _____

_____

City: _____

State: _____ Zip: _____

Phone Number: _____

Docket Number: _____

Email Address: _____

6. Total number of applications and patents involved: _____

7. Total fee (37 CFR 1.21(h) & 3.41) $ _____

☐ Authorized to be charged to deposit account
☐ Enclosed
☐ None required (government interest not affecting title)

8. Payment Information

Deposit Account Number _____

Authorized User Name _____

9. Signature:

_____   _____
                  Signature   Date

_____
        Name of Person Signing

Total number of pages including cover sheet, attachments, and documents: ☐

Documents to be recorded (including cover sheet) should be faxed to (571) 273-0140, or mailed to:
Mail Stop Assignment Recordation Services, Director of the USPTO, P.O.Box 1450, Alexandria, V.A. 22313-1450

Guidelines for Completing Patents Cover Sheets (PTO-1595)

Cover Sheet information must be submitted with each document to be recorded. If the document to be recorded concerns both patents and trademarks separate patent and trademark cover sheets, including any attached pages for continuing information, must accompany the document. All pages of the cover sheet should be numbered consecutively, for example, if both a patent and trademark cover sheet is used, and information is continued on one additional page for both patents and trademarks, the pages of the cover sheet would be numbered from 1 to 4.

Item 1. Name of Conveying Party(ies).

Enter the full name of the party(ies) conveying the interest. If there is insufficient space, enter a check mark in the "Yes" box to indicate that additional information is attached. The name of the additional conveying party(ies) should be placed on an attached page clearly identified as a continuation of the information Item 1. Enter a check mark in the "No" box, if no information is contained on an attached page. If the document to be recorded is a joint research agreement, enter the name(s) of the party(ies) other than the owner of the patent or patent application as the conveying party(ies).

Item 2. Name and Address of Receiving Party(ies).

Enter the name and full address of the first party receiving the interest. If there is more than one party receiving the interest, enter a check mark in the "Yes" box to indicate that additional information is attached. Enter a check mark in the "No" box, if no information is contained on an attached page. If the document to be recorded is a joint research agreement, enter the name(s) of the patent or patent application owner(s) as the receiving party.

Item 3. Nature of Conveyance/Execution Date(s).

Enter the execution date(s) of the document. It is preferable to use the name of the month, or an abbreviation of that name, in order that confusion over dates is minimized. Place a check mark in the appropriate box describing the nature of the conveying document. If the "Other" box is checked, specify the nature of the conveyance.

Item 4. Application Number(s) or Patent Number(s).

Indicate the application number(s), and/or patent number(s) against which the document is to be recorded. National application numbers must include both the series code and a six-digit number (e.g., 07/123,456), and international application numbers must be complete (e.g., PCT/US91/12345).

Enter a check mark in the appropriate box: "Yes" or "No " if additional numbers appear on attached pages. Be sure to identify numbers included on attached pages as the continuation of Item 4. Also enter a check mark if this Assignment is being filed as an Oath/Declaration (37 CFR 1.63).

Item 5. Name and Address of Party to whom correspondence concerning the document should be mailed.

Enter the name and full address of the party to whom correspondence is to be mailed.

Item 6. Total Applications and Patents involved.

Enter the total number of applications and patents identified for recordation. Be sure to include all applications and patents identified on the cover sheet and on additional pages.

Block 7. Total Fee Enclosed.

Enter the total fee enclosed or authorized to be charged. A fee is required for each application and patent against which the document is recorded.

Item 8. Payment Information.

Enter the deposit account number and authorized user name to authorize charges.

Item 9. Signature.

Enter the name of the person submitting the document. The submitter must sign and date the cover sheet. Enter the total number of pages including the cover sheet, attachments, and document.

Universal License Agreement

1. Parties and Summary of Terms:

Parties: This agreement is between:

Licensor: _____ ,

of _____ .

Licensee: _____ ,

of _____ .

Summary: Type of License: ☐ Exclusive   ☐ Nonexclusive

Invention Title: _____ .

Patent Application Ser. Nr.: _____ , Filing Date: _____

If Exclusive License, minimum number of units to be sold to compute Minimum Annual Royalty (MAR):

_____

MARs start first quarter of _____ .

☐ Option Granted: Premium $ _____ For term of: _____ months

Patent Royalty Rate _____ %   ☐ Know-How Licensed: Know-How Royalty Rate: _____ %

Total Royalty Rate (Patent Royalty Rate plus Know-How Royalty, if applicable): _____ %.

Estimated 1st year's sales (units): _____ x Estimated Unit Price $ _____

   x Total Royalty Rate _____ % = Licensing Fee $ _____

2. Effective Date: This agreement shall be effective as of the latter of the signature dates below written and shall be referred to as the Agreement of such date.

3. Recitals:

   A. LICENSOR has developed an invention having the above title and warrants that LICENSOR has filed a patent application on such invention in the U.S. Patent and Trademark Office, which patent application is identified by the above title, Serial Number, and Filing Date. LICENSOR warrants that LICENSOR has full and exclusive right to grant this license on this invention and LICENSOR's patent application. If the "Know-How Licensed" box above is checked, LICENSOR has also developed know-how in connection with said invention and warrants that LICENSOR owns and has the right to license said know-how.

   B. LICENSEE desires, if the "Option Granted" box above is checked, to exclusively investigate LICENSOR's above invention for the term indicated. If said "Option Granted" box is not checked, or if said box is checked and LICENSEE investigates LICENSOR's invention for the term indicated and such investigation is favorable, LICENSEE desires to make, use, and sell the products embodying such invention and covered by the claims of LICENSOR's patent application and any patent(s) issuing thereon (hereinafter "Licensed Product").

4. If Option Granted: If the "Option Granted" box above is checked, then (A) the patent license grant of Part 5 below shall not take effect except as defined in this part, and (B) LICENSOR hereby grants LICENSEE, for the option premium stated above, an exclusive option to investigate LICENSOR's invention for the term indicated above, such term to commence from the date of this Agreement. LICENSOR will furnish LICENSEE with all information and know-how (if any) concerning LICENSOR's invention in LICENSOR's possession. LICENSEE will investigate LICENSOR's invention for operability, costing, marketing, etc. LICENSEE shall report the results of its investigation to LICENSOR at any time before the end of the option term. If LICENSEE's determination is favorable, it may thereupon exercise this option and the patent license grant of Part 5 below shall become effective. If LICENSEE's determination is unfavorable, then said option shall not be exercised and no patent license grant shall take effect, all rights hereunder shall revert to LICENSOR, LICENSEE shall deliver to LICENSOR all results of its investigations for LICENSOR's benefit, and LICENSEE shall promptly return to LICENSOR all know-how (papers and things) received from LICENSOR or generated by LICENSEE in its investigations.

5. **Patent License If Option Exercised or If Option Not Granted:** If the "Option Granted" box above is checked and LICENSEE has investigated LICENSOR's invention and such investigation is favorable and LICENSEE has exercised its option, or if said box is not checked, then LICENSOR hereby grants to LICENSEE, subject to the terms and conditions herein, a patent license of the type (Exclusive or Nonexclusive) checked above. Such patent license shall include the right to grant sublicenses, to make, have made, use, and sell the Licensed Product throughout the United States, its territories, and possessions. Such patent license shall be under LICENSOR's patent application, any continuations, divisions, continuations-in-part, substitutes, reissues of any patent from any of such applications (hereinafter and hereinbefore LICENSOR's patent application), any patent(s) issuing thereon, and if the "Know-How Licensed" box is checked above, any know-how transferred to LICENSEE.

6. **If Know-How Licensed:** If the "Know-How" box above is checked, LICENSOR shall communicate to LICENSEE all of LICENSOR's know-how in respect of LICENSOR's invention within one month after the date of this Agreement and shall be available to consult with LICENSEE, for up to 80 hours, with respect to the licensed invention and know-how. All travel and other expenses of LICENSOR for such consultation shall be reimbursed by LICENSEE within one month after LICENSOR submits its voucher therefor. LICENSOR makes no warranty regarding the value, suitability, or workability of such know-how. The royalty applicable for such know-how shall be paid, at the rate indicated above, for a minimum of three years from the date of this Agreement if no option is granted, or for three years from the date of exercise if an option is granted and exercised by LICENSOR, and thereafter for so long as LICENSEE makes, uses, or sells Licensed Products and has a share in the United States of at least 15% of the competitive market for Licensed Products.

7. **Royalties:**

    A. **Licensing Fee:** Unless the "Option Granted" box above is checked, LICENSEE shall pay to LICENSOR, upon execution of this Agreement, a nonrefundable Licensing Fee. This Licensing Fee shall also serve as an advance against future royalties. Such Licensing Fee shall be computed as follows: (A) Take the Total Royalty Rate in percent, as stated above. (B) Multiply by LICENSEE's Estimate of Its First Year's Sales, in units of Licensed Product, as stated above. (C) Multiply by LICENSEE's Estimated Unit Price of Licensed Product, in dollars, as stated above. (D) The combined product shall be the Licensing Fee, in dollars, as stated above. When LICENSEE begins actual sales of the Licensed Product, it shall certify its Actual Net Factory Sales Price of Licensed Product to LICENSOR in writing and shall either (1) simultaneously pay LICENSOR any difference due if the Actual Net Factory Sales Price of Licensed Product is more than the Estimated Unit Price, stated above, or (2) advise LICENSOR of any credit to which LICENSEE is entitled if the Actual Net Factory Sales Price of Licensed Product is less than the above Estimated Unit Price. In the latter case, LICENSEE may deduct such credit from its first royalty remittance to LICENSOR, under subpart B below. If an option is granted and exercised under Part 4 above, then LICENSEE shall pay this Licensing Fee to LICENSOR if and when LICENSEE exercises its option.

    B. **Royalty:** If the "Option Granted" box above is not checked, or if said box is checked and LICENSEE has exercised its option under Part 4, LICENSEE shall also pay to LICENSOR a Total Royalty, at the rate stated above. Such royalty shall be at the Patent Royalty Rate stated in Part 1 above, plus, if the "Know-How Licensed" box above is checked, a Know-How Royalty at the Know-How Royalty Rate stated above. Said Total Royalty shall be computed on LICENSEE's Net Factory Sales Price of Licensed Product. Such Total Royalty shall accrue when the Licensed Products are first sold or disposed of by LICENSEE, or by any sublicensee of LICENSEE. LICENSEE shall pay the Total Royalty due to LICENSOR within one month after the end of each calendar quarter, together with a written report to LICENSOR of the number of units, respective sales prices, and total sales made in such quarter, together with a full itemization of any adjustments made pursuant to subpart F below. LICENSEE's first report and payment shall be made within one month after the end of the first calendar quarter following the execution of this Agreement. No royalties shall be paid by LICENSEE to LICENSOR until after the Licensing Fee under subpart A above has been earned, but LICENSEE shall make a quarterly report hereunder for every calendar quarter after the execution hereof, whether or not any royalty payment is due for such quarter, except that if an option is granted, LICENSEE shall not make any royalty reports until and if LICENSEE exercises its option.

C. **Minimum Annual Royalties:** If the "Exclusive" box above is checked, so that this is an exclusive license, then this subpart C and subpart D shall be applicable. But if the "Nonexclusive" box is checked above, then these subparts C and D shall be inapplicable. There shall be no minimum annual royalties due under this Agreement until the "Year Commencing," as identified in Part 1 above. For the exclusivity privilege of the patent license grant under Part 5 above, a Minimum Annual Royalty shall be due beginning with such royalty year and for each royalty year ending on the anniversary of such royalty year thereafter. Such Minimum Annual Royalty shall be equal to the Patent Royalty which would have been due if the "Minimum Number of Units [of Licensed Product] to Be Sold to Compute Minimum Annual Royalty" identified in Part 1 above were sold during such royalty year. If less than such number of units of Licensed Product are sold in any royalty year, then the Patent Royalty payable for the fourth quarter of such year shall be increased so as to cause the Patent Royalties paid for such year to equal said Minimum Annual Royalty. If an option is granted under Parts 1 and 4, then no Minimum Annual Royalties shall be due in any case until and if LICENSEE exercises its option.

D. **If Minimum Not Paid:** If this part is applicable and if sales of Licensed Product in any royalty year do not equal or exceed the minimum number of units identified in Part 1 above, LICENSEE may choose not to pay the Minimum Annual Royalty under subpart C above. In this case, LICENSEE shall so notify LICENSOR by the date on which the last royalty for such year is due, i.e., within one month after any anniversary of the date identified in Part 1 above. Thereupon the license grant under Part 4 above shall be converted to a nonexclusive grant, and LICENSOR may immediately license others under the above patent.

E. **Most Favored Licensee:** If this license is nonexclusive, or if it becomes nonexclusive under subpart D above, then (a) LICENSOR shall not grant any other license under the above patent to any other party under any terms that are more favorable than those that LICENSEE pays or enjoys under this Agreement, and (b) LICENSOR shall promptly advise LICENSEE of any such other grant and the terms thereof.

F. **When No Royalties Due:** No Patent Royalties shall be due under this Agreement after the above patent expires or if it is declared invalid by a court of competent jurisdiction from which no appeal can be taken. Also, if LICENSOR's patent application becomes finally abandoned without any patent issuing, then the Patent Royalty under this Agreement shall be terminated as of the date of abandonment. Any Know-How Royalties under Part 6 above shall continue after any Patent Royalties terminate, provided such Know-How Royalties are otherwise due under such Part 6.

G. **Late Payments:** If any payment due under this Agreement is not timely paid, then the unpaid balance shall bear interest until paid at an annual rate of 10% until the delinquent balance is paid. Such interest shall be compounded monthly.

H. **Net Factory Sales Price:** "Net Factory Sales Price" is defined as the gross factory selling price of Licensed Product, or the U.S. importer's gross selling price if Licensed Product is made abroad, less usual trade discounts actually allowed, but not including advertising allowances or fees or commissions paid to employees or agents of LICENSEE. The Net Factory Sales Price shall not include (1) packing costs, if itemized separately, (2) import and export taxes, excise and other sales taxes, and customs duties, and (3) costs of insurance and transportation, if separately billed, from the place of manufacture if in the U.S., or from the place of importation if manufactured abroad, to the customer's premises or next point of distribution or sale. Bona fide returns may be deducted from units shipped in computing the royalty payable after such returns are made.

8. **Records:** LICENSEE and any of its sublicensees shall keep full, clear, and accurate records with respect to sales subject to royalty under this Agreement. The records shall be made in a manner such that the royalty reports made pursuant to Part 7B can be verified. LICENSOR, or its authorized agent, shall have the right to examine and audit such records upon reasonable notice during normal business hours, but not more than twice per year. In case of any dispute as to the sufficiency or accuracy of such records, LICENSOR may have

any independent auditor examine and certify such records. LICENSEE shall make prompt adjustment to compensate for any errors or omissions disclosed by any such examination and certification of LICENSEE's records. If LICENSOR does not examine LICENSEE's records or question any royalty report within two years from the date thereof, then such report shall be considered final and LICENSOR shall have no further right to contest such report.

9. **Sublicensees:** If LICENSEE grants any sublicenses hereunder, it shall notify LICENSOR within one month from any such grant and shall provide LICENSOR with a true copy of any sublicense agreement. Any sublicensee of LICENSEE under this Agreement shall be bound by all of the terms applying to LICENSEE hereunder and LICENSEE shall be responsible for the obligations and duties of any of its sublicensees.

10. **Patent Prosecution:**

   A. **Domestic:** LICENSOR shall, at LICENSOR's own expense, prosecute its above U.S. patent application, and any continuations, divisions, continuations-in-part, substitutes, and reissues of such patent application or any patent thereon, at its own expense, until all applicable patents issue or any patent application becomes finally abandoned. LICENSOR shall also pay any maintenance fees which are due on any patent(s) which issue on said patent application. If for any reason LICENSOR intends to abandon any patent application hereunder, it shall notify LICENSEE at least two months in advance of any such abandonment so as to give LICENSEE the opportunity to take over prosecution of any such application and maintenance of any patent. If LICENSEE takes over prosecution, LICENSOR shall cooperate with LICENSEE in any manner LICENSEE requires, at LICENSEE's expense.

   B. **Foreign:** LICENSOR shall have the opportunity, but not the obligation, to file corresponding foreign patent applications to any patent application under subpart A above. If LICENSOR files any such foreign patent applications, LICENSOR may license, sell, or otherwise exploit the invention, Licensed Product, or any such foreign application in any countries foreign to the United States as it chooses, provided that LICENSOR must give LICENSEE a right of first refusal and at least one month to exercise this right before undertaking any such foreign exploitation. If LICENSOR chooses not to file any corresponding foreign applications under this part, it shall notify LICENSEE at least one month prior to the first anniversary of the above patent application so as to give LICENSEE the opportunity to file corresponding foreign patent applications if it so chooses.

   C. **If Licensee Acts:** If LICENSEE takes over prosecution of any U.S. patent application under subpart A above, and LICENSEE is successful so that a patent issues, then LICENSEE shall pay LICENSOR royalties thereafter at a rate of 75% of the royalty rate and any applicable minimum under Part 7C above and LICENSEE shall be entitled to deduct prosecution and maintenance expenses from its royalty payments. If LICENSEE elects to prosecute any foreign patent applications under subpart B above, then LICENSEE shall pay LICENSOR royalties of 50% of the royalty rate under Part 7 above for any applicable foreign sales, less all foreign prosecution and maintenance expenses incurred by LICENSEE.

11. **Marking:** LICENSEE shall mark all units of Licensed Product, or its container if direct marking is not feasible, with the legend "Patent Pending" until any patent(s) issue from the above patent application. When any patent(s) issue, LICENSOR shall promptly notify LICENSEE and thereafter LICENSEE shall mark all units of Licensed Product that it sells with proper notice of patent marking under 35 U.S.C. Section 287.

12. **If Infringement Occurs:** If either party discovers that the above patent is infringed, it shall communicate the details to the other party. LICENSOR shall thereupon have the right, but not the obligation, to take whatever action it deems necessary, including the filing of lawsuits, to protect the rights of the parties to this Agreement and to terminate such infringement. LICENSEE shall cooperate with LICENSOR if LICENSOR takes any such action, but all expenses of LICENSOR shall be borne by LICENSOR. If LICENSOR recovers any damages or compensation for any action it takes hereunder, LICENSOR shall retain 100% of such damages. If LICENSOR does not wish to take any action hereunder, LICENSEE shall also have the right, but not the obligation, to take any such action, in which case LICENSOR shall cooperate with LICENSEE, but all of LICENSEE's expenses shall be borne by LICENSEE. LICENSEE shall receive 75% of any damages or

compensation it recovers for any such infringement and shall pay 25% of such damages or compensation to LICENSOR, after deducting its costs, including attorneys' fees.

13. **Disclaimer and Hold Harmless:**
    A. **Disclaimer of Warranty:** Nothing herein shall be construed as a warranty or representation by LICENSOR as to the scope or validity of the above patent application or any patent issuing thereon.
    B. **Product Liability:** LICENSEE shall hold LICENSOR harmless from any product liability actions involving Licensed Product.

14. **Term:** The term of this Agreement shall end with the expiration of the last of any patent(s) that issues on LICENSOR's patent application, unless terminated sooner for any reason provided herein, or unless know-how is licensed, in which case the terms of Part 6 shall cover the term of this Agreement.

15. **Termination:** This Agreement may be terminated under and according to any of the following contingencies:
    A. **Default:** If LICENSEE fails to make any payment on the date such payment is due under this Agreement, or if LICENSEE makes any other default under or breach of this Agreement, LICENSOR shall have the right to terminate this Agreement upon giving three months' written Notice of Intent to Terminate, specifying such failure, breach, or default to LICENSEE. If LICENSEE fails to make any payment in arrears, or otherwise fails to cure the breach or default within such three-month period, then LICENSOR may then send a written Notice of Termination to LICENSEE, whereupon this Agreement shall terminate in one month from the date of such Notice of Termination. If this Agreement is terminated hereunder, LICENSEE shall not be relieved of any of its obligations to the date of termination and LICENSOR may act to enforce LICENSEE's obligations after any such termination.
    B. **Bankruptcy, Etc.:** If LICENSEE shall go into receivership, bankruptcy, or insolvency, or make an assignment for the benefit of creditors, or go out of business, this Agreement shall be immediately terminable by LICENSOR by written notice, but without prejudice to any rights of LICENSOR hereunder. This paragraph shall not apply so long as LICENSEE continues to pay royalties on time under Part 7, subpart B or C.
    C. **Antishelving:** If LICENSEE discontinues its sales or manufacture of Licensed Product without intent to resume, it shall so notify LICENSOR within one month of such discontinuance, whereupon LICENSOR shall have the right to terminate this Agreement upon one month's written notice, even if this Agreement has been converted to a nonexclusive grant under Part 7D above. If LICENSEE does not begin manufacture or sales of Licensed Product within one and one-half years from the date of this Agreement or the date of its option exercise if an option is granted, or, after commencing manufacture and sales of Licensed Product, discontinues its manufacture and sales of Licensed Product for one and one-half years, LICENSOR shall have the right to terminate this Agreement upon one month's written notice, unless LICENSEE can show that it in good faith intends and is actually working to resume or begin manufacture or sales, and has a reasonable basis to justify its delay. In such case LICENSEE shall advise LICENSOR in writing, before the end of such one-and-one-half-year period, of the circumstances involved and LICENSEE shall thereupon have up to an additional year to resume or begin manufacture or sales. It is the intent of the parties hereto that LICENSOR shall not be deprived of the opportunity, for an unreasonable length of time, to exclusively license its patent if LICENSEE has discontinued or has not commenced manufacture or sales of Licensed Product. In no case shall LICENSOR have the right to terminate this Agreement if and so long as LICENSEE is paying LICENSOR minimum annual royalties under Part 7C above.

16. **Notices:** All notices, payments, or statements under this Agreement shall be in writing and shall be sent by first-class certified mail, return receipt requested, postage prepaid, to the party concerned at the above address, or to any substituted address given by notice hereunder. Any such notice, payment, or statement shall be considered sent or made on the day deposited in the mails. Payments and statements may be sent by ordinary mail.

17. **Mediation and Arbitration:** If any dispute arises under this Agreement, the parties shall negotiate in good faith to settle such dispute. If the parties cannot resolve such dispute themselves, then either party may submit the dispute to mediation by a mediator approved by both parties. The parties shall both cooperate

with the mediator. If the parties cannot agree to any mediator, or if either party does not wish to abide by any decision of the mediator, then they shall submit the dispute to arbitration by any mutually acceptable arbitrator. If no arbitrator is mutually acceptable, then they shall submit the matter to arbitration under the rules of the American Arbitration Association (AAA). The arbitration shall take place in _____ _____ (City and State) and the law of _____ (State) shall apply. Under any arbitration, both parties shall cooperate with and agree to abide finally by any decision of the arbitration proceeding. If the AAA is selected, the arbitration shall take place under the auspices of the nearest branch of the AAA to the other party. The costs of the arbitrator shall be advanced by all of the parties or in accordance with Part 3 above and the arbitrator may make any allocation of arbitration costs he or she feels is reasonable. The final costs of the arbitration proceeding shall be borne according to the decision of the arbitrator, who may apportion costs equally, or in accordance with any finding of fault or lack of good faith of either party. The arbitrator's award shall be nonappealable and may be entered as a judgment by the prevailing party in any court of record and shall be enforceable in any court of competent jurisdiction.

18. **Assignment:** The rights of LICENSOR under this Agreement shall be assignable or otherwise transferrable, in whole or in part, by LICENSOR and shall vest LICENSOR's assigns or transferees with the same rights and obligations as were held by LICENSOR. This Agreement shall be assignable by LICENSEE to any entity that succeeds to the business of LICENSEE to which Licensed Products relate or to any other entity if LICENSOR's permission is first obtained in writing.

19. **Jurisdiction and Venue:** This Agreement shall be interpreted under the laws of LICENSOR's state, as given in Part 1 above. Any action related to this Agreement shall be brought in the county of LICENSOR'S above address; LICENSEE hereby consents to such venue.

20. **Nonfrustration:** Neither party to this Agreement shall commit any act or take any action that frustrates or hampers the rights of the other party under this Agreement. Each party shall act in good faith and engage in fair dealing when taking any action under or related to this Agreement.

21. **No Challenge:** LICENSEE has investigated the validity of LICENSOR's patent and shall not challenge, contest, or impugn the validity of such patent.

22. **Rectification:** In case of any mistake in this Agreement, including any error, ambiguity, illegality, contradiction, or omission, this Agreement shall be interpreted as if such mistake were rectified in a manner that implements the intent of the parties as nearly as possible and effects substantial fairness, considering all pertinent circumstances.

23. **Entire Agreement:** This Agreement sets forth the entire understanding between the parties and supersedes any prior or contemporaneous oral understandings and any prior written agreements.

24. **Signatures:** The parties, having carefully read this Agreement and having consulted or having been given an opportunity to consult counsel, have indicated their agreement to all of the above terms by signing this Agreement on the respective dates below indicated. LICENSEE and LICENSOR have each received a copy of this Agreement with both LICENSEE's and LICENSOR's original ink signatures thereon.

Licensor: _____ Date: _____

Print Licensor's Name: _____

Licensee: _____ Date: _____

Print Licensee's Name: _____

How to Use the Downloadable Forms on the Nolo Website

This book comes with forms that you can access online at:

www.nolo.com/back-of-book/PAT.html

To use the files, your computer must have specific software programs installed. Here is a list of types of files provided by this book, as well as the software programs you'll need to access them:

- **RTF.** You can open, edit, print, and save these form files with most word processing programs such as Microsoft *Word*, Windows *WordPad*, and recent versions of *WordPerfect*.
- **PDF.** You can view these files with Adobe *Reader*, free software from www.adobe.com. Government PDFs are sometimes fillable using your computer, but most PDFs are designed to be printed out and completed by hand.

A. Editing RTFs

Here are some general instructions about editing RTF forms. Refer to the book's instructions for assistance in completing the forms.

Underlines. Underlines indicate where to enter information. After filling in the needed text, delete the underline. In most word processing programs you can do this by highlighting the underlined portion and typing CTRL-U.

Bracketed and italicized text. Bracketed and italicized text indicates instructions. Be sure to remove all instructional text before you finalize your document.

Optional text. Optional text gives you the choice to include or exclude text. Delete any optional text you don't want to use. Renumber numbered items, if necessary.

Alternative text. Alternative text gives you the choice between two or more text options. Delete those options you don't want to use. Renumber numbered items, if necessary.

Signature lines. Signature lines should appear on a page with at least some text from the document itself.

Every word processing program uses different commands to open, format, save, and print documents, so refer to your software's help documents for help using your program. Nolo cannot provide technical support for questions about how to use your computer or your software.

> **CAUTION**
> In accordance with U.S. copyright laws, the RTF forms provided are for your personal use only.

B. List of Forms

To download any of the files listed here go to:
www.nolo.com/back-of-book/PAT.html

The following files are in Portable Document Format (PDF):

Form	File Name
Invention Disclosure	Form3-2.pdf
Provisional Application for Patent Cover Sheet	Form3-3.pdf
Application Data Sheet—PTO AIA/14	Form3-4.pdf
Declaration for Utility or Design Patent Application Using an Application Data Sheet	Form10-1A.pdf
Declaration for Utility or Design Patent Application	Form10-1A2.pdf
Supplemental Sheet for Declaration	Form10-1B.pdf
Utility Patent Application Transmittal	Form10-2.pdf
Fee Transmittal	Form10-3.pdf
Credit Card Payment Form	Form10-4.pdf

PDF files continued

Form	File Name
Information Disclosure Statement by Applicant	Form10-6AB.pdf
Nonpublication Request	Form10-7.pdf
Design Patent Application Transmittal	Form10-11.pdf
Request for Expedited Examination of a Design Application	Form10-12.pdf
Petition for Extension of Time	Form13-4.pdf
Pre-Appeal Brief Request for Review	Form13-5.pdf
Request for Continued Examination (RCE) Transmittal	Form14-1.pdf
Certificate of Correction	Form15-2.pdf
Maintenance Fee Transmittal Form	Form15-4.pdf
Recordation Form Cover Sheet	Form16-4.pdf

The following files are in Rich Text Format (RTF):

Form	File Name
Nondisclosure Agreement	Form3-1.rtf
Positive and Negative Factors Evaluation	Form4-1.rtf
Positive and Negative Factors Summary	Form4-2.rtf
Consultant's Work Agreement	Form4-3.rtf
Searcher's Worksheet	Form6-1.rtf
Drawing Reference Numerals Worksheet	Form8-1.rtf
Information Disclosure Statement Cover Letter	Form10-5.rtf
Request Under MPEP 707.07(j)	Form10-8.rtf
Petition to Make Special	Form10-9.rtf
Design Patent Application	Form10-10.rtf
Amendment	Form13-1.rtf
Submission of Corrected Drawings	Form13-2.rtf
Supplemental Declaration	Form13-3.rtf
Request for Certificate of Correction	Form15-1.rtf
Maintenance Fee Reminder Sheet	Form15-3.rtf
Joint Applicants—Statement of Respective Contributions	Form16-1.rtf
Joint Owners' Agreement	Form16-2.rtf
Assignment of Invention and Patent Application	Form16-3.rtf
Universal License Agreement	Form16-5.rtf

Index

U

⚖ NOLO   *Online Legal Forms*

Nolo offers a large library of legal solutions and forms, created by Nolo's in-house legal staff. These reliable documents can be prepared in minutes.

Create a Document

- **Incorporation.** Incorporate your business in any state.
- **LLC Formations.** Gain asset protection and pass-through tax status in any state.
- **Wills.** Nolo has helped people make over 2 million wills. Is it time to make or revise yours?
- **Living Trust (avoid probate).** Plan now to save your family the cost, delays, and hassle of probate.
- **Trademark.** Protect the name of your business or product.
- **Provisional Patent.** Preserve your rights under patent law and claim "patent pending" status.

Download a Legal Form

Nolo.com has hundreds of top quality legal forms available for download—bills of sale, promissory notes, nondisclosure agreements, LLC operating agreements, corporate minutes, commercial lease and sublease, motor vehicle bill of sale, consignment agreements and many, many more.

Review Your Documents

Many lawyers in Nolo's consumer-friendly lawyer directory will review Nolo documents for a very reasonable fee. Check their detailed profiles at **Nolo.com/lawyers**.